VISIONS OF TIME

Cover art by

Jane A Evans

Experiments in Psychic Archeology

DAVID E. JONES

*This publication made possible
with the assistance of the Kern Foundation*

The Theosophical Publishing House
Wheaton, Ill. U. S. A.
Madras, India/London, England

This is a Quest book, published by
The Theosophical Publishing House,
a department of The Theosophical Society in America.
Inquiries for permission to reproduce all,
or portions of this book
should be addressed to:
Quest Books
306 West Geneva Road
Wheaton, Illinois 60187.

Library of Congress Cataloging in Publication Data

Jones, David E.
Visions of time.

(Quest books)
Bibliography: p.

1. Parapsychology and archeology.   I. Title.
BF 1045.A74J66   133.8   78-64909
ISBN 0-8356-0525-6
ISBN 0-8356-0523-X pbk.

Printed in the United States of America

For Jane.

CONTENTS

ACKNOWLEDGMENTS

I would like to express my deepest respect and gratitude to Albert Bowes, Diane Davis, Marjorie Niren, and Noreen Renier, the psychics who freely gave me their time and cooperation during three years of research. I would also like to thank Raleigh Powell, Karen Smyth, and Stewart Lilie for the original photography appearing in this book. Expert research assistance was provided by Grace Langlotz, Stephanie Kindel, Joel Causey, Michael Tennyson, and John Coonfield. Deborah Harding of the Florida State Museum proved invaluable in providing the artifacts and photographs for my experimentation. Archeologist, Ronald Wallace, offered aid at many junctures: in collecting artifacts for double-blind experiments, in cooperating with psychic research subjects during a site excavation he led, and in the general high level of his contributions to research designs, and evaluations of experimental results. A number of social scientists and psychologists, including Wayne Burroughs, Philip Staniford, Shirley Lee, David Barker, Joseph Long, Ida Cook, and Allyn Stearman, gave me crucial advice, support, criticism, and feedback as my research was developing. I would, of course, like to thank my wife, Jane, and my son, Ian, for their unique contribution to the supportive environment needed to conceive and execute the book you are about to read. Although this project could not have been completed without the help of the abovementioned individuals, I must take final responsibility for the manner in which this research was carried out, and for the conclusions reached.

I.1 Albert Bowes

I.3 Marjorie Niren

I-5 Dr. David Jones

I.2 Diane Davis

I-4 Noreen Renier

I

INTRODUCTION

In the fall of 1972 I took a position teaching anthropology at a university in central Florida. During my general orientation to the area by an anthropological colleague, I was taken to Cassadaga, Florida, a church camp community and retirement center of the Spiritualist Church. The village of Cassadaga intrigued me for several reasons. My previous research among the Comanche Indians of southwestern Oklahoma had focused in the main on Comanche shamanism and supernaturalistic beliefs.[1] Sanapia, the Comanche shaman, or native doctor, that I worked with for three years, believed that spirits existed which could be contacted by mortals for good or evil purposes. She acknowledged and practiced clairvoyance and ritual healing techniques; and, although she did not admit to doing it herself, she also claimed that "certain old people" had the ability to travel with their spirit guardians in time and in space over prodigious distances. These notions are typical of shamanistic belief systems found in all parts of the world. A similar set of assumptions, I came to learn, was also part of the loosely organized cognitive world of American Spiritualism. These magico-religious ideas were not strange to me due to my experience with the Comanche and my training as an anthropologist. What I did find exciting was the unique situation of discovering in America a community entirely composed of shamans. Quite naturally I set about considering how I could study the community of Cassadaga.

One of the initial problems that an anthropologist faces when entering the "field" is establishing rapport; that is, in making positive contact with the people to be studied, getting to know them as human beings and allowing them the same access to the anthropologist. As one means of making such contacts in Cassadaga, I engaged in the custom of having "readings" from many of the resident Spiritualist psychics.* A "reading" is a claimed psychic encounter in which the psychic, for a fee or donation, describes to the clients certain events in their past, present, and future and counsels them on appropriate behavior. The psychic generally will entertain specific questions asked by the client concerning the reading or any other topic of concern to the client. The perceived paranormal nature of such readings stems from the good psychic's ability to relate to the clients specific things about their life, thoughts, and feelings which the medium could not

---

* A problem with language is encountered here. Spiritualists refer to the individuals with psychic talents who work, counsel, and teach in that tradition as "mediums." However, in that three of the four people I worked with were not associated with the Spirtualist Church, I will use the more neutral term "psychic" to refer to all experimental subjects in the body of this text.

1

possibly know no matter how expert they might be as observers and interpreters of human behavior.

During one reading a psychic asked if he might hold a ring I was wearing. The ring was a silver and torquoise Navaho piece which was given to me by a non-Indian friend. This exchange had taken place several years earlier. The psychic held the ring for several minutes and then in great detail described my friend and the surroundings and specific circumstance of the gift-giving situation. I was very impressed, to say the least. After the reading I asked the psychic if he had ever performed readings on objects from other parts of the world. He described several instances in which clients had brought objects to him for his psychic appraisal. The last such occurrence entailed several figurines which were brought to him by an individual who had acquired them while traveling in South America. He recounted what he had seen and felt while handling the figurines. After leaving the psychic's residence, an archeologist who had accompanied me to Cassadaga mentioned that the description of a burial vault seen by the psychic while in contact with the figurines was very precise.

The burial vault description was, on the surface, not that astounding. The entire account could have been gleaned from some popular account. But the startling accuracy of the description of the circumstances of the gift of the ring stayed with me and instilled in my mind a caution about dismissing too lightly the burial vault description. I forgot about the incident in a few days, but it was to come back in sharper focus a month or so later while I was preparing to lecture in an Introductory Anthropology course at the university.

The topic under discussion in my class that day was the nature of archeology — its contributions and its limitations. Archeology is that branch of anthropology which attempts to reconstruct the lifeways of people no longer in existence by the careful excavation and analysis of their cultural and material remains. Archeology is of crucial importance in its contribution to our knowledge concerning how human kind has developed into its present form biologically and culturally. Its reach into the past makes academic history pale by comparison. Written accounts, which form the bulk of the historian's working materials, have existed only about 5,000 years. Even these earliest written records, coming from the Near East, tell us little about the nature of life at the time. For the most part, the most ancient writing systems were designed to keep records of animal and plant production and trade. England was non-literate until the dawn of the Christian era, and the native peoples of the New World were unaccounted for in written records until the coming of the Europeans in the late 15th century.

Humans, however, have been around and leaving behind evidence of their passing for millions of years. From an archeological site near Lake Rudolph (recently renamed Lake Turkana) in East Africa, human remains have been found in association with stone tools which date to 2.6 million years. West of Lake Rudolph, at the Lothagam site, human remains have been dated to 5.5 million years ago. Using the date of 5000 B.P. (before present) as the starting point of written history and the Lothagam date of 5.5 million years B.P. as a very early date for the presence of humans, we can observe that academic history deals with only 1/1100th of human existence. In other words, if we imagine that humans have been around for 1100 years, written records could exist for only one of those years, leaving 1099 years blank as far as written accounts are concerned. That incredible gap in the cultural-historical record of humanity is the special hunting ground of the archeologist.

The major question is: "What can the archeologist tell us about the cultural development of humankind from the excavation and study of material remains?" The answer to this question is debated even within the field of archeology. Some archeologists feel that the objects and traces left by ancient people offer relatively little basis for making inferences about the kinds of intangibles—cosmology, morality, values, law, philosophy, ethics, etc.,— which comprise the cohesive of day-to-day existence. M.A. Smith[2] for example, has stated, "Since historical events and essential social divisions of prehistoric peoples don't find an adequate expression in material remains, it cannot be right to arrive at a knowledge of them through archeological interpretation." In the opposing camp are archeologists who believe that physical remains can be the source of the entire range of information needed to understand a culture. Binford[3] wrote, "...data relevant to most, if not all, the components of past sociocultural systems are preserved in the archeological record."

It is true that modern archeology is capable of an amazing depth of interpretation derived from advanced analytic techniques. Archeologists are able to draw strongly supported inferences from archeological features like pot sherds, burials, post hole patterns, stone tools, and ancient firehearths about everything from the settlement distribution and trading cycles of a people to basic descriptions of social rank and status. Still, the most elaborate attempts by archeologists to reconstruct a culture amount to little in comparison with the kinds of accounts obtainable by even an untrained observer of a living cultural group. The archeologist is also thwarted by the fact that he may not be able to find the burial remains which would allow him, using modern techniques, to make inferences concerning rank, status, and family type. The anthropologist studying living societies, on the other hand, could derive the needed information concerning that aspect of human life every time he entered a socio-cultural system. Then again, there is that several-million-year span of time closed to the first-hand observer of human behavior. This forces us to understand that we must not chastise archeologists for what they cannot do, but rather praise and assist them in what they can do. Knowledge of the history of our species' existence is largely in the archeologist's hands.

It was in the context of lecturing on these points that the experience with the Cassadaga psychic returned with clarity. The psychic claimed to have the ability to handle an object and to enter into the world of the object's maker and user. The description of the gift situation surrounding my ring had been highly specific in detail and accuracy, like nothing that any archeologist could do by simply observing the artifact. The psychic's claim, if it could be demonstrated rigorously enough, was precisely what archeology needed to make it an historical tool capable of generating cultural descriptions comparable to primary, or first-hand, observation. It would be even better, perhaps, than a written history because, whereas you cannot question a history book, you can question a psychic. The research project which suggested itself was obvious: I would simply construct a series of experiments to see if the psychic could do what he had in fact done once with my ring, and which he claimed he could do repeatedly although, he assured me, not with 100% accuracy.

Once the idea for a psychic archeology project developed in my mind, I began to feel uncertain because the notion was so entirely strange and alien with respect to my educational background. I had been trained as a social scientist, and my doctoral dissertation had involved a criticism of a particular branch of anthropology from the point of view of the philosophy of science. As I searched for some firm ground from which to conceptually launch my investigation, I hit upon a classic distinction in discussions of science which enabled me to define in a traditional manner my entirely non-traditional research goals. Students of science make the distinction between theoretical and applied science. It is often a fine and hazy distinction but I seized upon it. The theoretical scientist is oriented to delve into the inherent qualities of whatever the object of study is: its nature, history, structure, function, etc. This kind of approach develops knowledge for the sake of developing knowledge, although the research rationale may be pinned to its ultimate application for human good. The applied scientist stresses practical application of knowledge to human affairs. His question is not so much "what is it" as "does it work?"

The field of parapsychology, the scientific study of psychic phenomena, is basically theoretical in its make-up. Parapsychologists strive to understand what the psychic potential is, how it works, what natural features of the universe govern and limit it, what its principles are, and how it fits with the more conventional modes of sensing in the human being. The field of applied parapsychology seems little developed at the moment. In fact, Dr. Gertrude Schmeidler,[4] a leading authority in parapsychology, has in her book *Extrasensory Perception* indicated her opinion that ESP (extrasensory perception) "...cannot, at present, be put to practical use." It was precisely the possibility of the practical application of ESP in archeology that intrigued me most. I decided that I would model my experimental search in an applied direction. The question of the inherent nature of ESP phenomena is fascinating, but I chose to ignore it and stress the practical potentials of ESP. The shovel provided me with a short-hand rationale and model. It is simple common-sense that one does not have to know the principle of the lever to pick up a shovel and dig a hole. If the tool works, use it.

However, science—and archeology is a science—does not operate in the practical world. Science exists in a very special world which it both creates and authorizes. This rigidity is why sciences in their growth do not so much evolve as explode. The tools of discovery in science must not only work, but they must also pass the test of scientific understanding. Discovery procedures in science are rational, predictable, and replicable. For example, carbon-14 dating techniques in archeology are not like flipping a coin. It is known that all living things contain a radioactive carbon known as carbon-14. At the death of the organism the carbon-14 begins to decay at a known rate. It is therefore possible to date the time of death by determining the amount of carbon-14 remaining in the organism. In this fashion a piece of charcoal from an excavated fireplace, because it once was living material, can be dated and the time of the use of the fireplace can also be dated. This dating method can accurately produce dates reaching from 50-75,000 years in the past. But the field of parapsychology is lacking in a consensus opinion, and the psychic practitioners themselves generally arrive at highly individualistic explanations of how they do what they do. This is indicated by the many labels used by individuals with psychic abilities to identify themselves. Some prefer to be called mediums, others call themselves seers, or clairvoyants, or psychics. Each title represents a slightly different philosophical orientation.

I realized that, due to the absence of a theoretical understanding of the psychic ability, it could not at this time be argued as belonging in the arsenal of scientific discovery procedures in modern archeology. Still, it is a common-place among those who actually do scientific research that more times than most scientists would care to admit, they resort to guesses, hunches, intuition, and plain blind luck when they reach the end of the orthodox scientific tether. These non-scientific methods or procedures, of course, play no part in the nature of scientific explanation, but in the real world of research, they are ever-present, constituting the art in science.

With my feet planted in the applied camp and with a sympathetic understanding of the non-science that goes along with science, I felt that if in fact my experiments in psychic archeology produced any strong results, I could simply suggest a new tool for archeologists to try when their traditional procedures had proved futile or impractical. I knew from first-hand experiences with friends who were archeologists that they were generally operating with research problems that demanded more time and money than they had. For the archeologist working with this chronic shortage of time and money, any offer of assistance, even from such a bizarre direction as parapsychology, would prove interesting. My emphasis would be on practicality and application.

Another academically derived set of conceptions that proved helpful in delimiting the experimentation I was planning concerned the "etic/emic" distinction as it is called in anthropology. The distinction, invented by the famous linquist Kenneth Pike,[5] is based on an analogy with phonetic and phonemic approaches in linguistic theory—hence "emic" and "etic." The complexities of the etiology of these concepts are not important here. Basically, an emic approach to the description of a particular form of behavior is to present what the actors feel to be the nature of the behavior. For example, when I was studying the Comanche, I encountered a curious affliction found in a small percentage of the population which was characterized by the paralysis of one side of the face. They felt that it was caused by contact with ghosts. The explanation was therefore emic; that is, from the Comanche point of view. The etic approach, on the other hand, is to describe behavior from the point of view of the scientific observer. In the case of the ghost sickness of the Comanche, I concluded that it was a form of conversion hysteria — a conceptual category foreign to the Comanche but common in my frame of reference as an anthropologist. What this digression is leading to is the manner in which I decided to handle what could have proven to be a major problem in the research I was contemplating. I knew from my preliminary field survey in Cassadaga that psychics had a disconcerting way of using language as they worked in their mediumistic roles. For example, they would say that they were "seeing" something which occurred when the client was a small child. What exactly is "seeing" in this context? What do they in fact *see*? How can they use a present tense in conjunction with a past event, as in, "I am seeing you as a small child." What, in fact, were they saying when they spoke of "reading" this person or object or photograph or letter?

I decided that I would skirt the issue of language by simply using the language of the psychics uncritically. I was opting for an emic stand with regard to the language with which I would be confronted as I collected data. If a psychic reported "seeing" something, I would simply record that they saw whatever it was that they were describing. If they referred to a "reading," I would record that use of language. My feeling was that to the degree that I was seeking simply to discover if they could do what they claimed to do with respect to objects, it was unimportant to quibble with the language the subjects used. I was looking for results. What was producing the results and the language in which the results were conveyed seemed problems of secondary importance to my primary research goal.

The next step was to examine the basic criticisms that have been leveled against this kind of research. By becoming familiar with the traditional pitfalls of parapsychological research I could better design simple, persuasive and effective experiments. Schmeidler,[6] when referring to the lines of attack that have been used against parapsychological findings, neatly sums up the basic avenues of criticisms of the experimental dimensions of the field. In order of importance she lists: (a.) criticisms of statistical methods; (b.) criticisms of experimental controls of such variables as sensory cues, recording errors, and the like; (c.) criticisms that reject positive ESP results by claiming that the findings violated *a priori* the basic framework of mechanistic science; that is, they could not be logically explained as consistent with natural law; (d.) criticisms of an *ad hominem* nature; that is, criticisms which questioned the integrity of the experimenter, perhaps even claiming fraud, and (e.) criticisms which cite the failure of ESP experimenters to present a truly repeatable experiment.

The criticism concerning statistical methodology did not pertain to my research because I did not attempt to use quantitative methodology of any kind. My approach was to be exploratory in nature.

The second criticism mentioned by Schmeidler, the problem of the control of such variables as sensory cues, was an area I could do quite a lot about. I decided that as much as possible I would use a double-blind type of experiment in which the correct response was unknown both to me and to the subject. This would preclude the criticism that I was cueing the subject in the direction of the correct response consciously or unconsciously. If I did not know the correct response, I certainly could not lead the experimental subject to it. As for recording error possibilities, I chose to tape record every experiment and to work from verbatum transcriptions of these tapes. The complete record of my experimentation in psychic archeology is on tape and the transcript of all tapes are to be found in their unedited entirety in the Appendix of this book.

In addition, the use of the "non-diagnostic" artifact would permeate my research. A non-diagnostic item is one which is impossible to identify out of its context. Most "arrow heads," for example, are non-diagnostic in that a mere physical appraisal of a particular projectile point could not lead even the most expert archeologist to be able to locate the origin of the artifact. Again, the non-diagnostic test item would help eliminate the "cue" criticism.

My general methodology also included, where possible, the use of control groups. This means that I would select ten individuals to repeat each of the experiments on which I had worked with the psychics. In this fashion I would have at least a crude indicator of what chance accuracy might look like in a given experiment.

The next two lines of criticisms described by Schmeidler—the illogical nature of ESP phenomenon and the *ad hominem* arguments—seemed of minimal significance to me. I knew, as an anthropologist, that what appears to be logical is merely the reflection of a culturally conditioned manner of looking at the world. One of the reasons that I was drawn into research in such a non-traditional area as parapsychology and anthropology was precisely because I sensed in this interdisciplinary mingling a way to escape the tyranny of a Western "logic" of the universe which had more to do with the culture doing the perceiving than with the universe perceived. Ideas about the earth being round and speculation that perhaps the earth was not the center of the universe were all considered illogical and opposed to natural law in their time.

The *ad hominem* argument is one that has no rational potency. This type of argument is a signal of defeat by the attacker, though the one on the offense generally does not understand this. I felt that if my findings drew mainly *ad hominem* complaints it was a sure sign that I had done something right! Further, I planned to present my research in all its aspects regardless of success or failure. The tape recordings of my research would be kept on file and open to responsible scrutiny. The subjects with whom I worked, and who are named in the book, are easily accessible to the public. If someone accused me of fraud, I could invite them to see my files and hear the relevant tapes. If they persisted, I would suggest that they repeat my experiments with the subjects and reach their own conclusions. There is little more that can be done to protect oneself from the accusation of fraud, except not to care.

The "repeatable experiment," the fourth criticism did not apply. In any case it is a slippery area to define succinctly. Even the sun does not precisely repeat its daily "rise." I felt that I was more involved with "discovering" something than with "proving" something. In other words, if the existence of a demonstrable psychic archeology could be shown, no matter how crudely, then later the compulsion of science to explain and to replicate could be exercised. I did not believe that the "repeatable experiment" dilemma was part of the task I saw before me.

My next problem was to investigate the nature of the phenomena I would be encountering, to find the right terms and correct definition for its many manifestations. J. B. Rhine, the Father of Modern Parapsychology, believes that extrasensory perception falls into special categories, which include not only telepathy and clairvoyance, but also information arriving outside the linear time sequence we all know. He designated information received from future time "precognition" and from past time "retrocognition," linking these together under the category of general extrasensory perception, or GESP.[7] "Clairvoyance" means the awareness of things or objects that is acquired without known sensory means. Clairvoyance included both precognition and retrocognition. Telepathy, in parapsychological research, means the transfer of mental images between two individuals.

A further distinction of great importance for the work I was preparing to enter included special categories of ESP behavior related to objects. Archeological artifacts and the physical remains of ancient peoples would play a key role in my research. The ESP ability in which objects are involved is called "psychometry." The word comes from two Greek words—"psyche" meaning "soul" and "metron" signifying "measurement." The term was invented by an American geologist named Denton. In the late 1800s Denton performed a series of experiments with his sister, Ann Cridge, in which geological specimens, carefully wrapped so as to hide their identity, were presented to Mrs. Cridge. After placing the wrapped specimen next to her forehead, Mrs. Cridge was able to give an accurate description of the geological nature and history of the specimen. Denton had been motivated to attempt this type of experiment after reading of the work of Dr. Rhodes Buchanan. Buchanan had found that some of his students were affected by the physical reactions associated with the drug contained in glass vials they held—vials which were unmarked except for numbered labels.[8]

The term "psychometry" has a confused history because a branch of psychology dealing with psychological testing also uses the term but in a very different sense. In scholastic psychology "psychometry" means the theory or technique of mental measurement. Perhaps because of this historical confusion, J. B. Rhine chose to refer to the ability to convey information about objects not obtainable by the ordinary sensing faculties, "clairvoyant free association in connection with a token object," or "object association."[9] This particular type of ESP has received little attention from modern parapsychology.

I also learned of another variety of a psychometry-like ability once I started working with my subjects. As part of their services to their clients, psychics often work with letters and photographs, as well as with objects. The ability to psychically deal with photographs was to prove to be a very fertile area for investigation.

The key ingredient in the success of any parapsychological type of investigation is, of course, the subject attempting to produce the ESP effect. The psychic I referred to earlier as stimulating my initial interest in this field was Albert Bowes. Bowes was to be the major subject in my experimental program, though as my experimentation progressed I was to meet and to incorporate into my research Diane Davis, Margie Niren, and Noreen Renier.

I considered it a good indication of their integrity that all four subjects worked with me without financial recompense and with no promise of notoriety or financial reward in the future. In fact, at the outset of this research I told them that they would be anonymous, as is the custom in the majority of anthropological investigations. They agreed to these conditions. It was not until I became more familiar with the parapsychological literature that I discovered that in that field it is the custom to use the real names of subjects. Bowes, Davis, Niren, and Renier consented to be my experimental subjects because they believed, as I did, that an investigation into the potential uses of psychic abilities in archeology was inherently valuable and worthwhile.

Since the bulk of this book hinges on the reports of Bowes, Davis, Niren, and Renier, I would like to introduce them to the reader. The introductions that follow are, in each instance, of a different origin. For Albert Bowes I will include an excerpt from a discussion between us which followed the first experiment. For Diane Davis I will reproduce passages from a tape she sent me after I requested some biographical information from her. For Margie Niren, I will present a letter she wrote to me after I had asked for additional background information concerning her psychic history. Noreen Renier also presents her story in a letter.

Albert Bowes was born in Hackensack, New Jersey, on November 27, 1948. He grew up in central Florida and completed the twelfth grade. He is at present a licensed heavy equipment operator, landscape gardner, and professional psychic.

JONES: Do you ever read objects just for the fun of it?
BOWES: Yes, I do it with antiques and I do it at Flea Markets, or places that may have special exhibits. Like one a few weeks back where they had bullets from the Civil War and clothes from the same time. I touched them and picked up their backgrounds, their stories. Another thing that may sound funny but I can hold the steering wheel of a car or truck or jeep or motorcycle and tell about the people who operated the vehicle. It can be obvious. Bones are more strong. You can tell if the person was healthy or sick, or things about the personality of the person when they were alive.

JONES: While working with you, what are some of the things I should not do if I want to keep on working with you?
BOWES: Taking my time when I don't want you to and asking questions and being sarcastic when I give you my answer. That would aggravate me and I would probably tell you to leave. If you were out to disprove me or make me into a fake, if I felt that, I would tell you to leave. To ask, to try to understand, that's good, that's wonderful. I spend maybe too much time trying to help people understand. I get very involved in this. I enjoy helping people. I love people. I think people are wonderful. And another thing, everybody is capable of being psychic; except perhaps a mentally disturbed person or a person who is like a vegetable.

JONES: Do you mind me asking you more questions the next time?
BOWES: No! You should ask more questions to help me. It helps me to break through. It makes it more fun for me too, more interesting and more involved. The questions you ask help me get through the symbolic part of the message to the more technical information that you want. You ask me a question and I concentrate on, "Really, what am I seeing? What am I really seeing?" I ask myself, "Why?" You should not get thrown by my vocabulary. You have a much wider vocabulary than I do but mine is all I have and that means that when I see something and tell you what I see, I will be telling you only in the words I have to tell you. I start with my mind like an onion, and then I strip it until there is only one thing left and then I strip that out and my mind is like a void. I'm not thinking of anything. Then directions come in as I wonder or feel toward a question being asked me. That's the way I work. But there are different abilities and different mediums will work in different ways. There's the conscious, the subconscious, and memory. Between the subconscious and memory there is a void. You use another part of your brain. You have to believe that it is good, or of God, or of benefit, or you might start peeling and you won't get hold

of it. You might be too selfish, too quick to grab, too aggressive. You've got to stay with God, or love, or some higher vibration. Be sensitive and do it very, very gently. You must relax to gain this response.

JONES: So there is a role for the ego there?

BOWES: Yes! You must believe in yourself. If I didn't believe I could do this, I couldn't do it! You have to believe you can do it, and have the ability to relax your mind and you can do it. Faith is the key and that's your own thing. God is the universe, the energy. I don't put God on a throne, because that is not the way my faith is. That's why I'm not a Spiritualist. This is my own belief. I don't have to go to church, God is all around me all the time. If God is everything and everywhere, why do you have to go somewhere in particular?

JONES: Do you feel it is a legitimate question to ask where the psychic is?

BOWES: It's like another dimension. It is not limited by space or time. If your brother was trapped in a cave-in in California and he cried out for help and you picked it up psychically, you wouldn't pick it up yesterday or tomorrow or twelve o'clock central time, you would pick it up at the time he thought it. No matter if you were on top of the roof or in the basement or in the shower. Distance, space, time: no effect on the psychic. There is no way to answer your question. The psychic is something outside this stage we live on. This is only temporary. Our lives are only temporary. The psychic is real and not of space, time, and distance. It isn't anywhere, or somewhere.

JONES: Do you feel you work with spirits?

BOWES: No. Working with spirits is like the sugar sprinkled on the top of a pie; it is a taste but no substance. That's the way I feel about it. I don't respect it much because I don't feel it is a very high level. I'm not a Spiritualist, if you get down to the nitty-gritty of it all. Labels. Why have a room? Why have a building? Why have a cross? They are doorways to get up there, but I'm trying to find a more direct route.

Diane Davis was born in Phoenix, Arizona, November 2, 1949. She lived in many parts of the United States because her father's occupation in the hotel management business kept the family moving. Diane has completed five and a half years of college and at present works in a secretarial position in central Florida.

I learned about cocktail parties before I learned about dolls. Perhaps that's too strong. I had a lot of nice things when I was young. A lot of nice introductions to social things, and I learned an awful lot about people by watching. People were very transient in my life. I was isolated from neighbors and children. I spent a lot of time to myself though I never enjoyed it, or learned how to cope with it. I never had any psychic experiences that I remember during childhood. I was always very sensitive and people used to tell me I thought too much about things. I always thought my sensitivity was just emotional. I never knew until I started studying psychic things that it was a positive force that I could use in a constructive way.

I went to high school two years in Arizona and two years in Florida. I moved to Florida when I was fifteen. My life changed a great deal over that change. I was very active and had a lot of friends; many activities in and out of school. I went away to college, but left two years later. School was a trauma for me. I never was much of a book learner; even to this day I don't read a lot. I don't like to intellectualize my experience, it's a heartfelt thing. Life is just that way to me. I flunked out gracefully from college. Then followed a period of turmoil.

What was I going to do? Where was I going to go? I went to business college for a time and kind of got my head on again. I went through a lot of emotion about how I hadn't done what was expected of me and how I had been a bad daughter and etc., etc. "Woe is me." "Aren't I rotten." You know, that kind of trip. During that time I was talking to a girl and she said she had gone and gotten her fortune told. I thought, "Oh, what a kick." At that time in my life I had never thought much about psychic phenomena.

In 1971, I went to Cassadaga for a reading. I didn't know what to expect. The medium told me a lot of things he had no way of knowing but most importantly, he made me feel worthy of living. He showed me direction. During the reading he told me my grandmother was present, and he said, "She lays three roses in your lap." For a moment everything went blank. I didn't faint, but everything went blank and I got very calm. I thought, "How nice." I went back to see him several more times, and one time he said, "You know that you could do this." About a year later I started studying with him. He was a Spiritualist medium. Several years later I felt I was ready to do platform work because I was very confident in my ability. I knew that I could do it, but I felt very restrained. Through the fall and into the following spring I worked almost weekly for various churches. In July of 1975 I was doing platform work in Cassadaga. But in the fall of 1975 I began to feel compelled to move away from the Spiritualist Church, because I felt the Infinite Intelligence was more important to me than the spirit of my deceased grandmother.* I began to feel that there was too much emphasis on spirit entities and I began to feel there was a lot of trivia involved there. It made me unhappy. I was too enthusiastic and too impatient. I learned a lot. But I stopped working so publically, and I found that I touched a lot more lives off the platform than on. I tried to stay flexible and open. Then in spring of 1976, or thereabouts, is where you know me from.

Margie Niren was born on August 5, 1948 in Grand Rapids, Michigan. She completed the twelfth grade. Margie is married and the mother of two children.

It was in the summer of 1973 that I really realized something was different. My husband and children and myself went on vacation. While we were driving in Tennessee, I knew there would be two wooden bridges up ahead about one mile. We went over two wooden bridges about ten minutes later. I would think about things that would happen on the trip and they did. It just seemed like these thoughts would come to me and it would be correct. I felt somewhat strange yet excited. So I started going to study what it was. Everytime I would meditate I would see this blinding white light. I could hardly stand to look at it. Also I had deeply religious experiences which changed me completely. I had incredible energy. That was a most memorable time in my life.

Psychic people seem to experience a feeling of unbelief that you can actually do it. Then unbelievable excitement. Then it changes to 'it doesn't matter' and you get bored with the idea and the subject. Then something happens and you get excited again.

What do I feel when I hold an object? When I hold an object it is either of two ways; through the head chakra (third eye) or through the rest of the body chakras. When using the third eye it's as if the impressions form just the same as an idea. Where does thought come from? Electrical impulses, as all things have, are collected and formed back into forms. Through the solar plexus and the heart, I get feelings of a certain object; compassion, the heart, the place of emotion. I usually get a feeling around my heart on the right side, kind of tingly feeling. I feel a great security and the presence of a higher teacher. When feeling a disorder, like a heart attack, I get the feeling of pain just as if I was getting one. I'm not quite sure how this works, but perhaps it's a transfer of the entity's energy into my own. When seeing objects, it's like you see a telephone; close your eyes and you still see it. Then it feels as though the eye moves slightly upward

---

* Miss Davis has since realigned herself with Spiritualsim and is now an ordained minister of the Spiritualist church.

and it intensifies, like shifting into another gear. I hope this helps. It's about the best way to describe it, for me.

Noreen Renier was born in Turners Falls, Massachusetts, January 16, 1939. She worked a number of years in the central Florida area in the fields of public relations and advertising. The mother of two daughters, Noreen now lives in the Charlottesville, Virginia, area.

Until last October (1976), I was a total skeptic about psychic phenomenon. I still am skeptical to some degree. Last September an Indian woman who had studied the psychic for many years introduced a friend and myself to meditation. The first few sessions were interesting and relaxing but nothing startling happened until the third session. I remember feeling a surge of energy vibrating through me. My stomach hurt terribly and I cried from the pain. The next moment a voice that sounded somewhat like mine came out of my mouth and said things I had no control over. I could see pictures and images while the words flowed. This experience repeated itself. The Indian woman was excited but my friend and I just didn't believe it.

I'm not a Spiritualist and do not belong to any group or organization. My studying and development has been by myself. I hope working in clinically supervised conditions will help me grow and understand more of psychic phenomena.

It is important to note that none of the subjects had anthropological or archeological histories. Further, neither Bowes, Davis, Niren, nor Renier fell into the category of "Indian buff" or "pot hunter"; that is, they had no special interest in archeology or anthropology as a hobby prior to their work with me. This made the information they presented during several years of experimentation all the more remarkable.

After acquiring cooperative subjects and after much background reading and thought about the research I was to do, I discovered that I was not alone in this field of investigation. As I read more I came to understand that I was merely a modern-day experimenter in a field of study that has been around for many years and which was, at the time I was preparing to enter it, in a kind of contemporary florescence in many parts of the world. For example, in a symposium held during the 73rd annual meeting of the prestigious and conservative American Anthropological Association in Mexico City in 1974, three papers on psychic archeology were presented. Dr. J. Norman Emerson, then head of the department of archeology at the University of Toronto and president of the Canadian Archeological Association, chaired a seminar at the Association's annual meeting in 1975 devoted entirely to modern research in psychic archeology. At the most recent meetings of the American Anthropological Association (1978), several major symposiums were held on the general subject of parapsychology and anthropology.

Further, I found that psychic archeology, or intuitive archeology as it was called earlier, had a fascinating, though not too complex or deep history. Several notable figures appeared in the 1800s. Using intuitive approaches, J.J. Winklemann discovered the city of Pompeii which had been obliterated in the eruption of Mt. Vesuvius in 79 A.D.; Stephens and Catherwood revealed the first knowledge of Maya civilization after their excavation in the Yucatan in 1848; Boucher De Perthes discovered ancient tools in the Somme River Valley in France in 1859; Henri Layard, in 1845, openly acknowledged his use of clairvoyant dreams in his discovery of the palace of Nimrud in Assyria; and in the latter part of the 19th century, Heinrich Schliemann discovered the remains of Troy and Mycenai.[10]

Jeffrey Goodman[11] offers a concise account of two major pioneers in psychic archeology in his description of the work of Frederick Bligh Bond and Stefan Ossowiecki. Frederick Bond was a British archeologist who excavated the Abbey of Glastonbury, the first Christian church in England. What made Bond's Glastonbury excavation somewhat unusual is that he claimed it was directed by information gathered from the automatic writing of Bond's friend, psychic John Bartlett. Automatic writing is a putative paranormal ability in which subjects allow their hands to write without consciously willing them to do so. Who was writing through Bartlett? The written materials introduce "The Company," a band of spirit entities and phantom monks once associated with the famed abbey. The important point is that through the efforts of Bartlett and "The Company" Bond was led to hitherto unknown archeological features of the abbey which were unearthed in subsequent excavations at locations specified by the psychic Bartlett.

Another well-documented example of psychic archeology concerns the Polish psychic, Stefan Ossowiecki. His abilities were tested by anthropologists from the University of Warsaw in the 1930s and the 1940s. For example, in October of 1941 Ossowiecki, in the company of six professors from the University, was handed a nondescript stone tool and asked to give his psychic impressions of the artifact. The artifact was, in fact, a projectile point from the Magdalenian culture, a tradition that flourished in Europe over 15,000 years ago and which represented the most advanced Paleolithic (Old Stone Age) culture. In this blind test Ossowiecki correctly indicated the origin of the artifact and offered accurate descriptions of the house types and subsistence patterns associated with the tool. In a series of carefully controlled experiments spanning four years, Ossowiecki and the professors from Warsaw worked with artifacts dating to 40,000 years ago. Ossowiecki maintained an extremely high success rate as he located artifacts in time and space, described accurately the environmental situation at the time of the making of the implements, and as well offered massive documentation of the life-styles of the users of the tools he psychically examined.

I found as I perused the sources desribing early intuitive archeology that for the most part the accounts were uncritical and not very persuasive due to the slipshod manner in which the experiments had been executed and reported. Though I was not the first in the field of psychic archeology, I felt that I could make some contribution by attempting to demonstrate the existence and potentials of psychic archeology through somewhat more carefully wrought experiments. I felt the perogative of the explorer to enter an almost unknown area with relatively large steps and a broad sweep. An explorer simply indicates that there exists in some domain something worth further investigation. After the explorer come the specialists who painstakingly and minutely map the area. Though my experiments would lack sophisticated statistical and quantitative methodology, serious lapses to the most modern parapsychologists, I hoped that I could, by creating a number of different experiments, compel the critical observer to acknowledge that there was something there; that in fact psychic archeology had real promise for advancing human knowledge.

Further, I choose to stress the successes of my subjects rather than their failures. Since the complete transcripts of the various experiments are included in this book, the failures are there to see and are not hidden. When an archeologist colleague and I were preparing for the first experiment, a test in which ten artifacts wrapped in cotton and placed in cardboard boxes were presented to the psychic subject, an archeological specialist at the state museum commented, "If he gets even two of these right, I won't sleep for a week." I took this as a kind of very rough indication of what "success" would be from the point of view of an archeologist.

The entire thrust of the work that follows is suggestive in my opinion. There may be points in the design of the various experiments which can be criticized, but taken in their entirety I feel a positive conclusion is unavoidable. There are individuals who have abilities which we now refer to as paranormal or psychic. They can help the archeologist, and all historical sciences and disciplines, to recapture in great detail human events heretofore lost and frozen in time.

References

1. David E. Jones, "The Medicine Kit of a Comanche Eagle Doctor", in *Bulletin of the Oklahoma Anthropological Society*, Vol. XVIII, 1969. _____, *Sanapia: Comanche Medicine Woman* (New York: Holt, Rinehart & Winston, 1972).
2. M.A. Smith, "The Limitations of Inference in Archeology", in *Archeological Newsletter*, Vol. 6, 1955, pp.1-7.

3. L.R. Binford, "Archeology as Anthropology", in *American Antiquity*, Vol. 28, No. 2, 1962, p.217.
4. Gertrude Schmeidler, *Extra-sensory Perception* (New York: Atherton Press, 1969), p.23.
5. Kenneth Pike, "Language in Relation to a Unified Theory of the Structure of Human Behavior" (Glendale, California: Summer Institute of Linguistics, 1954).
6. Schmeidler, *Extra-sensory Perception*, pp. 60-63.
7. Thelma Moss, *The Probability of the Impossible* (New York: New American Library, 1974), p.197.
8. W.E. Butler, *How to Develop Psychometry* (London: Aquarian Press, 1971), pp.7-8.
9. Richard Cavendish, *Encyclopedia of the Unexplained* (New York: McGraw-Hill, 1974), p.168.
10. Maxine Asher, "Digging into the Past with ESP", in *Psychic*, June, 1976, pp.10-11.
11. Jeffrey Goodman, *Psychic Archeology* (New York: G.P. Putnam, 1977).

II

PRELIMINARY EXPERIMENTS

In the preliminary experiments I was attempting to discover if Albert Bowes could repeat the kind of success he had exhibited when handling my ring. His task would be made more difficult in the first several tests due to several factors. The objects he was to deal with would not be visible to him in the first stages of the experiment. Each of ten test items was wrapped in thick wads of cotton and placed in a box. He was not allowed to lift the box or move it around, though he did ask and I did permit him to touch the container. Another proviso suggested, or rather insisted upon by Bowes, was that he would later be able to read the artifacts out of their wrappings. I felt this to be a fair request, and it became a part of the method used in these experiments.

A further feature of importance was the double-blind nature of the experiment. Neither Bowes nor I would know exactly what was contained in the boxes. The only information known by both Bowes and myself was that they each contained one item, or set of associated items, of human manufacture or human association, and that each item could come from any place in the world and from any historical time frame. The double-blind requirement necessitated the use of a research assistant. I enlisted the aid of Dr. Ronald L. Wallace, an archeologist in my department at the university. Wallace's task was to acquire well-documented archeological materials from the state museum, wrap them individually, and place them in boxes, numbering them from one to ten.

I took the boxed artifacts to Bowes' residence for the first experiment. A tape recorder was in operation as I placed one box at a time in front of him with the instructions, "This item could come from anywhere in the world. Tell me what you can about it." As Bowes relayed impressions he was experiencing, I would often ask questions that seemed to be obviously pertinent. Also, from time to time, as the transcripts indicate, he would say, "Do you want to ask me a question now?" In this way, Bowes and I would engage in lengthy question-and-answer exchanges concerning an object totally unknown to both of us. Of course when describing an experimental object as "unknown" from his perspective, it must be noted that here I mean "unknown" in the conventional sense.

In the first double-blind experiment the following objects were used: (1) A pine needle basket made at St. Petersburg, Florida in 1916; (2) toy combs from Boston, 1845; (3) A Seminole weaving heddle collected at Big Cypress Reservation in 1952; (4) A baseball signed by

18

baseball greats J. J. McGraw and Christy Matheson, dated 1919; (5) A Sioux Indian burial moccasin for children, made about 1900; (6) A Seminole leather pouch from a medicine bundle dating to 1857; (7) A slate hoe from the Garfield site in Georgia; (8) three pieces of chalk carved by a sociologist colleague; (9) several vertebrae from a Georgia site, dating to about 960 A.D.; (10) A hair ribbon crocheted by the secretary at the state museum.

As for what I would consider evidence of an accurate object description under the double-blind test situation already outlined, I decided to look for descriptive passages which would specifically and exclusively identify the object, as opposed to generalized descriptions which could apply equally well to many different objects. Before the experiment I told Bowes that I was looking for this specificity, and he responded that he would do his best to relay only information essential to the identification of the object.

First Experiment: Part I

Box Number One contained the toy combs from Boston. Bowes' response to the box before him was:

> The first thing I picked up in relationship to Number One I seen a pin or a long...something almost like a tooth-pick. It may have been a bone. But I kept seeing something that was long and thin or skinny. I keep seeing an object that may have almost been like a comb or it may have had something like a ...it could have been bone...like a fish's rib or ...it could have been like a comb that was in somebody's hair, or...that it was used as an ornament or maybe it was like something they blew through or...I don't know what it is but I kept seeing that...in connection with this...I keep seeing a woman or a man with long black hair and I feel as though it was very...extremely oily or it could have been an Indian. I don't know what location it would be...I keep seeing some sand and some beaches or some sand. This could have been desert or the beach but I kept feeling as though that was something in relationship to...I wouldn't feel that the people were very educated. O.K.? I didn't pick up very much about that.

I have included the entire reading of the boxed comb as a means of explaining how I will present succeeding object readings. The important feature of this reading in my opinion is the specific identification of the object. Of the countless millions of objects which could be mentioned after I say, "This object could come from any time and any place in the world," Bowes focuses on combs and their features. He was also correct in his impression of an object of bone. The association with beaches is also accurate, though the Indian identity briefly mentioned is not correct, nor is the passing suggestion of a desert environment. The startling fact, however, is the identification of the comb.

In the many other readings I will present my subject's accurate identifications and not labor the misses. The error factor is present for the reader to see in the transcripts appearing in the Appendix.

Box Number Two contained the hair ribbon made by a secretary at the state museum. There appeared in Bowes' reading of this masked object nothing that could be construed as specific identification of the item. Box Number Three contained the Sioux child's burial moccasin, and, as with Number Two, Bowes offered no identifiable accuracy.

Box Number Four contained the antique baseball. In his reading of this item Bowes stated:

> I keep feeling something that would pertain to a game, and I don't know if it's like a ball or…like some sort of sport of some kind. I keep seeing somebody talking or little groups of people watching each other…

Box Number Five contained the vertebrae from the burial of an American Indian man whose remains indicated his violent death. Five projectile points were found embedded in vertebrae not used in this experiment. Bowes touched the edge of the box and said:

> I kept seeing something almost like it was a bone or something that was crushed or broken. I see people running, and I kept feeling as though there was a disaster or that they were afraid of something.

Box Number Six contained the leather pouch from the Seminole medicine bundle. In reading this box Bowes commented:

> I felt as though this may have been kept inside a house or kept by someone for a period of time. I keep seeing an older woman or I see a china cabinet…I would feel it was very small.

The item is less than two inches in length and would therefore be "very small" as compared with other items read by Bowes in this experiment. The reference to the "older woman" might pertain to Mrs. Octavia Stephens who had this object in her possession after her husband, the collector, was killed during a Civil War Battle near Jacksonville, Florida in 1864.

Box Number Seven contained the ancient stone hoe from the Indian site in Georgia. Bowes reading included:

> I keep seeing a stone or a stone hatchet or something somebody was using to cut something with. I don't know how this associated with it but I keep seeing somebody of the early… like early pioneer days or something associated with what I would say would be digging or a hatchet or a maddock or something, but I kept seeing somebody digging, I would feel these were farm people or somebody who was digging canals or making drainage.

Box Number Eight contained pieces of blackboard chalk which had been carved into fanciful shapes by an academic colleague. One of the pieces of chalk hidden in the box was carved into the shape of a bony human hand. This is important to point out because Bowes, in relaying the impressions received from looking at Box Number Eight, said:

I would feel that Number Eight is associated with a bone...I don't know why but I would feel that it could associate with something that bent or a knuckle or a hand or something that was...I see a joint of some sort.

Box Number Nine contained the Seminole weaving heddle. Bowes' reading of this box was not conclusive, nor was his reading of Box Number Ten, which contained the pine needle basket.

As this experiment was coming to a close I spontaneously put boxes one, two, four, and eight in front of Bowes and asked him to order the boxes sequentially in terms of the age of the materials present in them. Note that I asked about the materials the objects were made of and not the objects. Bowes considered the boxes for a moment and said, "From oldest to newest, I would say eight, one, four, and two." He was accurate in his response. The chalk of box eight was oldest, followed in successive order by the bone of the combs secluded in box one, the leather of the baseball in box four, and the synthetic fiber of the hair ribbon found in box two.

To appreciate exactly how impressive Bowes' performance in this first test was, a "control group experiment" can be performed by the reader. Select ten small objects from your own home, wrap them in thick wads of cotton, or any kind of available masking material, and then ask family members to guess what is contained in the boxes. You will find that typically none of the items will be guessed. Bowes was presented with boxes containing objects not from his own home, or even necessarily his own culture or his own historical time frame, and he managed to offer specifically identifying information on fifty percent of the sample.

First Experiment: Part II

In the second stage of the first experiment, which took place a week after Part I, I presented Bowes with the actual items which had been disguised in the first part of this experiment. As can be seen from glancing at the complete transcripts of the readings of the objects in this second phase, Bowes' readings are much longer and richer in detail relative to the readings in the first part of this test when the objects were masked from sight and touch.

The first object I placed before him was the stone hoe. The museum information identified the hoe as coming from the Garfield site in Georgia and dating between 500 B.C. and 1 A.D. Though I could see and touch the hoe, it was impossible for me, or any anthropologist, by simply observing this artifact, to date it or place it in its cultural and environmental context. This fact makes Bowes' reading of the artifact even more interesting, in that he was dealing with a non-diagnostic artifact.

The hoe artifact comes from a type of native American cultural context known to archeologists as Early Woodland. It was a time when Indians in the Southeastern United States were just beginning to incorporate some farming into their basic hunting and gathering way of life. Much evidence also suggests that it was also a time of major population movement. The sites that produced hoes like the one used in this test are typically found along river valleys. The particular site which produced this hoe is located on the piedmont fall-line of northern Georgia.

References to population movement abound in Bowes' reading of the object.

> I keep seeing a man who hunted or traveled near water...it may pertain to something that was at a time when people were traveling...but I see travel. I would feel this belonged to someone who may have done a lot of traveling...I would say its more like a migration. That these people continued to migrate...visiting people as they went along and possibly ended up here...on a trip or continued to travel...migrating...

The emphasis in the diet of Early Woodland peoples rested mainly in products of nature with some domesticated plants. With regard to this aspect of the life of the makers of the stone hoe, Bowes stated, "...I would feel that he ate corn...I would feel his diet pertained mainly to meat..."

The artifact itself is misidentified at first as a "tomahawk" or a "spear," but later Bowes correctly stated, "I kept seeing something almost like a shovel or a maddock or something that you dig with."

The riverine environment of the inhabitants of the Garfield site was described in several ways by Bowes.

> I keep seeing a man who hunted or traveled near water. There may have been a lot of swamps or water...I keep seeing the ground slopping off...I see a stream or water around there...a bubbling stream...I did see clay...like clay and a lot of water, or a lot of moisture in the ground...But I feel like there was a lot of water leaking out of the ground.

Bowes had some difficulty in locating the site, but considering that the artifact could have come from anywhere in the world, his location comments are very good.

> I feel that if this was in Florida...it came from another state, or another area, O.K....I would feel north of Florida...north of Florida for sure...if it pertained to Florida it could be palmettos or palm fronds but I wouldn't feel that it was that.

The reference to "palmettos or palm fronds" in the above quotation refers to Bowes' description of houses at the site. Archeological finds at the Garfield site indicated the presence of circular houses made of a mixture of pole foundations with thatching and mud packing. When speaking of the houses associated with the makers of the hoe, Bowes described "...some sort of round building..." and indicates the use of "...like branches and more like clay or dirt over the top...." He also indicated that the houses were elevated. There is no evidence that the houses were built off the ground at the time of the Garfield site occupation, but what is significant is that many later Southwestern Indian

II-1: *A stone-hoe maker's house.*

houses were elevated. Further, the particular house drawn by Bowes, and believed by him to be the house-type of the makers of the hoe, is an Indian house-type only found among Southeastern Indian peoples.

The second object presented to Bowes in this session was the baseball. In his reading of the antique ball he described several people, but I was unable to document anything he said concerning those associated with the artifact. This is typical of a problem that was to occur repeatedly. In setting up these early experiments I was not prepared for the depth of information Bowes was capable of generating. Often I had only a several line "bio" on the artifact from the museum with which to compare a reading on the object from Bowes that could run for several single-spaced type-written pages.

After the baseball was removed, I set the vertebrae before Bowes. The bones from the burial found at a Georgia site was an adult male. Projectile points imbedded in other vertebrae not shown to Bowes suggested a violent death. There were several obvious points here to measure Bowes' accuracy. Would he identify the remains as coming from an Indian man who died a violent death? Would he indicate the coastal environment? With respect to the individual Bowes stated:

> If this was a person I would feel that it was a fairly large person...it was a man...I keep seeing someone who is having problems...I would say escaping from someone...I would feel that there was a lot of bickering or fighting....This person died in great pain...a feeling of triumph.

In attempting to question Bowes concerning the racial characteristics of the individual, I asked, "What color was the hair?" Bowes responded, "Black. I would feel as though he was very dark skinned." When I asked Bowes to draw the man, he correctly drew an Indian.

His statements as to location of the coastal Georgia site contain two significant points. He stated, "I don't know why, but I feel that this was somewhere other than Florida" and "...a place where there was access to the water."

II-2: *The "vertebrae" man.*

The next items shown to Bowes were the pieces of chalk carved by an academic colleague. Bowes' reading included the following:

> I'm not very impressed with this for some reason. I felt like it was just chalk and I felt like someone made this very recently. That's the feeling I have…I would feel that the person who made it could have been inside a building, or…was at school, or was inside a building…either in jail or inside something….I do feel as though he is in school, and he may have had a deep desire as a young man to be a teacher or to something with his hands, and he may be a little bit frustrated and need this as an escape…he picks on chalk or picks on something to let out his frustrations or to let out his anxieties with, but I would feel that he could be an artist if he wanted to be. I would feel as though his parents may have goaded him or pushed him into this. I feel as though he feels he is in a prison or a little bit trapped….If that belonged to an Indian, I still feel as though it was an Indian who was in school, or an Indian who was trapped or felt held back.

Bowes was correct in indicating that a man in school made the pieces. The feelings of frustration and immobility with his position, the early desire to be an artist, and the pressure by his parents to go into "something respectable" are all correct according to the maker of the pieces. Further, at one point in the reading Bowes stated, "…he picks on chalk, or picks on something to let out his frustrations." The producer of the carvings is also an accomplished banjo "picker."

The next artifact used in this stage of the experiment was the Sioux child's burial moccasin. In his reading of this item, Bowes identified the correct environment of the Sioux makers who lived on the northeast periphery of the Great Plains. He even described the movement of these people from the lushness of their original environment further north into the relative dryness and aridity of the Plains. The child's death is noted at several points, plus indication of the "mummified" state of the body. Bowes even drew a picture which depicted a desiccated child's body. The relevant portions of the reading included:

> I keep seeing the west. Either the west or the north. I feel as though it was very dry wherever this came from…I seen a child and I seen like what you might call a mummy…something dried out like a…like something that would scare somebody if they seen it…I kept seeing something to do with corn. I would feel that would be in the north. Generally I kept seeing horses, and I would feel that this would possibly be more recent. I didn't feel that this was from Florida… I feel that it could have been in a place that was very very dry or like there was a desert or mountains. Now it could have been from the north because I see people who were …it was cold. Like cold at night…I feel as though they may have moved from a place that was like Oregon or a place that was like New York state or a place that was cold and

had a lot of trees, a lot of animals alot of people that ate and were free...it is as if they moved to the desert...This was belonging to a child. I feel as though it may have died because of it having to be moved...I did see a mummified person or child or like a little child or like a little doll, but it was like it was petrified...like a doll...but I kept feeling it was like a little short doll or a little short girl or maybe I'm seeing it as a girl because it has long hair but I would feel it was a girl and I felt its lips were tied together with ...I can draw you a picture of it... very rotten or it was like a mummy...It's an

II-3: A Sioux child.

ugly looking thing! ...But I still feel there was a little girl, or it was a young girl...died in sadness...left behind.

The next artifact in this series was the hand crocheted hair ribbon of modern origin and materials. In his appraisal of this artifact, Bowes accurately described the object as modern and the maker as a young woman—two deductions which may be so highly probable as to be obvious. There is nothing further in the reading of this item that can be construed as uniquely and specifically related to the object. Likewise, with the next artifact, the Seminole heddle, Bowes seemed unable to offer precise information.

It is relevant to note a pattern which had already begun to appear at this point in the experiment. Bowes' lack of accuracy and specificity is associated with being "bored" or "unimpressed" with the object. His lackluster readings of the heddle, hair ribbon, and baseball are characterized by their brevity, relative to the length and depth of more successful readings of the hoe, vertebrae, chalk, and moccasin. It is almost as if Bowes knew when he was "on" and proceeded at length, whereas knowing that he was "off," he cut the reading short. This trait, discernible within the first several weeks of the project, remained throughout the several years over which this research continued.

The Seminole leather medicine pouch was the next object. Before researching the object in some detail, I felt that Bowes' reading was relatively inaccurate, or at least, non-demonstrable. However, I discovered that the object had been collected by one Winston J. T. Stephens during a Seminole "uprising" in 1856. In attempting to find out more about the non-Indian collector, I discovered that Stephens had been involved with horses all of his life.

During the Civil War he was a Confederate Captain of Cavalry and died in that role during an engagement near Jacksonville, Florida on the first of March, 1864. This association of a white man, horses, and leather pouch helped make "sense" of Bowes' reading of the artifact.

Early in his reading of the item, Bowes, almost in passing, correctly identified the object when he stated, "I kept seeing something in here of good luck...pertaining to medicine...." Immediately after that and for the rest of the reading, his focus shifted to a white man and a continual reference to this man's relationship to horses. The following excerpts show this.

I see him worried about his horse or worried about his transportation...an animal of some kind...I don't know if this was owned by a frontiersman or if it was owned by an Indian... I felt more with a man...a man's vibration...I kept seeing long hair...It could be blond. It could be light colored... bleached...like he could have been a cowboy or somebody who rode a horse...This could be a white person because I seen a moustache and a beard and long hair...like a frontiersman...like a cowboy...I kept seeing mostly him either on a horse or traveling again...I would feel he loved animals. His life was surrounded by animals.

The next object Bowes read was the pine needle basket. His reading produced no information which could be verified.

The last item in the series was the duo of bone combs from Boston which dated to 1845. Bowes' reading of the combs was full of references to a mid-1800s Boston complete with suggestions of prowed ships in the harbor, men in slicker raincoats with whaling harpoons, large population, advanced architecture, cold winters, etc. Remember that the combs could just have easily come from Omaha, Nebraska, thus negating the major points brought up in the reading. Bowes in this reading constructed an image of Boston, the origin of the test objects.

Highlights of Bowes' reading included the following passages:

This could have been Eskimos or people from the north, but I would feel it may not be that far north...like Eskimo territory, but I see water that was frozen over. I keep seeing boats and I feel like it would pertain to boats or water...Hey, I just picked up something. I see a boat and in the front it may come up, and it may have something up here, a bird or maybe something with arms or something up here (prow), but I felt as though there was people standing up here and they were like in a dress or in something long. I feel as though they had a long pole in their hand or spear...I would feel that they were river people or people who lived near the water or lived with water, or something in association with water ...Several hundred or a thousand people or a large...I see large groups of people...lots of houses and building. These people are more permanent...they are in one place...they (houses) were quite solid but they were always near the water...there's a building here and another building here and another building up the hill aways. I felt they were always associated with water...I keep seeing them eating a tremendous amount of fish and using fish for everything...

II-4: Toy-comb related impression.

fertilizer, eating fish and using fish...I felt like everything
was water oriented. I see as I go into buildings...steps...
walking up and steps coming up. I would feel that these were
actually steps...more like that rather than a straight ladder
...but I feel like there are big platforms in front of the buildings...and they went inside. Like a porch...a porch sticking
out...It was a mixture of lots of different kinds of Indians
or lots of different kinds of people, rather than just one kind.
I would feel that these people would have made fire places
out of rock. These people were very advanced. They were
not primitives...I don't feel that they went to the bathroom
in their own house. I feel that there were rugs on the floors.
It was clean in there and not filthy, dirty. Like some of these
other things I held (referring to earlier artifacts), I felt dirty.
But I felt that these people had a lot of pride, a lot of feelings
of accomplishment.

SECOND EXPERIMENT: PART I

The reading of the toy combs completed the first experiment state. I
felt the results of the first experiment were very positive and exciting and I began to prepare for another double-blind experiment

using more museum pieces. The one new feature that will appear in this second early experiment is the presence of Bowes' drawings of every test item. Bowes had not often utilized sketches in his psychic work prior to the first experiment, but once it became clear that his drawings were of some importance in describing the images and impressions he received while psychically operating with people and objects, they became a staple aspect of all succeeding experiments. In fact, due to his new found fascination with sketching his visions, the emphasis in the first phase of the second experiment is decidedly visual as the transcripts indicate.

The design in the second experiment, conducted a month after the completion of the first experiment, was the same as the first. The procedure was double-blind. The items selected by Wallace from the museum were wrapped, boxed, and numbered by him. I had no knowledge of the contents of the boxes. I took them to Bowes, presented them to him one at a time, and tape recorded our conversations as he attempted to identify the artifacts hidden from his sight and touch.

Wallace selected the artifacts for the second experiment based on a statement by Bowes concerning the kinds of objects he felt he could best read. It was Bowes' opinion that metal objects of emotional value to some individual were easiest to read. All of the artifacts used in the second experiment followed those criteria. As will be seen, Bowes' performance with this collection was similar to the level of information given in the first experiment where the objects were not selected for emotional value or metallic composition.

The artifacts used in the second experiment included: (1) handcuffs found on the grounds of Chattahoochee State Hospital, Florida, probably belonging to the time when the facility was used as a prison; (2) an antique dental instrument called a "pelican-" or "turn-key" (American); (3) a sewing bird from the turn of the century used to hold cloth for hand sewing (American); (4) a pair of false-teeth made for a citizen of Edinburgh, Scotland in the late 19th century; (5) a silver pocket watch; (6) a necklace made from human hair with a gold clasp from Boston dating to 1835; (7) iron knuckles (American); (8) handmade corn husker (American); (9) a World War II German badge awarded to a soldier who had been wounded in battle on several occasions; and (10) a straight razor from the early part of this century (American).

The first box set before Bowes contained the pocket watch. Before touching the box he said, "I am absolutely sure there's something metal in there and you can put your finger in it." After offering descriptions and drawings of many objects he stated, "I kept seeing a slab and it could have been like a piece of lead, like melting down bullets or lead of some sort...I like something heavy was in there... someone valued it." When I asked him to emphasize on his drawing which shape pertained to what he most strongly felt to be hidden in the box, he picked up a ball-point pen and outlined an oval shape he had indicated earlier in pencil; he then paused and also inked in a semi-circular band. A glance at the picture of the object he was psychometrizing will indicate the nature of his accuracy here. The watch, a dull grey "lead" colored slab in appearance, had a metal ring at the top.

The second box contained the hair necklace with gold clasp. He never directly identified this object, but there are several things he did do with this object that are interesting. For example, this artifact

II-5: Contents of first box.

was the only artifact containing gold that was used in the several years of research, and in his reading Bowes mentioned the word "gold" four times. He also correctly drew the shape of the necklace, still not identifying it verbally. Further, he appeared to indicate the museum identification marks on the necklace's clasp when he stated, "I kept seeing something like a square...like made of brass or a flat piece of gold or brass...I see a lot of little decorations or little scribblings on it."

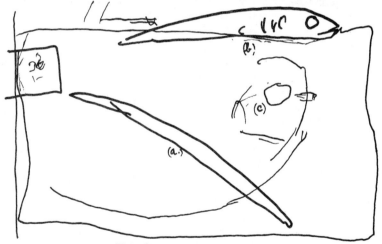

II-6: Contents of second box.

The next box contained the sewing bird. After describing various objects he stated, "...I keep seeing something metal...it might screw together but I don't know what it meant. I don't know if that was made for carrying something or holding down something...this metal ...I kept seeing it almost like it would swivel." The sewing bird was metal, did operate on a screw principle, swiveled, and was used to hold something down. What is most striking, however, is the shape he emphasized in his drawing of this box, and its resemblance to the tiny screw-handle on the sewing bird.

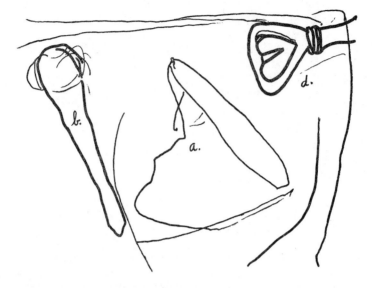

II-7: Contents of third box.

The fourth box contained the Nazi wound badge. Bowes offered nothing to specifically indicate this object. He did note that it related to "...ugly people; the bad side of people."

II-8: Bowes' reaction to fourth box.

In the fifth box was the hand-made corn husker. Bowes indications of shape once again command attention. He did not offer persuasive identification of the object, but he did stress in his drawing a shape which he felt to be present with the hidden object, and he was correct. The dark loop he drew is the dark leather loop on the object itself, as a comparison of Bowes' drawing and the photograph of the artifact indicate.

The next box held the broken handcuffs from the Chattahoochee site. The artifact was found laying on the grounds of the old prison. Bowes stated when he was presented with this box that he had unusually strong feelings about it. It will be seen that his accuracy with this object, both in Phase One, when it was hidden and unknown to both of us, and in Phase Two, when he could actually handle the item, was relatively high. The Chattahoochee facility has a long and colorful history, having been used at various times, as a fort, a prison, and a mental hospital. In his reading in Part I of the second experiment,

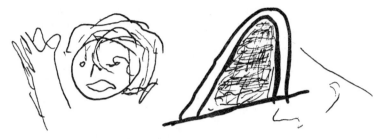

II-9: *Contents of fifth box.*

Bowes described a Florida-found artifact of metal characterized by hinging which was associated with violent people. The following excerpts are important:

> This I would feel is like something that people picked up... early artifacts of Florida...I would say this was quite heavy...the feeling I had was that there was a gun belt near or associated with this. I don't know if this is a piece of something...like a piece of a fort or a piece of a building like a hinge, or it's something of steel. I kept seeing something look like a piano hinge...I felt it was metal, and I would say this was related to early Florida...Something that bends back and forth...I kept seeing violence dealing with the building...I see violence inside the building...a lot of noise, violence...I felt like there was a lot of violence before they abandoned it. People without organization like alcoholics or violent people...

II-10: *Contents of sixth box.*

In his drawing he stressed the hinging of something metallic. The next box contained the false teeth from Scotland. What seemed to attract Bowes with this hidden artifact was the spring that held the teeth together. He never identified the artifact as false teeth, but his drawing and a statement from his reading of this box appeared to suggest this "spring" focus. In his reading he said, "I feel this spiral shape was made to hold something...this metal...like a spring...it could even hold bones together." When asked to indicate on his drawing which shape he felt to best represent what was in fact in the box, Bowes emphasized the spiral shape connecting two layers of some unknown material. The close-up of the false teeth will show what Bowes was seeing.

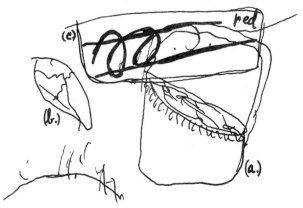

II-11: Contents of seventh box.

The next masked artifact presented to Bowes was the pair of iron knuckles. Once again, Bowes did not produce an overt identification, but what he did offer was intriguing. In the reading of the boxed object, Bowes related:

> ...the feeling I had was that it was metal and round. I would say it was held in your hand...it was held in your hand and it was steel...I would feel that that was like a ring or like scissors...like it was held in your hand.

In his drawing of this object, he immediately drew a ring-shape which he felt circled the fingers. He started to draw a pair of scissors, as the drawing shows, but stopped and instead reinforced the dark, thick oval area. Of further significance was the motion and shape of his hand as he gave his reading. As he talked of something that was held in the hand, he made a fist; not the hand position of holding scissors, but very much like the hand position for wearing "brass knuckles."

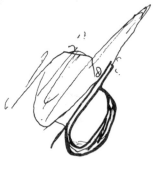

II-12: Contents of eighth box.

held in the hand, he made a fist; not the hand position of holding scissors, but very much like the hand position for wearing "brass knuckles."

The next box contained the straight razor. Here again, the narrative offered no identifying information, but the drawing did. He did not name the object; but when asked to emphasize the shape he felt to be relevant, he drew over the outline of what he thought to be a ship. The outline was the approximate dimension of the razor's blade.

II-13: Contents of ninth box.

The last object in this experiment was the pelican key, the antique dental tool. This object would be inserted into the patient's mouth, affixed to a tooth to be extracted, and then operated with a twisting motion. Bowes, while not naming the tool, described its basic function.

> ...it was like some sticks to relate to like stretching a shoe or stretching leather. I really wouldn't know what it was but...it could be something that was wound up. I don't know. The feeling I had was that it was used for stretching or winding something like...it may have sticks on both ends to wind something apart...could be like a crank...like it cranks or turns...there could be something to do with leather ...I thought I was drawing a boot, but it doesn't even look like a shoe or boot at all...it looks more like a bag or something that you would look down in...open up and look down in...I did see something like a crank and the wood was rotted and it may have a piece of steel through it and it may be a

spool or some sort of crank...something that was made to
turn around...it was used for turning.

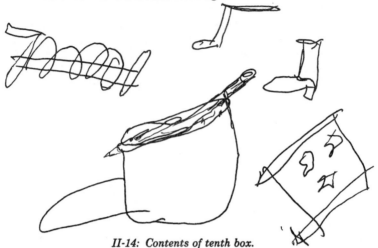

II-14: Contents of tenth box.

The results of Part I of the second experiment were even more
astounding than the first experiment. In an experimental situation
where neither Bowes nor I knew the content of the boxes and where
the artifacts were heavily layered in cotton, Bowes was able to offer
specific and correct data on practically every object. He drew the
outline of the pocket watch and indicated its color and density.

In the case of the hair necklace with the gold clasp, he indicated his
sensitivity to the presence of gold in the box, plus describing the
minute museum "scribblings" on the gold clasp piece. His drawing of
the heart-shaped screw-handle of the sewing bird matched exactly the
indicated section of the object itself. The dark loop on the cornhusker
showed up clearly in his drawing of the contents of that box. The
handcuffs from Chattahoochee elicited an accurate description of the
nature of the artifact (metal and hinged) and its setting "among
violent people." His reading of the false teeth produced statements
and a drawing which showed that Bowes was able to clearly indicate
a major feature of the hidden artifact, the spring that held the two
plates together. The iron knuckles were described as metal and related
to something held in the hand. The outline of the razor blade was
drawn in the same dimensions as the razor itself. The pelican key was
concisely described as an object whose function it was to turn in association with "something that you would...open up and look down in."

SECOND EXPERIMENT: PART II

A week after the completion of the first phase of the second double-
blind experiment, the same objects were brought back to Bowes and
he was allowed to read them while in direct physical contact with the

artifacts. It should be reiterated here that even in the second phase of the first two experiments, I was not informed as to the correct identification of the objects. I knew as much as anyone else could know simply by viewing and handling the artifacts. The objects Wallace selected for the second double-blind experiment were puzzles. Even when holding the object in my hand, I could not identify the antique dental tool, the sewing bird, or the corn husker. There was no way of immediately perceiving that the necklace was human hair or that the clasp was gold. The fact that the Nazi badge was a Nazi badge was obvious from the swastika, but that it was a wound badge was not obvious. It was also impossible for the casual observer to indicate the Scottish origin of a pair of false teeth simply by touching them.

The first object I handed to Bowes in this, the second phase of the second experiment, was the corn husker. The stick portion was held in the hand while the loop was pulled over the ear of corn. Similar to my reaction, and to everyone's reaction when I later showed them the picture of the corn husker, Bowes was unable to specifically identify the artifact or its function. He came close, in general terms, in the following short segment from his lengthy reading of the item.

> I don't know why but I kept feeling that this leather piece was around something...it fell down on something...I keep seeing a round pole or a spear or something in this leather...I see somebody grinding meal with a big stone and I see it going around and around and its grinding.

He was unable to accurately locate the artifact's origin.

Next I showed Bowes the iron knuckles. He offered no information that I could verify, but something did happen in this reading, which would happen repeatedly in the coming experiments. Bowes and I, after the three preliminary experiments were complete, would note what we called "contamination" as a major factor in producing error in this kind of object reading experiment. In short, what would happen was that Bowes would begin to offer specific information on object #1, for example in a consecutive series, which in actuality pertained to an object also in the series but one which he had not yet seen. The first instance of this took place in terms of the reading of the iron knuckles. I knew from the museum information that the knuckles were in fact from the southern United States, but Bowes in his reading begins talking about an entirely different context.

> I keep seeing violence with this, and the feeling I had was a relationship with an Italian person...something either to do with Germany or with Italy. The feeling I had was I kept seeing an association with either...maybe they were German people, but I felt they were violent...I would say it was associated with something political, and I see groups of men and felt these groups of men were someone who was very cruel like Gestapo or people who were hard.

Unknown to Bowes at the time was the fact that on this day, several artifacts later, he would be holding the only Nazi artifact used over the

entire course of our research together. I will point out "contamination"
as it occurs in subsequent readings. Bowes felt it occurred because the
objects were kept in a single large box for transport and storage, and
that this physical proximity was resulting in the contamination of
his psychic impressions of individual objects.

The next item he touched and read was the false teeth from Edinburgh, Scotland. In this reading he correctly identified the origin of
the teeth in Great Britain by the novel impression of hearing them
speak with a British accent. He also accurately described the often
humid and cold climate of the harbor town which produced the teeth.
Bowes stated:

> I kept seeing Boston or like up north somewhere, and this
> again could have come from Europe...I kept seeing a ship
> but I didn't know what it meant...it could have been just at a
> distance...Humidity. Where this was and in association with
> this in some way I kept feeling it was in a cold climate...this
> road went down hill and went down to the river, or down to
> the water, like down to the docks...I felt there was water here
> and I felt it would be very cold at times, or there could be
> whaling, water, boats, or something.

At one point I asked about the racial characteristics of the teeth's
owner and Bowes responded:

> I kept seeing red hair. He could have even been from England
> because I see an accent...He could have been from Canada,
> but I felt almost like an English accent...in Great Britain.

After Bowes mentioned that he was finished with the false teeth, I
removed the teeth and set the pocket watch before him. As the transcripts indicate, he went into great detail about the owner of the
watch. However, since I had so little information about the watch, I
was unable to verify or reject the bulk of his reading of the watch. The
one point of accuracy which could be verified has to do with the time of
the watch's use. The watch dates from the early decades of this
century, the time of President Theodore Roosevelt. In his reading of
the watch Bowes stated:

> I don't know if Teddy Roosevelt, or at that time had any
> association to it but I kept seeing someone very loud in
> political power. Like somebody who was very loud, saying,
> 'Bully for you,' very loud or something.

The next artifact Bowes read was the straight razor. While no verifiable information about the razor was offered, Bowes again, as with
the iron knuckles, began to mention Germany and Hitler. The Nazi
badge was to appear one artifact later.

After the straight razor I presented Bowes with the human hair
necklace. No verifiable information was produced. In fact, Bowes did
not mention gold, such a major point of his blind reading of the boxed
hair necklace, nor did he indicate that it was made of human hair.

Then came the Nazi badge, and Bowes laughed and said, "Oh, this
is the one I been waiting for." Bowes then launched into a reading

involving German soldiers in World War II, most of which was impossible to document due to the scant information supplied by the museum. He did, however, mention the wounding, the necessary prerequisite for the awarding of this badge. "I see some metal shrapnal getting into one of his shoulders...this could have knocked him out...."

Before I replaced the Nazi badge with the next test item, Bowes mentioned that he had felt that I would have something relating to the Nazis from the moment I had entered his house. He said he felt disturbed by the Nazi influence and he was having a difficult time working with the objects I was presenting to him during this session. However, with the very next object presented to him, he produced one of the more detailed and accurate readings of the day. Then again, the impressive accuracy of the following reading may not be due so much to the inaccuracy of his earlier readings as to the fact that the Chattahoochee artifact was one that I could document in great detail. I could not gather the information needed to document many of the other artifacts due to the museum's policy of protecting the privacy of the donors—a policy that was no doubt correct, but one which frustrated me continually in my research. In retrospect, I should have anticipated this problem and found a different source for my test materials.

As already indicated, the next artifact read by Bowes was the fragment of broken handcuffs from the Chattahoochee site. As can be seen by glancing at the photograph of the handcuffs, there is nothing about them that would indicate their origin. To appreciate the high degree of accuracy demonstrated by Bowes in his reading of this artifact, some background information on Chattahoochee will be offered.
chee will be offered.

The Chattahoochee site has had a long and often violent history. Located near the junction where the Chattahoochee and Flint Rivers form the Appalachicola River, it was a militarily important position for over a century, contested for by the French, Spanish, British, Seminoles, and the United States Government. The key factor in deciding the importance of the Chattahoochee site was its strategic position at the junction of a river offering access to the Gulf of Mexico. The Seminole Indians, with black freedmen and runaway slaves, held the garrison during the Seminole Wars. Andrew Jackson liberated the fort and built a garrison for federal soldiers. From 1866 to 1876, the facilities were used as a State Penitentiary, being turned into a mental hospital in 1876.

In the following reading of the artifact, Bowes notes the association of the artifact with Indians. Also, the presence of ships is noted several times. These two relationships, in particular, are not obvious in any way from a casual handling of the handcuff fragment. As Bowes handled the object he said:

> I did see something in association with a ship, water...I kept
> seeing a building burning, or falling down...In another
> association I see something to do with a boat, and I kept

seeing them on this boat...I don't know if there were people like Indians, or there were people like someone who was abused...but I felt as though they had dark hair, but I felt they were abused and abused and moved and treated very badly...I see someone screaming in the background...I don't want to get personal but I see someone raping someone in the backgrond so I would say there were men and women together. I see them in lines...I would say that they are prisoners. They were chained together, held together either on a ship or this was held...or this was bolted to a ship or to some sort of transportation...I would say it was somewhere where it was damp, and it could even have been in south Florida, or they were moving from a damp area to a place where they didn't want to go...I keep seeing a lot of screaming and a lot of...I felt negative...I felt like this could even have been made for slaves, but I didn't feel that way...I just felt very much about a ship, o.k.? They may have been just moved or kept in a ship, but I kept seeing this ship or this boat, and this could pertain to Key West or a place that associated with water, islands, but I felt there was a prison...
I would say they kept women and men together for a period of time and I felt it didn't work out.

During the time that Chattahoochee was a mental hospital, men and women were kept on the grounds, as Bowes alluded to in several places in his reading. Further, the Seminole Wars were a result of the attempt of the Federal Government to move the Seminole from Florida. Bowes noted, with respect to the Indians, that they were "...abused and abused and moved and treated very badly..." and "...they were moving from a damp area to a place where they didn't want to go...." The site is in Florida, though not in southern Florida as Bowes suggested.

The last two objects presented to Bowes in this session were the pelican key and the sewing bird. A comparison of the scant museum information on his pieces with Bowes' lengthy reading on each item showed no correspondence.

The results of Part II of the Second double-blind Experiment produced some interesting results. The phenomenon we called "contamination" began to appear during this experiment. Bowes also demonstrated an ability to accurately locate an artifact by noting the language he hears as he touches the item. The identification of the false teeth from Edinburgh being the case in point. Bowes' reading of the Chattahoochee manacles was also impressive in its specific accuracy.

THIRD EXPERIMENT

I decided to try one more experiment involving the reading of a number of artifacts from widely scattered locales in time and space. In order to use more exotic items, materials that the museum would not allow to be removed on loan, we moved the third experiment to the museum premises. Wallace acquired from the storage room of the museum the following artifacts: (1) a willow basket from the Mono tribe of east-central California; (2) an embroidered hat from the Ibo tribe of Nigeria; (3) a painted prayer wand of Hopi origin; (4) a Japanese dried-fish grater; (5) a Seminole woman's hair board; (6) a slate *ulu*, or Eskimo woman's knife; (7) a silver Navaho bridle; (8) an adze handle made by the Nootka Indians of British Columbia; (9) a silver stirrup from Brazil dating to the 19th century; and (10) a food basket from the Bontoc tribe of the Phillippines.

These artifacts were presented to Bowes one at a time while he sat in a museum seminar room with his wife. I was not in the room during the reading, nor was Wallace. In this experiment I gave Mrs. Bowes a list of questions that I wished her to ask her husband as he read the artifacts. A tape recorder was operating throughout the readings. As Bowes would finish with one artifact, his wife would bring it into the hall, where Wallace would then hand her the next artifact which he selected at random from a shelf where the test items were placed. In this fashion the reading of the ten new objects was completed and tape recorded without the direct presence of the investigators.

The test items in the third experiment were too large to be wrapped so we simply dispensed with that phase of the experiment. The items selected, however, were esoteric in the extreme. It would take a highly trained and experienced expert to differentiate a piece of primitive basketry as being Bontoc or Mono in origin. Nevertheless, it would be a legitimate criticism of this particular experiment to note that since the object was visible to Bowes and since there did exist identifying information on the object, then Bowes' accuracy could be feasibly accounted for by other than appeals to paranormal methods. However, the most rigorous critic must admit that the probability of Bowes being able to make instant and accurate identification of these rare and alien artifacts is very low.

The first item brought to Bowes was the silver bridle made by Navaho Indians of the American southwest in the late 1800s. The Navaho have had a long and complex historical and cultural involvement, not only with the older Pueblo peoples of New Mexico and Arizona, but also with Mexican and Spanish cultures of the area. As the transcripts show he wanders quite a bit in his attempt to identify this artifact. However, the following excerpts indicate at least an approximate accuracy on various points. The Spanish association is noted at several points, and though suggesting various origins from India to Egypt, he does note the possibility of American Indian origin. The arid environment of the Navaho is indicated also. His accuracy continues when, in noting the predominantly desert environment, he mentions fertility near the mountains. The Navaho took advantage of this fact by establishing their farms near mountains. Bowes also correctly suggests that the composition of this artifact included material from "another country." The silver was from

Mexico. The pastoralism and animal husbandry of the Navaho is indicated. The settlement patterns of the Navaho, in which a kin group rotates among a number of dwelling sites, appears in one reference in the reading. A comment about enemies produces an allusion to people with "large knives" carried in sheaths. The "Long Knives" were, of course, the United States Army. The meat and grain diet of the Navaho is described. The relevant excerpts from the reading of the bridle include the following:

> The first thing I picked up with this is something to do with a horse. I kept seeing someone who is Spanish or someone who is in a uniform. I don't know if this was a person who rode this horse or related to someone in the west, but I keep seeing a very dusty place...I don't know if it would be Indian, but I kept feeling this was very, very old. I would say that it could even be from India, but I feel the people may not be very civilized. I don't feel like this was made by a machine... more like something that was beaten, hammered or beat into shape...I would say either parts of this or the whole things originated in another country, and I don't feel so much with the United States...I don't know if they were ranchers, but I would feel that they did move or they migrated. I see them having one home base or one area which I would say relate to a confidence, in other words a place where they stopped or stayed. I saw a line of horses; or a line of people moving. I did feel they needed to rest their animals or whatever. I don't know if this was in the desert, but I kept seeing something to do with people who were very hard people. I don't know if this was Mexico but I kept seeing something in relationship to some people who...I see a lot of sand blowing. I see open land...I seen something pertaining to the mountains and I would say it was much more fertile around the mountains...I would say it was very extreme. It was hot during the day and cold during the night...I would say in relationship to conflicts...I see large knives or something that they would hold in harnesses or in sheaths besides them...I see small groups because I don't feel large groups could be sustained in a small area. Now they may get together as large groups every so often, but basically I kept feeling as though they were in smaller groups. I see large areas of land and then mountains in between. I keep seeing these people with very yellow teeth, like their teeth were worn from chewing dry...this could be dry meat like eating jerky or like chewing grain of some sort...I would say they were dark skinned people. I do see a moustache and black hair...I keep seeing like Mexico or Spaniards, or Mexican people...

The reading of the next object, the Hopi prayer wand, produced the contamination effect again, plus indication that Bowes was aware that he was having a difficulty in his reading of this artifact. The Hopi are a Pueblo Indian tribe of the Southwestern United States. The culture that began to intrude on Bowes' reading of the Hopi artifact was that of the Nootka Indians of British Columbia. It is important to note that at no other time in the years in which I worked with Bowes did I present him with an artifact from the Northwest Coast. In this experiment a Northwest Coast artifact, the adze handle, would be presented to Bowes as Number six in a series of ten artifacts. At the time Bowes began to report images specifically relating to Northwest Coast culture, he was dealing with only the second item in the series.

Bowes notes as he reads the artifact that he is having difficulty separating two powerful impressions; one of a western Indian group living in a hot and dry environment, and one a northern Indian group living in a watery environment characterized by coolness and humidity. This is a fair description of the Hopi domain in the first instance, and the Nootka location in the second. Bowes' confusion is seen in the following excerpts from the reading.

> I don't know if these were Indians from the west, but I still felt they originated in a colder area that associated with fishing or trapping. They may have been in the north and then later moved south...I was confused about two environments, one hot and one cold...also torn between north and south.

The dominant cultural impression that emerged in this reading of the Hopi artifact is of a people dwelling in a northerly climatic zone, depending on fishing and the water, and living in wooden buildings. This is the Nootka Indians, represented by artifact number six in this series. Further, Bowes correctly indicates that these people possessed "shields," "helmets," and "head gear." The Indians of the Northwest Coast were among the few native American peoples who employed a type of armor. Also uncharacteristically for American Indians, they wore basketry hats much of the time. Significant passages from the reading included:

> The feeling I had with this was a feeling with something to do with Indians. I don't know if these are Indians of the north. The feeling I had was something associated with Indians who did fishing or fished, or was around water...I would say they were Indians. I did feel as though they wore heavy clothing...I see them practicing with sticks...like they were practicing with shields and sticks, and they could have even worn something like a helmet or a head gear, but I do feel as though they may have lived in wooden buildings, or made of logs...I would say they were in the hundreds. I do feel as though they were more permanent or permanent people...I would say they ate fish or raccoons or animals that pertain to something associated with water...I would say it was very cold and possibly humid.

Bowes' awareness of his mistake with this artifact was seen in another context. After all ten artifacts had been read, I entered the room with Wallace, and together with Bowes and his wife, we listened to the tape of the readings. As the section of the tape covering the reading of the Hopi prayer wand was playing and the description became more and more like a Northwest Coast cultural description, I mentioned aloud to Wallace that this description sounded more like it related to another one of the artifacts in the series. Bowes immediately indicated the Northwest Coast artifact by saying, "You mean that thing with the bird's head on it."

The third artifact presented to Bowes was the small basket from the Bontoc of the Phillippines. The Bontoc are wet-rice farmers of the jungle mountains of Luzon. They live in villages with populations sometimes reaching over the five hundred mark. The Bontoc buried their dead in two ways. Important people were buried in pine coffins, while the less important and the unmarried were interred in graves which were walled on the sides, roofed with slabs of rock, and lastly covered with earth. Bowes, as will be seen makes several references to such structures. It is interesting that Bowes makes a fleeting reference to ritual structures made of concrete, though he quickly changes his mind. In one reference to the Kalinga, a Bontoc group, the anthropologist Edward Dozier[1] writes, "At present, some Kalinga bury their dead in concrete tombs; this is especially characteristic of the well-to-do in the Lubuagan region." Bowes also correctly alludes to weaving among the people who made the basket artifact. Further, Bowes is accurate in his indication of the presence of outrigger canoes; and though I could find no reference to Bontoc religion dealing with volcanoes as ritual foci, it is true that there are several active volcanoes in the Bontoc environment. The Bontoc, however, were headhunters, and this activity was central in their religious orientation. When Mrs. Bowes asked her husband about religion he responded, "I would say that they believed in violence....". In his reading of the Bontoc basket Bowes stated:

> I don't know if this was in an area of country where there was a lot of grass or an area of it being wet...I see water or areas of grass land...I would say that there were several hundred or several thousands. There was large groups of people. I don't know if there was a pyramid or a...something made of concrete...I wouldn't say concrete, but I would say stone ...I see stone structures. I felt very strong about something being underground...buried underground like a cave or pyramid or caravan, or buildings...could even be buildings in the wall, but I kept seeing stone or caves. I would say they are more religious quarters. I keep seeing stairways going down into a cavern or into a cave...jungle area, like Africa or South America...a jungle place...I would say they had long hair...I thought it was hot or warm...I felt something to do with material, and I felt it could have been woven...I do see a boat, and I felt this boat was something with a pontoon, like

pontoons on it. I didn't see it as a very large boat...
pontoons, and a sail. In other words, like a canoe...like a
large canoe with a little canoe on the side, and maybe a sail...
I would say they believed in violence, or believed in fire. I saw
them dancing on fire...volcanoes...religious worship of fire.
Something that's very loud. They may be even afraid of
lightening, but I kept seeing something of fire or movement. That is all I get.

The fourth item read by Bowes in this session was the *ulu*, or
Eskimo "woman's knife." This reading had a certain amount of carry-
over from the previous reading. The house he described ("...like a
grass hut...a ladder or something going up inside..."), of course, was
not accurate for the Eskimo, but it was specifically correct for the
elevated thatched houses of the Bontoc which were reached by
ladders. Also, not Eskimo, but very Bontoc, were Bowes' allusions to
attackers and the preventative measures of setting up bamboo
warning devices ("...little bells...made of bamboo...hanging in the
woods and when these people came to attack them, or invade them, it
was like an alarm and I felt these things rattled.") When asked about
the clothing of the makers of the *ulu*, Bowes accurately described the
clothing of the Bontoc when he said:

I would say that they originally didn't have very much on,
but as time went on I see them wearing clothes, or in other
words, they could be something that associated with
clothing like robes or long clothing. At one time I felt as
though the leaders of the people could have worn this. I
felt normally the people just wore leather...a very small
piece of it.

The accuracy in his reading of the *ulu* is keyed by Bowes' references
to seals, fat scraping, and the role of women in association with this
artifact, which is specifically a woman's tool. He also noted the
association of water and "wet ground" several times, though he
felt it may relate to Florida. However, the Florida identification disappeared as soon as he mentioned the presence of seals. The reading
included the following sections:

A wet place. I keep seeing a relationship to water and wet
ground. I do feel as though in association with this...I see
this used for scraping...like scraping fat off of skin. I saw a
lot of fat...I felt that it came from Florida, or a place that
was very wet...I would say they were Indians, or people
like early...I would say they were Indians, but they may
have settled an area of ground...I kept seeing very wet
country...I would say they did move by water...I would
say they scraped or separated fat from the leather or it was
involved in scraping something...I would say they ate
oysters or shellfish or something involving something
around the water. I did see them having a war-club, or some

sort of club. I felt it had a spike on it or a rock, or something pointed. They could have beat...like hit something like a seal or otter with it.

MRS. BOWES: Do you see anything about who was using this?

BOWES: I see a woman...I would feel it was a man, but I keep seeing a woman leaning over and pulling on something, and scraping something with this...I see them quite primitive, the actual people who made this. I would say a woman made this or someone made this, and I see them sitting with their legs crossed and I see them carving something. This could have been an old man or woman...I keep seeing the west. This could have been west of Florida, or west of the country...I would say before white settlers came in.

The next artifact brought to Bowes was the Seminole woman's hair board. This object was used as an interior structure for various complex hairdos. Bowes' reading was scant on this item, but he did make several valid points in his reference to the artifact being the "interior to something" associated with women wearing long dresses. The hurricane reference would also be correct for the Seminole experience.

...the first thing I picked up was that it was like the brim of a hat, but I didn't feel it was. The second feeling I had was that it was a part of a wagon, or part of an interior to something...I keep seeing an association to women...I would say she wore a very long dress down to her ankles, or clothes that were very long...I keep seeing a hurricane or a storm.

The sixth artifact was the adze handle from the Nootka Indians inhabiting the coast of British Columbia. This artifact was not diagnostically Northwest Coast in nature which means that Bowes' correct identification of climate, environment, subsistence, etc. was very striking. He even indicated the artifact's function. Further, Bowes pointed out the prosperity of the Northwest Coast Indians, a prosperity not experienced by the majority of other native American cultures.

I did see someone holding it and pushing it back and forth ...I did feel this was from the north, and I feel as though it would associate with people who...with water. I see mountains or water, like swift running water. I would say this bird, or whatever it is, is on the front for decoration but I keep seeing it in association...like with a hawk, or with a bird that catches fish...I don't know if they ever lived in a ship, but I kept seeing a boat...I would say in the north...I would say it was cold and foggy at times...I would say that there's lots of prosperity.

The seventh artifact in the series was the Ibo hat from Africa. Bowes demonstrated no accuracy with this piece. This was to be typical of all African artifacts or pictures of artifacts Bowes worked with during our research project. He produced accurate readings on materials from cultures in all parts of the world, except Africa. What does occur in this reading is another contamination effect related to the Japanese. The only Japanese artifact Bowes ever worked with was the tenth artifact in this series, but references to Japanese culture begin to show up on artifact number seven, the Ibo hat, three artifacts and a half hour away from his actual physical contact with the Japanese item. Since we were selecting the artifacts from the museum at random and we were not in the room during the actual readings, Bowes' "correct incorrect" response, or contamination responses, are puzzling to account for by any design error in the experiment itself.

> I do see a very small man and I feel he is bowing to some-one else. I don't know if they are sitting on the ground, or they are all sitting or squatting or cross-legged, whether they're Japanese or from another country. I felt generally that they were all talking. Maybe discussing something. This could be testing tea or testing liquor...they could be oriental...I keep seeing him bowing or holding his hands in front of him like he's praying or bowing...I don't know if they are vegetarians but I see them either working with... chop-sticks, or picking things up with a little spoon...it could have pertained to an island...I would say there were a great number of people.

The eighth artifact placed before Bowes was the Mono Indian basket. The Mono who made this artifact are located in east central California. The Mono, like the Nootka, sometimes wore basketry hats, as Bowes noted. They also used tumplines in which baskets were attached to bands that crossed the carrier's head and/or chest for easier carrying. This was suggested at one point in the reading. Pinon (pine) nuts were dietary staples. The environment of the Mono in-cluded mountainous areas, as well as the dry western portions of the Great Basin, which the Mono moved through as they sought the seasonally available edible plants and animals. Suggestions of Japanese origins appear again in this reading, although Bowes also indicated that the makers of the artifact may be Indians. Of particular interest was Bowes' inference that the artifact's manufacturers may have used hallucinogenic drugs. The anthropological record for the Indians in this area contains accounts of the hallucinogen, *Datura inoxia*. Peter T. Furst[2], when writing about the use of drugs among native American Indian cultures, states:

> California and Southwestern tribes...employed *Datura inoxia* in initiation rites. The Yuma took this drug to gain occult powers during these rituals, and the Yokuts valued it in a spring ceremony to insure good health and long life to adoles-cent initiates. The Luiseno gave it to youths who danced, screamed wildly 'like animals' and finally fell into a stupor to find their adult life.

The Yokut Indians, mentioned by Furst, are the western neighbors of the Mono, and it is known that the Mono used the drug in a ritual context also. What is most important is that of all the cultures with which Bowes worked during the first phases of this research, the Mono were the only ones who possessed a cultural affiliation which stressed the ritual use of psychoactive drugs, and it was in association with the Mono that Bowes offered the only reference to the use of such drugs appearing in the preliminary series of experiments.

> The feeling I had was that they had something that went on their head, and they may have had a basket or...not a basket but like a big hat, maybe a hat that was made of similar things to this (artifact). I don't know if this is oriental people or Japanese or Indian...I would say that there is an association with something that they are breaking open with their teeth like peanuts. I don't feel that's the only thing they eat, of course...I would say these people stayed in one place that they may have been seasonal, in other words if they were seasonal...that's very strange. I keep seeing something around the woman's chest. I don't know if it was like a basket or like it was a woven bra, but the feeling I had was like it was something she carried on her back, and I felt like she...like the woman may have carried up and down mountains there. I see grasses, but I didn't pick up too much on that...I would say that they had black hair. I see a lot of dust ...I see a lot of people swaying back and forth...I see a man smoking marijuana or poppy or something that would make him like...having hallucinogenic drugs, or like smoking something that would make him sick. I wouldn't say so sick physically but mentally...I would say he hallucinated or had mental problems, like mental visions.

The ninth artifact in the series was the silver stirrup from Brazil. The makers were of Spanish descent which Bowes correctly indicated. He also alluded to the political and social climate of the country at the time in which a powerful elite held power over a majority of lower class citizens.

> I would feel as though this is a shoe. I would say that it associated with armor or something that was either on a horse, or something that was on a person's foot, or their toe ...I would say they either had dark skin...I don't know if they traveled but I kept seeing a horse, horses. I would say they lived in stone buildings...Could even be a castle, but I would say more like a stone building. Again I kept seeing something with France or Spain, I didn't know what it meant...I would say there was many different people but this was more of a select few...in other words, these people were in royalty or in a position or like in the army or something like that...I would say there was the very rich or the people who were ahead of other people, and then I didn't feel there was any...I kept seeing India or like something to do with

very, very poor people, masses of them. I felt like there was
one rich, or one superior person.

The tenth artifact in this experiment was the Japanese dried-fish
grater. There was nothing on the object to indicate Asiatic origins,
and as the photograph shows, the artifact looks very much like a
simple carpenter's plane with a small attached box. As the complete
transcript indicates, Bowes said very little that directly related to the
function of the artifact or its place of origin, except noting at one
point, "I keep seeing somebody interested in studying the Japanese..."

Conclusion

This experiment concluded the series of three preliminary experiments I had planned as the first part of my psychic archeology project.
I learned a number of things during this time, perhaps the most important thing being that the medium—Albert Bowes—could, with
varying degrees of success and in ways that I could never predict,
relay accurate information in double-blind situations about human
artifacts from many different times and cultural settings. The preliminary experiments also introduced to both of us the phenomenon
we called "contamination." In succeeding experiments, we attempted
to overcome this problem by never mixing artifacts of diverse origin
in the same sample.

Contamination and Time Displacement

As I continued my background reading in general parapsychology
I encountered references to a phenomenon in parapsychological experimentation which seemed of a kind to the contamination effect discovered while working with archeological materials. When it occurred
in the preliminary experiments, it always involved Bowes' impressions
of an object he would be handling in the particular session but one to
which he had not yet been exposed. Only once, did a kind of carry-
over contamination occur and that was the instance in which after
reading the Bontoc basket, he continued to relate accurate Bontoc
information as he read the next artifact, the Eskimo "woman's knife."

A similar occurrence in parapsychological testing was noted by the
English parapsychologist Whately Carington, of Cambridge University. Carington asked several hundred experimental subjects to draw
their impressions of targets that Carington placed on his desk each
day. For example, Carington, on each day of a ten-day experimental
run, would open a dictionary at random and choose the first noun on
the page that could be easily drawn. Carington would render the
image himself and place his drawing on his desk before leaving for
the night, locking the doors behind him. His subjects were instructed
to attempt to "tune in" on Carington's drawing and send their
drawings of the target the next day. Carington obtained results in
eleven such studies which exceeded chance expectations, but he also

noticed something else. Sometimes he would receive a correct drawing of a Monday target, for example, on the several days following. It was as if somehow the receivers had unconsciously anticipated the target or delayed picking it up. Carington called this effect "time displacement."[3]

At about the same time, Dr. G.H. Soal, an acquaintance of Carington, had been performing card-guessing experiments with Basil Shackleton, a noted psychic. On 800 trials, Shackleton had performed no better than chance. Carington persuaded Soal to go over his data with the notion of "time displacement" in mind. Soal found that his subject, Shackleton, could be scored with impressive accuracy if each of his calls were paired, not with the card the transmitter was actually sending, but with the card the transmitter was to send next, a card the transmitter had not yet seen. Thelma Moss[4] comments:

> This 'displacement effect' so intrigued Soal that he asked Shackleton to tackle another, longer series of trials. Shackleton agreed, and in 1941, a total of 3,789 trials were completed. Shackleton scored only at chance with the usual direct pairing, but if each of Shackleton's calls was paired with the card which was to come next, his score was 1,101 hits. The odds against this happening by chance are an astronomical 10^{-35} to 1.

When, after the preliminary experiments, Bowes and I discussed the nature of the contamination effect and time displacement, Bowes commented at length as to the nature of the effect as he experienced it. For some unknown reason, according to Bowes, certain artifacts have a stronger "vibration;" that is, they impinge psychically on him more so than do other artifacts. Bowes said that he did not feel that he was moving forward and backward in time, but rather he was reacting to more powerful influences at the expense of less powerful influences as he was confronted with a collection of diverse artifacts. He could not explain why one cultural context would contaminate another; why, for example, in the last experiment, the Japanese context would appear at the expense of the Ibo context.

It is my opinion that the nature of the contamination is keyed not to the artifacts but to certain personality traits in the psychic. For example, the non-existence of Africa in all of Bowes' responses throughout the project and the incursion of the Japanese and Nazi Germany impressions noted in the second and third experiments may simply indicate a personal sensitivity or aversion on the part of the psychic, rather than a simple psychic anticipation, as in Carington's "time displacement" demonstration. "Time displacement" and "contamination" are certainly similar but since cultural materials can elicit emotional responses, and since the figures on a deck of cards do not, this experiment shows us something novel about the problem of attempting to study in a scientific manner, a phenomenon which can easily violate the time frames assumed to be valid and unchanging in the world of science.

The contamination effect is also instructive with respect to developing methods to more successfully use the abilities of psychics in archeological research. Obviously, random collections of artifacts from many different times and places are poor materials to employ, due to contamination, when attempting to obtain the best kinds of information from psychic colleagues. I found that contamination did not occur in later experiments as long as I only presented to Bowes artifacts from a single context. In other experiments I found that Bowes' accuracy rose even higher if, in addition to being relieved of the problem of dealing with artifacts of multiple origins, he was also informed that the materials he would be working with were of one historical type, or from a single cultural environment.

The Problem of Language

The preliminary experiments produced a number of findings which would help me to work effectively with Mr. Bowes and other psychic subjects. The awareness of contamination was one such discovery. Another had to do with the nature of Bowes' language. Ironically, he had warned me about the problem of language in our very first meeting, and I had not paid attention to his warning. As noted in Chapter I, Bowes had said:

> You should not get thrown by my vocabulary. You have a much wider vocabulary than I do, but mine is all I have, and that means that when I see something and tell you what I see, I will be telling you only in the words I have to tell you.

As I transcribed hour after hour of taped interviews and experiments with Bowes, I came to notice several features of his manner of communication during his readings which would help me more clearly understand the nature of his subsequent readings. For example, one such linguistic trait of Mr. Bowes occurs when, for example, he says "I don't know if this is Oriental...." The phrase usually hangs unfinished. My problem was that the subject of Bowes' "lack of knowing" often was correct, though Bowes seemed to be stating his uncertainty as he offered the correct response. One day during an experiment Bowes said, "I don't know if this is Oriental, but that's the way I feel." Suddenly it made sense. As a quick perusal of the experimental transcripts indicate, Bowes uses many variations of the verb "to feel," as in "My feeling with this is...," or "I felt that this was..." or "My strongest feeling is...", etc. To Bowes, there is a great difference between "knowing" and "feeling" in his psychic performance. "Knowing" is intellectual, and "feeling" is psychic, in Bowes' opinion. When reading the phrase, "I don't know if this is from a cold climate...," it is a psychic affirmation from Bowes' standpoint that the object in question is from a cold place no matter how negative it may look linguistically.

Another difficulty in the realm of language involved the use of metaphor and simile. This was especially frustrating at the outset with respect to Bowes' indication of the place of origin of an artifact. As the transcripts show, he would often indicate the place of origin as being "...like New York or Oregon or Colorado." If the object in question was from Wales, I naturally had to conclude that Bowes had missed in his bid to locate the artifact. But it gradually dawned on me that Bowes was not attempting to identify the place as much as he was attempting to indicate something they all had in common with the target object point of origin; in the case of the example just given, the commonality to Bowes was "cool, humid mountains" and in this he was correct.

This led to another problem—Bowes' relative lack of knowledge of world and national geography. His "New York" and "Oregon," for example, have "cool humid mountains," but each state also possesses a variety of other environments also. His meaning for "South America," for example, is "southerly jungle environment." "South America" also includes Mexico and Central America. Bowes also seemed unaware of the fact that in "South America" one could find all the environmental habitats found in North America. "South America" means "jungle." I had to conclude very early that I should not pay too much attention to Bowes' indications of national origin or his geographical references, although on occasion he was correct on these points. Bowes' continuing accuracy was in his ability to describe basic climatic and environmental features.

Another tantalizing aspect of his run-on simile trait was that often one of the several guesses was correct. For example, in dealing with an American Indian artifact he might say, "These people were like Orientals or Indians, or like people from Egypt." One of the three indications would be correct; and further, the "Orientals," "Indians," and "Egyptians" share certain gross physical traits in common. Bowes is saying in this kind of phrase that he is not sure of the ethnic or geographical origins of the artifact in question, but he is sure that the people in question had black hair and a swarthy complexion.

The language problem was sometimes very straight forward. For example, it was not until late into the preliminary experiment that I noticed that Bowes felt that "artifact," meant "Indian made." Bowes assumed that the items he was dealing with were made by Indians, because that is what he heard me telling him. Especially, in the first experiment, the reader can see Bowes often relaying correct information, though attempting to relate his impressions to Indians. Note his confusion with the combs from Boston, as still believing that the item is Indian made, he describes houses with porches, fireplaces, rugs on the floor, and sewage systems. After I noticed the problem and mentioned to Bowes that by "artifact," I meant any object of human manufacture, the tortured inferences to Indians stopped. This incident brought two points home to me: first, the specialist cannot assume that his language is understood by the non-specialist, and second, it was apparent from this episode that the experimenter has quite a responsibility in the production of the results of experiments in psychic archeology. Bowes had attempted to give me what I wanted, although this produced some strange "Indian" descriptions until the problem of "artifact" was straightened out.

Direction Finding

The problem of direction-finding was also dealt with in a unique and puzzling way by Bowes. Fortunately in this case, he was aware of how he did it, and he made it clear to me at one point early in the first experiments. An indication of his method appears in the reading of the Eskimo "woman's knife" in the third experiment just reported on. When asked about the location of the makers of the artifact, Bowes responds by saying, "I don't know if this was the west coast, but I kept seeing the west...This could have been west of Florida or west of the country." When Bowes is asked about compass directions, he receives impressions of varying degrees of clarity. With the Eskimo artifact, he only could indicate that it originated north and west of where he was sitting, but he could not focus more sharply. When Bowes is having some difficulty with direction, when it is least clear, "west," for example, means to him either west of a north-south line running down the west coast of Florida (his home), or west of a north-south line, paralleling the west coast of the United States. As the direction becomes more clear to him, he will next locate the target, still using "west" as an example, either between the west coast of Florida and the west coast of the United States, or west of the United States. The next phase in location is the association of environmental features to his impression of direction, which allows him to indicate his final appraisal of a westerly location. For example, in the Folsom experiment (Colorado site) described in Chapter III, Bowes psychic research method can be clearly seen as he correctly notes the western origins of the test materials and finally the precise geographic location by keying it to specific geographical and environmental features such as the presence of mountains, plains, cold winters, fast or slow growing trees, etc. Bowes is fond of indicating location and climate by reference to the density of wood, and the growth rate of trees in the area. "Light wood" and "fast growing trees" mean a relatively warm climate, while "dense wood" and "slow growing trees" indicate a relatively cold climate.

Bowes often used the analogy of a picture developing to explain the feeling he experiences as he receives his impressions from objects, people, and places. An experimenter working with Bowes would have to be sensitive to this in order to allow him to wander psychically as he seeks to develop his picture. The results are often worth the wait.

The Researcher's Role

An awakening to the fact that I was more than just a bystander, passively tape recording Bowes as he handled artifacts and talked about the impressions he received as he did so, alerted me to the kinds of effects I was having on Bowes in other areas of our work together. In my years of field work among the Comanche Indians of southwestern Oklahoma, I had developed a dead-pan approach to interviewing which stood me well in working with Bowes. As a field anthropologist, I had consciously worked at not leading an informant by word or by gesture—a passive and relatively expressionless technique was the result. Bowes found this approach to be most helpful as he both attempted to relate psychically to the artifacts and at the same time listen and respond to my questions. Bowes complained on several occasions when we were working with others present about how their mannerisms distracted him. For example, one colleague had the habit of nodding his head as Bowes was speaking. The individual was signaling continued interest, but Bowes found the motion to be irritating. As all this became clear to me, I attempted when working with Bowes and other mediums to sit in a relaxed posture and to limit bodily movements as much as possible—no head bobbing, no finger tapping, no fidgiting. Further, I attempted to deliver my questions to Bowes in a monotone voice, because unusual vocal inflections or characteristics also proved annoying to Bowes as he attempted to do psychometry with the test materials. In short, I had to be as inconspicuous as possible for maximum effectiveness.

There is also another point to make while on the subject of correct behavior for the experimenter. Individuals have a rhythm and a flow to their speech and to their thoughts. The pattern is unique and is, in a sense, part of the perceived personality of each person. By hearing Bowes read objects, and then listening to the tape of the readings, I quickly came to get a feel for Bowes' linguistic and conceptual rhythm. As part of my attempt to become as invisible as possible while working with Bowes, I tried to insert my questions, ask for clarification, or change topics only as I perceived in the movement of Bowes' voice and thoughts "permission" to do so. The effect of this conscious effort on my part was positively commented upon by Bowes, and by various parapsychologists who have read copies of my interviews and experiments with Bowes.

In noting the positive and negative effects of language, body and speech attitudes, and interviewing technique, I am addressing the larger question of the most effective environment for this type of research. That decision must always be left to the psychic colleague. Whatever the mechanism is that allows an Albert Bowes to do what he demonstrably can do, is extremely sensitive to surrounding variables. Such features as room color, lighting, arrangement of furniture, odor, outside noises, the physical deployment of the experimenter, the presence of others in the test rooms, and the attitude or mental state of the psychic prior to the experiment all have a marked effect on the results of the experiment. The rule-of-thumb is simple: for best results, the subject must be as relaxed and at ease as possible. This relates not only to the physical environment, but also to the psychological environment. There must be trust, understanding, and rapport among all present. Since each psychic defines the requirements for that state differently, it is obviously not intelligent procedure for an investigator to insist that a psychic subject enter a sterile laboratory setting and then complain when the desired results are not forthcoming.

It is my distinct impression, after working with a number of psychics over the years, that an experimenter must develop a relationship with the psychic that is more than merely professional. The working relationship must be that of friends. In some way which is difficult to pinpoint, Bowes and I truly worked together. He commented on this point several times during our research. My job was to study the situation until I could provide Bowes with the best possible environment for the task I was continually asking him to perform. It is not the case that one simply observes a psychic perform through his or her special ability. The success of the psychic is complex and interconnected with the entire environment in which the psychic operates. Success or failure in a card guessing experiment may rest on the traffic flow in the street two stories below the room where the experiment is taking place, or on the presence in the vicinity of someone who is vehemently opposed to, or just as strongly supportive of, parapsychological experimentation.

One last factor to list is the continuing need for reward, positive feedback, and reinforcement. All my subjects were very interested in the results of the various experiments, and found it frustrating when, because of the design of the experiment, I could not immediately inform them about the quality of their performance. When it became possible to share results with them, I found that what was most appreciated was a point-by-point rehashing of the experiment with successes and failures specifically noted. An unusual aspect of this debriefing was the demonstration of the detachment with which my subjects observed their performances. They often seemed to react to the results almost as if someone else had been the producers of the results. I remember, for example, when I told Bowes about his success in identifying the Scottish false teeth by noting the language that was spoken through them, he smiled and with sincere bemusement said, "Isn't that interesting. Isn't it funny how that works."

It should be emphasized that individuals with psychic ability are still individuals, and that the certain shorthand rules for working with Albert Bowes may not be applicable to working with Diane Davis, Margie Niren, or Noreen Renier. They are each unique personalities. I have attempted in the preceding pages to indicate some general areas I found to be crucial in understanding, interpreting, and successfully and effortlessly working with the psychics who cooperated in my research and their products. The points about language, for example, will help to make more clear the previous readings, as well as those still to be presented.

Appraisal of Preliminary Experiments

As the third experiment came to a close, I paused to consider what, if anything, had been accomplished. Did Bowes produce information that would suggest the real utility of psychics in archeology? Could he have tricked me? There were many professionals who felt that all so-called psychic results could be reproduced by talented magicians. In my approach of stressing positive results and underplaying negative results, was I fooling myself?

I had to conclude that Bowes had, in fact, produced anthropological and archeological information of startling clarity. I did not know why certain images, no matter how accurate, would be reported at the expense of other possible images, nor did Bowes understand why he would pick-up certain impressions and not others. I also did not know why he would be correct with one artifact and incorrect with another, nor did he. After much consideration and discussion with colleagues, I also had to conclude that because of the double-blind nature of the experiments and the complexity of the "correct responses," Bowes was not resorting to trickery. I was concerned about this possibility, not because I distrusted Bowes, but because if any of my results could be shown to be producible by other than paranormal means, it would in my mind invalidate or seriously challenge my results. I can understand how a magician is able to bend a key in the fashion of certain stage psychics who claim to do it by occult means, but I could not understand, or collect data to suggest, how a magician could in a double-blind experiment indicate diagnostic specifics of the Early Woodland culture of the native Americans of the Southeastern United States, as Bowes had done. This was altogether a different order of phenomenon than the potential stagecraft of bending keys. As for my emphasis on correct responses selected out of a complex reading, I concluded that it was significant. If, out of the countless millions of possibilities in the cultural record of human kind, Bowes indicates three possibilities and one of them is right, I am impressed. I decided to continue the project.

References

1. Edward P. Dozier, *The Kalinga of Northern Luzon, Philippines* (New York: Holt, Rinehart & Winston, 1967), p. 52.
2. Peter Furst, *Flesh of the Gods: The Ritual Use of Hallucinogens* (New York: Praeger, 1972), pp.46-47.
3. Thelma Moss, *The Probability of the Impossible* (New York: New American Library, 1974), p.213.
4. *Ibid.*, p.214.

III

SITE LOCATION AND CULTURAL RECONSTRUCTION EXPERIMENTS

Since the preliminary experiments convinced me that my subjects could, in fact, produce archeologically significant information beyond the capabilities of existing archeological techniques, I decided to test for two possible uses of this ability. On the one hand I wanted to ascertain if a psychic subject could, when confronted with a collection of artifacts from the same site, locate that site in space and time. Prior to this experiment, I had been using single artifacts from many times and places. Further, I was interested in the extent to which a psychic could offer verifiable information about a cultural system no longer in existence. Could psychics reconstruct a life-way otherwise lost forever because of the lack of sufficient archeological materials or the absence of written records? If they could do this, what would be the nature and quality of their impressions?

Methodology

A necessarily basic feature of this test was that I would present the subject with a collection of artifacts from a single site whose origin was unknown to me. Wallace secured ten artifacts and delivered them to me without any identifying comments. I took them to Albert Bowes on the following day. The artifacts were arrayed on a table and tape recording equipment was positioned. After these initial procedures I left the room, leaving Mrs. Bowes with the following list of questions to ask her husband as he psychometrized the artifact collection displayed before him.

1.) Where is the site?
2.) What does the countryside look like?
3.) What is the nature of the climate?
4.) What kinds of tools and implements do the people have?
5.) What kind of houses do they live in?
6.) What is the nature of their religious beliefs?
7.) What is the nature of their family life?
8.) How can you describe their political situation? Leadership?
9.) How did they get their food?
10.) What did they eat?
11.) Did they move around or stay in one place?
12.) What kinds of people lived around them and did they get along?
13.) Where did the ancestors of these people come from?

The absence of the investigator during the time of reading of the artifacts was to negate a common criticism of such experiments that the investigator is giving various unconscious nonverbal cues to the subject. I felt that though I had not been instructed as to the origin of the collection, a valid criticism could be that my training as an anthropologist would allow me to make certain inferences about the artifacts. These inferences could then be communicated to the subject by means of the cues mentioned above.

With Bowes a second taping method was employed. After the reading of the artifacts at which only Bowes and his wife were present, I entered the room, started a second tape recorder, and played the tape of the first reading while I questioned Bowes further about various responses he had given on the first tape.

Two months later a second subject, Diane Davis, was presented the same artifact collection, with the exception of the musket-ball described below, in the double-blind manner. With Davis, I was present and directly questioned the psychic as the reading was in progress. No second taping method was used at this time. Both subjects were encouraged to draw pictures of things they saw during the readings. Discussions surrounding the drawings often produced additional information regarding the artifacts in question.

The Artifact Collection

The artifacts were selected from an assemblage excavated from an early historic Georgia coastal culture called *Guale* (pronounced: Wally). The only criterion used in selection of the materials by Wallace, in addition to their protohistoric stratigraphic context, was that all of them should be products of human use or manufacture. I believe that the artifacts, which are listed below, conform to these criteria. Further, since the Guale are a little known people described only in unpublished manuscripts, graduate student dissertations, and translations of the accounts of several little known European explorers, this would preclude the criticism that Guale were a widely known and therefore easily identifiable target culture. In addition, the artifacts used in the experiment are non-diagnostic to the degree that celts, beads, pottery fragments, bone awls, and musket balls have worldwide distribution. This means that even an expert could not, simply by looking at the artifact collection, identify its source as a Georgia sea-island site of the sixteenth to seventeenth century.

The test collection is composed of the following items. (1.) *Slate Celt.* The artifact, both in its design and lack of wear, appeared to be of ceremonial rather than functional significance. It was made of slate not available on St. Simon's Island, Georgia, the location of the site. (2.) *Clay Pipe.* This was an expanded-mouth clay pipe fragment. (3.) *Musket Ball.* In the northwest portion of a protohistoric human burial complex at the site, a fully intact dog burial was found. The dog burial was removed, and fine-screening of the otherwise sterile soil in the pit yielded the ball. (4.) *Burial Stone.* To the south of the mound structure, a group of several human burials were encountered. In direct association with the skull of the seventh burial, two stones and three projectile points were arranged in a headdress fashion. The stone used in this experiment was one of the two stones found. (5.) *Shell Beads.* These were small cylindrically shaped beads encountered in direct association with a human burial taken from a protohistoric burial complex. (6.) *Broken Clay Pipe.* This was a fragment of an expanded-mouth clay pipe. (7.) *Greenstone Celt.* A small celt with a pecked, roughened surface encountered in direct association with a bundle burial. (8.) *Ceramic Bird Effigy.* This was a molded-clay representation of a bird's head, apparently broken off from a larger clay artifact. (9.) *Bone Pin.* This artifact was found in direct association with a burial. (10.) *Columella Beads.* Found in association with a burial.

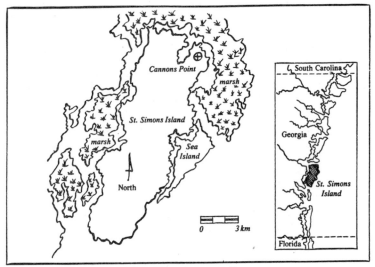

III-1: Map of target site.

The site dates from 1500-1650 A.D. Saint Simon's Island is a part of a chain of ecologically similar barrier islands extending from just south of the Florida-Georgia border along the coastlines of both Georgia and South Carolina. The physical environment of the site is, in the main, flat and wet. A major archeological feature is Taylor Mound, a ceremonial mound with associated burials. A central characteristic of the mound, which will have importance when a consideration of the double-blind psychic reading of the artifacts is presented, is that there were several steps on the southern side of the mound. In association with the mound, eleven burials were discovered. Two other features of the site include two burial complexes in association with mortuary structures, or charnal houses.

From the time of the 1526 visit to the Savannah River area by
Lucas Vásques de Ayllón, a Spanish auditor from Santo Domingo,
until the final collapse of Guale culture during the late 17th century,
these coastal people were exposed to almost continual contact with
European cultures. The historical record of the Guale is broad, but
fragmentary. Ayllón was concerned with the problems of establishing
a colony; the French Huguenots of Rene Laudonniere's 1562 expedition were preoccupied with finding enough to eat; the Jesuit Father
Juan Rogel faced problems of converting a semi-nomadic population;
while the later Franciscans (as well as their political allies, such as
Governor Canzo and Governor Ibarra) were primarily involved with
problems of rebellion and the consequent necessity of understanding
at least something of aboriginal political organization. This brief
listing of the basic historical sources naturally chronicles non-
Indian contact during the occupation of the site. This list will become
more significant when we describe how Bowes and Davis responded
to questions concerning the presence of other people in the vicinity
of the site.

At the time of European contact, the Guale Indians inhabited the
region between St. Mary's River and the Savannah River as well as
the adjacent inland areas. In all, the territory they occupied extended an unknown distance inland between 75 and 100 miles along
the coast. This region is characterized by multiple habitats—the
inland pine forest that borders the tidal flats, the inland valley forests,
the tidal flats themselves, the high-hammock forests of the barrier
islands, and the beach-and-dune habitat of the eastern side of the
island chain.

The Guale were a hunting, collecting, and fishing society practicing
an incipient cultivation of maize and other cultigens (such as peas), a
cultivation that was becoming more extensive at the time of European
contact. This technological organization involved seasonality, terri-
toriality, and resource redistribution. The yearly-round of the Guale
would find them gathered in settled villages during the spring and
summer of the year. During these months, the planting and cultivation was occurring in conjunction with other subsistence activities.
Foremost among these were hunting and fishing. Until the maize
ripened and provided them with grain, the Guale would rely on the
food sources provided by the forests, the marsh, the rivers, and the
sea. Many kinds of fish, such as sea catfish, sheepshead, drum, and
the huge Atlantic sturgeon were taken, as well as small mammals such
as raccoon and opossum. The white-tailed deer was the primary forest
staple.

In the fall of the year, the Guale entered upon a somewhat more
comfortable time. The maize was harvested and the surplus was
placed in the village granaries. After redistribution ceremonies and
religious observances, the Guale became dispersed in what can be
called "central-based nomadism." Small groups of Guale would, in the
late fall and winter, move into base camps, repair them, and remain

only as long as there were nearby resources of fish and game. When the resources waned, they would move to another base camp. As the winter came to an end, the Guale would once again gather in their agricultural villages.

As is typical among Indians of the Southeastern United States, the Guale were very female oriented. When a couple married, they established their residence in the vicinity of the wife's mother. Descent and inheritance were also reckoned through the woman's line. The position of territorial chieftain, or *mico mayor,* was transmitted along matrilineal kinship lines from the chieftain to his sister's son. This is all to say that women were not considered to be the lowly and inferior sex. Their position in Guale society was very powerful.

The religion of the Guale centered around the chief gods who lived at the antipodes—Mateczunga in the north, Quexuga in the south. The Guale's beliefs regarding origin and fate, as well as their symbolization in ritual activities, were inextricably linked with the directional orientation of the gods. Souls had their origin in the cold regions of the north where Mateczunga rules, passed their time on earth, and then departed. Prestigious groups (and young infants) went directly to Quexuga. After an appropriate eulogy was delivered by priests, the body would be interred in a ceremonial mound and never disturbed.

For other groups, however, less honorific in life, a markedly different ritual was observed. These individuals were placed in a mortuary structure, or charnal house, attended by shamans who provided them with food, while their souls existed in a temporary state in the region of Mateczunga until their expiation was fulfilled. At that time, they were removed from the mortuary charnal house and reburied, with kin attending.

This brief outline of Guale culture is of course needed to evaluate the following psychic reading of the Guale artifacts.

Experimental Results

Environment

In the following excerpts from Bowes' reading of the artifacts, the sea-island environment of the Guale site is described.

> I kept seeing low ground, almost like it was water or wet ground.
> I would feel as though it may have been humid or hot in one area...I kept seeing streams and I kept seeing, like low land, but I kept seeing these streams, like with rocks in them, so it could have been like in Georgia or north of Georgia, but I do see a relationship with the people in that area....
> First I felt as though I seen turtles or something near the water...I kept feeling that when they moved inland that there could have been a lot of bugs and mosquitoes.... In other words, I didn't feel it was desirable inland.*

* Inland was undesirable due to the lack of extensive faunal resources. Larson (1969) has referred to the area as the "great green desert."

I would feel as though this could have been in Florida or that there could have been connections with the water.

These people traveled by water.

Something like a flounder or a stingray.

I see them...running back away from the coast-line or away from the water, and this could have been an inland lake or it could have been something quite large.

I see mud flats.

I kept seeing the ocean.

The following are several passages concerning environment and location from Davis' reading of the artifact collection.

I pick this up: I say shells or something that would have to do with water...Maybe they ate more food from water, and I get 'sea'...the sea, sea creatures.

So I feel there was more of a tendency to get the protein you need, you would get from the fish, or some sort of weed or some sort of green thing that would look to me like some sort of sea weed or grass....

Its more of like Florida to me where I would see maybe cypress and palmy looking trees, and like citrus trees, but these have...these don't have citrus.

I'm seeing alligators again and snakes, lots of snakes.

Mound

In the passages cited below, Bowes makes reference to the existence of a mound structure in association with the site. It is significant to note that there was only one mound at the site, and both Bowes and Davis independently described a single mound. Bowes said, "I

III-2: A site showing burials, single mound and water.

kept feeling as though in the background as though there may have been a mound or...a mountain or a larger area."

In these passages Davis described the mound.

> I'm seeing something that would have like steps, and I'm going up. I feel that I would have gone up these steps and the steps are made of stone or they are hard, and they are on a hillside or like a place that I would have gone up. As I'm saying this I feel like an Aztec, like their great monuments or that kind of thing, but I don't feel these are Aztec...something of like a Mexican type of influence almost....No, that's wrong.

> I feel a mound, though; like a mound type of thing.

Davis was not entirely mistaken concerning the "Mexican type of influence." Temporally bracketing the Guale site date (1500-1650), there was massive Mesoamerican influence in the Southeast area (700-1700 A.D.). Her description of the steps on the mound was also quite accurate.

Charnal House

In the Bowes' reading is found:

> I would feel that this (artifact) was buried with someone because of...I keep seeing a large amount of possessions. I do see a room or a building full of soot...lot of smoke. I would feel like it was almost like it was underground or it was like a hole or a dip in the ground, and I see grass or something over the top of it.... I don't know if it was for smoking meat, but I kept feeling as though they had meat or something hanging in there. I see them using bamboo or something. Bamboo, reeds, like tall grass with pom-poms on top to block it off. I would feel that they could be worried about something getting in there...a opossum or a raccoon could get in there and I see these bamboo...I see it around the front. I didn't feel very good with that. I did feel that that was something of importance to the one man or several people but I didn't feel as though it was too outstanding with everybody.

The mortuary structures in the Guale area were sunken and covered with palmetto. Bowes' reference to meat may relate to the Southeastern custom of stripping flesh from the corpse. References to bamboo, reeds, grass, etc. as mortuary coverings are cited in the ethnohistorical literature. His comment about a "building full of soot...lot of smoke" is supported by the fact that much charcoal and ash were found in association with the skeletal remains of a former charnal house at the site.

House Types of the Guale

The archeological and historical record describes the Guale pavilion-type house as being basically a log and branch wall topped by grass and palmetto roofing. Andreas de San Miguel, a Franciscan priest involved in the mission effort in 1595, writes concerning Guale houses:[1]

> All of the walls of the houses are of rought timbers and covered with palmetto...all of the houses are small, because, as they have little to keep in them they make them only for shelter, and for this reason the houses of the chiefs are also small.

With regard to questions about house types of the people Bowes responded:

> Generally I didn't feel too much with houses with these people. I see something that was more like grass or more like something near the water...grass shacks or something.

Davis commented on the houses she sees in this manner:

> I'm seeing wood, like branches that are on top of each other ...kind of a thatched, not simply roof, kind of an overlap of branches and things. I don't feel as though living with this, I feel some place that would have been a shelter. As though it would be some place that would be built out from a hill or a piece of ground or maybe even a tree.

In her reading Davis also described a structure covered with hides or "fibers" sewn together and stretched over a frame. There is no archeological record of this type of structure among the Guale.

Yearly Subsistence Rounds

The semi-nomadic horticultural/hunting and gathering activities of the Guale are suggested in the following extracts from the psychics' statements.

Bowes commented:

> I do see them (the ancestral population) stopping in this area because of either fresh water or a stream or a place where they could rest.

> I do see people living there for quite some time, and this could be an area where there's either brackish or fresh water or a place where they could move by water, but I kept seeing that.

> I do feel as though when they were near the water, I see them eating meat or eating something to do with a furry animal, and I felt like it could have been a raccoon or something like that. I kept feeling that when they moved inland that there could have been a lot of bugs....

Excerpts from Davis' reading include:

> There's a lot of travel with these people as though they would have traveled around and then come back.

> I keep feeling this circular motion as though they would have left and come back, and they would have kept a lot of freedom somehow, like they would have kept leaving and coming back, back and forth.

The men went out to get the food and they not only planted but they also drew from nature as though there were natural ...maybe berries or something that they drew from a various times of the season, and I feel that there were times when they would go beyond...I keep wanting to say 'the river.'

Black Drink and Healing Circles

"Black drink" was a culture trait typical of many peoples of the Southeastern area. Hudson[2] describes it in the following:

Black drink, a ritual beverage, was a necessary part of all important council meetings...Black drink purified men of pollution, served as a symbolic social cement, and it was an ultimate expression of hospitality...Black drink is a tea whose bitter taste and caffeine content increase as it is made stronger. In addition to being a stimulant, the beverage also acts as a diuretic, causing increased perspiration. And the Indians sometimes used it as an emetic.

Compare Hudson's description of the Black drink with Davis' statement below.

There is also something special that they drank and it's like a tea or soup of some type that they would have made from a concoction of things...it was very good for their bodies, and they used it quite often like we would consider today that we would fast, but they would drink this three times a day and it would act as a cleansing...as a fasting type, cleansing purification.

Davis seemed to be particularly interested in describing health practices, as the transcripts in the Appendix indicate. For example, at one point while talking about health customs she began to describe a kind of circular pattern. "I'm seeing something that would look round with designs around the borders." She then produced a drawing. Later in her reading she saw another circle and continued her commentary on this phenomenon.

III-3: Davis' impression of a "healing circle"

This one is about three feet. And I would say it's probably made either on top of clay or stone or something, but it's things that were put on top and carved or beaten but somehow there is a design in there, and there is a line that separates light and dark, symbolism of light and dark somehow and then there's things that are set across what I would consider a meridian or an equator or something...something set across a middle portion of it and that would be the focal point of the center.

The kind of circle described by Davis is in fact depicted in an obscure drawing by the French artist Jacques LeMoyne, one of the

settlers at the French installation, Fort Caroline, in 1564. Fort
Caroline is within the Guale cultural sphere, and the time of the
drawing also falls within the time span of the site under study. The
drawing (shown below), titled "Chief observing his sorcerer," por-
trays Indians and French soldiers watching a scene in which an Indian
man is kneeling and contorting within a circle approximately four
feet in diameter and fashioned on the ground. Clearly depicted in the
LeMoyne drawing is a series of esoteric designs arranged along the
border, just as Davis had indicated.

*III-4: Chief Outina observing his sorcerer, being the twelfth of the engravings
of Jacques Le Moyne de Morgues in his book* Brevis Narratio [Frank-
fort, deBry, 1591].

Osteoporosis

Osteoporosis, a bone disorder, was found manifest in several of the
burials at the St. Simon's Island site. Wallace[3] describes one burial in
the following way: "Burial eight was a highly pathologic individual
exhibiting premature closure of cranial sutures, billowed and unfused
cranial condyls...."

Compare Wallace's statement with the following section from
Bowes' reading. Note Bowes' focus on the "vertical forehead."

> I keep seeing a man with a headache or dizzy or having a
> problem with breathing. I didn't know what it meant but I
> felt it was an illness in connection with the man who possibly
> could have owned this (artifact).... I keep seeing someone

with a very tall forehead, or like possibly a receding hairline. Something flat about the head in front. I keep seeing someone with quite a tall forehead...I feel as though with this person this is the distinguishing mark.

III-5: An osteoporosis victim.

Women

The earlier account of the matrilocal/matrilineal orientation of the Guale suggests the positive status of women in Guale society. In Davis' reading of the Guale materials the following comments appear:

Women were important not only in the home as childbearers, but also with the healing, and with the foresight to know when to act and when to move.

I still would say that women were important.

They (women) were sensitives, they were healers, they were seers, they were very important, but I feel it was almost like not an equal thing; certain men and women.

The Great Storm

There are several references in the records of the 1565 voyage of the Frenchman, Rene Laudonniere, which describe an extraordinary storm in the vicinity of Fort Caroline, near the modern-day city of Jacksonville, Florida.[4]

On August 29 there fell on the fort such a stroke of lightening that I think it more worthy of interest and of being recorded than any unusual thing that has yet come to pass, more strange than historians have ever written about. The fields were at that time all green and half covered with water, and yet the lightening in one instant consumed about 500 acres and burned with such a bright heat that all the birds which lived in the meadow were consumed. This thing continued for three days. It left us in wonderment, because we could not guess where all the fire came from.

The Laudonniere account states that this fire was followed on September 10 by a storm "with such heavy winds that the Indians assured me it was the worst that had ever come to the coast."[5]

Compare the above with Davis' reading.

There was a time when these people were very threatened by a storm, like a great wind, rain came, and I feel this was followed by a period of almost like a drought where they were worried about their food. I feel that this storm was something very awesome..... It was heard of in legends of these great storms and winds, almost like what I would consider as a hurricane but they had never really experienced one that deeply and I feel destruction as though things were blown and scattered and this happened within thirty-five years of the fire. So there were many negative physical things that occurred. I feel this fire was almost a thing of combustion due to heat when it was really dry out and something occurred that ignited it. I don't feel it was something set by errors or accidental. I feel like it was almost a nature freak thing.

The Expeditions of Jean Ribault and Rene Laudonniere

Though there were a number of other European contacts in the Guale area from 1500 to 1650, the history of the expeditions of Jean Ribault and Rene Laudonniere is important because many of the references by Bowes and Davis to "outsiders" appear to bear a striking resemblance to the particulars of the French exploration and settlement of what is now the South Carolina/Georgia/Florida coastal regions. The 1562 expedition, captained by Ribault with Laudonniere second-in-command, first made landfall in the Guale territory about fifty miles north of St. Catherine's Island. Ribault had been expressly ordered not to contact areas where France was not established. Basically this meant that he was to avoid the Spanish. He was well received by the native population and was thus able to erect a base which he named Charlesfort. After establishing this foothold, Ribault left twenty-six soldiers with provisions for six months and sailed back to France to recruit more colonists.

During the succeeding months supplies ran out and, with no news of Ribault, conditions at Charlesfort became desparate. Two of the men drowned in an accident, and the captain of the fort was killed in a struggle with one of his men. The twenty-three remaining men decided to build a ship and sail for France, though none of them knew how to construct a ship, nor was there one among them who knew how to navigate properly. An account of the sailing of the Charlesfort survivors is found in Bennett's[6] translations of the expedition's records.

> They used a kind of moss with which to stuff the cracks and for caulking. Then they made sails out of their clothing and bedclothes. They set out to sea on the first good wind. The calms and erratic gusts soon held them captive and the fresh water and victuals gave out. Since in three weeks they had advanced only 25 leagues they were restricted to eating not more than twelve grains by weight of corn meal per man per day. But even this gave out, and they devoured their shoes, leather collars, straps, and dried animal skins. Those who tried the sea water suffered with swollen throats and scorched their guts with strange torment. So others drank their own urine. Suddenly, after the vessel's hull burst, a huge tidal wave and a gust descended on them with such force that the boat was thrown against a rock.

One of the garrison, a fifteen-year-old boy named Guillaume Rouffi, chose to remain with the Indians rather than to risk his life in such an ill-equipped craft. Rouffi ultimately married the daughter of a Guale chief.

Two years later, Rene Laudonniere led a contingent of French Huguenots to the area. The accounts grow confusing, but it is clear that Laudonniere established Ft. Caroline at the mouth of the St. John's River in northern Florida, and explored in the vicinity of the Guale. In 1565, the Spanish built the fort of St. Augustine and proceeded to destroy the French colony at Ft. Caroline.

Many of the historical specifics so briefly outlined above re-emerge in the readings of Bowes and Davis.

Outsiders

When questioned about the presence of intruders or outsiders in the environment, Bowes stated:

> I don't know if they were Spanish-speaking people...I would feel as though they were Quakers or people...possibly people from another country other than Spain. Now they could have been like the French or people from a country not normally here because I didn't feel them having experience either with the Indians or experience with the terrain....

Concerning the same subject, Davis responded:

> I feel 'northern'....maybe these people had more of the French, or English...no, no, Portuguese...I'm feeling like close to a French dialect, but I'm not French. I feel they would have come from the northern part of the United States, or a northern region from this area where these (artifacts) were found as though they would have been there some time and were moving on...were looking further. I see them with water, like maybe a boat or a ship...that they would have, I get 'parked' it north and then traveled south.

> These people are dark haired people with more of an olivey Spanish type of influence, but I'm not hearing Spanish, I'm hearing French, or maybe it's Italian. It might even be Italian.

General Comments About the Outsiders

In the following series of excerpts Bowes and Davis touch upon many of the points described in the preceding survey of the Ribault and Laudonniere expeditions.

From Bowes we hear:

> I don't feel they were educated or talented people. Could have been convicts or they could have been people who were ...I would say inexperienced, the actual passengers, people

on the ship were actually inexperienced to traveling over the ocean. They may have been collecting Indians for slaves ...there could have been something associated with slaves.

...this was a poor attempt to establish a colony in the United States. This was the strongest feeling I had.

I would say they were trying to get north. I didn't feel they liked the area where they were at, but I felt a storm or a miscalculation brought them into an area where there was a lot of shoals or a lot of sand. I would say they probably had problems with their sails because I felt that the ship was very ill equipped. I would say it dealt with a hurricane or storm. It may have blew all their sails, ripped all their sails up. I would say they were very afraid.

I would say that they were afraid of the Spanish. They had been blown south and were afraid of St. Augustine or the south...I don't feel they came from the south at all, in fact I felt they fell off course, and I feel that they fell way south of where they should've, but I felt they were very afraid and not knowing where they're at. I don't feel they wanted to go to St. Augustine. That's one place they knew they didn't want to go. They were trying to get back north, but the whole thing was a failure. I just felt the whole thing was a big failure.

The feeling I felt was that they were fairies, who weren't normally in this association. I feel the captain or the person normally in charge was either sick or ill or not there. I don't feel they had authority. In other words, they were very confused.

I thought these people were very, very confused. They were not prepared for this. I would say there was a very small amount of them left because of illness. Could have been because they were lost or they were getting scurvey or problems with vitamins. I see them getting sick...I felt they may have gone to shore but I feel that, at the time the ship was wrecked, there was no life boats or no real transportation to get back and forth. I felt they went to the beach and it was covered with bugs and there was a lot of sand flies and mosquitoes and I don't feel they found any food to speak of. In other words, they were just really inexperienced people.

Davis' reading includes:

I feel the influence of non-Indians there but I don't feel they stayed there, but I think they came back.

...there's lots of people in here and half of the people went one way and half the other. I feel like they had so many days they were traveling and then they were to meet again. I felt some of them stayed behind.

The ship had slats and the slats were fairly far apart. I'm surprised to say, and I don't know what's keeping it up but there are beams or something that go across under the bottom of it and you had to be very careful when you walked because I think the floor surface of it wasn't complete. It maybe had some sort of places dug out of something, but there was something underneath it that filled it in, that got wet and would absorb some of the moisture and then the rest of the moisture would have to stay out somehow. And I wonder what that could be? I could see spaces in between the slats, which really surprised me, and I don't understand how it stayed afloat myself.

I said they split in two. I feel like one of the groups didn't go away far. I feel like they settled there waiting, waiting for word to travel because I see the boat completely up on the shore, it's not like docked, it's like there...and it's like stuck on the shore or like pulled way in...they didn't pull it to sail out again.

It's funny because when I think about it and I see somebody dressed like a Quaker.

I feel like they came in search of something...I feel that these men came here to where the Indians were and then they went back, and I feel later that they would settle near there, but it might have been later, later, like a generation later.

Firearms

III-6: Impression of gun.

When psychometrizing the lead ball in the artifact collection, Bowes gave a very detailed description of the gun he saw firing the ball (Drawing #4). The description of the firearm does not follow in any obvious fashion from simply looking at a lead ball because such balls occur from the 15th century into present times and in all parts of the world. Further, the study of primary ignition systems of lead ball firing guns is quite complex. In the period stemming from 1400 to 1700 there existed three major ignition systems, plus several varieties of each. The drawing Bowes made of the gun he saw was given to a firearms expert for a blind analysis. The gunsmith identified the picture as a rough drawing of a French snaphaunce type of firing mechanism. As has been noted the French were predominant in the area during the Guale occupation. There is also record of Captain John Smith using a French snaphaunce in a fight with

Indians in 1606.[7] The major point here is that Bowes described and drew in specific detail a type of firearm which can be dated, and that date corresponds in fact with the date of the site at which the ball was found.

The Ship

Both Bowes and Davis described the presence of a ship moving off the coast. As the transcripts indicate, Bowes returned several times to the subject of the ship. This is noteworthy because there is nothing in the artifact collection related to or suggesting the ship they both describe. Further, their descriptions of the ship are accurate enough that the ship can be dated.

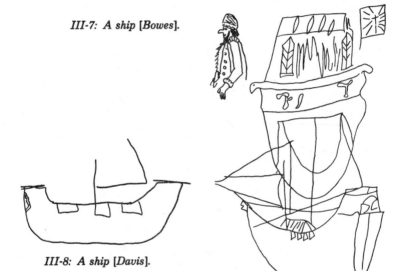

III-7: A ship [Bowes].

III-8: A ship [Davis].

Relevant ships of the period include the cog, the carrack, and the caravel types. For example, Columbus' ship, the Santa Maria, was of the carrack variety, while the Nina and the Pinta were caravel types. Comparing Bowes' and Davis' descriptions and drawings of the ship with other accounts and drawings of ships, it appears that the type that Bowes and Davis independently described is a carrack or caravel. This would temporally place the vessel anywhere from 1450 to 1550, and possibly as late as 1600. In fact, their account best fits at 1475 to 1525. Interestingly enough, both Davis and Bowes describe a phenomenon, the ship, not represented in any way in the artifact collection before them at the time, which dates precisely in the range of the Guale occupation of the site under investigation.

The description of the clothing of the passengers on the ship also offers a dating possibility. The man's clothing in Bowes' drawing definitely fits the 16th century. The doublet and jerkin that he drew could be used almost any time in the century. The rolled shouldered sleeve was used more or less throughout the century with many variations. He described the man he saw as having long hair and a "baby bonnet" hat. These two features narrow it down much further to the last two decades of the 16th century. Once again, the date fits the time span of the Guale occupation.

Another fascinating detail related to Bowes' discussion of the ship involves a woman that he saw. He stated:

III-9: Captain's woman.

> I keep seeing a woman looking out of a cabin...looking out of a window.... This could have been the back window of the ship or something, because I kept seeing this person looking out the window, and down below was like a rudder, so it may have been a captain's cabin or something in the back of the ship.... This was a very sad person, and I felt it was a dark skinned person. She could have been Italian, she could have been an Indian, but I felt she was very, very sad. I felt she was afraid or sad. This is emotion, a lot of emotion that I felt there.... I would feel she wore very rough clothing. Either a dress that was just sewed and thrown over her or it was something that was...an Indian woman with no clothes or just a piece of leather or a burlap bag over her because I felt it was just sewed on the tops over her shoulders.

Bowes' mention of a woman in the captain's cabin is supported in the accounts of the first Laudonniere expedition. Laudonniere's detractors accused him of bringing a mistress on the ship to New France and later living with her at Ft. Caroline. Laudonniere wrote in his defense, "The woman was a poor chambermaid which I had taken up in an Inn to oversee my household business, to look to an infinite sort of divers beasts, as sheep and poultry which I carried with me to store the country withall."[8]

Bennett's[9] translations indicate that there were "Moors" and "paroled criminals" forming a substantial portion of Laudonniere's crew. In his reading Bowes commented:

> Generally I felt that they had someone aboard who was like a slave or someone who had done something wrong, because

...they could have even been prisoners, or they could have
done something wrong....

These people could have been Indians or Negroes or whoever that was put there as prisoners or slaves....

Shallop

On board the ships of the French explorers were several small boats
of the shallop type. A shallop is a small open boat propelled by oars
or small sails and used chiefly in shallow water. The early expeditions
in this area often used such craft to explore water courses too shallow
for larger vessels. There are several references in the readings of
Bowes and Davis that seem to indicate a boat of the shallop type. For
example, Bowes made the following series of references to a kind of
boat that seemed to confuse him.

In other words, these people had gotten this ship and
brought it over here to the United States and really it was
not something I would say was really set-up for travel in
the ocean...just a poorly made ship for the ocean.

It wasn't made to actually be out on the ocean.

The feeling I had was that it was not a ship that you would
normally expect to be traveling at that distance. I would say
it came from France or Europe.

Davis also reported confusion upon seeing a certain kind of boat.

I'm seeing something that would have...it reminds me of a
Viking ship to tell you the truth...there's something sticking
out and I feel oars and a sail but the sail isn't that tall...the
sail is small though...its strange. I don't know.

Guilliume Rouffi

The presence of the fifteen-year-old French boy, Guilliume Rouffi,
who chose to live with the Guale rather than risk an uncertain voyage
back to his home country, may be indicated in the following comments
from the reading.

Bowes reported:

...I don't know if this would be a Pilgrim or an Indian but I
kept seeing him as being somebody.... I keep seeing him
having clothes on.... I kept feeling that the idea of clothes
was something that may have been a little different. I don't
know if this man would have a brass button, or buttons on,
but I kept seeing that. I kept feeling as though it was a
jacket...it may have had round buttons or something tied
onto it. The collar was torn off the jacket.... I feel as though
that the man who owned this pipe may have been different or
or like a character or somebody different. Could have been
like a sole survivor or someone not an Indian like these
people.

Davis mentioned:

> ...maybe this person came in and eventually infiltrated their group or lived with them to bring them these new ideas.

In the context of this experimental time span, the "sole survivor," "someone not an Indian," "having clothes" could have been Rouffi. It is conjecture, of course, but perhaps the presence of Rouffi may "explain" why Bowes and Davis seemed to focus almost entirely on the expeditions surrounding the fate of Rouffi while they largely ignored the massive presence of the Spanish in the Guale territory both before and after the Ribault and Laudonniere expeditions.

Additional Comments

There are many instances in the readings of Davis and Bowes in which they reported various pieces of information not amenable to a major discussion in the text, but nonetheless significant in their accuracy. In the following section several such points will be briefly noted.

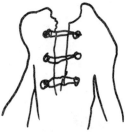

III-10: Brass-button jacket.

(1.) Bowes at one point described a man wearing a jacket upon which was sewn six brass buttons. As he talked about this man he drew a picture of a jacket with six brass buttons prominently displayed on the front. There were no buttons in the collection he was viewing during the reading, but six brass buttons were in fact found during the excavation of the Guale site.

(2.) In response to a question concerning political organization and leadership, Bowes responded:

> I would feel as though the leadership could have been prejudiced. I kept feeling as though there were like some outside influence...very strong...it could have been the Catholic religion...or a religion that dominated the people.

As the ethnohistorical record shows, the Jesuits and later the Franciscans were a major influence in the Guale area utilizing the military might of the Spanish garrisons in the vicinity to coerce conversion to Catholicism and to suppress rebellion against the missionizing efforts of the Church.

(3.) While holding the greenstone celt, Bowes stated, "I see it being buried...I don't know if this was in a cave or underground." The celt he was holding at the time was in fact found in direct association with a burial.

(4.) After touching the large slate celt, Bowes said, "I kept feeling that this was not from this place." Once again, he is correct. The celt in question was made from slate not available on the island.

(5.) In Davis' reading she described a rather unusual figurine. "I'm seeing one and I want to say it has the tail of an alligator, or the body of an alligator, and the head of something else more like a cat...."

Hudson[10] points out that Southeastern Indians were particularly interested in anomalies. Animals that fell into two different categories at once were singled out for special symbolic value.

(6.) When Davis picked up the two celts, the only trade items in the collection, she said, "I sensed that somehow new influences would come in periodically."

Summary: St. Simon's Island Site

The performance of Bowes and Davis in this experiment, though perhaps not entirely conclusive, is, nonetheless, highly impressive. Confronted with a non-diagnostic artifact collection in a blind experimental situation, they offered accurate descriptions of environment, race, specific pathology, contact situation, and various cultural traits such as the black drink, curing circles, charnal houses, and the elevated role of women. The place of the gun, the ship, the costuming of the ship's passengers, and the specific details comparable to the actual occurrences of the Ribault/Laudonniere expeditions is of particular significance, both because the descriptions could be dated, and did in fact fit the correct time range, and because the actual physical material handled by the subjects during the experiment in no way indicated the generated and datable responses.

THE FOLSOM EXPERIMENT

In the follow-up experiment, the research goal, as with the St. Simon's Island test, was to explore the possibility of site location and cultural reconstruction *via* assistance from psychic colleagues. Albert Bowes was asked to read a collection of stone tools and tool fragments from the Lindenmeier site, a Folsom site in Colorado. He was not told the nature or origin of the materials. The major difference between this experiment and the St. Simon's Island test was that with the latter massive documentation could be marshalled to demonstrate the accuracy of the subject's reading, but with the Folsom context the documentary possibilities were practically nonexistent owing to the nature and extreme antiquity of the Folsom culture. Therefore, the probable accuracy of the Folsom reading depends on the demonstrated accuracy of the St. Simon's Island reading. In my opinion, the Folsom reading stands not as a proof, but as an example of one of the more fascinating promises of psychic archeology—the highly detailed reconstruction of extinct socio-cultural systems.

Ancient Man in the New World

In order to place the information given by Bowes in the Folsom experiment in proper context, a brief account of the early history of man in the New World must be offered. To begin, the dating of man's arrival in the New World is very problematic. Some archeologists assume that humans did not enter North America before about 12,000 years ago; other suggest 30,000-40,000 years ago; while a minority argue that the first humans appeared in the New World as much as 500,000 years ago. Very little is known about the most ancient of these immigrants from northeast Asia. The first New World people that can be described in terms of life-style are the big game hunters belonging to what archeologists refer to as the Clovis tradition. The Clovis complex, named after an archeological site near Clovis, New Mexico, dates to about 11,500 years ago. The Clovis hunters specialized in the hunting of the Columbian mammoth. Their artifacts are found from the North American southwest to Nova Scotia.

Beginning about 11,000 years ago, North America became drier and warmer and northern glaciers began to recede. As climatic and environmental conditions changed, the mammoth became extinct. The big game hunters of the New World turned their attention to the abundant bison herds which thrived at the time, most plentifully in the Plains area of North America. It is from that area, dating between 11,000 and 9,000 years ago, that we find the most abundant remains of the Folsom tradition, hunters of the now extinct bison form, *Bison antiquus*. *Antiquus* differs from the modern bison in a number of ways. It was about 20 per cent larger in body proportions, while its head and horns were more than twice as large.

Folsom materials are found from Alaska to Peru, and from the Rocky Mountains to the east coast. The area of maximum concentration, however, forms a wedge shape with its base along the front ranges of the North American Rockies, and its tip touching into New York and Pennsylvania. The diagnostic, or identifying, artifact which defines the complex is a characteristic type of projectile point called the Folsom Fluted point. Archeologist W. R. Wedel[11] describes the Folsom point in this way:

> They are more or less leaf-shaped in outline, broadest toward the tip, which is either rounding or tapering, and have a concave base. The base frequently has two sharp rearward projections and sometimes nipple-like protuberances in the center. Highly characteristic is a broad groove on one or both faces, which runs from the base two-thirds or more of the distance toward the tip, and results in two lateral ridges paralleling the edge of the blade. In cross section, this gives a biconcave appearance to the points. The edges have a fine secondary retouching, after which the base and the edges, for about one-third of the length of the blade, were blunted. In length, Folsom Fluted points range from less than one inch to about three inches.

The Lindenmeier Site

The Lindenmeier site, about thirty miles north of Fort Collins, Colorado, is a Folsom site of great importance. It is not only the single major source of knowledge about Folsom culture, but also one of the largest and oldest ancient Indian sites ever discovered. Because of its singular significance, materials from this particular site were used in my research with the psychic, Albert Bowes.

The site was originally in a valley, but subsequent erosion over thousands of years has produced a geological situation in which the former valley appears now as a terrace on the side of the first foothill ridges of the Rockies. Wilmsen[12] one of the most recent commentators on the Lindenmeier site, notes that when standing on the site, one sees seemingly endless, gently undulating plains extending to the east and south. Westward, the foothills rise in a series of tilted uplifts to the crest of the Rockies. The surrounding topography is today not markedly different from the time when the ancient Folsom hunters inhabited the area.

Though the geophysical condition of the area has been relatively unchanged, the climatic changes have been drastic. At present the area is arid and semi-desert in nature. However, at the time of Folsom man's occupation of this territory it was cooler, and many lakes were scattered through the environment. Springs and ground water soaks produced large wet meadowlands. Spencer and Jennings[13] envision Folsom hunters "...camped along the shores of the shallow marshy lakes or beaver meadows that dotted the country during the glacial ages."

The ancient environmental conditions were ideal for the large assortment of animals which were hunted by Folsom people. From the strata containing human tool remains come the bones of jackrabbits, foxes, coyotes, *Bison antiquus*, antelope, and the American camel. Elephant bones were also found at Lindenmeier, but not in direct association with human artifacts.

The tools found at Lindenmeier are quite varied. Besides the characteristic fluted points and fluted knives, a variety of stone scrapers, chopping tools, and drills were found. Hammerstones, grooved sandstone blocks (presumably used to smooth wooden shafts), small sandstone bowls and tablets used for mixing paints, red and yellow ochre, and bone artifacts including awls, needles, and incised beads have also been taken from the site. In addition, one small piece of fossil resin and a number of unidentified artifacts have come to light at Lindenmeier. A dramatic blank exists, however, in that no human remains have ever been found anywhere in association with Folsom stone tools.

Putting these bits and pieces of information together, what can conventional archeology tell us about the Folsom big game hunters at Lindenmeier? Very little actually. A picture emerges of bands of big game hunters wandering in a restricted area characterized by a cool, well-watered environment. They specialized in hunting *Bison antiquus*. They probably had a complex skin industry judging from the many kinds of scrapers, awls, punches, and needles found at the site. From the presence of the red and yellow pigment, we can guess that some form of decorative art probably existed. As for the rest—social organization, values, political philosophy, etc.—we can only infer by analogy with known hunting and gathering societies. We do not even know what Folsom people looked like. We can only assume that these ancient early Americans were ultimately Asiatic in origin.

In the following I will present what Bowes saw as he handled ten artifacts from the Lindenmeier site. However, several issues must be addressed before I present Bowes' description of life in a Folsom hunting camp.

A basic and inescapable criticism of this particular experiment is that Folsom fluted points are identifiable out of context. I can only respond that those of us who have taught New World Prehistory are very aware of how difficult it is for a student, even one with a solid grasp of the relevant lecture and reading materials, to differentiate such closely related artifacts as Clovis points from Folsom points from Plano points, etc. Consider the odds against Albert Bowes, a twenty-nine-year-old high school graduate with no special interest or background in New World Prehistory, looking at an artifact collection and identifying it as Folsom. Further, consider the amount of expert knowledge needed, even if the identification were made, to spontaneously construct a plausible account of an ancient hunting and gathering society and to maintain an internal consistency in such an account over a two-hour period (the length of the Folsom reading). What professional archeologist and anthropologists take for granted regarding Folsom point identification and the generic traits of a hunting and gathering society, is often not that obvious.

Further, and this is much more impressive, no one, not even the most expert New World archeologist, could look at a Folsom point and tell that it came from Lindenmeier. As Wilmsen[14] reports, there are tens of thousands of such points in the collections of amateurs alone. It is quite remarkable that Bowes, as will be shown below, could describe the specific past and present geological and climatic conditions of Lindenmeier, even locating the site in the west-central area of the United States, simply by handling one complete Folsom point and several fragments and scrapers. The same kind of materials could just as easily come from sites in Alaska or Peru, as well as from very different environmental settings.

Folsom Ethnography

An *ethnography* is a written account which purports to present a description of a way of life, or culture. Such an account traditionally begins with a description of the physical environment and location of the culture being described, and then moves into a consideration of anthropologically relevant categories of behavior such as kinship, subsistence, politics, economics, religion, etc. In this experiment it is as if a traveler in another culture is being debriefed by an anthropologist who never visited the people in question. Of course, Albert Bowes is a traveler of quite an unusual kind.

Location

In the following, Bowes described impressions he received of the location and environment of the artifacts' origins.

I feel an association with the west. I don't know if this is an association with California, or the west, or the mid-west. I keep feeling that around where this was there was petrified wood, or something like the climate changed. But the feeling I had was the climate was completely different from where they found that (artifact). If they found it in a desert, if they found it in a cold place, I feel it was different at the time it was made, and I felt the animals were different too. I would say it was cold. It could be a desert now, but I felt it was cold then. A lot of water there, and lakes.

JONES: What does the terrain look like?

BOWES: I felt that when you looked at it now that this could have been washed out. The feeling I had was it may be desert or a lot of clay hills. I felt there were humps, and it could be out in California, or out west, or mid-west, Nevada, or something. I felt you'd be going along and it would be flat ground and all of a sudden there would be this big hump and then the water washing down and eroding it down...I felt it was very swampy around these lakes.

I felt like they were running through water, or running through rocks. The feeling I had was the reason they (archeologists) did not find the actual...for example, amounts of other objects in the area or in the area they found this (artifact) is this is not, and I repeat, not an area that they lived in. I do feel as though it is a retreat or an area where they were hiding. I don't know if this was up a valley or at the end of a valley or group of mountains or group of rocks, but I do see fresh air and some animals. I don't know if this is out west, but I kept feeling as though the area in which it originated was in an area where there was running water and possibly very cool up in the mountains, or...I first felt in the New York state area, or an area that was in the mountains, but I could be associated with the west because I kept seeing something of a different territory, a different atmosphere as they came down out of the mountains... I see a lot of erosion where red clay and dirt had been washed away, like in Georgia or like in Tennessee...mountains where the water is washing very fast. It could be... could have been in the desert where the water was washing very fast... a sudden surge of water in the rainy season, like flash floods. This (artifact) was buried for a long period of time.

III-11: Target site.

Though Bowes hedged as to his opinion concerning the state in which the site is found, his description of the environment at the time of the occupation and now is quite accurate. In an attempt to elicit a more specific response as to location I asked him to indicate on a rough map of the United States which he had drawn, where he most strongly felt the site to be located. He looked at the map and said:

> I would say they moved east, and I don't know...I would say they either lived here (indicates east central area of the United States), or they lived here (west central area of the United States). I felt basically here (west central).

Dating of the Occupation of Lindenmeier

As for the dating of the Folsom materials used in the experiment, Bowes made these statements, all excerpted from the tape recording of his reading. (a.) "...before Christ, they were in Canada." (b.) "I would say this was before Egypt. Way, way back." (c.) "Again, I would say they don't have horses." (d.) "I don't feel they associated with bringing pottery along." (e.) "Basically I didn't see any fire-power, guns...I don't see any metal." (f.) "I don't feel so much toward corn, but I felt more with things in the ground like radishes, or roots or something."

The references to Christ, Egypt, the invention of pottery and metallurgy, and the domestication of horses and corn are all datable, and Bowes was correct in asserting that the makers of the Folsom artifacts existed prior to those events.

Origins

In this exchange, Bowes talked about the origins of the makers of the stone tools before him.

> JONES: Do you get any feelings about where these people came from?
>
> BOWES: I would say that they were there a very long time, maybe even hundreds of years. A long time in that vicinity, but I would say that they were pushed down from the north. I would say they came originally from Canada, or north.
>
> JONES: How far back can you get in terms of where they came from?
>
> BOWES: I would say before Christ. In other words, before Christ they were in Canada.
>
> JONES: Can you move back in time and space any farther than that?
>
> BOWES: I would say they moved east and I don't know...I felt parts...in other words, this would be Alaska and Canada (draws # 11), and California and down this way, and I would say they either lived here (east central) or they lived here (west central). One of these two places. I felt basically here (west central). I keep seeing them coming from the north and I would say there were a group of people who came this way (from the south), and they were associated together. At that time they were much more advanced then they were there.

JONES: More advanced earlier?

BOWES: Yes! Yes. I would say that this group of people (from the north and from the south) derived...divided. I would say they ran out of resources and they maybe came toward the Great Lakes or this was (east). But I do feel as though the people in the south were people from a different, either different origin or different responsibility. I felt they were possibly more advanced. These people (touches artifacts) were more like Eskimos.

JONES: These people (touches artifacts) **are which of these people** (touches north and south arrows on Bowes' map)?

BOWES: Both. A combination of both, because I see these people (artifacts) trading, an association or a group of two. In other words, these (north) were more like Orientals and these (south) were more like something else.

JONES: A combination of the Orientals and the 'something else'?

BOWES: 'Something else' would be a longer face...a little different. I feel originally in South America. I feel a group came, or coming from the south would...I see them coming by boat, but I feel these people up here (artifacts) came from land. From Alaska, coming south. And these people (from the south) came by boat. I would say this (artifacts) was before Egypt. Way, way back.''

Physical Appearance of the Folsom People

JONES: What did these people look like?

BOWES: I would say they were much more advanced than all the people around them where they lived. They may have been Indians, or people from another country...not Indians in the sense of the people in this country, but I felt west, west. Could have been like Eskimo people...I felt they were like Indians. I would say they had very long, long faces, and maybe sunken cheeks. I felt they were very, very powerful people... very strong in the legs especially....

III-12: A Folsom man.

JONES: Do you see these people as being tall or short or thin or fat or....

BOWES: I would say they were taller and healthier than these other traveling people, but basically they were very wide shouldered and short in comparison to us. Basically I wouldn't say they were tall, but they were maybe tall for Indians. I felt good health.

JONES: Could you draw a face?

BOWES: This is going to be hard. (draws #12) I felt their face was quite long. It wasn't...I really couldn't tell you too much. I'm not too good at picking up something like that."

Population of Site at Time of Occupation

Questions concerning the population of the group he was psychically observing drew from Bowes not only his feeling about population numbers, but also the first of many references to the existence of two separate localities considered by Bowes to be of crucial importance to an understanding of these ancient people.

I keep seeing the women, or woman, not being there. Basically I see a large group of men. You see, I'm torn between two different places. One of them is in the mountains where I see big tall trees and very solid wood, and then I see another place where there was either swamp, or a place that was like a desert today. What I am trying to say is that the people lived in one place and I felt they went somewhere else.

JONES: How many people do you see?

BOWES: I wouldn't say too many with these people. I would say fifty to seventy-five, but I don't see large amounts. Now there could be more than that. There could be a couple hundred of them, but I would say they were in smaller groups. I wouldn't say there were over seventy-five. I would say they were quite established. I see them on a river and I see them going back and forth like that down below like south of where they lived. I felt as though there were two territories...two areas that were quite different.

Some insight into why Bowes may be drawn to two different physical environments in his reading is offered by De Garmo.[15] In a study of early big game hunters in the New World, De Garmo posits that the presence of most Folsom materials in a plains environment, on the one hand, and in a more mountainous environment, on the other, is due to the seasonal migration of the bison, the staple of the Folsom hunters. Touching upon the earliest accounts of the habits of bison, De Garmo notes that the traditional seasonal activity of the bison in western North America involved wintering and summering ranges divided between the plains and the higher elevations. This is approximately what Bowes suggested when he described being "torn between two different places...one...in the mountains" and the other "...either a swamp or a place that was like a desert today." The issue of the two locations will be echoed again when Bowes described two separate, though sympathetic, groups of hunters exploiting different environments, but coming together periodically at Lindenmeier, the target site.

Flora, Fauna, and Subsistence Patterns

With no suggestion or lead from me, Bowes quickly established in his 'reading' that he was dealing with a very ancient group of Indian hunters once located in the western United States. Obviously, I had to ask questions concerning the nature of food resources in the area. In the excerpts listed below, Bowes responded to the question.

> I would say they would shoot bison or something very large with it (artifact)...something very big.

> These (artifacts) were big, like to shoot a bison, or an elephant or mastodon or something.... I felt it was different at the time it (artifact) was made, and I felt the animals were different, too.

> I do feel they used bees.

> **JONES: Bees?**

> **BOWES:** Yes, and I felt like this was something...like, if they knew that there was bees around, they would upset these bees with it (artifact)...that they would shoot the tree or upset the bees. I don't know what it all means, but I'm going to give it to you. Again, this could be bees and fire, or something that would aggravate the bees.

> I had the feeling they shot fish, and the arrows had to be very sharp. These (artifacts) were for mammoths or something that was huge like a buffalo or something like a bison.

Bowes mentioned emphatically the presence of bison at one point, and several passages later he conditioned his description by describing some large game animal "like a buffalo," or "like a bison." At another point he denied the presence of bison. This issue is important, because according to New World archeologists, "Folsom" is almost synonymous with "ancient bison hunters." This is due to the massive presence of bison remains at practically all Folsom sites. The confusion here may be that the bison in existence at the time of Folsom man was very different looking in certain key respects from modern bison, as was noted earlier. Accepting the very premise of this book, it can be suggested that Bowes' difficulty with the question of the bison may be due to the fact that the bison he saw was not the modern bison, but was in fact "like a buffalo" or "like a bison."

> **JONES: Do you have any feeling about...when they hunted animals, did they hunt a few animals or large amounts of...**

> **BOWES:** I don't feel buffalo. I don't feel that at all. I do feel they would hunt one or two deer, but I didn't feel any more than that. I would say there was two methods. One would be almost respecting the dignity of the animal, like if they shot something...(TAPE ENDS) ...But I see them hunting something else and crushing it...like no dignity, like hating it. It could even be a bear. They crushed it into the ground. they lured it into an area and then they crushed it. I would say that the bear was their most feared enemy. I don't feel they feared these other people as much as they did bears, or some association with bears. Especially around the water

like at a time when there was a lot of fish in the water, when the bears would come up through there. I would say that they wouldn't run away from other men, but sometimes they would run away from bears. I feel the bears would kill women. They wouldn't give them any notice. They would come up there and kill them at night, or kill them at a time when they were moving.

I don't know if there were pigs there, but I kept feeling something...even wolves...something that they crushed, like I said before. A deer, I felt, they would just shoot.

JONES: Did they have any plant foods?

BOWES: I would say mostly roots. I didn't know what kinds of roots these were. I don't feel so much toward corn, but I felt more with things in the ground like radishes or roots or something. I would say definitely berries. I seen something round, like this (indicates object about the size of a golfball). I don't know if they were green or brown, but I felt it was round and had an outer shell to it and maybe they put it in the fire and broke these open. It was like a nut or something and I felt it broke open. I felt like they cooked this and they may have made like a butter, or smashed it, but I didn't know what it was. I would say they ate fish. I don't know if they planted these berries but I would say that every so often they did move or they moved possibly closer to where there is something growing along the shore, because I see them walking back and forth and I see the shore line or something get very muddy or sloppy or whatever.

Clothing

JONES: Do they have anything on their feet?

BOWES: I would say they had something similar to a sandal but they could have had moccasins. I would say they possibly wore moccasins for awhile, but I don't feel...I feel there was something and I'm not trying to be a smart-alec but it was something that was similar to a "flip-flop"...it went between your toes your big toe and the rest of your toes, and I would say they used this more in the mountains. I felt they had tall boots to protect their legs up about to the calf... something crossed like thread or leather. But I felt their legs were bare when they were running in these mountains and it must have been summer time or a warm period of time. I felt their muscles were very...very like a race horse's muscles...very tense, and sweating, but I could see clear up to here (indicates upper thigh). I see that part of them. They may have had just a breech cloth or whatever, but the feeling I had was like later in the winter time...they had this full set of clothes, because I see them wearing a jacket.

JONES: Did they wear anything that had a meaning?
BOWES: I feel that they either wear bear claws or something in relationship to respect...I would feel that they wore like the teeth of a bear or the claws of a bear by a religious respect of gaining their strength, or showing their...like an ego trip, or an attitude of strength, like with every bear they would keep the teeth or the claws to show they were stronger than the bear. In fact I even feel they took the skin or the head of a bear and used it. They could have used it for a headdress or used it for a ceremonial, or used it...

War

The subject of warfare comes up often in Bowes' reading of the Folsom tools. The following are some relevant sections from the reading.

I do feel as though they were in a big hurry as if a whole group of people were moving, or were in war. If this (artifact) was found in the mountains or in an inaccessible place, I would feel very strong with it being a place that associated with war, as if they ran way up to this place to build a lot of ammunition, like arrows and spears and such... I don't know if they took drugs or something like to get drunk or excited but I felt them screaming and yelling and screaming. I keep seeing them calling 'hah-kahf' or 'hah-tuka' or 'ho-toko'... something to do with 'tee' or 'toe' or something like that. I see them screaming and running around. I see violence with them. I don't know why but I felt the people were destroyed or something like, they died. I see people coming in and taking women away, or like while they were away, the women or the families were destroyed or shot or something, but I felt very bad with it. I would say it was a massacre. Basically I would say they took the women away or they raped them or they took them for hostages or prisoners. I don't feel they saved the young children, the boys. If they did, they used them for slaves. Basically I didn't see any firepower, guns...I didn't see any metal. I did see them with

...something that had a stone here and a stone here and it had a piece of leather on it and they swung it over their heads (draws #13), but I don't feel they used it so much. I felt like they worked more with something being above somebody and attacking or throwing things from the top...up high. Their way of attack would be from the roof, or from the heights of the mountains. In other words, 'Come and get me.' They fling rocks and stones and bees and...down on top of them. I would say

III-13: A bolo-like weapon.

they were great fighters, but I would say that they either became extinct through not having...possibly because of wars or because of something that associated with the people who were their enemies kept going after their children or their wives or after their basis of reproduction.

JONES: What kind of people were their enemies?

BOWES: They could have been white people, but I felt they were Indians. I would say they outnumbered them, or they were...they hit them where it hurt. They hit them where the women and children were. Basically I would say that the people were someone who wanted this water or wanted this territory but I don't feel they took advantage of it, they went on. This river that went down through there it meandered along or it was winding...and they (artifacts) were right there at this place where the water was shallow, and maybe the fish were going up the river and coming down. I felt it was a perfect place where all these fish, or all this food was. These other people were coming up the river and down the river and they just said, 'Well, we're going to have to get rid of them. This is the way we go, and this is the way we are going to continue to go.' That may sound like a simple explanation but the feeling I had was that these (artifacts) people were there for many years and years, for a long period of time, but I felt these other people were someone who always was traveling like they traveled in circles...all the time. In other words, they did go back to the same place but it took them a year or six months or whatever to go around.

JONES: Why were they (the artifacts) involved in this war?

BOWES: I would say they established a place that was near the water, or near a place that was valuable, like for example a place where there are canoes or a place where there was food...valuable. I kept seeing this other tribe going through there, or like traveling. These people (artifacts) may have been more established. In other words, they may have just lived in one area or established one place. There was enough food to where they could stay in one place.

JONES: Were these people involved in war a lot?

BOWES: No! I would say that these may not have been warring people, but I would say they were continually attacked. They were satisfied with the area where they lived. Their area supplied them with enough food. They may have gone after wives or went after something that they really needed but I don't feel so much with war, except them being attacked. I would say these other Indians were not relatives, or not like these people (artifacts). They were quite different. The enemy could have looked different or been different. They could have had rounder faces...stockier.

After the reading I mentioned to Bowes my confusion over the continual references to war in his reading, but his denial of a war focus when I directly asked him, "Were these people involved in war a lot?" Bowes responded that he believed the problem was related to his own confusion over an emotion he was feeling and attempting to interpret. He felt that the hunters he was seeing did not so much hunt an animal or certain animals, as make war on them. In his perceptual categories, a hunter stalks a deer, for example, in a cold and calculating manner; but the people he was viewing behaved more as if they were preparing for a major attack on an enemy group. In our discussion after the reading he reiterated his feeling that other groups did attack the people from time to time, but that the intensity of the feelings of war were more related to game animals than to human enemies, and particularly the game animals that were "crushed, without dignity, from the heights."

Technology

In his reading Bowes touched upon many areas concerned with the manufacturing techniques and general technological level of the people he was observing. For example, he described the use of a travois.

> I felt as though they had things that they would pull behind them, behind horses...but I didn't feel they had horses. I feel they pulled them by two people. In other words, over their shoulders. Like this (draws #14). I would say there were sticks, or two people would carry it or pull it. I felt they carried most of it on their backs. they carried stuff on their backs like a pack. I see bags hanging from their sides.

(a.)

III-14: A Folsom travois.

In the succeeding passage Bowes attempted to describe an *atlatl,* or throwing stick, which he saw being used by the Folsom people. The identification of the *atlatl* did not happen during the reading, but later, while touring the museum where the experiment was conducted. As we passed an ethnological exhibit, Bowes pointed to an unmarked throwing-stick in an Eskimo display and said, "That thing, I saw that but I couldn't make sense of, that thing where an arrow was on a board and it would fling it. That thing right there (points to Eskimo *atlatl*) is just like it."

The confusion of images, seen in the passage immediately following

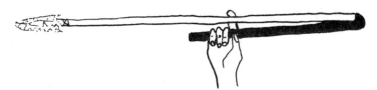

III-15: Author's drawing of a Folsom hunter's throwing-stick.

which occurred as Bowes struggled to describe an *atlatl*, an object absolutely new to him, is a good example of the kinds of impressions, pictures, images, and feelings that come to Bowes as he is confronted with the problem of reading an unusual artifact from a culture unknown to him.

JONES: You mentioned arrows. Did you see how these arrows were fired? Did they use spears at all? How did they shoot these big animals you talk about?

BOWES: I felt...this may sound strange to you, but I felt there was something strange about one of these weapons, and I don't know...I would say somebody used a bow and arrow, but I would feel they did use something more similar to a cross-bow (makes motion of a shaft reclining on a flat surface). I don't feel that people give them credit for this, but I keep seeing something other than a bow and arrow... something they would pull back and fling, almost like a tree.

JONES: Could you draw this?

BOWES: I really don't know. I don't know what it would be. I don't have any idea. I would say it was more of...of a cross-bow or a bow that goes sideways instead of straight up and down. The feeling I had was, almost like a tree, or it was almost bigger. It could even fling rocks. The feeling I had was, it was something that threw things. Much more effective than a bow...not in accuracy, but of hitting something or killing something.

JONES: Would one man carry this or...

BOWES: I really can't get back to that. I feel as though there could have been a board or log, and it may have almost been like an avalance or something going down, but I felt it was like a hole and it had something in it...it was a projectile...pushing something, or shooting a spear...it wasn't so much like an arrow, or bow and arrow, but it was more like something that layed in a trough, and something hit it. More like a cross-bow. More like something that was dugout, like a log, or stick, and this spear was laying on it.

House types of the Folsom people were also touched on in Bowes' reading.

JONES: You mentioned tents. Do you feel they lived in tents?

BOWES: I don't remember saying 'tents'. I said 'logs.' I

don't know if these are dugouts or whether they had something associated with something on the side of the bank. I
would say they did have tents, but they lived in something else.

JONES: **What did they live in?**

BOWES: I would say it was like a lean-to. It was among a
bunch of logs, or it was something of logs stacked. I would
say there was dirt over top of it. There was something
leaning against it...I would say they did live in this. I don't
feel like it would be a tipi that they would put up and tear
down...I do feel they definitely lived in caves at the time
they were working on this (artifact).

Since the Folsum Fluted point is the major diagnostic characteristic
of these people, it is interesting to note Bowes' description of how
the points were made.

JONES: **Do you have any feelings about how any of these
tools were made?**

BOWES: O.K. I would say they had extremely hard rock. I
would say they made a hammer, and that they set this (projectile point) down and they shoved it into a piece of wood,
or like something that would strike it and strike it and
chip it off in layers. The feeling I had was that they had to
have it braced or put into something solid before they can
do this, but I would say that they concentrated on it very
much. At the time these were made was a time of need. They
were in a hurry. They did cause things to mess up. I would
say the elders or the older men did this (making of points)
through experience. They were craftsmen. I did feel that
when they put this (projectile point) in here (shaft), they
either put the wood through a treatment or put it through
fire or through something where the wood would shrink
and become very, very hard. I felt like they put it (point) in
there (shaft) and it was like wet, and then they dip it in the
fire and keep dipping it or putting this in this liquid,
whatever it is, like resin, like something that would...I felt it
was almost like a varnish or like a glue that they keep dipping it in there. I see like a little bowl, or like a little something with a fire going. I felt they even did it at night.

I see the wood that they were using and I felt it was very
hard, and that it bent...you could bend it. I see them putting
it in the water, or putting it in an oil and they dipped it in
there and then they bent it, almost like they were tempering
it or doing something but I keep seeing them bending it.

JONES: **What are they doing with this wood?**

BOWES: I would say that they were either going to make a
bow out of it, or an arrow. I do feel as though part of an
arrow...if it was split or if it was empty, they soaked this

thing in this... I see this, like resin, kind of wax, or something but I see them dumping it in there. Could even be fire arrows...they keep dumping it in there, coating the arrow with something.

JONES: What other kinds of tools or weapons do you see?

BOWES: I would say they had clubs, or they have like a hatchet...it could be like a club on their side, but I don't feel they used that. I would say they had knives of a sort, and I would say they were extremely sharp.

In the last two passages Bowes twice mentioned the presence of resin at the site in the treating of arrows. Wilmsen,[16] in describing the nature of the artifact assemblage at the Lindenmeier site, states that besides a few pieces of mineral pigment, bone debris, and the characteristic Folsom stone artifacts, the only other item of importance found was one small piece of resin.

The Calendar

In the most recent study of the Lindenmeier site, Wilmsen[17] writes:

Fluctuation in seasonal and long-term cycles of productivity in both plant and animal communities must have been as great then as now. The survival of a hunting group depends upon its ability to predict food conditions in different parts of its territory and to take advantage of these predictions. That these late paleolithic hunting and gathering peoples were successful is demonstrated by the fact that their descendants populated two previously unoccupied American continents in addition to vast areas of the Old World.

Perhaps the Folsom people had a means of keeping records on the productivity of localized resources. Bowes seems to suggest this in the following.

I do see them carving in trees, and I felt like they carved in trees, stories, or carved in wood, and this could even be a totem pole but I felt they made marks or stories that associated with hunts or months of the year.

JONES: Can you draw what these carvings looked like?

BOWES: It could be something like circles or dots, but I felt most of them were slanted.

JONES: When the lines touched?

BOWES: Some of them were like this ($\swarrow$), but more of an angle like this ($\vee$) I felt meant more happiness or more success in the hunt or success in the...

JONES: When the lines touched?

III-16: A calendar tree.

BOWES: Yes. Generally, I feel these(◯)were like moons, like something that they seen in the moon. And these lines (◯)were something where they didn't see the moon. This could be like a calendar...I felt they went back. In other words, when they went up the river they went back and measured these or they talked about these times by looking at that tree. There could be a lot more than that but that's all I seen. Because of the digging into the trees, this was outstanding...you could see it. I feel they worried about their enemies seeing this, but I don't feel their enemies knew what it meant.

Social Life

In his reading of the Folsom materials, Bowes discussed many areas relating to the social life of the people—their family and marriage customs, divisions of labor, customs relating to crime and the elderly, games, political organization, etc.

JONES: Did you get any feelings about family life?
BOWES: The first thing I felt was that...more like a relationship of a man having more than one wife, or having more than two or three wives, or they could have had their sisters or daughters as family, but I would say they do have a family. These other people that attacked them, I don't feel they had that. I feel they were more changing all the time. With these people (artifacts) I felt they took care of the elderly, the older people. The other ones, they left the older people behind...when they were sick, they were weak. I keep seeing something that caused these people (artifacts) to leave their wives and children or whatever behind. I don't know if they valued their children until they got to a certain age. I wouldn't say they valued them...in other words, they felt they were a handicap, but...I don't know if the people who attacked them had a tremendous advantage over them. They may have had more people, but I felt it caused them to be desparate. They tried to go up there (site) as fast as they could to get stuff ready for this attack, and this put them at a disadvantage. If they had stayed and fought, these people would not have probably really never conquered them, or took over or destroyed them.
JONES: Did you get any feeling about whether there were certain jobs that men did and certain jobs that women did, or did men and women have the same jobs?
BOWES: I would say that men and women were different because I kept seeing the men up there putting these arrows together, or putting war things together. Generally I would feel the women worked with wood, cut down trees and did a lot of physical labor. I don't know if they tore into

beaver dams, or whether they made dams in the water or whether there was some sort of...like they were blocking or holding water back with a dam, but I would say the women were more associated with making camp...setting up tents, cooking, doing a lot of physical labor. I would say the men associated more with war. I would say the men were away at times, but basically I felt that these people stayed in one place, that they lived in one area.

Bowes' mention of beaver dams is supported in Spencer and Jenning's[18] *The Native Americans*, when they hypothesize, based on archeological evidence, that Folsom man at Lindenmeier "...camped along the shores of the shallow, marshy lakes or beaver meadows that dotted the country during the glacial age."

When questioned about the nature of crime in the culture under study, Bowes responded:

I would say they could banish. Basically I would say that they challenged the person with fire or combat, like killing each other. In other words, they were continually improving their skill at fighting to defend themselves. I would say the worst thing which they felt was bad was in association to someone who was born crippled. They didn't like that at all and they banished this person or ran them off, or killed them. This could be being paralyzed or it could be anything that is associated with something physically or mentally handi- capped. Especially more physical, like being born with one hand, and I did see this association like marrying among or having sex relationships with their own mothers and such. I felt that associated with it. Something that would not be so much stealing but stealing and getting caught at it. Not so bad if they don't get caught. In other words, making a ruckus and disrupting the harmony of the group. Another thing I felt like being associated with the eyes, or like facing someone straight in the eyes, not looking away, in other words like weakness if a man can't look in another person's eyes. I would say another thing is to wander too far away and then not come back for a long time. In other words, they didn't trust the person after they had been gone for a long time. Not so much with a hunt, but for no apparent reason they came back with no game or especially if they went down the river, they didn't trust them.

JONES: Why?

BOWES: I would say because they came down and looked at these trees (calendar trees), and they came back down where the enemy was. They felt they would be swayed one way or the other by going down that way.

JONES: **Did the men and women hunt together?**

BOWES: I would say that women would only catch small

animals like rabbits or fish. The men would shoot the big game such as deer and elk and whatever. I didn't feel buffalo at all. I didn't feel that at all. Deer and larger animals. I don't know if the men had nets but I felt they were out there in the stream or out there in the water, wading in the water. I felt like the women more like caught rabbits or a mouse or something smaller...they would do more of the skinning and tanning or working with leather. This may have been almost their full time...I would say it did get very cold.

JONES: Do you see a camp scene or a village?

BOWES: I keep seeing it but it is very blurred. I couldn't associate to it clearly. I do see like a sandbar and I see all this smoke coming up like from the tents, or lean-tos and such, but I didn't see it real clear because they possibly kept moving or changing it. I don't know why but I see them having a hoe or like a rock or something through it, but I keep seeing the women digging holes in the sand, and I felt it was right where the river went by, and they keep digging it and water followed them, but I didn't know what they were doing. Maybe they were going to trap fish in there. I keep seeing them digging these little ditches. I didn't feel they were very wide. They were about a foot wide.

JONES: How did they relate to children? What did they think of their children?

BOWES: I would say that the men only seeked in children what would benefit the tribe or them. In other words, if it was a girl they would say that it was something to trade, something to use. But a boy would be more of something that they felt they could...would this boy be crippled? Would this boy be potentially strong? They could even destroy a young boy who was crippled, or leave him out, like the spirits have rejected him or...there was something wrong with him. If the boy seemed healthy and strong, then he watched him...in other words, as being proud, feeling a value in that boy. I felt as though they pulled the young girls by their hair. I don't know what it meant. To cause them to move.

JONES: You mentioned that a girl would be considered something to trade?

BOWES: I didn't feel trade outside the community, but it was like a trade, a horsetrade or something. I didn't feel a son would be traded. A son would be kept for pride, like to become a warrior himself or become subject or become close to his father. The father and son would fight later on, but I still felt pride. With the daughter, I felt it was horses or animals or trade...of arrows or valuables. Again, they don't have horses, so it would be trade.

JONES: Do you have any feelings about marriage with these people?
BOWES: I would say the pride of women...the value of a woman may be very high, very high. But when they get older they may be used for nursemaiding, than being a wife by their side. In other words, they could find a new wife or a younger one, especially a man who had strength in battle or strength in respect in the tribe. I would say the old people were valued but they were valued more as doctors or nurses or people who help people when they were sick. If they were strong enough to live and not get sick, to live long, then they were considered powerful or strong, and then they were given to the people who were sick to help them or to help children.

In this passage Bowes described what appears to be a kind of rite of passage, or ritual of transition, from childhood to adult status. Such rites are very common among known hunting and gathering societies.

I did feel the boys—they may have had games or been made to run, run a distance or something. Play a game. Have to go through things about...like the age of twelve. I did feel as though they could castrate boys, that there was something wrong with them or they were weak.

JONES: Are there any other things that the men would make the boys do?
BOWES: I would say they had to learn to make a bow and arrow or make things. I see them doing something to their head and I don't know if they shaved the head down or they put a band around the head, but I would say they had to... they tied them down or they left them behind, like to prove their manhood, or whatever. I don't feel that the father would tie them down too strong. I felt it was just something more or less...the father was there, he would, you know ...I kept seeing the boys laying flat and then getting up and then going like chasing after them or following them back to camp. I feel an association with the idea of a bear. Everything is bear. An association with danger or fighting. If they can kill a bear, then they are real strong.

JONES: Did you get any feelings about games or children playing?
BOWES: I felt they had many different games. One game was to chase something and I don't know if it was like chasing rabbits or chasing something, but I felt children chased something, or like a mock hunt. With the girls I see them making something, wrapping something, making a doll. I see them wrapping stuff and pulling or stretching things. I don't know if they had a dog or dogs but I felt they played tug-a-war, or they pulled against something...an

animal, a dog. A type of hide-and-go-seek, almost like a hunt again. I felt the men had a sport of throwing something into a tree or splitting something, like a spear contest. Another thing, I felt they had wrestling games, and someone would try to run across the water and the other one would catch him.

JONES: What about leadership? Do you have any feelings about what kind of authority was there?

BOWES: I would say there were two brothers, or two men that worked together. They may have worked in a pattern that they always worked with, but I would say that these two were either warriors of the time or people who everybody respected through past experiences. Basically, I would say that these two people were respected by the group, or tribe, or whatever. They were like brothers. Two men who worked together. In other words, I didn't feel one leader. I felt there may have been a group of people, or like two men. I felt they always broke it up in two groups. In other words, there's two groups and one relied on the other.

JONES: Interesting. Do you get any more about that? About the idea of two groups or why they did it that way?

BOWES: I would say that it was because of their terrain, or because of the knowledge, like one of them knew a certain way to defend something and they felt that was a credit to him, or a credit to him in the way he won that battle, or the way he maneuvered, or like one of them was a great hunter and he knew how to run through the woods and shoot the arrow or shoot the deer. The other one was knowledgeable about rocks, or the up high. I would say the man who was up high, or dealt with rocks, may have been an elderly man, or an older person than the other. I felt as though he knew, possibly how to escape or how to go out of the mountains or the rocks. He may have known caves or something in the rocks. I would say that through their experiences one of them knew more about the woods and one of them may have known more about the rocks. If there was no woods there, then again, it could be desert or any area of open plains, but I felt there was definitely a difference in the way they fought.

This reference to two leaders and two groups resonates with Bowes' reference earlier to the duel environments of the people. Bowes' theme of the "two leaders/two groups/two environments," which appears throughout his reading, is supported in the most modern analysis of the Lindenmeier site by Wilmsen[19] in which he also suggests the existence of two Folsom groups at Lindenmeier, drawing his conclusion from highly sophisticated statistical and computer methodologies. The following quotation is from his conclusion.

There appears to have been a social as well as an ecological reason for the occupations in the Lindenmeier Valley. The territorial range of *two semiautonomous groups* (author's emphasis) probably overlapped here. Periodically, as conditions permitted, these groups scheduled their movements so they would meet in this valley. They did so to cooperate in bison hunts — which neither probably could carry out alone — and to continue a series of social transactions upon which both depended for continued existence. Mates could be exchanged, adolescents initiated into adulthood, the sick and recently dead given proper ceremonial attention, and the natural environment given whatever ritual care that may have been thought necessary.... They would then move in their separate directions to exploit other parts of their own territories from other locations. ...There is at present no way to test these statements (Wilmsen, 1974:116).

Religion

Bowes had many things to say about what he felt to be the religious orientation of the Folsom hunters.

I keep seeing them associating to something of a god, or a certain kind of association with a person out of the past, or a god. I see them yelling up at a mountain, or a valley, or a mountain range and I see them hearing voices, almost like echoes, but I felt they associated this to the gods, or to a religion...I thought they could have worshipped a bird or something that was in this valley. But I see them yelling out into these mountains, or this valley, and thinking that the god was over there on the other side, or like it was over there...like up in the mountains. I keep seeing a man going like this (extends arms forward and upward), over the mountain like he was someone who was contacting a spirit, or contacting people from the past. I do feel they respected their old, old people. I felt good with that. I see them saying something like over the mountain or into the Grand Canyon, or wherever they're at. I would say they could have had totem poles or they could have had certain gods for certain seasons. I see the bird as being very important. I would say there was an owl or an eagle or some bird. I would say birds were one of the biggest things. Again, the mountains and the flying bird up over the mountain...like over the mountain where the bird goes is where the god is. This bird was like a messenger that goes over to the god.

JONES: Do you get any feelings about what they thought the nature of this god was?

BOWES: No. I would say they thought this god was something...in other words, the mountain gave life to the valley, the water came down from the mountain down. The storm came from the mountain and then came down. Lightening came from the mountain down, and this is what I associated with.

JONES: Do you feel these people believed in a soul?

BOWES: Yes. I felt they believed everything had souls...
except the ground. Everything living had a soul. In fact I
felt they ate things and felt they consumed their soul. They
became more stronger by consuming and eating things.

JONES: Do you feel they had an idea of life after death?

BOWES: They would either put him in a cave or throw him
off into a canal, or this mountain, throw him down. But I felt
something falling. I don't know what the difference is here,
but I see them putting a body in a cave. I see it sitting up
almost like it was sitting like this. But then I seen another
body and they threw it off the mountain. They threw it off
into the cavern or down off the mountain.

JONES: Why would they treat one one way and one the
other?

BOWES: I would say possibly death through sickness may
have been something like they put them in a cave because
they might have thought they could re-live. But someone
who had died in battle they may have thrown them off this
mountain, almost to sacrifice him, or throw him into the
mountain, down in this valley, or this hole. I felt that was
more of a sudden thing, something they did suddenly.

JONES: Would they do it again?

BOWES: I wouldn't know. They may have done that only in
war, like when there was wars they threw the body down
there, but...I don't feel they ever showed how many people
they lost. To show that you had somebody killed was a weakness, and this was the feeling I had with it. I don't know if
they scalped people, but I did feel they took part of their
body or they revered part of their body. In other words, to
remember that person...maybe their possessions.

JONES: Do you mean the enemy or their own people?

BOWES: I don't know. I see them saving a part of the body.
Maybe the eyes or the skull or the head or something. It
could have been the skull, like the scalp. I don't feel hair. I
feel part of the skull, like they chopped into the head.

JONES: Do you feel anything about the stories they told, or
maybe the myths they had?

BOWES: I would say they had a myth about a giant bear,
and I felt they were always talking about it being in the
north, and I felt there was truth in it. This bear could have
even been like a polar bear, or a huge...like a kodiak bear,
huge bear, and I felt they always talked about this story of
the bear in the north.

JONES: What was the story about?

BOWES: I would say that this bear that they talked about,
if they went north, or this place where they originated, like
this was their birthplace, and everything was more severe
there, everything was something to brag about. I felt they

talked about this great bear, that no one could kill and that
nobody could destroy. I would say that they had very, very
serious problems with bears in some association.

JONES: Do they have anybody like a doctor?

BOWES: I would say they did have a doctor. I don't know
if he was the one who was standing on top of the mountain
with his arms out but I would say that the chief and the
doctor were very similar, or that one was a power. He may
have decided on battles, or decisions.

JONES: Can you describe the bird you mentioned earlier?

BOWES: It had a curved beak. I kept feeling as though it
was like a hawk or eagle. I definitely feel the dead was something important to them...I would say definitely caves but
that is neither here nor there. I would say the mountain or
the ground was their god, or more relating to the ground,
rocks, solid...rather than air, or the outside of nature. I
would say more that the gods were in the mountains, or the
noises of the mountains. Solids. Anything that's solid. They
may have had a lot of value in water, and may have felt that
the mountain gave them water. I see them continually
crossing water, like streams or water, like rushing water.

Summary: Folsom Ethnography

It is true that Folsom points are diagnostic, but it is also true that
it would be highly improbable that an individual not schooled in New
World Prehistory could be capable of making the proper identification.

Another issue of relevance is the internally consistent description of the Folsom hunters which Bowes offered. Anthropologists
assume that these ancient bison hunters formed themselves into social
groupings called "bands." Bands are kinship-based social units with
low population density. Leadership in bands is typically based on the
personal appeal and magnetism of the leader, and not on heredity or
election. Religion tends to be shamanistic, which means, among other
things, that it would involve animism, or the belief that spirits inhabit
the world. Rites of passage in which children, through dramatic ritual,
are quickly initiated into full adult status are also characteristic of
band society. Warfare, as we know it, is not found among the band
cultures, but raiding, in which short-term forays are made against an
enemy, is found. Often the object of these raids is to capture women
and children. In bands, lacking as they do police, courts, and prisons,
punishment is often typified by banishment, ostracism, or ridicule.

Bowes described the people he was seeing as living in groups of fifty
to seventy-five, which is typical of band populations. He noted that
leadership among the people was based on respect, not on inheritance
or election. When discussing religion, he delineated an animistic view
of the world when he stated, "I felt they believed everything had
souls....". His description of male rites of passage was coherent in the

context of a band people. The kind of war Bowes described is also characteristic of band behavior to the degree that the emphasis seemed to be the stealing of women and children instead of the destruction of the enemy population and occupation of their territory. Infanticide, or the killing of unhealthy or impaired infants, was also suggested by Bowes. This trait is also a custom most often found among hunting and gathering band peoples confronted with periods of dangerous food scarcity. Another point of accuracy is Bowes' reference to the ability of older men to obtain the youngest wives. It is common in band societies for older men to be married to young women. Also, Bowes correctly indicated a band's reaction to crime when he noted the role of banishment among the people he was reading.

A more persuasive issue has to do with the characteristics of the Lindenmeier site. It is suggestive of the possible, though non-demonstrable, accuracy of Bowes' cultural description of the Folsom hunters that he was able to do several things that would be impossible, not specifically knowing the archeological site from which the Folsom materials came. For example, he accurately described the location of the site and its physical features at the time of occupation and at present. To make the point again, not even an expert archeologist could look at Folsom materials and identify the site of their origin. He also indicated, in several ways, the existence of two Folsom groups occupying the Lindenmeier site; a conclusion that has only been reached in the past several years through the use of advanced statistical and computer methodologies.

Conclusion

The St. Simon's Island test and the Lindenmeier site* test show that psychics are able to describe with specificity the nature of the physical and cultural environment from which an artifact collection has originated. Further, as the St. Simon's Island experiment demonstrates, the cultural reconstruction can be detailed to an incredible degree and quite beyond the present capabilities of archeological reconstruction.

It was after these experiments that I felt I had solved one of my original research problems. I had wondered if psychics could, as they claimed, reach back into time and retrieve cultural and historical materials outside the domain of conventional systems of knowing. Even after I had the St. Simon's Island data well in hand, I found it

---

* Portions of the St. Simon's Island material have been published in the *Phoenix* journal (Volume 1, Number 2, 1977) under the title "Experiment in Non-Scientific Discovery Procedures in Archeology"; and sections of the Folsom material have appeared in *Phoenix* (Volume II, Number 1) under the title "Folsom Ethnography." My thanks to the *Phoenix* publishers for permitting the use of those materials in this more expanded format.

difficult to accept what it indicated. While delivering a paper concerning this particular project to a scholarly meeting of anthropologists, I recall asking the audience in attendance at the symposium to criticize my research, to tell me where the flaw was, to relieve me from confronting what I was being forced to confront about the nature of the perception of time and space. Though I repeatedly asked for a rational means of negating the St. Simon's Island findings, I found none. There was only one strong inference to make: certain human beings are able to violate the accepted norms concerning space and time, to in effect travel in time.

At this point in my research I began to explore other ways in which psychics could be used to further the aims of archeological investigation.

References

1. J.R. Swanton, "Indians of the Southeastern United States", in *Bureau of American Ethnology Bulletin*, 1946, p.405.
2. C. Hudson, *The Southeastern Indians* (Knoxville: University of Tennessee Press, 1976), pp.226-227.
3. Ronald Wallace, "An Archeological, Ethnohistorical and Biochemical Investigation of the Guale Aborigines of the Georgia Coastal Strand". A dissertation, Dept. of Anthropology, University of Florida, Gainesville, Florida, 1975, p.70.
4. C.E. Bennett, trans., *The Three Voyages of Rene Laudonniere* (Gainesville: University of Florida Press, 1975), pp.88-89.
5. *Ibid.*, p.161.
6. C.E. Bennett, trans., *Laudonniere and Fort Caroline: History and Documents* (Gainesville: University of Florida Press, 1964), p.81.
7. H.L. Peterson, *Arms and Armor in Colonial America: 1526-1783* (New York: Brinhall House, 1956).
8. Bennett, *Laudonniere and Fort Caroline*, p.26.
9. *Ibid.*, p.26.
10. Hudson, *Southern Indians*, p.139.
11. W.R. Wedel, *Prehistoric Man on the Great Plains* (Norman: University of Oklahoma Press, 1961), p.61.
12. E.N. Wilmsen, *Lindenmeier: A Pleistocene Hunting Society* (New York: Harper & Row, 1974), p.17.
13. R.F. Spencer et al., *The Native Americans* (New York: Harper & Row, 1977), p.19.
14. Wilmsen, *Pleistocene Hunting Society*, p.13.
15. G.D. DeGarmo, "Big Game Hunters: An Alternative and an Hypothesis". A paper presented at the 35th Annual Meeting of the Society for American Archeology, 1970.
16. Wilmsen, *Pleistocene Hunting Society*, p.69.
17. *Ibid.*, pp.10-11.
18. Spencer et al., *Native Americans*, p.10.
19. Wilmsen, *Pleistocene Hunting Society*, pp.10-11.

IV

EXCAVATION EXPERIMENTS

The opportunity to carry out a series of experiments related to the excavation of an archeological site presented itself in the spring of 1976. At that time archeologist R. L. Wallace directed anthropology students in an archeological field-school out of the university with which I was affiliated. The focus of the activity was the excavation of an Indian mound site on the St. Johns River in east central Florida.

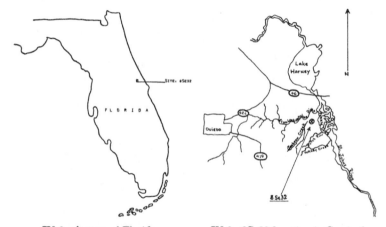

IV-1: A map of Florida.

IV-2: 8Se32 location in Seminole
county, Florida.

The site is listed in the archeological records of the state of Florida as 8Se32. "8" is the code designation of Florida. "Se32" indicates that the site is the 32nd officially excavated site in Seminole County, Florida. The site is a low, flat mound ten feet high at its highest point and covering an area of approximately 6000 square feet. 8Se32 is located in Seminole County about three miles south of Lake Harney and one mile west of the St. Johns River which flows into Lake Harney through Puzzle Lake from the Everglades. The surrounding environment is typical of the inland riverine areas in this part of Florida. The soil is poorly drained thus creating marshy conditions around much of the mound, especially from the borders of the mound eastward to the banks of the river. On the mound and immediately to the west and south, trees such as the red maple, southern red cedar, and live oak suggest somewhat higher and drier soil conditions.

The completed excavation of the site indicated that below the levels bearing evidence of human habitation, there existed a slight natural rise. It is probable that this small area of elevated ground in the otherwise marshy environment of the site attracted human attention thousands of years ago, and that continual use of the area contributed to the gradual accumulation of refuse which today is represented by the mound itself.

Due to limitations of time and money, the entire site was not excavated. The total excavation of a site is, in fact, rare in American archeology. A trench 3 meters wide and 43 meters long was placed in a north-south line through the center of the mound. In addition, two test pits were excavated to the east and west of the main trench. This partial excavation method contributed to some interesting problems when evaluating the psychics' reporting concerning the nature of the mound. If the psychic subject stated that a particular artifact was present in the site, the lack of its discovery during excavation would not disprove the presence of the artifact. It could mean that the item in question, though perhaps present in some part of the site, may not have been found. Then again, the artifact suggested by the psychic to be present in the site, but not found by the archeologists, may in fact not exist.

8Se32 is composed primarily of the remains of freshwater shell-fish deposited by the long extinct shellfish-gathering cultures of the area. Later analysis proved that the site was not a ceremonial or burial mound, though two burials were discovered in the site. Essentially, 8Se32 was, as Bowes would correctly surmise, an ancient pile of garbage. Additional study of the mound's archeological materials would also show that the site, during the peak phases of its occupation, was in the main a seasonally occupied shellfish-gathering area used by Indians who moved from habitat to habitat on regular rounds of exploiting the various food resources of east central Florida.

The higher conditions of the mound also made it an attractive campsite for Indians traveling north and south along the St. Johns River. This important river has been a food resource, a highway, and a refuge area for the native peoples of eastern Florida from earliest times. The site was also probably used as a butchering area at which big game kills could be processed for food and hide in the relative comfort of the mound's dry elevation. The many chopped and charred animal bones at the test site indicated this interpretation by the archeologists.

The animal resources available to the ancient populations of this area included such big game as the black bear, white-tailed deer, alligator, and manatee (or sea cow) as well as raccoon, bobcat, rabbit, grey fox, opossum, and turkey. In addition there were many varieties of edible turtles, fish, birds, reptiles and amphibians. Notably present was a wide sampling of freshwater shellfish species and snails. Plant life was likewise rich. Among the edible plants and plant products in the area are acorns, blackberries, cabbage palms, cat tails, deer moss, ferns, persimmons, pine, red maple, saw palmetto, water lily, wild plum, and wild grape.

The human artifact and bone remains taken from the test site by the archeologists yielded only a tenuous interpretation of the mound's history. A major factor impinging on the researchers' ability to be more certain of the cultural history of the site was the extensive root action in the upper zones of the site. Many centuries of plant life on the site had served to confuse and disrupt the stratigraphy, or consecutive layering, of the cultural materials. Therefore, a single spadeful of earth from 8Se32 could contain pottery pieces of a type dating to 1000 B.C., other pieces dating to 800 A.D., and still other fragments related to 16th century cultural activity.

An indication of the antiquity of the site is found at the very lowest levels, well below the midden accumulation. There, intruding into the sterile zone (soil yielding no evidence of human occupation) was found the burial of a young female in a flexed, or fetal, position. Small human cranial fragments were found in direct association with the torso of the young woman leading the senior archeologist at the site to suggest death during childbirth. Due to the fact that this burial was found well below the shell mound itself, it is very possible that this is a Paleo-Indian (ancient Indian) burial dating as much as 8-10,000 years into the past.

The Paleo-Indians entered Florida about 10,000 years ago. They came mainly from the western United States, being drawn into Florida by the herds of horses, camels, mastodon, bison, and deer which grazed and watered along the numerous lakes and rivers of the state. The watercourses also provided them with fish and manatee, though their primary subsistence activity centered around big game hunting. Farming was totally absent among these ancients, and gathering played a minor role in their search for food. The Paleo-Indian populations left little behind them due to their highly nomadic life way. They are witnessed by very old campsites usually found near river crossings, lakes, and savannas. It is believed that these areas attracted them because of the ease with which game animals could be hunted in such environments.

In the later phases of the Paleo-Indian period the climate began to shift toward drier conditions. Many big game animals became extinct about that time. Food sources previously available became increasingly scarce, and the ancient Indians were forced to change their patterns of obtaining food. This modification in subsistence activity from big game hunting to a mixed technology of hunting, fishing, and gathering marked the beginning of what archeologists refer to as "The Archaic Period." It was during this time that native Floridians began to exploit the abundant shellfish populations of the areas' rivers, and to leave behind them shell middens such as 8Se32. This first occurred about 5000 B.C. along the St. Johns River.

Approximately two-thirds of the mound, directly overlaying the burial of the young female, was found to be predominantly shell

IV-3: *Timucuan Indians.* Reproduced by permission of Smithsonian Institute.

debris. The absence of pottery and the presence of bone and shell tools, beads, and a flint cache suggest that a major occupation of the site occurred during the early, or "pre-ceramic", Archaic Period which persisted until about 2000 B.C. Since the test site demonstrates extensive Archaic occupation, some amplification of this cultural phase might be useful. Hudson[1] describes the Archaic Period in the Southeastern United States in this way:

> Instead of a primary reliance on hunting large animals, the Archaic tradition was more diversified and efficient, being based on the gathering of vegetable foods, particularly acorns and hickory nuts, fishing, and the hunting and trapping of small woodland animals. People in the Archaic became increasingly sedentary, making their living in smaller and smaller territories, and they became increasingly efficient in exploiting all the food resources the environment had to offer. The Archaic tradition left its marks on all subsequent cultures of the Southeast.

Another important feature of the Archaic is the apparent importance associated with the ritual burial of the dead. It is very common to find red ocher, weapons, tools, and often the bodies of dogs in Archaic burials.

The invention of fired clay fiber-tempered pottery occurred about 2000 B.C. in the Southeast. All ceramic pieces found at the site were found in the top several feet of the mound. One hundred and forty-three fragments of fiber-tempered pottery were recovered. This type of pottery is datable and indicates occupation of the site between

2000 B.C. and 500 B.C. In the later stages of this time period the economic life of the inhabitants of this part of the St. Johns River came to be characterized by the addition to their food inventories of cultigens like maize and squash. This time-span also marks the beginning of a new cultural period in the Southeast which archeologists call "The Woodland Period." This cultural phase is typified by the widespread use of pottery, the introduction of rudimentary agriculture, the continued elaboration of burial procedures, and, in various places, the construction of monumental earthworks.

However, of the 5,862 ceramic pieces found at the test site, 5,011 were of the "St. Johns I" type. This kind of ceramic dates from 500 B.C. to 800 A.D. It may be assumed, therefore, that there was intensive human activity at this site during this time frame.

Also found at 8Se32 were 108 fragments of check-stamped pottery, a type termed "St. Johns II" and dating from 800 A.D. to 1565 A.D. St. Augustine, the oldest city of non-native American origin was established in 1565 A.D. on the northeast coast of Florida. It is probable that the Indian people stopping at 8Se32 on their subsistence rounds were aware of the presence of the early Spanish invaders at St. Augustine.

The following list notes relevant historical events occurring after the founding of St. Augustine which would have affected the native people who used 8Se32 from the 17th into the late 19th century.

1656: Indian rebellion against the Spanish lasting eight months. English pressure directed to remove the Spanish presence from Florida increases at this time. Pestilence claims half of the "mission" Indian population mainly around the St. Augustine area.

1700: Members of the Creek Indian Confederacy (forerunners of the contemporary Seminole) begin moving into northern Florida due to the growing hostilities with English settlements in Carolina and Georgia.

1763: British take Florida.

1783: Spain retakes Florida.

1814: Andrew Jackson defeats the Creek Nation in the Battle of Horseshoe Bend. The defeated Red Stick faction moves into Florida. At this time they outnumbered the Creek Indians already there.

1818: Andrew Jackson enters Florida in punitive raid against the Seminoles. The term "Seminole" is a derivation of a Creek word meaning "wild" or "renegade."

1821: United States acquires Florida.

1830: United States Congress decrees that all Indians should be removed from the east to lands west of the Mississippi River.

1835- First Seminole War. Various groups of Seminoles refused
1842 to be removed, thus drawing military attention from the U.S. Army intent on enforcing the orders of the Congress.

Throughout this time the Seminole people continued to drop southward using the St. Johns River as a major north-south migration route.

1855-   Second Seminole War. By this time most of the military
1859   action was taking place in south Florida.

1860-   Civil War. Military action on the St. Johns River.

1864-   From the end of the Civil War to the present time, the area
present immediately west of 8Se32 has been used mainly for cattle
        and citrus production by white land owners. To the east of
        the site the marshy conditions still prevail to the waters of
        the St. Johns River. Looking to the east one sees today
        what the ancient Indian inhabitants at the site would have
        seen thousands of years ago—flat, wet prairies covered
        with wax myrtle, leatherfern, wire grass, and sea myrtle
        stretching miles toward the coast interspersed with the
        convoluted flow of the St. Johns River as it finds its way
        through the many bodies of water collectively and aptly
        called Puzzle Lake.

In addition to the burial of the female at the bottom of the mound and the ceramics already noted, the test site also yielded the following items:

a.) Eleven projectile points.

b.) A flint-cache consisting of forty-two pieces.

c.) Several fire hearths.

d.) A number of conch shell tools. Suggesting possible contact with the Atlantic coast.

e.) A highly disturbed burial occurring in the top portion of the mound which consisted of tibia, fibula fragments, carpals, metacarpals, and phalanges.

f.) One small shell or bone bead, round to oval in shape.

g.) One small, flat, white bead made from shell.

h.) A worked, rectangular, smooth, flat stone about 2" by 1" in size.

i.) A rectangular piece of iron, flat with one edge thinned, measuring 2½" x 1½" in size.

j.) Several pieces of worked bone, possibly pins, awls or hooks.

k.) A fragment of nail of non-Indian manufacture.

l.) A number of small, thin iron flakes of unknown association.

m.) One small piece of white glazed ceramics of European manufacture.

The absence of any sure evidence of post-holes further suggests that 8Se32 was not a major habitation site, but rather a shellfish gathering area, butchering platform, and temporary campsite throughout its long history.

8Se32 did not prove to be a very dramatic site by layman's standards, or by archeologists' standards for that matter. However, its very ordinary nature made it a perfect laboratory for the type of testing in which I was interested. Since the test site is typical of the kinds of sites most archeologists deal with most of the time, the reactions of the psychics to it would best indicate what an archeologist might expect in working with psychic assistants during the excavation of a site.

As the experiments related to this site are discussed in the succeeding sections of this chapter, additional cultural and historical information will be added to amplify the context of many of the statements made by the psychics as they dealt with materials from 8Se32. Remember that neither the contents of the mound nor its cultural-historical association could be known prior to the completed excavation of the site by the archeological team from the university. As will be seen, however, Albert Bowes was able to make an impressive series of predictions (many later proved to be correct) about the site before its excavation and many months before even a preliminary site report was possible using conventional archeological reporting and analytic methods.

First Experiment: 8Se32

The first experiment related to 8Se32 was based on an observation I had made while collecting general background information on the psychics involved in my research. Several of them had mentioned their ability to psychically read photographs. In fact, this was quite a common feature of their relationships with clients. People who were arranging for an interview or reading with the psychic might be asked to bring photographs of individuals who would be the subject of the client's questions to the psychic. My own experience with psychics, using photographs of family members and friends, had indicated that indeed many of these photograph readings, about people never met by the psychic, were often amazingly accurate and specific.

Several months prior to the excavation of 8Se32, and without warning Bowes in advance of the nature of this particular experiment, I mailed to him four photographs that I had taken of the site. In the accompanying letter I simply stated that the pictures were of an actual archeological site, and that I wanted him to attempt to tell me about the site's location and cultural-historical context. Bowes kept the pictures for three days, reading them, tape recording his impressions, leaving the task and returning to it again as his busy schedule permitted.

It would be tempting to dismiss this experiment by observing that Bowes had three days in which he could take the photographs to local museums or departments of anthropology for some "expert" opinions about the nature of the site. In response I can only state the obvious. The pictures do not in any way show that the site is located in east central Florida. The environment the photographs reveal could be found from South Carolina to South America; from India to the Texas Gulf Coast; in short, in any sub-tropical location. Further, the photographs do not indicate the ten-foot mound, because that was a fact known only after the excavation in which it was found that the bottom eight feet of the mound had literally sunk into the moist earth, leaving a gentle rise only two feet high in a kind of "tip of the iceberg" effect. Also, I purposely took the photographs from a vantage point well onto the mound to further mask the "mound" nature of the site. What Bowes had to work with in this phase of the testing were four poorly exposed and badly focused photographs of a sub-tropical forest clearing. All he knew was that some cultural activity had occurred on the spot shown in the picture.

Environmental Statements

In the first half of the first page of the tape transcript of his reading, Bowes correctly located the site in the vicinity of the St. Johns River, and also described its shell mound status.

> I did feel as though these people lived away from the St. Johns, or away from the primary river source...I keep seeing the ground being round almost like a spoilbank or like a pile of shells....

Water animals and shellfish also appeared early in his reading.

> The first thing I picked up was something about an otter, or an animal that they skinned, and then I picked up something about shellfish, or like a raccoon, and I picked up something ...either a shellfish or a turtle.

The following are excerpts from the reading in which Bowes repeatedly described the wet, marshy locale of the site and the flat expanse of savanna extending eastward to the water's edge.

> The feeling I had was there was a low area, or a place or grass that possibly had water near there, and I felt it was almost like a round circle, or almost like a little swamp or something, but I felt water near there.

> I kept seeing something about people wading. I kept seeing them wading up to their knees.

> I still see it as a slope or an area where there was water.

> I do see saw grass or mud.

> I would say these people talked about passing or crossing the river... They ate shellfish, but I did see them associating with the salt water or the beaches...or traveling in that direction. I keep seeing a large turtle or like a big shell, and I don't know if these are soft shell turtles, but I do feel as though there are shells there.

> I don't feel so much with a place with a lot of mosquitoes. I keep seeing more of a place that was open and lots of grass and I see the wind blowing.

> I keep seeing a place where there's like a little dock or a place where they set up a wood walk-way or something over the grass or over the water.

I would say that this ground was higher, away from the water, away from the river front. With something to do with grass... I kept feeling if there was a lake or like an ancient lake near there that associated with...like you could walk out to the edge of this bank or to the edge of this mound and look and I would say there was a grass lake....

I keep seeing several of them talking about traveling or traveling on the water and I feel as though this was the best way they knew how to travel, or the thing that they enjoyed or did more than traveling on land. I don't know if they worked around with alligators or something, but I keep seeing them scaring or throwing something or chasing something away, and I keep seeing eggs, like almost as if they were alligator eggs or something like huge or large eggs.

A few miles due north of the site is Lake Harney, one of the largest lakes fed by the St. Johns River. Perhaps Bowes was indicating the presence of Lake Harney in the following excerpt concerning a large lake north of the site.

I kept feeling like they were talking about or associating with a large body of water, and I would say that was north of the direction the water flowed. I would say it was a large lake. They keep talking about rough water, like they called it 'hah-toda' or 'ta-toa', or something, some name, and I felt with this name there was a meaning and the meaning meant 'rough water.' I don't know if this was Lake Monroe (the next large St. Johns lake north of Lake Harney) or north of where they lived but I kept seeing them not going beyond there.

Bowes' reference to 'rough water' is significant. A university fish biologist recently told me that Lake Harney was well-known for the unusual severity of its chop, especially in late afternoon. Another excellent indicator of the location is offered by Bowes when he stated, "...when they left this place I see them going to higher ground, like rolling hills or hills of sand, and I would say it was located toward Titusville, or towards the south, maybe southeast...". Titusville, Florida is, in fact, about thirty-five miles southeast of the test site on the Atlantic coast.

There are several remains of old sugar mills north of the site on Lake Harney and at New Smyrna Beach, Florida. Bowes touched upon this when he said, "I don't know if there was...like sugar mills or something that associated with the north, but I keep seeing it up the river and I see them talking about or associating something with somebody living north of them...".

Nature and Physical Composition of the Site

His identification of the site as a mound came early and casually when he was making a statement about the number of women he saw at the site.

I kept seeing mostly women associated with this mound.

In the succeeding passages of the readings he identified the site as a mound several times. Of equal importance, he never offered any alternative description of the site's basic character.

He again proved correct in his opinion of what the site essentially was.

> I felt like it was a pile of debris, almost like it was a pile of shells or a pile of bones or garbage...like a garbage dump. I do feel as though later on dirt may have settled in there or there may have been dirt associated with it...I feel basically that this area is nothing more than a garbage dump.

More specifically, he offered the following observations about the types of soil found in association with the mound. Soil analysis is a basic aspect of almost all modern archeological excavation work. The archeological site report described the bulk of the mound's soil type as "dark gray-brown fine humic soil." Sandy soil was not found until the bottom-most layers of the mound were exposed. From his photograph reading Bowes reported:

> But the feeling I had was I seen ground, like dark brown or black dirt, and I didn't see sand now. I didn't see sand at all, but I see dark brown or black dirt...

The completed excavation demonstrated that the original mound was approximately eight feet higher than the present mound contour. The original height of the mound was alluded to by Bowes in the following passage.

> I keep seeing almost as if it was at one time very high in a certain area and I keep seeing the ground being round almost like a spoilbank or like a pile of shells or something and I see it quite steep and then it drops off the other side.

Inhabitants of the Site

In the third sentence of his blind reading of the photographs Bowes identified the primary inhabitants of the site as Indians.

> Another thing I picked up was I felt the water was higher at the time the Indians were there.

He was also right about the direction from which the mound's users and makers came. "I kept seeing north, and I see the people coming from the north."

However, as the earlier description of the results of the mound's excavation showed, there were a number of different types of Indian cultures represented in 8Se32. The Paleo-Indian presence seemed indicated by the burial of the female. The pre- and post-ceramic Archaic cultures touched this area, as did the Woodland tradition and the later Seminole. In his reading Bowes pointed to the presence of the various Indian traditions which we know archeologically did exist at the test site. This is not an automatic assumption. There are sites in this area that are shell middens of the Archaic period. There are historical sites which reveal Spanish sugar mills and Civil War fortifications. There are Woodland sites and a few strictly Paleo-Indian sites.

Bowes suggested the "meat-eating" Paleo-Indians of the site and the later Archaic adaptation, which elevated the importance of gathering in the food quest, in the following sections from the reading.

> I would say that the original people who lived in this area, originally were very primitive. I keep seeing an association with people who may have not had any clothes, or people....
> I don't know if they were cannibals or if they were people who ate mostly meat, but I keep seeing them as people who were very primitive. Now as time goes on, I felt a little more... associated with gathering things in their area. I don't know if these are clams or whatever.

It was discovered after the archeological analysis of the site's materials that 8Se32 was not a permanent habitation site. The inhabitants moved in and out of the site over thousands of years for a variety of reasons. In fact this pattern of temporary subsistence exploitation of a site followed by movement to another food-getting area was typical of the Archaic Period, the era largely responsible for the shell and artifact deposites found at 8Se32. Bowes noted the nomadic tendency in the site's population.

> I don't know why but I felt as though they didn't live in this place permanently. I felt an association with movement, or change.

> I do see them continuing to move.

Evidence of the Woodland tradition existed at the test site in the presence of certain types of pottery which correlate with this cultural period in the Southeast. The pottery evidence of 8Se32 indicated a minor Woodland style adaptation at the site itself. Bowes did not stress this phase, though he did emphasize the preceding and succeeding stages of culture history in this vicinity. In the last sentence of his reading he mentioned a Woodland trait (cultigens) when he said: "...I did see them growing something, and I don't know if they were vines or blueberries or something."

The place of the Seminole was alluded to several times in Bowes' reading. Bowes, for example, was puzzled by his repeated impressions concerning the large number of women at this site.

> ...something I picked up about the people was an association with mostly women, and I don't know what it means, but I kept seeing mostly women associated with this mound.

> I did feel as though women may have been here for a period of time, but I see them planning on moving.

The allusion to women at the site was again mentioned in the following excerpts as Bowes appeared to be describing the Seminole Wars.

> I kept seeing people in gray uniforms or something in a blue or gray uniform and I would say there was something almost ...they almost looked like cavalry, but I felt they had funny hats. I did feel as though these people could have been some-

one who...I don't know if they captured Indians or whether they made slaves out of them, but I keep seeing chains or shackles and I kept feeling as though this may have caused the people to move. This could have been the last straw or whatever. I keep feeling as though that when they caused this to happen there were mostly women there and this is the last thing I picked up is an association with women. I see them moving and I kept feeling as though they moved south and I don't know if they moved to a place where there was sand, but I kept seeing them moving south and traveling on south.

Bowes' confusion over the inordinate numbers of women he saw in connection with 8Se32 and the female populations' relationship to the tensions with the men that "almost looked like cavalry" is possibly explained in an account concerning the behavior during the Second Seminole War of the Seminole chief, Coacoochee. In 1841 in a conference with Major Childs, commander of Fort Pierce, Coacoochee admitted that for months he had been busily engaged in moving women and children southward to the safe haven of the Everglades.[2] The test site, located in the forest edge along the St. Johns River, would have been a perfect temporary hiding place on the Seminoles' journey south.

Periods of Intensive Occupation of the Site

Bowes suggested in this experiment the presence of two major habitations of 8Se32. As will be seen, this theme continued in other Bowes' experiments related to the mound site.

I don't know if there was two different types of people living here, but I keep seeing two different times that they may have lived in this area.

I would say that this place was abandoned at some time and then someone returned there, but I didn't feel so strong with how long.

These spontaneous observations, based on Bowes' handling of four pre-excavation photographs of an unknown site, offer a novel kind of reinforcement of one of the most probable interpretations of the test site's culture history. In listing the site's contents it was mentioned that most of the shell midden is evidence of a pre-ceramic Archaic occupation with dates ranging from about 7000 B.C. to 3000 B.C. There is evidence of a continual utilization of the site after the introduction of pottery at about 2000 B.C. It is only in the St. Johns I Period (500 B.C.-800 A.D.) that we again find evidence of a massive human presence at 8Se32 attested to by the 5,011 St. Johns I potsherds found out of a total of 5,862 in the entire excavation. As Bowes suggested, there is a very strong indication of two different periods of intensive use of the site—one during the Archaic Period and one during the later St. Johns I phase.

Steamboats?

Viewing four pictures of a sub-tropical forest clearing, Bowes spoke of steamboats.

> I seen an association with something of the idea of a steamboat or some sort of a boat. I keep seeing it larger than a canoe. Now I don't know if this would be a boat that makes a lot of noises, or whether it associates with something that they would dislike or be afraid of, but I kept seeing that.

> …but again I hear noises, almost like it was thunder, or like something…like steam or like something very loud exploding, and I felt it was towards the water. This could be a cannon of some sort (Bowes makes a hissing and exploding sound).

I did not know what to make of these impressions until one of my research assistants came upon "The Journal of Lieutenant John Pickell: 1836-1837."[3] Pickell's journal shows that not one, but two steamboats, the *Santee* and the *McLean*, operated within a mile of 8Se32. The journal entry which noted the presence of the *Santee* and the *McLean* at the mouth of Lake Harney is dated August 22, 1837. Pickell's account also indicated that rocket-flares were in constant use as a means of signalling. Such primitive rockets could account for the hissing-exploding sound that Bowes heard as he read the photographs of the site.

Contents of the Site

Bowes mentioned at various points the kinds of things he felt would and would not be found upon excavation of the site.

> I do see a nail or metal in the ground. I don't know if this was metal that was carried there or whether it was dropped there by someone later on but I did see metal.

> I did see like pieces of metal in the ground…like little pieces.

> I kept seeing this chain and this nail and things that were metal in the ground.

As the earlier description of the mound's contents showed, several pieces of metal were in fact found; a fragment of a metal blade, a number of iron flakes, and a nail. Only one nail was found, and as the above passage indicated, Bowes predicted the presence of only a single nail. Further, Bowes represented a portion of a nail in the drawing that accompanied his reading, and it was but a fragment of a nail that was found by the archeologists.

IV-4 A nail fragment.

The excavation uncovered one complete burial and mere pieces of a second. Bowes stated in his reading, "I really feel as though this site or this area may not show that many bones or people."

A theme running throughout the reading dealt with a human skull separated from the body, or heads and necks damaged in some fashion. In his drawing accompanying the reading Bowes drew a single skull as well as depictions of severed heads impaled on poles.

I keep seeing someone with a broken neck or someone with a ...I keep feeling the neck. I don't know if someone was hanged or whether there was a problem with someone being attached but I keep seeing something like their neck was broken.

I kept seeing poles with heads on them. I felt like there was a skull on top, and I felt like there was black hair hanging from them. I don't know what that associates with but I would say they could be cannibals or this could be like a way of...like reward.

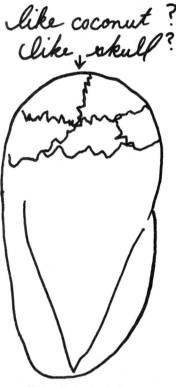

IV-5: A single skull.

The severing of body parts and the mounting of "war trophy" heads on poles was commonly described for the early Florida Indians, as was cannibalism. It should be noted that one of the two burials found at 8Se32 was lacking a head. Perhaps the head is at the site today but was simply not found. Animal or root disruption could explain why the head was not found with the remainder of the human bones. Or, Bowes may be right.

Conclusion: First Experiment Related to 8Se32

The photograph experiment proved fruitful. Bowes could, simply by looking at four photographs of a forest clearing, indicate the location and environment of the site, the site's nature and composition, and the general cultural history of the target location. He also demonstrated the ability to describe certain artifact categories which would be present at the site. Further, he appears to have been able to note various unique and obscure historical incidents related to 8Se32, such as the Lake Harney steamboats described in "The Journals of Lieutenant John Pickell" and the large number of women at the site

IV-6: Mounted heads at 8Se32.

potentially accounted for in the reference to Coacoochee's interview with Major Childs. Bowes also anticipated the possibility of two major habitation periods which the ceramic inventory and the ancient burial may suggest.

<h3 align="center">SECOND EXPERIMENT: 8Se32</h3>

Several weeks after Bowes had mailed his reading of the photographs to me, I arranged for him to actually visit 8Se32 with archeologist Wallace and me. I tape recorded Bowes as he wandered over the site and offered spontaneous readings as well as responses to questions put to him by Wallace and me.

Themes from Photograph Reading Reiterated and Elaborated

In this section I will note basic information areas that Bowes touched upon in his reading of the photographs of the site and again mentioned while physically present at the site.

(a.) *Nature and Composition of Mound.* The fact that the mound was basically a debris pile built upon an ancient natural rise and that it was much higher in the past was again indicated by Bowes as he stood on the site.

> **WALLACE: Do you feel we are going to find shells and pottery all the way down to the bottom or do you think this is just some kind of natural dome formation and we will just find sand underneath and evidence they camped on it?**
> BOWES: I felt they camped on top of it. Basically I really don't think they made this hill but they did pile debris here. As time went on...like a garbage dump. As things were broken or finished like a shell they had eaten or did something with a bone, they threw it out.

JONES: Is this rise natural or is it a garbage dump?
BOWES: I would say it was high here and it was a place
where they could stop and rest, but I would say that they did
make a garbage dump out of it.

I do feel this area in here was higher, much higher... In other
words...the mound was higher.

The relative lack of sand in the mound, noted by Bowes in the first
experiment, was once again mentioned.

I don't feel there is any sand anywhere around here. I'm
talking about white sand, and I said that in the tape (referring to his earlier reading of the four photographs of 8Se32).

(b.) *Burials.* In the first experiment Bowes stated that he felt very
little evidence of human skeletal remains would be found at this site.
Again, while on the site, Bowes stated, "if you find skulls here, it
would surprise me. Basically I felt this (potsherd) is what you're
going to find." As has been noted only one skull was found, while over
5000 pieces of pottery were recovered.

For the reader who may feel that Bowes could produce his apparent
accuracy concerning lack of human physical remains simply by
making generalizations about known mound builder cultures of
Florida, it should be noted that the Browne Mound, excavated by
William H. Sears[4] on the lower St. Johns River produced, like 8Se32,
a preponderance of St. Johns I potsherds, but very much unlike 8Se32,
evidence of forty-four burials.

(c.) *Heads on Posts.* The burial without a head at the test site could
possibly have produced Bowes' descriptions and drawings noted in the
first experiment. Toward the end of the walk-over of the site Bowes
once more returned to this subject.

What I picked up when I first seen the first picture is that
people were hung here or were killed, and again it could pertain to that head that was on the post. In other words, whoever was searching for them if they found some people here
they might have killed them...put their heads on the post to
scare the other ones... The first thing I seen with the picture
and the first thing I felt when I walked up here is death...like
death through the neck. So does that give you anything? I
don't know if it makes sense or not.

His continual references to severed skulls and damaged necks of
course made no sense until the burial *sans* cranium was unearthed
about a month later.

(d.) *Women at 8Se32.* As Bowes stood on the mound he stated, "...I
see mostly women here for some reason." At another point during
the afternoon at the site, when the subject of women again appeared, I
asked, "When you talk about seeing women associated with the site,
is that in terms of the earliest people or the later people?" Bowes'
response was:

I really don't know. I really can't tell you about that. I felt it was more toward the last, but I felt they stayed here and they stayed busy doing something.

The Seminole Wars would be "more toward the last" in the great span of the mound's temporal existence.

(e.) *Two Major Habitation Periods.* As in the photograph experiment related to 8Se32, the actual visit to the site produced a number of references to the possibility of two different habitations of the site, one by a very primitive people, and one by more typically "Indian" types.

BOWES: No trees. Just all grass like this and there was water about this deep (indicates several feet) in the grass that went in there (north). If you had a topo (topographic) map you might be able to see a circle in here, or like a place where possibly water came in.

JONES: Why is this so important?

BOWES: It's important because I felt this is the way they came into the mound. This is the way they came in and out.

JONES: For the people who came in here, was this a regular stop?

BOWES: Yes. The feeling I had was the other place was up that way (points to the south-south-east). They came down the river and they could come in here... They knew this was high ground. They came in and stayed here and then they went on. They were travelers.

JONES: These people didn't have a home base around here?

BOWES: But the original people may have stayed here. The original people...the real primitive people may have been here in this area.

JONES: So to the earlier people this may have been home?

BOWES: Right.

JONES: And then later this was just a stopping off point for some people moving through?

BOWES: Yes. Going down the river, or going here and there. Let me ask you a question. Is there a large lake right up there (points north)?

JONES: Yes. Lake Harney is about two or three miles up that way. How many people do you feel associated with this mound?

BOWES: I would say the original people...there would have been a couple hundred. But I feel the last group I wouldn't say was over fifty people.

JONES: The original group...do you get a feeling of where they were?

BOWES: I felt they walked all over this place. I didn't see them going in and out with the water so much, but I felt they were naked...walking in the woods, walking between the palm trees. I thought they were real strong in the buttocks, and their legs were real strong. The other people I felt were thinner and skinnier...the last ones I felt were associated with the water. I felt they had stronger arms and I felt they were more...thinner. Taller maybe.

JONES: Did the last people have clothing?

BOWES: Yes. Yes.

JONES: What did it look like?

BOWES: I would say that it would be leather and I kept seeing these other uniforms I was telling you about. And I felt there was something associated with black...something of black with lines of red and green and all colors...like lines. (Suggestive, of course, of the colorful and well-known clothing of the Florida Seminole).

WALLACE: Do you have any feelings about any kinds of ornaments that the people who lived here might have worn—

BOWES: I felt like bracelets and things around their neck, and I felt they were mostly bones and teeth. The funniest thing...I kept feeling like the first people who were here, their faces were funny, like they were ugly, almost like they were cavemen or like they were real ugly, like their faces were real big, like big jaws. I felt like they were real primitive, but these last people I felt were more like typical Indians, like Seminoles or like a round face. I felt they were more like a civilized person...a more civilized type. These other people were humped over and may have had very poor health.

I did feel that they collected alligator teeth, especially the first original people, and I felt alligators were the big things ... This could be a long, long time ago. This could be two or three hundred years...long, long ago. It could be longer than that. Very huge reptiles. Alligators. But the last people, I didn't feel they would associate with alligators, maybe see them or something...maybe to shoot them or something, but I didn't feel that was anything real important. The other people (original people), I felt they were rattling or making a noise, a thumping or pulling something back and 'thud', or making a thud noise while going out through there (points to the north).

*   *   *

BOWES: (referring to the original populations' fascination with alligators). I felt they said something about the eyes, and they always taught the young boys to poke the eyes out, like they were afraid the animal could still see them. Like superstition...because I see them poking at it and it's got something real heavy over it. They might have nightmares about the eyes...opening up after it's dead or something. I'm trying to give you as much as I get and these things sound funny but it's what I pick up. People, like primitive people like that, they might think that's real special. These last people I don't feel they even thought of any of that stuff. It wasn't important to them.

(f.) *Metal at the Site.* During the site visit, Bowes again spoke of metal fragments. Also, in this interchange with Dr. Wallace, Bowes correctly identified where one of the metal artifacts, the nail mentioned earlier, would be found.

> I did feel the nail and I drew a picture of it...it was square, got a square head on it...like a concrete nail. I felt this nail was beat with a hammer. It wasn't...in other words when the rust broke off it may have broke off in like layers. It was made that way... The chain I felt the same way with. Not something recent. The chain I felt when it rusted it broke off in layers...in square looking pieces. I felt that was here somewhere.
>
> **WALLACE: You aren't sure where the chain is?**
>
> **BOWES:** No. I wouldn't be able to pick that up. It could be to the left (east). I felt the nail was in the middle. (It was found in the central portion of the trench which the archeologists had excavated across the middle of the site.)

General Comments by Bowes

Bowes made a series of observations while at 8Se32 which subsequently proved to be accurate. For example, at two points in the reading of the mound, and in almost identical language, Bowes correctly indicated that the trees at the site were not the same kind of trees which existed in that place at the time of Indian occupation.

> This is strange but I don't feel these trees were here. There was a different kind of tree here. I felt oak trees.

> That's funny. I really don't feel these trees (refers to cedar trees) were here. I felt more oak trees.

Later more extensive exploration of the area would reveal a spring-fed stream several hundred yards west of the mound. Bowes noted this in the following:

> **BOWES:** I still don't understand it but I keep seeing clear water or something clean there (points to the west). Is there a stream or something over there?
>
> **WALLACE: Its low and marshy over there. I haven't seen any streams over there yet. Very low and mucky, though.**

In the first exchange between Bowes, Wallace, and me at the mound, Bowes described quite correctly the location of the nearest associated site to 8Se32.

> **BOWES:** ...but I felt back in this direction (south-southeast) there was a high ridge, and that they had a village or there was more people living there...
>
> **JONES: And you felt a village was that way?** (points to SSE)
>
> **BOWES:** I felt as though it was on a higher ridge, a higher area.
>
> **WALLACE: And this could very well be that higher area?**
>
> **BOWES:** Yes. What's ever back up in there (points SSE)...I

don't know what's up in there, but the feeling I had was that
it was a high ridge. Now this could be the ridge, but I would
say it was considerably higher than this. In other words you
could stand up on the ridge and at that time look out over
grass, and it was sitting up high and there was a lot of palm
trees (Bowes turns and faces toward the SSE). The feeling I
had was they almost had a vantage point of who came in or
went out and I would say it was in that direction (SSE). Is
there an area over there that could be higher?
WALLACE: **There are quite a number of shell rises over
there that are fairly close to the river and they are quite high.**
BOWES: The feeling I had was you could see the river
from it.*
WALLACE: **You can.**
BOWES: And you could stand up on the ridge and see out
over there and see people coming or leaving. I felt as though
they landed, from what I pick up right now, I feel they landed
here, but I felt like they didn't stay here very long. That over
there (points SSE) was more of a place where they stayed.

Bowes spoke of cocina rock during the reading of the photographs
and again while at the mound. Cocina is formed by the consolidation
through time of shell masses. In this excerpt Wallace asked Bowes his
impressions concerning the depth of the cocina layer that the excavation team had only recently hit and had not yet penetrated. Since this
reading took place only several days after the excavation had begun,
Wallace was naturally concerned.

WALLACE: **Do you have any feeling about how far out this
heavy stuff may go?**
BOWES: I felt its going to be a layer...I don't feel it would
go out too much farther than this (indicates crown of mound)
...could be a thin layer of it all out in here.

The completed excavation proved Bowes to be right about the
nature and extent of the cocina cap.

It was during this experiment that Bowes predicted the discovery of
the single, round, white bead.

WALLACE: **Do you see any shells used as ornaments, like
shell beads?**
BOWES: I felt there was a little bead, like a pearl, like a little
round bead, but I felt it was something from shells, but I
didn't see the shells being used.

Wallace was interested in what Bowes might have to say about the
possibility of locating structures at the site. Bowes, at the time the
question was asked, did not appear enthusiastic about the possibility
— and none were found.

WALLACE: **Do you have any feeling about the shape of the**

---

* It should be noted that Bowes was not told the exact location of 8Se32 prior
to his interview at the site. This means that he could not have "boned up"
on local geography ahead of time.

structures or any kinds of patterns that indicate what they
look like in the ground that we might find when we dig?
Round? Square?

BOWES: No, I didn't feel you would find them in the
ground. You might find logs, things laying like logs, but the
feeling I had was there was posts in the ground and this is
what you would find and I felt it would be about four feet by
ten feet or something like that...and you might find the posts
in the ground. I did feel this was all burned off...that there
was a fire here, so you might just find a log or a stump that
high (indicates about twelve inches) that was burned off at
the top.

Conclusion: Second Experiment Related to 8Se32

The visit to 8Se32 by Bowes resulted in his reaffirmation of several
themes first developed in the blind reading of the photographs of the
site. The chief differences were in his refining and amplification of
these themes from the first experiment to the second. The "little
pieces of metal" from the first experiment, for example, became the
precise and accurate description of metal that was "...broke off in
layers...in square looking pieces."* He also greatly expanded his description of the two different types of Indian peoples he felt occupied
the mound. In addition, the site visit produced some new accuracies in
his indication of the change in tree types on the site over time and in
his location of the stream adjacent to the mound to the west. He also
located the closest related site, correctly described the cocina rock cap
on the mound, indirectly suggested his opinion that few structures
would be located, and predicted the finding of a single, white,
round bead.

What I found most striking in this experiment was that Bowes'
accuracy while actually on the mound was not appreciably greater
than when he was reading the site photographs blind. This experience
with Bowes proved to be one of several factors which would lead me to
attempt a more ambitious experiment later in my work involving
photographs of archeological materials.

Third Experiment: 8Se32

In the third experiment I worked with Marjorie Niren. I was interested in the nature of psychic reporting that resulted when the artifactual materials were presented to the psychic fresh from the archeological excavation. In the two Bowes experiments with the test site
just described, he never actually handled or even saw the mound's
contents. The materials from 8Se32 were presented to Niren under
blind conditions. I refrained from locating the site for her until after
her phase of the mound site experiments was completed. Furthermore,

---

* All the artifacts of metal found at the site were found undisturbed in the top
  three feet of the mound.

I presented Niren with the most nondescript bone and artifactual materials the mound produced. In this I was attempting to duplicate the conditions under which archeologists work. In the majority of cases most of what comes out of an archeological site is, by layman's standards, not very impressive. Small, broken pieces of crude pottery, charred animal bones, and stone tool fragments are not the stuff of dreams.

I presented bags of 8Se32 material to Niren over a period of several months. Later, I would use the same materials with Bowes and Davis. The combined accounts of Niren, Bowes, and Davis give an incredibly rich account of life at 8Se32 covering thousands of years. At this time the collected descriptive reporting, the "psychic history" of the test site, is so vast that I have been able to process only a small portion of it. However, in that Niren's work was blind and she was the first psychic subject to deal with the materials, her impressions are the more significant experimentally.

Site Location and Environmental Statements

At out first meeting, working under blind conditions with the artifacts and general refuse remains from the mound, Niren offered the following very precise statement about the site's location.

> **JONES: Are there any major environmental or geographical features around this place that would identify it? Where is this site?**
> NIREN: I see...I feel Florida. I see water all around and of course the palm trees and that kind of scrub stuff. Like a stream going by. I don't feel mountains. The water is very close to the ground. Very damp kind of feeling.
> **JONES: How far away is this site from where we are right now?**
> NIREN: I get 'twenty-five miles.' (she points east)

She was within only a few miles of absolute accuracy in her indication of the distance from her home, where the reading took place, to the test site. 8Se32 is also east from her location during the experiment, as she rightly noted.

During the second session with Niren, she drew a map locating the site in relationship to other surrounding environmental features. On this map the essential relationship between the site, Lake Harney, and the St. Johns River is strikingly illustrated. There is also a suggestion of the "circular lake" that Bowes insisted was at one time adjacent to the site on the north.

The stream to the west of the site was noted by Niren as she described a man working to the west of the mound.

> I don't know. He is part of this group, but perhaps the location is better for him to work in, maybe he needed something that was nearby. I also feel...I see a very small stream on the side by him, over this way (indicates west of mound), it's like a small stream. I don't see this huge river or anything like

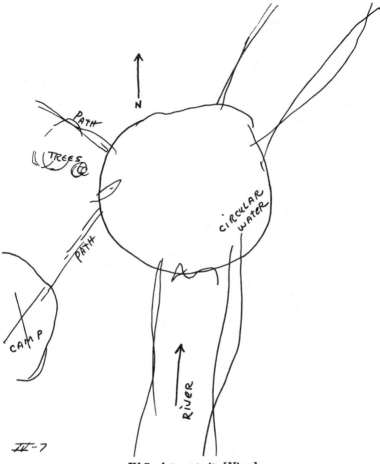

IV-7: A target site [Niren].

that (again she indicates west of mound)...I just see like a
small trickling thing going by.

The Site's Inhabitants

At each of the sessions with Niren, as she touched the artifacts and
bones placed before her, she made comments concerning the physical
characteristics of the makers.

JONES: Do you see what kind of clothes these people wear?
NIREN: I see this gentleman and he is wearing...a skirt. He
has got beads on. Not wearing pants, just wearing a skirt.
JONES: What does his hair look like?
NIREN: It's black and its forward...like some comes down
like this...like bangs or something. Kind of greasy looking.

Like some kind of pomade or something on it, you know.
JONES: What does he look like? (referring to adult male mentioned by Niren)
NIREN: I see more or less on the thin side. I don't feel he was very short, you know, maybe about five foot ten, that size. I feel like shortish hair, I don't see long hair. The cheek bones would be high, and the nose would be...I don't feel his nose would be close to his face, or anything like that, but, you know, his nose isn't small. Not large, you know, a little bit straight. He is tan looking, dark hair.

Early descriptions of the inhabitants of Florida coincide with Niren's observations in the main. Short hair, bangs, and "skirts" are commonly described in the early European accounts. It is also true that some ancient Florida peoples are depicted with long hair. Further, Florida Indians at the time of the early French, British, American, and Spanish contacts are generally pictured as barefoot and shirtless. At one point in her reading she spoke of an Indian man and said, "I see long dark hair, and I don't see a shirt on him, and barefoot." Her suggestion of black hair and tan skin tones completes the picture.

A suggestion of two habitations, strongly noted by Bowes, also appeared in Niren's reading of the test site's artifacts.

JONES: Do you think these people are the first people who came to this area?
NIREN: As far as they were concerned, like when they moved and when they went to these areas it was new to them, you know...not like coming into somebody else's territory. I feel it was clean coming in there, but before that ...I am not...I think that there was others there but...quite a way away...long ago. I don't see anyone new, I don't feel newness with this area. It looks like it just was old, like nothing's been there when they move into it.
JONES: But there was a long time ago? Is that what...
NIREN: Yeah, I feel like a long time ago there was. But not real recently.

The archeological interpretation of the site's bone and artifact assemblage demonstrated that 8Se32 was a temporary living site. Bowes noted the movement of the people through the area. Niren made a similar observation.

JONES: Did these people live at this place all the time, or did they move around, or are they recent, or have they been there for...
NIREN: I feel like this area is a place where a lot of people have passed through, but I also feel that there were times when they have to leave.
JONES: Do they come back or do they go some place else?
NIREN: It is really weird, as I'm looking here (straight ahead) my eyes go that way (she looks to the south).
JONES: Is there something important about that direction?

NIREN: I guess it would be like they would have to move on on. I feel like an anchor point at this...like it was the hub of something. Do you know what I mean?

JONES: **Why would this site be the 'hub' of something? What was it that made it that way?**

NIREN: I feel like these people traveled in the water there. It was like a stop-off. It was like a point between two other places or it was...you know, the time of day when it would be time to rest and that would just be the place where everybody kind of went and then moved on. Traveling through there. But I feel they knew these people.

JONES: **I don't understand? 'They' knew 'these' people?**

NIREN: These people that lived there would know these people that traveled through...most of them, I would say. It would be their friends that would come through.

JONES: **Do you have any feelings about where they originated?**

NIREN: These people? (touches test collection).

JONES: **The people at the site?**

NIREN: The words I'm getting are like 'migration.' Like a southerly migration...moving.

Several times during the 8Se32 work with Niren I asked about the origins and general movements of the peoples associated with the test artifacts.

JONES: **Do you get a feeling about whether they move around a lot, or stay there all the time, or stay there some of the time, or leave and...**

NIREN: I don't feel that this is the first place that they have lived. There have been other places. They moved many times I think.

JONES: **Do you have any feeling about where they might have come from?**

NIREN: I feel more northerly, and I feel they are moving south each time they move.

JONES: **Do you have a feeling of why they move?**

NIREN: I think they more or less exhaust the things they have around that area. So instead of going out further and further to get things they need, it was just easier to move the whole camp like further down, and...

JONES: **Further down?**

NIREN: Down south. Just moving further south.

JONES: **Why not east, or why not west, north?**

NIREN: I don't know. I feel like there is something around them, something that...I also feel they thought it was better for them to move, not only for food supplies, but I felt something on the sides, like closing-in somehow.

JONES: **Something on the sides closing in?**

NIREN: I don't feel people...their own people. I feel somebody else that would be trying to move in.

JONES: What about the people they could speak to? Where would those people be? People who spoke their dialect or language?

NIREN: I feel further north than they are. Up in north Florida and Georgia, you know, that area, the southern states up there. I feel they had come down from there.

JONES: Are there any descendants of these people still alive?

NIREN: Yeah. I feel they are further south. Like you have the Seminoles down, further down in the Everglades. I feel they just moved down. I think a lot of them were killed, but I think a few got out.

While handling a white ceramic shard of European origin found at the site, Niren elaborated upon the connection the people at the site had with peoples from Georgia. It is worthwhile to reiterate that the vast majority of historic Indian inhabitants of Florida, especially after the Spanish presence, came from cultural centers located in Georgia.

NIREN: I don't feel this (white shard of European origin) belonged to these Indians...I feel that outsiders brought it somehow. I almost feel like it belonged to something that was fancy.

JONES: Fancy?

NIREN: I don't know. That was just a word that I got. But it's like...some kind of container or something. It had a top on it that was kind of a little bit fancier.

JONES: Outside influence?

NIREN: Like from these other people?

JONES: Who were these other people?

NIREN: Now it seems like I'm going to a different state.

JONES: Where?

NIREN: Georgia.

JONES: How did you get to Georgia?

NIREN: I don't know. It feels like...this came from outside Florida. (Niren laughs) How about that! I don't know if it was...I'm not sure if it came down here from them to this campsite (touches artifacts).

JONES: From Georgia?

NIREN: Yeah. I just don't feel like this is...It's got a foreign feeling.

JONES: Did Indians make it? (referring to white shard)

NIREN: I don't feel they did. No.

JONES: Did the people in Georgia make it?

NIREN: Didn't feel Indians did, either one.

JONES: Where did it originate?

NIREN: It came to the Indians. It was either given to them, or...I see it like in...I feel like from Georgia it was brought down. In Georgia it was given as a gift somehow.

JONES: What is the relationship between these people

(touches artifacts) **and the people in Georgia? Why would it come here? Who would bring it and why?**
NIREN: I feel like a division of Indians, and...because of the population. Some moved further south. Like this was taken with them.
JONES: **Where did they move south from?**
NIREN: From Georgia...Tennessee. I'm not sure about Tennessee.

(The following passages seem to suggest the Seminole War situation.)

NIREN: I feel this is also one of the reasons why they moved south. I just...it is like they're running, they're going...all they do is want to have a place to stay and stay there and I feel all these kinds of anxieties, and people being killed and trying to reproduce and have more children and they just can't seem to find a place to settle down.
JONES: **Are these people passing through?**
NIREN: It's like they feel they are going to be gone, and there's just nothing they can do about it. They fear these people that are coming through. It's like they knew that this was their territory, and these people coming through were just going to push them out, and I feel like a need to...just stay there and try to get things going, but I just don't feel that...like they are always being pushed out somehow, and these people...I see uniforms on them and some with blond hair, and...
JONES: **Where are we now? With the people associated with the artifacts or with these later people?**
NIREN: The people that are coming into their sites as they move.
JONES: **Associated with these people with uniforms?**
NIREN: Yeah.
JONES: **What kinds of feelings do you get about them?**
NIREN: I feel like...I'm in sympathy with the Indians. I feel that...like I'm being threatened by these people. I don't like them. I don't want to have anything to do with them. They won't leave me alone. They just want to...and I feel like with these people coming through, I see drinking...just wanton destruction. They just don't care. I see these people (Indian artifacts) really appalled by the sight of them. They can't imagine people being like that.
JONES: **What kind of language were the men in the uniforms speaking?**
NIREN: I feel it's a foreign language of some kind, and this adds to the Indians' fear of them. They can't understand them, and they just see what's going on.

During a discussion about invaders in the area, Niren made the following succinct observation.

I feel it was somebody from across the sea, somehow, that was there. I don't feel like a large number of them or anything like that, but I don't think...these people (artifacts) even knew they were down there. They never got down there that far away.

JONES: **From across the sea? Where do you feel they were from?**

NIREN: Spain, or some place like that, or France, or some place like that area, but I don't see a whole lot of people there. I feel like kind of new, new to Florida...new experience, but I don't think the Indians even knew they were down there.

Repeating Themes

At the time Niren read the 8Se32 materials, she was unaware of the nature of the experiments with Albert Bowes. It is intriguing, therefore, to note the themes that Bowes presented which Niren also touched upon.

(a.) *Skull.* Bowes made a number of statements, both in his first and second experiments with the test site, concerning skulls. He drew a picture of a single skull, as well as depicting several heads mounted on poles at 8Se32. He also said that the first impression he received upon walking onto the mound was a feeling of "attack" through the neck. Niren began her third blind reading session with the test materials by saying:

NIREN: I'm seeing a river bank...o.k. I also saw a skull of some kind.

JONES: **Of some kind? What do you mean?**

NIREN: I just got 'skull,' you know, and then my rational mind comes in and I see all these different things...

(b.) *Burial Near The Water.* In Bowes' blind reading of the photographs he made several references to his impressions that burials occurred near some closeby water course.

I did see teeth or bones and I keep seeing it near the water. I really feel as though this site or this area may not show that many bones or people. But I would say that there is an area closer to the water, or closer to an area I would say...I keep seeing it being a lower area, almost like a grass marsh.

I picked up something about where we could find something to do with teeth or bones, and I kept seeing it near the water, almost like near the water's edge.

Niren stated, as she handled a collection of potsherds from the site:

I see...I feel, like animals, but...a bunch of animal bones and things like that and then I think of a burial site, but I don't see why there would be a burial site for animals, or things like that...close to the water. Not too far away from the water.

(c.) *Butchering and Ritual.* The many cut and burned animal bones at
8Se32 were evidence that the site was, among other things, a butchering site. Independently, both Bowes and Niren, after accurately describing the butchering scene, proceeded to suggest some ritual
significance to the act. In his walk-over of the mound Bowes made the
following comments.

> I felt alligators, and, I don't know, this sounds strange, but
> I kept feeling almost like they sucked something out of the
> vertebrae, almost like they did something with the vertebrae
> or they were doing something with the tail of it, but I see
> them pulling on it...looked like strings...long strings like
> you'd pull them out...like it was inside the vertebrae.
>
> I did definitely feel that they, too...these alligators...or they
> did something with the alligators, and I felt with the back-
> bone, like the vertebrae and they split it open or split their
> back open and I see them getting long things that look like
> tendons or strings, and I felt they were pulling them out of
> the backbone of them. What could that be? Would that be
> anything? That thing in the back?
> WALLACE: Some sort of tendons, nerves. I don't know.
> JONES: Could be sinew in the back.
> BOWES: I felt they used it for string.
> JONES: That sounds like sinew.
> BOWES: They pulled it out of their backbone or they pulled
> it out of their back, but I felt it was a celebration or some-
> thing real important... They were all excited about it...they
> thought it was real important.

Niren's observation of this scene is described in this exchange
with me.

> NIREN: What I'm getting...I feel there was a particular
> area where they...where certain animals were killed. I'm also
> seeing animal bones being broken, as if it was like to release
> the spirit of it, or something... I see this man there and he's
> bending down, and these animals that they had...I don't
> know what these particular things are (indicates bone frag-
> ments before her), but like I see small animals...any animal
> they used, the bones they broke. It was like to release a spirit
> of that animal, or something, and they felt it was like a
> necessary thing to do.

(d.) *Alligators.* In Bowes' reading of the site photos he reported:

> I don't know if they worked around with alligators or some-
> thing but I keep seeing them scaring or throwing something
> or chasing something away, and I keep seeing eggs, like
> almost as if they were alligator eggs or something like huge
> or large eggs.

In the visit to the site, Bowes added more information about the importance he felt the earliest native peoples at the site gave the alligator.
Niren, during her first experiment with the site materials, offered

the following:

> Alligator eggs were sacred to them somehow. Shells were
> used as medicine of some kind. Eggs were very important to
> them. The alligator was important because it could go on
> water and land, it was somehow singled out to them. They felt
> it was very strong. Same kind of feelings with Indians and
> the buffalo. They would use the alligator egg shells in their
> food...or they would just grind it up. It was given to males
> in particular. It was supposed to do something for them...
> The alligator was a big part of their environment. They could
> see its great strength...the males felt they would get strength
> by eating the shells. It wasn't medicine exactly. It was like a
> superstition. They felt it was the alligator's land as well as
> their land. They didn't hunt the alligator...it was sacred.

Niren made a very specific "hit" when she stated, "Because it (alligator) went on water and land, it was somehow singled out to them."
Hudson [5] writes:

> Like preliterate people elsewhere, the Southeastern Indians
> were particularly interested in anomalies and abominations,
> beings which fell into two or more of their categories. These
> anomalies and abominations were singled out for special
> symbolic value, and they played important roles in their oral
> tradition. The alligator is a creature of the land domain and
> the water domain, thus an anomaly in the Southeastern
> Indian scheme of things, therefore very special.

(e) *Dwindling Population.* In Bowes' photograph reading of 8Se32 he
noted, "I kept seeing sadness about their numbers." Independently,
Niren, during her stage of the test site work, elaborated on this topic.

> They felt like if they were to do certain things, you know,
> that they would be able to conceive easily. That's what they
> need. They need, they need to have more people among them.
> I feel their numbers getting smaller and they're praying to
> the gods, or whatever, to help them...to do certain things.

> They wanted to keep all this stuff going and it was impor-
> tant to them to have children, but I also see like a...I don't
> feel they lived too long, you know...that's why they feel it's
> very important to get these children going, to get these
> children out. I also feel that there are more men than women,
> and this is a concern of theirs also. Their whole thing here is
> for population. This isn't something new, because of sickness
> ...I feel it's been going on. I feel more male children being
> born than female, and so they want to take steps before...
> they feel they have to put more children out to keep the
> thing going.

(f.) *Belt and Knife Image.* When Niren picked up the rectangular
piece of metal that was found at the site she made the following
comment:

> ...that couldn't be. I don't feel these Indians had this...like

it was...I keep seeing a belt, and...but it wasn't the Indians, it was somebody else...like it was on these other people.

JONES: Who were these other people?

NIREN: Someone who was in some kind of army type thing. By looking at it (metal piece), I don't see how that could be, but...

JONES: How does that piece of metal go with the belt? What is that?

NIREN: It's like...it's like on the belt, it's like a part of the belt...like a decoration. I don't feel...I believe it is a part of a knife. That's what I'm seeing.

Bowes, in an experiment not herein reported, drew the following picture while reading materials from the test site. He explained that the items on the tarp or blanket were trade items. Prominently displayed in the lower right quadrant was a belt and a knife. At this point he had not yet seen the metal piece which was later archeologically identified as a knife or sword blade fragment. The following passages contain Bowes' description of what he had drawn.

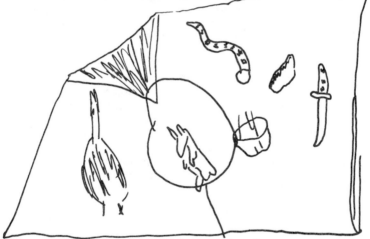

IV-8: A trade scene [Bowes].

JONES: Do you see anything else sitting on this piece of material? (refers to Bowes' drawing of 'trade items'.)

BOWES: Could have been a metal knife (draws knife... pauses, then adds belt). I felt like that was something like a belt with like something brass or something metal on it. There was a belt buckle here and then there was little things on the leather. There could either be brass or metal but I felt like they were all hooked through this belt, and I would say this belt and that knife go more together.

(g.) *Few Human Bones.* Bowes proved correct in his statement that few human burials would be recovered from the test site. Niren also made this type of observation.

> I felt this woman sitting back and dying, and she wasn't put on the mound or anything like that, so I think you'll find peoples' bones scattered. I don't see a whole bunch of them, just a few of them...scattered around that were not on the mound.

Burials

Niren's ability to relate valid information about mere fragments of the one complete and one partial burial at 8Se32 was impressive. At one point I handed Niren several potsherds to read which I later discovered were found in direct association with the partial burial found at the site. I did not know this at the time of the Niren sessions. She, however, immediately noted the relationship of the pottery fragments to a burial. Further, as with Bowes, she focused on damage to the head region of the individual she observed as she held the shards.

> JONES: This is Number Six. ("Number Six" was a code which signified a collection of potsherds found approximately five feet below the surface of the mound.)
> NIREN: As soon as I saw this, I felt a burial site of some kind. A grave site.
> JONES: Can you give me any particulars?
> NIREN: As I hold this, I get the feeling it's a male, and this was a piece of jewelry that was decorated on him. And I feel as though that when someone was buried they put things with them.
> JONES: Like what?
> NIREN: I'm seeing this woman placing...like pieces of pottery in there with him...I just got the words...like I saw this woman putting pottery in there and then I got the words 'listening to the sounds.' And I was trying to figure out, what kind of sounds. What are they trying to listen to?
> JONES: How do you see the body arranged?
> NIREN: Like it's on its back and...I see beads and...this thing that I'm tuning into...there's a problem with the head, I feel...why this person died.
> JONES: What kind of problem?
> NIREN: I don't know. I feel something to the left side of my brain, or skull, like a blow or something.
> JONES: Did it kill the man or...
> NIREN: I feel it was suddenly and I see people wailing and I felt like they felt the loss of this person but the wailing went beyond that. Their voices were to help the spirit of this person somehow.

When Niren, at a different point, was handed a few non-diagnostic bone fragments of the human bone from the burial with which the above potsherds had been recovered, the following impressions ensued. Interestingly enough, the potsherds from the burial and the non-diagnostic bones from the burial both produced impressions in Niren having to do with a reclining human figure being approached by a woman carrying pottery.

JONES: This is Number Four (Code for human bone fragments.)

NIREN: As I hold this I get the feeling of laying back on the ground looking up at the sky. I almost get like a very restful feeling, and as I look up I see a bird going over head. Like now I'm almost getting feelings, you know.

JONES: What kind of feelings?

NIREN: Like a comfortable kind of feeling, a relaxed feeling, like a lazy afternoon type feeling. As I look to the left I saw some people walking up...it was a woman and a child...they were carrying some type of pottery to hold water in, walking down towards the water. As I hold this...I...it's real strange ...today I'm mostly getting feelings. It's like feelings of unity with the people, that they had for one another, like a family type of feeling. I don't get violent reactions to holding these things...just like a drifting feeling.

One of the most dramatic moments in my work with Niren came when I placed before her several non-diagnostic fragments of the infant cranium taken from the ancient burial found partially below the mound. As will be remembered, the archeologists judged that this burial of a young female with associated infant bones in her pelvic and torso region was the result of death during childbirth. As the following transcripts show, Niren reacted violently when the impression she was receiving from the bone fragments became too powerful for her to tolerate. It was a startling experience to be watching a normally positive and cheerful young woman suddenly become hysterical for no apparent reason. When she touched a particular portion of the bone, her face instantly contorted in terror and pain. She jumped up from her seated position directly across from me, knocking over the table upon which the artifacts and tape recorder sat, and ran from the room. Several minutes later she came back into the room and the reading continued. This scene was enacted during the following exchange relating to the bone fragments just discussed.

JONES: This is Number Seven. (Code for Burial II bone remains of infant cranium.)

NIREN: As I hold this I get a female vibration. I'm seeing a young girl.

JONES: What is she doing?

NIREN: I saw her standing next to a woman I take to be her mother. It's very strange. All of a sudden I was seeing light, and then dark, like a dark shade being pulled. Like darkness, just coming down.

JONES: **What do you feel it means?**

NIREN: I feel like it would be her death. I feel like sickness. I don't feel any kind of violent death or anything like that... violence. But the lights are going out.

NIREN: It's like a very tired feeling. All the energy is depleted. It's like I'm seeing the moment before death, I guess, and it's just like letting go. It was easy to do, just let go and ...beyond.

JONES: **What is the relationship between this dead girl and the mother?** (As soon as I said this Niren started sobbing hysterically. The interview stopped as Niren left the room to compose herself. She returned within five minutes and her reading continued.)

JONES: **Do you want to stop?**

NIREN: No, go ahead.

JONES: **What happened?**

NIREN: I don't know. It's like I saw a picture of a little child, like a brother, and...you know how when people start to cry their faces get all screwed up? Well, when I saw it I just felt the vibration. I guess, and I just felt all the sadness and everything. It was the grief this brother was feeling for this other person in the family...you know, the death. It was like this child that died was very close to many of the kids there, and they had felt a great love for her, and they felt very close. I felt like there hadn't been a death for a while, you know, among the children. It really upset them a great deal.

In an experiment not reported here which related to the psychic's ability to determine age and sex of human bone remains from non-diagnostic pieces. I presented Bowes with the infant cranial fragments which Niren had psychometrized. Bowes' impressions of the bone pieces coincides in the main with Niren's as well as the interpretation of the chief archeologist at the site.

BOWES: The first thing I picked up was something about a small animal.

JONES: **What kind of animal?**

BOWES: Like a small mouse, or rat, or some small animal, like a raccoon...like there was a child, and this was different than these, but I felt 'child'...or a small child that died. I felt it was a girl.

JONES: **Do you feel any more about that;**

BOWES: I kept feeling as though she had troubles breathing and that she was in the mud, almost like sinking in quicksand, or stuck, or drowned. 'Breathing' is what I felt very strongly. I would say she was speaking a language so she must have been over a certain age, but the feeling I had was like a child, like a little baby, maybe not old enough hardly

to talk, but the feeling I had was I did see a young girl
talking.

General Observations Concerning Niren's Reading

Scattered throughout Niren's reading of the test site artifact and
bone remains are numerous examples of her accuracy with these
materials.

(a.) As was noted when I presented a description of all the materials
taken from 8Se32, a flint cache of forty-two pieces was discovered.
During Niren's phase of the experiment with the mound site, she was
handed one of the pieces from the flint cache. She touched the flint
item and said, "I saw a pile of rock in a flash, all of a sudden...a bunch
of things like this."

(b.) Post-excavation analysis of the projectile points found at the
site showed that the flint points were all made of flint imported from
outside the site area. During one session Niren was discussing her
feelings that some of the objects before her were not from the vicinity
of the site. To more precisely record these impressions I began to point
to each object in turn and ask, "Is this one from the site area?". When
I pointed to several projectile points and asked this question, she
correctly responded, "I don't feel this was (from the site area). I just

(c.) The diet of the site's makers was correctly described when she
said, in response to my question about diet, "I saw fish, and berries,
and birds and rabbits...and shellfish, some kind of shells, small
animals, you know."

(d.) When I asked Niren about her feelings concerning the religion
of the makers of the artifacts, she said, "I think there was something
greater to them, but I think that they looked to the moon to help them
somehow, and for some reason I think of reproduction." In this regard, Hudson[6] writes, "In the Southern belief system the Moon was
sometimes associated with rain and with menstruation, and with
fertility generally, but it was not as important a deity as the Sun."

A Fair Woman at the Site

The following episode is intriguing, not because any evidence was
unearthed to verify the historical reality of the incident to be described, but because the same incident was described under three
separate experimental conditions, at three different times, by three
different psychic subjects. The general impression is of a European
woman at, or near the site. Niren's notice of this event is illustrated in
the following passage offered as she handled potsherds from the
mound.

NIREN: I see women in long dresses and...like they're...like
they're...like they came from across the...water, and I don't
know why women...I don't understand this...I don't know
all this history and like that...

JONES: **Just tell me whatever you feel.**

NIREN: Like I see women in flowing dresses, and like, with a parasol, and she is fair. I wouldn't figure that she would be there, like this doesn't really make sense.

JONES: **Why is she there?**

NIREN: I feel like a number of people came. I feel like wealthy people, and like they had heard that there was land there, and they went to see it and what could be done with it...I don't know. This just doesn't make sense.

In a separate experiment with Bowes dealing with 8Se32 materials, he described a similar event. This experiment is not completed at this time.

BOWES: With this here (potsherd), again I felt the ocean, near the water with it. I felt it was quite old, but I would say that white people made it. I see an old, haggy-looking woman, and I see her very troubled. I see her stuck. I don't know if she is stuck in a wagon or stuck in a car or what she is stuck in, but I see her stuck, and feeling trapped, and again I seen the ocean, the water.

JONES: **Where do you think that originated?** (Pointed to white shard of European manufacture.)

BOWES: I would say it originated from the north. I would say it was broken when it was in the ground...I felt a woman owned it. It could have been a white woman...or a Spanish woman. I felt they punched her eyes out.

JONES: **At the site?**

BOWES: No, near the beach again.

JONES: **How did it get from the north to the site?**

BOWES: I would say they were stuck, like I said, on the beach or stuck where they couldn't go anymore. Whether the boat was stuck on a sandbar or whether they were in a wagon and they were stuck on the beach or whatever it was, but I see them stuck. And this woman was alone, and she was carrying this stuff. I felt like some of it was like woman's stuff like powder and valuables.

JONES: **The people who were stuck, what did they look like?**

BOWES: I would say that there is a man there who had dark, curly hair, black hair, and he could have been Spanish, but I see him talking in a different language, and I see this boat as not being like a seafaring boat, but I felt it was a smaller boat, like a sloop, and the feeling I had was that it needed a lot of depth in the water, and I felt it was stuck on a sandbar...and this man was giving orders, screaming at everybody, and nobody would listen to him. Everybody wanted to go to shore, and then after they got to shore I felt like he left, he was gone, and this woman was on the shore with this stuff.

JONES: **What does she look like?**
BOWES: I would say she was a Caucasian woman with light
brown hair, and she was ruffled or messed up. With a long,
long dress.
JONES: **Where is this taking place?**
BOWES: I would say near the Cape (Canaveral) or New
Symrna. (Twenty to thirty miles east of the test site on the
Atlantic coast.)

In another experiment I presented a group of students of a Spiritualist medium with the site photographs that Bowes read. Their
accuracy was impressive, but continuing tape malfunction prevented
me from using the transcripts. However, one of the student mediums,
while viewing one of the four site photographs indicated the presence
of the "fair" woman.

When I saw all the spirit faces around, they looked different.
They weren't all the same. I saw one lady with fair skin and
blond hair, and then over here I saw a darker man, so I don't
know if this goes with all this or not. These spirits that I saw
…they didn't look like it was all the same people. I saw that
white skinned lady with the blond hair.

Conclusion: Third Experiment Related to 8Se32

Marjorie Niren, reading an assemblage of materials from the test
site under blind conditions, was able to locate the site within two or
three miles of absolute accuracy, as well as present much verifiable
informaion concerning the site's inhabitants, their cultural behavior,
origin, and subsequent dispersal. Further, she independently reiterated themes that Bowes had introduced in his stage of the test site
experimentation. As the account of her experiment showed, she was
particularly sensitive to, and accurate in relationship to, the burials
at the site.

FOURTH EXPERIMENT: 8Se32

The fourth experiment was totally unplanned. In fact it took place
several years after the 8Se32 sessions with Bowes, Davis, and Niren.
One afternoon after finishing a non-related experiment with psychic,
Noreen Renier, I spontaneously placed a sealed package before her,
started the tape recorder, and asked her to describe the impressions
she received as she held the package. In the package, wrapped in
layers of plastic, were numerous bone materials and several artifacts
from 8Se32. The wrapped items were sealed with glue and tape in a
heavy manila envelope. I had packaged the materials to return them
to the archeology laboratory. There was no way for Renier to feel or
to see the contents of the package. Further, at the time Renier read
the package, there were in my office artifacts and artifact collections
from around the world and many times periods. For instance, a
Comanche arrow sat on top of a sealed box containing fake "Mayan"

ceramics. In my desk were numerous fossil bones dating millions of years into the past. On the wall behind my desk, a Cheyenne beaded hatband hung next to beads from Greece. In my filing cabinet, which sat about five feet away from Renier as she read the sealed packet, were projectile points and ceramic materials from California, Arizona, Georgia, and Virginia. I mention this brief list of the wonders often found in a cultural anthropologist's office simply to indicate that, even if Renier had known about the 8Se32 experiments carried out years before we met, it would not have been an obvious guess to identify the sealed items as coming from the test site.

Environmental Statements and Site Location

Renier located the site from which the packaged materials originated in these passages.

JONES: **Then where is this** (touches bag) **place?**
RENIER: I feel it might be Florida. I just see tree tops right now.

In the middle of her reading Renier described a feeling of hovering over the site. In response to a question I asked at that point she again located the site correctly, and also rightly indicated its direction from her.

JONES: **Still over the site, turn and face the west. What do you see?**
RENIER: It is Florida. I don't know why, but I feel that I am blocked with structures toward the west.
JONES: **In what direction from this spot where you are right now is the site?**
RENIER: That way, (turns and points to the east).

Mention of a river and a distant large body of water appeared in her short reading of the masked 8Se32 items.

RENIER: ...there must be some distant large body of water, but I feel it is distant, distant.
JONES: **Large body of water?**
RENIER: It's more like a ...it flows like a river. More like a river.

*   *   *

I see a lot of land and then some water. I see a lot of land and then at quite a distance water, big water.

As in Bowes' and Niren's reading, the image of an alligator also appeared for Renier.

I feel the water. Something running. What is it? What is it? I got an alligator, or crocodile. I don't know which.

A Mound

Renier suggested the mound nature of the test site in the following sections from her reading.

I feel an incline...I see this person, and behind her I feel an incline (with both her hands she makes a dome shape motion) ...I don't know if that's a dwelling or just stone or...but I feel it is made of...probably clay, water...goes up, goes up. It is high. It is not like little. More height to it. Structure. Tall.

I feel him up high. I feel there is some height to this land (touches package)...could be height that he is standing on.

Seminole

Renier made several references in her reading which appear to point to the presence of the Seminole. The heavy and multi-colored costume of the Seminoles are suggested in this series of statements.

JONES: What do the people look like?

RENIER: I feel long clothes on them. I feel more layered or more...clothes. Covered bodies. The woman I am seeing looks quite broad. I feel broadness. Not that short.

JONES: Can you tell me some characteristic of her clothing?

RENIER: Colored. A lot of color or brightness around this individual's clothing...different patterns of color.

The historical overview of the Southeast presented earlier in the chapter noted that the development of the Seminole was spurred by the grouping of a number of tribal fragments of the Southeast. In this context, Renier's response to the following question was pertinent.

JONES: What about the numbers of people?

RENIER: At one time they are joined by another group and they get large. I feel growth or strength at an early period. Other tribes or other people getting with this group here, and making them strong.

She never directly identified the inhabitants of the site. She did demonstrate accuracy as far as she went.

JONES: Do you see these people very clearly?

RENIER: No, because I am high up.

JONES: What color is their hair?

RENIER: Dark. Straight. Some of them might have bangs.

Diet

JONES: What would the people at this place eat? What would their diet be like?

RENIER: I feel sort of grainey stuff. It looks mushy. Maybe it's meal with some liquid in it. A mushy substance that they might do several things with. Let me see food, food, food. I feel like fish.

She was right about the fish. As for the "mushy stuff" she described, read Hudson's[7] description of *sofkee,* a staple dish of all Southeastern Indians.

Cracked hominy was one of the most important items in the

Southeastern Indian diet... From cracked hominy the Indians made a kind of soup by putting it in a pot of water cooking it about four hours, stirring frequently and adding enough water to keep the mixture thin. For flavor, they sometimes added a little wood-ash lye until the hominy began to turn yellow.

Invaders

Spontaneously during the reading Renier began to speak of invaders.

RENIER: ...Somebody is invading their land very shortly... or coming into a territory where they never been before. I don't know...people from a different land invading. A different land invading, or from a different territory? No, I feel from a different land.

JONES: What land?

RENIER: I see these people from across the ocean. I see an ocean. I feel waves lapping up. I feel more of...like from England.

Earliest Inhabitants of the Site

JONES: See the very earliest people at this place. Try to feel when that would be, and who that would be.

RENIER: With the very earliest inhabitants there was much more water and rain in that period of time because I am seeing a lot of grass where there is not grass now. I feel more rain. I feel very short, but with a great deal of strength, with ornaments or things near the ear (makes motion along side of head down jaw line). This area (upper jaw) seems very predominant on the male for some reason.

Renier was right in stating that the earliest inhabitants lived at a much wetter period of time in the site's history, as the brief discussion of the Paleo-Indian era noted. Her mention of the "predominant" area along the upper jaws echoes Bowes' description of the earliest inhabitants obtained when he visited the site. At that time Bowes reported, "The funniest thing, I kept feeling like the first people who were here, their faces were funny, like they were ugly, almost like they were cavemen or like they were real ugly, like their faces were real big, like big jaws."

Niren also noted something peculiar about the side of the face. Her mention of this trait appeared in the following passages from her reading of a bone from the site.

Something around the head, and...there's something on the right side of my head. Maybe it's something that would go around their heads (motions along her jaw line)...I just keep getting a feeling of around in here (right side of head)...it was

used for...
JONES: A piece of bone used for something around the side of the head?
NIREN: I just keep feeling around this side. I don't know. It doesn't make much sense.

Frederick W. Pau,[8] in his survey of the physical remains of the most ancient inhabitants of Florida notes that these Paleo-Indians were unusually heavy and massive, especially in the jaw area.

Sadness

Bowes and Niren, under different experimental conditions, spoke of the sadness they felt when in psychic contact with the site's inhabitants. Renier, too, spoke of this.
JONES: What about the religion of these people?
RENIER: More than one god. They aren't so happy right now. I guess the gods aren't doing too well, because I feel very...negative and downcaste among the people. For some reason I feel very low energy. Very great sadness.

Water Cougar

Early in her reading Renier offered the following observation.
...I'm switching to a statue. I feel it like a statue. I feel like an animal statue. I don't know if it's in the cat family or not, but I see its arms and legs and it is up right. Not like this (four feet on the ground), but it is up right, up right.
JONES: How big?
RENIER: I don't know.

Several years earlier, Bowes, in an unpublished experiment with 8Se32 artifacts, drew a picture of a figurine he felt to be related to the test site.

As I probed for information about this figurine, Bowes presented the following series of comments.

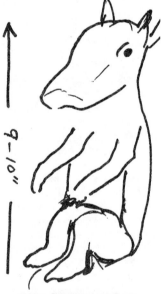

IV-9: A statue at 8Se32.

The feeling I had was this thing, whatever it is, the feeling I had was the legs down here was like a dog... In other words the heel of it was here, and then it stuck out (comments are being presented as Bowes draws the figurine), and the legs were like a dog or something, and then I seen it's eye but I couldn't figure out the face of it too much, but I felt it's hands were sticking out like this, and I would say it was like a cross between an alligator or a bear or something. But I would say that this pertains to weather, or time of year.

*   *   *

JONES: And it's (the figurine) **from the north, you said, but but you said it really meant something to these people at the site.**
BOWES: Yes. I felt it was a trade object. Something of trade.
JONES: **I forgot. You said it had something to do with the weather?**
BOWES: I would say that it pertained to months of the year or weather. Like good luck or like religious or almost like a good luck charm. I felt this person, whoever came from the north, was like a medicine man and someone who was religious. I felt like he sat that (figurine) out and this made everybody respect him more. Something to do with medicine. I keep seeing with these...I kept feeling as though they were afraid of becoming extinct, or like their people were dying out. And this man may have come, like a special person, or like he came to solve the problem.

*   *   *

This (touches face of figurine) could have been an otter...a statue of an otter. Nine or ten inches tall.
Davis, in her reading of the St. Simon's Island materials, culturally and historically similar to the later occupational zones at 8Se32, also mentioned a peculiar figurine.

I'm seeing one and I want to say it has the tail of an alligator
I'm seeing one and I want to say it has the tail of an alligator, and the head of something else more like a cat, or an animal that cures.

These references from Bowes, Renier, and Davis were of interest only in their approximate agreement, like the case of the "fair woman," until my researches in the ethnology of the Southeastern Indians uncovered accounts of the mythic Water Cougar of the Seminole Indians, a later day outgrowth of a more ancient Southeastern mythical character, the Uktena. The Uktena of the Cherokee, for example, was described as having the combined attributes of a snake, a deer, and a bird. It was believed to inhabit deep pools of water and also high mountain passes where it would wait to kill luckless travelers. Some Uktena are depicted as having the head of a cougar. It is also from the Uktena model that the Water Cougar was derived; a creature having four legs, no feet, long hair, a long fish-like tail, and a cougar's head. The Seminole believed that the Water Cougar had control over water and all creatures of the Under World.

With regard to Bowes' feeling that the figurine he saw was related to the weather, it is significant that one of the major categories of beings contained in the Under World, and controlled by the Water Cougar, were the thunderstorm spirits.

Conclusion: Fourth Experiment Related to 8Se32

Noreen Renier, working under blind conditions, was able to locate the test site, and to present many specific and verifiable pieces of information about the site's populations, their history, and their culture.

Summary: Site Excavation Experiments

The 8Se32 experiments suggest that psychics, even under blind experimental conditions, can (a.) access the physical nature and general contents of a site prior to its excavation; (b.) locate related sites; (c.) indicate the indigenous or extraneous nature of the materials found at the site; (d.) describe the physical appearance of the site in its pristine and native state, as well as the physical and cultural traits of the inhabitants; (e.) note the presence of aliens and their origins; and (f.) account for the origins of the site's users as well as the route and means of their later dispersal.

To truly grasp what Bowes, Niren, and Renier have done in the series of experimens related to 8Se32, it must be constantly remembered that they were working blind in all cases. Further, since my potential targets could, because of my museum access, range extremely widely in space and time, the psychic subjects had no conventional method of predicting a pattern to my experimental offerings. The 8Se32 materials were presented to Bowes, Niren, and Renier in different manners, in randomly staggered order over a two-year period interspersed with a variety of dissimilar experiments dealing with artifacts and photographs from many other parts of the world and many diverse temporal periods.

During this period of experimentation a standard response to my description to a colleague of a documented "hit" was this typical dismissal: "If you could find that out, so could they." The crucial difference, which must not be lost, is, of course, that I knew the nature of the target site, but the psychics never knew—in the conventional sense.

References

1. C. Hudson, *The Southeastern Indians* (Knoxville: University of Tennessee Press, 1976), p.44.
2. Edwin C. McReynolds, *The Seminole* (Norman: University of Oklahoma Press, 1957), p.225.

3. Frank White, ed., "The Journals of Lieutenant John Pickell: 1836-1837", in *Florida Historical Quarterly*, Vol. XXXVIII, 1959.
4. William H. Sears, "Two Weeden Period Mounds", in *Social Sciences*, No. 5, 1959.
5. Hudson, *Southeastern Indians*, p.139.
6. *Ibid.*, p.126.
7. *Ibid.*, pp.304-305.
8. Frederick W. Pau, *Florida: Old and New* (New York: G.P. Putnam's Sons, 1934), p.206.

V

PHOTOGRAPHY EXPERIMENTS

Due to a variety of external problems confronted in relationship to this experiment, I at first decided not to present it in this book. However, the psychic subjects did produce accuracy far beyond that demonstrated by the control group, and this factor caused me to consider including the photograph experiment with an accompanying description of the nature of the problems that were encountered.

The first series of difficulties came as the result of certain logistic problems. One of my main informants moved her residence at this time. Several others were involved in a variety of personal and business matters which caused the experimental schedule to be disrupted. Because of these incidents, all of the research subjects were not able to read all the photographs used in this experiment. This makes for a lack of uniformity in the results.

Another problem related to the double-blind design of this test. I asked an associate to acquire from the state museum photographs of a number of artifacts.* Further, I requested that the artifacts photographed be as non-diagnostic as possible. The associate was to give me the photographs while retaining the identity of the objects until the completion of the experiment. The problem came in the nature of the artifacts which were photographed for this test. Many of them were artifacts from cultural/historical contexts that were practically impossible to document. For example, a series of the photographs showed stone blades found in South Africa, dating to 200,000 years ago. It was almost impossible to verify, or refute, cultural data offered by the psychics as they viewed these photographs because so little is known of the culture of the makers of the stone tools in that place at that time.

Informant fatigue was a big problem. All of the subjects reported varying degrees of boredom with this experiment. It is a common observation in all fields of parapsychological experimentation that a bored subject is a poor psychic subject. Bowes, for example, was so uninterested in looking at "pictures of rocks" that he began to read the photographs face-down or while they were still in the envelopes to interest himself in what he was being asked to do.

One of the photographs, Number 23, produced striking effects in Bowes and Renier, the two psychics to read it. The museum information that came with the photograph simply identified it as: "One

* All photographs used in this chapter courtesy of Florida State Museum.

chipped stone celt. Loho Liang, Komodo, Lesser Sunda Islands, Indonesian Republica. Surface find." When Bowes read the photograph he appeared to physically wilt. His body slumped slightly forward and his eyes suddenly showed strain and exhaustion, and his voice level dropped and became monotone. After looking at the photograph, he told me that he was finished reading for the day. At the end of the session that day, the following conversation ensued with relationship to the marked change that had come over Bowes when he was attempting to read Number 23.

JONES: It seemed like you hit one photo (referring to Photo 23) and it sort of turned you off. Do you know why?

BOWES: Yeah, it drained me for some reason, and then I didn't pick up hardly anything. Almost like I wasn't receptive. I thought I was giving out a lot of information about the objects, but once I got to that one I felt really drained. Like it wasn't that important. Like it was something that was just cast in there, but I didn't know what it meant.

The same physical sensations struck Renier. She began the session that day with her usual enthusiasm and continued to read the photographs with interest until Photo 23 appeared. Immediately she appeared exhausted and somewhat agitated, and reported that she was bored and tired with this experiment. We stopped at that point for the day. Neither Bowes, nor Renier, could offer any reason for the particular affect that photograph produced in them.

As will be seen, the control group did not make a single "hit", or correct identification of a test photograph. In evaluating this test I interpreted "hits" as accurate reports which located the origin of the object, or described some unique characteristic feature of the artifact's context, or portrayed a complex of accuracy, such as a valid series of statements regarding, for example, the race of the maker, climate of the artifact's origin, environment, diet of the makers, etc. In some cases a control group subjects would say of an artifact later to be identified as African, "It was hot there." I did not accept that alone as a "hit" from the control group, or from the psychics, because it was but a single correct statement that would operate with the same chance as flipping a coin. Head it's hot, tails it's cold. A "hit" would be noted, for example, if the subject correctly stated that it was not only hot, but also that it was arid and rocky with low mountains in the distance and a small lake to the north.

I presented the photographs to the subjects in mixed batches. A typical collection might include photographs 33, 27, 10, 9, 8, 7, 5, and 3, the grouping which was in fact used with Bowes in his first session of the photograph experiment.

The nature of the experiment was somewhat different with each of the four participants. The photographs were mailed to Davis and Niren for their reading. I personally took the photographs to Bowes, and I saw them at the same time he did. The design with Renier was much more rigorous. In selecting the photographs she would read, I began by shuffling the pack of photographs face-down and randomly selecting fifteen. Without looking at the photographs, I handed them to a colleague who shuffled them again and placed them in manila envelopes numbered one to fifteen. In the test area I created a board barrier about a foot and a half high between Renier and me so that I would be unable to see the photographs she was reading. I would hand her a sealed envelope, and she would open it and place the photograph against the barrier facing her. As the tape recorder ran, she would begin by stating the number of the envelope and then proceed with the reporting of the impressions she was experiencing. I would ask obvious questions aimed at eliciting specifically identifying information. As soon as I felt that she had said enough for me to ascertain her accuracy or inaccuracy I would suggest that she go on to the next envelope.

The original museum collection numbered thirty-six photographs. I pared down this number prior to presenting them to the test subjects for a number of reasons. In one case the photograph was very out of focus. Several other photographs were of objects from places I simply could not locate. In other instances, the photograph of the object was too diagnostic to be used. For example, I took one photograph out of the experiment collection because it was of the distinctive black-on-black pottery of Maria of San Ildefonso. The final photograph sample used for this experiment amounted to thirty pictures. The psychics missed, or did not read, fourteen of that number, while having relevant things to say about sixteen of the photographs, while the student control group missed on all thirty photographs.

In the following I will present under the photographs used in this test the scant identifying information that came with the photograph from the museum. I will then list the results of the control group, Bowes, Niren, Davis, and Renier, and indicate either "miss," "not read," or "hit". If accuracy was suggested, I will present the statements that I feel suggest that the psychic was accurate.

Because of the timing and scheduling problems mentioned earlier, ten of the thirty test photographs were not read by the psychics. The four that were totally missed by the psychics included photos of an Acheulean trimmed flake from South Africa, and dating to 200,000 B.C.; a 50,000-year-old stone projectile point, and a 2000-year-old stone blade, both from South Africa, and a Babylon clay tablet from Jokha.

Control Group: Miss
Davis: Not read
Niren: Not read
Renier: Not read
Bowes: Hit

When I asked Bowes about the race of the makers of the object pictured in the above photograph he said:

First thing I seen was blue eyes. But the feeling I had was that most of them were like natives, or Indians, or people who...not really Indians, but I felt they were dark skinned and their faces flatter. Not orientals. Didn't look like orientals.

"Natives" means an individual of African ethnicity, when Bowes uses the word. He makes his identification more clearly when he reports that the makers were not Indians, not Oriental, but were dark skinned individuals with relatively flat faces. If the makers are described as "natives," people who are "not really Indians," and "not Oriental," Africa is strongly suggested. As for the "blue eyes", I am most interested when Bowes begins, "But the feeling I had was that most of them were like natives..."

In his short reading of this photograph he mentioned the word "volcano" several times. My research showed that there had been no major volcanic action in this part of Africa since many thousands of years prior to the advent of the humans who made the tool pictured above. I considered Bowes' "volcano" reference a total miss until I found a reference by the two famous archeologist/anthropologists F. C. Howell and J. D. Clark[1] which stated that it was typical in the Acheulean tool industries of South Africa to make stone tools out of lava and volcanic obsidian. Perhaps Bowes was responding to the material from which the cleaver shown in the experimental photograph was made. It is noteworthy that "volcano" references recur whenever Bowes viewed photographs of South African Acheulean artifacts.

Control Group: Miss
Davis: Not read
Niren: Miss
Bowes: Miss
Renier: Hit

I will include Niren's entire reading of Photograph #2. Though Niren does not directly indicate the Vaal River area of South Africa in the following reading, she does come very close to a complex of particular accuracies. She speaks of a "black haired man" in a place that is "very arid". If we grant that her phrase "the feeling of like Nevada" describes a type of environment and not a specific place, then Niren's impressions are consistent with what we know of the ancient environment of the artifact picture above.

I see a black-haired man sitting cross legged holding this object (artifact in photograph) point side down scraping it towards him. It's some kind of dark material. When scraped it leaves a white mark. I see a lot of sand and very arid. People sweating. I also see trees and a lot of wooden sticks. Houses were made of sticks. As I see it now, also bushes. I get the feeling of like Nevada...and I got that really fast. I also see creeks or lakes where they get fish. Also berries were in their diet. I feel reptiles were also eaten. I feel birds were important to them. Feathers. I also feel this object was used as a weapon. I feel very protective of land and people, as if people were trying to encroach on them. They would not hesitate to protect themselves. I feel they used everything available to them for survival as it was a hard life. Their survival was most important.

The following is Renier's reading of the photograph of the 200,000-year-old South African hand axe.

I feel so beautiful. I feel like a lot of hours, a lot of time, a lot of pride went into this object. I feel...nothing on my chest or arms. A short cloth or something around my waist. With this one...I know this can't be verified, but I feel a young boy. Not a man but a young boy. I feel like a warrior. I feel he wants to be a warrior. I feel in this tribe, which is a long time ago, I feel like they had specific people to be warriors and specific people to have different ranks...but the warrior was the highest. There is a river that is flowing through this area. I don't know direction. I can't tell you whether it's flowing north or south or...Let's leave that.

JONES: Can you tell me anything to identify the makers of the object or where it came from?

RENIER: Hilly environment. I don't know if they lived in caves or they had a lot to do in caves, but I feel hard rock areas. High.

JONES: What does the climate feel like?

RENIER: I feel like it could get cold. I am not cold now. The boy has no shirt on, and the wind is pushing his hair back. Hair not touching his shoulder area.

JONES: As you look at this boy, what color is his skin?

RENIER: It's brown. Light brown, not a black. Tan. Could possibly be like an American Indian skin or even a Mexican Indian skin.

JONES: What about the place where this came from? (Indicates object in photo)

RENIER: As you said that I just saw the river and I saw the heights going up, and I saw little caves up on the mountain side. Fish. Oh, wait a second, I'm getting mixed up.

JONES: Where is this place?

RENIER: I don't know if this is my conscious mind or not... I'm going to say it, but I want to have stars around it because I think it might be me saying it. I would say...Africa... but I don't feel all that good about it.

JONES: Can you tell me what other kinds of things were going on in the world at the time this object was made?

RENIER: I feel like not too far away some land went into the sea. I feel like some land being covered with water. I don't understand it. I don't know if it breaks off and goes into the water or if the water...I don't know. I just don't see much going on.

JONES: What did these people eat?

RENIER: Fish. Fish was very strong in the diet. Something I could chew on and throw away after a while.

JONES: Do you feel you are with these people strongly? Like could I ask you questions about their culture?

RENIER: I feel like I am just with this boy. We are just walking in the woods. I want to go to his village. I want to go to where they live. I feel like I am in a very small village of Indians. I feel like I am more like...it looks more like...it looks more American Indian from what I know. I don't know. There are cliffs in the background and then lower plains. They are scouting. I don't think scouting for war but scouting for a new place.

Renier notes the river flowing through the area. As the museum information stated, the site producing this artifact was on the Vaal River. The area is characterized by broad flat plains, The Great Escarpment, and dry barren hills, as Renier correctly noted. Douglas Hey[2], in describing South Africa's countryside, states:

Much of South Africa consists of mountains and rocky hills which cannot be cultivated. Large areas are too dry, receiving only a few inches of rain each year.

When questioned about the climate, Renier said that "it could get cold, though I'm not cold now." Does it get cold in South Africa? Yes. Hey[3], again speaking of agricultural problems in South Africa, substantiates Renier when he writes:

There are also localities which are too cold and others where the soil is too poor...Even in the relatively good agricultural areas farmers have to contend with frost, hailstorms, and periodical droughts.

At several points, Renier spoke of caves. "I don't know if they lived in caves or if they had a lot to do in caves....As you said that, I just saw the river and I saw the heights going up and I saw like little caves up on the mountain side." Inkeep[4] and Bordes[5] both note the cave occupations of the Acheulean peoples of South Africa.

When I first asked, "Where is this place?", Renier's correct response was "Africa". Also, like Niren, Renier stated her opinion that fish were important in the diet of the tool's makers. She also is no doubt correct about the dark skin of the tool's maker. Her response to my question, "Can you tell me what other kinds of things were going on in the world at the time this object was made?" proved significant. Renier's feeling that some land was being covered with water could relate to the fact that at that time the melting waters of the retreating glaciers in the north were raising the sea level and indeed covering land hitherto exposed. She is also right in saying that at the time the object was made—200,000 years ago—not much was going on in the world. *Homo sapiens* (modern) was not even present at this time.

Her excellent hit with the Acheulean hand axe from South Africa was somewhat marred in the last several sentences when she stated, "...it looks more American Indian from what I know. I don't know."

Control Group: Miss
Bowes: Miss
Davis: Miss
Niren: Not read
Renier: Not read

Though I gave both Davis and Bowes a "miss" on this photograph, there is an observation to be made. When I asked Bowes where the site which produced the pictured artifact was, he responded: "I hear the roar of the ocean, and I don't know if these people are near the water, but I kept hearing that, like waves, like the ocean." Davis began her reading with, "I'm very much aware of water...a large body of water." Davis continued with a description of Western style gold prospector and Bowes spoke about Spanish invaders, both incorrect cultural/historical descriptions. However, the congruence on the subject of the proximity to the ocean or a "large body of water" by the psychics when reading a photograph of an object coming from a river in the interior of South Africa struck me as peculiar. While researching South Africa in order to evaluate the readings of Davis, Bowes, Renier, and Niren in this experiment, I came upon this statement by R. R. Inskeep[6]:

> ...the slender ethnographic evidence available to us, and indeed some archeological evidence in the form of rock paintings and engravings of marine animals and the occurrence of marine mollusks in inland shelter sites, suggests that our Late Stone Age population may well have practiced a seasonal migratory way of life, moving at times to the coast to take advantage of sea food, and at other times moving inland to hunt and collect.

Control Group: Miss
Niren: Not read
Renier: Not read
Bowes: Hit
Davis: Hit

Though Davis never directly identified the location of the object, her comments concerning environment and climatic variation are correct. She also may be reacting to the cave habitats of many Stone Age South African peoples in her allusions to mountain-side dwellings.

> I do sense like mountains in this area. I'm seeing an area that is mountainous as well as flat. It looks dry. There is not lot of greenery. More of a desert-type terrain...

As she observed a "tall, lean" man she spoke of the climate he experienced:

> ...where it would be very hot for him to wear that in summer time when he hardly wore anything. In the winter times they wore a blanket-like woven substance...

The mountain dwelling comments came in this passage.

> I sense buildings and things put up against the mountain. I

don't know if they are in the mountain itself. I can't really
distinguish that...

In Bowes' reading of the South African material he made his characteristic "volcano" reference as he did when reading just about all
South African items. He correctly noted that the object in the photograph originated outside the United States. Like Davis, he felt
impressions of mountain dwellings. He is also correct in characterizing
the object's maker as "native" ("African" in Bowes' vocabulary). His
description of the house he saw is not inaccurate. Several Stone Age
dwellings have been unearthed in South Africa and they are typified
by an oval arrangement of large boulders which served as a base for
a branch and stick roof. The relevant passages from Bowes' reading
follow.

> The first thing I picked up with this was the north, or
> volcano action. I felt as though this could have come from
> another country...But this I felt was like on the floor of
> a building.
>
> JONES: Do you have a feeling of what the building looked
> like?
>
> BOWES: I felt it had open windows and it was build in
> blocks. I felt like the windows were open. I didn't know...
> big windows, big solid walls. Real thick and massive.
>
> JONES: Do you get any feelings about the environment?
>
> BOWES: I felt it had open windows and it was built in
> canic rock, or island, or a place where the ground is very
> desolate and drops off very quickly...I felt a stone building
> and it was vacant and the wind was blowing. I felt it was like
> on a volcanic rock, or island. I would say that if it isn't on an
> island, it could be on a mountain, or it could be like those
> stone buildings that the Indians made into the walls, or
> shelves of the mountains. That's the feeling I picked up. But
> I would associate it more with water, because I kept seeing
> people who looked like natives, like on islands, and they ran
> down naked with no clothes on, or maybe they had some-
> thing around their head. I felt they all ran to the shore. I
> would say they were associated with volcanoes or earth-
> quakes...uncertain ground conditions.

Control Group: Miss
Niren: Not read
Davis: Miss
Bowes: Miss
Renier: Miss

With Bowes it should be noted that when he saw this photograph,
he immediately leafed through the pile of photographs set between us
on the table until he came to the picture museum-labeled as photograph number nine. He then told me that the above photograph and
"Number 9" came from the same area and same time. They were

today but very small, very minute. I want to say they are in
a backwoods area, or an area that has not become overly
civilized yet and they still have many of their primitive
customs although they are more modernized in dress, and
in attitude.

Control Group: Miss
Bowes: Hit
Niren: Not Read
Davis: Not Read
Renier: Miss

This was the photograph which produced the draining effects in
both Bowes and Niren. Bowes' most specific hit came while he was
reading this photograph face-down. He said, as he placed his hand on
the photograph and closed his eyes, "I don't know if they tried to grow
something in terraces but I felt that they had very poor luck." The
Lesser Sunda Islands are located right in the middle of the major
terrace farming area of the world. The tropical environment of the artifact is described in this passage from Bowes.

I felt that some of the trees when they chop into them got a
lot of water out, like in the south...like a swampy area. Like
they would cut into a tree and it could be real juicy, and it
wouldn't hold up.

Control Group: Miss
Bowes: Hit
Davis: Not Read
Niren: Not Read
Renier: Miss

In his reading, Bowes located the environment and described the
nature of the artifacts before he had seen the photograph, while it was
face-down under a manila envelope. The many references to mud are
valid because the Key Marco Site is famous for the rare finds of
wooden artifacts discovered there which have been preserved for many
hundreds of years due to their emersion in the mud encompassing
the site. Bowes is also correct when he connects the site producing
these artifacts with the "site along the St. Johns River," 8Se32. Both
sites were occupied simultaneously and they shared basic culture
patterns, especially during the Woodland Period.

(photograph is face-down under a manila envelope) I don't
know if there is something here that relates to a culture that
is around water, but the feeling I had was something around
the ocean or something near Georgia, or near water. I felt
"Indians". This could even have been from the site along the
St. Johns River. Somewhere where there's water. It is something that they were digging with. I keep feeling a picture of
a goblet, a scooper, or something that digs. I would say this
could be a shell. This could possibly be a shell with a hole in
it. I feel as though there is more than one object. I would say

two shells or two bones, or two something. I see a lot of shells, and I see a lot of bones, but I felt they are mixed in. I did feel there was a lot of mud there. I felt the area was smelly or there was a lot of dead animals there. I would say that whatever is in this picture it is white, or...like bleached bone, or shell that's white. (Bowes now turns the photograph face up). This was something they used to tie things down (indicates pendant). I felt it was a shell...almost like they hung it. I don't know if this was some sort of weight...almost like for fishing, but I felt it held a net down. This here (pick), I felt was like a goblet, or something that was used to dig with. I would say this hole is there for a purpose. I wouldn't know what it was. But I feel the ocean, or near the water. Now I don't know if this is near Georgia. I felt some people's teeth missing.

JONES: What did these people wear?

BOWES: I would say fur. I keep seeing fur. I keep feeling something tied over their shoulders almost like they were carrying water bags or carried something. I don't know why, but I felt this (pendant) here could have related to a civilized people, a more advanced or more important people wore this. I felt they had a bunch of them like hanging around their waist. I don't know if this is a weight for like nets, but that's the feeling I had. I felt mud flats, like areas where there's a lot of water. I felt like white beaches. And in behind was all marsh, swamp, like the ground or mud was clay. Almost like it was grey clay or there were dead trees sticking up from it. There could have been cocina rock sticking out. I do feel as though someone tied their hair back. I kept seeing a red cloth, or something red around their head.

Control Group: Miss
Bowes: Hit
Davis: Not Read
Niren: Not Read
Renier: Hit

The Poverty Point culture (1500 B.C.-1200 B.C.) was characterized by the possession of mound and earthwork building, maize horticulture, extensive trade networks, and a lamellar flake industry reminiscent of the Olmec culture of Veracruz.[7] The type site at Poverty Point is located on a bayou. At the site is a massive bird effigy mound plus many raised ridges presumably built as house platforms.

Bowes' reading of the photograph follows.

(photo still face-down) I know this will sound strange to you, but I felt that whatever is in here is something that relates to almost something that was rough like...like it had big lumps or bigger lumps. I felt it was almost like a huge tooth, or like a mastodon's tooth, or something that was rough. Now I'm explaining the looks of it, rather than what it is. I felt it could be white, or light colored. I kept feeling the outside of it was in lumps, or roughness. Almost like it was rough or rounded like...and it was almost like a cow's tooth. Now I may get more as I see it. (Bowes turns the photo face-up) Hmmm. That's what I seen. I don't know what it is. I do feel with this here (clay object) that it was man-made, like holding it with their hands, or like to grab it. I felt very old with this. Very, very old. I don't know if these are like cave men, or very primitive people, but I felt like this (slate gorget) was almost like a breast plate, or something that was tied onto a person, or tied onto something...flat, like on their chest here. I keep feeling as though they are farmers or people who dug in the ground. I keep seeing an association with wood...making things of wood and I felt like they were quite...carpenters. I kept feeling the houses or the buildings were up high...I felt they used pegs...wooden pegs, and they may have been square on the outside. The houses were off the ground. I don't know what they were like. I felt that they came there at a time that was then cold weather or a change of weather, but I felt they changed. They were very basic, and could be travelers but gradually they grew into more of a farming group of people.

JONES: What feeling did you get about the environment?

BOWES: I really didn't pick up environment that much. I picked up...could be a warmer climate, but I would say that they were originally people who followed weather patterns or seasonal changes. Eventually, because of the weather changing, they may have moved south, or toward Georgia, or toward Florida, or toward the south, and stayed there and made a home out of that area.

JONES: (pointing to objects in photograph) Do you feel these are from Georgia or Florida?

BOWES: I would say they originated from the north, and they could have brought these things from the north. That's what I picked up. I would say that whoever owned that was in war. Continuously warred. Fight people. I wouldn't have any idea what it is. This here (clay object) could be a bone, or it could associate with crushing bones, or...I'm just picking up 'bone, bone, bone'. I would say that it is a stone but again it could be used to crush something. O.K. I would say the people who owned that were very primitive but because they stayed in one place they improved on their ideas and they could have made these houses or made some structures. I keep seeing the man who owned these things with one eye missing or a problem with his eye. The eye was very red and yellow inside. No way of proving that, of course.

He described a population that "stayed in one place," and that could be true for the people who built Poverty Point Site. Bowes' reading contained references to "farmers" who lived "south, or toward Georgia, or toward Florida, or toward the south". The house ridges at Poverty Point were suggested at several points by Bowes: "I kept feeling the houses or the buildings were up high..." "The houses were off the ground." All of the peoples, of historical record, who lived in sites like Poverty Point were extremely war-like. Even though the Poverty Point population was too early for historical observation, Bowes is probably right in characterizing the Poverty Point builders as people who "continuously warred." The complex requirements of their slash-and-burn horticulture, large population, and complicated trade-networks would almost oblige warfare to exist.

This is Renier's reading of the photograph of the Poverty Point materials.

I am picking up a large body of water, but I feel it is more still. I feel it is not...it is either an inlet or a lake. I don't feel it is as rough as the big ocean. These objects were found in a heap, or a pile. I'm seeing more of a mound effect.

JONES: Do you feel climate?

RENIER: I feel warm, but I feel like nice breezes. I feel like there would be a breeze. Let me see what part of the country I am in or what country I am in...I feel like I want to say 'south'...perhaps even South America...I would be in a tropical part.

JONES: Do you see the people associated with this? (referring to photograph).

RENIER: More short, square built...short fingers...smaller feet. Sturdy but short. Native...

JONES: Can you give me some identifying characteristics what would tell me who the makers of these objects were?

RENIER: A high...either chieftains, or...the tribe...high headgear but it doesn't look...it is high, but it doesn't come down. Possibly a band or something around the head. Head. I felt also shiny material...on this. I don't know if it is gold or what but I felt the sun would reflect on it. I think it might be a country plentiful in gold.

JONES: What is the race of the makers?

RENIER: Language...there would be reserved for this tribal group. There are variations of this language, but not...as exact as in this one place. This one place...I feel like I am being attacked...attacked.

JONES: By whom?

RENIER: We are up higher, and there doesn't look like there is that many of us, and people are coming from below. I feel there are more whites involved.

JONES: Again, what is the race of the makers?

RENIER: When you say 'race,' do you want me to say 'Korean' or something like that?

JONES: Yes.

RENIER: I feel like I want to say 'In-' but that could be 'Indians.' I better try harder. I just got 'In-'. Is there something like "ingrius" or ...whatever I said. I'm getting confused.

JONES: As a way to help date these things I want to ask you what other kinds of things were going on in other parts of the world at the time these things were made?

RENIER: To the left I feel some earth disasters. Earth disasters to the left. I feel like at this time...I'm picking up a boat with people on it but I feel the boat or the people are more American or more civilized looking. I don't know what this is all about. They are searching. They are looking for something. I don't understand. They are over water but they are looking or searching. I don't know if that is in conjunction with these artifacts or not. Let me try to answer your question...In the European era...in the European countries possibly France, England, were involved in some traumatic ...it started verbal but it's some sort of war, but I don't know how major it is. I feel it was in the 13th or 14th century at that point.

Renier was wrong in her dating attempts. However, she did describe a site by an "inlet or a lake" possessing "a mound effect." The elevated earthworks may account for why she felt the people were "up higher" being attacked by people "coming from below." Renier shared Bowes' image of conflict stemming from the Poverty Point artifact photograph. "I feel like I am being attacked...attacked." Renier also noted the warm climate of the site. She also described "Indians" as the makers of the items.

Control Group: Miss
Davis: Not read
Niren: Not read
Renier: Not read
Bowes: Hit

These items were made by Neanderthal peoples. These cousins to modern-day humans lived from about 100,000 to 35,000 years ago. I gave Bowes a "hit" on this one due to his dominant impression of "cave men". Here is Bowes' reading of the Neanderthal items:

I felt death with this. I felt north, and I felt they were scratching for something that wasn't there. I don't know if these people who were in caves, or where there was granite or very hard rock, but I felt like they were very primitive. And I felt that someone fell from the rocks and died. I felt...down.

JONES: Do you have any feelings about what they might have looked like?

BOWES: I feel that none of these objects have any real value to people, but I feel these are rocks or something they took off the floor of a cave or off the floor of a...I felt chips of stone, and I felt the ground was very desolate, and it was either cold or very sharp rocks...almost like you'd go along and you see kind of a desolate valley or like...something... you'd go down in the bottom of this valley and they would pick up all the parts...maybe on the bottom of a cave or ravine or something, but I felt they picked up all the parts. I would say these people could have been cave men, or somebody very primitive.

JONES: What makes you feel that they are primitive?

BOWES: I would say it was a primitive people because they may not have worn clothes or they may have just had things hanging over the middle part of their body. I felt a very primitive, an extremely primitive, spear. Real...tied with string or leather. Very primitive. The point wasn't even sharp. It was blunt.

JONES: What kinds of things did they eat?

BOWES: I keep feeling as though they hit rocks, or throwing rocks off of something or hitting animals down below. If this is near the water...I would say that they did eat things from the water, but I would say they walked along the cliffs. I really don't pick up that much from this. I'm sorry. I would say there were later people there, but they didn't associate with these parts (touches artifact photograph) as valuable. I see a woman in a bonnet...like the Pilgrims who came to this country from another country. I see a woman with a little bonnet on. I felt like it was New England, or came from Europe, but I feel that was later people.

JONES: These were the later people?

BOWES: Yes. I felt like they had like buckles on it. I felt they had something like leggings or white leggings...showed the calf of the leg, but it was white looking. I don't know. Maybe they were pirates or something. I don't know. This thing (touches photograph) was very primitive. They were like Indians or cavemen, or somebody very primitive. Later these people came (later people) and lived in the same area or are familiar, but they (touches photograph) were very old people, of the past. They (later people) could have even built buildings, or built something that was made of stone, or white chalk or clay, but I see them crushing stones or crushing shells and mixing sand and shells and making like mortar out of it. But these people (touches photograph) were extremely primitive. They could have been Indians, or cavemen, or somebody basic, very, very simple.

Bowes directly described the major geomorphic feature of the site area, the Vallee de la Vezere, when he said, "...you'd go along and you see kind of a desolate valley...you'd go down in the bottom of this valley..."

Control Group: Miss
Bowes: Hit
Niren: Not Read
Davis: Not Read
Renier: Not Read

The items pictured here are artifacts from the St. Simon's Island site (Chapter III). These materials were an excellent selection on the part of the colleague who acquired the photographs because it enables a comparison between Bowes' double-blind reading of artifacts from this site, and his double-blind reading of a photograph of more artifacts from the same site. This is Bowes' reading of the photograph.

In assocation with this picture I felt 'survivors'...something associated with something near the water. I kept feeling salt water or something where something was all washed away... almost like in a hurricane or a storm...something where there's water. I kept seeing sticks sticking out of the mud and that's all that was left. I don't know if there was malaria or disease, but I felt very sad with that button right there. I don't know if it's near Mississippi, or the pan-handle of Florida or Georgia, but I kept feeling 'near the water and in the south' ...I kept seeing a place where there was an island. I don't know if there is a river or something going this way. There was a place where there was a sandbar and mud. There are raccoons and animals...something up in there all furry. In here, along the coast, I felt they collected oysters or something like shells. I don't feel it would be below Georgia. With this button, I kept feeling somebody had died...could be drowning, but I kept seeing the chest.

JONES: What kind of people were involved here?

BOWES: I felt dark skinned, and I don't know if they spoke French but they had an accent. I would say they had very dark hair. They had a moustache...some of them. I felt that in dealing with this button and this spike, you know. The beaches, but there were mud flats where it would just stink. The oysters and the shells would lay on the ground. I felt there were sand dunes somewhere around here. Most of it was flat ground, and very long, flat stretches of mud.

Bowes accurately described "a place where there was an island" that was "in the south" but not "below Georgia." He may be echoing the accounts of the great storm described by Laudonniere, for example, in his mention of the destruction of land "almost like in a hurricane or a storm." The French expeditions of Ribault and Laudonniere appeared in his reference to "survivors," and in his comment, "I don't know if they spoke French but they had an accent."

Control Group: Miss
Niren: Miss
Davis: Miss
Renier: Not Read
Bowes: Hit

Bowes' double-blind reading of the photograph of the Florida artifacts.

I would say that this was from Florida. They could have been
from the coastal area, or a place where...could have been
from Georgia...but I felt more with Florida. I kept feeling it
was from a coastal area. I did feel that when they laid this
down (potsherds), when it was clay, it made these marks in
the back of it. I feel as though these people had a boat. I feel
with these people that they moved south. I don't know if this
was found in the Brevard area, or a place around where there
was a lot of water, but I would say that this (points to
stone pieces) was brought from a different area, possibly
Ocala or the north...traded down, O.K. I felt this was almost
like two cultures. This (pottery) and this (stone tools) was
different. I keep seeing a man with a nose that looked large.
JONES: What kind of diet do you feel this group had?
BOWES: I would say that these people here ate very poorly,
and whatever they ate, they could have eaten something they
needed to crunch, or crush, or grind their teeth, because I felt
their teeth were worn. I felt they had good teeth, but I kept
seeing their teeth worn, and they could have eaten oysters,
but I see something related to that. Now these people may
not have lived in Florida, but they may have lived near the
water.
JONES: When you said 'these people' you indicated the
pottery?
BOWES: This pottery...this (stone tools) could have been
found with this stuff, but I would say it was traded from
some other place. I feel these people (pottery) were very poor,
and these people (stone tools) were running from somebody,
but I felt all this stuff was together. I felt they could have
found with these things, or very near there, a hinge...a steel
hinge, but it didn't belong with that (artifacts in photograph). That could have been from the Georgia site (probably
referring to St. Simon's Island Site), but I would say it
related more to Florida, or a place that was near Florida. The
way they made this (pottery) was familiar to the way Indians
made things in Florida. It was very brittle and didn't
last long.

Bowes correctly located the target site in Florida and even more
specifically "in the Brevard area." The materials came from about a

mile from the Brevard County line. Similar materials can be found many hundreds of miles north and south from the Hawthorne site.

Control Group: Miss
Niren: Not Read
Davis: Not Read
Renier: Not Read
Bowes: Hit

Interestingly enough, Bowes' accuracy with this photograph came while the photo was still sealed in its envelope. His accuracy waned when he took the photograph out of the envelope to read it. Here is the section of the reading presented prior to Bowes' visual contact with this test photograph.

I'm going to pick up photograph number one, and I feel very strong with a feeling of people in a cold climate. The first impression I got was like Vikings, or Indians, or people in a climate. I keep seeing a relationship to something symbolic. I don't know if this thing is a tool or its significance is a religious purpose or use. I keep seeing the claws of a bear, or like claws of something. The feeling I had with this is a bird, or something that carried something. The feeling I had was a bird's head. I would say that this could be a very old object. I would say it could be made of brass, or there could be bone or ivory involved with it. I would say the front of it, or there's an end, almost like it's round, and it's almost like a goblet or something round, and then it comes to a point, and on the end of the point there could be...the first thing I picked up was an arrow head, but then I picked up an Indian, or some person. I felt fur on them. Another feeling I picked up was a bird's head, or something with a beak. I kept feeling these people were traveling a lot. It could be in the northern part of the United States, or it could be somewhere around where there's water, but that's what I picked up. O.K.?

Conclusions: Photography Experiment

Though this experiment was not, in my opinion, a complete or finished piece I included it here because it does suggest that psychics are capable, with varying degrees of success, to look at photographs of a variety of artifacts, some diagnostic and some non-diagnostic, and offer accurate complexes of information concerning the environment of the artifact, time of its manufacture, race of the makers, cultural characteristics, and related historical events taking place in other parts of the world. The control group composed of university students did not produce a single hit in this experiment.

All of the psychic subjects found this experiment to be the most tedious and boring of the entire experimental series. Bowes' comment presented below, was voiced by all the subjects in their own way.

> I don't know why they would give me pictures of things I don't understand. These are rocks. They are not important or valuable. If I could only touch these things I could tell you much more about them.

References

1. F. Clark Howell, and J. Desmond Clark, "Acheulean Hunters-Gatherers of Sub-Saharan Africa", in *African Ecology and Human Evolution*, F. Clark Howell, and Francois Bourliere, eds. (Chicago: Aldine Publishing Co., 1966), p.513.
2. Douglas Hey, *Wildlife Heritage of South Africa* (London: Oxford University Press, 1966), p.20.
3. *Ibid.*, p.20.
4. R.R. Inskeep, "The Late Stone Age in Southern Africa", in *Background to Evolution in Africa*, Walter W. Bishop, and J. Desmond Clark, eds. (Chicago: University of Chicago Press, 1967), p.572.
5. Francois Bordes, *The Old Stone Age* (London: Wedenfeld and Nicolson, 1968), p.69.
6. Inskeep, *Late Stone Age*, p.572.
7. Robert F. Spencer et al., *The Native Americans*, second ed. (New York: Harper & Row, 1977), p.403.

VI

PALEONTOLOGY
EXPERIMENT

Paleontology is the science which attempts to understand prehistoric life forms through the study of plant and animal fossils. The time range in which the paleontologist investigates is immense—the oldest known traces of life dating to over 3,500 million years. Paleontological investigation usually stops at a boundary arbitrarily marked at about one million years ago; hence to the paleontologist, one million years ago is the beginning of recent time.

Paleontology is an important field to consider when experimenting in psychic archeology for several reasons. Archeologists often use animal and plant remains unearthed at archeological sites to aid them in interpreting the history of the site. This is such a common factor in archeological analysis that I had necessarily planned to create some type of "bone" experiment, though I had not intended at the outset to utilize the bones of extinct animals. When the opportunity to experiment with fossil bones came up, I was immediately intrigued, both because of the bone experiment I had scheduled and because the great antiquity of the fossils would help me to evaluate the degree to which psychics might be able to accurately reach backward in time. Albert Bowes had demonstrated in the Folsom experiment that he could touch events over ten thousand years in the past. But could he go back several million of years?

I acquired fragments of fossil bones from ten extinct animals. The bones were numbered one to ten. An accompanying list identified the items by number. I perused this list briefly upon receipt and filed it for future reference. This experiment is not technically double-blind because I had pre-experiment access to the "answers"; though to a non-paleontologist like myself, the glimpse of a few words like "Gomphotherium" or "Megalothere" on a slip of paper is approximately equal to never having seen the list at all.

The fossils were from Polk County, Florida. Extensive phosphate mining in that area over many decades has produced a great number of fossil remains from the Miocene, Pliocene, and Pleistocene geological epochs. The fossils in the test group presented to Albert Bowes were from the Pliocene, dating to twelve million years, and the Pleistocene, dating back about two million years.

164

The Experiment

Generally, Bowes found this experiment to be extremely difficult. All the fossils which were very stone-like in appearance produced responses like the following which came as Bowes handled a piece of fossil Pleistocene manatee rib. The manatee (sea cow, dugong) resembles a warm water, tusk-less walrus with a broad, flat, rounded tail.

I don't know why but when I picked this up, I keep feeling 'no'. Like it wasn't a bone. I do feel it was a bone, but now it isn't...in the feeling about it. Again I felt a clay pit. I didn't pick up much from that at all. It's just like picking up a rock. I thought it was very, very old, and in the ground for a long time. I felt something stepped on it and broke it into a lot of pieces. I wish I could help you more with that.

Another extremely lithified manatee bone elicited a similar report. However, in this response, after denying that he could accurately identify the nature of the animal which produced the bone, Bowes proceeded to correctly describe the marine environment of the long extinct creature.

No. You see these things have lost their vibrations because they turned to stone. This is just a piece of stone to me. I pick up nothing about it. I just pick up pressure and heat. There was an ocean around it. Maybe a water animal that swam in the ocean. I just don't get much from these pieces... like rocks.

The tooth of a Pliocene horse led Bowes to state, "I don't get anything from that but teeth." A Pliocene rhinocerus tooth was incorrectly described as coming from a sabar-toothed tiger. As he touched the rhino tooth he exclaimed:

Boy! These things are old. Animals don't look that way now. It's hard.

However, when he was presented with a bone of a twelve-million year-old capybara, he correctly said, "I felt like a pig-like animal... more like a little tusk." This animal is so "pig-like", in fact, that it is sometimes referred to as a "water hog."[1] The modern-day capybara is the world's largest living rodent, averaging twenty-four inches in height and forty-eight inches in length. Bowes' emphasis on the "little tusk" could relate to a definitive trait of all rodents—pronounced incisor teeth.

Another accurate observation came while he was reading the ancient capybara tooth. He pointed to the fossil bone collection and said, "I would say that all these things you have here today came from Florida." He was right.

Two of the larger specimens in this experiment, a vertebrae from a Pliocene whale and a heavily fossilized Pleistocene sea cow rib, were packed in the same container. I mention this because the following reading of the whale bone not only brought forth an accurate description of, and drawing of the whale (complete with the diagnostic horizontal flukes), but also a description and a drawing of a sea cow. This again suggests the contamination phenomenon noted earlier. It is doubly interesting because when Bowes was presented with the sea cow rib separately, he denied that he could read what appeared to him to be merely a piece of rock. The following exchange between Bowes and me came as he touched the Pliocene whale vertebrae.

> The first thing I picked up was...like a mammoth, or like an animal with a lot of fur. I kept picking up something about it being stuck, or stuck in the mud or walking for a long distance over grass lakes. I felt there was like big elephant ear plants or big leaves. Lots of...very wet, humid, wet. But then I picked up something about the ocean, or water, and then it was on top. This thing could have died and been buried in the ground and been buried under the water, over the land. The feeling I had was that this was found in Florida and in a canal...of clay. The first thing I picked up was something down its back almost like it had a fin down its back, or like its back was real humped up in the back. O.K. Do you know what this is?

JONES: No. This really isn't my field.

BOWES: I felt like...the funniest thing is that I felt like that animal originally had hair on it. The feeling first of all was like an animal in real swampy...like half in and half out of the water. Real, real swampy, and jungle. More jungle than anything on earth today. Just more jungle. I felt like you would push on the plants and they were real mushy, real soft. Big plants, great big plants. And this elephant, or big animal that had fur on it. Then I kept seeing it in the water, and then I seen like a big shark, or a big animal in the water...like smooth looking skin. Would be like a whale or a shark... something with smooth looking skin. It had a big hump on its back. I would say that it's not like a whale today. Like a sperm whale...had a great big mouth. A big mouth. I didn't feel it had any teeth. I felt its mouth was going through the top of the suds...sudsy water. I don't feel I'm wrong on this one. It's good. Interesting. I'll try to draw (produces DRAWING: VI-1). That's strange. The feeling I have is a big sea cow. This was the first one I got (points to figure 1). I don't know what this looks like (head on figure 1), but...it's big. It may have had hair on it...brownish hair. Then I picked up this one (figure 2), something with more like a fin. It had the same shaped head, but this here (points to mouth area on figure 2) was not teeth...something else. Like it ran something over its mouth. Like it came through the suds, like the waves or something and it kind of skimmed the top. That's number 2. It was real big, and humped back, and it (points to figure 1) was like a sea cow, and it had kind of an elephant's

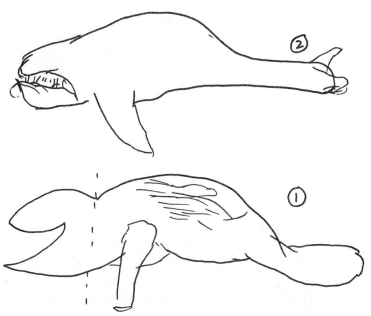

VI-1: Bowes' impressions from vertebrae. Pliocene whale vertebrae.

foot down here. Kind of stubby and round foot, and it just
sloshed around in shallow water...mud, shallow water. The
feeling I had was it propelled itself along with its feet...like
a seal. Kind of bounced along on its stomach. Then I felt like
...the plants were real soft, full of water, real soft. This
(figure 2) was in the sea, in the ocean. It was real, real
smooth.

One of the Pleistocene fossil specimens given to me for this test was
a piece of fossil bone unknown to even the paleontologist who produced
the fossil collection. Bowes offered the following reading as he touched
the bone.

(Bowes begins by drawing. DRAWING VI-2.) The legs
aren't exactly right. The feeling I had was like it was a
raccoon-like animal, and this is the vertebrae from it...in
the back.

JONES: Do you feel the environment?

BOWES: I felt the animal was like a raccoon or opossum...
that kind of thing way, way back in time.

JONES: Anything about temperature? What do the plants
look like?

BOWES: Around the water. It ate things out of the water
like shell fish. I felt if (the fossil) had been in the water and
washed around. O.K. Do you know what this is?

JONES: No.

VI-2: An animal of an unknown fossil bone.

BOWES: Maybe they don't even know what it is. I felt real strong about the face (refers to his drawing) I drew of that thing. I'm sure that's what the head looked like. I was real confident about the little ears and the face. Not really a raccoon, you understand, and not really a cat, but it was kind of something along those lines...an ancestor maybe. Had a longer face, and it was bigger. Definitely not a reptile.

One does not generally think of raccoons living in Pleistocene times. However, Murray[2], in a discussion of Pleistocene animals writes, "The list of early carnivores includes dogs, cats, raccoons, bears, skunks, and several others." Bowes was also correct in the above reading when he stated with reference to the fossil before him, "Maybe they don't even know what it is."

The next fossil set in front of Bowes was the molar of a mastodant called *Gomphotherium floridans*. In most respects this animal looked like our modern-day circus elephant, with the exception of a few subtle variations in the head, tusk, tooth, and jaw conformation. Bowes offered many correct images in the following reading of the fossil tooth. He noted the "ripping" motion of a feeding elephant—and its great size. He was also right in saying that the animal was a land animal and mainly a vegetarian. The bathing and spraying of elephants is a common and daily occurrence. Bowes may be describing this behavior in the last part of his reading.

I don't know. The first feeling I had was that this was an animal that ate more than one thing. I don't know if this would be a dinosaur or a sloth kind of thing, but I felt it grabbed things and ripped them out. I felt it was very big, or very tall. I could not say it was out of the water. That it is not an animal in the water. I don't pick that up.

JONES: A land animal?

BOWES: Yes. Even if they said it was something else, I wouldn't believe it. I would feel it was from the land. I would say it was very, very big. I would say it had very many teeth that grew in, when it broke teeth off...new teeth grew in. It ate grass, mostly, or vegetation, and it ripped it. It could have eaten some meat too. I felt it had a big square head. That's the one thing I picked up real strong was the ear. Something like that. It had rows of teeth. I picked up water, but it went mainly on the land. It may swim and blow water out of its nose, but then it would go back on the land. Would somebody know what these things are?

JONES: I am going to get them described.

One of the direct "hits" in this experiment came when Bowes was handling the non-diagnostic fragment of the tooth of a now extinct bison type known *Bison antiquus*. As soon as I handed the tooth piece to him, Bowes began to move his jaw in a horizontal motion. I asked him what he was doing, and he responded with the following reading.

VI-3: A pliocene bison.

I felt this was a cow's tooth, or a buffalo's tooth. It felt like eating grass and chewing cud. Its jaw went from side to side. It may have had an unusual jaw, but I felt its jaw went back and forth, and just kept chewing on things. I felt like a bison, but not like we know it. It had big horns on it. Like the horns...let me show you (draws his bison picture). Great big horns like those long-horned... I would say bison would have more small horns but this one was much bigger and had long horns.

His indication that the ancient bison had longer horns and was generally larger in body size than modern bison precisely identifies the two most obvious differences between the extinct bison *antiquus*, and the contemporary bison *taylori*.

The last bone given to Bowes in this experiment was a piece of the left front shoulder of a Pleistocene mammoth. The contamination effect may be occurring again in this reading as Bowes seems to be simultaneously describing certain basic characteristics of the Pleistocene mammoth and the horse. There was a horse fossil in this collection which brought forth no significant response when set before Bowes earlier in the experiment. His references to a very large, vegetation eating, stiff-legged animal with a curiously sloping profile strongly suggests the mammoth. At the same time, however, he spoke of horses, hooves, and animals that did "a lot of running."

One unmistakable accuracy was in Bowes indication of the location of the bone in the animal's body. In that this was a non-diagnostic bone, not even a paleontologist could, without knowing the context of the fossil find, correctly place the bone's location in the animal. Bowes marked the origin of the bone with a small oval shape on the animal's left front shoulder.

The feeling I had to start with was a leg bone of a horse, or like this animal, whatever it was, I felt was stiff legged. Like giraffe or a horse, stiff legs, but it was huge, and much, much larger. I don't know if it had short back legs and longer front legs, but I felt it was weird looking. The rear-end was down low and the front was kind of long. The feeling I had was that it did a lot of running or physical activity. I felt it... I don't know if it broke its leg, but I kept feeling like it was running from something and it broke its front leg.

JONES: What are your feelings about the environment climate?

BOWES: I would say something where there are caves, or big places where there's water, but I would say that where this animal was there was a lot of grass. That's all I picked up. (starts to draw his impression of the animal that produced the bone). I don't know if this animal had feet or hooves, but I felt...kind of like a horse, but bigger. Hmmm. Doesn't look like a horse when I try to draw it. It had a big massive chest. Then its body went down like this in the back. Its back legs were kind of short. I'm not doing too good a job on this. It had a large head. This bone (fossil) was right here (makes mark on left front shoulder). I know that looks silly. I feel its front legs were real big and strong. Its chest was real big, but the back legs were kind of lower...like a hyenna. You know, the way they slope down in the back. That looks silly but that's what I picked up. It ate grass and vegetables. Not meat. I feel real strong about that. (he draws line across animals neck). I'm not sure about what the head looked like.

VI-4: Bowes' "mammoth".

Conclusion: Paleontology Experiment

This experiment suggests that psychics, like Albert Bowes, can offer valid and specific information under blind conditions concerning non-extant animal forms which existed many millions of years ago.

Further, in that Bowes in this experiment spontaneously offered background information about vegetation, climate, landforms, and the ancient placement of oceans, the potential application of psychic abilities in the fields of paleobotany, paleometerology, geology, and geography is indicated.

References

1. Stanley J. Olsen, "Fossil Mammals of Florida", in *Florida Geological Survey,* Special Publication No. 6, 1959, p.56.
2. Marian Murry, *Florida Fossils* (Tampa: Trend House, 1975), p.23.

VII

PSYCHIC ARCHEOLOGY
OF THE MAYA

As the body of this text has shown, I attempted during the several years of experimentation with Bowes, Davis, Niren, and Renier to use as target materials artifacts and photographs of artifacts from a great variety of places and times. I believed that this random selection of materials would help to preclude the criticism that the psychics consciously or unconsciously had begun to predict, in quite a rational fashion, a pattern in the nature of the items presented to them. However, a number of circumstances resulted in four separate experimental encounters between the pyschics and Mayan materials.

The first Mayan experiment was purposely designed to probe an area that I felt may be a problem in evaluating the work done with Florida artifacts. I felt that a valid criticism of those experiments may center on the probability of Florida residents, in this case the psychics working with me, "guessing" Florida environments when confronted with ambiguous experimental materials. I was of the opinion that such a criticism would be weak because the psychics had demonstrated their ability to locate sites and cultures through ambiguous artifactual materials found in a great variety of locations over the earth. Still, I decided to try an experiment with Bowes when an unforeseen set of occurrences presented me with the possibility of using a series of unique photographs of a natural feature found in the Mayan territory.

One afternoon at the university I stopped by the office of an anthropologist and Latin Americanist colleague who had recently returned from a trip to the Yucatan to visit and photograph Mayan ruins. She was separating slides on a display board. As I casually scanned the photographs I noticed what appeared to be what Florida residents call a "sinkhole," or spontaneous natural well that occurs when a limestone surface plat crumbles and falls into an underground water course. These sinkholes can be no bigger than a table top or they can reach sizes large enough to swallow a good-sized house. The main point was that the "sinkhole" in the slide I picked up from the display board was not from Florida but rather it was a picture of a *cenote*, or natural well, found in the Yucatan outside the ancient Mayan city of Chichen Itza. I looked closely at the slide and saw that there was no cultural material in the photograph that would indicate the location of the "sinkhole," nor did the plants growing around the edge of the well differ significantly from the vegetation found around many sinkholes in northern and central Florida.

When I had asked Bowes to read the photographs of the unexcavated 8Se32 site, he had been able to locate it and describe the environment in great and specific detail. What would he do when asked to read a picture of a "Florida sinkhole"; in fact, the sacred Mayan *cenote* of Chichen Itza.

The second experiment relating to Mayan culture centered around my curiosity concerning a psychic's potential ability to read pictures of ambiguous monumental architecture. With a few exceptions, such as the famous and unique massive stone walls of the Inca cities, a stone wall is a stone wall whether it is located in China, north Africa, Germany, or central Mexico. Likewise, the technique of making a doorway by topping two upright stones with a lintel stone is universal wherever stone architecture was practiced.

In this second Mayan experiment I placed before Bowes two non-diagnostic photographs of parts of buildings in Chichen Itza—one of the doorway of the Temple of Kulkulcan and one of the interior of a building called The Observatory. In the first case Bowes would be looking at a non-diagnostic stone door and in the latter he would be reading an interior of a non-diagnostic stone building. I interspersed several experiments centering around unrelated cultural and historical materials between Bowes' reading of the Mayan *cenote* and this experiment, which would also deal with Chichen Itza. Could Bowes, simply by looking at non-diagnostic photographs of monumental architectural features, locate these structures and offer verifiable cultural, historical, and environmental information concerning them?

After Bowes read the two experimental photographs, I continued to present him with a variety of photographs from a number of Mayan sites. I did not deem this aspect of the session an experiment because the photos were not of the non-diagnostic type. As with the reading of the equally diagnostic Folsom materials (Chapter III), I was simply curious to hear what he would say.

The third Mayan experiment was truly outside my control. When an archeologist at a local museum asked me to present some of my findings, stemming from my research with psychics, to his archeology class, I saw the opportunity to arrange another double-blind type of experiment. I asked the archeologist if he would acquire for me several non-diagnostic artifacts from a single site. He was not to inform me of the site location until after I had presented the test materials to the psychics for their reading. I was informed at the conclusion of the experiment that the materials had come from a late Mayan site in the Peten, or jungle lowlands of the ancient Mayan territory.

The fourth experiment that I did with Mayan materials was the final experiment I performed in the series reported in this book. The fact that the materials to be used were of Mayan origin bothered me because I had studiously avoided such a focus on any one cultural setting in my experimental series. However, an intriguing issue was at stake.

Some psychics, probably most, argue that psychometry has to do with a kind of psychic residue left by the humans who have handled or made an object. Most psychics also feel that there is a kind of "vibration" left in bones that can allow the sensitive individual to identify features of the one-time owner of the bone. However, others feel that the ability to read objects has not so much to do with some type of "vibration" emanating from an object as it is concerned with the generalized psychic potential of the one doing the reading. My own research has inclined me to the latter view.

In the fourth Mayan experiment, I was given several pieces of ordinary rock picked up at three Mayan sites by a colleague. These pieces were not artifacts. They have never been "worked" in any way by human hands. To make this experiment even more interesting I was not informed of the precise location producing the rocks, though I did know they were from three different Mayan sites. There are, however, thousands of Mayan sites.

What would the psychics do when given a handful of rubble to read? Would they deny their ability to offer psychic impressions due to the lack of intentional human physical contact with the stones, or would the familiar descriptions of terrain, culture, and history still be forthcoming as they had been in the many unusual experimental situations already described.

First, so that the accuracies and errors of the psychics in these experiments may be evaluated, a brief overview of the Maya is in order. The classic Maya were a truly amazing people. As Stuart and Stuart[1] write:

> Between A.D. 250 and 900 the Maya created one of the most distinguished civilizations of all antiquity. Soaring pyramids and imposing palace complexes rose in a network of populous cities that stretched across the mountains and rain forests of Guatemala to the parched plain of the Yucatan Peninsula. Brilliant art styles, a sophisticated astronomy, and the most complex writing system in the New World marked the age of Mayan splendor.

Mayan social organization was so precise and well-modulated that they controlled a domain of 125,000 square miles which included such modern-day states and regions as Guatemala, Yucatan, Campeche, Tabasco, the eastern half of Chiapas, Quintana Roo, and Honduras. Their large sea-going canoes plied the Caribbean for trading ventures and war, further expanding their influence. Mayan ceremonial centers, masterpieces of planning and monumental design and execution, were cultural pivots of large populations. Tikal, for example, was the center of a population of about 40,000 Indians. They also built the most sophisticated road system in pre-Columbian America, linking interior cities with the coastal towns. The Mayan skill in building permitted them to create underground cisterns and reservoirs to deal with the chronic water shortage found in much of Mayadom, as well as to con-

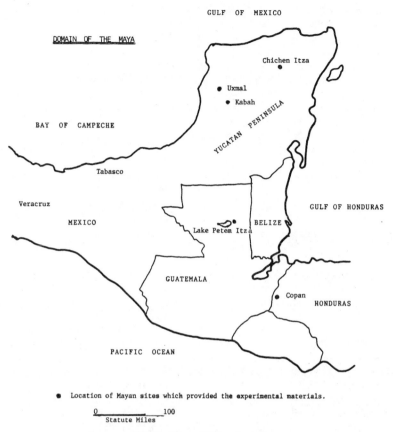

GULF OF MEXICO

DOMAIN OF THE MAYA

Chichen Itza

Uxmal

Kabah

YUCATAN PENINSULA

BAY OF CAMPECHE

Tabasco

Veracruz   GULF OF HONDURAS

MEXICO   BELIZE

Lake Peten Itza

GUATEMALA

Copan

HONDURAS

PACIFIC OCEAN

● Location of Mayan sites which provided the experimental materials.

0 _____ 100
     Statute Miles

VII-1: Map of Mayadom.

struct terraces and elevated farm plots to maximize the production
potential of their horticultural base. Their calendar and astronomy
made the similar achievements in Europe at that time pale by comparison. Further, they managed these great feats as a Neolithic people,
without the knowledge of metallurgy, the wheel, or domesticated draft
animals.

The Maya first entered history in 1502. Christopher Columbus, on
his fourth and final voyage to the New World, was anchored off one of
the Bay Islands along the coast of Honduras when he met an immense
Indian dugout canoe ladened with trade goods including cotton, foods,
and weapons bladed with obsedian. When Columbus asked the leader
their point of origin, the leader replied, "Maiam".

Who were the Maya? Where did they come from? What was the
nature of their culture? Why did they so quickly abandon their great
cities? What became of them? Modern archeology is beginning to offer
some initial and tentative answers to these questions.

We now surmise that the ancestors of the Maya were part of a cultural complex which developed in the highlands of the area now known as central Mexico, Guatemala, and El Salvador. Between 2000 B.C and 1000 B.C. the precursors of the Maya began to filter out of the more mountainous regions of the interior into the jungle lowlands and onto the Yucatan peninsula. Part of the cultural inventory they brought with them were plants and growing techniques first developed in central Mexico. They knew how to make pottery, and they hunted with the spear, the bow and arrow, and the barkless dog. Little else is known about these proto-Mayans. In fact, the archeological record remains relatively silent until about 200 A.D. when in the Peten—the lowland jungles—the cultural traits of the classic Maya began to appear rapidly. In 200 A.D. the city of Uaxactun was in existence, and several miles from Uaxactun, the great temple city of Tikal was under construction. Until about 1000 A.D. there was continual construction of the dramatic Mayan ceremonial centers throughout the Mayan domain. Hundreds of such cities were built complete with temples, palaces, governmental buildings, warehouses, ball courts, roads, cisterns, and pyramids.

Then something happened which is still not completely understood. In 1000 A.D. these great cities were simply abandoned. There is no universally accepted evidence that the cause of the decline of the classic Maya was related to either large-scale war, traumatic climatic change or disease. The most widely accepted theory relates the abandonment of large Mayan centers to the exhaustion of the surrounding farm lands because of the primitive methods used by the Maya to grow their crops. The only thing that is known for certain is that the population that remained began to relocate, first centering in the Guatemalan highlands and in the northeastern part of Yucatan. After 900 A.D., for some unaccountable reason, the Mayans concentrated in the northern reaches of Yucatan. This brought them into direct contact, and conflict, with the Toltecs, who were invading out of central Mexico, and a variety of Mayan and non-Mayan speaking intruders whom the Mayans called collectively, *Itzas*.

The infusion of Toltec-Itza vitality caused a revival of Mayan culture, a sort of Mayan Renaissance. Building resumed. Old roads were repaired and lengthened. New roads were built. Art and architecture reached new peaks. During this period Uxmal, thought by many to be the most beautiful city of all Mayan cities old or new, was built.

Though the causes of the first decline of the Maya in 1000 A.D. are obscure, we know at least the symptoms associated with the final decline. In 1194, the Mayan chronicles tell us, there occurred a civil war between Mayapan and Chichen Itza, the two most powerful cities of the Yucatan. Mayapan won. In turn, Mayapan met its end in 1441. The Maya proper viewed Mayapan as an Itza city, and apparently in the heated atmosphere of the times, utilized that sentiment to sack the city and kill its inhabitants. After this attack, Mayapan was abandoned, never to be reclaimed.

During the civil unrest in Yucatan, it is believed that many Itza-Mayans migrated southward back into the Peten region. It was here that Cortez contacted them during his march from Mexico to Honduras in the early 1500s. After this period the Spanish, who had only recently conquered the Aztec, turned their attention to the Maya. The Maya, seriously weakened by their own internal problems, were no match for the Spanish. The last stand of the Maya took place at Tayasal, a site on Lake Peten Itza. On March 14, 1697, the Spanish armed with cannon and individual firearms defeated the stone-age Maya, thereby effectively destroying a high culture that had existed for over three thousand years. The final blow for historians of the Maya came in the succeeding years when Spanish priests and monks in their attempt to civilize the Maya burned thousands of priceless Mayan books dealing with such diverse subjects as astronomy, architecture, history, and medicine. In more recent times, looters continue the destruction of the remains of the Mayan legacy.

During the time of their flourishing the Maya did not function as an empire. There was never a single ruler of all the Maya, nor was there a true Maya capital. The analogy of the Greek city-state may be useful. The Maya were a people lightly bound together by a common culture, language, religion, and an advanced system of communication most strikingly illustrated by their writing system and complex of roads. Further, they were a people with a bountiful environment and much to trade, which also served to make them rich and powerful. The foundation for all this, however, was the possession of a territory which provided the climate and soil to produce great maize crops, the key to Mayan culture. No matter where one looks in the Mayan world, whether to astronomy or to the attributes of the gods, the themes of maize growth and water permeate.

The natural environment of the Maya ranged from the mountains of the western edge of their territory to the lowlands toward the east called The Peten, an area of swamps and rain forests. Moving farther east the land becomes increasingly flat and dry as the Yucatan peninsula is encountered. In the north is Campeche and Tabasco, environments of lush tropical jungle and swamp. In the southern reaches of the Mayan country is modern-day Honduras.

Geologically a potent resource was limestone. It underlay the plateau jungles of the Peten as well as the flat, dryness of Yucatan, giving to both the soil fertility which produced such great quantities of maize. Further, limestone rock for building was easily quarried with stone tools. It also could be reduced to lime by burning, thus providing mortaring materials.

Additional resources included volcanic glass, or obsidian, from which they fashioned razor sharp knives, mirrors, and points for a variety of projectiles and thrusting weapons, and jade which was more highly prized by the Maya than gold. In the lowlands they cut giant cedars to make their canoes, some of which were eighty feet in length. They bred stingless bees in hollow trees for honey. The list of animals

that provided them with food, and manufacturing and decorative
materials, for trade and domestic use is long and impressive—quail,
woodpecker, pheasant, turkey, puma, deer, tapir, armadillo, agouti,
opossum, coatimundi, frigate birds, cormorants, herons, egrets,
muscovy ducks, iguana, turtle, crocodile, manatee, and fish. Besides
the crucial maize plant, they also grew cotton and cacao in addition to
many other domesticated and semi-domesticated fruits and vegetables, including beans, squash, pumpkins, chili peppers, sweet
potatoes, sweet cassava, papaya, avocado, gourds, and hemp.

Nevertheless, as Von Hagen[2] notes: .

> Water, however, was the one element the Yucatan Maya
> could not command. Although water was everywhere, there
> was often not a drop to drink. Great quantities of rain fell...
> Still, there was no way to hold the rain. There are no rivers
> on Yucatan peninsula. To meet the water problem the Maya
> constructed reservoirs and cisterns. At their greatest city,
> Tikal, they hollowed out an immense reservoir between two
> temples, cementing the porous limestone so it would hold
> water...Water, or the lack of it, was the curse of the Mayan
> paradise.

The nature of the Mayan social organization explains much when an
attempt is made to understand how a stone-age people could achieve
the material successes that the Maya reached in such a short period of
time. The great majority of the Mayan population lived much as their
descendants do today, as rurual maize farmers. Modern estimates
suggest that upwards to 97% of the Mayan population lived outside
the splendid urban centers, and though they were ruled from these
centers, the average Mayan citizen visited them only on special
religious and political occasions. The cities were made for ceremonial
and religious functions and did not house large populations. Studies
of the city of Uaxactun, for example, show that an elite class of about
two hundred lived in the city, and served as the administrators of a
total outlying population of about 8,700 people. Of the two hundred
elites, probably about thirty were in direct charge of all civil affairs.

The common man's function was to provide food through farming
activities and to serve as a labor pool for the construction of roads
and buildings. They also served as the source of the Mayan military.
The elites functioned as coordinators of labor and wealth, as redistribution centers. As in all early state-level societies, they protected
the privileges of their political power by hereditary transmission of
office, and by wrapping themselves in the guise of spiritual leaders
and purveyors of arcane knowledge; in the Mayan case, astronomy,
astrology, and the rituals of the gods.

Mayan religion was extremely complicated. Though it mainly centered on reverence to such natural elements as sun, moon, stars, and
earth, the representation of these elemental supernaturals could be
very elaborate. For example, the Great Itzamma, or Lizard House, the
supreme being of earth and sky, had four aspects, each a double-

headed iguana dragon, which framed the heavens. There were, in the Mayan cosmology, a variety of levels of heavens and hells. In fact, it can be said with literal truth that each day was a separate god to the Maya. Chac, the rain god, was no doubt the most important Mayan god. He was always depicted as having a long nose and T-shaped eyes. The eye design suggested tears which stood for rain. In the three surviving Mayan books his name is evoked 218 times. While the majority of Mayan gods were seen as at least potentially dangerous if not downright malevolent, Chac was viewed as benevolent and a friend of mankind.

The Maya believed that one of the functions of the priest was to contact the spirits of the past rulers in the hopes that they could control the often dangerous gods. When all else failed, the Maya turned to sacrifice—human sacrifice. The citizens of Chichen Itza felt that the rain god Chac lived at the bottom of the sacred *cenote*. In order to assure a continuing fall of rain, or in an attempt to stimulate a failing water supply, the priests of Chichen threw selected people, usually young women, and precious material items into the *cenote*. At other times, a sacrificial victim, always painted blue as in all Mayan human sacrifice rituals, was tied to a wooden frame, lifted off the ground, and then shot full of arrows. The most infamous method of Mayan religious sacrifice involved the ripping out of the still beating heart from the victim's chest.

But what did the Mayans look like? How did they dress? Did they use money? What did the houses of the common man look like? There are, of course, thousands of particulars that could be presented in this brief survey of Mayan culture, rendering it ultimately not so brief. The broad outline of Mayan culture and history has been presented in the immediately preceding pages. It will be much more intriguing to allow the analysis of the psychics' responses to the Mayan experimental materials to fill in the details.

FIRST EXPERIMENT: BLIND READING OF PHOTOGRAPHS OF THE CENOTE OF CHICHEN ITZA BY ALBERT BOWES

The point of this experiment was to see if Bowes would be led to make a "Florida" response by a photograph of a geological feature which appeared to be in all ways a typical Florida sinkhole. The two photographs were all of the sacred *cenote* of Chichen Itza. I took them to Bowes wrapped in several layers of typing paper and taped for protection, just as they had been delivered to me. Bowes began to read them while they were still in front of me, still taped and wrapped. As the first few minutes of the interview presented below show, he even resisted my offering of some potential helpful information to him in his eagerness to convey his first impressions.

JONES: These two pictures are of the same place.

BOWES: Well, just set them down here and maybe I can tell you about them.

> JONES: Since these are slides and it may be difficult to get a visual fix, I can tell you it is a natural setting...
>
> BOWES: Don't say anything, o.k.
>
> JONES: Sure.
>
> BOWES: The first thing I picked up was something stone. I felt grey stone. I don't know if it's like a cliff, or something sticking out of a mountain. The strongest feeling was it was a cliff that stuck out, and then there's a stream down below it. Could be even a building with a balcony sticking out. But I felt cold stone. That's what I was picking up. Could be a stream there. I don't know if it's in the mountains or looking down, but I felt one of the pictures could be from a mountain looking down, or something high up looking down. I don't know if there's a building in one of the pictures, but I felt it had been vacant for a long time.

His initial impressions of "grey stone," "a cliff," water "down below," and "something up high looking down" are all correct as a glance at the *cenote* photographs will demonstrate. Not appearing in the photographs are the ruins of a structure with a protruding platform from which the Mayan priests threw their human and non-human sacrifices into the *cenote*. Bowes quite distinctly described it. At this time the pictures were still wrapped, sealed, and in my hands.

After making a passing mention of an image of a "barn with hay in it," Bowes asked to see the pictures. In his first response after viewing the slides he accurately described the function of the *cenote*.

> I don't know if this had to do with an Indian, or something that had to do with a ceremony, but I kept feeling something was pushed into this hole. There's a spring in this water, or water down this hole. I would say there was no way to come up. I don't know if they ever pushed a woman in there, but the feeling I had was a young girl or woman, or they put a basket with fruit and threw it in there with a rock on it.

He is right about who would be sacrificed. Skeletal evidence shows that young women were the major sacrificial victims. Fruits and other foods were also typically sacrificed.

He went on to add, concerning the young women sacrificial victims:

> I felt like the woman could have even had blond hair. I kept picking up a very beautiful young woman. It looked like an Indian woman with blond hair...I felt she had blond or white hair. A young girl.

After the session Bowes returned to the puzzling image of the "blond Indian" and concluded that he was seeing an albino Indian girl. In my research into Mayan culture history, carried out after the Mayan experiments, I did not find any references to albino sacrificial victims. However, Dr. Allyn Stearman,[3] Latin American ethnologist, reported to me that there is a very high incidence of albinoism among Panamanian Indians. The Cuna of Panama, for example, considered albino youths to be sacred and called them "moon children." Further,

Von Hagen,[4] in describing the range of the Mayan canoe trade, noted that they traveled the entire Gulf Coast "from Tabasco to Panama." Slaves, used for labor and as sacrificial victims, were a major part of Mayan trade. Also, Stuart and Stuart,[5] when detailing the material items recovered in modern times from the *cenote*, state, "The material found here comes from as far away as Panama....". This information, supplied by Stearman, Von Hagen, and Stuart and Stuart, may make some sense of Bowes' confusion concerning the albino Indian girl being thrown into the cenote, and witnessed by Bowes.

In the next passage Bowes began probing for the site's location.

I would say that it was a religious place, and it had a ceremonial or religious background. If it was like England, I would say there was a lot of savage people there, like the Vikings. If it was not England, if it was up north...I would say there is still something strange about the Indians, or wild people. If this is South America I would say there's something buried in the bottom of this water. Could be in any case. The feeling I had with this place is...desolate. I would say the people were afraid to go in the water..they couldn't get out, or there was something fearful in the water. Could be today. Like even now people feel that. I felt 'northwest,' like toward Gainesville or towards the north. 'Northwest, northwest.' I felt like people died out and there wasn't people around for a long time. At one time it was all beaten down at the side.

"South America" to Bowes means the western hemisphere south of the United States. Predictably, the "Florida" reference that I was baiting Bowes toward appeared in his mention of the city of Gainesville. Though he feels a similarity to the Vikings, which is not that far-fetched in that both Vikings and Mayans were warlike, seagoing traders, Bowes ultimately finalized his location of the sinkhole in the final sentence of the reading when he touched the pictures and stated, "I felt mainly with South America." Bowes was also valid in his impression that there were things beneath the water, and also that a person who went into the water could not get out. Stearman[6] said that if the victims could stay afloat until midday, they would be pulled from the water. A common reason for such behavior is the assumption that the gods refused them as a sacrifice.

Bowes' statement that modern-day people feel that there is "something fearful" in the water is supported in this comment by the first archeologist to excavate the cenote, Edward Herbert Thompson:[7] "The present natives of the region believe that big snakes and strange monsters live in the dark depths of the Sacred Well."

The sacrifices to the rain god were intended to bring rain and to insure good crops. Note Bowes' response to my question, "Why do you feel those people felt that place was important?"

It was a place where they could put people in there, or put something in there and it wouldn't come out...I would say

that they may have thought there was a god in there. A god
in the ground. I felt like they thought if they put things in
the water it would help the crops, or help things naturally because the water was in the ground.

The succeeding lengthy passage contains many correct impressions.

JONES: Do you see any design or...

BOWES: I would say that they could have built something
and I don't know if they built things in the sides of mountains, but the feeling I had was they were like Aztec people
who built things. I would say they were very religious and
very organized.

JONES: Do you get any more about the culture? About the
kind of society they had?

BOWES: Again, I'm working with a picture of a location and
it's lately, probably in the last few years is when this picture
was taken, and I'm not speaking of the past here. I'm only
talking about a place. I would say it was far removed from
where the people were. I would say that they were pottery
makers. People who made lots of things...may have made
buildings, or things that were structures. The feeling I had
was that they stored things in clay pots. They may even
have mummified or cremated people...I see little jugs of
ashes, or preserved things like in a pyramid. Little bitty
rooms...and caves. Does any of this make sense?

JONES: I guess so.

BOWES: I would say a king fell in there at one time, or
somebody who was...I felt 'king'. Now, I'm not talking
about...I kept feeling like Vikings, that kind of people...kind
of aggressive. Like—wanted to war all the time.

...To them wealth was women...women was wealth...how
many women they had, and like young children. Women...
twelve, thirteen...that's wealth to them...And I felt a king
fell in there (touches *cenote* picture). Somebody of royalty...
fell in there and I felt they felt that was a very bad omen...
like it poisoned the water, and I felt they left. They may
have never went back.

JONES: What kinds of things would these people eat?

BOWES: The first thing I picked up when you said that...I
picked up berries. I felt they grew things in fields, and they
may even have had irrigation. Like they may even have had
canals or ditches where the water came into the ground. But
I felt the ground was dry there now.

JONES: Interesting.

BOWES: Extremely dry.

JONES: Are there any descendants of these people?

BOWES: I don't feel so, but if it's true, they went north.
And if it's in South America, or...in the west...I felt they

went north and there may be a few distant, distant relatives
but that's what I picked up. Because I felt like they ran into
opposition going north. I felt these people could have had
boats...which is not common...which wouldn't be expected
to happen.

In his first response, Bowes is certainly correct when he made the
analogy between the Maya, and "like Aztec people who built things."
The Maya were also very religious and very organized, as he mentioned. His reference to a people "who built things in the sides of
mountains" may relate to the temple pyramids of the Maya. Then
again, he may be erroneously seeing visions of actual mountains in the
flat environs of Chichen Itza.

In his response to my second question in the above passages, he
stated that "it (referring to the *cenote*) was far removed from where
the people were." The *cenote* is about one-fourth of a mile from the
main settlement area. The Maya were exceptional pottery makers, and
they also constructed "buildings," as he correctly noted. With regard
to Bowes' comment concerning cremation and his impressions of
"little jugs with ashes," It is an ethnographic fact, particularly associated with the Maya of Yucatan, the location of the *cenote*, that
nobles were cremated and their ashes placed in small urns.[8] I could
find no references to mummification among the Maya.

Bowes' statements about "pyramids," "little bitty rooms," and
"caves" all ring true. The pyramids are characteristic of all Mayan
ceremonial centers. The reference to small rooms may indicate an
aspect of the self-limiting nature of the corbeled arch architecture
practiced by the Maya. For example, a Maya pyramid may be composed of 250,000 square feet of fill but have at its pinnacle a structure
of only one or two small rooms with a total area of about 150 square
feet. We also know that certain nobles were interred in pyramids. This
was the method used in the burial of the Maya king, Pacal, at the
Palenque site. Further, caves were considered sacred by the Maya. As
Stuart and Stuart[9] state, Mayan priests of ancient and modern times
sought out dripwater from caves for ritual use because they considered
this "virgin" water to be the most sacred and pure of all water.

In Bowes' third response he described his feeling that the people
associated with the site in the photograph were "kind of aggressive.
Like—wanted to war all the time. Wanted to fight all the time."
Von Hagen[10] writes, with respect to this aspect of the Maya:

They were also warriors; 'for any little causes they fought.'
They never knew peace,' said a chronicler, 'especially when
the corn harvest was over.' The old myth of a peace-loving
people, passionately dedicated only to erecting dated monuments, tracing the planets in their flight, and preoccupied
with writing complex glyphs, has been fully exploded. At
every turn the scholar is confronted with sculptures
showing Maya lords sitting on the necks of slaves, or battle
captives being seized by the hair. The murals of Bonampak

bristle with the sound and the fury of battle. Yet one reads
again and again about the peace-loving Maya. This has the
odor of exquisite archaism. War was continuous. It could
not be otherwise.

Bowes' comment about "women as wealth" may be suggested in
this observation by Edward Herbert Thompson:[11] "The lords and
principal personages of the land had the custom, after sixty days of
abstinence and fasting, of arriving by daybreak at the Cenote, and
throwing into it Indian women belonging to each of these lords and
personages, at the same time telling their women to ask for their
masters a year favorable to his particular needs and desires."

Bowes' use of the word "king" is pertinent. He did not use words
like "chief". Mayanist refer to Mayan rulers as "kings"—as in "King
Pacal of Palenque." The behavior directed toward these men by the
Maya themselves also suggest royalty. The Mayan kings sat on
thrones, wore elaborate ceremonial costumes, and were carried in
litters by slaves and elite body guards.

Bowes' feeling that someone of royalty fell into the *cenote* cannot
be substantiated by extant Mayan materials. However, in the account
of the first archeological dredging of the sacred *cenote* of Chichen Itza
by Mayanist Edward Herbert Thompson, he describes the discovery
of the skull of an old man, and how he considered that find highly
unusual. C. W. Ceram[12] dramatically comments:

...the gold of the Cenote was fished out from among the
bones of young maidens who had been hurled, screaming,
into eternity by cruel priests as offerings to cruel gods. Had
ever one of the girls pulled a priest into the water with her?
Among the many female skulls Thompson found one of a
man, a skull with the protuberant glabella of an old man. A
priest?

Bowes' feeling of "canals or ditches where the water came into that
ground" are true for the lowland Maya, especially after 600 A.D. The
Maya in that area had the ability to drain swamps, control water, and
terrace hillsides. As for the Yucatan Maya, irrigation methods are uncertain. Bowes was correct when he noted that the land surrounding
the site was "extremely dry." He was also not off the mark when he
stated, "I felt they grew things in fields...".

In Bowes' reaction to my question concerning the possible descendants of the people associated with the site, he commented, "I felt
they ran into opposition going north." Again, generally speaking, a
major historical marker of Mayan history is the movement of the
Maya, especially after A.D. 1000, in a northeasterly direction out of
their homeland center with subsequent confrontation with the invading Toltec-Itza peoples coming from the north.

The last sentence of the long passage being analyzed is, "I felt
these people could have had boats...which is not common...which
wouldn't be expected to happen." Von Hagen[13] writes that the Maya
"...and they alone of all the great civilizations of the ancient Americas

were maritime people, going out in large ocean-going dugouts, traveling over thousands of miles of coastal sea."

Bowes' impression about the homes of the people associated with the site in question being beside a mountain is wrong; but again, the great pyramids of Chichen Itza could give that impression. He goes on to say "…or that they were made of stone." This would be true for the elite. The common man's home was composed of withes, adobe, and palm thatch.

In an attempt to elicit dating of the site, I followed up Bowes' statement, "I would say this was a long, long time ago," with the question, "Before or after the time of Christ?" He answered, "I would say it was the same time that the Vikings were in Great Britain." The Vikings were particularly active in raiding the British Isles during the early Middle Ages, or approximately from 500 to 1000 A.D. The occupations of Chichen Itza by the Maya occurred three times: A.D. 432, 964, and 1185. Using the unusual method of historical connection with Viking activity in England, Bowes very neatly dated the *cenote* site associated with Chichen Itza.

My questioning concerning the presence or absence of domestic animals produced this exchange:

JONES: What about domestic animals? Do you see…

BOWES: I felt they had llamas.

JONES: These people had llamas?

BOWES: Yes. Or that they were something similar to that. I kept seeing it looking like a camel with a big lip but it was softer and more docile than a camel. I felt they herded them like goats.

My research in the Mayan literature produced no evidence that the Maya possessed llamas. However, the Maya did have semi-domesticated deer. The reference to the llamas may not be that far-fetched. It is well-known that the Maya were energetic traders and that their southerly reach was impressive. The Maya may have gone farther south, toward the land of the llama, than we now suspect. Also, the high civilizations of central America were interested in zoos with varieties of exotic animals, as well as botanical gardens. The Spanish report being extremely surprised by the quality of the zoos and gardens of the Aztec .

As the previous historical overview of the Maya pointed out, the major enemy of the Maya were the Spanish. The Spanish destroyed the Maya, not because they outnumbered them, but largely because the Spanish were better armed. This series of historical facts is alluded to by Bowes in his answer to the following question.

JONES: Did these people have metal?

BOWES: There could have been an adversary, like the Spanish, or adversary people who had something better than they did…like war materials…because I don't feel they won all their wars. I felt every year they lost a lot of people in war.

When I asked Bowes to tell me the feeling he had concerning the kinds of myths the people told, he offered these impressions:

I felt they talked of like dragons from the ocean, or people from the south. I felt they talked of a dragon that came out of the ground or out of the water. I felt they talked about the sky becoming fire, like the lights from the sky...I would say this was a real thing they seen. It may have been in Alaska or in the north, but this was...like people came from the north and went down south and then came back. Hundreds of years, or a hundred years later and talked of this...they seen fire in the sky. Like the sky was red with fire, and it could have been during a volcano, or a time when there was a lot of smoke in the air...like the sky was red.

JONES: Where there volcanoes in the area?

BOWES: There could be volcanoes in the area, or volcanoes at the time they were there. Yeah. But I felt red smoke or the sun was shining through the smoke and it looked like the sky was on fire.

The image of the ocean-dwelling dragon may relate to a principal god of the Chichen Itza Maya, Kulkulcan. In fact, one of the major structures at Chichen is the Temple of Kulkulcan. Kulkulcan is a borrowing from the Toltec-Aztec pattern of Quetzalcoatl, "The Feathered Serpent." The Maya at Chichen Itza believed that Kulkulcan fled into the ocean.

As Bowes continued his impressions, he spoke of the possibility of these people talking about a volcanic eruption, and he added, "I would say that this was a real thing they seen." Volcanoes do exist in the Maya range. They rim Lake Atitlan, a center of highland Maya culture. Of possible relevance here is the eruption of the volcano Ilopango in the extreme west of the Maya domain in central El Salvador sometime between A.D. 100 and 300. Payson Sheets of the University of Colorado has specialized in the study of the effects of this phenomenon. Stuart and Stuart[14] write:

'We've seen the ash fall,' Payson told us. 'It covers much of central and western El Salvador, and its effects probably reached much farther. Near Ilopango, plants and animals directly in the path of the ash flows would have been killed instantly by the heat and suffocation; survivors would face the immediate problem of shock, injury, and choking dust, soon followed by those of fouled water and a disrupted food supply. Things simply stopped, and as many as 30,000 people may have left this area. Probably many of these survivors moved north, into the Maya lowlands.

Toward the end of his reading of the photographs of the *cenote*, Bowes commented:

I felt like, in a religious ritual, that they may have problems with hearing or they did things to their ears. I see them clapping sticks together, or doing something with sticks and then I felt they slapped each other's ears...or something they did that made problems with hearing. I didn't know what it meant.

Bowes may be referring to two characteristics of Mayan aesthetics. To achieve a long-headed shape, which they considered to be beautiful, they wedged infants' heads between two narrow boards for long periods of time. The method produced the desired result, but we do not know if it affected hearing. The ears were the focus of much attention. The Mayan people expanded their ear lobes to a size which would permit a turkey egg to be passed through the resulting hole. Again, whether this would produce hearing problems is unknown.

These are the last series of images Bowes presented in this experiment:

JONES: Is there anything unique or characteristic of the kinds of outfits they wore?

BOWES: As soon as you start talking I pick things up...I was picking up something that was very strange and I kept feeling they were almost like cannibalistic, or...they had a lot of things around their...or like...bracelets around their legs. For some reason the bottom parts of their legs was empty or...clothes. I see bracelets and scars on their legs. That's what I picked up. It could have been cannibalistic, or it could have been...I felt that they...people bled, or they bled people, or they sacrificed people, or...kind of ugly, ugly people. To them blood, war and blood and violence to them was religion...religious things. Ugly. I would say the only thing you could find of these people was the rocks that was left, or the stones or the clay pots. Not very much more than that. I felt mainly with South America.

Bowes' reference to cannibalism is noteworthy. Stearman[15] states, "Lately a good bit of very controversial evidence is coming out suggesting that Mesoamericans engaged in rather large-scale cannibalism, not only of a ritualistic nature, but also to supply dietary needs." Bowes was also correct in his observation that "the bottom parts of their legs (were) empty of clothes." Mayan men wore neither trousers, nor leggings of the American Indian type. As the majority of murals depicting Mayan life show, men wore nothing on their legs except an occasional "bracelet", as Bowes reported. For example, leg bands are clearly seen on several glyph figures at Yaxchilan and Dos Pilas.

Bowes' many mentions of blood and bleeding in the last few sentences of his reading and his indication that it related to religion is a valid observation. Again, Von Hagen[16]:

The Maya...'offered sacrifices of their own blood. They pierced their cheeks, their lower lips, 'and their tongues in a slanting direction.' Blood so obtained was smeared on an image of the god that was being propitiated, or onto their hair and bodies...So obsessed with blood and its magical

qualities were the Maya that 'they even,' wrote Diego
deLanda, 'split the superfluous part of the virile member, cutting it and fraying it as they did their ears to obtain blood...'.
Bowes is sadly correct, when in conclusion he stated:"I would say
that the only thing you could find of these people was the rocks that
was left, or the stones or the clay pots. Not very much more than
that."

Conclusion: First Mayan Experiment

This was one of Albert Bowes' more complexly accurate photograph readings. Still an obvious observation must be made: the sacred
cenote of Chichen Itza has been photographed before and those photographs published. Nonetheless, not a single control group member
could locate the site, most guessing its location to be in Florida as I
had expected. Even if Bowes could have recognized the site when he
saw the photographs it would have taken an expert Mayanist to spontaneously create such an accurate series of impressions of Maya
culture and history. Further, remember that Bowes was able to describe the setting, including a structure at the site but not pictured
even before he touched the photographs and before they had been
removed from their protective wrappings.

Second Experiment: Blind Reading of Two Photographs of Non-Diagnostic Architectural Features

This test was an extension of the photograph experiments. Instead
of using photographs of artifacts, or of natural settings, as in the use
of preexcavation photographs in the 8Se32 experiment and the *cenote*
photograph experiment, this test focused on photographs of non-
diagnostic architectural features. It was carried out approximately a
month after the *cenote* experiment. As mentioned in the introductory
remarks to this chapter, I was careful to intersperse other test sessions
using a variety of materials between the first and the second Mayan
experiment. The question investigated was:*Can a psychic, by viewing
a photograph of an architectural feature, relay accurate information
about the people who made and used the structure?* For experimental
purposes the photographs were non-diagnostic and the materials were
presented to Bowes in a blind fashion.

The first photograph whic Bowes viewed showed a simple stone
building technique, no symbols or designs, no evidence of environ-
picture which would specifically identify its location—no unique
building technique, no symbols or designs no evidence of environment. It would even be impossible to identify the type of stone from
this photograph. The picture is of the door to the small temple on the
summit of the pyramid of Kulkulcan at Chichen Itza.

Bowes' reading of the temple door will be presented in its entirety,
although I will interrupt the reading with comment from time to time.
Bowes began:

The first thing I picked up was something where this had been repaired. Another feeling I had was there was someone with a uniform. I don't know if it was a Spanish uniform, but I kept feeling a uniform. I keep seeing them walking through here (indicates door). The feeling I had was inside there I felt 'cold'...or a cold feeling. I would say that there was something up here (indicates over door). It may have been some sort of statue or some sort of image, but it was over the doorway. I would say there was some drawing on the wall.

JONES: **Was this room important or unimportant? If you went in there what would have been...**

BOWES: I would say in there that there was a storage of something. I kept feeling 'cool.' Cool. Cool. But I felt like a cold feeling. The strongest feeling I would say was that there was bodies laying in there. At one time, I would say there was storage. They stored wheat or, like stored bags or bowls of grain. But I felt there was a stack or a pile of bodies in there at one time. It might have been soon after a war and they didn't belong in there. I felt mass death. I see decomposed bodies.

Bowes was right about the repair to the total structure. The temple that is visible today was built over an older one. His mention of the Spanish was also accurate. The interior of the temple is in fact relatively cool due to its limestone construction which traps water causing the interior to be moist. Bowes' impression that there was an image, or statue, over the door area and decorations on the walls is substantiated by Von Hagen[17] in his account of the temple.

The walls were muraled and still survive to show many aspects of Maya-Toltec life. An open-mouthed plumed serpent is on the balustrade on each of the four stairways ascending the pyramid. On top, at the temple, the serpents appear again, this time as sculptured columns... To make doubly certain that people knew it was the Temple of Kulkulcan, the top of the building is decorated with the symbol of the sky god, Quetzalcoatl.

Bowes' impression about the use of the temple for storage is uncertain. We do know that such buildings were sometimes used to house sacrifices and served as temporary holding areas for "tax" offerings which were often in the form of grain. His report of war and mass death was much more verifiable with respect to Chichen Itza. The Mexican Toltecs invaded the city twice.

I next asked Bowes, "What do you feel this total structure would look like? He replied:

I would say that it could be underground, or that it was below ground level. I would say that there was worry of leakage or water dripping. I would say that the soil was very dry...even though I picked up something about moisture. I

kept feeling very dry in there. There could have been something that was kind of square. I'm picking up something like
this. (draws picture of structure). I felt there must be a lot of
trees and things around the outside. I felt there was a vent
or an opening in the top right here (indicates middle of structure). Kind of a hole. Of course it could be filled in.

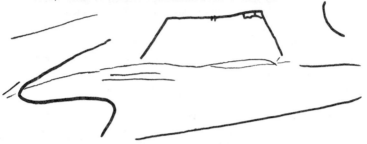

VII-2: Door structure.

Interestingly enough, even though he stated, "it could be underground or that it was below ground level," he proceeded to draw a
very close approximation of the general shape of the flat-topped
pyramid of Kulkulcan and also noted that its exterior was at ground
level ("I felt there must be a lot of trees and things around the outside."). He was also correct about the vent running from the middle of
the temple vertically through the pyramid.

His confusion about "moist" and "dry" is understandable. The
environment of Chichen Itza is very dry. However, the interior of the
dark limestone buildings are cool and damp.

Next I asked Bowes, "What did the people look like who were going
into this room?"

I would say they had a lot of jewelry on. I would say they
were dressed like this (draws human figure). They had some
sort of hat on. They may have had feathers on, or something
in their hat. I felt lots of jewelry, or lots of gold or something
hanging down here (neck) like...I don't feel they had much at
the bottom (legs). They may have had like a skirt or something hung down here (from waist), but I felt their legs were
plain.
JONES: And this man (indicates drawing of figure made by
Bowes) would go in there? (Touches photo of door)
BOWES: In and out of there. I felt that they could even have
something hanging down like a breech cloth, but I felt the
ones who were important had lots of jewelry or things
hanging around their neck. I felt like big plumes or flowers
or feathers...pink ones. I felt these little bumps here (indicates shoulder area of upper-garment).

Referring to the first human impression he received which was related to the structure in the photograph, he remarked:

VII-3: Man associated
with stone door

VII-4: Mayan warrior
[Bonampak murals].

The other one I felt was like a soldier, and I felt he was in
uniform or in some sort of unusual regalia...could have been
Spanish...some sort of uniform. If this was on an island, I
felt a ship definitely visited there...with cannons.

Bowes' drawing of the man he saw entering the doorway combined
with his narrative account produced many accuracies. The abbreviated
upper-garment can be found in Mayan murals showing male attire, as
well as in ceramic figurines and statuary. For example, such a vest-
like garment is seen in the section of the famed Bonampak mural
which deals with a Mayan war chief holding judgment over a number
of captives. The same mural can be used to illustrate Bowes' comment
concerning the amount of jewelry worn by the elite, the decorated
"hats", the plain "legs," the breech cloth/skirt image, and the "big
plumes." This mural is one of thousands of pictures the Maya left of
their day-to-day affairs in which Mayan clothing styles can be seen.

He again mentioned the Spanish presence, and in so doing also
added mention of a ship with cannons visiting the area. The people of
Chichen Itza would have known about happenings on the coast due to
the fact that there was a Mayan road running from Chichen Itza to
Izamal to Pole on the coast. The Spanish also moved through the
Yucatan in their wars against the Maya.

groups...large groups of people there. I would say that this
could have been a place where they could look out...a group
of people looking or watching for something. That's what I
picked up. I would say this door was very secure at one time,
or secured. It wasn't always open.

JONES: Where is this place?

BOWES: The first thing I picked up was 'island,' and then I
picked up...I picked up an island, then England, then South
America. The strongest feeling I had was that they were very
primitive people and they were people who were like Vikings,
or people who were like...very crude or hard. I feel they
carried spears, but that's what I picked up. They could have
been people who went by boat...like big boats like Viking
boats...long boats.

Several things can be said about Bowes' reading of the Observatory
photograph. He mentioned "well" several times in association with
this place. The relationship of Chichen Itza to "wells" has already
been described in the *cenote* photograph experiment. Further, steam
baths and pools were quite near the Observatory in Mayan days. He
was also correct about the presence of flooring in the structure. His
reference to the structure being defended makes sense in terms of the
history of Chichen Itza. The Observatory is part of the Old City, that
is, the city built prior to the Toltec invasion. Given its elevated position it would have been a logical place in which to seek refuge and a
perfect location to defend.

Bowes' suggestion that there may have been a cliff at the point he
marked as (d) on his drawing of the entire structure is validated by a
glance at the photograph of the exterior of the Observatory. In the
front of the structure, as depicted in the photograph, one sees the
sheer drop Bowes may be alluding to.

He was right when he said that "hundreds or even thousands" of
people were present at the site, and he was also probably correct when
he stated that the structure was a place from which people were involved with "looking for something, or watching for something."
Among other things an observatory is a place for "looking" and
"watching".

As with the temple door photograph reading, Bowes spoke of
"people who were like Vikings," an "island"; and "then England, then
South America" when asked to locate the site. The Maya did fight
with spears, and they were people who "went by boat...like big boats
like Viking boats...long boats."

He elaborated his impressions of the "long boats" in these passages
after first drawing a picture of the boat he saw.

I'm uncertain about the front here. But there was oars, or
things like this (a). This was a large boat (main vessel body),
and this was smaller (pontoon). And it had boards or something in here (interior of main vessel body).

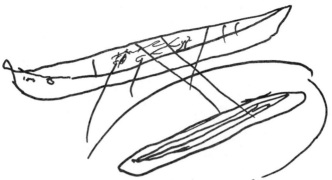

VII-6: A type of boat of target people.

JONES: How many people could be in this boat?
BOWES: Maybe up to twenty or thirty...a large group...
This here (pontoon) was not something people would ride on
...there could have been something in here (interior of main
vessel body) where people slept or went inside. But I felt it
was pretty big.
JONES: How was this boat constructed?
BOWES: I would say long logs. That there (touches main
body) was long logs, and there may have been bracing in
here (interior). I still see them carrying spears. They may
have had an interest in skulls. Skulls...skulls or something.

I could find no ethnohistorical evidence that the Mayan canoes had
pontoons. However, the Spanish accounts and various Mayan murals
depict canoes made of hollowed logs, with interior struts and central
shelters, capable of easily carrying "twenty or thirty" people. His
reference to "an interest in skulls" is witnessed by the fact that the
human skull was a major Mayan design motif occurring in many
contexts.

At this point in the session my experiment was completed. I was
interested to see if Bowes could offer valid cultural and historical information simply by looking at photographs of non-diagnostic architectural features. He could. The rest of the session that day can in no
way be construed as an experimental situation. The remainder of the
photographs used were diagnostic, at least to a Mayanist or anyone
who had ever studied Mayan literature. Still, I was interested in what
kinds of impressions Bowes would relate when confronted with a range
of photographs of many Mayan site features.

The first photograph I showed to Bowes after the initial test ses-
sions was a picture of a broken Chac Mool located at Chichen Itza. The
Chac Mool statues are believed to be a result of the Toltec invasion.
During human sacrifices, human hearts were placed in the cupped
hands of the semi-reclining Chac Mool figure. As Bowes looked at the
Chac Mool photo he had the following things to say.

VII-7: Statue of Chac Mool.

Hmmm. This used to be a statue. Very interesting. This marked a boundary. This marked a boundary of a group of people. When you went into that area it was like a signpost. It was telling you that you were going into a different group of people. There was something that looked like...ah, something that looked like...I'll show you what I see (draws figures). Their lips were thick for some reason. There were several statues of people or things sitting around. One of them was stolen. The one that was back here (indicates smaller figure on drawing).

JONES: Did anything special go on around this place?

BOWES: I would say it was a boundary marker and I would say that...the strongest feeling I had was that there may have been games around there...where people went along and kicked things. This part here (b) is uncertain to me. But I would say that there was more than one statue.

JONES: Do you have any feelings about why it was broken?

BOWES: I would say it was broken because of war. I would say somebody destroyed it. Because they were destroying the border.

JONES: Do you have any feelings about these destroyers?

BOWES: I would say they were local people. That over the years local people stole whatever they could try to sell...that they carried it away in a wagon. I would say that during a war or during a group happening that this was destroyed because of resentment of the border...saying that they didn't like the border of a particular area...that they wanted to take the whole place over. This statue was a warning of a sort, to say that you are now entering this country or this group of people. It was more like a country, not really a particular country...more like a county or a state.

JONES: What about the direction from...

BOWES: I would say there was much more there...much more of it there.

JONES: There were three statues you said?

BOWES: Yes.

JONES: All three of them were boundary markers?

BOWES: Yes. One of them might have looked something like a totem pole...may have had a lot of pictures or round things on it, or faces...stood up straight.

JONES: The people who were angry about the border, from what direction did they come?

BOWES: I felt they came from...the first word I got was 'south.' I feel that they came from the north. I pick Mexico ...going south...north to south. They may not have been from the south, but they may have been going south.

Much of what Bowes had to say about the Chac Mool might be understood by noting that the Chac Mool is a Toltec symbol in a Mayan world. It did indicate a "different group of people." Further, to the classic Maya the Chac Mool may have literally represented boundary markers. He was correct when he suggested that there were more than one such statue. Bowes was also specifically accurate when in response to my question—"Did anything special go on around this place"—he responded, "...there may have been games there...where people went along and kicked things." Within sight of the Chac Mool are several ball fields upon which the Maya exercised one of their abiding passions, a ball game that seems to have been a cross between soccer and basketball complete with body padding and a hoop, on a vertical instead of a horizontal plane, set thirty feet off the ground.

Bowes' statements about warfare, destruction, and looting are all correct. One of the major Mayan art forms is the stelae, a columnar sculpture covered with glyphs often depicting a human figure, standing up to fifteen feet in height. Bowes may have been reporting such a thing when he stated, "One of them might have looked something like a totem pole...may have had a lot of pictures or round things on it, or faces...stood up straight." In his last statement he succinctly noted the origin of the Toltec, and the direction of their invasion route when he stated, "I pick Mexico...going south...north to south."

This photograph shows a stelae at Copan, the second largest of Mayan cities, which is located in what is now Honduras. Copan was a center of astronomy. Periodically astronomers would meet there to correct the Mayan calendar and to study and discuss issues related to the bark cloth used as paper by the Maya when he spoke of "pieces of parchment or wood, or like wood with writing on it."

This wall decorated with the death's-head motif stands in Chichen Itza. After I removed the photograph of the Copan stelae from the table, I took the photograph of the wall from its envelope and handed it to Bowes and his reading began immediately.

I would say this depicts death. It is telling you that death is sacred. I would say that it is almost like a threat. I would say that these faces were depicted as skulls...and there is a burial around there somewhere, and it's in the ground. There may have been thousands or hundreds of people buried there...a graveyard. I would say inside this there was buildings that were like pyramids...at one time. The strongest feeling I had was that this was depicting death...almost glorifying it. I would say that what it was saying was that the people who died, that their spirits or death was laughing...laughing at people who were living. In other words, like the people who were dead were better off than the people who were alive. They were laughing, but it was like giving power...almost like a threat. I would say that these people worshipped death. Death to them was very powerful. It was like the more people they had die, or who were in the spirit world dead, that was more strength. I would say they probably killed girls...killed women. They may have picked virgin girls, or young girls to die.

JONES: **Would this death occur in association with this place?**

BOWES: Yes. This was a place saying 'don't go beyond this point,' or 'this is where death is.' But I feel they worshipped death.

JONES: **Do you see them building this thing?**

BOWES: I don't feel they built it, but I felt they moved it. They moved these stones. A lot of these...I felt they moved these...they made these and then they moved them there as time went on. I see them dragging them along the ground on wooden sleds. I felt they built it gradually...that they didn't build it all at once. They built it piece by piece and it took a long time to build it...like they were counting. It was like a thing that they wanted to count...it wasn't all built at the same time. These different stones could have been built within a year or in the same year or whatever, but I would feel that they were counting something, and they were building it. Each of these faces signified something.

JONES: **Something different? Each of them?**

BOWES: Each one was an identity in itself. Each one meant something different. Like each one of those could signify a person, or ten people, or a family. A number or unit...not particularly a person...because I would say there were many more people buried there than it shows. In fact, I would say that they might find a place that was like ten-foot deep in skulls or burials...like the ground was sunk down with so many thicknesses of bodies.

Death was certainly a major aspect of Mayan religion, though it is doubtful that they worshipped death. The Maya, in fact, were disgusted by death. Dying, for example, was considered an anti-social act. Bowes was correct in stating that young girls were often sacrificial offerings.

Bowes' account of how the wall was built cannot be substantiated. A theme that Bowes returned to several times in this reading is related to counting ("...it took a long time to build it...like they were counting. It was like a thing that they wanted to count...I feel that they were counting something...each of these faces signified something...a number or unit... Like each one of those could signify a person, or ten people...") The Maya considered numbers to be gods. For example, Number Nine was depicted as a young man with a magical mark on his chin. Number Five was an old man with a peculiar drum-like headdress. But of greater significance for this reading is Number Ten, the number noted by Bowes in connection with a wall which he felt "depicts death." Number Ten was the death god.

This photograph shows the main ball court as Chichen Itza. It is the largest such field in any Mayan city and measured 545 feet in length and 225 feet in width. The ball game played was called *pok-a-tok*. Although no account of the Maya ball game exists, the Aztec version was described. The court was similar, in most respects and the description of the Aztec ball players equipment matches Mayan ceramic figurines of Mayan ball players. On either side of the ball field were placed stone rings, likened to millstones by the Spanish, set vertically in the walls sometimes up to thirty feet off the ground. Two teams with an undefined number of players competed, and the winner was the first team to place a solid rubber ball about six inches in diameter through the ring. The trick to the game was in the required technique for delivering the ball through the hoop. The players could not use their hands. They had to strike the ball with their buttocks, or elbows. They wore thick leather belts around the buttocks as well as heavy gloves. The feat of scoring the winning shot was apparently so stupendous that the scoring player often had the right to receive all clothing and jewelry worn by the opposing team as well as the spectators.

These are the impressions Bowes related upon seeing this photograph.

> This place was very, very busy at one time, a very busy place. There may have been hundreds and thousands of people there at a time...lots of people. This was a pretty advanced place. There were places where they stored water. There are a lot of things missing here (touches photograph).

A lot of disease there. Like death through pneumonia, or like a disease that made people very weak, or they breathed hard. They abandoned these areas, or ran away, but I felt somebody was hiding out here, or like the last of the people, or storage of...I don't know what it was. More like death. There may have been a last ditch stand here, or there was a war there, or like people literally starved to death, or died there. I felt they just abandoned this and ran away.

I still felt this was the last place where they were at. Like they were worshipping or there still trying to calculate things at the very last.

Bowes returned again to his impression that a war had forced some people to take refuge in the Observatory. He was right about the war. It is also significant that he connected "worship" and "calculating" in connection with the Observatory.

Photo of Chac Mool at Chichen Itza

"This was like a political move, more like 'you are now entering' a certain city or area."

Referring back to the photograph of the interior of the Observtory, Bowes said, "I felt they just abandoned this and ran away." These comments then ensued.

JONES: Why?

BOWES: Invasion.

JONES: Is this related? (touches photo of Chac Mool).

BOWES: Yes. Invasion. I would say these (chac mool) were not that originally totally destroyed when they were pushed over. I would say this signified a midget, or the little people, or strong man. When I first picked this up there was something about an owl...night. Watchman over the night. Owl.

JONES: Why midget? Why strong man?

BOWES: I would say it was signifying a powerful midget, or like somebody who was strong. Like supernatural or like in the spirit world. Midget. Little people. Powerful. Like a warrior.

Bowes was historically and culturally correct when he connected the abandonment of the Observatory in the pre-Toltec section of Chichen Itza with an invasion leading to the establishment of the Toltec Chac Mool. Bowes' mention of midgets may relate to "dwarfs". Dwarfs were a common element in the artistic motifs of the Maya, as they had also been for the more ancient Olmecs. The Maya believed that a race of dwarfs lived in the lower world, the place of death.

Photo of Stelae at Copan

This was something religious. It was like a statue of Lincoln or something. It signified an ancient important person, ruler, or religious person. I would say he was more religiously based, more like a religious figure, like Jesus or more like Buddha. I don't feel there was anything in the statue that signified a violent death.

Photo of Ball Court at Chichen Itza

This had the feeling of...like Rome, lot of competition, general hub-bub, lots of people. There was like a political basis to it...like Rome...like that attitude.

A spontaneous question from me brought forth more information from Bowes concerning the structure in this photograph.

VII-9: A Mayan ball field figure.

JONES: Did these people have a supreme deity?
BOWES: Yes. The sun. The planets. Associated with, like astrology, and I felt they talked of the earth and the sky. Like they felt the planets had a big influence on the people, time, and future. And these things (draws figure associated with ball court photo.) It had arms like this and it was sitting up here (indicates top of near-wall in photograph). They carried these (indicates figure) along. It was like their mascot. I felt they were made of...could be more like a lion, or like a thing that was like 'this is our team. Football. Bulldogs.' Then another one had things and another one had that. They carried these. They were huge and heavy, and some of them stayed there, but I felt they were sitting all over the place. And they were like of marble, and they were pink, and white. Very beautiful. Expensive looking. This glass or this marble was so well made that it was almost like you could see the depths in it...almost like see through it. I felt a lot of them were broken. Crushed. They may have been pink or white, or they may have been green and white.
They may have been pink or white, or they may have been green and white.

ceptacles for burning incense, upon which were modeled representations of the gods. These were quite common, especially at the time of Spanish contact. The Spanish friars, who for the most were somewhat more than a little biased in their reporting of Mayan religion, described this religious expression as involving homosexuality, human sacrifices, burning people alive, and impaling skulls of victims on stakes.

As I did with the reading of the St. Simon's Island materials by Bowes and Davis, I will present the readings of the late Mayan ceramics by Bowes and Renier together, first stating a category of response, such as "Environment," followed by relevant excerpts from both their readings and concluding with any comments I can offer to elucidate the readings. The complete uninterrupted readings by Bowes and Renier will be found in the Appendix.

Environment of the Target Site

The environment of the island site is noted at numerous points in their readings.

From Bowes:

...I felt water near there. It may be a river, or maybe at one time they used water to travel.

I don't know if there was a stream or river near here, but I kept picking up water. I see them down near the water, and I see them digging into the sides of the bank.

All this has something to do with a peninsula going out into the water, like the Baja peninsula, or something were there was a peninsula sticking out in the water. Like the ocean was here, or water was here, and then the ground went way up high. You could walk out to the edge and look down. It was real high.

I would say humid, or hot weather...I still felt tropical.

I see them going right out into the waves or going right out into the water in canoes. I see them spearing both fish and turtles.

I see people carrying things in big baskets. I feel they even had monkeys, or had little animals that they could sell or trade. Again this could be South America or some place that had an association with another influence from some other place.

I see lines of them going down through the woods carrying things. May not be woods, it may be swamps. Maybe jungle. I picked up 'woods'.

They may even had baskets with monkeys in them...or mice.

I would say South America or another place where it was very tropical.

...could be an association with islands, because I picked up islands a lot of times...an association with jungles and beaches.

Bowes correctly described a tropical area complete with "monkeys" and "jungles" and an "association with islands" with respect to the target site. The archeologist was struck by Bowes' correction, "Maybe jungle. I picked up 'woods.'" The Maya researcher wrote to me:

The site is in a tropical deciduous forest area of Peten. It's called 'jungle' in the vernacular, but the term brings frowns and worse from botanists.

Renier's environmental statements include the following:

I feel the land is flat but as it goes into the distance there's mounds...not like mountains, or not like flat desert all over...

I see mounds in the distance. In the background I see like sand mounds or...I don't see any vegetation on it. There is a large body of water. I'm facing it this way. A large body of water and I feel small...more of a stream...river cutting across the land.

JONES: You said mounds?

RENIER: More like hills...sand hills.

JONES: Sand hills. What do you feel the air temperature to be?

RENIER: I feel like I would sweat. I feel sun...very bright.

I see an animal that's more like on the ground...crawling. I feel like it might be some sort of a lizard. I feel it long and bulky with very short legs...animal...long body, short legs.

I got a woman this time. I feel her barefoot...and she is in this sandy place. I almost feel like different levels behind her. She is down near the water. I feel she might be gathering water.

There is a shore like shallow water.

Oh, good, good, good. I'm by this water again. I feel the slope down...the water must be down...of course, it's low...I feel a gentle sloping to this water.

It is warm though. It is hot. The sun is very bright. There is sand.

Very peaceful water. I feel peace and quiet. Quiet water. I don't feel waves. I feel quiet water.

I keep feeling like these things relate to two different locales. I felt like one was more in a very dry, hot climate. Very dusty. Almost barren. And then when I would go to the boat,

I would see more green, more lushness. I would feel more pretty things. I don't know if I'm speaking of two different things or if they are somehow the same.

I don't see a lot of vegetation around. I didn't see very much vegetation at all.

I see a lot of things to do around water. It is very sloping.

I feel a kind of Mediterranean type of heat. White...again I feel the desert and very lush growth. I feel water is important although there is a large body of water near them.

It would be cold occasionally, but I don't see snow. I feel mostly heat.

I feel the land has changed since this time when the people were on this site. Some strange relationship about the land being replaced by water, or water by land.

Renier's initial comments are very accurate. The surrounding territory is characterized by low, hilly terrain. Also, Lake Peten, a "large body of water," is near, and there is also a "river cutting across the land." Her statement, "I see mounds in the distance," could relate to the fact that there are numerous ruins of classic Maya temple pyramids in the vicinity of the target site. She was also correct about the climate being characteristically very hot; however, as she noted when she said, "It would be cold occasionally, but I don't see snow," the Peten region may experience temperatures dipping into the forties at night during January and February.

Renier's statements about the large lizard she saw may relate to the alligator populations of the area or to the iguanas which abound in the area of the site. Thompson[19] states that the iguana was a prized food source of the Peten Maya.

Renier made several comments about the nature of the water she saw. The archeologist who worked the site stated that there is a shallow slope to the lake bottom from the beach on the north and east edge of the island. Renier noted this feature of the lake several times. She was also accurate in her repeated comments about "quiet water." The lake upon which the target site is found does experience marked fluctuations in water level. This made Renier's report concerning "some strange relationship about the land being replaced by water, or water by land" meaningful. The changing water level of the lake is directly alluded to when she said, "...the water must be down...of course, it's low...".

As the reading showed, and as Renier admitted, she appeared torn between a "barren, dry" locale, and a more lush environment. Three possible explanations arise. One is that she was simply not receiving good impressions of the floral environment, although her description of water and climate are very accurate. A second factor is that both her conflicting images may be correct. Especially in the late Mayan period, the Maya in an effort to feed larger populations slashed-and-burned more and more land to create additional farmlands. The surrounding forest was also exploited for building materials. It is possible, therefore, that the Maya could have denuded large areas in the middle of the jungle simply as a result of their heavy construction and horticultural techniques. A third possibility relates to the suggestion that the late Peten Maya were recent immigrants out of the Yucatan.

II-5 Seminole medicine bag

II-4 Human vertebrae, A.D. 960

II-2 Crocheted ribbon

II-1 Toy combs

II-7 Carved chalk

II-3 Child's burial moccasin

II-6 Indian hoe, Georgia

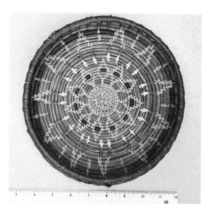

II-8 Pine needle basket

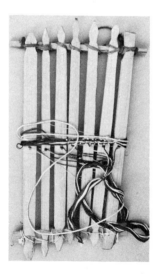

II-9 Seminole weaving heddle

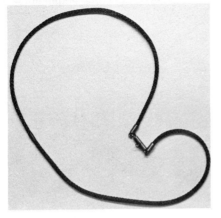

II-11 Hair necklace

II-12 "little scribblings" on clasp

II-10 Pocket watch

II-14 Sewing bird's screw handle

II-13 Sewing bird

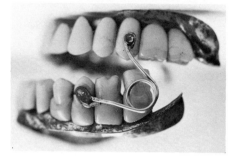

II-18 False teeth

II-16 Corn husker

II-19 Iron knuckles

II-15 Nazi wound badge

II-17 Fragment of old handcuffs

II-22 Navajo bridle

II-25 Eskimo ulu

II-23 Hopi prayer wand

II-21 Pelican key

II-20 Straight razor

II-24 Bontoc basket

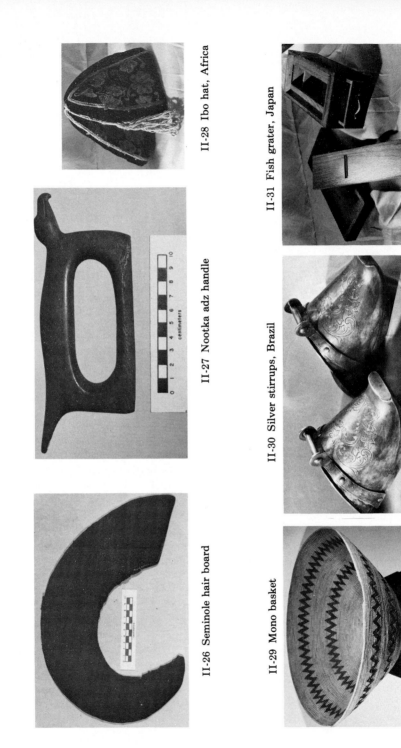

II-28 Ibo hat, Africa

II-27 Nootka adz handle

II-31 Fish grater, Japan

II-26 Seminole hair board

II-30 Silver stirrups, Brazil

II-29 Mono basket

III-1 St. Simon's Island artifacts collection

III-2 Folsom collection read by Bowes

IV-1 View of 8Se32 from opposite bank of St. Johns River

IV-2 One photo sent to Bowes to "read"

IV-10 Mikasuki Seminoles - *Reproduced by permission of the Smithsonian Institution*

IV-9 Package of artifacts for Renier to "read" blind

IV-3 Seminole chickee - *Reproduced by permission of the Smithsonian Institution*

IV-4 Rusted nail compared to dime   IV-5 "Square looking" pieces of metal

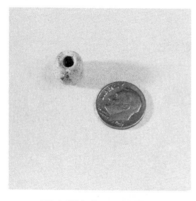

IV-6 "Little round bead"

IV-7 Knife blade fragment

IV-8 Experimental collection

"read" blind by Niren

V-1 Experimental Photo #2

V-2 Experimental Photo #7

V-3 Experimental Photo #10

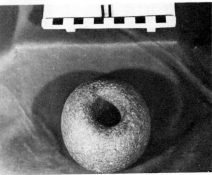

V-4 Experimental Photo #11

V-5 Experimental Photo #25

V-6 Experimental Photo #26

V-7 Experimental Photo #27

V-8 Experimental Photo #32

V-9 Experimental Photo #33

V-10 Experimental Photo #35

VI-i Fossils used in paleontology experiment

VII-1 Third Mayan experiment, Ceramic collection

VII-2 Mayan stones

VII-6 Stone door to Temple of Kulkulcan

VII-5 Stellae at Copan

VII-3 Cenote picture shown Bowes

VII-4 Stone interior

VII-7 Choc Mool statue at Chichen Itza

VII-9 Temple of Kulkulcan

VII-13 Ball field, Chichen Itza

VII-8 Statue at ball field

VII-12 Kabah, The Palace

VII-14 Uxmal, Main Temple

VII-10 Death's head wall

VII-12 Observatory, Chichen Itza

Renier's impressions of a flat, dry, barren environment may be a "memory" of the late Peten-dwelling Maya.

Renier's comment "I feel water is important, although there is a large body of water near them" is probably accurate. Though there is a definite rainy season in the Peten, the area is karst, with primarily subterranean drainage. Aside from the lake surfaces, water is rare. The Peten city of Tikal, for example, built reservoirs to store water.

Location of the Site

An interesting facet of Bowes' location of the site is his gradual approach to the target site starting in Alabama. As the succeeding passages and his related drawing will show, he ultimately located the general vicinity of the site, but the route he traced is one which suggests a possible explanation for the temple-mound cultural phenomenon found appearing in eastern North America beginning during the Mayan cultural period and ending several hundred years after it had fallen. Truncated pyramids, human sacrifice, corn based economy, the caste system, and the presence of a special class of priests, all very much like Mesoamerican cultural patterns, such as was exhibited by the Maya, did occur in Alabama. Of course, the accepted opinion of modern archeology is that the influence moved from Mesoamerica to the north—not from the north to the south. Keep in mind that Bowes was tracing the route in a double-blind, non-diagnostic test situation.

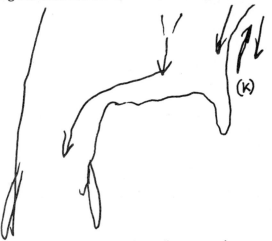

VII-12: *Migratory "route" to target site.*

It would start north of here (central Florida). The first thing I picked up was something about Alabama, or toward...I picked up toward the west, like northwest from here.

I picked up something about Spanish, or Spanish-speaking toward the south of where they lived...I kept picking up more like...Spanish-speaking people, or they may have spoken to someone from a Spanish-speaking...it may not have been Spanish but it may have been from the Mexico direction.

The reason for that is I picked up something from an outside influence, and I picked up a narrower part of this country, or a narrow part of another continent.

I kept picking up 'west,' and then I picked up 'peninsula,' or I picked up 'west' and then something jutting out into...this could be a mountain range, but I picked up more like water. I keep getting up about Alabama and then saying 'west'. Toward Mississippi, toward Mexico, toward the west.

From a Spanish-speaking place...or people of another language, or another culture.

I would say this may have had an association with this area, or this area (draws arrow south along Mississippi). It may be from up here, but I felt down here...like down the Mississippi, and back this way (arrow moving to the southwest.)

...it could be from another continent.

I would say from South America or there could have been a connection with these people and people from another continent...like South America.

...again, this could be South America...again if this is from South America, and it may be...

I would say South America, or another place where it was very tropical.

Renier was not specifically accurate in her location of the site.

I want to say 'in the east.' I don't know if it is Asia I'm seeing. I don't know.

JONES: I want to ask you about the location again.

RENIER: I just want to say 'east.' I don't feel like it is in the United States.

JONES: Do you have to cross an ocean out of this country?

RENIER: That would be one way. But I feel you could get there by land, or you could at one time.

On Renier's behalf it can be noted that she is right in stating that the site is not in the United States and when she remarked that one could reach the site from the United States by water (Gulf of Mexico) and by land.

The People

A variety of peoples played a part in the cultural experience of the late Maya of the Peten. Though the account of various ethnic groups in the Peten is based on much inference drawn from archeology, Spanish documents, and local myth, a generalized picture does emerge. A number of non-Mayan Indian groups lived in the vicinity with the Maya who were remnants of the early Maya culture prior to the relocation of massive segments of the Mayan population northward after 1000 A.D. Added to that were the late Maya immigrants out of Yucatan, and the Spanish who contacted the immediate area of the target site in the early 1500s.

Bowes had much to say about the people associated with the non-diagnostic potsherds he read.

These are pretty advanced people from what I can pick up. They may have worn unusual helmets or hats. I kept getting that they had visited on a trip, dignitaries or religious people. These people could have walked on mounds. There could have been great huge mounds where they worshipped. I kept feeling very beautiful countryside. I see a lot of vegetation.

But I felt these were pretty advanced people. They knew how to preserve food. They stored food in jars, or in bowls. I felt they were capable of making stone buildings.

I picked up that the lower class people, or the lower group of people, could live in wooden or shack type things...I felt some higher priests...the higher people may have lived in mounds where there was stone.

I kept feeling they were short and stocky and they had real round faces. They chopped their hair right here (bangs across forehead)...flat across and kind of round shaped (indicates shoulder length hair)...I felt the common hard working people had real heavy clothes down to here (waist)...real heavy clothes (draws picture of "hard working people")... kind of chopped hair.

Didn't have real long hair. They had kind of an Oriental look to them. Round looking faces, and these long heavy clothes. Real heavy. The clothes came down to their hands. These were like workers. The priests wore much more beads and jewelry, and lots of things hanging...like layers and layers of beads, or jewelry. I would feel they were something more like this (draws picture of "priest"). This...I saw a tie in front (returns to picture he drew of "workers")...but these people (priests) had something...lots of beads...layers and layers of beads. This is more like a person who is very religious or of a high position. These (workers) are more like women or like workers...people who carry big baskets...big round baskets. They may have carried stones or carried clay, or carried things in big baskets.

JONES: How many people occupied this site?

BOWES: Could have been over a thousand. These people wore different shoes, too. These people (workers) wore a shoe more like...rugged shoes, real coarse. These people (priests) wore more like a sandal, and it was more like something open. I can't explain it. It was like straps where this (shoes

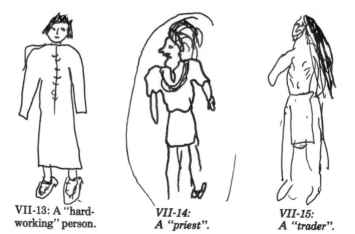

VII-13: A "hard-working" person.

VII-14: A "priest".

VII-15: A "trader".

of workers) was...like solid leather, and just tied together. Quite a difference between these two peoples. These people (workers) didn't go anywhere. They always stayed at home. These people (priests) would do some traveling. They (priests) would be studying things, and visiting and investigating. These people hide things...maybe gold, maybe valuables...in caves south of where they lived. I feel they sealed it up...probably still there. Things hanging from walls. Skulls and skeletons, and like people hanging...like a burial cave or something, because I see a lot of skulls.

JONES: **You mentioned another people when you touched this** (Indicates a particular shard).

BOWES: From a Spanish-speaking place...or people of another language, or another culture.

JONES: **What did those people look like?**

BOWES: The first thing I picked up was that they were naked...just had breech cloth, or just...and they may not have...this piece of pottery may not have been made by them but whatever they got from them. This is (draws figure).

They just may have had something tied around their waist.

JONES: **What about the hair on the traders?**

BOWES: I felt black hair. They were more like in the water, or around the salt water, or...real nature people, outdoor types. These people (workers) were more like workers, or very much more serious. The people who associated with this (potsherd) were more like savage people. They got things out of the ocean, or things out of the water. They had bows and arrows and they shot under water, or shot fish. They did things more like in nature. These people (workers) were almost like slaves...where they all worked together carrying these baskets.

JONES: Who were the masters of these people (workers)?
BOWES: These people (priests). These people (traders) talked another language, and these people (priests) had very little respect for these people (traders), but they did trade with them. They (traders) had long hair.

These people (workers) lived in these shacks...these grass shacks or these wood shacks. These people (priests) lived here on the mounds. These people (traders) lived on the river or on the water. They were more like savages, or more like people who were fishermen, or people who were close to nature. These people (priests) talked about religion. These people (workers and traders) did not live as long as them (priests).
JONES: As a culture?
BOWES: Yes. These people (priests) were much healthier. These people...
JONES: What is the relationship between all these heavy clothes (referring to "workers") and the humid climate?
BOWES: It sounds like it contradicts...but I kept seeing the heavy clothes as a cultural thing or as a worker, and I kept seeing it as heavy leather, or heavy clothing, but I picked up that they were like suppressed...that they were workers.

JONES: Were these people (priests) and these people (workers) of the same racial background?
BOWES: Yes. They had the same racial background. These people (indicates priests) may have actually looked different ...in the face. These (workers) looked more oriental. These people were oriental but they had a long looking face (priests). They may have not been interbred...These people (workers) may have just stood there and watched these others (priests) worship. These people (traders) would worship nature, fish, and animals, and the tides and health, and things more like nature. These people (priests) felt there was a god, gods.
JONES: I am interested in the nature of the family.
BOWES: I felt these people (workers) had a very poor family group. In fact, when they may have begun to get a family they may have been used like slaves, or separated or sent to particular places to learn certain trades...These people (priests) were considered royalty and when they had children, they were very coddled or taken care of, but young women from here (workers) may have at times taken care of these people (priests), but they (priests) were considered like kings, or royalty.

I keep seeing a lot of people walking with limps. This is strange, because I see a lot of people walking with, like hip problems, or knee problems—these people (workers)...the

workers. Maybe like scurvy or something with the lack of
nutrition. These people were limited in the kinds of food they
had and were pushing for trade. I would say...again if this is
from South America, and it may be, but I picked up these
people (priests) could have rode
and they (workers) may have
carried them in things like this
(draws following image)...like a
box on poles. The man sat in
here. The man is out of proportion. A lot of feathers, lot of
plummage, lot of color.

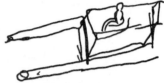

VII-16: A royal Palanquin.

God, this is strange! I keep picking up them limping,
limping. I felt joints...problems with their knees, and their
hips...like stiffness, like a problem with malnutrition. I
didn't see them eating right...I seen them (workers) sick...I
would say these people (traders) ate very well, in comparison
to us. They could get to the food.

JONES: **You mentioned these** (priests) **people traveling...**

BOWES: Yeah. They would get away. Go places and meet
other people...in other places. They even visited a place
where people live up in the sides of hills...like they have
adobe buildings, or buildings up in the sides of mounds or
hills. I hear them saying they are going to visit the water,
which to them was a sacred place.

JONES: **When these people** (priests) **left, what kept these
people** (workers) **from leaving?**

BOWES: All of them (priests) didn't leave. The workers
were like cattle, or like dedicated, or brainwashed, or like
robots...they were kept working. What's strange is that they
kept carrying things. Trading is probably what it was...they
were carrying things. I see lines of them going through the
woods carrying things.

Bowes began his double-blind reading of the non-diagnostic ceramic
fragments correctly with a general statement concerning an "advanced people" who had "great, huge mounds where they worshipped" and were capable of "making stone buildings". In passing he
noted an environment with a "lot of vegetation."

He immediately zeroed-in on the marked class differences of the
Maya and rightly identified a lower class group who lived in "wooden
or shack type of things" and the "higher people" who lived "in
mound where there was stone." His description of the "workers" or
"common people" with "chopped off hair" and wearing "real heavy
clothing" fits closely with Von Hagen's[20] description of the slaves of
the Maya:

> They were used for heavy manual labor, as fishermen, pad-
> dlers, and cargo carriers. Women slaves helped to draw
> water, grind maize, and dye cloth. Men slaves had their hair

cut short and were given ragged mantles to wear.

Bowes' description of the "priests" is very accurate. He also noted an interesting physical trait of the Maya when he remarked, "They had kind of an oriental look to them." Von Hagen[21] writes, "Maya eyes, dark and lustrous, appear to be more Mongolian than those of most 'Americans,' because the eyes being placed obliquely in the face emphasizes the epicanthic fold that gives them that 'slant'."

Bowes' comment about the caves to the south with things hidden in them and his reference in the same vein to "skulls and skeletons and like people hanging...like a burial cave or something...a lot of skulls" stimulated several pertinent comments from the archeologist who worked at the site. He noted that there are, in fact, caves to the south of the site which contain artifacts as yet not systematically studied. Further, he stated that skull burials were found all around the site area.

Bowes was right again when he touched a potsherd and noted that it came from another area. The piece in question was made at or near an island site northeast from the target site. He related the item to traders who "got things out of the water." His watery locale was correct for the particular shard, and we do know that the late Mayan people in this vicinity were very much involved with trade throughout the region. In addition, Bowes noted that the "priests" and "traders" had a somewhat tense relationship. This, too, is supported in several ethnohistorical reports.

The issue of health appeared in several places in Bowes' observation of the people connected with the pottery pieces. He stated that the "priests" lived longer and that there were differences in the food available to various social groups. This has been substantiated by modern archeological techniques. Adams[22], for example, writes:

> Diet of the elite was improved by the meat of a small deer that was semi-domesticated. We have been able to determine this superior diet through study of Maya burials. The average height of individuals buried in formal tombs is consistently greater than that of individuals buried elsewhere... under the pole and thatch houses for example.

Bowes' drawing of the "priest" in a "box on poles" which was carried by "slaves" is true to Mayan custom with respect to their rulers. He noted at many points that the "slaves" were involved in carrying things much of the time. Two of the more common functions of slaves in the Mayan culture, lacking in draft animals, were to serve as beasts of burden and to carry the rubble around with which the Maya built their great monumental structures.

At the end of this reading Bowes began to describe a counting device which seemed to resemble an Oriental abacus.

> I would say they had some form of money or a calendar, or something that they looked at. They would barter on this calendar. They may have even counted things with these beads. Like, when they were bartering or trading, they may

have had, like pieces of wood on both sides and a lot of little beads that they shoved back and forth. I don't feel anyone knows about that...I keep seeing them counting beads, or pushing beads across...counting.

Stuart and Stuart[23], reconstructing a day in the life of a Mayan mathematician, describe a Mayan calculating tool.

The box is divided into three compartments, each containing a set of carved wooden 'counters'. The longish ones, painted black, represent fives; the small brown cubes, ones; and the pellets of white shell, zeros. Working with these on the grid scored on the box lid, the old priest can add, subtract, divide, and multiply—into the billions if he needs to.

When Noreen Renier read the ceramic pieces she had the following things to say about the impressions she experienced concerning the target people.

I see a very broad-faced individual and I feel like there's a bang, or bangs on this man's head. I feel like bangs...hair. Bangs.

JONES: You mentioned hair. How long does this hair come down?
RENIER: About to the shoulder. It wasn't black. I'm not that good on hair color, but I felt light. For a moment I thought I might have picked up the man who touched it (referring to potsherd before her).

I've got this person who has something very high that peaks at the top, but it is very solid. It looks like...this man looks like he might have been a priest...a religious individual at one time. I feel it might be gold or heavy material in his cap. Alright, this man has more dark hair...dark hair and curls around his hair. Ouch, ouch, ouch. Can I tell you? He had a back ache. Oh, dear, this is ridiculous. I'm getting a back ache...lower back to my right side. I'm getting a lot of pain ...in my back.

JONES: Why don't you see what he is wearing.
RENIER: O.K. A long thing...ouch...long, long robe. Full sleeves. Indentation in the sleeves. It is not straight across. I feel either embroidered or again...ouch...felt, riches.

Oh, I have some people on horses now. I feel negative toward these people. I don't feel the people on horses live in this area. They are not from that town or that city. I feel destruction with them. I feel fight. I feel the people on the ground are helpless. I don't see any...they don't have any protection. These other people are coming in force. I feel they are coming in from the...I don't see any men. Just women and children around there. Oh, dear, I'm bleeding. I am dark, not black. The features are flat and broad. I don't cry that much. I don't know why I'm not crying.

JONES: **What do these people look like who just came in on horses?**
RENIER: Dark hair. Dark eyes. I feel bigness in their size. Bodies very strong. Their head is wrapped in something.
JONES: **What direction do they come from?**
RENIER: They had to travel over a green and more mountainous area to get to where we are. I feel they live in a higher altitude and a cooler climate than we do. I don't know why they are hurting us.
JONES: **What do they want?**
RENIER: They are killing people, and they are looking for some male. But they are not there. The males are gone. This place is almost deserted now.
JONES: **Are the people who are in trouble praying to anyone or anything?**
RENIER: No. I don't see that with them. I feel water.

In touching this (potsherd) I feel more like a young body. Again, the hair. The hair is that cut again (indicates bangs and shoulder length). Straight...I feel there is some thing on his body. I don't know if it's a scar or it it's painted on.
JONES: **What is he wearing?**
RENIER: His chest is bare. I feel color. He is not an American Indian, I don't think. He is wearing a brief thing on the lower part of his body, and his legs are bare too. Most of the time there in nothing on the feet. The horsemen again. I can see his boot. He has a boot on. But I feel lightness in the material. I feel lightness in texture. The horse is light colored. I feel a blanket or something before the saddle. I feel again nice colors. A nice weave or blend of colors. Thick belt, or something thick around him.

JONES: **Are there any designs on his clothes that are important?**
RENIER: One color. I just get one color.
JONES: **Do you hear them speaking?**
RENIER: I feel it would be some kind of funny...I see all kinds of twisted things. It is not English, or Italian, or French...it's a funny kind of language.
JONES: **Spanish? German?**
RENIER: It is something that I don't know...I've never seen it before.
JONES: **Do you get the origin of the people on the horses?**
RENIER: There is a lot of traveling involved with these people. I still feel higher altitude around them, and I see green...green hills and green grass. I see some rock in the hills...heavy stones, thick stones. Might go down into the ocean, but I am higher up. I don't see the water, but I can feel it...feel the ocean.

JONES: How many people lived at this site?
RENIER: Small. Like hundreds, or fifty. Not big. Maybe fifty.

First of all they are a small people. I feel smallness in their structure. Smaller than five feet. I almost feel like I would have to bend when I walk into their houses. I feel like a giant.

No, they are slaves. They weren't black. I don't see them as black.

Renier described the people she saw as short, "smaller than five feet", and "broad faced." Von Hagen[24] writes of the Maya:

...the Maya's average height was five feet, one inch. Still, he was robust and strong. The Maya were brachcephalic, one of the most broad-headed people in the world.

She described independently the bangs and shoulder-length hair style that Bowes described when handling the same objects. Renier, also like Bowes, spoke of slaves, and priests with embroidered robes. Embroidered *mantas* were well-known for the time and place of the site and were at the time of the site's occupation widely traded throughout the area.

Of particular significance are the "horsemen" Renier described. Horses were not native to the Maya. The Spanish, however, proved to be a major military challenge to the Maya due in large part to the fact that the Spanish were mounted. Cortez marched through the vicinity of the target site in the mid-1500s. The archeologist who worked the site feels that the site is over a hundred years too early to have experienced Cortez. Still, while looking at non-diagnostic pottery fragments Renier began to speak of large, dark-haired, dark-eyed horsemen. She mentioned that they came through a mountainous area to arrive at the site. It is factual that Cortez crossed the highlands of Guatemala and Honduras in his march through the Mayan area. When questioned further about the horsemen, Renier accurately noted that fact that there was much "traveling involved with these people." Also, she stated that in the "higher altitudes" associated with the origin of the horsemen, she could feel the presence of the ocean: the Pacific Ocean is visible from the Guatemalan highlands.

When I asked Renier about the population of the target site, she spoke of a small population numbering about fifty individuals. The archeologist succinctly noted in the margin of the transcript of Renier's reading of this site next to Renier's population estimate, "Probably about right."

Trade

One of the traits associated with the late Mayan peoples in the Peten is an elaborate trade network. They had a trade system that included both coastal and overland routes. Their connection with the Yucatan as well as coastal access came via the series of lakes which included Lake Peten Itza and the rivers, such as the Belize, which ultimately carried the Mayan traders to the coast. In the preceding section concerning the people of the site, Bowes in paticular emphasized the role of the trader. His comments about trade included the following. In fact, the image of "a trade route" was the second image he relayed in this reading, within seconds after touching the ceramic pieces.

I picked up something about a trade route...or trade...I felt they had a religion that was quite involved with the idea of planets, or something that has to do with trade or navigation. The feeling I picked up was that these people were actually relying, and based on the idea of trade...something having to do with trade. In other words, I don't see them being totally self-sufficient.

JONES: Could you draw a map to help locate this place?

BOWES: You see, one thing that is confusing me is the idea of trade.

I would say from South America, or there would have been a connection with these people and people from another continent...like South America. There could have been trade in that direction.

JONES: So you feel with these people that a crucial fact of their life had to do with...

BOWES: Trade.

JONES: Is that why they are there or did the trade happen later?

BOWES: No. That was the reason they are where they are. I would say originally they came to farm, but as there came to be more and more people, they would relate to trade to keep the people going. I would say they depleted their soil.

I see a lot of people talking and milling around. I see a lot of trading going on...outside. These buildings here (mounds) are off in the distance. I see people carrying things in big baskets. I feel they even had monkeys, or had little animals that they sell and trade.

JONES: These people (priests/workers), what do they have that people would want in terms of trade?

BOWES: Pots. Things made of clay. These little idols, these little figurines, things made of wood where they were making things like clubs that were very, very polished...I felt dark red wood.

JONES: What would these people want from other people?

BOWES: Fish, animals, things of trade. They may have had baskets with monkeys in them...or mice. I don't feel that the people who dug this up realized the trade involved. What they got there (indicates ceramic collection) may have only been like an outpost of the actual civilization. Like a colony of the original. Like Columbus, like the pilgrims came over from England. These people were like the pilgrims in this particular place.

Bowes' suggestion that trade increased as the soil became depleted due to over-utilization is a commonly held opinion among Mayanists. His reference to monkeys is accurate, and the other "little animals that they sell and trade" could relate to coatimundis, small raccoon-like animals that were kept as pets by the Maya.

Bowes' response to my question about what the people of the target had to trade to others brought forth a correct picture of the items traded in fact. Pottery ("Pots. Things made of clay.") was a key trade resource. His reference to "like clubs that were very, very polished" could relate to the greenstone traded out of the Peten that was used for making celts—polished stone axes. The reference to "dark red wood" would be right for two items traded in this area, brazilwood used for red dye and cedar.

The image of trade in "these little idols, these little figurines" is very accurate. The figurines at another point in his reading were described in this way:

> What I'm dealing with is little statues and one of them was a statue of a man with his hands up, and the other one was like a little dog sitting down. I picked up an association with those statues and this piece (indicates particular shard). I picked up a bunch of little artifacts, or a bunch of little statues or little animals, or different objects.

As noted in the introductory comments about the culture related to this experiment, figurine censers were associated with a religious cult in this area and were a main trade item. Bowes was specifically designating the censers when he reported seeing a "statue of a man with his hands up." Many of these censers were constructed in such a way that the piece of incense rested on the upturned palms of the ceramic figure.

From what has been already stated about the origins of the late Maya in the Peten, Bowes was certainly correct in characterizing the people he was seeing as "like an outpost of the actual civilization. Like a colony of the original."

Renier, too, seemed to be very interested in the trade behavior of the people she experienced as she handled the test shards. Her reaction to one of the shards, a piece manufactured in the Tabasco region of the Mexican gulf coast, elicited this exchange concerning trade.

> JONES: You indicated with one of these pieces (later identified as having come from Tabasco area) that the people came from somewhere else. I am interested in that.
>
> RENIER: When I picked this up (indicates shard from Tabasco), I get travel and I get that boat again. That same boat...the long smooth lines of it. It is beautiful. I feel riches. It is not an ugly boat. It is very pretty. I am going on the boat. We are loading. There's food and things being put on the boat. I feel quietness. I don't feel hostility. I feel peace ...around it. God, doesn't anybody wear any clothes around here? I feel nakedness again. It is warm though. It is hot. The

sun is very bright. There is sand. The boat is not that deep. It doesn't go down that far. I feel shallowness in the boat structure. It is wood. Very long planks. I see very defined lines going laterally. Long. I can...

JONES: **Where is this boat going?**
RENIER: Very peaceful water. I feel peace and quiet. Quiet water. I don't feel waves. I feel quiet water. How can it...oh, it's more by a city or something. It must be an important boat because I feel like people sending it good wishes, or love. I feel that it is very important where it is going.

JONES: **How long will it take to get where it's going?**
RENIER: I feel several days at least. There will be one stop before we get to our destination. Our destination is more northeast. We will go up, not down. Up. I feel differences from these people (touches shard from Tabasco).

JONES: **How do these people** (indicates Tabasco shard) **feel toward the people in the boat?**
RENIER: I feel the people in the boat are more privileged, more important. Again, men, no women, are on the boat. Just men.

Renier was correct about the external origin of the nondiagnostic ceramic piece she was holding as she delivered the preceding impressions. Her observation that the loaded boat would travel for several days in a northeast direction is also interesting because that would put it on the Caribbean coast, one of the major destinations of Mayan traders. Renier was right once more when she stressed the absence of women in such trading ventures.

Her reading continues with respect to trade:

This old woman says not to worry so much. The men go off all the time. They may go up to the higher ground to hunt, or to get things that they can't get at home. She says they go all the time. That I shouldn't worry. They come back. Many things to be done while they are gone.

JONES: **How long is it before the men come back?**
RENIER: Many weeks...long periods of time that they are gone because they have to travel so far...to higher ground.

JONES: **When they return, do they bring anything with them that they didn't have when they left?**
RENIER: I felt more with meat.

The custom of trade behavior patterns in which men leave periodically for extended periods of time is known generally for Mesoamerican high cultures.

Religion

The religion of the Maya has been sufficiently discussed so that the readings of Bowes and Renier related to that subject will, for the most part, stand without additional comment. The special additions in the case of the late Mayan site being read involved the aforementioned figurine censers and an apparent emphasis on skull burials, both mentioned in earlier contexts by Bowes.

Bowes' statements about the religion of the people associated with the test shards included the following.

I felt they had a religion that was quite involved with the idea of planets...

There could have been great huge mounds where they worshipped.

JONES: The religion...

BOWES: Again, it has to do with the direction in the stars or dealing with something that has to do with religion...like something that has to do with talking to the gods, or they would sacrifice, or they would work with the gods.

...to them there was, like layers that they spoke of that signified evolution or growth.

Renier had these comments about the religion of the people she was experiencing:

Oh, I see a tree. It is bare. It doesn't have lots of leaves on it. It is just sort of sticking up there bare. I feel like there is a big nest up there. It is not a little nest...big nest. This is higher up, as you go higher (indicates elevated area behind living area of people). A big bird. Brown.

JONES: Do the people think anything about this bird?

RENIER: Oh, it is a bird that likes death. I don't know why. A bird that likes death. I feel like they burned their people.

JONES: Do these people feel that something happens after death?

RENIER: They talked about something that came in the sky. Not that much sorrow. I don't feel that much sorrow. I feel very matter-of-fact...to what we have to do.

JONES: Do these people tell myths to each other? What would they speak of?

RENIER: They do feel their soul or spirit has to be released. Something that was up in the air. It came many, many years before this old man. He tells the younger people that something in the sky came...very big. They felt it was one of the gods. Gods. Not only one god. Gods. They believed that some animal holds the soul or the spirit of other people. An animal that looks more like a dog or a wolf. I see his stomach being cut open.

JONES: Why?

RENIER: He is dangerous. If he is skinny...he is not well fed. I feel skinnyness.

JONES: Being with these people...if you wanted to act in a religious manner, what would you do?

RENIER: Act. Birds. Fire is very important. In a house.

Before the men leave there is a ritual. The men have to leave
at certain times. There is a ritual...women...second rate.

**JONES: What kind of designs would they associate with
their religion?**

RENIER: There's that triangle shape. Like energy coming
out of it, but it is an open triangle. I don't see this part (bottom) being closed. Oh, dear Jesus! Somebody's tongue is
being cut out. He has done something. I feel punishment.

**JONES: If these people were making a religious appeal of
great importance, how would they do it?**

RENIER: Sacrifice. To the different gods.

**JONES: Do you feel any of the characteristics of these
entities?**

RENIER: They sacrificed to these gods to bring luck to the
hunters, to have the good I see a very big pit, very deep. I
don't know if I am on the edge of a volcano or not, but it
could be. It had a very wide opening, very, very big, and
very, very wide.

JONES: How many feet?

RENIER: Fifty feet at least. Very big.

In the context of a question concerning religion, Bowes spoke of
"layers". The Maya in fact believed that the skies were structured in
terms of thirteen layers, terraced like a pyramid, each pertaining to an
aspect of the gods. The Underworld, they felt, had nine layers.[24]

Renier's relating of the "bird that likes death" to the Maya is appropriate. Renier, like Bowes, mentioned volcanoes several times. Perhaps
the reference to the tale of something dramatic happening in the sky
may relate to the earlier eruption of Ilopango. Then again, she may be
responding out of a "chariot of the gods" type of orientation. There is
also a suggestion in Renier's reading of a ritual theme among the
Maya which related sexual abstinence with men to preparation for
major ritual events like religious ceremonials, hunting ventures, and
trading expeditions.

The open-ended triangle she spoke of was not found in any of my
Mayan research. It is curiously like the "wedge" shape Bowes mentioned in his reading of the ceramic pieces.

Renier reported an image of a tongue being cut out when I asked her
about religious symbolism. Producing blood for ritual purposes by
lacerating and piercing the tonque is widely reported for the Maya.
The theme even appears on a stone lintel at Yaxchilan, which shows a
woman pulling a thorn covered cord through her tongue.

When she spoke of sacrifices she described seeing a very wide pit,
suggesting that it could be a volcano. The custom of sacrificing by
throwing victims downward to their death was known among the
Maya. The behavior surrounding the sacred *cenote* of Chichen Itza is a
good example. Thompson[25], for example, wrote: "In Yucatan, the
victim was sometimes bound and hurled from a height onto rocks
below."

Diet

We can assume that the Maya at the target site were mainly involved in maize horticulture, while at the same time attempting to augment their diet with other plant and animal resources. Here is what Bowes had to say about the food of the site's inhabitants.

JONES: **What was the diet of the makers of these materials?**
BOWES: The first thing I picked up was something about grain, or something about things that were grown in fields. Then I picked up long strips of something, and it may have been almost like the insides of a plant, or something that was stripped, and I picked up strips of meat that were smoked. But I felt these were pretty advanced people. They knew how to preserve food. They stored food in jars, or in bowls.

They might get berries, or purple or black colored berries, and cook it. I seen them (priests) giving it to them (workers). I would say that it would keep them working, keep them going like a stimulant.

Bowes was correct about the "grains," and "things that were grown in fields." His description of the "long strips" of "the inside of a plant" may refer to a food source described by Thompson[26] in which a tuberous plant was cut into strips and then roasted. Bowes may be describing cacao, a drink to which the Maya were almost addicted, in his reference about the stimulant beverage.

Renier had this to say about diet:

JONES: **What does she eat?**
RENIER: Chews something a whole bunch of times. I see her chewing something a great deal of the time. It has to be chewed a lot.

JONES: **Do you see it before she puts it in her mouth?**
RENIER: It's tough...tough, dried.

They have either something they chew...they chew it and I feel like it sort of relaxes them. Maybe like some sort of dope. What we might consider a dope. But I do feel like they chew it. It is what I tasted before. I don't know why I want to laugh. It just feels so good. I feel very relaxed. I feel very good.

Renier may have been describing, and apparently experiencing, a relaxant chewed by the Maya which, among other things, was composed of tobacco mixed with lime.

JONES: **What do most of these people eat?**
RENIER: Two basics...I feel like I got meat but it doesn't look fresh meat. I feel more dried meat. I also feel some green stuff around too...some stuff that can be...I feel as I put it in my mouth there is moisture in the thing. I don't feel like it's cooked...raw and freshness coming out...she is picking up something by the water.

JONES: Do these people plant or do they gather or...
RENIER: I don't feel like it's harvest crops. I feel like things that are growing wild or...I feel more wildness. I don't feel like a garden.

I feel pounding.
JONES: What are they pounding?
RENIER: To make food with. Making a meal or mush. They do this all the time. Everybody has to do it.
JONES: Can you see the woman putting something underneath the pounder? What does it look like?
RENIER: It's gathered...from the more wooded or the more ...not green, not green, not green. More like brown. Not green. I don't see green. Fire is open. It is shallow. Shallow fire.

Preparing and storing some strange grain. Mashing.

Renier is certainly incorrect when she denied the presence of gardens. Then again, a *milpa* plot of a Mayan farmer would not look like what Renier would know as a "garden". However, her several references to "mashing" and "preparing and storing some strange grain" could relate to a daily chore of Mayan women, the grinding of maize grain on *metates* to produce flour used in making torillas, a staple meal item of the Maya. She was also right when she stated with reference to this food preparation, "They do this all the time. Everybody has to do it."

Miscellaneous

Bowes had a number of interesting comments to make about the specifics relating to the shards he touched. When handling a piece brought to the target site from another site called Topoxte, Bowes remarked, "I feel as though these people may have traded this from a different location." Another one of the pieces, considered by archeologists to be a line sinker since the site is on a lake and fish were presumably a major protein source, brought this response from Bowes: "This I picked up was tied...something tied onto it, or something separated...I felt it was stretched, or dealt with...stretched." When Bowes picked up a tubular fragment of what was probably an incense burner he commented, "I picked up a man with this, and I felt him smoking, or smoke inside a building." When he touched a fragment from the Tabasco region, not native to the target site, he said, "Now this I felt came from a different group of people." Another item in the test collection was a fragment of a mold used for making the figurine censers mentioned earlier. Bowes immediately responded, after touching this piece, "I picked up an association with those statues and this piece."

Another fascinating observation came when Bowes was talking about the differences between the "priests" and the "workers". I asked him, "Were these people (priests) and the workers of the same racial background?" He responded:

> Yes. They had the same racial background. These people (priests) may have actually looked different...in the face. These (workers) looked more oriental. These people (priests) were oriental but they had longer looking faces. They may not have even interbred. These people (priests) were like royalty.

His feeling that the "priests" and the "workers" were of the same race but that the "priests" may have "looked different...in the face" might be explained by a brief description of the kinds of things the Mayan elite, not the slaves, did to their faces and head region in the name of beauty. Noses were broken and remodeled with putty making them very hooked to conform to the accepted norms of attractiveness. Eyes were purposely made to cross by techniques initiated during infancy. Teeth were filed and inlaid. Earlobes were widened, noses pierced, and bodies scarified and tatooed. In addition, the custom of the elite in which an infant's head was artificially flattened and elongated may account for why Bowes saw the "priests" having "longer looking faces."

When describing the footgear of the "priests" and "workers", he noted that the "priests"wore sandals. He was correct. In response to my question—"During the time that the people were making these things, what other kinds of things were going on in the world?"—he spoke of Indians traveling in the southeastern United States at a time when no white men were present. The target site dates between 1100 and 1400 according to the archeologist working with it, and at that time Bowes would be right about the absence of whites in the southeastern United States. At another point, in passing, he noted that the materials may be from five hundred years ago. Again, this puts him approximately into the known date of the site.

The Maya did not have knowledge of metallurgy. When I asked Bowes about his impressions concerning the use of metal by the people under investigation, he said:

> I felt a little round disk...a little metal thing. But I felt...I didn't understand that. I felt it was added later. It was among this stuff (shards) but it was added later by a different people.

In the reading he stated that he saw the people spearing both fish and turtles. The fish relationship is assumed due to the island location of the site. In addition, the archeologist associated with the site noted that turtle carapaces are fairly common at late Mayan island sites in the area. Bowes in the last few sentences of his reading stated that the people had both money and a calendar. The Mayans are, of course, famous for their calendars. Further, they also had a form of money, a culture trait not that common in the world of stone-age peoples. Von Hagen[27] comments:

> Cacao seeds are almond-sized and -shaped and when dried in the sun they become dark, chocolate-colored, with a dry,

parchment-like skin. It is these beans that were used as money. A rabbit was worth 10 cacao beans, a pumpkin 4, a slave 100 (the same amount of cacao that would make about 25 cups of chocolate)...

Renier also seemed to be particularly sensitive to items not indigenous to the target site. When she touched the potsherd from the Mexican gulf coast at Tabasco she said:

I feel this piece migrated into this place...or it got carried around a lot. I feel travel with this piece. I feel it traveled. I don't know where it went, but I see bigger water.

When I asked her what the walls of the houses were made of, she stated:

RENIER: Cool. Cool. Clay, mud, clay. Is it solid? It is not set rock, not stone. It is either clay, or...smooth. It is cool inside.

JONES: When you see this from the outside, what color is the structure?

RENIER: I feel almost like a very dull orange, dull like yellow, orange. It is not painted.

The walls of the common people's houses at the target site were covered with lime plaster. The "dull orange, dull like yellow, orange" coloring may be a result of the organic resin that was sometimes put on the lime plaster to harden and protect it in the moist, humid environment.

Renier, like Bowes, described the elite wearing sandals. She added two more correct times—the occasional wearing of long robes, and the growing of beards by some older Mayans.[28] Two important questions concerning culture level were answered correctly by Renier in the following dialogue.

JONES: With these people, do you feel the presence of metal?

RENIER: (nods her head in a negative gesture)

JONES: What about domestic animals?

RENIER: Maybe they had dogs. I wanted to see a cow but I couldn't.

Another significant feature is revealed in this passage from Renier's reading.

I feel an unnatural disaster. I feel sliding, I feel crumbling.

JONES: This sliding and crumbling, is that on this site?

RENIER: Yes. The one we have been looking at.

JONES: Before or after the men on horses?

RENIER: After. I don't see people there. It's funny. I see belongings but I don't see people there during the sliding. There was a land slide and destruction. An earthquake and water. I don't know. I just feel...trembling. I felt they knew it was coming.

The archeologist stated that there is no archeological evidence that he knows of concerning an earthquake at the site. Still, it is interesting to remember that the site is located on an earthquake fault-line in the

Peten. Further, Stuart and Stuart[29], in commenting on the Guatemalan environment, states: "Far below the rocky soil lie complicated systems of fault lines that often cause the land to tremble."

When Renier touched a piece of copal, one of the items in the test collection, and a resin widely used by the Maya as incense, she stated, "This piece has been hot." Her "date" response to my standard question—"At the time these people were alive and making these things, what kind of things were going on in other parts of the world?" —brought forth this remark:

> Let's see…in Europe at this time I see boats with sails that sort of remind me of Columbus. Europe was more or less in a dark state, or dark ages.

She was right in the correct time period of the site's date (1100-1400). The European scene she noted would date around 1300 to 1400.

Conclusion: Third Mayan Experiment

In my opinion, this experiment was the most complete of the several Mayan experiments reported here. It was truly double-blind and of the non-diagnostic type. Yet, Bowes and Renier were able to describe the site and locate it with impressive accuracy. They also described such characteristic late Mayan traits as the social class differentiation, celestial emphasis in religion, trade focus, censer figurines, physical appearance of the citizens, diet, and even the Mayan relaxant that Renier seemed to "psychically" enjoy so much. In addition, they proved able to identify which items were non-native to the site and which were in truth indigenous. They also accurately dated the site within the "plus-or-minus" range used in the orthodox archeological tradition.

FOURTH MAYAN EXPERIMENT: BLIND READING OF STONES FROM THREE MAYAN SITES IN YUCATAN

A colleague had acquired the items used in this experiment during a trip to Yucatan. The rocks from the sites were not artifacts. They were simple ground debris. The blind aspect of this experiment was that the psychics were of course not apprised of the origins of the rocks prior to the test, though I was. A double-blind feature of this test was that I was not told of the specific source of the rocks, that is the cities from which they were gathered. I was told that the debris came from three different sites. Of particular interest is that one of the stones was from Chichen Itza, a site already "visited" by Bowes. Neither of us knew that fact at the time the experiment was in progress.

The Mayan stones were read independently by Bowes, Davis, and Renier. The nature of the experimental session, as in all cases, was not divulged to the subjects prior to the session. In addition, the subjects were not told if others had worked with the same materials.

The two other cities, besides Chichen Itza, which were represented in the test collection were Kabah and Uxmal. One of the pieces was from the Kabah *sacbe*, or road, while another piece was picked up from the ground inside the city of Kabah. Since the story of Chichen Itza has been adequately presented in prior section I will focus on a brief overview of Kabah and Uxmal as a means of offering some preliminary background to the readings that follow.

Kabah was a center of Mayan population in Yucatan in the 11th and 12th centuries. Kabah also possesses, aside from the typical monumental forms of the Maya, a huge underground cistern, or *chultun*, utilized as a central collection point for rain water collected from the roofs of the city's buildings. The *sacbe*, or road, which produced one of the stones in this experiment, runs from Kabah to Uxmal, which lies about nine miles northwest of Kabah.

Uxmal sits in an area of low hills about fifty miles from the coast, and approximately one hundred miles from Chichen Itza to the northeast. Uxmal, like Kabah, has cistern structures, as well as the usual compliment of Mayan monumental forms. It was built by the Mayan-Toltec groups during the Mayan renaissance after the Toltec invasion. Like Chichen Itza, Uxmal was built near a natural *cenote*.

Site Location

First, Bowes located the general point of origin of the stones. His "method" of locating sites under blind and double-blind conditions involved, as has been seen throughout these experiments, a kind of tracking of the site beginning at some point usually far removed from the target. However, by the end of his tracking, he was usually in the right vicinity of the site.

> I picked up North Carolina, but I would say south of there. I would say it was a place with underground limestone caves with water.

> I get Florida, but I get Texas or south...going south... southern part of the United States.

> I would say from the south...southwest. I don't pick up Florida now...when you ask about direction, I pick up another place...could even be in South America, or...I felt different. I didn't feel Florida. I see a peninsula. I feel stuck in the water. Cliffs near the water.

> Again if this was like Florida, again I didn't feel so much Florida, but I felt it was near the water.

> I picked up people were migrating from South America to the north.

Davis had the following things to say about her impressions concerning the location of the target sites.

> I am very drawn to say that there is a large body of water to the north...like a big lake. I see something almost like Lake Erie.
> ...suddenly the feeling of Louisiana, Missouri. I get 'connection'...

...I feel there was a larger body of water that could be faintly seen on the horizon, but...it wouldn't be that people could stand there and (snaps her fingers) be on the beach.

JONES: **Where were these people before they were here?** (Indicates stones)

DAVIS: Well, I said that man had been there all his life... But then I felt they came from the west, as though coming from the west and south, like coming up from perhaps Mexico, or somewhere that way. I see Louisiana again.

JONES: **Feel like you are going backwards on their route.**

DAVIS: I am in central America. An orientation around a large body of water.

JONES: **What do you mean?**

DAVIS: My first impressions were of a large body of water, and I feel these people would always migrate around a place where there was lots of water.

Renier's reading produced the following comment with regard to her feelings of the target site's location. She never directly indicated a location. Then again, by some interviewing lapse on my part, I never asked her to locate the origin of the test materials.

The water is not that close. I don't think I can go to the water...just go to the water...this big water...everyday, but I feel like I can see it. Maybe I'm too young, but I can see big water in the distance.

Bowes, in a manner very similar to that employed by him in the last experiment, began his discussion of the target location by an indication of a potential location in the southeastern United States. Then, he dropped south as the reading progressed until the last location he indicated was "South America." He also spoke correctly of a "peninsula" location. Again, he was correct in stating that the target area is a "place with underground limestone caves with water."

Davis, too, migrated in her reading from the north to the south, ending with, "I am in Central America." She, like Bowes, felt a proximity to water. More specifically, Davis correctly described the water as "big water" with "beaches" lying to the north. Davis, like Renier who also talked of "this big water," felt that the body of water was close but not immediately accessible. Both Renier and Davis are accurate in their descriptions of the "big waters" proximity.

Environmental Statements

Bowes' general environmental statements included the following:
I kept picking up something about a well, or like a sinkhole, or something that goes down in the water. I kept feeling water way down below.

I keep seeing a coastal area, but then I keep...I keep seeing coastal areas, but then it says 'no.' Coastal areas, then 'no'. I would feel there is water underground in this area.

After I pick this up (A-21), I get a dry countryside.

I felt a lot of dust.

I keep picking up forests and stones, or jungle and stones. Great differences. Not like Florida...I felt like 'jungle and stone' and like 'high and low'...ground.

I see a lot of dust...lot of dust.

They may have been superstitiously afraid of these people because they kept saying they were like pygmies, or short people because they came from the jungle...they came from what they called a 'wild place'.

I would say that food was diminishing. Less, and less, and the ground was getting drier, or the weather was changing.

Davis had these comments about the stones' environment.

Here I am with the mountains and the water. And now I'm feeling pine trees, but I...but there's still not...woodsey... you know, thick...they are, like sparse.

JONES: What does the climate feel like?

DAVIS: Cool. It is not real cold there. I don't see snow, but I get a real crisp effect, like in the fall. I see pine needles, and I see green...and again, there's the water.

There are mountains or hills behind the house, and an occasional pine tree right around the house but the trees are tall.

I felt these were one of the types of animals that would be in the wooded area. It would thrive nearer swampy water, or water that was in a swampy area where there were heavy trees...dampness.

...a lot of water around there was stagnant. That was one of the things I was talking about in terms of the natural killing off of some of the children. They did not know protection from stagnant water.

I sense again a large body of water that was nearby and the fact that I am around what looks like a steep incline, or a mountain, or a cliff or something that's not huge like the Grand Canyon, or anything, but it's...I mean I can see the top of it if I stand and face it. It's not so overpowering that I have to step back from it to see it.

I don't see the sun shining a lot, and I don't see them out in a real clear area. I get this feeling about dampness, and this wall of rock, or whatever it was, and it wasn't impregnable or anything like that.

Renier's impressions concerning the environment:

Let me go up and see the scenery. I don't feel a lot of brush and trees around this area, but I see more tropical trees in the distance.

I feel very deep water underneath the ground. I feel like there

is some running water underneath their ground. Very deep.
Very cool.

I'm getting some scraggly looking bushes and trees. They
look thin and the leaves are flat. It's scraggly...not like big
thick trees. It grows under very unusual conditions.

The comments about deep running water from Bowes and Renier
are echoes in this statement from Stuart and Stuart[30] concerning
Yucatan Mayan sites.

There are no rivers here. But underground, the hidden movement of water has caused great caverns in the porous limestone.

Bowes' reference to "something about a well, or like a sink hole,"
was significant because at the time he made the statement he was
holding the stone from Uxmal, a Mayan city built in proximity to a
cenote, or sinkhole well. Bowes' major impressions of the countryside
associated with the sites was very accurate. It is a dry, dusty land for
the most part. He was also correct when he noted that the citizens
would have been aware of an enemy coming from a jungle environment.

Davis' statements concerning mountains are incorrect. However,
there is a suggestion in her reading that what she was perceiving as
mountains may be the monumental Mayan structures. The reading
segment which may indicate this is the one in which she spoke of the
"steep incline, or a mountain, or a cliff or something" that was "not
huge like the Grand Canyon." As if she were viewing a Mayan pyramid she said, "I mean I can see the top of it if I stand and face it. It's
not so overpowering that I have to step back from it to see it."

Both Renier and Davis independently described an extraordinary
storm. Davis stated:

I feel that some of the children have been killed. When I say
'killed,' I feel there has been a natural disaster.

I see a lot of rain, and I'm back to the natural disaster...the
water. I felt a lot of rain and wind, but I didn't feel hurricane,
or anything like that. I just felt storm and water. I feel a fear
of what would happen to their natural water supply and a
fear of a natural disaster concerning rain or water...

Renier commented at several points about a storm.

JONES: What is the climate and weather like?
RENIER: I saw some storms coming up as you said that.
They would have unusual storms and very strong winds. The
winds are coming from the water...they seem to be sweeping
over a large body of water. I feel like there is a lot of destruction to this land due to weather conditions.

Everytime I pick these things up I feel a very violent storm.
I feel a lot of rain in this storm and I feel that for a long
period of time rain came. I feel water rising, too. I don't
know what all this is.

Again I get 'wind and rain.' Everytime I touch one of these
things I get 'wind and rain.'

Prior to even looking at the still wrapped stones set before her, in
the beginning of her part of this experiment, Renier began to convey
impressions stimulated by the package on the table between us. One
of her first images may relate to what later was developed as the impression of an unusually violent storm.

JONES: **Why don't you open the pieces and look at them?**
RENIER: I won't look at it first. Oh, dear. I have a great
deal of activity of people running around and yelling. Got a
whole bunch of people running around. I see people and they
look like they are panicking. Something unusual, something
very fast must have happened, and it has taken these people
by surprise. They look like they are going in all directions,
and not understanding what is going on. I feel something
very sudden happened. Very fast. Very quick. Some sort of
disaster.
JONES: **What is the nature of the disaster?**
RENIER: I feel like it was...I don't see an enemy. I just see
people running. A good amount of people. I'm not just alone.
I see the sun about half way down near some water here, and
there is higher stuff behind me (makes step-like motion behind to her right).

Von Hagen[31] described a singular event in the Yucatan which may
relate to the storm images experienced and related by Davis and
Renier.

Now only a high brush grows in most of Yucatan, yet there is
evidence, botanical and traditional, that trees, and even
jungles, once flourished there. There is a Maya folk tale—
which might well be pure history—that in 1467 after the fall
of Mayapan, the capital of Coastal Maya, '...during a winter's night about six o'clock there arose a wind, a hurricane...
There followed a great devastation—villages, temples, game,
trees, were all destroyed...and it lasted until noon next day...
there were thousands killed... So much was lost (on that
night) and so much changed,' said Diego de Landa, 'that
even the name of the land disappeared, that land which was
once called 'The Land of the Turkey and the Deer.'

The People

Bowes' impressions of the people who related to the rocks set before
him.

JONES: **What did the people look like who associated with
these rocks?**
BOWES: I feel big round faces. I picked that up very, very...
pronounced. Real round faces, almost like Japanese, or
oriental, but I felt real round looking, and real kind of fatty
face with kind of slit looking eyes. I would say they may
have traveled previously by boat.

JONES: **What do you feel about body decoration?**
BOWES: I don't know if there was something like armor, or
something hanging, but I would feel that they would have
had straps. I felt almost like straps that protected them or
something hanging down. I felt a lot of leather. Very round
faces and very dark skin. I feel whoever was doing that, was
working and there may have been someone else there dictating. I don't know if it was Spanish people, but I would say
there could have been armor or something on them. I see
them carrying things and...I just keep feeling 'piles of
stone.' ...that were dug out of a cave or out of a hole.
JONES: **What does their hair look like?**
BOWES: I felt short, cropped. Not that long.
JONES: **What color was their hair?**
BOWES: I felt black. Indian looking people, or Oriental
looking...people. I can't say beyond that.

...they could have had purple scars on their body.

I would say there could have been slaves involved.
JONES: **Did these people ever see or interact with Caucasian
people?**
BOWES: I would say there was a chance of it, but only at the
last part when these people were living. I would say that
they could be afraid or be very unsettled with people with
light skin.
Renier's description of the people.
JONES: **What do the people look like?**
RENIER: I got a very large mouth on this person, and I see
a lot of teeth. Maybe a little bit protruding...lots of teeth.
Shortness, and broadness in the face itself. Broad features on
this person. I'm seeing a man.
JONES: **What is the hair color?**
RENIER: Dark. Straight. I feel there is something they do
with the hair, and it is something they put in (she is twisting
her hair as she speaks). Maybe a braid of hair around here
(indicates back of her head).
JONES: **Eyes? Nose? Ears? What do they look like?**
RENIER: Let me see the eyes. Dark. I feel intelligence with
this person. Nose...not sticking out. More on the face, but
not spread out all over, though. Oh, that's not defined
enough, I can feel it. Oh, oh, wait a second. There is something with the ear. I don't know if it is like a hole in the ear,
or they do something to the ear. I feel like there is a hole in
my ear.
JONES: **What is this man wearing?**
RENIER: He wasn't wearing much when I looked at him.
Let me check him out again. I see a very strong climber...
more of, like a hill, not trees. More agility around him. I
seem to be focusing on one individual in particular. I feel
something going around him that could be a cape or blanket
...something of warmth. Either a cape or blanket.

JONES: **We still haven't gotten a good description of clothing?**
RENIER: I feel a piece of cloth...longer than it is wide, with designs on it. (Renier indicates with hand movements that this cloth is related to the waist region of the body.)

If I had a voice level I feel it would be a monotonous voice. I feel more monotone voices. What do they look like? I feel the ear, or something on my ear, or something done to my ear. I feel that very strongly. Children...I see designs going on young people.
JONES: **Let's go back to the man you saw.**
RENIER: The first shot I got of him was naked. I don't know if this nakedness is all the time or not. I don't see much hair on his chest.
JONES: **Is he wearing anything on his feet?**
RENIER: Something that comes up around the ankle, and it would tie...I don't see a sandal. I feel more of an over-covering...I feel more covering. More covered. I feel it comes up quite close...low to the ankle in some way.
JONES: **What about from the waist down?**
RENIER: There are things which are hanging from the waist.
JONES: **What are they made of?**
RENIER: Seems like I got some feathers. Little feathers though, not big feathers. And it's got designs and looks intricate...lots of them and they hung down. I see this man outdoors. I see him climbing this (makes step-motion)...this hard thing...I don't know what it is. I feel like he is looking, or watching for other people to come. I feel just watching.
JONES: **Is there any other kind of thing that these people did to their bodies? You have already mentioned something to do with the ear.**
RENIER: I feel this young person would have something done on his body. Might even be painful for a few moments. I felt pain would be inflicted for a few moments with what is being done to his body. I just feel pain on his body. It is something he looks forward to...not hides from.

Davis' reading produced these observations about the target peoples.

There was like a platform of some sort and it wasn't very wide...maybe three feet wide and six feet long. They weren't that tall. Short.

Very weathered people. I have the old man again, and he has some scars, but they were marked. They were identification marks of some sort, or they weren't...they were identification marks. He had some on his body. I'm touching the right shoulder, and then along the shoulder blade. It was like... they were identification marks from some sort of ritual, or something to do with his position.

There is something around his neck. He has got a cape on, and...there is something around his neck of feathers. I don't see a headdress on the head. I see feathers or something as a collar. Something that would force him to put his head up. I see it coming off the shoulders like sleeves. I feel they were created for a special...it is not something you wore very often, or it was not something that was worn that often. It was almost like made for this special occasion.

I feel like this group of people might have infiltrated into a group that was largely and widely known. Eventually set- tling on some reservation or some piece of land. I'm having difficulty with that. Because the group of people I picked up were small, but I feel they are connected to a larger group of people. I get this land that has been set aside, or whatever, is something connected with their culture but I don't feel it is directly their name.

I feel there was like a hierarchy type set-up. Like I get three leaders and then two above them and one above them. A pyramid kind of thing. I get a strong feeling it wasn't one from one group and one from another.
JONES: Who were their enemies?
DAVIS: I get 'other Indians.' Another group. It was some- thing to do about the land.
JONES: Something to do about the land?
DAVIS: Just as I said that I saw cavalry again coming in... horses. I see someone pointing 'go', and these people are walking or being marched away. I feel there was some sort of strife that took place, or some period of time that was very stressful between two different groups of Indians, and then I felt that shifted and they were not...or later they were forced to leave and confined to a certain area.

In describing the people, Bowes noted the "big round faces" and "slit looking eyes," already shown to be valid characterizations of the Maya. He was also right in his impression that the people used armor. In fact, one kind of Mayan armor, involving quilted cotton jackets soaked in salt-brine to make them stiff, was so superior in the humid climate of Mesoamerican that the Spanish borrowed the style to re- place their more cumbersome and less efficient European armor. His mention of "someone else there dictating" and his suggestion of the Spanish presence was also correct. As happened in earlier Mayan ex- periments of the blind and double-blind type, Bowes spoke of "short, cropped" hair that was black in color. He also spoke of slaves. The cropping of the hair of Mayan slaves has been previously described. His comment about the "purple scars on their body" could relate to either tatooing or cosmetic scarification, both of which were common with Mayan peoples.

Renier, too, immediately spoke of short, broadheaded people with dark straight hair. In addition she suggested two traits associated with Mayan hair styles. When talking about the hair of the people she stated, "something to do with hair, and it is something they put in" while at the same time she twisted a portion of her own hair. She next made a motion behind her head and said, "Maybe a braid of hair around here." This passage from Von Hagen[32] touches upon the item that was placed in the hair as well as the braid she described and located.

> The hair was long, black, and lustrous, wrapped around the head, and 'braided like a wreath, leaving the queue to hang down behind like tassels.' Tied to the hair was an obsidian mirror disk, 'All of the men wore mirrors,' but the women wore none...

Renier was also right concerning her several references to mutilation of the ear, a standard cosmetic practice of, particularly, the elites. Her comment about the "cape or blanket" was right. Again Von Hagen[33] writes, "Around their shoulders the Maya wore a covering like a pancho; it was elaborated according to one's life station." The foot covering Renier described is clearly seen in the Bonampak mural figure presented in the beginning of this chapter. Correctly she noted "cloth" and a breech cloth arrangement of the cloth. She also accurately spoke of the decorative use of feathers hanging from the waist. Her reference to "designs going on young people" and the fact that though the "something" was painful, it was not avoided but rather looked forward to may relate to the Mayan atttitude about tatooing.

> 'They tattooed their bodies...'. (which has been confirmed by archeology since quite a few sculptured stone heads show tattooing) 'the designs being pricked in the skin with a sharp bone into which pigment was rubbed, accompanied with great suffering.' For this reason, the more tattoing one had the more one was thought brave and valiant.[34]

Davis noted that the people were relatively short. She related this to a six-foot long platform which she suggested would be taller than the average man. Davis also described tattooing and scarification, and she was correct when she noted that said marks would have "something to do with his position."

Her reference to the "cape" and "feathers...coming off the shoulder like sleeves" relates very specifically to the elaborate featherwork mantas made by the Maya and worn on special ritual occasions. Diego de Landa, who witnessed the Mayan culture, described "the lords of the land (who) went clothed in certain *xicoles* of cotton and feathers woven into a kind of jacket.[35]

Davis accurately described the political organization of the people in her reference to a "pyramid kind of thing." She could be speaking of the Toltec invasion into Mayadom in her noting of a group of people "who infiltrated into a group that was more largely and widely known." The relationship between the Toltec and Mayan civil wars and the coming of the conquering Spanish was also suggested in her final statement about the strife between two Indian groups followed by the "cavalry" which forced the Indians to go.

Another Davis' accuracy related to the Mayan people concerns their love for jade. They valued jade more highly than gold. The topic appeared in this exchange between Davis and me during the experiment.

> JONES: Did their trade have any form of money? Or currency?
>
> DAVIS: When you asked about metal before, the only sensation I got was a crude sensation of metal. Like they could distinguish some sort of metal in rock, and like stone. When you said that I saw a little bag of...or money pouch and there was these little rocks in it.
>
> JONES: What color?
>
> DAVIS: I get green like a malekite or a jade kind of thing that would have little lines through it.

Mayan Monumental Structures

A dramatic culture trait of the Maya is their massive stone and masonry monumental architecture including temples, administrative complexes, cisterns, etc. The following are portions of the readings which seem to indicate the psychics' awareness of this feature of Mayan life.

Bowes had these comments.

> I really don't get much from rocks...I felt piles of stone. I would say there was a structure near there but it would have been abandoned. I felt a lot of dust. I feel the structure was very low, and the doorway was very low, and there was not a top on it. Like it may have been underneath a cave, or...but there may have been a roof of wood, but I felt that all that was left was just the structure. Like the walls were very low. Like white stones down low.
>
> I see them carrying things and...I just keep feeling 'piles of stone'...that were dug out of a cave or out of a hole.
>
> I would say there was something in caves, or something in stone.
>
> I would feel they were digging to extract something that they were using for building materials or they were using to build something.
>
> I don't know if it was like a pyramid or like a stone pile, but I kept picking up them possibly carrying something in a basket...and I see them dumping stones.

Renier's first impressions concerning a man-made structure seems to resemble a cistern.

> As I go underground I feel more...made...man-made. There is water there. It is dark and damp, and...looks like hard stuff, rock or cement on the top, and this water is going through this area.

Many times during her reading, Renier would refer to "high" things "going up," usually behind her, and she would make a step-like motion with her hand. When I asked her if she could be more specific about that impression she said:

I felt height, but I felt very hard, a little bit of dirt, and hardness going up. Might be like caves in this place, caves going in. Caves might lead down into where the water is underneath. Caves. Wideness. Lowness. Caves.

Davis never directly identified the massive Mayan stone buildings, but she did continually relate to behavior around a large pile of rocks. For example:

I am suddenly around big rocks. I'm with a man. I feel an Indian. I feel him on these rocks and there is some connection with this community.

I feel they would stay with the (dead) body. Somebody would guard the body while the person went out of the body. They let the body sit. It was up on a high place, and it went through a decaying process.

I see a platform like in the movies, except this is on a rock. Remember those rocks I was talking about? Well, this is with those rocks...and I saw this chipped stuff and it might have been the way these rocks were formed...down around here (base of rocks). Little pieces of stuff.

This young fellow I felt was watching over someone's body. It was like a relatively high place, but it wasn't the highest point on these rocks.

I'm looking up at...more rocks. I am removed from those other rocks though I am looking up at them.

I am very conscious of this cliff-like wall that I have been talking about with the rocks, and then this spot below it... it's like an area of land within a protective setting. It's like a wall.

I can't understand why the women aren't there. I feel this area I've talked about was used but mostly by men, and I want to go behind these rocks...this wall of rock, or whatever it was, and it wasn't like it was impregnable or anything like that.

Religion

Bowes' reading concerning the religion of the target site people. They could have beheaded a girl, or taken a virgin, or taken someone's head off, but I felt it was a young child. Especially if it was like an albino child, or someone very light skinned. I felt they were afraid of that. Felt people with dark skin had power.

JONES: What was the single most important religious ceremony in which these people would become involved?

BOWES: I would say it was something on top of this

mountain or hill, and it could be like a cross or like something sticking up in the air. I kept feeling like they would climb up this thing...I would say it was at a certain time of the moon, or like it was a full moon or at a special time of the season, and I would say it was religious significance to animals or food, and to them it was the most important thing because of the value of eating. Again they may have actually looked at the stars, or moon, or the sky.

They may not have had a crucifix but they had some sort of thing that stuck in the ground and they may have hung a person on it or there was something in the air.

These are Renier's statements on the religion of the people associated with the stones.

RENIER: There is more than one god.

JONES: **What are the characteristics of these gods?**

RENIER: These gods...there is either a statue or some symbolic thing that they pray to, or give to...maybe even giving sacrifices, offerings, or food. I feel they moved something to look like a god.

JONES: **What does the god look like?**

RENIER: He is scary-looking. He's big and I feel stone. He has a big nose...flat nose. A mouth that is closed. I feel something about his hands (she puts her hands together with palms up at the waist as if to receive something)...I feel the hands are open and there is an indentation about the waist, or around this area (indicates waist). I feel this is a statue or a thing of stone. I feel stone with this.

Oh, this is interesting. I feel more like a heart, and it looks like death. What are they cutting out! Oh, Lord!

JONES: **What are you seeing?**

RENIER: They got to cut out the enemy heart or liver...I don't know which it is but I feel it is very important. It's the heart. It's so the enemy...for this man I've killed...like a soul...I don't know, David, I'm getting confused. I just see them cutting something out.

It is interesting that Bowes, who had described the sacrifice of an albino youth in an earlier experiment dealing with photographs from Chichen Itza, should months later and under double-blind conditions describe again the killing of "an albino child" while touching A-5, the only stone in the test collection from Chichen Itza. Also fascinating is the fact that Bowes, while "unknowingly" touching the stone from Chichen Itza, spoke of "crosses" and "crucifix" images, though not associating those symbols with the obvious Christian referent. Chichen Itza was heavily influenced by the cult of Kulkulcan introduced by the Toltecs. One of the major symbols of Kulkulcan was the cross. The cross symbol associated with Kulkulcan, or Quetzacoatl as the Toltec called him was one of the reasons why Montezuma II did not resist Cortez when he arrived carrying banners and wearing in-

signia showing the cross. Montezuma II assumed Cortez was a god—
Quetzalcoatl returned.

Bowes was correct when speaking about worship occurring in
association with a high place and focusing on "the stars, the moon, or
the sky." His references about "a crucifix," or "some sort of thing
stuck in the ground" from which a man was affixed, may relate to one
of the main forms of Mayan sacrifice. Von Hagen[37] states:

> If he was to be sacrificed by the arrow ceremony, he was tied
> in crucifix fashion to a wooden frame high off the ground, and
> they 'danced a solemn dance about him.' ...Then at a given
> signal the dancers one by one as they came in front of him,
> released their arrows; 'in this way they made his whole chest
> look like a hedgehog of arrows.'

Renier's reading on religion hit several significant points. The
"scary-looking" stone statue of a god with a "flat nose" and "a
mouth that is closed" holding its hands together, palms up, at the
waist and related to sacrifice is none other than Chac Mool, the recip-
ient of the human heart during the Toltec-inspired human sacrifices.
Renier, in fact, described the cutting out of the heart. Both the Chac
Mool and the human sacrifices based on the removal of the heart are
almost diagnostically Mayan-Toltec in nature.

Davis never specifically identified key religious behavior, but she
did make a series of accurate observations of typical Mayan religious
traits. For example, when I asked her to signify an important religious symbol of the target people, she said, "O.K. I just got a circle
and I got the word 'tree,' and I feel a design in a little circle that was
like a tree." At another point she stated:

> When you asked about religion I felt that this symbol is
> somehow used with the death process...or was looked upon
> about life. I feel like 'tree of life.'

In writing about Mayan religious beliefs, Stuart and Stuart[38] note:

> In the very center of the earth stood the Tree of Life, the
> *ceiba.* Its roots reached into the Underworld, and its towering
> foliage brushed the heavens.

Davis' very accurate statement about the "tree of life" included her
feeling that the symbol was involved with the "death process." She
was correct again. Von Hagen[39] writes:

> The Maya believed in immortality and a form of heaven and
> hell. Those who kept the rituals, that is, 'the good,' went to a
> place shaded by 'the first tree of the world'...

The Mayan custom of ritual bleeding was described earlier in this
chapter. In Davis' reading she stated:

> And then I got the word 'bleeding' as though at one point
> there is something to do with bleeding...bleeding to purify
> the soul, and where the body is cut. I feel that could be possi-
> bly the one on the shoulder. That one is not clear to me. I feel
> the process of purification.

When I asked Davis what the major content of mythology would be
for the target people she responded:

I felt they would talk about...sensation like a lion...it was a
cat. Stories having to do with hunters. And I think there was
stories about birds. I feel a story about fire, a hunter, and a
cat, or an animal of some sort that was the size of a mountain
lion. I felt a lot of images had to do with animals or man...
they didn't deal a lot with...you know, about plants or
terrain.

Her image of "an animal of some sort that was the size of a mountain
lion" in response to my inquiry on religious mythology may be accounted for by this statement from Adams.[40]

The most powerful animal known to the Maya, the jaguar,
was also regarded as divine. The jaguar's skin was a symbol
of a king's divine status.

Davis' feeling that religious images had mainly to do with "animals
and man" and not much to do with "plants and terrain" is absolutely
correct. Indeed, Mayan scholars have always been puzzled by the fact
that an often jungle-dwelling, horticultural people would pay so little
attention to botanical motifs in the thousands of carvings and mural
paintings they left behind. As Davis stated, almost all Mayan art
dealt with animals and human subjects.

Davis may also have been responding to the smell of copal incense
in her reading. The Maya used copal incense, a sweet smelling resin, in
all state and religious ceremonial functions. Davis reported:

They are sitting around a fire. The fire is smoky. It's not...
it's not burning, it's like...smoky burn. There is some
smoke that is also important to the group.

...a man sitting by the fire...when I said the fire was
smoking. I feel it is applied to the fire and then as if the fire
smokes. I don't know...somehow, the fire would produce
the smoke.

Renier also may have been responding to the ever-present burning
copal incense. Her copal-like images include the following:

I'm getting a lot of burning.

I'm getting a burning sensation...I almost smell burning. I
don't know what I'm smelling.

JONES: What are you smelling? (She is sniffing the air constantly at this point)

RENIER: I felt like leaves and wood and natural things are
burning.

JONES: The man dressed in the 'strange way,' what is he
going to do?

RENIER: I think he is going to take care of his spirit or his
soul, and I think this is why I'm smelling things because he
is putting stuff in the fire to make things smell a color.

JONES: A color?

RENIER: Yeah. I feel things went in the fire and small
clouds would poof up. Looks like a lot of theatrics to me, but
I don't know. I shouldn't say that. I don't know.

They smoke. They smoke something. I feel smoke inside this man's lungs, and I don't think it is like a cigarette, but there is some form of inhalation of something that would be smoky.

Diet

My question concerning diet and subsistence patterns brought the following responses. Bowes conveyed only one impression about subsistence.

I don't see them growing things...right where that was at (A-21)...somewhere else they may have grown things.

Of course, A-21 was taken from downtown Uxmal, and it is doubtful that any farming took place there. The Maya of Uxmal, naturally grew things "somewhere else".

Davis offered no information about diet, nor was she asked to. Renier had the most to say of the three on the subject of food habits and subsistence behavior.

JONES: What does he eat?
RENIER: I feel something dried. I feel they must have knowledge of how to dry things because I feel something dried. I feel that some of it is meat. There are also some fields out around there that are being cultivated...I see some fields around there that...small fields. Small farm or garden. Oh, I'm picking up the dirt and I'm dropping it again. It is not good dirt. Not rich. I'm feeling more like sand to...just falls through my fingers dead-like. Needs rain, or something. It just doesn't look good. It's got more gray than black or yellow.
JONES: What is in the garden?
RENIER: Berries, whatever it is, it doesn't grow very good.
JONES: Is it big or little?
RENIER: When I first saw it I saw tall plants growing. Now I get close and it seems things are withered up and dried, and close to the ground.

I feel a lot of grain going into my stomach.

The Maya knew how to preserve their corn by drying it and keeping it in underground storage bins. Further, as Renier noted, the Maya did farm "small fields" called *milpa*, and families also had private gardens. The "berries" she mentioned may be corn. This possibility is enhanced when she described seeing tall plants associated with things that "were close to the ground." The Mayan custom was to plant squash and pumpkin on the ground intermixed with their corn.

Domestic Animals

It is assumed that the only truly domestic animals that the Maya possessed were dogs and Muscovy ducks. It is also reported that they had a semi-domesticated deer, as well as semi-wild bees. They made pets of a variety of wild animals. Bowes had one comment to make concerning the question I asked about the presence or absence of domesticated animals.

> I felt like sheep or an animal that had long hair. Could have been like a pig. I felt they caught it and tied it by its back legs. It could have been like a sheep or a pig, or an animal with long fur on its body...on its back especially. I picked up 'goat' to start with.

Davis' one impression concerning animals that associated with the target people was this:

> I keep picking up dogs. Something about the importance of dogs. They used dogs.
> JONES: Used dogs?
> DAVIS: Yes. I feel like watch dogs, like hunting dogs. I feel like they would keep dogs around them.

Renier's comments about animals are as follows:

> JONES: Did these people have, or did they not have, domestic animals?
> RENIER: As you said that I got a long-legged, it's not that high...it looks like it has long legs and medium-sized body. I don't know if it's a dog or a goat or what. It looks sort of scraggly. I don't know what that thing is. Got sort of long hair instead of short hair.
> JONES: How long?
> RENIER: Medium long. I can see something from the stomach area. As I'm looking at the animal I see the long legs and I see about this much hair (three to five inches).
> JONES: Do you see horses here? (touches stone)
> RENIER: Not now (touches stone)...not at this time (touches stone again.)
> JONES: What about cattle?
> RENIER: Maybe more to the south. There are small herds of ...I don't think we would call it a cow. It looks like a small... you use a stick to keep them in order. They don't look like cows that I know about...if it is a cow. Small quantities of them. I feel like these animals could almost be domesticated.

Bowes' and Renier's impressions are remarkably similar. Bowes had described a similar animal in earlier Mayan experiments. It sounds as if both Bowes and Renier were perhaps describing a llama. Maybe the "long legged" goat-sized creature was the semi-domesticated deer referred to in the early Spanish accounts of the Maya.

Davis was correct when she noted the presence of dogs, as was Renier when she rightly denied that the target people possessed the horse.

Metal and Writing

The Maya are famous for their glyph system of writing. Metallurgy was apparently unknown to them although they did possess hammered gold ornaments. The question concerning metal is of course archeologically important in dating a people and in characterizing their culture. These are the responses received from Bowes, Davis, and Renier when I asked questions concerning writing and metallurgy.

I asked Bowes if the target people possessed a written language. He replied:

> I would say they had...not a written language, but sort of a symbolic thing that were added together. Now I picked up a tablet with writing on it so I would say they had something like a written language.

At another point I asked Bowes about the presence of metal and he said, "I didn't see that." Likewise with Davis. When I asked her about metal she said, "I'm not feeling any."

When I touched the stones and asked Renier, "Did these people write their language?" She responded, "There was some things...they looked more like designs than words to me...not like the English language." I neglected to question Renier concerning her impressions about the presence or absence of metal.

Dating of the Site

Bowes' reading with regard to the dating of the target materials:

> JONES: About what time did these people live here? (touches stones)
> BOWES: I picked up '14' or '1400' or '14,000' or '14-something'. I picked up people who were migrating from South America to the north and something was happening in Italy. A change in 'owners', I say, but I don't know what it means. At the time these people (touches stones) were alive, the people in power were changing in Italy, or the Mediterranean Sea at that time.

These were Davis' comments with regard to dating.

> JONES: At the time these people were vital, what other kinds of things were happening in the world?
> DAVIS: I get the feeling of Italy. I get the word 'Magellan.' I have no concept of time with that. Then I saw these people pushing and I saw this cavalry kind of. The association with Italy is I see a man with a telescope. I feel a lot of things happening in Italian history. In and about Rome, but not way back. I see blossomy type clothing with a beret type hat.

Renier's only "date" response was a passing comment that the target people had only recently seen "some sort of guns" along the coast with a strange group of people.

Bowes' emphasis on "changes in Italy" correlates best with his date of "1400". Renier's date would fall in the early 1500s. Davis' reference to Magellan is easy enough to date. Ferdinand Magellan was born ca. 1480 and died in 1521. The "man with a telescope" associated with Italy could be Galileo, of course (1564-1642).

The dates are too late for the specific target sites. Chichen Itza was founded three times—432, 964, and 1185. Kabah was established in 879, and Uxmal was built around 900 A.D. However, the psychics' dates do fall in the upper Mayan period, and it is true that the Mayan culture would have been alive during the time of Magellan and Galileo, as Davis suggested.

Double-Blind Features of the Fourth Experiment

As mentioned at the outset of this experiment, there was a double-blind aspect of this test. The specific Mayan locations were not revealed to me. Would the psychics be able to not only locate generally and describe the target people, but would they also be capable of offering specific information related to the individual cities?

When Renier touched the piece of stone taken from the road at Kabah she said:

> O.K. I'm getting a foot. I don't know why I'm getting a foot, and a big toe. I just see a foot and a big toe. Must mean something.

Bowes' reaction to A-5, the rock from Chichen Itza, offered the best set of specifics about one of the test cities. It was in association with this rock that Bowes again described the killing of an albino child, as he had done earlier while looking at a photograph of the *cenote* at Chichen Itza. At no other time in any experiment did Bowes speak of albino children except in relationship to Chichen Itza materials. Further, at the time he dealt with those materials, he had no way of knowing their origins.

It was also at Chichen Itza that the Toltec quickly established the cult of Kulkulcan, Bowes touched A-5 and said, "I would say there was, not like a Christian religion, but some sort of certain religion that was pushed on them by another group." Toward the end of his reading, while handling A-5, the subject of sinkholes came up. Not only did Bowes allude to the Chichen Itza *cenote* again, but also to the fact that artifacts were to be found in the sinkhole.

> They could find a lot more about these people in caves or... like sinkholes. I would feel there is a lot of evidence in sinkholes. I would say that they (archeologists) are missing out on the most valuable things. There could be like a hole and down below is water. And below that is grey sand or clay, and if they took a pump and took that out of there, used wellpoints, they could get numerous...I felt the layers were like this...like a sinkhole...down in the bottom there is a layer of real soft mud, and clay, grey clay...and then down below is silt and sand and dirt and then down here there is rock, and then gravel, and just above the gravel is all kinds of artifacts. All kinds.
> JONES: What kinds of things?
> BOWES: Jewels. Pottery. Things. This (top of sinkhole)

could be real sharp or almost closed in, with just a little opening showing, or it could be like sunken-in. It settled in one place. Does this make any sense? There is much more stuff down there.

Kulkulcan

The story of Kulkulcan begins in the early 900s. At that time, the priest-ruler of the Toltec at the capital city of Tula, north of Mexico City, was Quetzalcoatl, son of Mixcoatl, conqueror of the Valley of Mexico, destroyer of Teotihuacan, and founder of the Classic Toltec dynasty of central Mexico. Quetzalcoatl inherited his father's domain and ruled until sometime between 987 and 999 A.D. when he was forced to flee his capital due to internal strife in the city. With groups of his followers, he moved to the Veracruz coastal area. He stayed there for a while and then disappeared, being last heard of moving east. At that time, Kulkulcan appeared at Chichen Itza. "Quetzalcoatl" means "feathered serpent" in the Toltec language. "Kulkulcan" means the same thing in the Mayan language. By the time Quetzalcoatl appeared in the Yucatan he was thoroughly deified.

This tale may or may not be history. Certain authorities accept it as generally correct while others describe the "invasion" of the Toltec as being more like a slow leak as opposed to a sudden flood lead by the great Quetzalcoatl. The story remains, however, and it seems to have appeared in the readings of the psychics.

In a discussion of political organization, Davis remarked:
I get this old man, and he is very important and I feel this old man is famous and written about or something. He was known for his contributions.
JONES: Do you feel this famous old man would be an identifying characteristic of these people? This leader would be known?
BOWES: Yes. There is something around his neck. He has got a cape on, and...there's something around his neck of feathers.

It is another aspect of the double-blind feature of this test that Bowes, while handling the stone from Chichen Itza, began talking about an invading group led by a man who was considered, "almost like a god," who worshipped on high places.

JONES: What is the religious inclination of these people?
BOWES: They may have had an established religion or idea. I would say they talked about the skies or weather and I felt it was part of their religion. I would feel they had an association with water or when it rained, or weather. I would say there was, not like a Christian religion, but some sort of certain religion that was pushed on them by another group. I kept seeing a very heavy set person who was very dark skinned. I see him being a leader or someone who they felt

was almost like a god. I feel like they actually worshipped other people, like they may have worshipped the leader of the group after...like a king or a god. The biggest man. The biggest man. I felt he was very dark skinned. Almost like a Black man, but not quite. I keep feeling as though he lived in the mountains or worshipped in the mountains. He lived in the mountains...or up high.

JONES: **What did the people feel the characteristics of this man were?**

BOWES: I felt a man like this (he raised his arms and held them horizontal to his shoulder at his sides with the forearms bent at ninety-degree angles pointing directly up)...his arms like pipes or out like this. I see them putting this man aside from everyone else.

JONES: **Did this man...**

BOWES: I keep seeing him doing like this (posture described above) to the sky and talking to the weather, or to the sky, I would say that they really felt he had results...I felt like he would go to the mountains, like that was where he worshipped, or like going up high. It may not have been so much a mountain, but there may have been something built that was like a hill, but I felt 'up high'.

A possible "Kulkulcan" response came from Renier in the following response to my question about supernaturals.

JONES: **What about some of the other gods they worshipped? You mentioned 'gods'?**

RENIER: Oh, dammit! They had this one leader, but he is very ferocious and he wears a lot of things on his head. I feel some ferociousness as his character trait.

Conclusion: Fourth Mayan Experiment

The impact of this experiment may be difficult to appreciate since so much Mayan material has preceded it in this chapter. Remember, however, that those five nondescript stones could just as easily have come from an Eskimo site in Greenland, or a Bedouin site in Yemen, or a Papuan site in highland New Guinea. Again, the psychics showed the ability to describe cultural patterns, historical sequences and environment, and to date the target site accurately within the time-span of the target culture's existence.

References

1. G.E. Stuart, and G.S. Stuart, "The Mysterious Maya", in *National Geographic Society* Special Publication, 1977.
2. Victor von Hagen, *World of the Maya* (New York: New American Library, 1960), p.25.$
3. Allyn Stearman, *Personal Communication* (Orlando, Florida: 1978).
4. von Hagen, *World of Maya*, p.192.
5. Stuart and Stuart, "Mysterious Maya", p. 98.
6. Stearman, *Personal Communication.*
7. Edward Herbert Thompson, in *Gods, Graves and Scholars*, C.W. Ceram (New York: Alfred A. Knopf, 1959), p.386.
8. von Hagen, *World of Maya*, p. 109.
9. Stuart and Stuart, "Mysterious Maya", p.530.
10. von Hagen, *World of Maya*, p.125.
11. Thompson, in *Gods, Graves and Scholars*, pp.381-382.
12. Ceram, *Gods, Graves and Scholars*, p.389.
13. von Hagen, *World of Maya*, p.190.
14. Stuart and Stuart, "Mysterious Maya", p.50.
15. Stearman, *Personal Communication.*
16. von Hagen, *World of Maya*, p.138.
17. *Ibid.*, p.163-164.
18. R.F. Spencer et al., *The Native Americans*, second ed. (New York: Harper & Row, 1977), p.460.
19. J. Eric Thompson, *Maya History and Religion* (Norman: University of Oklahoma Press, 1970), p.152.
20. von Hagen, *World of Maya*, p.32.
21. *Ibid.*, p.38.
22. Richard E.W. Adams, *The Civilization of the Ancient Maya and Its Collapse* (Norwalk: Reading Laboratory, 1974).
23. Stuart and Stuart, "Mysterious Maya", p.56.
24. von Hagen, *World of Maya*, p.38.
25. Thompson, *Maya History and Religion*, p.179.
26. *Ibid.*, p.109.
27. von Hagen, *World of Maya*, p.91.
28. *Ibid.*, p.38.
29. Stuart and Stuart, "Mysterious Maya", p.94.
30. *Ibid.*, p.94
31. von Hagen, *World of Maya*, p.23.
32. *Ibid.*, p.38.
33. *Ibid.*, p.40.
34. *Ibid.*, p.38.
35. *Ibid.*, p.76.
36. Ignacio Bernal, *Mexico Before Cortez: Art, History and Legend* (New York: Doubleday & Co., 1963), p.66.
37. von Hagen, *World of Maya*, p.137.
38. Stuart and Stuart, "Mysterious Maya", p.54.
39. von Hagen, *World of Maya*, p.110.
40. Adams, *Civilization of Ancient Maya.*

VIII

SUMMARY

"Experimenting...
I hung the moon
on various
branches of the pine."

-Hokushi

Originally the heading "Conclusion" set at the top of this page. But as I worked on the body of this section, I became uncomfortable with the chapter heading and changed it to "Summary." That apparently insignificant change, however, expressed more accurately the attitude I had concerning the assembled results of my many experiments with Bowes, Davis, Niren, and Renier. I do not feel that these experimental findings warrant conclusion or some claim as final proof. It is my intention that they be considered exploratory in nature, roughly hewn suggestions of what may or may not, upon closer and more minute scrutiny, prove to be an important contribution to the methods and techniques of the many scholarly disciplines which focus on human behavior in time. My wish is that these spare experiment-suggestions stimulate the "closer and more minute scrutiny" of which I speak.

With the perogative of the explorer, I arbitrarily selected a number of positions from which to evaluate and present my findings. I stressed the subjects' accuracy, but at the same time I printed the transcripts of the experiments so that the nature and rate of inaccuracy would also be recorded. I selected an Applied as opposed to a Theoretical research orientation. I was not specifically interested in *how* Bowes, Davis, Niren, and Renier did what they did. I was most concerned with the fact *that* they did what they did. Neither was I oriented to develop my own notions of the "how" of the behavior recorded here. My aim was always to conceive and design experimental situations that would in some way suggest parallel applications specifically in the field of archeology. I also, in like manner, attempted to recreate the atmosphere of relationship between an archeologist and a psychic colleague. By this I mean that I was nonchallenging to my research subjects and attempted in every way to help them do what I had asked them to do, within, of course, the parameters of the experimental environment and its controls. However, I also endeavored to remain critically aware and to anticipate certain types of criticism about the various tests.

252

These experiments suggest that psychics can, with better than average results (as established by control group response), convey valid information about objects masked from their view, even under double-blind conditions (Chapter II); locate archeological sites and reconstruct physical, cultural, and historical environments by means of the psychometry of artifacts (Chapters III, IV & VII); describe artifactual materials buried in a site prior to its excavation (Chapter IV); locate a site and describe its cultural experience by viewing photographs of the target site (Chapters IV & VII); identify, locate and describe in rich detail the cultural context of an artifact simply by scanning a photograph of it (Chapters V & VII); identify now-extinct animals from bones over ten million years old (Chapter VI); identify the physical, cultural, and historical context of monumental structures from viewing non-diagnostic photographs of the structures (Chapter VII); and relay accurate identifying information about a cultural situation by handling non-diagnostic rubble from the particular site (Chapters IV & VII).

I know that there will be some who will believe almost everything said by a psychic simply because a psychic said it, and that there will be some who will accept nothing a psychic says simply because a psychic says it. Both positions are unwisely extreme. An overly quick move to embrace a psychic explanation for some event leaves one open to the unknown error factor that good psychics will admit, and also seduces that individual to abandon perfectly sound conventional and rationalistic life-managing techniques. The immediate and absolute leap to the psychic conclusion is often simply an unrecognized abdication of responsibility. On the other extreme, those who blindly deny the psychic hypothesis seem foolishly enslaved by the undefendable position that a particular notion of space/time/cause, prevalent now, is in some magical way a once-and-for-all explanation of the way things are. A study of the history of science would do wonders toward softening up that position.

I would like the reader of this work to remain free and critical in evaluating the experiments reported here. Read the total transcript of the session. Note the context of the apparent accuracies and inaccuracies. Be alert to possible inadvertent "leading" in my questioning. Consider other ways that the results might be obtained or explained. Ponder the method and approach I used in presenting the materials. Look at the total picture suggested by the entire range of tests, but also closely observe each claim for accuracy and relevance. It is dangerous and inefficient to too readily accept or deny what these experiments may indicate.

I have always been charmed by Sir Isaac Newton's simple and unpretentious preamble to the "Theory of Gravitation" presented before the Royal Society. I offer it in conclusion. In one sentence, Newton said all that a researcher can ever really hope to say about his or her work: "I beg leave to present to you the results of certain experiments for your contemplation."

APPENDICES

Herein is included the transcribed tapes of all relevant experimental sessions. If the transcript does not appear here, it means that the entire transcription was utilized in a particular chapter. This would be true, for example, for the reading of the Folsom materials in Chapter III.

Appendix A—Chapter II

First Experiment, Part I: Objects Wrapped and Boxed.
Double-Blind Reading by Albert Bowes.

Toy Combs [Boston, Mass.]

The first thing I picked up in relationship to Number One was, I see a pin or a long...something almost like a tooth-pick. It may have been a bone. But I kept seeing something that was long and thin and skinny. I keep seeing an object that may have almost been like a comb or it may have had something like a...it could have been bone...like a fish's rib or...it could have been like a comb that was in somebody's hair or that was used as an ornament or maybe it was like something they blew through or. I don't know what it is but I kept seeing that in connection with...I keep seeing a woman or a man with long black hair and I feel as though it was very...extremely oily or it could have been an Indian. I don't know what location it would be. I keep seeing some sand and some beaches or some sand. This could have been desert or the beach but I kept feeling as though that it was something in relationship to...I wouldn't feel that the people were very educated. O.K.? I didn't pick up very much about that.

Crocheted Hair Ribbon [Gainesville, Fla.]

I picked up a different vibration from this. I kept picking up something that was related to something square. It may have been almost like jewelry or it could have been something that was like a ring or something that was put on someone's finger or hand. I keep seeing a man shouting and I would feel that it pertained to a war or it pertained to something that would associate with someone who was impatient or became angry. I see cliffs or rocks and I see the shoreline as if that is very high...like high ground. It could have pertained to, like South America or it could have been like in Italy or...Europe, or in a place where there was people who...I keep seeing them traveling. I keep seeing this shoreline or cliffs...like it dropped straight off. I see grass on the tops... like grass fields where they had animals that they brought along on caravans or groups of animals in relationship to grazing. And then I see this straight drop-off...very steep rocks. I don't know if there is...I kept picking up that and then I felt as though there may be something to do with Number One (the first artifact in experiment), but I felt as though it was associated with Indians in Florida or in a place that was very wet...swampy.

Sioux Child's Burial Moccasin [Northern Plains]

(Bowes appears to be upset)
BOWES: Could you turn that off a minute (referring to tape recorder)?
JONES: Sure (Discussion follows concerning Bowes' reaction to this box).
   (Tape Running Again)
JONES: You said that you didn't think Number Three was very old?
BOWES: I felt that there was something wrong here. I didn't understand what it meant. I kept seeing that...like it was a part of something else. But I kept seeing a long tube almost like something that somebody would look through, or like it could have been a bracelet or it could have been something round. I see a man who is trying to commercialize on something. I didn't know what it meant but I felt as though this may pertain to something that somebody was doing previous to the actual value of this merchandise. I really don't understand what it means. I'm sorry. I wish I could give you more about that.

Antique Baseball [Atlanta, Ga.]

This is very strange. I get a completely different feeling from this. I keep seeing teeth and pottery. I keep seeing something that would pertain to a game, and I don't know if it's like a ball, or...like some sort of sport of some kind. I keep seeing somebody talking or little groups of people watching each other or watching...almost like they have have been...it could have pertained to people like the Incas or people in South America or in association with a game that they played. I keep seeing a man with a scar on his face or like his cheek-bone or his jaw or something is broken or crushed. I kept seeing something that was associated with...it could have even been like Egypt, or it could have been a place like where there was a mummy or something buried, but I kept seeing caves and rocks...and it could have been like inside a building or inside a cave or inside a pyramid. I felt as though there was maybe one supreme ruler. One person who thought very little of human life...and that's the feeling I had. I seen bones and teeth like tops of the teeth or jaws or bones.

Human Cervical Vertebrae [St. Simon's Island, Ga.]

I don't know why but I felt something was broken here, and I don't know why but I kept seeing something almost like it was a bone or something that was crushed or broken. I see people running, and I keep feeling as though there was a disaster or that they were afraid of something. I didn't know if this pertains to something that was a long, long time ago, like maybe when there was mammoths or...in the past. But I keep seeing groups of people and they may have been afraid of volcanic action or like tidal waves or...I keep seeing disease or something that would...a little bit superstitious. I'm really not able to pick up as much as I could I could hold the object itself. This is a little confusing. I do feel disease...like groups of people died or they were superstitious or afraid of something about disease.

Seminole Medicine Bag [Florida]

First thing I picked up was something about jewelry. I felt as though this may have been kept inside a house or kept by someone for a period of time. I keep seeing an older woman or I see a china cabinet or a...almost as if it was a cabinet...it was behind glass. This could be teeth or something pertaining to a bone or like an artifact or something...I keep seeing a little thing that was like a piece of brass..or like it was a leaf, or about the size of your fingernail...and I see something that may have been chipped or flaked off or it may have almost been like an emblem of some kind. That's what I picked up. O.K? I don't know what it means. I would feel that it was very small.

Stone Hoe [Georgia]

I felt that this was very heavy. I don't know if this was made of brass. I keep seeing someone sitting it up and I kept feeling like there was a man who made this...and I see him studying it and I felt as though he had a very sunken face or he was a person who may have been very thin. I kept seeing a face and I kept seeing this face almost like it had a beard on it or it could have been like an emblem on the hood of a car or it was something like an animal or something ready to jump or a facing-out of something. I didn't know what it meant. I did feel as though that whoever made it had a lot of pride in what they made. I keep seeing a stone or a stone hatchet or something somebody was using to cut something with. I don't know how this associated with it but I kept seeing somebody of the early...like early pioneer days or something associated with what I would say would be digging or a hatchet or a maddox or something, but I kept seeing somebody digging. I would feel that there were farm people or somebody who was digging canals or making drainage...and that's what I picked up.

Contemporary Carved Chalk Pieces [Orlando, Fla.]

I would say that Number Eight is associated with a bone or associated with something that was...I keep seeing something and the first symbolic feeling I had was a cannibal or somebody who ate other people or other...could have ate other animals or other people, but I keep seeing them...(pause). I don't know why but I would feel that it could be associated with something that bent or a knuckle or a hand or something that was...I see a joint of some sort. I don't know why but I kept seeing that and then I see something that was almost like a...I see somebody in a uniform or wearing something that was like a clip and I kept feeling as though it was a clip that slid down into a pocket or something that I felt like it could have been somebody like a Spaniard or someone like a cavalry person or someone who shot Indians or shot someone. I keep seeing them thinking very little of the people they were shooting...but I see somebody running away. I kept seeing somebody who lived in the water or lived around where there was a swamp or where there was a place they traveled by water or where they traveled like by canals. And I feel like the countryside or where they come from was very, very different than it is now.

Seminole Weaving Heddle [Florida]

Something I picked up here was almost like it was a picture of someone. I keep seeing like a very, very old...like an old photograph or something that was...as if it was a family heirloom or it was handed down from one to another. I keep seeing someone who...I don't know if this was from another country but I feel that whoever owned it would have been aggravated or mad because these people owned it.
JONES: The people who own it now?
BOWES: Yes...or like they wouldn't want the people, possibly in this country, or like they may not have had much respect for a Caucasian person or that they may not have wanted somebody...this could have been in someone's grave or it could have been like an heirloom or an antique of some sort. I see something that pertained to like gun powder or some sort of powder or something that someone would throw in a fire. I keep seeing it go "poof", or a very large...almost like an explosion. Once again it could apply to an old photograph...like during the Civil War or during that period of time. And I see them holding this trough up and I see them lighting this trough and I felt like when they lit this trough this exploded or like powder exploded and it took a picture ...but I kept seeing that. O.K.?

Pine Needle Basket [Florida]

This is very strange. I keep seeing something in the ground, and I keep seeing like round or square holes in the ground and I see them picking at it, almost like they got little...like a little hook or like a little shovel...something ...they keep picking at it...and it could be like an Indian or somebody in a grave or somebody laying there and it could apply to archeologist or somebody digging out somebody in clay or in volcanic rock. I felt as though they were encased in this rock or maybe it was like a volcano...like lava or something, or like rocks but I see, actually the bones are like protruding in the rock. With this...(pause)...I keep seeing people with beads around their neck...or like silk or layers of clothing. I would feel that this would be royalty or something of value...like silk and it could have been from China or India or from another country.

FIRST EXPERIMENT, PART II: OBJECTS UNWRAPPED.
BLIND READING BY ALBERT BOWES

Stone Hoe (Georgia)

In relationship to this I keep seeing the north. I keep seeing a very big man. I kept feeling as though he was someone who...I see him very boisterous. I keep seeing very hard rocks, and I don't know if he traveled south or related to ...I keep seeing clay and I keep seeing, like that they're moving south. I keep seeing a man who hunted or traveled near water. There may have been a lot of swamps or water...I keep seeing the ground sloping off. I don't know if this was a tomahawk or if it was a huge spear but I do feel as though it was thrown. I don't know if this pointed end was more pointed at one time but I feel it was buried in the mud...buried at some time. I do see a man with very wide shoulders, and I feel he would be very strong through the chest, and I feel as though he was a person who might have been very stubborn or hard to deal with. I keep seeing a relationship to a wagon so it may pertain to something that was at a time when people were traveling, or it could have been in the early west times. I keep seeing a spring and I keep seeing something thrown into the spring...thrown into this water, and I would feel that there was religious background to this spring or water. It could have been like a lake, or it could have been a spring where there was a round area there, but I would feel that they felt youth with this or something to do with medicine or...something to do with water. I don't know if this has ever been in Florida, but I do see pottery buried with this. I feel that if this was in Florida...no, it came from another state or another area.

JONES: **What do you feel about the people who made that...like their life. Do you have feelings about what kind of food they ate or how they made a living?**

BOWES: I feel as though the man...I keep seeing one man separated from the others. I keep feeling as though he was a hunter and a trader. I keep seeing buildings or little grass shacks or little shacks up off the ground. I keep seeing something like...like little tipis or some sort of a round building up on stakes. I don't know if this came from northwestern Florida, or whether it came from west of there, but I keep seeing west, and I keep seeing this man or these people being separated, and I feel that the relationship to this...I keep seeing a musty cave or a place...this might pertain to where it was buried. I would feel that the man...I would feel that he ate corn or ate something off...like he could have eaten some fish but I keep seeing him eating something off of a stick. I would feel his diet pertained mainly to meat because he traveled.

JONES: **Do you have any feelings about what these people looked like?**

BOWES: I would feel that this man was much bigger...physically much bigger than the other people that lived in the area where you found this. I keep seeing with this man...people in the background and I feel they were very short, squat, short and stocky, but I feel as though he was bigger, and I would feel that he was very wide through the shoulders, have a very massive chest. I see a woman and I keep seeing something wrapped around her head. I do see a farm but I feel that this was something that would have made this person mad, or like something that pertained to a building or he didn't feel too good with it. I would feel that this (artifact) would be very, very old. It was buried. I don't know...I kept seeing this being with some other tools and I kept seeing something almost like a shovel or a maddock or something that you dig with. I see these all piled together. I kept seeing a stick involved and something wrapped around...

JONES: **This object...?**

BOWES: It may not have been so much this object. I keep seeing something that was being cleaned on a big piece of slate or a big piece of rock. I keep seeing them cutting open an animal or cutting open a fish...on something like a big piece of rock. This could have been something they used to clean the meat off the back of something...kneading the skin or something. But I keep seeing them scrapping at something with this. I did see a person who had a crippled foot, and I felt it was a club foot.

JONES: What about the environment? Do you get a feeling of what the territory would look like?

BOWES: I felt that where it originated may have been...it could have originated in a colder climate. There may have been mountains or...clay or mountains or...I kept seeing mountains and then I kept seeing them going south or going to a lower country or area, and I see rivers or swamps and grass. But I see travel. I would feel that this belonged to someone who may have done a lot of traveling. I would feel that where it may have originated there was some canoes or boats but...I mean where it ended up. I didn't feel that it originated there. I do see people carrying things on their back...like children and packs on their back or things that they carried over across their backs...poles across their backs or something. Almost like a...something like a basket...something across their shoulders...wood stakes or something, but I see them carrying... bent over carrying things. They could have been carrying a deer or carrying something. It could have come from the west, but I feel as though the animals were much bigger than they are today...during the time the Indians or the people were there. I felt that this person looked different than the Indians in the area...that possibly this was found by...I feel as though he had more a thin face. He may have been around people with more of a round face.

JONES: Is that what you feel about most of the people associated with this artifact?

BOWES: I would feel that most of the people in the area that he went to was kind of short and squat with a round looking face. But I feel that he was from ...like an outsider.

JONES: I don't understand this. What you are reading is the maker of this artifact?

BOWES: The maker and possibly the owner, the user, but it could have been used by other people. I see it either being lost or buried with pottery...maybe when he died they buried it with him. I see a stream or water around there...a bubbling stream, and this again could have been a religious place. A lot of mist or a lot of...it could have been a place where it was very misty in the morning. It could have been a cold climate.

JONES: Do you feel like there were white people living around the maker of this object?

BOWES: I don't feel that so much. I would feel as though this person would have hated white people or avoided them, but I didn't see them so much. I did feel as though he went by what I would call a log cabin or a shack or a building. But I see him afraid or not liking it. I picked up something about someone being killed, and I would feel that the last thing that this man remembered was a loud noise. I felt as though it was like a whip...a loud "pop". I don't know...it may have been a gun shot, but I felt as though it was more like leather popping, but I felt it was very sudden. I would feel it was a violent death like a fall or something breaking or making a loud noise just before he died. I felt as though it was over his right shoulder. It happened from the back. I do see them dealing with feathers. A lot of feathers. This could deal with somebody who was like in the Everglades or like in a swamp, but it's a lot of feathers. These big long feathers. Not the feathers like out west, but more like a plume or a large feathers. I keep seeing something around their head, almost like a bandana or something. In connection with this building, I seen it was straight and then round at the top. It may have poles or something under the floor. I see smoke coming out of the top. I don't know why this would be up in the air. Now this building I seen, that this person avoided, I felt was up on a kind of hill and I would say that this was a structure set up on a hill. It was more like a cabin. It was very sloppily made. I would feel...it may not have been made by a white man. I feel resentment. I don't feel good with it. I keep feeling like it was like a lean-to or up against a mound or up against rocks. I would feel that this roof was peaked. It is not. I would say that this is more like leaning against something. I don't feel that these people had much jewelry, or...I feel that what they owned was leather...I don't feel too much with jewelry.

JONES: In the sense of decoration? Or in the sense of metal, or...?

BOWES: I don't feel too much metal around them. I would feel that they were primitive, but I see trails...like trails that were down...like they'd walk back and forth from some place many, many times. I did see clay...like clay and a lot of water or a lot of moisture in the ground, and I would feel that it was north of Florida, or northwest, or north of something...north of Florida for sure. But I feel like there was a lot of water leaking out of the ground. The place where this originated or where he started. I would say it was more like a migration; that these people continued to migrate...visited people as they went along and possibly ended up here (indicates artifact). In other words he was on a trip or continued to travel or migrate...migrating...but I feel like he went by that house on stakes and avoided that place on the hill or mound and ended up here (touches artifact)...he was killed there. These people could have turned against him because of his size or because of his...something about his strength. But I see him disregarding that structure on the hill or hating it or resenting it...that more squre looking building.

JONES: What about numbers of people?

BOWES: I would feel that the people he was visiting at last would have had more sweets in their diet than he did originally because I see them having some trouble with their teeth...or I would feel more sweets...maybe more tropical or more abundance of fruits. I also see them eating more meat. I kept seeing twenty-five...a number like that but it was...but I would feel that it wasn't any more than a couple hundred. A hundred and twenty-five or a hundred and fifty. A small group like that. I feel that the group that was with him may have just been his family...like he may have had two wives or something but I feel that part of the time he was alone.

JONES: The structure you talked about...do you have any feelings about what they were made of?

BOWES: If it pertains to Florida it could be palmettos or palm fronds, but I wouldn't feel that it was that...I would feel that it was more like branches and more like clay or dirt over the top...over this round part. This could be buried ...or pertain to burial, but these buildings had smoke coming out of them so I would say they were more like something they would live in. I keep seeing the west side of Florida...this could have been up towards Crystal River or west... west of United States or west of Florida. That may sound very general but you see the coast of the United States is on the west side and the coast of Florida is on the west side and this is the way I always get it...in other words west of Florida. I keep seeing more of a westerly direction. I don't feel east too well. It may have started in the east but I keep feeling more westerly.

Antique Baseball

With this, I keep seeing something to do with a memory...something to do with a young man. I don't know if there was a friend of his that had red hair or light colored hair but I keep seeing him laughing or giggling or like being a jokester. I do see another man who had black curly hair. I did feel that this was in the north...north of Florida, or it may get cold or it has cold weather. I

noved to a desert, or moved to a place where they had a lot of
they kicked the can around...I would feel it was before a can
g of, like they are restless because they have anxieties to do
used to do. But I feel that over a fifty or a seventy-five, or
fifty-year period, that these people changed very much, but
being adaptable, possibly intelligent or being able to change,
le may have moved from the cold, mountainous, or a place
a lot of trees to a place where there was a desert. I would feel
ut there to get them out of the way. They were held back or...I
y were on an Indian reservation, this is the feeling...but...the
touches moccasin) belonged to a child. I feel as though it may
se of it having to be moved...in other words they were pres-
to move...under pressure, not in the normal way. I did feel
ee a mummified person or child or like a little doll, but it was
petrified.

lo you see it?
a doll...but I kept feeling like it was a little short doll or a little
aybe I'm seeing it as a girl because it has long hair, and I felt its
ogether with...I can draw you a picture of it (draws). I don't
eyes because this is dark (indicates upper face). I see the hair
like a little dress made of leather. It may have been a doll, or
t...I really didn't see its arms very well, and I really didn't see
uch. It may have pertained to a medicine doll or something but
the legs. I would say that this could have been something like
es the neck region).

nd the neck?
er around the neck or a stalk that would stick out of here (neck).
a doll, but this right here (dress) was very, very, very old. Very
s like a mummy. And this was dark (indicates upper face), dark
u really couldn't see it. I see this (mouth) like it was tied together
ke leather. It's an ugly looking thing...to me...from what I seen
scare somebody to see it. I would feel it was propped up and put
place where it was dark or musty...very dusty. Maybe it be-
tle girl. The feeling I had was that it was more an instrument like
ething of a meaning. They would leave this there to protect the
something like that. But I still feel there was a little girl there or
girl.

Crocheted Hair Ribbon
an to throw you off again, but again I didn't get much from this.
hat the person who made this may not be very talented, but I
was from very long ago. That it was from very recent. I don't
one made this when they were sick but I see a woman making it.
d of losing her job or losing...I don't know if this was a recent
t as though it was not very old.

old do you think the woman was?
would say she was heavy set and she could even be a young
t she wasn't very good. That's the feeling I had. Someone who
in a hurry to make something. This could even have been some-
on a Indian reservation or at a place where she was pressured to
essured to do something to make a living, but she really wasn't
n other words, she was making beads and making this maybe to
make up something...she was trying to be a so-called quote
t I don't feel she was good at this. Her parents never taught her
d maybe she was separated from Indians or separated from other

see an older man and a woman. I don't know if this is this person's mother and father or...I see somebody coughing or having a lot of concern about somebody's health, and other than that I didn't see anything. I did see a red uniform.

JONES: What about the time period? Do you feel anything about that?

BOWES: I would say it may pertain to teenagers or somebody. I see somebody being involved in Little League or a grown-up helping young people. I don't see them getting paid for it though. I do see somebody having problems with their front tooth or having a problem with teeth, and this could have pertained to something...being hit in the mouth or something pertaining to the teeth.

Cervical Vertebrae

I don't know if this was human vertebrae but I keep seeing someone hit in the head, and I keep seeing them having a problem with their eye. I kept getting the word "death". If this was a person I would feel that it was a fairly large person, but it was a man. I do see a young teenage girl. I keep seeing a cave and...and I don't know what it is but I keep seeing someone who is having a problem...and I would say escaping from someone. The feeling I had was possibly they've captured a young girl, or they could have even been cannibals, but I kept seeing them capturing a young girl. I would feel that there was a lot of bickering or fighting. I do see a dog or an animal and I would say that this bickering or this problem came in result of, like hunting territory or a problem with that. I would feel that he...or this person was a very large person. I do feel as though this could have been a chief or somebody who was buried with ceremony. I feel as though a lot of the people who died may have died and was thrown in a hole, but I feel as though that this person was set aside from others. I don't know why but I feel that this was somewhere other than Florida. I do feel as though there was a lot of ceremony, and I keep smelling perfumes, or something smelling. Hopefully this box isn't a perfume box (touches box containing vertebrae). The feeling I had was a relationship to a lot of ceremony and possibly incense or something that was smoking, like purple smoke or something. I would see a lot of women wailing or chanting, or making noises and I keep seeing them swaying back and forth clapping their hands and something like that. I see these pots that are hanging from...like clay pot with leather thongs and I feel they're hanging there...maybe this is where this smoke is coming from. I would feel that when this person died...it could have been someone who was walking through what you might say was bramble bushes or saw grass...because I see the man or people with cuts or sores...like almost like they've cut their face...maybe to scar the face for war... or to make themselves look ugly. A lot of this cutting...a lot of sores like cuts, like down their chest and on their face and on their forehead. This man had markings on either side of his chest and on his face...I don't feel there's any clothes from here up (draws Indian figure). Then a band on his arm. I kept seeing these scars and I felt that everybody was in a frenzy or all upset or excited. With these scars I feel like they could be in a pattern but I feel as though several men have these same cuts on their face and on their body. I do feel they had a hooked nose. Their nose was hooked or curved rather than a slanted nose.

JONES: What color was the hair?

BOWES: Black. I would feel as though he was very dark skinned.

JONES: You mentioned pots on leather thongs...?

BOWES: This may not be this man. This may be the people who were there at the ceremony...where he was buried. That was the feeling I had.

JONES: Do you think there were white men around at this time?

BOWES: I don't know why, but I kept seeing something...I kept seeing a man with blond or red or orange hair, but I don't feel it's in with this (vertebrae) at all. I did see this was something far away. That man may have discovered this or gotten involved with this, but I don't feel as though he was there at the time of this (touches vertebrae).

JONES: Do you have any feelings about the environment? The kind of country it might have been? Or how these people might have made a living?

BOWES: I kept seeing an animal. I kept seeing its stomach bloated. Or whatever. Like an animal that could have been like a steer or like a buffalo, but the feeling I had was it was something with long horns...and a buffalo doesn't have long horns, but the feeling I had was it was something that they ate or killed. The feeling I had from that was...I would feel that these people were in a group...like there was little groups of people here and there, and they was always fighting among themselves. I didn't feel too good with that. I felt like a war to them was like a game...like football. I felt they were all fighting among themselves, and this could have been like up in New York state or a place where there was access to the water, but the feeling I had was that these people was almost warlike...that they played these games and they actually hurt each other...killed each other or hurt each other with these games. I don't know why but I kept seeing something wrong with the person's ear, and this may be like a punctured ear drum. I don't know what it meant. This person died in great pain...a feeling of triumph.

Contemporary Carved Chalk

I'm not very impressed with this for some reason. I felt like it was just chalk, and I felt like somebody made this recently. That's the feeling I have. I didn't get much from that. Like chalk they used on the black board. The feeling I had was somebody who...I don't know if it was a game or something like it was just thrown in there with this stuff (referring to artifact collection). (In fact it was an afterthought addition by Wallace after a museum piece became unavailable.)

JONES: Do you have any impressions about the person who made this?

BOWES: I would feel that the person who made this could have been inside a building, or...was at school or was inside a building...either in jail or inside something. In other words, secluded or isolated. I wish I could give you more. I do feel he is an artist and takes a lot of pride in his work. This is very strange. I don't know why this would be in here (refers to artifact collection).

JONES: What do you mean?

BOWES: I don't feel it belonged in there (collection).

JONES: All those things were things people made at different times or things that related to people.

BOWES: The feeling I had was, was that somebody threw this in there to see frustration with or to let out his anxiety with but I would feel that he could be may have had a deep desire as a young man to be a teacher or to do something with his hands, and he may be a little bit frustrated and need this as an escape. When he becomes nervous being indoors a lot or being in Gainsville or being indoors at his job, he picks on chalk or picks on something to let out his frustration with or to let out his anxiety with, but I would feel that he could be an artist if he wanted to be. I would feel as though his parents may have goaded him or pushed him into this. I feel as though he feels as though he is in prison, or a little bit trapped. Let me say this...if that belonged to an Indian, I still feel as though it was an Indian who was in school, or an Indian who was trapped or felt held back. I still feel who does that (touches chalk) is held back either by being in jail or being held back in some way. I do feel as though he could be very creative if he wanted to be. I do feel that this person may write a book or write something involving his creative abilities, not just art. (The carver of the chalk has published several scholarly articles related to music and sociology.)

Sioux Child's Burial Moccasin

I get a completely different feeling from the west. Either the west or the north. I fee this came from. I do feel in relationship to what you might call a mummy...somethir that would scare someone if they seen it. was a child or a woman. It may be a small cates beading) was made afterwards, but I involved with somebody being killed...like with white people. I see the people being like they had to move a lot. In dealing with ment or like she has to carry her child and s I don't know if this came from...if it were ev were a different time than this (touches lea have been displayed behind glass at one tim plaining about something or being very gre she could be a person who...like you migh apply her ability toward something...tryin belonged to her, I don't know. I don't feel very much. I felt this was used, the leath (touches beaded areas). I do feel that whoev last. In other words, very durable and some very, very handy with their hands and creat

JONES: What did these people eat? How d

BOWES: I keep seeing something to do would be in the north. Generally, I kept se this would possibly be more recent. I do fee with white people or fight with them or arg suppressed by white people...made to chang proud people. I would feel they ate a mixed keep picking up a sea-cow and that would that this was from Florida. It may pertair (touches moccasin) could have been a plac there was desert or mountains. Now it could I see people who were...it was cold. Like col like archery for accuracy with a bow...accur that they were like killing time...like there didn't hunt or couldn't hunt. I see them bo this. And I would feel over a fifty-year peric dominance of something...it could have ever see them dominated or like they were held ba

JONES: What kind of structures did they ha

BOWES: I feel rock and clay...adobe. If it c could have been logs...or log cabins or build in the north. They grew very slow...maybe very hard trees. Then I seen like a desert or l lived like in the side of a mountain or like moved, pressured to move for political rea people or because they had a problem in conne not getting along or not understanding each

JONES: Do you have any feelings about wl they moved to?

BOWES: I feel as though they may have m Oregon or a place that was like New York st had a lot of trees, a lot of animals, a lot of pe

as though
spare tim
but I'm s
things lik
generally
because o
that these
where the
that they
just felt li
outcome.
have died
sured and
sadness. I
just like it

JONES: I
BOWES:
short girl,
lips were t
know if it
and then I
don't know
its legs th
...I didn't
layers (ind

JONES: A
BOWES: I
Maybe it w
rotten or it
in here like
with bone.
of it...it w
in a cave c
longed to a
voodoo...s
spirit or to
it was a yo

Contempor

I didn't
I would fe
didn't feel
know if so
She was a
thing but I

JONES: H
BOWES:
woman. I
may have
one who w
do this or
that kind.
surprise...
"Indian,"
to do this

people, but generally it may not even be an Indian. Maybe just a woman who made this for this purpose. I don't know. I didn't get much from it. It's like those chalk pieces or whatever...but the feeling I had was that it's something to do with a woman or to do with a person who felt that their job or this job was not really their kind of work. I see her in the back room doing this and I felt she was a little bit nervous on how it could come out. I didn't feel happy with her. I see her worried about a man...a relationship with him.

Seminole Weaving Heddle

Again with this, I didn't feel it as old as possibly some of the other things. I do see with respect to...either the north or the west. This person's ancestors or this person may have moved from the north or the west. I felt that this thread was possibly older than the rest. This leather here may not have been really like the original. I would feel that this was made to impress someone. I don't know if this was used as a breast plate, or whether it was used as an instrument. I wouldn't say they made music with it, but...I kept feeling as though there were something hung...maybe it was hung...might support something. I didn't get much from that. I'm sorry. I would feel that the string and the nails don't belong on it. I would feel that it should be tied with leather...been made that way. This could have been an imitation of something out of the past. But I don't feel that the person who made it was very talented. In other words, an imitation of what it is supposed to be...not really what it is. The people who made it could have been from the west, or in association with something like that but I didn't feel this was very old or it was ever buried. I wasn't too impressed with that, but that's neither here nor there. I kept feeling a little disappointed or bored. I didn't have much vibration with that.

Seminole Leather Medicine Pouch

I do see a man or a person on the run or on the travel. I kept seeing them either in the west or in Texas or someplace that could have been desert. I see a lot of frustration, like he was riding a horse or maybe he was clutching this. His relatives were sent out west. I kept seeing something here of good luck... pertaining to medicine, or...like I felt there was a little ball in here (in pouch)... like a rock or whatever, but I see them putting this in their mouth...either in the desert, or something to hold, to keep the moisture in their mouth. In other words they may have put a pebble or a stone or a little something in their mouth to hold moisture in the mouth. I felt with this...I see him worried about his horse or worried about his transportation...an animal of some kind. I do feel with this person...I do feel like there was something wrong with his stomach or something wrong with something inside him. I would feel that it pertained to not eating or that sort of thing. I keep seeing there being something in his eyes or his eyes hurt.

JONES: Do you have any feelings about what this person looked like?

BOWES: I don't know if this was owned by a frontiersman or if it was owned by an Indian. I kept feeling as though it may have pertained to someone who was...I kept feeling like Texas or the Alamo or something like he was going somewhere to prove a point or to accomplish something. It could be a man or a woman, but I felt more with a man...a man's vibrations but...I kept seeing long hair.

JONES: Do you have any feeling of the color?

BOWES: It could be blond. It could be light colored...bleached. But this could even be a man who traveled with this person for a short period of time. I see him coughing or having congestion or problems with his breathing. I felt like there was a lot of dust, like he could have been a cowboy or somebody who rode a horse and leaned over and breathed a lot of dust. I do see him smoking something of some kind.

JONES: How was he smoking?

BOWES: Could have been a pipe, but I feel like he was inhaling dust or smoke. This could be like a white person because I seen a moustache and a beard and long hair...like a frontiersman...like a cowboy or somebody who was very rugged. I don't feel as though he took very good care of himself. Could have been an Indian who was covered with leather. He traveled. I did feel him traveling for a while and seeing him having something over his shoulder or this could have been a gun or a spear or something...over his shoulder.

JONES: When you say "covered in leather," how specifically are you seeing this leather?

BOWES: I would feel as though this thing could have been a leather saddle right there...but I kept feeling as though this person actually had a leather outfit tied with leather...strung together with leather.

JONES: What do you pick up about this person's diet?

BOWES: Jerky. Something of dried meat. He pulled it out of his mouth. I felt a rabbit.

JONES: Do you see other people around this person?

BOWES: I would say occasionally but I kept seeing mostly him either on a horse or traveling again. I see something about a mountain. I see him going through this mountain or this place, and it echoing. This could even be a swamp or...I just don't feel it is so much of a swamp. I feel more dry country... or in the north. I kept seeing him going through this mountain and saying something and hearing it echo. I would feel he loved animals. His life was surrounded by animals.

JONES: Do you have any feelings about what he may have done for a living?

BOWES: He may have had a moustache and a beard, but I see him looking up and seeing a hawk, or bird, and I felt he just sat there and looked at it. In relationship to this (artifact), I do feel this person had another occupation and this may have been a past time. I do feel as though he could have had a problem with...feeling like he belonged, almost like being a frontiersman or cowboy or like someone who is a little of an outsider...in other words he really didn't get along with people that well...he wasn't right in among a lot of people. Now I do feel as though he had a friend or someone who related to a medicine man or somehow who dealt with medicine or prepared something. This person could have been someone who related to leather goods...buckskin and otter pelts and again this could be in the north. I do feel him going southwest or something more toward open plains or open areas.

JONES: You mentioned that he was looking at a hawk. Why was that significant?

BOWES: I would feel that this was proving a point. The man wouldn't stop to watch a steam train. He wouldn't watch man-made things but he would sit there and watch a hawk for an hour. He would see the hawk dive and then it would come up. It may have been like in the mountains where the air stream of the mountains or the air coming through the mountain kept the hawk suspended there but I felt he watched this for hours and hours. This is the personality of the person. I feel as though he was someone who wanted to be free or someone who enjoyed nature rather than man-made things.

JONES: What about the medicine man association?

BOWES: I would feel that this could have been his father or it could have been a man who ran a trading post, or someone who ran something in dealing with trade goods. He could have been a frontiersman...someone who went out in to the wilderness and then came back with his pelts. That's my association with that. He went back to his tribe or back to this trading post or whatever to trade his...what he'd been working for for months and months. I felt he started maybe in spring time and then worked that way and then...the other part of his life I didn't pick up too well. I felt boredom with that or I just felt blank with that. He may have stayed in a cabin or stayed...because of the winter or whatever. I felt as though his aim was to come back and talk to this medicine man or this man who had goods...like medicine and food and can goods, or something to trade. I wouldn't feel so much can goods, but I feel more like a bag...like a big bag of flour or a bag of something...could have even been ammunition. I do feel that he abused his health by breathing in a lot of dust...possibly smoking a pipe.

JONES: **When you are reading dust or smoke, do you clearly feel that...**

BOWES: It was a problem with his lungs. Eventually in his life...this would affect his lungs. Eventually this is maybe what he died of...problem with his heart or lungs, something in his chest. I do feel that this man could have been someone who was very unique or different. I do see him teaching or talking to people. I feel that was when he was very old or when he was knowledgeable.

JONES: **What do you feel he would be teaching or talking about?**

BOWES: His travels or his experiences.

Pine Needle Basket

With it, I do feel as though it's held something of value. It could have been... something that was very, very small. It could have been like food of some sort, but I felt it was a basket and this was the top of it (artifact). I felt in connection with this that it had been repaired many times. I do see a woman bending over or leaning over something, and see this being over in the corner (referring to artifact). I don't know if this was sitting down and something was sitting in it or that this was like a lid, but I feel the inside was protected and the outside was kind of brushed and abused. In connection with this I keep seeing a woman and I see her having a lot of pride in her children, or pride of what she was making. I don't know if she had yarns or grasses, but...I see her having problems with her legs, like her legs being very fat...or like problems with circulation in her legs. I would feel as though it took a great deal of time to make this. I do see forests or trees. I would say they were pine trees or in relationship to forests. I did feel northern. I don't feel swamps or humidity.

JONES: **Can you give me a physical description of the maker of this thing?**

BOWES: The maker could have been a man...someone like a blacksmith or someone who specialized in making things. I feel that this woman who owned it may have bought it or traded it from this person. I do see a man standing there or sitting there and I felt he was very old and possibly very thin. I felt like he nodded his head or went this way (nods his head back and forth) all the time...like his nerves were...like he's nodding his head. I see the inside of a tipi or the inside of something...could have even been a concrete building at one time, but I felt it was very cramped or small there and I felt that there was clay pots or something clay or like they...I thought they had a board or log and I felt there was pots hanging from it. I kept seeing them carrying water. I felt this person spent a lot of time indoors. I keep seeing someone having a lot of problems with his back. I do see them climbing ladders. I see a building and I see little round holes where they crawled down in these holes and maybe it's just a little small cave...could even be a cave...but I felt it was a building and they climbed through these holes, and they may have this ladder on the outside. I kept seeing them going in from the top.

JONES: **What race was the maker of this basket?**

BOWES: Could have been a black woman...could have been an Indian. I don't feel a white person. I see them having a lot of time. They could have looked a little like a Japanese because it was an Indian of that sort...in other words, round face and slanted eyes. I see them having a lot of time and a lot of dexterity with their hands...being able to duplicate the same thing over and over. But I would feel that this was something to be used...not ceremonial...not to be pretty but to be used.

JONES: **What did the countryside look like?**
BOWES: Before I got something about forests or pine trees. Then I felt as
though it may have been something that pertained to rocks or clay. I kept
seeing a clay building or a round or square building and I see people sitting on
the floor. That would be more like a desert and not so much up north, but I
kept seeing forests...where it originated. I keep seeing somebody limping or
having problems with their back...carrying things a lot. Felt they were in a
rush but I see prosperity around this...not boredom or unhappiness. I would
feel this woman, or the person who owned this or was around was very, very
proud of her family or proud of her children...a lot of pride in connection with
that. I felt this may have been given to several different people. All of a sudden it was given away from the people who owned it. It was babied and taken
very good care of. Originally it was treated very rough or used for the reason it
was originally used for...to carry things, to store things. I kept seeing something beside it which I felt was a real tall basket...very tall, and very thin...
round like a big pipe. They could have put sticks in there or put arrows in there
or...I felt it was a cane because of this person's back. But I felt as though there
was an eagle's head or like it turned this way with a face on it and I see them
sticking it in this basket. I did see a canoe or water and I keep seeing her
husband or somebody leaving and going down the water...a stream or going
out on a lake and never coming back. I kept seeing it stopping...went off in the
water and didn't come back. I didn't get too much of a future with this. The
person may...I don't know if they're still living. I didn't see so much in the
future about it.

Toy Combs [Boston]

I feel as though this could have been made from a bone. I felt that it was
made to hold something in place. This could have been hair or it could have
been...hold something in place until it was sewed together or held together. I
see somebody putting that in their mouth. The feeling I keep getting is ivory...
like it was made out of teeth or bone, but...could even be plastic but the feeling
I had was that it was something that was used to hold something in place.
JONES: **Where did they come from?**
BOWES: This could have been Eskimos or people from the north. I would feel
it may not be that far north...like Eskimo territory, but I see water that was
frozen over. I keep seeing boats and I feel like it would pertain to boats or
water...like where they originally got it. I would feel that originally whoever
made this was very skilled. I do feel as though it was buried at one time, in a
very musty place or it was possibly involved in...hey, I just picked up something...I see a boat and in the front it may come up like this (draws) and it may
have something up here (indicates prow), a bird or maybe something with
arms or something up here, but I felt as though there was people standing up
here and they were like in a dress or like in something long. I feel as though
they had a long pole in their hands or a spear. I feel large groups of people were
poisoned with relationship to that. I see people either poisoned through the
meat they ate, or something they smelled in the air...like a disease.
JONES: **At the time these were made and used?**
BOWES: Possibly. There may have been pollution in the air or pollution and
somebody could have poisoned them through the meat they gave them but I
see large groups of people dying of a disease.
JONES: **What do the people look like?**
BOWES: I would feel that they were dark skinned people...have very long
hair. Straight hair. I would feel that they were river people or people who lived
near the water or lived with the water or something in association with water.
JONES: **What do you feel about their numbers?**
BOWES: Several hundred or a thousand people or a large...I see large groups

of people...lots of houses and buildings. These people are more permanent
...they are in one place.

JONES: What do the buildings look like?

BOWES: I would feel they were quite big. I would say they were like a log
cabin. From what I seen of them. The roofs of them or the wood or the logs
were crossed at the top and I would say they were quite solid but they were
always near the water. Like layers of them, or they were...there's a building
here and another building here and another building here and another building
up the hill a ways. I felt that they were always associated with water. This
may have been...originally they may have been forced to move or change. This
is where the people originally were.

JONES: How long ago was this (referring to artifacts)?

BOWES: The feeling I got is that it could have been associated with the north
...like in Virginia or a place where there was Indians there or they were
around the Great Lakes or they were around a place where people...I guess the
white people came over, the settlers came over. People moved in that disturbed
their way of life. They were people who may have had to move as time went by
but I feel as though they could have been there...I would feel that they could
have been there at the same time that white people were there, but of course
they were way before that. I still don't understand quite what that's for (refers
to artifacts). I don't understand it but I do feel as though it was something to
hold something until something else is sewed or like they pushed it in there to
hold it until they could do something with it. I kept seeing them eating a tremendous amount of fish. I see them using fish for everything...fertilizer,
eating fish and using fish. And I feel that they would deal with making things
out of beavers or like otters or things that was from the water. I felt like everything was water oriented. I see as I go into the building...steps...walking up
and steps coming up. I would feel that these were actually steps...more like
that rather than a straight ladder, but I feel like there are big platforms in
front of the building...like this could be up on stakes or whatever, but I felt a
platform in front and then they went inside. Like a porch...a porch sticking
out. I don't feel like they would leave these buildings behind if somebody came
over to run them off...I feel that they would burn them. They would burn them
before they would leave them. The only thing I seen left is just posts...burnt
posts and wood piled up.

JONES: This did happen at one time?

BOWES: Yes. These people are not still there...where they originated.

JONES: And at one time these buildings were burned?

BOWES: Yes. They were burned rather than left.

JONES: Do you have any feelings of who or what would make them do this?

BOWES: Possibly the influx of other people. I see people destroying or
making a dam or changing the water or changing their ecology. I would feel
that these kind of people died...I don't feel that they were as a whole there. I
feel that them and their ancestors may have died...died out. There was a large
...in other words, the only ones left are a mix of other people, not the real
strain of these people. It was a mixture of a lot of different kinds of Indians, or
lots of different kinds of people, rather than just one kind. I would feel that
these people would have made fire places out of rock. These people were advanced. They were not primitives. They are much more advanced than what
people really give them credit for. But I feel that they stayed there and they
had a way of disposing of their sewage and such. They had a place to put it,
they used it for fertilizer. I don't feel they went to the bathroom in their own
house. I feel there was rugs on the floor. It was clean in there and not filthy,
dirty. Like some of these other things that I held (referring to artifacts), I felt
dirty. But I felt that these people had a lot of pride, a lot of feeling of accomplishment.

Pocket Watch
JONES: This is Number Eight.
BOWES: Very strange. (Draws picture). Like a gun, and then I seen pieces of
...pottery or pieces of white clay or white...something white as if it was over
top of it. Now maybe what I picked up was something in association with a
case that it was in and maybe there was pieces of pottery and then a gun below
it in another shelf, but I felt like this was pieces of something but I felt this
gun was below it in some association with it. I don't understand it that well.
JONES: What do you feel is in this box? These pieces?
BOWES: Yes. The pieces may be in the box.
JONES: What do you feel they are made of?
BOWES: There's either clay or metal in this box. I don't know if it's of the
recent but I didn't feel any age to speak of (adds oval shape to drawing). So
this is confusing me. I don't understand it.
JONES: You said pottery...?
BOWES: It could be pottery...I kept seeing a slab and it could have been like
a piece of lead, like melted down bullets or lead of some sort. I don't know but
this is the feeling I had...like something heavy was in there. But I really didn't
pick up anything else...the feeling I had was like it was a little derringer or a
gun that was the first picture I picked up. Absolutely that there is something
metal in there you put your finger in. Someone valued it. (Emphasizes oval
shape and semi-circular shape).

Hair Necklace
   The feeling with this was...was, I seen something that was shaped like this
(draws long thin oval shape). I don't know if it was used for sewing or like it
was a rib-cage of a fish...the feeling I had was I seen a fish, and the eye...like
the eye was gone...and it was partially decayed. I don't know if it pertains to
something that was in with this (indicates box)...or like it was buried or something, but I kept seeing something pointed and I felt like it was a bone or like a
rib-cage or like a long slender bone. I see a bone and I kept seeing it like a skull
...And I see like a hole...like a bone in the face...like it sticks out from the
nose. Something around the head.
JONES: You mean it was stuck in the head or part of the head?
BOWES: I kept seeing something like a square...like made of brass or a flat
piece of gold or brass...I see a lot of little decorations or little scribblings on it.
This would be an association of more where it came from. This was associated
with whatever this was, either alive or dead at the time it was being used. This
other was I felt where it was found. I see dead fish or things like...things that
were cast aside by a culture or a people. I see people wearing turbans. The
feeling I had was that it was like a turban. The man was walking and it had
something on his head. He was either carrying something...I don't know...I
felt like he was either carrying something on his back or carrying something on
his head like in the Bahama Islands or a place where they carry things on their
head or back.
JONES: Do you get any feelings about the designs on these things?
BOWES: I would say it was on the ground or that it was layed on the ground.
I felt it could have been some sort of barter, but I felt it was about an inch
thick or half an inch thick, and that it was layed down. It could have been gold
because that was the color of it. Now this could pertain to Inca Indians or a
place of barter...like they used it...like the Spanish people or somebody melted
this gold down and made it into these bars or these...I felt like they were flat

pieces of steel or gold or they were made...I kept seeing them valued. This could even be like a pirate or someone who would take it or barter or trade it but the feeling I had with this was something like with South America...somewhere where there was a lot of jungles grown over.

JONES: Do you feel the main object in here is this long...(Indicates the long oval shape that he keeps tracing as he talks).

BOWES: Like bones or rib-bones...it could have been like a piece of bone from the nose or like a bone of some sort but this was the feeling I picked up. I don't feel like I'm doing very well with these boxes because I'm not actually holding or surrounding the object when I work with them.

Sewing Bird

The feeling I had with this is it's clay and it is pottery. I keep establishing the box as an isolation. I keep seeing something round sitting at an angle. I would say that is broken like this (a.), but it used to be a pot or piece of clay or it could be a piece right in like that...I kept seeing it as being clay. This pot could be laying in the other direction, but the feeling I had was...I keep seeing something like this (b.)...maybe it was made for stirring...it could have been bone or it could have been something that was bigger and rounder at one end, but the feeling I had was it was made for stirring...or turning something.

JONES: Do you feel that these (a. & b.) are in here together or they were associated with...

BOWES: Yeah, like they were at one time together. Either buried in the ground or they associated with each other. I wouldn't say these things (a. & b.) are in there (box)...I wouldn't say the bowl was in there at all. It could even be a piece of it, but I would feel like I kept seeing this stick or this thing that a pharmacist would use to crush a powder or make a powder.

JONES: Like a mortar and pestle?

BOWES: Like a pestle...that was the feeling I had. I kept seeing somebody crushing bone, or crushing something to make like powder.

JONES: Do you have a feeling about somebody doing that? Like what they looked like? Where they came from or what their area looked like?

BOWES: I kept seeing this person's face. I see a lip and then I see a tooth. missing. I'd say they had a lot of trouble with their teeth. I don't know if this was like from people who would come from the west or from a desert place that's hot...I keep seeing something metal (draws figure in upper right of box shape)...might screw together, but I don't know what it meant. I don't know if that was made for carrying something or holding down something...this metal ...I kept seeing it almost like it would swivel.

JONES: Do you see it in association with these pieces (a. & b.)?

BOWES: I don't understand what it was but I would feel it was in association with it some way...this metal thing. I see something threaded or screwed together. It could even associate with something to do with a gun because I kept seeing something spring loaded or "click" like that...makes a noise...something that would hook something together.

Nazi Wound Badge

I see two young men laughing or something to do with that, and I see a little sign or something and it said, "help". And then I see a piece...like a piece of pottery or piece of something and I see some markings like they were round and I see some markings like this (draws). This piece of paper could be on someone's desk or like it was...I don't know why but I felt like someone was like missing or lost...like they didn't have something to put in here...like they ran out of things to put in there (collection of artifacts) or there was some reason for it. I don't know what it was. I did see something that pertained to like a piece of something. I would feel that it was very small. Again it could be like little, little things...like round things, like a string went through them.

JONES: **And that's what you feel is in here** (indicates box)?

BOWES: I feel as though these things were in here, yes. But I kept seeing the association with...the first thing I seen was this piece of paper, it was a piece of paper...they dealt with paper. They may have put a piece of paper in there saying something...like a newspaper or there could be this note or whatever... it could have been saying something on there.

JONES: **Is this old? Recent?**

BOWES: I would say the artifact or things were very old. I kept seeing white for these.

JONES: **The little things on the string?**

BOWES: Yeah. But the feeling I had was like there was nothing in there (box). The first thing I picked up was there was nothing in there, but then I picked up this piece of paper that said, "Help"., and then I seen these other things. So what I picked up, I don't understand exactly what it means, but I'm going to give it to you.

Corn Husker

In association with this I see something broken again and I would say it was either clay or this could have been with this at some time. I felt this was burnt inside (draws). If this was clay, it was broke...something burnt or something that's been burnt inside. I kept seeing a child and the child was reaching up. This child could have had a hat on or a bonnet...could have been a woman or girl. I kept seeing death or fire...like the child was left alone. I kept seeing a skull or skeleton or teeth, and I keep seeing the teeth like broken or...this child was left behind dead or like it was exposed for a period of time.

JONES: **What do you feel to be the race of the people?**

BOWES: I would say they were Indians or like people who were afraid or in travel. They could have been early Spanish or early people who didn't know their way...they were lost. But I see the body laying there and I felt it was associated with an arm bone or some bone. Could even have been one of the bones in the arm...but that's something I picked up. This sounds strange but I keep seeing a green chalk board, and I see someone talking to someone else. I felt like it was somebody investigating something. This was something I felt like someone was discussing.

JONES: **This object in here** (indicates box)?

BOWES: Yeah, something about this object. I would say there was more than one piece in here...more than one thing in here or this could associate with being together with something else. I keep seeing like someone's back is broken or like their back is humped over, and I kept seeing this again with this travel. But I feel someone was lost and someone was lost by fire.

Fragment of Antique Handcuffs from Florida

I would say this was quite heavy. I see this as being something...I don't know if there is more than one picture but I picked up sand. I see something large and flat...I kept seeing a gun belt and I don't know how that associated with...this (gunbelt) isn't here (in box), but the feeling I had was that there was a gunbelt near or associated with this. I don't know if this is a piece of something...like a piece of a fort or a piece of a building or like it's a hinge or it's something steel. I kept seeing something looking like a piano hinge...it had holes in it. Then I seen a brick, a piece of brick from the side of a fort or the side of a building but I didn't know what it was. I kept seeing pieces of something.

JONES: **And the object that is in here you would feel to be a hinge?**

BOWES: It could be a hinge or it could be whatever this is here...flat and square...like a piece of concrete or a...I felt it was metal, and I would say this was related to early Florida or like...I don't feel it's very, very old...there could be a round flat rock in there, but I still felt as though it was something round and flat and it was used as a tool or used to shave or clean something or to move something like it was hinged in the middle, it was tied together with something...like a rock that was tied onto a stick where they swung it around and hit somebody with it. In general I felt like it was something that was left over from a building. Really, that's what I picked up.

JONES: Hinging seems to be the...

BOWES: Something that bends back and forth...The hinging of this moving back and forth. It was what I was seeing before, this flat thing or stone...it was flat...it was low. The feeling with this was that it was hinging. This here (makes rectangular shape in drawing) was like a stone or like a corner of a building. It was like one of the stones from out of the sides of the building. It could even be a stick like a rock was tied to it and swung around it. I just felt it bent or hinged...that's the only thing I had so...I kept seeing violence dealing with the building...dealing with the association of it, and I see violence inside the building like a saloon, or a place that's violent...a lot of noise, violence.

JONES: Do you see people associated with this object?

BOWES: I would say it was early Florida or...people who...I would say it was like a ghost town that somebody abandoned. I see glass and I see things that are broken or run down.

JONES: So you don't feel it would be an Indian thing?

BOWES: It could associate with an Indian thing but I would feel that they... from wherever it came...this place was abandoned for years and years. This was like a ghost town even if it was an Indian village...that it was abandoned and I felt like there was a lot of violence before they abandoned it. People without organization like alcoholics or violent people...it could have been destroyed by flood or hurricane or storm.

False Teeth

Felt like a little bag or something leather. I would say there was bones in here, and I kept seeing this bag and I felt it was owned by a woman or a girl. I don't know if there is a piece of skull or something round, but the feeling I had (draws)...I see an adobe building or a concrete building or some sort of building. I see either clay or dirt and then I see bones and then more clay and dirt and maybe more bones and I felt as though this could be way out in the country or it could be nowhere near a building, but I still see layers and layers of civilization or people. Like I keep seeing this building or this wall, and down behind this wall I see layers of clay or dirt. I wouldn't say it was Florida, but...I see the real floor or original floor where this building was made...it may have been quite a bit deeper but over a period of time it was filled in. I kept seeing red clay...this could be in association with something other than where this is from. There could be salt marsh or sand. I kept seeing sand or sand dunes or something to do with rolling hills or grass. I would say this could be something associated with Indians or something that was buried...I still feel something to do with bones, but I felt something to do with metal, and I see something like this (draws c.). I don't know what it means. It was the feeling I had. I didn't understand it.

JONES: What do you feel is the connection between the leather bag, the buried house floor, the piece of skull, the sand hills and this (refers to c.)? Do all of these connect in some way?

BOWES: Yes. I would feel this here (indicates spiral shape on c.) was made to hold something. This metal...it's like a spring...like a spring you put in a gas can neck so you can't get a siphon in it, or it could be one to hold something...

it could even hold bones together. But I keep seeing these other associations with something that was around that (refers to c.)

JONES: Which of these shapes do you feel most strongly?

BOWES: I would say that this right here (c.) is in the box, and this...I kept seeing these other things associated with it...I hope that doesn't sound confusing but I felt like this (c.) was on someone's desk at some time...this spring here. It could be modern art of some sort...but I kept seeing these other things as being made as a hobby or artifacts or things of value. I seen some real bright colors...orange or green or red or something.

JONES: The color of the metal or associated with it...?

BOWES: Associated with it and I felt there could be something to do with imitation wood or a base of some sort...didn't know what it meant. I do feel there was something like a spring...something that held something together, and I really don't know what it was. It could have been...it could have been associated with weaving or pushing like an old, old machine or something like an old backward way of doing something. I kept seeing a spring like it was putting tension on something.

Iron Knuckles

This could be a pair of scissors. I don't know but...this could even be a piece of a gun...I felt like it came to a point here (draws) or was round here...could be another one of these (indicates round area) on the other side, but I didn't see that so much...the feeling I had was that it was metal and round. I would say it was held in your hand...it was held in your hand and it was steel. Could be a pair of scissors.

JONES: Is it recent or old?

BOWES: I would say it was...if it's worn in here in this loop, and if it's brass or worn...it's very old. If it's silver as I first picked up...like chrome...I don't feel it's old at all. In fact this may be a new artifact, as they say, and that isn't something that's valuable, but it could be something like a gun or like the ring of a gun or round or like you held it or something. I really didn't feel it had too much value. It's very strange I felt like I picked this up once before. It could have been like this here (indicates round area on drawing related to reading of pocket watch)...round, a ring, like...I don't know, but the feeling I had was I kept seeing this ring (touches drawing made of box contain iron knuckles.) Like a ring, or like scissors, or like something that was held in yor hand.

Straight Razor

I felt like there was an old book in here or paper. I would say it could have even been a child's book or like...I keep seeing Roman numerals...something to the corner. Could even have pertained to religion or a bible or like a school book or something that's more valuable. Could be like a newspaper but I felt it was yellowed or old, and it was a book or something of value, not just a piece of paper. I see the letters being real big and maybe in color or standing out and then I...later on there was something else. This could be proclaiming something that would pertain to food or teaching something.

JONES: Do you have any feelings about where it might have come from?

BOWES: I felt it was almost like a family heirloom or something that was handed down. I did feel like it was found by someone in an old house.

JONES: What about the people who may have owned it?

BOWES: Would that pertain to an artifact?

JONES: Sure. Anything associated with human beings making objects...

BOWES: This may be part of that book or the information could pertain to books, or talk about study of something, but...I would feel this could be something like one of the original school books like in Florida or in the United

States, or it was something of long ago like they even wrote or talked different in here...in the writing then now.

JONES: Do you get anything about who may have owned it?

BOWES: That's very strange. I just picked up something about World War I, and I didn't know what it was and this might not even associate with...this might be a book that was with this, and I seen one of the old-fashioned ships that had the front like that (draws a.)...and the water was down here (on bottom side)...and there was an advertisement for like joining the war. It may have been advertisement of some sort. There was this man and his face and all, and I just felt like this was showing him as proud to join the U.S. Army or join something. At that time...the time this book was made there could have been a war or it could have been something it was promoting or you may have been seeing this big posters to join the war to join something. This could have been like Teddy Roosevelt time or it could have been the first World War, but the feeling I had was the book was much older than that...although I did see this association with something different, maybe another book that was with it, or other information. This could have been something of this here (traces over the "ship"). I would say it was in someone's possession for a long period of time rather than being in the museum or something. They may have lumped this together with these books and all this other stuff together like they were a collector of some sort.

Pelican Key or Turn Key [Antique Dental Instrument]

I don't understand what this is...don't understand what it could be but the feeling I had was it could be a bag or a shoe or something. I kept seeing something sticking out, and I felt like it was a bone or like a piece of wood sticking out. It could be even something that was like a loom or something that was made to stretch leather or stretch cloth across. It could have flowers on it or whatever, but the feeling I had was that it was something that was...that had a stick through it...it pulled apart or something that was rounded that you stretched something with. It could even be like stretching a purse like to knit or it was like some sticks to relate to like stretching a shoe or stretching leather. I really wouldn't know what it was but...it could be something that was wound up. I don't know. The feeling I had was that it was used for stretching or winding something like...it may have had sticks on both ends to wind something apart or stretch them.

JONES: Do you get any feelings about where it was from or the kinds of people who used it?

BOWES: I would say it was very old. I see a very old woman or a very old person, set in their ways or very stubborn, and she could have white hair but the feeling I had was it was someone who...I would say the woman was alone or far away from other people. This could be like a crank (indicates box)...like it cranks or turns or something. I wish I could give you more but I didn't understand what it was. I don't know what this is. It seems strange. There could be something to do with leather...like leather boot or like a boot of some kind. It could be associated with that but I drew this (indicates shape on drawing) and I thought I was drawing a boot but it doesn't even look like a shoe or a boot at all...it looks more like a bag or something that you would look down in...open it up and look down in. I don't know what it is. I drew all that mess and I'm giving it to you. I did see something old like a crank and the wood was rotted and it may have a piece of steel through it and it may be a spool of some sort or a crank. I almost felt like it cranked electricity or cranked something, but again this could be cranking something that was stretching something...something that was made to turn around or something that was like wood rods. The feeling I had was that it was used for turning.

SECOND EXPERIMENT, PART II: OBJECTS UNWRAPPED.
BLIND READING BY ALBERT BOWES

Corn Husker [Albany Township, Pennsylvania, 1870]

I keep seeing a relationship to something being carried. I don't know why
but I kept feeling that this leather piece was around something. I felt as
though this stick was holding something up or it fell down on something. I
don't feel this was used very much. I don't know if this was owned by an
Indian or owned by someone who was a traveler, but I kept seeing that. I did
see something swinging and I did feel that whatever this was, it was swinging,
or I heard leather almost like a horses' saddle or something squeaking. I kept
seeing a round pole or spear or something in this leather. I don't know why I
kept feeling the feeling of someone's vest and I kept seeing this vest tied together with pieces of leather. I keep seeing someone have trouble with their
eyes. I kept seeing one of their eyes…this could be their right eye actually
crossed. The strongest feeling I had was this was holding something and it
went down so far on a pole or down on something and then it stopped. I don't
know if this was every part of a weapon or used in something that was ceremony but I felt it was used as a purpose. It wasn't so much as decoration. It
had a purpose. I keep seeing a man and I felt he was very primitive and I see
him humped over. His back hurting and I didn't know what this pertained to.
I kept seeing him having very long hair. I don't know if this was from Europe
but I felt like it could have been from another place other than the United
States. It could even be made of a special wood, but I would say that it was
near mountains where the wood grew very slowly. Very, very hard wood. I do
feel this wood was made or used for something other than this, and when it
broke, it could have been a lance or something, but they made it into this later
on because it was so strong.

JONES: Do you have any feeling about the use of it or what it is?

BOWES: I would say that maybe it tied a saddle bag together, tied something or held something together. But the feeling I had was it wore, it
squeaked a lot, kept feeling like leather. I see somebody grinding meal with a
big stone and I see it going around and around and it grinding.

JONES: What do the people look like?

BOWES: I would say that the person I seen before could have been a humped
back or somebody with problem with their back, but I kept seeing long black
hair. Then I felt there was someone with blond hair. This could have been
someone who discovered it. I see them as travelers so I would relate more
to black hair.

JONES: Do you get a feeling about what kind of places they might have
lived in?

BOWES: I see stone. I would say that the people who owned this may have
related to a place where there was stone or it was in the rocks, but I felt they
traveled a lot.

JONES: Do you feel the presence of many people or few people?

BOWES: This is very strange, and I don't know what it means, but I would
say that there could have been a thousand or a group and then areas with
groups of hundreds, but the feeling I had was there was something in someone's nose. I don't know what this means. Like there was a bone or something
in their nose. I see their teeth missing and I see them laughing. This could
even be Africa…a lot of noise and music. But I would feel that the person who
owned this was very serious. They weren't friendly or happy people. The
African people are more friendly or laughing or happy people, but I would feel
more with Indians or people who were serious. I kept seeing this wheel turning
and I hear a grinding sound. I wouldn't say this was from the south. I would

say it was from the mountains or from the north where trees grow very slow. The wood is very, very hard. That's funny. I kept seeing like a wooden door and I felt with the door like there was a wooden latch. It latched this way (sideways), and this could be somebody from Europe, but the feeling I had was it was something...could have even been like a cabin, but I would say that whoever made this door was a Caucasian or someone who knew carpentry... pioneer or somebody like that. I kept seeing something associated with a latch or a door that was latched...a dead bolt, or something that was made of wood. I do see somebody fishing, or something with water but I would feel that it was far from this.

JONES: The wood door—it is a door on the stone houses?

BOWES: I felt it was very musty inside. But I would say houses were very low and they may have thatched roofs or they're at an angle, up like this and then they're made of stone, but I would say that they're built on the side of a hill. They are very low or could be down underground, like you'd have to walk down underground because I felt it was very cold and damp.

Iron Knuckles [Gainesville, Florida, 1943]

I keep seeing violence with this, and the feeling I had was a relationship with an Italian person...something either to do with Germany or with Italy. The feeling I had was, I kept seeing buildings or barracks, and it could have been like in a city. I kept seeing an association with either...maybe they were German people, but I felt they were violent. I see a lot of violence in dealing with someone who is arguing or disapproving of...I would say it associated with something political, and I see groups of men and I felt these groups were someone who was very cruel like Gestapo or people who were very hard. I see this laying for a long time on the floor of a building...wood floors.

JONES: Do you have any feeling about what kind of building or where it is?

BOWES: I felt it was like barracks, or like buildings...it could have even been a concentration camp...buildings that were partially concrete but I felt the windows were way up high, and they could have had bars on them. I would say this has been used. I don't feel it was used to any great extent. I felt as if somebody could have been hit with it. Now, wait a minute. I picked up something about a big, heavy-set man with a moustache, and I felt he was very cruel. Something else I picked up was a younger man, but I felt he was someone who coughed a lot.

JONES: What about the time period this came from?

BOWES: This could have been very, very old. The feeling I had was...I don't know how old it is. I see other metal lying around, and I see a lot of these being made. In other words, they were made in a factory or made somewhere where there was a lot of them being made. I would say the man was wearing something that looked like clothes they wore in Europe, a little cap or a round cap, flat cap, and it could be in a big city or in Europe, like sewers in the streets.

JONES: What about the building it was in?

BOWES: I would say there was several buildings all together and I kept seeing the windows up high. I thought they were barracks, or warehouses. They were all one after another. It could have been a prison. I would say it was a very trying time. I would say this was brass knuckles or something to do with...I would say this was made for that purpose, not an imitation.

JONES: Is that the real thing?

BOWES: Yes. I don't feel they punched people in the face with it. I see them punching them in the side or the stomach, or in their shoulder. I kept seeing them pushing people, pushing people, pushing people, and this (artifact) was more of a bluff or threat, but I kept seeing them always pushing people, making them move, and this could be like a concentration camp or in a place

where they more or less showed this (artifact) and threatened somebody with it
...more so than it was actually hitting. But I do feel it did protect someone's
hand so they actually did use it. I see this big heavy-set man with this big
round heavy-set face and small moustache. I felt he had a very large neck, very
heavy and big man. I see them making two sizes of this (artifact). I see them
making a small and a large and this was a large. They made quite a few of
them. That's strange. I felt this was made from another piece of metal and the
metal could have been made from a piece of armament like a gun or a cannon or
a tank. It was melted down or it was used because something was wrong with
it. But I would say that it was in that period of time...with guns and tanks. It
wasn't metal that was taken out of the ground for that purpose. I felt it was
reused. I did feel a lot of violence with that, and I felt the man had a lot of
troubles or worries. I would say that thing made me very nervous.

Antique False Teeth [Edinburgh, Scotland. Late 19th-early 20th century.]

I keep seeing this sitting on a dresser, and I felt as though whoever made
it...I felt as though it was used but I don't feel it was used that often. I kept
feeling as though it was made or used for ceremony. I don't know if this man,
and I do know it belonged to a...at first I seen a woman, but I felt it was
maybe worn for a woman. I see this man in a lot of travel. He was a person of
high position. He could have even worn a uniform. I see a building that's
fallen down. I don't know if it was bombed or if it had fallen down, but I kept
seeing all his belongings were left behind. I do feel death with whoever
owned this.

JONES: **Do you have any feelings about the location?**
BOWES: I don't really know but I kept seeing Boston or like up north somewhere, and this again could come from Europe, but I kept seeing somebody as
a policeman or somebody with authority and I kept seeing them relating to a
feeling about telling people about something or warning them about something. I don't know if this would be an army officer or somebody in uniform. I
would say he could be in politics. I keep seeing this man having a problem
with his neck or his back. I didn't know what it meant.
JONES: **Around where this thing was, were there a lot of people or a few
people?**
BOWES: The feeling I had was like it was left behind, and this man may have
went to war or went somewhere, and I kept seeing a ship but I didn't know
what it meant...it could have been just at a distance. I felt this person was
very wealthy, could have owned ships or could have owned a business, but I
kept seeing a ship but I didn't know what it meant...it could have been just at
a distance. I felt this person was very wealthy, could have owned ships or
could have owned a business, but I kept seeing him dictating to people. I
would say that where he lived or where he was there wasn't very many people,
but I felt he went away and died. He died. He could have even died in action,
and his possessions were left in a...I see a...like a dresser, for a long period of
time. I keep seeing a cave or rocks or like a mountain or like caves like somebody was hiding in a cave, and this could have been like Japanese or it could
have been like something to do with an island. I see mountains and I felt
it was like islands, could have been Japan or something.
JONES: **What kind of climate do you feel?**
BOWES: Humidity. Where this was and in association with this some way I
kept feeling it was in a cold climate, but I see this person traveling or going
into a warmer, hotter climate. This is where he could have lost his life. I would
say the man, whoever this was, I felt he was in control and wore a uniform or
he did something that dictated to other people. He could have been a policeman, a politician, or in the army, but I felt like he traveled south to islands
or I felt it was undesirable...could have been like caves, and then I felt he lost

his life or he never came back. I felt he could have had more than one set or more than one. I would say how old it is, is in association with...I would say sixty years old but that would be very hard to say.

JONES: About the race of the man who owned it?

BOWES: I kept seeing red hair. He could have even been from England because I see an accent.

JONES: Can you reproduce the accent?

BOWES: He could have been from Canada, but I felt almost like an English accent...in Great Britain. He could have been like an explorer and interested in exploring something. I keep seeing him seeing or being interested in, like the White House, or some political setting...almost like he was interested in something political. I did feel this was stolen.

JONES: From him, or sometime later?

BOWES: From after he was already passed away. I felt it was from his grandchildren or his wife or an old woman. I see his house tore down or broke down and then going in.

JONES: Did you get a feeling about the sort of town he lived in? What did it look like? What did the houses look like?

BOWES: I would say it was a small village. The feeling I had was this road went down hill and went down to the river, or down to the water, like down to the docks or down, like slanting down. It was going down and there was a lot of little houses. I felt this was a small community, a small area. This is going down and there are houses all along the road. I felt there was water here and I felt it would be very cold at times, or it could be whaling, water, boats, or something. I really didn't pick up too much with that and that surprised me because I would feel that that (artifact) was something that would have been valuable to the man or to the person. But I felt he only used it...like ceremonial, like he took it out in everyday life or on the ship or when he was working.

Pocket Watch [*Silver, Made in Springfield, Illinois*]

I don't know if this person was an immigrant, but I would feel that this watch was very old, or was used by more than one person, but I felt this man. I see him waving at someone. I felt like he left his country. I would say that this watch has been repaired many times. It was used for a long time. I felt it was buried, or it was underground or it was buried in something for a long period of time. I keep seeing a man hiding money or gold or hiding something in a wall...brick...and I felt no one ever went back for it. I don't know why, but I felt this person was suppressed, like he was an immigrant into this country or an immigrant into some country, and this may have been something that was very valuable to him. I see it in the weather or outdoors or like associated with something that was abused, like it was abused. I see this man struggling with authority, or struggling with...he could have been somebody who worked around equipment or a train or a ship or around something but I kept seeing him in a hurry like he was a dock worker or somebody working, but ...I would say he had a very bad temper. I don't know if he was an immigrant from another country, but I see him having a...hard of hearing...maybe because of the equipment or the noise. I see a whistling train, and I see mountains like in Europe but I kept seeing mountains, steep mountains and this train going around this hill. Another thing I seen is someone who was involved or interested in sports like baseball or interested in some sort of sport...and I see men like in Germany or England, and I see them wearing like knee...like shorts, and I see them running around like playing a game like hitting a ball on the ground, like croquet or something. I see them speaking in another language, it could be Polish or German, or some foreign language.

I see this man being a little dogmatic...or dominated by the idea of who he was, or like he was prejudiced and maybe he was unhappy because they treated him bad.

JONES: In this country or in Europe?

BOWES: I would say, if it was in this country, it would be someone who was dominated because like he was Polish or a German person, but I would say in the other country he may have moved from then...once in Europe...I don't know if I said this about another object but I kept seeing someone not being able to hear very well. I kept seeing like he couldn't hardly hear this...hold it up to his ear. I see him either smoking a pipe or chewing on tobacco, and I felt in relationship to him he may have been someone with heavy eyebrows, or like he was someone who was kind of like heavy and fat, but I felt he was the typical immigrant-type of person in relationship to owning his own shop or business...a little bit narrow-minded about a new idea. He may have held onto old ideas. I don't know if Teddy Roosevelt, or at that time had any association to it, but I kept seeing someone very loud in political power. Like somebody who was very loud, saying, "Bully for you," very loud or something. I didn't know what it all meant, but he could have been like right for this person.

JONES: Do you get a feeling about what part of the country this person could have lived in?

BOWES: I would say New York or the north. He could have moved south, but I don't feel that much. I felt like he was...I'm not, of course trying to hurt his memory, but I would say he was narrow-minded, like once he moved to a place he stayed there, but he may have felt persecuted because of a change of political power. I do see him having a daughter and I felt like she either had blond hair or light colored hair, but I felt as though he didn't have a wife. I didn't know what that meant.

Straight Razor [Belonged to Ford family]

The feeling I got was that this was not ever used very much, but it was something more ceremonial, or something that was used for, like more to talk about and more for something that was fancy. I would say that this was either made in Germany or made in a country where they made this steel part of it, and I keep seeing a relationship to someone who had money or someone who wanted to show off something. I don't know whether this pertained to a German person or whether it was imported into this country. In association with this, I see death, like disaster or death, and I felt like what this person owned was given out to many different people, like Hitler, or somebody in a high position...that was blamed for something. But generally I felt they were very rich. They had a lot of money or they had a collection of things, and this may have been used but I don't feel it was used for a long period of time.

JONES: Do you have any feeling about where it may have come from?

BOWES: Where it was made? I felt the metal was made in Germany, but I don't know where the other parts of it was made. I see a lot of people in a lot of physical activity, like the whistle of a train and a lot of people loading, a lot of people migrating around. This person I felt wanted to stay in one place, this person was quite wealthy or something.

JONES: And you don't have a feeling about where that person was from?

BOWES: I don't know why, but I kept seeing lights, and I keep seeing shields over the lights. Maybe they couldn't see it from the air, like there was gas lights or kerosene lights but I kept feeling that they were shielded, and I don't know what that would mean but...I would say that this was possibly quite recent. I would say World War II or soon after. I wouldn't say it was older than that. I don't pick up too much from it. I don't feel it's very important. I did see somebody who was Oriental when I first picked it up, but I don't know what it meant...could be a woman. I do feel that that was used for cutting a sheet at one time...material. I kept seeing them cutting it and unrolling it, rather than like a shaver, rather than something you would shave with. I see them cutting material with it and unrolling it and I felt it was white or it was cotton. Maybe there was a shortage of cotton or a shortage of material. In other words, they may not have grown that material in that country, but I felt them cutting it and I felt they were trying to invent or create a synthetic. I would say that was a razor, but I would say it was made for cutting things... like there was a pattern, and they cut it. You know, it could have been used for that on a side line, or something. I don't know.

Human Hair Necklace [Boston, Massachusetts, 1835]

This is very strange. The first thing I pick up is that it was part of a uniform. I kept seeing something hanging from a pocket, and I felt first it was a dark uniform, and then I seen a red uniform. I keep seeing it holding two things together. I see whoever owns it being very chauvinist or very hard. Could be like in the army, but...I see a chain taking place of this...like a small chain. I do feel that was used. It was used for quite a period of time. I keep picking up weird shapes. I don't know what it was used for but I keep seeing something on this little eye here and I felt it was like a handkerchief, something that was very fine, but I didn't quite understand what it was. I don't know if this goes on the shoulder or holds something like a metal, like a decoration but that's the feeling I had about it. May even be a brim of a hat but the feeling I have is that I keep wanting to put it over my head...might go around the neck. The feeling I had was it held something together. I wish I could pick up more from it, but I really didn't pick up too much about it. I don't feel it was that valuable to the person who owned it.

JONES: Do you have any feelings about where it might have come from? Or what the person who owned it might have looked like?

BOWES: No. I see them getting off an airplane or a ship...navigation, a boat, something that would open up the door and it was like a hatch door, it sealed, and it opens up and they walk out and maybe walk down the plank or walk down the runway or down the walkway off an airplane. I did see this a real long time ago and I felt there was an old woman, and with that old woman I see her with very high shoes.

Nazi Wound Badge [German. World War II. Equivalent to three single badges]

Oh, this is the one I have been waiting for (laughs). I don't know if this is an imitation of something...but the feeling I had, whoever this belonged to was a soldier...someone in the German army in World War II. This person, whoever it was, was in the army but was associated with submarines, and I see them getting into a submarine and never coming back. I see them either coming to South America or like the Gulf of Mexico and I see the submarine going down. I did feel with this that this was somebody who was in infantry, but...I see a woman who had blond hair. I feel this person was a craftsman or someone who was talented, like a machinist. I see him very afraid. I feel his name was "Dutch" or "Ducko" or something like that. I see somebody with blond hair, or tall, and had a very thin head. He didn't have to have blond hair but he could have had light colored hair. I see another man who associated with going in the submarine. I see his hair being shaved, like bald, or a crew cut.

JONES: So there are two men...submarine and infantry...and this was given to the infantry...

BOWES: Yes. I see it associated with this person. These two could have been brothers. I don't know but I almost felt this an imitation of something.
JONES: **Who is giving it, or why is it being given to the man in the infantry?**
BOWES: I would say he was given this because of either something he did in a tank battle or something he did in association with being a marksman, being, like hand-to-hand combat, but I see him later going into tanks or equipment, like being a machinist. He had the association of something like a drive-shaft. I see some metal shrapnel getting into one of his shoulders, this might have knocked him out or something (Bowes touches right shoulder). I do see somebody talking about airplanes, or something flying. I didn't get too much from that. I keep seeing a woman who keeps nodding her head, but she doesn't say anything...like she is deaf. I kept feeling like she really doesn't approve of war, or violence, but I see her nodding her head...could be this person's mother. I see a lot of rubble, like bombs dropped or something. I see a lot of grey brick or red brick laying all over the road. This could have been associated with a tank or bombing. I did see a man with a patch over his eye or something to do with his eye, and this thing that we brought in before (human hair necklace) could associate with like having a spectacle on it. Like glass. Could have been holding up glasses or something made of glass. Sometimes I pick up about things that have already been brought in and then just comes to me very suddenly and I just give it to you.

Hand-Cuffs. [*Found on grounds of Chattachoochee State Hospital, Florida. Probably belonged to Old Penitentiary*]

I would say this was hand-cuffs, but I would say they were very, very old. I did see something in association with a ship, water. I didn't know what it meant. I would say this right here (key hole) could have unlocked it, or something was there to unlock it. I see someone drowning, or dying, falling down and not being able to come back up. I would say that this was only used for a temporary time. It wasn't used for a long period of time. I kept feeling as though this was snatched or pulled on...this chain. I don't know if this held something down or held some people together, but I felt it was in association with chains, things that were held together, and I kept seeing a house or a building burning, or falling down. I keep seeing a dirt floor and I see people, like a person dead or died, and I kept feeling like they were buried in the floor of the building. I keep seeing that being concrete. I see someone, I don't know if their hand is in here (cuff) or whether their wrist is but I see them pulling their hand out and laughing or showing someone else but I don't feel that did them any good. In another association I see something to do with a boat, and I kept seeing them on this boat or this could even associate with holding something down. I would say that this was buried or that this was something that was very old. I don't know if these people were like Indians, or these were people like someone who was abused like the Jews or Indians, but I felt as though they had dark hair, but I felt they were abused and abused and moved and treated very badly. I would say this was actually, literally worn by a person's wrist...like it was around something round. This chain moved... somebody living with it is the feeling I had. I see somebody screaming in the background...I don't want to get too personal but I see someone raped...raping someone in the background, so I would say there were men and women together. I see them in lines. I wouldn't say this was associated with Oriental people, but I did see someone with either black hair or slit, their eyes were slited, or more of a...could be Japanese or Oriental...or it could even be Indians, but...
JONES: **Why are these people in association with this object?**
BOWES: I would say they are prisoners. They were chained together, held

together either on a ship or this was held...or this was bolted or hooked to a ship or to a boat or to some sort of transportation...even to a wagon, but I felt as though it was chained together, one piece after another.

JONES: Do you have any feeling of location?

BOWES: I would say that it was somewhere where it was damp, and it could even have been south Florida...like moving Indians from south Florida to the west, but I kept feeling as though they were moving people, or they were moving them from a more damp area to a place where they didn't want to go.

JONES: Do you get any feelings about emotions? Or the kinds of people that are...?

BOWES: I would say these people didn't care about each other as much after they moved. I would say they threw people in together. I felt it was a suppressed group of people. I keep seeing a lot of screaming and a lot of...I felt negative. I would say that they were in a truck together or wagon together. I would say more like a wagon, or that would be of the time. It may not even be that far past but I see something made of wood, but I felt as though this could even have been made for slaves, but I didn't feel that way. I felt that this chain may have been changed, this chain as being more recent than this part (cuff). I felt the way the shape...it slid, it doesn't hang as easy. Another thing, I felt as though these people abused each other. They didn't care about each other so much. I did feel very strong about this woman being raped, and I felt ugly with it because, of course, she didn't want to be. I see a lot of screaming or whatever going on. I just felt very much about a ship. They may have even been just moved or kept on a ship, but I kept seeing this ship or this boat, and this could pertain to Key West or a place that associated with water, islands, but I felt there was a prison or a place where people were kept out on an island. I would say they kept women and men together for a period of time, and I felt it didn't work out. I didn't know what they did but I see problems about the way they ate or the way they fought with each other.

Antique Dental Instrument. [Mid-late 19th century. America.]

The feeling I had with this...the first thing I felt, the first thing I picked up, and it may associate with some of the other things, but I felt almost like there was a finger in here like that (places finger in area of artifact that would be attached to teeth for extracting). I felt as though there was something leather, and this could have been leather straps around their wrists, but I felt this tightened something up, this little hand here held it (indicates clamping portion of tool). I feel this was used. I see them tightening, maybe tightening a bottle, tightening something with it. I would say it had tremendous leverage, whatever you wanted to do—tighten or whatever you wanted to do...persuade somebody into something. In other words, if you grabbed that and pulled it, it would break their finger...pull something. Again I seen something about a boat (laughs). I would feel as though this was a tool, and I would say it was very old.

JONES: How old is it? Do you get any associations that would tell us that?

BOWES: The feeling I had was they looked like a pirate, or they look like that time. I see like the Mississippi, or like a period of time of the past. I see a lot of things made of brass, like on a ship to keep from rusting. This could be harnesses on a wagon, or a horse drawn something. I see a lot of people drunk. I would say this was a well-kept tool, that it was used. I felt like they almost took something off the top of a bottle, or they pulled something. They did this (applied griping end to his finger) and then they tightened up and then they turned it or something. The feeling I had was that they was kind of hard people. They drank a lot or they were cussing or hard type of people. I would say it was of the past and it could have been like 1837 or 1850, or something.

JONES: Do you get a feeling about where it might have come from?

BOWES: I see someone calling somebody "Swede"...like "you're a Swede." I really can't find the location. I would say that it traveled, that it was on a boat or on a wagon, like one of these large wagons with a lot of horses. I felt it was traveling, traveled a lot. This could have even been from Europe because I see wagons and people who were on the wagons blowing horns, or like there was a horn blowing, and like noises. This could have been a horn like in a building or a business, like every so many hours it blew. Could have been on this wagon and they blew it every so often to warn travelers, like they passed people going very fast with this wagon and there's a young boy on the top blowing a horn. That's funny. I keep seeing something to do with a phonograph, one of those things you crank up and it makes music. And I felt this was either in the museum with it or it associated with something along with something old like that...you cranked it up and it played and it made music. I see music with it. Kept seeing an association with something that would be adjusted or cranked. I don't feel so much that this really belongs with it but I felt it was more like something in with all this other stuff. Maybe this is in a museum or in a collection with this thing that cranked up and then made music, or like you cranked it and I don't know what this would be. I felt it was like rolls of brass and it had dots on it and maybe you cranked it and made noise or made your voice or something...you talked into it and it recorded it and when you played it or turned it, it made noise. This was with that (artifact), or near it. I keep seeing somebody rubbing somebody down with liniment, some sort of oil on their back and on their body. I felt like that was maybe a cure-all or something but I kept seeing it being like Ben Gay, like a rub that's supposed to remove like some muscle pain or something. I don't know what all this stuff means, but I'm going to give it to you and hope it makes sense.

Sewing Bird. [Late 19th-Early 20th century. America. Used for holding cloth for hand-sewing].

First thing I felt was I kept seeing a desk, and I seen this woman and I felt she was in a hurry, that she was rushing from one place to another. The feeling I had with this was that it was on a desk or it was on a board, and I felt like there was paper in there or leather, and it was holding something and I don't know if this was in like a factory or it was in a place where...in association with something being stretched. I felt that with that crank thing, and I felt that with this, too...to a degree. I see something being held like to something solid with a screw. The bird shape, I have no idea why that is there. I would say that it associated with something that was held. The feeling I first got was the thing about the desk. I felt something later on about a car or transportation, and I don't know why. Maybe this leather is being punched or held together in some way. I did see something...I felt like the company or the people who made that also made guns. Somebody made guns around them, or had guns around them. I don't know if anybody's fingers were ever pinched in here, but the feeling I had was...but the feeling I had was in association with holding things together. I would say that this was either in a blacksmith's shop or on a man's desk, but I felt things were held inside here (clamp portion) like a paper weight.

JONES: You mentioned a woman very quickly in the beginning...

BOWES: I felt this woman...like this might have been something that belonged to Benjamin Franklin, some inventory, or some business man, and I see them walking in and out. I would say this person was interested in making ...it could have been making an airplane or making a gun or making cars, but I kept seeing a factory or like interests in making things. But I felt this woman was kind of a nagger or a person who nagged, or somebody who was like a secretary or a landlord, but I keep seeing her walking in and walking out... every so often.

JONES: **What is the time period?**

BOWES: I don't know. I get the number "16", but I didn't know what it meant.

JONES: **Do you have any feeling about location?**

BOWES: No. Again I didn't feel this was valued. I keep getting the word "north," due north. I don't know if this went along with that other thing out there, the crank thing, but it could be of the same age. Is there a possibility of that?

JONES: **I have no idea.**

BOWES: I didn't pick up too much from that. I don't know if that thing was on a boat, or something but I kept seeing something rocking back and forth like it was holding something and I felt it was rocking back and forth.

THIRD EXPERIMENT: OBJECTS NOT WRAPPED.
BLIND READING BY ALBERT BOWES.

Navaho Bridle. [Arizona]

The first thing I picked up with this is something to do with a horse. I kept seeing someone who is Spanish, or someone who is in uniform. I don't know if this was a person who rode this horse, or related to someone in the west. I keep seeing a very dusty place. I keep seeing a relationship to a man who...I don't know if this is...whether it's from Spain or whether it's from a place that...I see large groups of people and I don't know if they wear white uniforms or white clothes, such as peoples in the desert. I kept seeing them riding with covers over their faces, or clothes that were...could even have been white clothes like in Egypt. I keep seeing them riding very fast. I see the horse, or an animal, and I keep seeing a relationship to something which I felt was like an animal that was sick, or like had foam coming out of its mouth. I don't know if there is another animal involved, but I keep seeing something chained to something almost as if it was a bear or a dog, or something and I kept feeling as though that...I keep seeing some sort of sport, and I don't know if they have a long stick or a long...like prod or something but I see them running around or running by something sitting on the ground and them hitting it, or sticking it with a spear or stick. I would say that the people involved in this may have eaten a lot of very, very spicy or greasy food. I would say that it could even have been garlic, but I see them...like their bodies reeked of this smell.

MRS. BOWES: **Do you get anything about where they lived, or what the dwellings looked like?**

BOWES: I would say their dwellings were made of rock.

MRS. BOWES: **You said something about "dusty". Do you get anything else about the country?**

BOWES: I kept seeing mountains and I don't know if this is like Europe or Spain, but I kept feeling...I kept seeing someone...I don't know if it would be an Indian, but I kept feeling this was very, very old. I would say that it could even be from India. I feel that the people may not be very civilized. I don't feel like this was made by a machine. I would say it was made...more like forged, and made more like something that was beaten, hammered, or beat into shape. I don't feel it was made in a factory. I keep seeing a man beating something with a hammer to make it. I would say either parts of this or the whole thing originated in another country, and I don't feel so much with the United States.

MRS. BOWES: **Did these people move around or stay in one place?**

BOWES: I don't know if they were ranchers but I would feel that they did move, or they migrated. I see them having one home base or one area which I would say would relate to a confidence, or, in other words a place where they stopped or stayed. I saw a line of horses, or a line of people moving. I did feel like they needed to rest their animals or whatever. I don't know if this was in the desert, but I kept seeing something to do with people who were very hard people. I don't know if this was Mexico but I kept seeing something in relationship to some people who...I don't know if there was a boat involved but I did see some salt, like salt air, or salt water, and I didn't know what this meant. I would feel that whatever this is, this silver, or metal was at one time very corroded, or it could have been around the salt air. I would say that their houses were made of rock or stone, and that their windows were very small or open.

MRS. BOWES: You said something about them wearing robe-type clothing?

BOWES: I would say that this was protection from the elements or protection from sand, because I see a lot of sand blowing. I see open land. I don't know if there is clay, I keep seeing white clay, like a white chalky looking clay, or sand, and I seen something pertaining to the mountains, and I would say it was much more fertile around the mountains.

MRS. BOWES: What about the temperature or climate?

BOWES: I would say it was very extreme. It was very hot during the day and cold during the night. I don't know if these people ever lived in caves, but I did see some caves where they may have stayed or hid things.

MRS. BOWES: What about anything political or any type of conflicts?

BOWES: I would say that with relationship to conflict...I see large knives, or something they would hold in a harness or a sheath beside them. I would say these people were either very hard or very violent. I would say they fight among themselves. I see small groups because I don't feel that large groups could be sustained in a small area. Now they may get together as large groups every so often, but basically I kept feeling as though they were in smaller groups. I see large areas of land and then mountains in between. I keep seeing these people with very yellow teeth, like their teeth were worn from chewing dry meat, like eating jerky, or like chewing grain of some sort, but I felt they had poor teeth.

MRS. BOWES: What about their race?

BOWES: I would say they were dark-skinned people. I do see a moustache, and black hair. I did feel as though this (artifact) was...something that was used very much. It maybe was ceremonial or something that was used for ornaments. I do feel it was used very much. I keep seeing like Mexico, or Spaniards...Mexican people, or from Spain or whatever, but the feeling I had was if this was...I would say it was from another country, but basically I would say it could have been from a country where the people may have been very hard on someone else. There could have been slaves involved. People that they thought very little of.

Hopi Prayer Wand [Arizona. 1900. Used in Maran Ceremony.]

The feeling I had with this was a feeling with something to do with Indians. I don't know if these are Indians of the north. The feeling I had was something associated with Indians who did fishing or fished, or was around water. I don't know if they had interests relating to something that...like this (artifact) was against a wall or against a post. I kept seeing it against something. I don't know if this was something like there was beads or leather hanging from it, but the feeling I had was that there was something laying on it. I would say this (artifact) is very primitive, or crude. I don't know if a child made it but I didn't feel too much with it. Basically, I did feel the person who made this was in a hurry. I don't feel so much skill with them. I would say that this meant something. It could have meant something that was like a ceremonial time, or a Period of time or weather...or a period of a certain area of time. This could have been a time of the year. Basically, I don't know if these were Indians from the west, but I still felt they originated in a colder area that associated with fishing or trapping. They may have been in the north and then later moved south.

MRS. BOWES: Do you see anything about what they looked like?

BOWES: I would say they were Indians. I did feel as though they wore heavy clothing.

MRS. BOWES: Do you feel anything about what they had on, or any kind of decoration...anything like that?

BOWES: I would say that they were violent people...if someone was on their territory or went into their area. I kept seeing something to do with South America, but I kept seeing something to do with someone who was very primitive and they could have been south of where they (artifact) were. I would say that these people could be of a warring sort. I see them practicing with sticks. I almost...like they were practicing with shields, and sticks, and they could have worn something like a helmet or headgear, but I do feel as though they may have lived in wooden buildings, or made of logs.

MRS. BOWES: What about their numbers?

BOWES: I would say they were in the hundreds. I do feel as though they were more permanent or permanent people.

MRS. BOWES: Do you get any more about what that (artifact) was used for?

BOWES: I would say they ate fish or raccoons or animals that pertain to something associated with water.
used for basically what it was made for. This could have been associated with something...I still see it being put on the wall and hung up. I did feel there was an association with someone who did a lot of coughing, or there was sickness. I see a room full of smoke or something like a tent or a room full of smoke. I didn't understand it.

MRS. BOWES: Do you see anything about what they ate?

BOWES: I would say they ate fish or racoons or animals that pertain to something associated with water.

MRS. BOWES: What about the countryside or climate?

BOWES: I would say it was very cold, and possibly humid. This is strange because I felt this wood was very light or a very soft wood. I don't know if this would be associated with Florida, but I felt this wood grew very fast. Warm weather. The temperatures were like...the trees grew very fast, like they were in a good environment. I was confused about two environments... one hot and one cold...also torn between north and south.

MRS. BOWES: Did you see any more about what they wore?

BOWES: I would say they wore something made of leather but I didn't pick up too much with that.

Food Basket. [Bontox. Mountain Province, Luzon, Philippines.]

The feeling I had with this is the feeling of something being hidden or stored. I don't know if this was in an area of country where there was a lot of grass or an area of it being wet. I keep seeing something being stored in here, and it could have been carried over a long period of time or an area. I don't know if a woman carried this, but I kept feeling as though it was something valuable. It could have been medicines. I don't know if this was Egypt or another country, but I kept feeling as though it could have been carried...like there could have been a strap through these little circles here on the ends and carried over the shoulder. I do see groups of people. It could have pertained to nomads. I felt as though these people may have kept this in a tent or in a building. I keep feeling medicine or some sort of herbs or something that was valued. They could even have been from Egypt, but the feeling I had was, I would say this was valued but it was made for durability, or it was made to be used, to be carried, something to be carried inside. I don't know if there was bones or something a little bit eerie carried in this. I kept feeling as though there was something that could have been magical or considered magical. I see water or areas of grass land.

MRS. BOWES: What about what they ate?

BOWES: I would say corn or wheat, but that's all I get...bread maybe.

MRS. BOWES: Do you get anything about what they looked like or what they wore?

BOWES: I keep seeing one of them either passed away or dead, and I don't know if this was left in there when a person died, but I see one of their eyes crushed in or rotten or like they're dead, like a mummy or something. I kept seeing something in here like food. I don't know if this would be made to be carried into the spirit world or into another life, but I kept seeing somebody passed away. I would say that this could possibly be an Indian, but I kept feeling it could associate with something that would pertain to...I couldn't understand it. I did feel as though there was a lot of hair around this person's face. I see them having troubles with something in their lungs or their heart or lungs. This could even be a person of value. I felt as though this sat in place for a long period of time.

MRS. BOWES: Are there large groups of people around this or small groups?

BOWES: I would say that there were several hundred or several thousand. There was large groups of people. I don't know if there was a pyramid or a... something made of concrete...I wouldn't say concrete, but I would say stone, but I see these people visiting a large city, or a group of people, in other words this could have been in South America, but I felt an association with people who related to a larger city, possibly for trading. I see stone structures. I felt very strong about something being buried underground like a cave or a pyramid or a cavern, or building...could even be buildings in to the wall, but I kept seeing stone or caves.

MRS. BOWES: Are you talking about living quarters or...?

BOWES: I would say that they are more religious quarter. I keep seeing stairways going down into a cavern or into a cave, and this could even be into a temple or a pyramid or something, but the feeling I had was...I wouldn't say so much with the desert, but I would say it may have changed since the times these people who made this were there. Jungle area, like Africa or South America...a jungle place.

MRS. BOWES: Did you see anything about what their faces looked like?

BOWES: No, I didn't pick up too much on that. I would say they had long hair.

JONES: You said something about a lot of hair around the face?

BOWES: I really couldn't say too much about that. It could be hair that was around their face after they died, but I didn't pick too much up about that. I keep seeing them...I keep seeing planks or wooden planks. I felt very strong about that, things that were like wooden idols, and I don't know if they were wooden...of animals. They deteriorated and rotted. I keep seeing these things put together with little blocks of wood. I felt that they were like totem poles or some sort of animal that was put together piece by piece, and this could be inside a pyramid or inside a building. I would say that these people traveled. I keep seeing an association with this (artifact) being something that hid something, or something was inside. Again, I felt it was almost shaped like a boat because it was supposed to travel, maybe through the spirit world.

MRS. BOWES: Did you get anything about what was in it?

BOWES: It could have been something like herbs. I felt there was something ...like something silver associated with it, but I didn't know what it meant, something like jewelry, but I kept seeing it being in a different area.

MRS. BOWES: Do you get anything about the political organization?

BOWES: I would say that whoever this associated with, whenever they died there was a disruption in politics or disruption in rulership. Basically I kept seeing problems with a dynasty, like a group of people who governed each other. I kept seeing a little bit of havoc. If this does relate to someone in South America...or it could associate with some who was involved in...could even be Africa. I kept feeling as though it was south, south of the continent or whatever. I keep seeing a lot of disruption. I do see a civilization. I keep seeing them making several of these but I feel they threw some of them away.

MRS. BOWES: What about the climate?

BOWES: I didn't pick up anything about that. I thought it was hot or warm.

MRS. BOWES: Did you get anything about what they wore?

BOWES: I don't know if these are robes, but I felt something to do with material...could have been woven. I keep seeing something like a loom that's pushing material together...weaving something, and when they weaved they pushed it down strings, but I didn't pick up too much from that.

MRS. BOWES: What about how they prepared food?

BOWES: I see a lot of...I see them sitting on the ground, and I see lots of bowls, and I felt all these bowls had different things in them. I kept seeing...it could be like frogs, it could be like fish, but I kept seeing things dried. I did see a boat, and I felt this boat was something with a pontoon, like pontoons on it. I didn't see it as a very large boat...pontoons, and a sail. In other words, like a canoe...like a large canoe with a little canoe on the side and maybe a sail.

MRS. BOWES: Do you get anything about their religious beliefs?

BOWES: I would say they believed in violence or believed in fire. I saw them dancing on fire...volcanoes...religious worship of fire. Something that's very loud. They may be even afraid of lightning, but I kept seeing something on fire and movement. This is all I get.

Woman's Knife. [*Eskimo, Alaska, Mid to Late 19th century.*]

I see this as being very, very old. I don't know if it was buried in the ground, but I would say that this could have even been Florida. A wet place. I keep seeing a relationship to water and wet ground. I do feel as though in association with this I see this used for scraping, like scraping the fat off of skin. I saw a lot of fat.

MRS. BOWES: Where did it come from?

BOWES: Like I said, I felt it came from Florida, or a place that was very wet.

MRS. BOWES: What did the people look like?

BOWES: I would say they were Indians, or people like early...I would say they were Indians, but they may have settled an area of ground. I keep seeing an association with things that were thrown away, or thrown into a hole and then covered up. I kept seeing very wet country...saw grass or a lot of wet ground.

MRS. BOWES: Do you see them moving a lot or...

BOWES: I would say that they did move by water. I keep seeing mounds of dirt or shell, and I keep seeing something on the top. I would say it was like a grass hut. I don't know if there was a ladder or something going up inside but I would say the opening is either in the middle or at one side.

MRS. BOWES: How do you see these people dressed?

BOWES: I would say that they originally didn't have very much on, but as time went on I see them wearing clothes. In other words, this could be something that would associate with clothing like robes or long clothing. At one time I felt as though the leaders or the people who lead these people could have worn this. I felt normally the people just wore leather…a very small piece of it.

MRS. BOWES: **What about their numbers?**

BOWES: I would say that there were two or three hundred at the most. I would say that there was something about their leaders on their religious groups, and I see them up on top this hill, and I would say that it was made of shells. I did see canoes or water. I do see something to do with the water or I see them traveling or trading with some people that were north of where they lived.

MRS. BOWES: **Do you get anything about their religious beliefs?**

BOWES: They were either Indians or early settlers, and the feeling I had was that they worshipped the weather or worshipped the seasons. I would say they were very stubborn people or that they didn't want to change.

MRS. BOWES: **You said something about that (artifact) being used to scrape?**

BOWES: I would say that they scraped or separated fat from the leather or it was involved in scraping something.

MRS. BOWES: **What do you see them eating?**

BOWES: I would say they ate oysters or shellfish or something involved with something around the water. I did see them having a war-club or some sort of club. I felt it had a spike or a rock on it, or something pointed on it. They could have beat…like hit something like a seal or otter with it. I felt like it was something …after they caught something they may have to hit it with a club. I kept seeing the water. I keep seeing them wearing something in their ears and I don't know if they punched holes through their ears or they had something hanging from their hair but I see something hanging on both sides, and I would say it pertained to beads or pieces of bone.

MRS. BOWES: **What about houses?**

BOWES: I would say it was more a ceremonial or religious up on a hill. The other houses I kept seeing are like little huts or something, like lean-to or something more like something they associated with staying for a short time. Something low to the ground. I felt this rock (artifact) may have come from farther north than the wood. I keep seeing a fire or something burning around this, but this may just be like treating the meat or treating something.

MRS. BOWES: **Do you see anything about who was using this?**

BOWES: I see a woman…I would feel that it was a man, but I keep seeing a woman leaning over and pulling on something, and scraping something with this (artifact). I felt this at one time may have been a color, like it was coated with something or it was…basically I feel that this is a tool, a tool they used, but I did see some color to it. I don't feel these people were very happy. They may have been pressured or pushed, but I see them quite primitive, the actual people who made this. I would say a woman made this or someone made this, and I see them sitting with their legs crossed and I see them carving something. This could have been an old man or a woman.

MRS. BOWES: **Do you get any feeling about the time period?**

BOWES: I don't know if this was the west coast, but I kept seeing the west. This could have been west of Florida or west of the country, but I keep seeing it in association with…I would say before the white settlers came, but I keep seeing an association with something that would be people who worried or people who weren't settled where they were. I did feel with them that they had bells, and I didn't feel as though they (archeologists) knew that, the people who found that. I see them having little bells. They may have been made of bamboo or some sort of wood with wood inside, and when the wind blew or when people came through the woods that these little bells or these things rattled. I felt like they were bamboo with holes in them. I see them tied and then another piece of wood inside, and I felt there was a hole here and it was tied…hanging in the woods and when these people came to attack or invade them it was like an alarm and I felt these things rattled. They were made of wood, or parts of them could have been made of clay.

MRS. BOWES: Do you know who might have been attacking them?

BOWES: I would say there were other Indians, or other people who were more of nomads.

Seminole Woman's Hair Board. [*Florida, 1942*]

The first thing I picked up with this is a woman. I felt as though this woman was traveling. I don't know if this was a woman or a man, but I kept seeing something of a religious sense. I did feel as though they were very worried or troubled. I don't know if they were Pilgrims or people who were…I keep seeing a carriage or a wagon. I didn't understand it well.

MRS. BOWES: Do you get anything about the countryside?

BOWES: No, not really.

MRS. BOWES: What was that (artifact) used for?

BOWES: I would say that it could be…the first thing I picked up was that it was like a brim of a hat, but I didn't feel it was. The second feeling I had was that it was part of a wagon, or part of an interior of something. I really didn't pick up too much about that. I don't feel this was valued very much. I keep seeing these people worried as if they were going to be attacked or something. I do feel that they were either narrow-minded or that they didn't want to change. I don't know if they were early settlers of Florida, or a place that they didn't feel welcome, but I see yellow fever or disease, and I didn't feel very good with it.

MRS. BOWES: Are these large groups or small groups?

BOWES: I would say they were small groups of people and they could have had wagons, but I kept feeling like…the wagons, like there was maybe a solid wheel or like a wheel that was repaired, but I kept seeing wheels turning. I see the people very worried. I would say that this person carried a book or carried a bible or carried something with them. I keep seeing an association with a woman.

MRS. BOWES: What did she wear?

BOWES: I would say she wore a very long dress down to her ankles or clothes that were very long, but other than that I didn't pick up too much.

MRS. BOWES: Do you see anything about the food they ate?

BOWES: I keep seeing a hurricane or a storm, as if it blew things away, and I just didn't feel too good with the people. I felt sad.

MRS. BOWES: What about their dwellings?

BOWES: I would say that if they had glass windows, they were very fortunate. I kept seeing them having burlap or something over the windows.

MRS. BOWES: Do you get anything about where they came from?

BOWES: I kept seeing a ship, like a boat from another country, but…other than that I didn't pick up too much. This could even be a piece of furniture or something, but I still see these people traveling or moving.

MRS. BOWES: Do you get what that (artifact) is?

BOWES: I seen a trunk, but I didn't know what it meant.

Adze Handle. [*Nootka. British Columbia. ca. 1860.*]

I keep seeing something that associates with something to be carried, and I would say to the bottom of this that there could have been something glued or stapled, or nailed together. I do feel as though that this was not used. I felt it was more like decorating something. I did see someone holding it and pushing it back and forth, and I didn't know why...or holding it or carrying it. I did feel that this was from the north, and I feel as though it would associate with something that would...with people who...with water. I see mountains or water, like swift running water. I would say it in association like with a hawk or with a bird that catches fish, or catches other birds. I would say that this bird, whatever it stands for, stands for eating meat. I do feel in association with this, I don't know if this is white people or who it is, but I see machinery, like a sewing machine. I kept seeing that associated with someone either with glasses or like early America or Pilgrims or something like that. I keep seeing something trailing out behind this (artifact), but I didn't know what it was.

MRS. BOWES: Do you see anything about where they lived or what they lived in?

BOWES: I don't know if they ever lived in a ship, but I kept seeing a boat. I did see people coughing or something with their throat. I did see somebody being a merchant or selling or trading things. I do see someone who could be in politics, dressed like Benjamin Franklin, or someone who was dressed up like a businessman. This could be someone who was trying to deal with people, in other words, convince them into selling their land or trading something... real estate, or something. This could associate with Europe because I kept feeling people, like Germans, like people who were very determined. There could even have been an association with white people who were trying to trade for land.

MRS. BOWES: Do you see where this land might have been? In what area?

BOWES: I would say in the north.

MRS. BOWES: What about the climate?

BOWES: I would say it was cold and foggy at times.

MRS. BOWES: Do you see what race these people were? Or what they were wearing?

BOWES: I keep seeing something else besides this (artifact), and I see a collection. I see something else made of wood and it's like a duck. I would say that this could be like early America. I kept getting a feeling like there was lots of things in a little shop, and there was like cuckoo clocks and I keep hearing "tick, tick, tick, tick." Ticking or noises, and I feel like it's novelties or something like a novelty. I see someone who is very particular, and they may have been talking about furniture or making wood furniture. I keep seeing a woman but I feel that she is in the background. I don't know if it was right after a war, but I would say that there's a lot of prosperity. In other words, people making things and this may, may have made gun stocks, or something. I keep holding it (artifact) and I kept feeling like it stuck against something, held against something. I don't know if this (artifact) is like a door handle, like hooked onto a door or whatever. I keep seeing cloth around it, and I felt it was like this but I felt there was cloth on it, and I didn't know what it meant. I don't understand. I do see someone who made this was once on a ship. I see everything made of wood...brass.

MRS. BOWES: Do you see anything about what the ship looked like?

BOWES: I keep seeing a door, and I didn't know what it was but I felt this person stayed indoors a lot.

MRS. BOWES: The person who owned this object or...

BOWES: Made it. I see it like being up in an attic or being inside a building for a long time. This could even be a museum or something somebody had. I see it sitting on someone's desk for a period of time, or sitting on something, and I felt things were lined up. Could even been decoys, or something. I keep seeing almost like there was another one, and I don't know if this was like a musical instrument or something that went in and out, but I kept seeing it being slid in and out, but I didn't know what it meant.

Ibo Embroidered Hat. [*Nigeria. Man's Hat. 1950*]

I keep feeling as though this was...the feeling I had was almost like a graduation gown, but I felt as though it pertained to religion or belief or something. I don't know if this was from India or a place where there was a belief of something, but I see an organization of people. I keep seeing people talking to one another. I do see a very small man, and I felt as though he's bowing to someone else. I don't know if they are sitting on the ground, or they are all sitting or squatting or cross-legged, whether they're Japanese or from another country. I felt generally that they were all talking. Maybe discussing something. This could even be testing tea or testing liquor or some sort of drink. I felt like it was a group of people celebrating something. I felt whoever wore this walked very fast. At first I did see a woman involved and then I didn't see her anymore.

MRS. BOWES: What did the person who wore this look like?

BOWES: They could be oriental, but again they could be something else. I keep seeing him bowing or holding his hands in front of him like he's praying or bowing. I would say that he was two-faced, or wasn't exactly the person he was talking about. He may have been desiring power or desiring something—influence. I keep seeing him blinking one eye and I felt like he had something wrong with his eye, or he could have been very old. I felt first he was very young when he got this or there was something young about it. I don't know if this was stolen or taken from a trunk, but...could have been from another country. I see them very set in their ways.

MRS. BOWES: What kind of foods did these people eat?

BOWES: I don't know if they're vegetarians, but I see them either working with...chop sticks, or picking things up with a little spoon. I keep seeing them talking. I do feel this person went to college or school.

MRS. BOWES: What kind of houses did they live in?

BOWES: I would say that they related to a feeling...I don't know if they went high or went up high but I see somebody with either a red beard or red hair, and I see them talking with someone else, and I don't know what that meant.

MRS. BOWES: What about the climate?

BOWES: I didn't pick up anything about that. It could have been cool, or misty, but I felt it may have been foggy. It could have even pertained to an island.

MRS. BOWES: Do you see anything else about their clothing?

BOWES: I felt like someone wore this for awhile or had this and thought it was a joke, or thought it was funny because I see them laughing. I see someone else talking to someone and I keep seeing lots of fire, or like a war, and I felt that this was hidden in a trunk, or hidden underground, hidden somewhere. I keep seeing it being on a boat for a short period of time, or around water, but I didn't pick up anything else.

MRS. BOWES: How many people are there?

BOWES: I would say there was a great number of people, but where he or she or whoever this person was...I would say they were looking for solitude of some sort. I don't know if this was in a military association but I see a lot of people in rows marching...like they were watching it.

Mono Indian Basket. [*Great Basin. Mid-19th century.*]

The feeling I had was that they had something that went on their head, and they may have had basketry or...not a basket but like a big hat, may have had a hat that was made of similar things to this (artifact). I don't know if this is oriental people or Japanese or Indians, but I kept feeling as though this hung up, and I kept feeling as though there was three or more ropes or strings. I did feel as though they suspended this from something. I felt they may have carried something in it or had something to dry out. I don't know if they had it off the floor to keep it away from rats or bugs or something, but I keep seeing it being covered by a piece of material. I don't know if this is a cover (artifact) to something, but I kept feeling as though there may have been another end or may have been something else to it. This may have been a cover over top of it. But I still see it hanging.

MRS. BOWES: Do you see anything about what they ate?

BOWES: I would say that there is an association with something that they are breaking open with their teeth like peanuts. I don't feel that's the only thing they eat, of course, but I see wheat, and I see a goat, or animals that they would milk.

MRS. BOWES: About their houses?

BOWES: I would say they were made of stone and rocks. I would say these people stayed in one place, but they may have been seasonal, in other words, moved if they were seasonal.

MRS. BOWES: What about their numbers?

BOWES: I would say they were in small groups but there was quite a few group areas. I would say there was more women...in other words, there may have been one man and several women. I felt as though that he had either sexual relationships with several women, or he may...could have been head of a religious group, or head of something but I still see him having more than one woman.

MRS. BOWES: What about the kind of clothing they had?

BOWES: That's very strange. I keep seeing something around the woman's chest. I don't know if it was like a basket, or like it was a weaved bra, but the feeling I had was like it was something like she carried something on her back, and I felt like she may have carried up and down mountains, or carried something on their back like maybe even a baby, but I feel these straps across their chest. It could have been around their breasts or something, but that's the feeling I had.

MRS. BOWES: Do you get anything else about what the area looked like?

BOWES: I would say there was mountains there. I see grasses, but I didn't pick up too much on that. I do see a large thing that looked like a kiln or something that they would shove bread into and this could even been in Mexico or in the desert. I see them shoving like a big scoop shovel in there with either clay or bread on it.

MRS. BOWES: Do you see anything else?

BOWES: I would say that they had black hair. I see a lot of dust. I see them sitting on floors in a concrete or adobe building. I kept feeling as though they were sitting on the floor...like there was dust around. I see a lot of blankets or maybe ceremonial or something of blankets on a wall...weaved.

MRS. BOWES: What about religion?

BOWES: I keep seeing them going (he chants), or making noise like that. They may have been singing or chanting. This could have been in Egypt or somewhere, but I felt as though they were singing or talking like that. I see a lot of people swaying back and forth like that. I see a man smoking marijuana or poppy or something that would make him like...having hallucinary drugs, or like smoking something that would make him sick. I wouldn't say so sick physically but mentally. I felt he was very skinny. I would say he hallucinated or had mental problems...like mental visions. I would say there could have been a policeman or a man who was a...this could have been a British soldier or a person with a white uniform, and I didn't know what this was. He could have come off of a ship.

Silver Stirrups. [*Brazil. Possibly 19th century copy of earlier
Spanish-Portuguese type.*]

I would feel that this was a shoe (although the photograph shows two stirrups, Bowes had access to only one of the pair while at the museum). I would
say that it associated with armor or something that was either on a horse or
something that was on a person's foot, or on their toe. I keep feeling as though
this thing at the top was hinged, and I don't know if this hole in the bottom
was for pulling it off the foot, but I feel like they would hinge it up and lift up
on it. I don't know if this is from Europe. I do feel that this was used, but used
possibly in association for something that was for ceremonial purposes. I don't
know if this is quite recent. I keep seeing something being hot. I see someone
complaining about it not fitting.

MRS. BOWES: What did these people look like?

BOWES: I would say they had dark skin...I see one of them who is very short
and stocky, and could have had blond or red beard, and basically I would feel
that they had...I keep seeing this man laughing and I didn't know what it
meant. I would feel that this associated with something more of riding or ceremonials, for decoration rather than something they would use every day. I did
feel as though they were riding. I see a brother of a man and it could have been
the person who used this, but I see his foot catching someone else's saddle or
catching something and breaking his foot.

MRS. BOWES: What kind of houses did they live in?

BOWES: I don't know if they traveled but I kept seeing horses or a horse. I
would say they lived in a stone building. That's all I can pick up. Could even
be a castle but I would say it was more like a stone building. Again I kept
seeing something with French or Spanish. I don't know if this is an imitation
of something but I kept feeling in relationship to something that it was not
used for everyday use. This may have been made to be used in everyday use,
but I didn't feel it was.

MRS. BOWES: Did these people move around a lot?

BOWES: I wouldn't say this was used very much (artifact). I do feel as
though someone was spoiled or someone...in other words this was owned by
someone who didn't use it very much.

MRS. BOWES: What about their numbers?

BOWES: I would say there was many different people but this (artifact) was
more of a select few. These people were in royalty or in a position or like in the
army or something like that. I didn't feel it was something that they used
everyday. I would say that this was very, very expensive at its time. I would
say it was extremely expensive.

MRS. BOWES: Do you get anything indicating the time period?

BOWES: No, I don't. I did see a shield with a lot of flowers on it or it could
have been something with something brass in the middle but I felt it was gold
or brass in the middle and I felt it was round. I felt as though that was in a
museum or that was in a building for a long time.

MRS. BOWES: What about political matters?

BOWES: I would say that there was the very rich or the people who were
ahead of others, and then I didn't feel there was any...I kept seeing like India
or something to do with very, very poor people, masses of them. I felt like
there was one rich or one superior person. I did feel like they wore loose
clothing underneath like dresses or loose clothing.

Dried Fish Grater. [*Japan. 1940.*]

The first thing I picked up before you came in the room is something about
somebody's eyes. The feeling I had was this associated with a desk or another
box. The feeling I had was something associated with sharpening something

or straightening something. I don't know if this is a tool or something to store
something in but basically I felt as though there was some value of...from
where it came and I don't know if it was from a ship or whether it was from an
office but I keep seeing a building and I felt it was very musty. I would say
this is very old. I see more than one of these or several kinds. I don't know if
there's something being shaved. I did feel as though...I keep seeing a man
with a beard. I do feel as though this could have been on a ship, or on some
sort of vessel or something that moved. I did feel as though with this man I see
him being very particular—stubborn—and I would say that possibly the time
that this was used...this man...may have had a lot of money or may have been
very particular.

MRS. BOWES: What did the man wear? What was the time period?

BOWES: I see him wearing this small cap for a while and wearing a uniform
or some sort of clothes. I see him being someone who had his arms crossed over
his chest. I would say he was in charge of a business. I keep seeing people,
someone working on very small pieces or small pieces of something. I see this
sitting alone (artifact)...like not being used. I don't feel it was used very much.
I don't know if there was something to do with this to be a trick or something
to do with this to be a something that was unexpected, but I keep seeing small
pieces of wood. I do see someone writing letters...or like something for printing
and I see little pieces of...like printer's ink or little pieces of...something in like
...I don't understand it too well.

MRS. BOWES: What about the type of place this was used in?

BOWES: I would say it was an office or a shop. I see some tools being kept
inside this drawer (artifact), or little pieces of something or wood. I do see
tools, or things made of brass.

MRS. BOWES: Do you see anything about the homes in the area?

BOWES: I wouldn't say this was extremely old, but I would way that it did
have some value. I keep seeing a lot of old...a lot of things being separated...
like separated in other words. Like a man died or someone died and everybody
got a piece of it everybody got an area or thing of it. I see this man collecting
guns, or collecting something made of wood, partially wood and partially
steel. I would say that it would associate with a business or a machine shop.
Could have been making guns or something.

MRS. BOWES: Did these people move around at all?

BOWES: No. I didn't feel that. It could have been on a ship, but I felt that
was where it came from, like there was some movement. I keep seeing somebody interested in studying the Japanese, or something to do with another
culture, but this may associate with a man. I don't know if this man is an in-
ventor but I see him being someone...whoever made this. I didn't feel it was
made with a lot of craftsmanship involved. I felt it was more to be used. I
didn't feel it was real expensive at the time it was bought.

MRS. BOWES: Do you get anything about where it came from?

BOWES: I would say the north, the north United States, or it could even be
from another country, but I felt more with the north United States.

MRS. BOWES: What about what they eat?

BOWES: I would say what an American would eat, like corn and turkey and
like Thanksgiving time and such as that. I would say it associated with the
United States. I do see a man flying or talking about a machine and this again
could be something to do with an inventory. I see him wearing a hat or a
helmet or something that had goggles like flying an early airplane. It could
even been riding a motorcycle or horse. I felt like more with the age of...Like I
see mechanical, something made mechanical...machines.

Appendix B—Chapter III

BOWES: The first thing ahead of me here are from what I pick up, bones. This is a number ten (Columella beads). I keep feeling as though they are related to shell or to very hard bone. I keep seeing a man and I keep seeing him confused about something. I see him throwing something down...or something pulled off his neck. I don't know if this was found underground or in a burial...like a burial ground somewhere. I kept seeing low ground, almost like it was water or wet ground. I kept seeing low ground and I see ditches or canals or something dug and I would feel that there was burial grounds or something...or people were buried in the ground. I kept feeling in relationship to this that whoever owned this may have been traveling or this was a religious or ceremonial gathering. I kept feeling as though there was someone who was sick or someone who had a problem. I kept seeing a man with a crushed skull or something where someone was either attacked from behind or abused in some way.

Now I'm going to number six (broken clay pipe). I don't know if this was like a spoon or a bowl, it could have even been a pipe, but didn't feel it was really a pipe. I kept feeling as though there was something in it, and it was maybe pulled or sucked through something. There could have been something in relationship to a handle or a string. It could have been put in the mouth. With this hole in here, I did see them drawing this string through it, and I felt it dangled or hanged something at one time. I don't quite understand what it was. I keep seeing this man with a headache or dizzy or having a problem with breathing. I didn't know what it meant but I felt it was an illness in connection with who possibly could have owned this (broken clay pipe).

MRS. BOWES: Do you get anything about what the people looked like?

BOWES: I kept seeing someone with a very tall forehead, or like possibly a receding hairline. Something flat about the head in front. I keep seeing someone with a quite tall forehead. But I see this as kind of bald up here over the forehead. I feel as though with this person this is the distinguishing mark. I do feel as if this person may have worn clothes, and I felt as though there was some people without clothes. I see him coming from the north. I do feel that in relationship to these people that they may have stayed in one place for awhile, but I felt that this man who had this did travel or move around, and I keep seeing him seeing a ship or a boat, and this could have even been a sailing ship, or it could have been a boat they were waiting for, but I did see it.

MRS. BOWES: What did the country look like?...or the climate?

BOWES: I would feel as though it may have been humid or hot in one area... that this person had traveled south, but I kept seeing streams and I kept seeing like low lands...but I kept seeing these streams, like with rocks in them —so it could have been like in Georgia or north of Georgia, but I do see a relationship to the people in that area, and they could have made trade with them or they could have...trade or friendship with people in the north...to the north.

MRS. BOWES: Do you get anything about what the houses looked like?

BOWES: Let me go to something else. Generally I didn't feel too much with houses with these people. I see something that was more like grass or more like something near water...grass shacks or something.

MRS. BOWES: What they lived in, actually?

BOWES: Yes. I felt that some of them were traveling people. Number eight (ceramic bird effigy fragment) caught my eye. First I seen something...I seen turtles or something near the water. Then I felt I saw something that would pertain to a bird, and I see it on the side of a cup, or the side of a bowl...like on the front of it. I do feel as though this relates to their religion. I don't feel as though this was something that was meant to be used everyday.

MRS. BOWES: Do you get anything about their kind of religion?

BOWES: I keep seeing a ship. I keep going back to that ship. It was a big thing in their life. I don't know what it means...in the water. I would say that they...on the ship...were a very strong religious people maybe like Pilgrims or people like Quakers that lived their religion very strongly. I keep seeing somebody arguing and I kept feeling as though there was a group of people. I see people that are squatting down.

MRS. BOWES: Do you feel anything about the tools they might be using?

BOWES: I kept seeing something with one of them and it could have even been a rifle. I kept seeing something sitting in his arms and...I kept feeling with this...it was like a spear with feathers on it, or it could have been a rifle, but I kept seeing that. I keep seeing a woman looking out a cabin or looking out of a window. I kept feeling as though the window was a square window... and this could have even been a window of a ship. The glass in the window wasn't clear like today. It was muddied. I kept seeing the window very crudely made or the window was blurred, but I kept seeing this woman or this person looking out. This could have been the back window of a ship or something because I keep seeing this person looking out the window, and down below was like a rudder, so it may have been like a captain's cabin or something in the back of the ship. I kept seeing these people living in a place where it may have gotten cold at certain times because I see them standing and sitting around this fire as if to warm themselves...there could have been someone there who had a uniform on...white people were colonizing this area and these people didn't like them. Anyway...I keep seeing a little bit of sickness or...I don't know if these people wore hats, round-looking hats, but I kept seeing someone there interrupting something or interrupting people. This could have been someone from another country or whatever. They may have had kind of a round-looking hat. I keep seeing this round, kind of round hat on top of their head. Having to do with that (artifact), I see a woman prizing that, or taking care of that. I didn't feel it was used everyday.

MRS. BOWES: Do you see anything about what they eat or how they got their food?

BOWES: I kept feeling that something to do with these people were new or there was some outsiders coming into the area. I see them hiding things and running off or running back away from the coastline or away from the water, and this could have been an island lake or it could have been something quite large, but I see them running back or running away from it. I see them hiding things. I do feel as though when they were near the water, I see them eating meat or eating something to do with a furry animal, and I felt it could have been a raccoon or something like that. I kept feeling that when they moved inland that there could have been a lot of bugs or mosquitoes or a lot of pestilence...In other words, I didn't feel it was desirable inland.

With number nine (bone pin), I kept seeing somebody sewing or holding something together. I keep seeing like a hide or like a skin and I see everything like it was pulled tight. I kept seeing this holding something together, or pushing this through something...I did feel that some of these things (artifacts) was in a junk yard or was in a place where they threw things away. I kept seeing people moving away and leaving things sit. I see it with a lot of other sharp things and I kept feeling as though it could have pertained to something that was like a spear or something that was like used for spearing or spearing catfish or blowfish or animals...water...in shallow water. Something like a flounder or stingray. But I see somebody spearing something in the water and I see this laying with a bunch of...like arrows or spears, or something very sharp. I kept seeing a large piece of leather and it could have been pulled tight from various areas.

With number four (burial stone)...I don't know what this is doing here. I don't know if this was a stone or good luck or this was something found in with the rest of it but I am not very impressed by it. I would feel if anything it might have been used to sharpen something, or run over something, but other than that I didn't feel much with it. I just felt it was a stone.

Number two (clay pipe)...I was very attracted to this. This may have been made in a hurry. I felt like there was more to it. I keep seeing a piece of wood stuck in the end, and this may have been like a mouth-piece or whatever. I do feel that this was a pipe and I kept feeling as though it may not have been of too much importance but I kept seeing it as something that may have been passed around. I see one man alone smoking this. One eye turned up in his head and the other eye looked straight ahead. I don't know if this would be an Indian or a Pilgrim but I kept seeing him as being somebody...I kept seeing him having clothes on...I kept feeling that the idea of clothes was something that may have been a little different.

MRS. BOWES: Do you see anything about what kind of clothes they wear... or ornaments?

BOWES: I don't know if this man would have a brass button or buttons on, but I kept seeing it. I kept feeling as though it was a jacket...it may have round buttons or something ties onto it. The collar was torn off that jacket. I don't know if there was a shipwreck but I kept seeing somebody having a big to-do about something along the beach. That ship was never heard from again. There was confusion on it and I felt those people on it were amateurs. Something to do with the water. I don't know what it means. It might even pertain to the shipwreck that I see or the ship that this woman was looking out of the window, and I kept seeing that. I would feel that this (artifact) was buried with someone because of...I keep seeing a large amount of possessions. I do see a room or a building full of soot...lot of smoke. I would feel like it was almost like it was underground or it was like a hole or a dip in the ground and I see grass or something over the top of it.

MRS. BOWES: Do you know what this room may have been used for?

BOWES: I don't know if it was for smoking meat, but I kept feeling as though they had meat or something hanging in there. I see them using bamboo, or something. Bamboo or reeds, like tall grass with pom-poms on top...to block it off. I would feel that they would be worried about something getting in there... an opossum or a raccoon would get in there, and I see these bamboo...I see it around the front of it. I didn't feel very good with that. I did feel that that was something of importance to the one man, or several people, but I didn't feel as though it was too outstanding with everybody. I feel as though that man who owned this pipe may have been different or like a character or somebody different. Could have been like a sole survivor or someone not an Indian like these people.

MRS. BOWES: Do you get anything about political organization or about leadership?

BOWES: I would feel as though the leadership could have been prejudiced. I kept feeling as though there was like some outside influence...very strong...it could have been the Catholic religion...or a religion that dominated the people, but I felt it was something that you may have to owe allegiance to. I do feel as though...that there could have been an Indian relationship with these people, but I keep seeing them interested in something from the east. I would feel as though this could have been Florida or that there could have been connections with the water. These people traveled by the water.

With number five (shell beads)...this is the funniest thing...I keep seeing teeth. I felt like people's teeth were rotten or they were broken off. I don't know if these pieces of bone or stone or whatever they are pertain to that. I see this as being a necklace. I would feel as though a young woman or a young person had this. I don't feel it was a necklace so much around the neck but I

felt it could have been draped on clothing or in connection with hanging from
something. Again I feel like there's somebody there who…didn't wear clothes
at all but I kept seeing possibly outsiders or someone who wore clothes.
MRS. BOWES: Do you feel any white people in the area?
BOWES: I would feel in relationship to this that there was something but it
may have been nearer the water because I don't see it so much near…like
inland. I would feel that this (artifact) was owned by a young woman. I see a
woman crying, and she may be pregnant. I see her leaning over and I felt she
was very large in front. I see her holding her stomach and I see somebody
making noise or leaning over her. Shaking a rattle. I see her bent over like
she's in pain. I see somebody dancing and holding something over the top of
her. It's something like a tambourine or a rattle, but I keep seeing them
shaking it over her.
MRS. BOWES: Do you get anything about the ancestors? Where the people
originated from?
BOWES: I would feel that they came from the north, and I kept feeling as
though they may have traveled along the shore line. I see two groups of people
together. I felt that in the past they were more of…travelers. I do see them
stopping in this area because of either fresh water or a stream, or a place where
they could possibly stop and rest. I keep seeing this as something that would
relate to a resting area. I do see people living there for quite some time, and
this could be an area where there's either brackish or fresh water or a place
where they could move by water. I keep seeing it as being quite swampy. I
don't know if there was palm trees there. This was an area where there was an
interest, but these would possibly be cabbage palms. I kept feeling as though
this land much lower, and there may have been like pools of water here or
there, or it may have been swampy…I kept feeling in the background there
could have been a mound or…a mountain or a larger area. I did feel as though
there was something different about this than inland. I see a stream of fresh
water. I keep seeing them being closer to the water in this vicinity.
    This number three (musket ball)…I don't know what this is but I kept
feeling like it was a ball that was shot or something that was like from a musket. I kept feeling as though there is something to do with a gun or a bullet. I
see someone cussing or screaming or making a loud noise. I felt as though
there was sparks or like this could have been like a musket or a flintlock or a
gun that…I don't understand this too well, but I kept seeing like a pan of
powder or like a little…something there and I kept feeling as though this
man really…I didn't feel as though he really knew what he was doing.
MRS. BOWES: What about his feeling?
BOWES: I would say as though he was surprised. I don't know why, but I
kept seeing it as very…very…like there was a lot of sparks involved and I
felt that the back of the gun was brass.
MRS. BOWES: Do you get anything what the man looked like or what he
was wearing?
BOWES: I wouldn't pick up that—but I kept seeing him being a little bit
humped over. He could have been carrying something on his back. I don't
know if this was a pistol or a rifle, but I would feel it was a pistol. If this was
an Indian who shot this, I don't feel he liked the gun. He didn't relate to it
because I felt it fired or went off too fast or it was something he couldn't aim
very well, but I felt as though something scared him, or something he didn't
like about it. I kept seeing something about a shipwreck. I don't know if
there is something pertaining to someone from another country but I kept
seeing people agreeing with them. I see them shaking their heads and smiling,
but I would feel that whoever this was, was not telling the truth. I felt they
were laughing.

MRS. BOWES: Do you get anything about where the ship came from or what kind of people were on it?
BOWES: I don't know if they were Spanish-speaking people...I would feel as though they were Quakers or people...possibly from another country other than Spain. Now, they could have been like French or people from a country not normally here because I didn't feel them having experience either with the Indians or experience with the terrain, but I kept seeing lots of bugs or torment. I seen them having problems with that.
With number seven (greenstone celt), I didn't know much about it. I see it being buried. I don't know if this was in a cave or underground, but I kept seeing it being in a place...I would feel it was used for pounding something or hitting something. It could have been something that was used to roughen something up, but I keep seeing it being used in the palm of the hand. It changed from one hand to another. This was used very much.
MRS. BOWES: Can you say anything about the people who used it?
BOWES: The word I pick up is "ballast". I don't know if this would be considered ballast or if there was something to do with the ship...the ballast of a ship or stones, but generally I would feel that this was from a different area. When the Indians saw that, they thought of ballast in the ship. I keep seeing the ocean, and I feel if you seen it from the air it would be like a sandbar or something...I see like an outline of rocks on the ocean or floor of this water.
MRS. BOWES: Why did you hit your head like that?
BOWES: I kept feeling as though somebody was hit in the head with it (slate celt). The feeling I had was that this end went in something...either covered with wood or covered with cloth.
MRS. BOWES: What about the people who used it? Anything about that?
BOWES: I see young people, and I felt like...either young women or young people...and I don't know if it was made to stir something but I kept seeing it being in...that's really all I pick up. I kept feeling that this object was not from this place and it was either outside of Florida or outside of a wet area...I did feel that these people (touches the slate celt) were more advanced. I feel, as I see them, being something from the north. I feel very strong with that. I want to say that I feel health problems with these things...there was a river... I see mud flats.
ONES: Could you tell me more about the ship you saw?
BOWES: With this ship, I would feel it was not a Spanish ship, but I would feel as though it were either a French or Dutch ship or something they put a lot of pride into. I see red wood and I see...like carving in the back of it...had all kinds of carving in the back of it...I don't feel they were educated or talented people. Could have been convicts or they could have been people who were...I would say inexperienced—the actual passengers—people on the ship were actually inexperienced to be traveling over the ocean. They may have been collecting Indians for slaves...there could have been something associated with slaves...I felt this ship was much more decorative than a normal ship that would be out to sea. In other words, these people had gotten this ship and brought it over here to the United States and really it was not something I would say that was really set for travel in the ocean. And I would say it may have been stricken with rot, or this could have been after it wrecked but I felt there was a lot of worms in the wood or something. Just a poorly made ship for the ocean. And this was a poor example of a poor attempt to establish a colony in the United States. This is the strongest feeling I have. I would say that this ship was something of a trade ship and they brought it and used it for this travel. In other words, everything was makeshift. It wasn't made to actually be out on the ocean.
JONES: Do you have any feelings about where they were trying to go?

BOWES: I would say they were trying to get north. I didn't feel they liked the area where they were at, but I felt like a storm or miscalculation brought them into an area where there was a lot of shoals or a lot of sand. I would say they were afraid. Generally, I felt like they had someone aboard who was like a slave or someone who they had done something wrong...They could have even been prisoners, or they could have done something wrong because I felt they were afraid. I would say this was a poor example of a ship but it was much fancier than a ship you would normally see on the ocean.

JONES: How long was this ship?

BOWES: I couldn't tell you that. The feeling I had was that it was not a ship that you would normally expect to be traveling at that distance. I would say it came from France or Europe...over there and it came over here, and I would say these people were misfits who had been in prison or people who had been in a debtor's prison or something, and they were trying to...possibly make up for it.

JONES: You talked about a woman looking through the window...

BOWES: This was a very sad person, and I felt it was a dark-skinned person. She could have been Italian, she could have been an Indian, but I felt she was very, very sad. I felt she was afraid or sad. This is emotion, a lot of emotion that I felt there. I would say the ship was round...short and round. I did feel it was made of red wood. Could have been teak wood or some sort of wood from a special forest, but I would say it may even should have belonged in the Mediterranean instead of the ocean, or it could have pertained to an area that was more secluded, not so rough of water.

JONES: What about cannons?

BOWES: No, that's the thing I was picking up that I didn't feel too...there was a cannon...kind of a small, short cannon on the front, or on the side. Now, the feeling I had before, I did feel...I did pick up cannons but I would say they were inoperable, that they weren't something that they used. This gun here on the top, a little short gun may have been the only gun that they had. I didn't feel as though it had many cannons. I would say that they were afraid of the Spanish, that they had been blown south and were afraid of St. Augustine or the south.

JONES: So you are saying that they didn't come from the south?

BOWES: No! I don't feel they came from the south at all. I felt that they fell off course, and I feel that they fell way south of where they should've...but felt they were very afraid and not knowing where they're at, and I don't feel they wanted to go to St. Augustine! That's one place they knew they didn't want to go. They were trying to get back north, but the whole thing was a failure. I just felt the whole thing was a big failure.

JONES: When you saw the woman on the ship, did you see her clothing?

BOWES: I would feel she wore very rough clothing. Either a dress that was just sewed and thrown over her or it was something that was...again I need objects to work with and I could give you much more technical information. An Indian woman with no clothes or just a piece of leather or burlap bag over her because I felt it was just sewed on the tops over the shoulders.

JONES: What about the men in charge of the ship? Did you get any feelings...

BOWES: The feeling I felt was that they were fairies, who weren't normally in this association. I feel the captain or the person normally in charge was either sick or ill or not there. I don't feel they had authority. In other words they were very confused. I see them very light skinned...who actually ran the ship. I felt that the person who had a hat that was much fancier than what you'd normally use in the ocean. It looked like a baby bonnet. It wasn't something that was for durability like leather or something. I felt it was silly. I would say they had puffy shoulders. Kind of wore clothes that weren't too durable in the ocean...I would say...I thought these people were very, very confused.

They were not prepared for this. I would say there was a very small amount of them left because of illness. Could have been because they were lost or they were getting scurvy or problems with vitamins. I see them getting sick. I felt that they may have gone to shore but I feel that at the time the ship was wrecked, there was no life boats or no real transportation to get them back and forth. I felt they went to the beach and it was covered with bugs and there was a lot of sand flies and mosquitoes. I don't feel they found any food to speak of. In other words, they were just really inexperienced people.

JONES: Did you get any feeling for their language?

BOWES: This is much too far after the fact. Generally I would say they were either French or...I don't feel it was Spanish. I don't feel that the actual people who made the ship or related to it, I don't see them as dark skinned as the Spanish. They were light complexioned and they had a lot of blisters on their hands and they just weren't experienced with any of this stuff. The ship could have floundered for a long time because I see a lot of rot in the hull...a lot of water that they just left in there. Through inexperience they could have gone through a storm and let the water get down into their drinking water. I do feel that one of the reasons they were in this area was because there was drinking water there and they may have come back into that area, but I would feel they were lost, and they ran aground there. Could have been during a storm. They may have been in the area for a short period of time. But I would feel that the Indians or the people who were on land were very hostile or mad at these people. They wanted to kill them. They could have even wanted to eat them...like cannibals. These people could have been Indians or Negroes or whoever that was put in there as prisoners or slaves but generally this was going against them because they had to feed these other people.

*   *   *

DIANE DAVIS' READING OF
ST. SIMON'S ARTIFACTS

DAVIS: I'm seeing something that would have like steps, and I'm going up. I feel that I would have gone up these steps...walked up these steps and the steps are made of stone or they are hard, and they are on a hillside or like a place that I would have...gone up. As I'm saying this I feel like an Aztec, like their great monuments or that kind of thing, but I don't feel these are Aztec... something of like a Mexican type of influence almost, or an influence from Mexico. No, that's wrong. Let me go backwards. My first impression is I wanted to go north of Orlando. I'm heading in that direction (points).

JONES: You are pointing northeast of Orlando.

DAVIS: Yeah. That would be northeast, wouldn't it? I feel "density" and I don't know what it applies to or what it means. With the people...illness or personal difficulty that just keeps interfering with time. I feel these people weren't scattered. Even if they spread out in physical proximity to one another, there was still organization to their...They were very flexible, but organized. I'm getting "organized". There were patterns. They understood the cycles that man can get into. Year cycles, monthly cycles, and moon cycles. They were very much aware of that. Something about women again. That women were important not only in the home as childbearers, but also with the healing, and with the foresight to know when to act and when to move. I feel pressure at different points in their existence. I feel there is something very significant with the women as though (noise interference).

    This thing looks like a bowl of a pipe (clay pipe). I get the effect of shoving things down it and cleaning it out. I still would say...that women were important...I feel that there was something different about these women, as though men were important, too. Women in this group were important. They were sensitives. They were healers, they were seers, they were very important, but I feel it was almost like not an equal thing, but certain ones it was an equal thing, certain men and women. These were lean people, as though they had more vegetables.

I pick this up: I say "shells" or something that would have to do with water. Maybe they ate more food from water, and I get "sea"...the sea, sea creatures. So I feel there was more of a tendency to get the protein you need, you would gain from the fish, or some sort of weed, or some sort of a green thing that would look to me like some sort of sea weed, or grass that would have been employed in the diet somehow. I see them crowded in between like rocks...no, it's not rocks, but there's not this feeling of great space. It's like they're clumped together. I get this feeling of very close together. There's a feeling of...not being cramped but close quarters as though not as much movement and freedom of movement because there is something that would not give me that flexibility on the sides of this area that I lived in and dwelled in. I feel a mound though...like a mound type of thing.

Again, I feel more relating to the sun. There was a feeling of the sun...but something more of a ritual or ceremony that would have been...would have taken place with these people. It's something where they lay on the earth and absorb the sun. I felt a woman might have held this pipe...somebody who was important within a group of people, not the leader, but somebody who would have been important or connected with a leader, and I feel this was made by a loved one. It was made for them by a man, because I feel a man's touch to be on there, as though modeling it and I feel it was given as a...love object. There was also sort of a ritual to give it. I'm seeing lots of trees and there are some really tall trees and then there are short trees and...it's more like Florida to me, where I would see maybe cypress and palmy-type looking trees, and like citrus trees, but these have...these don't have citrus...they bloomed and they get a seed on them that was used for something but they don't have oranges on them. I see them wearing something that would extend over the loin area. There was also a tendency to wear something that would have draped the sides and down the front...almost down to the abdomen, not past the waist...and this was draped over the shoulders and under the arm as though it was circular. I feel that there was something about a headdress or something that would have been made with...almost like feathers...but it's not like a headband or what I would call "an Indian headdress". It's like wide, very thick, and it would have been placed on the head and maybe feathers or something stuffed in one side of it...no, stuffed in a lot of parts of it. I get a lot of healing with them, too, because I don't feel they originated at this site. I feel like they came from another direction, but they had been there for a long time, where these things were found. I feel that there was healing because there was impurities in the body from...well, lack of something in the diet for one thing, but also because there was something nearby where they lived that was...stagnant or polluted or...I don't know if this is water...and I'm seeing an area of trees that would have burned down, or a place where there would have been a lot of...remains of fire...ashes and...there are trees where I don't see trees anymore. I felt something to do with the diet, as though maybe somehow they got into...animals got into that so the animals were impure and it was a carry-over from something. I'm getting water again, as though there are three bodies of water nearby. One, a lake, for sure. The others, I'm not quite sure about, but there's one more like a lake that was used for their main water supply, and I see springs that would be connected further on down. Maybe this is a river, but I feel like springs or something that bubbles, or you'd see this rapid movement in the water and it would be a spring...it's not a waterfall.

JONES: Do you have a feeling about the relationship between where these people lived and these three bodies of water?

DAVIS: I feel like it's almost a triangle, but two of them are closer together. I don't know what size they are. There's a lot of travel with these people as though they would have traveled around and then come back. I keep feeling this circular motion, as though they would have left and come back, and they would have kept a lot of freedom somehow, like they would have kept leaving and coming back...back and forth. I want to go back and say there was a ritual passed down...and there were little things...little statues and I feel maybe they would have worked with children to show them how to do things. They were like about four inches high.

JONES: Can you see what they looked like?

DAVIS: I'm kind of feeling like they were unusual...maybe unusual birds or animals. Im seeing one and I want to say it has the tail of an alligator or the body of an alligator, and the head of something else more like a cat, or an animal that cures. I feel like if I lived then I would have been happy. I feel these people were not oppressed or constantly under watch or in danger of invasion or disaster or disease or anything. They lived in harmony...pretty much. There were natural dissensions but I feel they worked very hard to create harmony. There were morning and evening rituals but I see prayers almost—like to the gods or whatever, and the sun was very important. I'm sitting there and I'm staring at the sun, and then there are times when I can't look at the sun, and I'm not supposed to look at the sun, and then there's times that I see it at dusk and I'm looking at it and there's peace and beauty, and again, I'm sitting at the water's edge, as though this could have been a very, very strong healing technique. I feel there are teas, teas that were made from leaves and bark, especially bark...and special trees that were nearby whose bark was used for a special ointment. I feel an ointment that would have been put on wounds and sores. I'm seeing something that would look round with designs around the borders.

JONES: What do you feel it is made of?

DAVIS: I feel shell or a substance that would be colorful. I don't know where it belongs. Yes, I do. I see figures, and there's something that goes through it like halving the circle...one side the sun and one side the moon...you know, like the balances of the earth. I don't know what this is but I keep seeing little statues and little things would poke up from the ground. But this pipe bowl... I feel like I'm sitting on the outskirts and I'm staring into the design and the set-up...something about the pipe. I'm talking and my voice is very low. My eyesight is very poor at this time. I'm staring at these things and it could be nighttime, but it's not nighttime, so it could be inside. I feel that there is an old person. This must be an old person. I'm very tired. I feel that I have lived many years. I feel that I have lived here all my life. I am a woman because I have raised many children, and there are times I feel I ask the sun for guidance to give my children and family if we should leave. There seems to be a lack of some sort of food supply at this time...there is no grain, no grain. I'm...it's like there's been no rain, and I feel the water is around but we can't get the water to the soil somehow. There is some sort of fear of starvation from the plant life. This circle and the pattern around the edges has the cross of the energies of light and dark. This woman would have been in her fifties, but that was very old for her at that time, although I feel she did live on...for a time longer. There is something in her dress that's different...more of a woven type of garment of some type that is a little bit heavy but light, or maybe the weave was big, or something because I am not hot. I don't feel as warm, and I feel that I lived under heat...a large part of the year. But in the winter I feel that something was put on underneath this right around the torso, like maybe a skin or a fur.

JONES: I didn't understand if that was an ornament or a design on the ground or exactly what it was?

DAVIS: It was something that was stared into...this person was sitting on the ground staring into this...different sizes. This one is about three feet, and I would say it was probably made either on top of clay or stone or something... but things were put on top and carved or beaten, but somehow there is a design in there, and there is a line that separates light and dark—symbolism of light and dark somehow and then these things that set across the meridian or equator...something set across the middle portion of it and that would be the focal point in the center. I would feel that they were very wise, very intelligent people. I feel, too, that they did studies with the ground...with, like they would have tested better means for better growth for better foods or healthier foods. They would have done something where they would have tried different methods...rather than say, "this is the old ancient way and we use it." I sensed that somehow new influences would come in periodically. I feel friendly with these influences almost like the people would almost speak the same kind of dialect, but not quite, but there would be a means of communication when they did this...that possibly these people would bring to them the new ideas, or maybe a person came in and eventually infiltrated their group or lived with them to bring them these new ideas.

JONES: Did you get a feeling of where these other people came from?

DAVIS: I get "due north".

JONES: What about the kinds of structures they might have lived in?

DAVIS: I'm seeing wood, like branches that are on top of each other...kind of an overlap of branches and things. I don't feel as though living with this, I feel some place that would have been a shelter. As though it would be some place that would be built out from a hill, or a piece of ground or maybe even a tree. Could be built up against a tree, and it would just be a whole pile of things. There's a feeling of something where skins or fibers were sewn together for...I get this expression "pulled together"...and placed on some sort of frame built from wood. I naturally think of a tipi but I don't think they were considered that. I think of a 'cone type' tipi but this wasn't that. This was different somehow, almost squared off at the top, but it wasn't squared off. I feel that there was something inside where you could have a fire, and it would not hurt the walls. They were very respectful of fire. There was a time when these people were very threatened by a storm, like a great wind; rain came, and I feel this was followed by a period of almost like a drought where they were worried about their food. I feel that this storm was something very like what I would consider as a hurricane, but they had never really experienced one that deeply. And I feel destruction as though things were blown and scattered, and this happened within thirty-five years of the fire. So there were many negative physical things that occurred. I feel this fire was almost a thing of combustion due to heat when it was really dry out and something occurred that ignited it. I don't feel it was something set by error, or accidental. I feel like it was almost a nature freak thing.

I want to go back into the people and say that these people later settled in a lower part of Florida, and I feel they still exist. I don't know if they do in name or tribe or whatever, but I feel they still exist. I feel too that there was something about kinship that was very important...where there was a strong sense of kin. I'm seeing alligators again—and snakes, lots of snakes. There were creatures and I feel they were possibly afraid of them. The men went out to get food and they not only planted but they also drew from nature as though there were natural...maybe berries or something that they drew from at various times of the season, and I feel that there were times when they would go beyond, and I keep wanting to say "river." They would go beyond the river, whatever it would be, the water, and perhaps get in the water and I'm seeing not a raft. It's like something that would have floated but you would have had to be very careful in it because of your sense of balance...if your sense of balance was off you could have easily fallen in and that's where the snakes and things are. I feel like there was something about going across the water and there was something very good for me. It's green and it's very good for me.

I want to go back to the healing, because I feel very strongly that they had many rituals that were followed, and many of these were by the moon also, not just by the sun, but by the moon, and I go into light and dark things again. I keep going into this ritual of light and dark. I feel there was something about smoking something very special, and this could be obtained and this, too, could be on the other side of the river because they had to go long distances to obtain it. There is also something very special that they drank, and it's like a tea or a soup of some type that they would have made from a concoction of things...berries and this green stuff they went to get and grasses and, it was just a conglomeration of different things but it was very good for their bodies, and they used it quite often, like we would consider today that we would fast, but they would drink this three times a day and it would act as a cleansing...as a fasting-type, cleansing purification. I feel, too, that there was something in the diet like bread, but I don't see how they baked it. I think, too, that they ate many birds. Birds were important. They were holy...or some of them were. I feel this one kind of bird would have been seen in other religious rituals somewhere else in the world.

JONES: Feelings about invaders in the area?
DAVIS: You mean now, or what?
JONES: During this time (points to artifacts).
DAVIS: I feel northern...I feel the presence of non-Indians there...but I didn't feel they stayed there, I think they came back.
JONES: Where did they come from?
DAVIS: "Northern" again...maybe these people had more of the French, or English...no, no Portuguese...I'm feeling like close to a French dialect, but I'm not French. And I feel they would have come from the northern part of the United States, or a northern region from this area where these (artifacts) were found as though they would have been there some time and were moving on... were looking further. I see them with water, like maybe a boat or ship...that maybe they would have—I get "parked" it north and then traveled south.
JONES: The ship traveling south?
DAVIS: They didn't travel in a ship south. They parked it north.
JONES: Do you get a feel of the ship?
DAVIS: Well, I'm seeing something that would have...it reminds me of a Viking ship to tell you the truth. It almost had a thing on the front, like the Vikings but the ship is heavier kind of. There's something sticking out and I feel oars and a sail but the sail isn't that tall...the sail is small as though...it's strange. I don't know. I get the color red, and there's lots of people in here and half of them went one way and half went the other. I feel like they had so many days they were traveling and then they were to meet again, and I feel some of them stayed behind. These people are dark haired people with more of an 'olivey' Spanish-type of influence, but I'm not hearing Spanish, I'm hearing French, or maybe it's Italian. It might even be Italian. What I keep seeing is like the panhandle of Florida, and I keep seeing it jammed in the sand, and I associated it with that area and then traveling south. I hope this is in Florida, but anyway that's the kind of thing I'm seeing. Like I'm in that general direction.
JONES: Can you get the ship you see in more detail?
DAVIS: The ship had slats and the slats were fairly far apart, I'm surprised to say, and I don't know what's keeping it up but there are beams or something that go across under the bottom of it, and you had to be very careful

when you walked because I think the floor surface wasn't complete. It maybe had some sort of places dug out or something, but there was something underneath it that filled it in, that got wet and would absorb some of the moisture and then the rest of the moisture would have to stay out somehow. And I wonder what that could be? I could see spaces in between the slats, which really surprised me, and I don't understand how it stayed afloat myself.

JONES: Do you see the people on the ship? What do their clothes look like?

DAVIS: It's funny because when I focus on it, I see somebody dressed like...a Quaker. A head piece that would look like a skull-cap. A bib-type front on the woman. Shoes that...leather shoes that look almost like ballet slippers...they would have fit closely to the foot...maybe it's stockings. I want to get back to the Indians and I want to leave the ship alone.

JONES: O.K.

DAVIS: I want to talk about recreation. There was something they done that was lots of fun. It was a game and it was done with leather straps and rocks. It was almost like I would say 'clackers,' but it was something that you would almost throw like a lasso or twirl around and around. They were thrown and they had a certain boundary. It was like everybody was a big kid some of the time. You know, maybe ceremonial type of things that would be enjoyable and harmonious for the people...the group.

JONES: Who were these people? (pointing to non-indigenous celts)

DAVIS: I really couldn't get much with that except maybe some people who came in very temporarily. I still haven't felt the separateness...like another people...yet...and I think that that is what has been...I do see the color blue and I do see mountains...O.K., it's not really mountains but larger hills than just a...kind of rolling type things. Larger hills. A somber type of people. O.K., I'm feeling the separateness now. I feel these people (associated with celts) would have been more land dwellers. Something very vital to the land, the earth, the soil.

JONES: You don't like the people on the ship?

DAVIS: It isn't that I feel good or bad about them...I mean, I didn't feel dangerous with them. I don't think they were there to hurt anybody. I think they were looking and they were fearful of what other people might do, but I didn't feel...

JONES: Excuse me. They were fearful of what?

DAVIS: I think they were just fearful of the unknown but I don't think they were looking for a fight. These Indians weren't war types but they were well prepared to handle that type of thing.

BOWES: The first thing I picked up in connection with these photographs was —I picked up something which dealt with a fire. I kept picking up something of dried branches, and palm fronds. The feeling I had was there was a low area, or a place of grass that possibly had water near there. And I felt it was almost like a round circle, or almost like a little swamp or something, but I felt water near there. Another thing I picked up was—I felt the water was higher at the time the Indians were there. I did feel an association with this—fire...and I kept seeing posts in the ground, and I felt like they were burned off almost level with the ground...only stakes or parts of them sticking up. Another feeling, or something I picked up about the people, was an association with mostly women, and I don't know what it means, but I kept seeing mostly women women associated with this mound. I did pick up something to do with animals and I don't know if this is something that they ate or whether it associated with something that they used. The first thing I picked up was something about an otter, or an animal that they skinned, and then I picked up something about a shellfish or a turtle. I keep seeing longer bones than any of those animals seem to have. I feel that it would associate with a deer or some sort of...animal that...ran on all fours. I did see...I kept seeing something about people wading. I kept seeing them wading up to their knees. I did feel as though these people lived away from the St. Johns, or away from the primary river source. I kept feeling...almost like they were hiding or away from the water's edge. Now when I look at the photographs...I keep seeing almost as if it was at one time very high in a certain area and I keep seeing the ground being round, almost like a spoilbank or like a pile of shells or something, and I see it quite steep and then it drops off the other side. I pick up...almost as if on the other side looking straight ahead...almost like you can see this palm tree over here in the sun lite...I felt like over there is more where people lived or more of where they associated with something in the ground or something associated with the water (direction marked on photo by circle). I did see something psychically, almost as if people were dragging sticks, or dragging something, where they dragged someone or dragged something towards the water or towards this tree (in circle). I keep seeing people with a lot of scratches on their ankles or their legs and I would say this associated with walking through stickers or saw grass. I don't feel as though they lived in this place permanently. I felt an association with movement, or change. I did feel as though women may have been here for a period of time but I see them planning on moving. I see an association with something of the idea of a steam boat...or some sort of a boat. I kept seeing it larger than a canoe. Now I don't know if this would be a boat that makes a lot of noise or whether it associates with something that they would dislike or be afraid of, but I kept seeing that. I keep seeing someone carrying...I keep seeing a wooden box buried or like something square...I felt it was in the ground. I did see something with teeth or bones and I keep seeing it near the water. I keep seeing someone with a broken neck or a someone with a...I keep feeling with the neck. I don't know if someone was hanged or whether there was a problem with someone being attacked but I keep seeing something like their neck was broken. The feeling I just picked up was an association with hundreds of years. This could be two hundred years old or older. Now that wouldn't associate with that ship, but again I hear noises, almost as if it was like thunder, or like something...like steam or like something very loud exploding, and I felt it was towards the water. This could be a cannon of some sort. I don't understand this but I kept seeing

311

rocks, or something that looked like a coconut, and maybe it's a skull, but I see it round and like pieces of it, almost like there was jagged pieces of it and I keep seeing something round...I'm going to draw a picture...almost like it was cracked or pieced together. I don't know what it means but this is the feeling I had with it in the ground. Now I keep seeing lances or sticks, and they're burned, almost like they were burned. I do see them near the water. I do see a nail or metal in the ground. I don't know if this was metal that was carried there or whether it was dropped there by someone later on, but I did see metal in the ground. I really feel as though this site or this area may not show the many bones of people. But I would say that there is an area closer to the water...I keep seeing it being a lower area, almost like a grass marsh. I still see it as a slope or an area where there was water. I keep seeing someone poling something, and I don't know if these people wore leather or whether there was different colors in their uniform...clothing, but I keep seeing them walking along with long sticks. I do see them talking about snakes or holding these... like a pole straight up in the air and I see them holding a snake or like pinning it down with a stick. I keep seeing somebody laughing and I felt like the front of their teeth were rotted out or they had problems with their teeth. I don't know if there was...like sugar mills or something that associated with the north, but I keep seeing it up the river and I see them talking about or associating something with somebody living north of them and...I don't know if there was two different types of people living here but I keep seeing two different times that they may have lived...in this area. I would say that the last time was near the water...or the original or where the water is now. I do see saw grass or mud. I keep seeing them putting something in a tree. I don't know if these are stones or whether they drilled or wedged something in a tree but I see them wedging it in the wood. I do see them having pieces of wood in the ground and I see it in a square shape. I would say the wood was burned out but it was stuck in the ground. I see them digging something or dragging something, and I kept seeing it almost as if it was dugout or like it was a paddle or a canoe...scraping the wood and scraping the wood, burning it or scraping it or slicing it off. I kept seeing that in the ground. I don't know where this would be but I kept seeing it near this site. This could associate with this building. I would say that this building was something that was peaked up at the center and I would say it had bent sticks, almost as if they had bent the wood or wet it. I see palm fronds on the sides. I keep seeing them talking about big people, almost like the big people were south, and I felt like they were taller or bigger than these people. I would say these people talked about passing, or crossing the river. I keep seeing them having problems with their teeth. They are shell-fish, but I did see them associating with the salt water or the beaches...or traveling in that direction. I keep seeing a large turtle or like a big shell, and I don't know if these are soft shell turtles, but I do feel as though there are shells there. I don't know if they have some sort of spears, but I keep seeing them carrying something with a belt...something slung over their shoulder. They could even have guns, because I kept feeling as though they...had something that was different then...I didn't see a bow and arrow. I kept seeing this wood, almost like the stock on a gun. I keep seeing someone smoking something or inhaling something, and...I just felt as though it was something that they breathed in or there was a lot of smoke...around the ground. This little house I have here...I don't know if they had them in the air because I kept seeing posts. I felt the walls were more of palm fronds. The top—I felt there was sticks inside of it and there was a skeleton of wood inside. I kept seeing someone throwing something, and I don't know if this is something to do with the water but I see them going after, like, a bird that goes in the water or ducks under water, I see them after their eggs, and I see them throwing something at this bird. I keep seeing them talking about a something made of stone, and I don't know if this is like a stone house, or whether it was a stone fortress, but I see them talking about something made of stone and I don't know if they made it, or you might even find it, but I kept seeing it like cocina rock and I would say it was towards the beach, towards the ocean. I don't know if the rock was squared but I see somebody flattening the stone out and I keep seeing them chiseling at it or digging it out. I do see them...I don't feel so much like with a place with a lot of mosquitoes. I keep seeing more of a place that was open and had lots of grass and I see the wind blowing. Everytime I talk about leather I keep wanting to associate it with Indians but I would say it was almost like a leather piece that would go from the butt of a gun to the barrel, or like a leather pouch or a strap, almost like it has a belt to it. Another thing I picked up was this could be like a fort, like St. Augustine or it could be like...it could be even Caucasian or white people in association with them investigating something. The feeling I had was they were mad or aggravated with something, and I kept feeling as though they were looking for somebody. I see them mad and wading through the water and looking. I kept seeing someone with a missing tooth in the front and the feeling I had was gold...almost like a gold-filled tooth, or like there was a tooth there that was gold. I don't feel, what I'm talking about here, I don't feel they would have stayed there very long, but they may have gone and killed someone, or was chasing someone. I would say these people were unhappy or mad or ugly or after...like to kill. They could even have hung someone. This is the feeling I picked up. The association with the water or the ocean...I kept seeing north and I see the people coming from the north. I would say that this place was abandoned at some time and then someone returned there, but I didn't feel so strong with how long, or when it was. I did see...like pieces of metal in the ground...like little pieces. I don't know why but I keep seeing these people...when they left this place I see them going to higher ground and I would say this was higher ground like mounds or like hills of sand, like rolling hills, or hills of sand and I would say it was toward Titusville,or towards the south, maybe the southeast. I do see them continuing to move. I keep seeing something like a pot and I don't know if this was a clay pot but I see it being suspended up by sticks or rods,. and...I see it hanging. The feeling I had was it was hanging above fire or hanging above something. The feeling I had about this site was generally there was somebody looking for someone or someone moving. I did feel as though some of the people there were very primitive. I don't know if there was an association with slaves, but I keep seeing an association with someone being taken away. This thing about them smoking could associate with a pipe. I keep seeing a lot of smoke, almost like they smoked up the inside of a building or a house or like a...lot of smoke. I picked up something to do with the number "fifty." I would say it associated with fifty years. I don't know if the people lived in this area fifty years or whether all together, off and on, they were around this area for fifty years, but I would say that the original people who lived in this area, originally, I felt very primitive. I keep seeing associations with people who may have not had any clothes or people who ate mostly meat, but I keep seeing them being people who were very primitive. Now as time goes on, I felt a little more...associated with gathering things in their area. I don't know if these are clams or whatever but I keep seeing a place where there's like a little dock or a place where they set up a wood walk-way or something over grass or over water. There could even be logs laying in the grass or laying on the water but I kept seeing something high. I did feel as though that originally the people that live...(tape ends). I did see, as time went on with these people, an association with something of other tribes or other people. I do see...I don't know if this the area of the ridge, or whether this is the ridge or whether this is the ridge or whether there is a ridge higher... as if there was a higher ground away from this area. This could even be the higher ground but it could be farther on down. But the feeling I had was I seen ground, like dark brown or black dirt, and I didn't see sand now. I didn't see sand at all, but I see dark brown or black dirt, and I see all underneath oak trees or underneath trees, I see a lot of...deep down or ground that was worn over years or places where it was like worn from people running, with bare feet, or running. I felt as though this was quite a big area, and I felt from this vantage point they could see the water or they could see a large amounts of grass or water, and I kept seeing them seeing a place where there was lily pads or a place where there was water. I felt more like it was a pile of debris, almost like it was a pile of shells or a pile of bones or garbage...like a garbage dump. I do feel as though, later on, dirt may have settled in there or there may have been dirt associated with it. I did feel as though there may have been water in there and out of there during times of hurricane or places when there was water moving around. I feel basically that this area is nothing more than a garbage dump. I do feel as though there was a ground higher, but this may be the ground I'm speaking of over on the other side. I kept seeing the ground higher. I would say that this ground was higher, away from the water, away from the river front. With something to do with the grass...I kept feeling if there was a lake or like an ancient lake near there that associated with, like you could walk out to the edge of this bank or to the edge of this mound and look and I would say there was a grass lake, a round lake and out in this lake...it may not even had water in it but I felt grass...just basically grass and then I seen like a little small island about maybe two- or three- or four- or five-foot wide, and kind of across this little lake and then on beyond that I felt there was grass and maybe water...maybe on farther there may be a lake there or a place where there's water. The feeling I had, at the time the last people lived there, I felt this was all grass but they could slide a canoe or slide a boat out of it. Now I picked up and I was quite startled with it, a little nervous with it, I kept seeing poles with heads on them. I felt like there was a skull on top, and I felt like there was black hair hanging from them. Don't know what that associates with but I would say they could be cannibals or this could be like a way of...like reward. I wouldn't say that this went on at the time the last people were there. I would say in the past, like in the history of these people they may have captured other people. I kept feeling like they were talking about or associating with a large body of water, and I would say that was north of the direction the water flowed. I would say that it was a large lake. They keep talking about rough water like they called it "Hahtoda" or "Tatooa" or something, some name, and I felt with this name there was a meaning and the meaning meant "rough water." I don't know if this was Lake Monroe or north of where they lived but I kept seeing them not going beyond there. I would say that there was an association with people there...might even associate with white people. I kept seeing them talking about that lake or that place being dangerous or real rough. A rough place to maneuver. I did draw a map or a picture...this is a very rough drawing of the area of where this canoe was sliding in and out. Basically what I did this for is so we can go and look and try to find this lake or this large grass...almost looks like a grass field of like a round kind of lake and I feel beyond that it almost looks like there was never water there but I do feel there was at one time. I would say there was a lake or river out beyond there. I do see an association with...as the people...as time went on, I don't know if they captured these Indians or whether they made slaves out of them, but I keep seeing chains or shackles and I kept feeling as though this may have caused these people to move. This could have been the last straw or whatever. I kept feeling as though that when they caused this to happen there was mostly women there and this is the last thing I picked up is an association with women. I see them moving and I kept feeling as though they moved south and I don't know if they enjoyed or did...more than traveling on land. I don't know if they worked south and traveling on south. I did see disease with them and I see some problems with breathing, or this could be like pneumonia, or...I do see them hanging something up off the ground. I felt like this was meat or something to preserve or save something. I did feel, in association with the people...I keep seeing several of them talking about traveling or traveling on the water and I feel as though this was the best way they know how to travel, or the thing that they enjoyed or did...more than traveling on land. I don't know if they worked around with alligators or something, but I keep seeing them scaring or throwing something or chasing something away, and I keep seeing eggs, like almost as if they were alligator eggs or something like huge or large eggs. This could have been associated with the bones I seen. I felt as though this alligator or this animal, was very large. I would say over fourteen feet long...I would say huge. I did feel as though there was like islands, or like large mud flats or places where the grass was all worn off and I see these big round areas or places where the...like these little small islands only ten foot or five foot or... wide or very short. I felt as though this ground was very worn from things sliding on and off it all the time. I did see them using turtle shells for a rattle, and I see them making music or making a lot of noise. I don't know if they were afraid of the lightning or loud noise, but I kept seeing them looking to... I would say to the west, and seeing these storms come up with lots of lightning, or thunder, but I felt I kept hearing this noise. They may have even worshipped that. I picked up something about where we could find something to do with teeth or bones, and I kept seeing it near the water, almost like the water's edge. Again, this is where the grass is. I don't know if the ground slopes off very suddenly and goes into this grass, but I kept seeing something associated with poles that were in the ground or these could be even spears but I felt like they had a spear with a jagged end on it like a fish hook, and I don't know if they stuck gars with it or some sort of fish, but I felt these fish were real long and they had teeth. They may have had like an alligator mouth or like teeth. I did feel as though...I see teeth and like a staff, or something buried in the ground and it was burned, but this is something I picked up and I felt this is where we'd find some bones. I kept seeing this chain and this nail and things that were metal in the ground...now, that could be in the vicinity of the area or it could pertain to something that was brought from another area. I felt that these people lived in a cocina or stone building, or they may have built something out of stone. I don't know if these were outsiders or whatever, but I kept picking that up. I keep seeing something being stretched. I don't know if this is leather or something that they made, like some sort of tool or something... like a sling out of, but I kept seeing that, too. I do feel a loneliness with these pictures. I kept feeling as though sadness or loneliness. I don't know if these people died but I felt like they may not be...I didn't feel they were Seminoles, I felt they were something else. I felt they were a group of people...this may have been hundreds of years ago, but I felt the original people who lived here... there may not be very much known about them, but I felt like they were people who rejected other Indians or other people, but I kept seeing sadness about their numbers. I did pick up that number fifty and I kept seeing fifty...fifty years and I don't know what it meant. I would say that these people not only lived in this area but they had small outposts or small groups of little houses or hutches or something spread out over the area, but I felt mostly these were people, and I did see them growing something, and I don't know if they were vines or blueberries or something, but I kept seeing vines or sticker bushes or vines.

Bowes—Visit to the Site

BOWES: ...out there was water (gestures north of mound) and I felt like the water was the way they come in and out. Now, I don't know why, but I felt back in this direction (SSE) there was a high ridge, and that they had a village or there was more people living there. This could be the ridge because the thing has changed so much. I felt like this was the place I picked up but that out there (to the north) had no trees, it was all grass.

JONES: And you felt a village was that way (pointing SSE)?

BOWES: I felt as though it was on a higher ridge, a higher area.

WALLACE: And this could very well be that higher area?

BOWES: Yes. What's ever back up in there (SSE). I don't even know what's up in there...but the feeling I had was that it was a high ridge. Now this could be the ridge, but I would say it (the ridge) was considerably higher than this. In other words you could stand up on the ridge and—at that time—look out over grass, and it was sitting up high and there was a lot of palm trees. The feeling I had was they almost had a vantage point of who came in or who went out and I would say it was to that direction (SSE). Is there an area over there that could be higher?

WALLACE: There are a number of shell rises over there that are fairly close to the river and they are quite high.

BOWES: The feeling I had was you could see the river from it.

WALLACE: You can.

BOWES: And you could stand up on the ridge and see out over there and see people coming or leaving. I felt as though they landed, from what I picked up right now. I feel they landed here, but I felt like they didn't stay here very long. That over there (area referred to SSE of site) was more a place where they stayed.

WALLACE: Do you feel we are going to find shells and pottery all the way down to the bottom, or do you think this is just some kind of natural dune formation and we will just find sand underneath and they camped on top of it?

BOWES: I felt they camped on top of it. Basically, I really don't think they made this hill but they did pile debris here...as time went on...like a garbage dump. As things were broken or finished like a shell they split or did something with a bone, they threw it out. The feeling I had was a real strong feeling about alligators, and I felt that they were out there (to the north of the site).

JONES: So you feel this rise here is a natural feature or a garbage dump?

BOWES: I would say that it was high here and it was a place where they could stop and rest, but I would say that they did make a garbage dump out of it.

JONES: So it was both?

BOWES: Both. In other words, I felt all this area in here was water (around mound), from what I pick up psychically that there was definitely a foot-, depending on the weather, but I felt it was a foot- to two-foot deep in areas all in here. But I didn't feel the palm trees and the trees...I would say where that oak tree is, from there down it started...beyond that oak tree there was grass, and there was no palm trees out in there.

WALLACE: Do you have any feelings about human burials? Do you think we will find any?

BOWES: I felt as though at the time of what I picked up, and I drew a map for him, out there somewhere there was skulls (north of site). I felt they shot or killed people and put their heads on poles, and they could be out in there somewhere. They could be way over there (north) or they could be right here (north), but the feeling I had...

WALLACE: Not here.

BOWES: I don't feel up here, no. I don't feel...if you find skulls here, it would surprise me. Basically I felt this (potsherds) is what you're going to find. I did feel very strong about a chain. I felt that there was a chain that was forged by hitting it with like a hammer. Not forged like you'd find somebody here that made a chain from Orlando or something. The feeling I had was...let me ask you a question. Is there a possibility of a boat or something out in that direction making a explosion or a large noise? Like a cannon or a noise of some sort?

WALLACE: The only thing I could think of was something moving on the river?

BOWES: That's what I'm talking about.

WALLACE: The river at present is about one or two miles from here? East of here? But there have been shore line changes, too, and where the river is now is not where it might have been.

BOWES: I felt it was right out there (northeast). I would say that it moved up and went back that direction and turned back that way (described a course curling around the site on the east then to the northwest and then north again above the site.) I don't even know where I'm at, seriously, but I felt the river was over there and came from that direction and then came over here and went back in that direction (his directions described above). I would say that this may not have been the river but it was water that could be used. Water that was deep enough for a canoe to get in and out.

WALLACE: Do you have any feelings about hearths, fire places, or anything like that?

BOWES: I would say that in here, in this area, I would say over there (west side) that there was fires, and I would say over there (SSE) was places where they slept. There could even be a building in that area, or a place where there was poles in the ground.

JONES: From the photos you drew a fire place and one structure.

BOWES: That doesn't mean there wasn't more than one but I felt palm fronds, it was made from palm fronds and the palm fronds faced down. But the feeling I had was the direction of the wind...I don't know if they wanted the wind to blow, like blow the smoke over them or blow it away from them but for some reason I felt the fire was over on this side (west), but they could have put fires all over here, but the feeling I had was maybe something was over on this (west) side. This is strange, but I don't feel these trees were here. There was a different kind of tree here. These trees were not here when the Indians were here. I felt oak trees.

WALLACE: Do you have any feelings about the shape of the structures or any kinds of patterns that indicate what they look like in the ground, that we might find when we dig? Round? Square?...

BOWES: No, I didn't feel you'd find them in the ground. You might find logs, things laying like logs, but the feeling I had was there was posts in the ground and this is what you'd find and I felt it would be about four feet by ten feet or something like that...and you might find the posts in the ground. I did feel this was all burned off...that there was a fire here, so you might just find a log of a stump that high (about a foot) that was burned off at the top.

WALLACE: What about animal bones? You have any feelings about the different kinds of animals that we might find?

BOWES: I felt turtles...I felt otters, not so much raccoons. I felt alligators, and I don't know, this sounds strange, but I kept feeling almost like they sucked something out of the vertebrae, almost like they did something with the vertebrae or they were doing something with the tail of it, but I see them pulling on it...looked like strings...long strings, like you'd pull them out...like it was inside the vertebrae. I kept seeing them doing this over here (east), I felt there might have been a lake or water over there (east), but I see mostly women here for some reason.

WALLACE: Do you think if we walked over the surface you might be able to tell us where we might find hearths or where we might find animal bones...

BOWES: I don't even know what a hearth is...

WALLACE: Fireplaces, ash, charcoal and animal bones. You usually find them concentrated in one place. Archeologists just call it a hearth.

BOWES: I might be able to. I don't know why I keep going over to this side. (We go to southwest corner of mound near column sample area.) I come over here and I get a different feeling once I come over here. But I see a lot of activity in this area. I don't know...I keep getting the impression that there was water, fresh water near here. I wouldn't say it was a spring, but...I kept feeling like this was pertaining to a stay-over, or a place where they stayed for a short time. But I do feel it was used...used quite often. I would say that there was a possibility of something right over here. I keep seeing something in here (center of mound)...again I felt over there (west), but...when I stood up over there (west) I felt a lot of activity was over there (east)...there may have been a building over there. I wish I could tell you more.

WALLACE: Do you see fire areas in here (Indicating center area)?

BOWES: Yes.

WALLACE: This is 500 North/497 east, right about at the apex of the mound.

JONES: You said you felt a house over here someplace (southeast corner of mound)

BOWES: There may have been a house over here (southeast). Can I ask you if you found a fire place?

WALLACE: We found a charcoal and an ash concentration right there (center of mound).

BOWES: That's funny. I seen it over there (west) but once I went there and touched the ground I felt like there was a little house there or something like they all met over there or something. I want to ask you, have you found anything that looked like cocina rock? Like something, like something of a structure?

WALLACE: Yes.

BOWES: I felt that.

WALLACE: We had to chop through it with a maddox or stop the excavation. I don't know how far down it goes. We will map the walls of this thing and see what it looks like. Yeah, we have been running into that.

BOWES: I felt that it was here and...

JONES: A cocina structure?

WALLACE: I think that it is...as yet I don't have an explanation for it.

BOWES: I felt like they took round pieces of cocina rock and actually chiseled squares out of it and made little blocks.

WALLACE: We haven't found evidence of that. But we are...following this along.

JONES: We are talking about a structure here and not just cocina?

WALLACE: I don't know about a structure yet. The only thing is that the shell is heavily concreted together. Now whether that is natural or whether that forms the floor of a house or whatever we won't know until we get the whole thing mapped. We only have a section of it from this unit and portions of it over there. The only thing we can say right now is that it is heavily compacted shell.

BOWES: Maybe it was shells that they beat down with their feet or something to build...the feeling I had was there was something associated. It doesn't have to be here. It could be to that other side. I felt there was men in uniforms here and I feel they associated with someone who was collecting slaves.

WALLACE: That sounds like it would be fully historic, so parts of this could be fully historic as opposed to prehistoric occupation.

JONES: When Al talked about the pictures he indicated two different occupations—a primitive one and a more recent one.

WALLACE: Do you have any feelings about how far out this heavy stuff (cocina) may go?

BOWES: I felt it's going to be a layer. The feeling I got from this is that it is debris. It was debris that they had. They made it, they layered it. The impression I got was almost that it was oyster shells, but I'm sure that there is no oysters in here. I don't feel it would go out too much farther than this (indicates crown of mound area)...could be a thin layer of it all out in here. I kept feeling as though it was packed...like they did this with logs...pounded it... compacted this. This people here (touches potsherds), I would say that these were the last people who were here. I would say that they were traveling and I don't feel they lived here all the time. I see these migrant...people moving a lot. But I do see them associating with this (mound) as a place where they know it stays dry like year round or it stays dry for a long period of time and I felt this is why they were attracted to this place. I still don't understand it, but I keep seeing clear water or something clean over there (west). Is there a stream or something over there?

WALLACE: It's low and marshy over there. I haven't seen any streams over there yet. Very low and mucky.

BOWES: Maybe it was a lake where they could...maybe it didn't have much in it like this did (north)...maybe it was clearer water, maybe it was deeper. I don't feel sand, but I do feel sand with that over there (SSE). I don't feel there is any sand anywhere around here. I'm talking about white sand, and I said that in the tape (referring to reading of pictures). The impression I got was that they were going to move south-southeast. I don't know if that's southeast (pointing to the southeast) but the feeling I had was it was higher ridges and it was sand, and they retreated in that direction—the last people who were here.

WALLACE: Do you have any feelings at all about this eastern section?

BOWES: O.K. Let me go over there. The impression I had was you're going to find wood in here. There's going to be something laying in here that's wood. I do feel this area in here was higher, much higher and I felt it silted out in that area (toward the east). I do feel like you will find more artifacts in this area... more of this (pottery) and more of like spears of something of sticks that are burned...not so much a fire but more like a stick that was burned purposely. I feel much better with this (east) than with that (west) over there...like things that were thrown out or things that were thrown on the ground. I don't feel you're finding the real level...in other words, that up there, the top layer is recent. Up there (top) is the true level of today, but I felt this here (east) had silted off. You could scrape a couple of feet off of this and this would be a lower level than maybe where you are at right now. In other words I felt that this mound was actually higher and like there was a ridge and I'll walk along the ridge...right along here. It's right along here (Al walks from SE to NW in the eastern quadrant of the mound) and it was washed out and went down there (to east). The feeling I had was that there was no trees here, and it was barren for years. Washed out for a long time. Do you understand what I mean? In other words, the mound was higher...even with that over there in here, but since there was no trees or maybe because the water, the wind was blowing in from this way (from southeast), it silted out. I want to walk out there (northeast). That lake is out there. Something is out in there. Is there something out there? A grass field or something?

WALLACE: There is an open area?

BOWES: That over there, I felt that was a marsh (north). I felt it was actually a lake at one time. There was water there. It could have come up in here, too (water up to north edge of mound). If you walk out in there I think you'll find it gets real, real wet. There's layers of muck that deep (indicates several feet). Like it was silted in there. This I felt was a lake (north of mound). This was the feeling I had. I don't know how much good it's going to do you.

JONES: (Kicking up dirt) It's much marshier.

BOWES: I don't feel that there was any trees out there (points to the north).

JONES: Might not have been at that time.

BOWES: No trees. Just all grass like this...and there was water about this deep (several feet) in the grass that went out in there (north). If you had a topo map you might be able to see a circle in here, or like a place where possibly water came in.

JONES: Why is this important?

BOWES: It's important because I felt this is the way they came into the mound. This is the way they came in and out.

JONES: For the people who came in here, was this a regular stop?

BOWES: Yes. The feeling I had was, the other place was up that way (SSE). They came down the river and they could come in here...they know this was good high ground. They came in and stayed here and then they went on. They were travelers.

JONES: These people didn't have a home base around here?

BOWES: But the original people may have stayed here. The original people...the real primitive people may have been here in this area.

JONES: So there was early people and this may have been home...

BOWES: Right.

JONES: And then later this was just a stopping off point for people moving through?

BOWES: Yes. Going down the river, or going here or there. Let me ask you a question. Is there a large lake right up there? (points north)

JONES: Lake Harney is three miles up there.

BOWES: I felt they were afraid of that river, or that part of the river, like there was big waves there and they felt there was danger there. I felt that they talked about it like there was danger or like a superstitious type of thing. It was a big body of water, like Lake Monroe...a huge big lake and shallow and when the waves got up, that they went a long ways and they was real high. I didn't even think there was a lake around here like that. I hope I'm helping you in some way. I hope it's making sense. (tape ends and conversation continued as we changed tape)...like stuck in the ground right near the water ...where they went out and went in.

WALLACE: Do you think there's possibility of burials along this northern edge of the mound?

BOWES: I wouldn't say there was burials because I felt there was bones. I wonder if there was a canal or something that went up in there? I felt that that out there was wet (east), but I don't feel that way now. When I got out there (east of mound) and saw that flat place I didn't feel water there...there may have been water there but not deep enough to move a boat in and out. This...I did feel that. This (north edge of mound) is where they came in and out.

JONES: Do you think that Wallace and the crew are going to find evidences of the earliest people who lived here?

BOWES: I would say that it's here somewhere. Again it could pertain to that other site (points toward the SE) or that other thing that I seen. I would say that you might find their fires. You might find the bones of what they ate...could even be bones of the people. I felt like the early people put their people above ground, not something below, but the last people who were here buried things...put it in the ground or put it down...like threw things down.

WALLACE: Do you think we are going to find very many historic artifacts at all?

BOWES: I really couldn't tell you, but I did feel there was a thing with rods that come up like this and I felt there was a pot hanging from it. They would fold it up and take it with them. I don't know who that would belong to, but I did feel it was around here somewhere. Now, that could be misunderstood as somebody from the 1920s or somebody just the last six years may have come here and cooked out with a cookstove and this may be impressions of what I get from it...but I did feel it was stuck in the ground and it was there and it was...and somebody cooked over a fire. The feeling I get is in the ground, down under. And whether they left that thing here or whether it was just sitting here, I don't know. I wouldn't say it was here but it could be, you know. I did feel the nail and I drew a picture of it...it was square, got a square head on it...like a concrete nail. I felt this nail was beat with a hammer. It wasn't...in other words, when the rust broke off it may have broke off in like layers. It was made that way. Not made like a hundred and fifty strips of it was made and stamped out, but I felt it was taken and beaten with a hammer. The chain I felt the same way with...not something recent. The chain, I felt when it rusted it broke off in layers...in square looking pieces. I felt that was here somewhere.

WALLACE: You aren't sure where the chain is?

BOWES: No. I wouldn't be able to pick that up. It could be to the left (east). I felt the nail was found in the middle.

WALLACE: It was found in that trench we are running across the middle.

JONES: How many people do you feel associated with this mound?

BOWES: I would say the original people...there could have been a couple hundred. But I feel the last group—I wouldn't say was over fifty people.

JONES: The original group, do you get a feeling of where they were?

BOWES: I felt they walked all over this place. I didn't see them going in and out with the water so much, but I felt they were naked...walking in the woods, walking between the palm trees. I thought they were real strong in the buttocks, and their legs are real strong. The other people I felt they were thinner and skinnier...the last ones I felt were associated with the water. I felt they had stronger arms and I felt they were more...thinner. Taller, maybe.

JONES: Did the last people have clothing?

BOWES: Yes. Yes.

JONES: What did it look like?

BOWES: I would say that it would be leather...and I kept seeing these other uniforms I was telling you about. And I felt there was something associated with black...something of black with lines of red, and green and all colors... like lines.

WALLACE: Do you have any feelings about any kinds of ornaments that the people who lived here might have worn?

BOWES: I felt like bracelets and things around their neck, and I felt they were mostly bones and teeth. The funniest thing...I kept feeling like the first people who were here, their faces were funny, like they were ugly, almost like they were cavemen or like they were real ugly, like their faces were real big, like big jaws. I felt like they were real primitive. But these last people I felt were like typical Indians, like Seminoles or like...a round face. I felt they were more like a civilized person...a more civilized type. These other people were humped over and may have had very poor health. I felt the people walked back and forth that way...going that way and they may have gone down the St. Johns or went to the St. Johns or crossed the St. Johns, but I felt they were walking back and forth that way (SSE from mound).

WALLACE: Do you have any feelings about changes in animal bones? Are we going to find less of it for the earlier people or are we going to find any changes in it? Will they stop hunting one kind of animal and start hunting...

BOWES: I would say that you are going to go into alligators...more alligators, or an association with something that would be like vertebrae or something...I felt huge alligators over fourteen or fifteen foot; and I felt as time went on there would be less and less of that. I didn't see any armadillos at all. In fact I didn't see very few opossums.

WALLACE: What about rodents, like rats or anything like that?

BOWES: I would say there are small bones. Some of them are from birds or from fish. I did feel that there was something here that was a gun...something that was metal..it was round...it was a gun. I really feel like the people who were here...somebody came here and either was looking for them or was chasing them or wanted them. What I picked up when I first seen the first picture is—that people where hung here or were killed...and again it could pertain to that head that was on the post. In other words, whoever was searching for them, if they found some people here they might have killed them...put their heads on the post to scare the other one...I would say that that was like a tragedy, like something that...the first thing I seen with the picture and the first thing I felt when I walked up here is death...like death through the neck. So does that give you anything? I don't know if it makes sense or not.

WALLACE: It suggests a lot of things. I don't know how to check it out by digging.

BOWES: I feel that this here (potsherds) was in the bottom of a boat at one time...a canoe or a boat. I felt it was made of wood that was honed out or sliced.

JONES: Does this (pottery) feel like the first people or the second people?

BOWES: Again, the second people, because I see the association of the first people walking in this direction...like there was a trail that went right through there (SSE) and they went back and forth through there. That's funny. I really don't feel these trees were here (referring to trees on mound). I felt more...oak trees.

JONES: When you were reading the pictures you said you saw the Indians talking about a fortress or a fort, or something made of stone.

BOWES: This was the cocina I was talking about. I felt that it's either associated with this site or with something north. I felt it associated with these people in uniform. I would say that it associated with that lake again. That lake or north, and it could even be St. Augustine. The feeling I had was that it was north. But this is the feeling...like a fortress or like cocina rock.

That's funny. I felt that somebody had a strap around their stomach and somebody was pulling something and they were digging in the ground with it. Maybe they grew something. I did feel there was lots of vines and I expected to see them when I came out here, but I didn't see them...like blueberries or vines, like sticker bushes. I felt they were over there (west of the mound), but they're not there. That would be in a real swampy place I would say...where there's a lot of blueberries or real stickery bushes. I don't see any at all, that's strange.

I feel these pieces were colored (referring to shards). I see them associating with a place near Titusville, south of here, I felt it was south-southeast of here. I see big sand hills.

JONES: What kind of association? What do you mean?

BOWES: I felt they were trading, and they went that direction. I felt these were very local people and they stayed in this place, this area.

I felt they chased each other...through the palm trees. I kept seeing them making a hissing sound. I don't know if they make a hissing sound...they throw water on the wood, or like when they put the fire out (Al makes hissing sound). They could have burned themselves and made scars, but I felt like they were playing with the hot coals, and they were screaming and running out there and running around. I felt they were always sitting with their legs crossed wrapping things and I thought it associated with the rattle I told you about (referring to mention on photo-reading tape)...and sticks with something between them. Always wrapping. Like when there was nothing else to do they were wrapping, wrapping.

WALLACE: Do you see any kind of worked shell—shell that would have been altered?

BOWES: I felt...I'm not trying to get you off the subject but I seen oyster shells, and I felt that they were at the other site, and they could even be from the Indian River (near Titusville). But the feeling I had was that it was at the other site...using as scoops, scraping something with it. This place here, the only thing I felt was shells which seemed surprising to me. I didn't even know there were shells in the St. Johns River. I didn't know there was things there that were shells. I always consider shells, like salt water, but I felt little clams, like little clams and they were purple...but I see them opening the, like with a knife, or something sharp. I did feel that they collected alligator teeth, especially the first, original people, and I felt alligators was the big thing. They went out there (north) and as they went out there, they went through little canals or like there was lakes and then it was narrow and they pushed through grass and then there was like another lake or something, but I felt like when they seen the alligators that there was areas of ground that was, like, slimey slime and there was no grass, it was just open, like worn off. This could be a long, long time ago. This could be two or three hundred years...long, long ago. It could be longer than that. Very huge reptiles. Alligators. But the last people I didn't feel...they would associate with alligators, maybe seen them or something...maybe to shoot them or something, but I didn't feel that was anything real important. The other people I felt they were rattling or making a noise, a thumping, or pulling something back and "thud" or making a thud sound, while going out through there (north).

WALLACE: Do you see any shells being used as ornaments, like shell beads?

BOWES: I felt there was a little bead, like a pearl, like a little round bead, but I felt it was something from shells but I didn't see the shells being used. I did pick up, when you asked me that, I did pick up scars...like scars on their face, or scars especially around their ears, because I was trying to pick up earrings or something like that but I kept seeing like blue scars on their face...like funny looking. I did feel like when they were living here—I don't know if this was the original people or the people I picked up before—but I felt there were oak trees or trees here but I felt they were hanging things from them...like leather or like they kept their food up in the air or hung it off the ground, maybe to keep animals from eating it, but I see them walking around and hanging things up. The original people, I felt the women, I didn't see them with any clothes but I felt their breasts were real long, like they did a lot of walking and they stretched or something.

JONES: When you talk about seeing women associated with the site is that in terms of the earliest people or the later people?

BOWES: I really don't know. I really can't tell you about that. I felt it was more toward the last, but I felt they stayed here and they stayed busy doing something...wrapping things or...I keep seeing them getting a...some sort of plant and I don't know if this is like a lily pad, a banana leaf, but I see them wrapping it up and putting something in it like fish, like they were smoking fish. Does that make sense? Would they do something like that? Maybe it's like a flavor or something, but I felt that...but there's no banana trees around here, but I would say it associated with water, like maybe they went and got some sort of...I felt it was almost like a...something that shot up out of the water and it was like a cone or like a...or like this (makes fist)...and they took this and they folded it and they put something in it.

WALLACE: What about snakes?

BOWES: I was picking that up before. I didn't feel there was very many snakes. I just didn't pick that much up about that. Obviously, there was snakes around.

WALLACE: I meant to say, if they were being used for food or something like that?

BOWES: I did definitely feel that they took these alligators, or they did something with the alligators, and I felt with the backbone, like the vertebrae and they split it open, or split their back open and I see them getting long things that look like tendons, or strings, and I felt they were pulling them out of the backbone of them. What could that be? Would that be anything? That thing in the back?

WALLACE: Some sort of tendons, nerves. I don't know.

JONES: It could be sinew in the back.

BOWES: I felt they used it for strings.

JONES: That sounds like sinew.

BOWES: They pulled it out of their backbone, or they pulled it out of their back, but I felt this was a celebration or something real important to them. It was like a long string and they were pulling that thing out and they were all excited about it...they thought it was real important. I felt they always knocked the eyes out.

JONES: Is this alligator we're talking about?

BOWES: I felt they said something about the eyes, and they always taught the young boys to poke the eyes out, like they were afraid could still see them ... Like superstition...because I see them poking at it and it's got something real heavy over it. They might have nightmares about the eyes...opening up after it's dead or something. I'm trying to give you as much as I get and these things sound funny but it's what I pick up. People, like primitive people like that, they might think that's real special. These last people, I don't feel that they even thought of any of that stuff. It wasn't anything important to them.

MARGIE NIREN/BLIND READING
FLORIDA SITE 8SE32 MATERIALS

NIREN: What are these—all bones? Pieces of pottery and stuff?

JONES: Pottery, bones, little piece of stone, a bead...

NIREN: I'm getting something about shoes. I don't feel like regular shoes, or anything on the top. I just see something on the bottom, with a strap of some kind around the top...very early-type shoes.

I see this very tall tree...very tall, very tall tree with just branches and greenery at the top, and I see this man who has some type of duty and this has something to do with shoes for some reason...going out and carving things off of trees, working with trees somehow. I feel that maybe his job could have been something like getting the supplies for people. I don't feel that he would be a hunter or anything like that...just like, I don't know what you would call him...providing things to be made, to be worn.

JONES: What is he carving off the trees?

NIREN: The bark. Now, this would be a palm tree...taking that brown stuff, you know, kind of like netty looking stuff.

JONES: Netty?

NIREN: Yeah. What do you call that stuff that's in the bark of palm trees? They have that burlap-looking stuff. That kind of stuff.

JONES: So he's getting that. Do you have a feeling of what for?

NIREN: I feel like he supplies things like for the clothes and for the shoes, things like that. I don't feel like they know of shoes that much. It was something that he was just thinking of. I just see it on the bottom of the foot and not coming up over the top of the foot at all...just on the bottom. Like an idea, or a new way to make something for the bottom of the foot. That type of thing ...This is a bone, right?

JONES: I don't know. Bone or pottery, I don't know. Maybe just a piece of fired clay.

NIREN: I feel this associated with a man, whatever this thing is. (She is holding a piece of pottery). I don't feel he wore any clothes on the top. I feel like a little thing on the bottom (indicates loin cloth). I feel I'm just kind of stuck with that tree thing.

JONES: What about the man you just picked up, is he related to that tree or is he related to something else?

NIREN: He's the one that works scraping the bark from the tree. The tree was very, very big, because I see him standing there and it's really a huge tree.

JONES: Tall?

NIREN: I see more or less on the thin side. I don't feel he was very short, you know, maybe about five foot ten, that size. I feel like shortish hair, I don't see long hair. The cheek bones would be high, and the nose would be...I don't feel his nose would be close to his face or anything like that, but you know, his nose isn't small. Not large, you know, a little bit straight. He is tan looking, dark hair.

JONES: After he was through working on this tree, do you have a feeling of where he would go?

NIREN: I see like a little place that he would work, that he had for himself, in the trees. I see like little scrub shrubs of some kind and I see a little place in the middle there that he would work. Also things being dried. Strange, because I would think that a woman would be doing all this stuff. But it's a man that's doing this.

JONES: Things being dried and then you said, "strings"?

NIREN: "Strange"—to me, because I thought that would be woman's work, but this is like his job, to supply these things.

JONES: What's he drying?

NIREN: I see rabbits. I don't see anything really big being dried. Just small animals and stuff like that, and things from trees. He had a little place cleared out for him to work in...and I don't feel that it is real close to the camp, wherever this place would have been, like I feel that he's off by himself almost.

JONES: Why do you think that?

NIREN: I don't know. He is a part of this group, but perhaps the location is better for him to work in, maybe he needed something that was nearby. I also feel...I see a very small stream on the side by him, over this way, it's like a small stream. I don't see this huge river or anything like that, I just see like a small trickling thing going by, and I feel like he used that in some way for the work that he did, and it was just more convenient for him to be closer to it.

JONES: You mentioned the rest of the group. How many are there?

NIREN: It's like I see pottery and bowls and...I'm looking at all this stuff and I can see like he's over here and the stream is there and the group is here, and the pottery is over in this area. I see it like all grouped together, like this is where they kept this type of stuff...the pottery and things like that.

JONES: Can you see what the pottery looks like?

NIREN: I just see like...like rounded, like a round one, and then there's one, almost like squarish kind of, it doesn't go in at the top, squarish. I also see some long things down there.

JONES: How many people do you feel are there? 5, 10, 20, 30, 100, 500, etc.?

NIREN: 50 to 75.

JONES: Do you get a feeling about whether they move around a lot or stay there all the time, or stay there some of the time and leave or...?

NIREN: I don't feel that this is the first place that they have lived. There have been other places. They have moved many times, I think.

JONES: Do you have a feeling of where they might have come from?

NIREN: I feel more northerly, and I feel they are moving southerly each time they move.

JONES: Do you have a feeling of why they move?

NIREN: I think they more or less exhaust the things they have around that area. So instead of going out further and further to get the things they need, it was just easier to move the whole camp like further down, and...

JONES: Further down?

NIREN: Down south. Just moving further south.

JONES: Why not east, or why not west or why not north?

NIREN: I don't know. I feel like there is something around them, something that…I also feel they thought it was better for them to move not only for food supplies but I felt something on the sides, like closing in somehow.

JONES: Something on the side closing in?

NIREN: I don't feel people…their own people, I feel somebody else that would be trying to move in. I also feel they have sent runners out to these different places and I also feel that there is a man who they listen to quite a bit who tells them what to do. I don't know if he was some kind of chief or whether he had some strange powers, but they would trust him and believe him. So when he said it was time to move, I felt that they moved. But I feel like they had men going out all the time, looking and watching these other people…whoever they were. Like it was their security system of some kind. I also feel they were very watchful of what went on around them…like I don't feel everybody sleeping down at night, I feel they would be keeping watch to make sure the camp was o.k. I hold this stuff. I feel the water around it and I feel…(Makes a mound shape with a movement of her hands). I feel like a sickness of some kind, and I see like, I don't know what kind of sickness they had, I feel like real achey kind of feelings, everything just aches…

JONES: What other kinds of symptoms go along with this sickness?

NIREN: I feel a fever and I feel a great deal of pain like in my bones, in the muscles and…like I've been run over by a bulldozer…that kind of feeling. I feel a lot of stress on the people, because I see this happening to them and they exhaust all the means that they have but there is just nothing can help them.

JONES: Means that they have for what?

NIREN: Their healing. All the different herbs and stuff…all the different natural stuff that they use. I feel like they just tried everything, and…

JONES: Do you have a feeling of what they think is going wrong? Is this like a sickness that a lot of people are getting?

NIREN: Yeah.

JONES: O.K. Do they have some idea of what is causing it, or why their methods aren't working?

NIREN: Well, I feel that these things have been brought in from other people, and they also feel that it is a white man's disease of some kind. It's almost like the women are the last to go, for some reason. The women somehow are stronger. I don't know if that is due to something in their body that…I also feel that in their diet there's a lack of certain things…like a lack of calcium, and when things did happen, like broken legs, and things like that…I think they needed calcium. They didn't get as much as they should have gotten.

JONES: What did they eat?

NIREN: Mostly fruits, berries, things like that. At certain times, meats, but I don't feel that often. I see fish, but I would say that most of their diet is berries and things like that.

JONES: Did they cultivate any crops? Do you get anything about that?

NIREN: I don't get too much of a feeling. I just feel like they use things that are already there, you know. I also feel a lot of singing with these people.

JONES: Is this like singing for the fun of it or religious singing or…?

NIREN: I would say both. I feel like there were certain rites that they did on certain times…religious rites of some kind.

JONES: What kind of rites? What are they doing?

NIREN: I feel they dressed differently, like they put this stuff on. Going out on the town, you know, and I feel like a lot of eating goes on. I feel that this is the time mostly when they eat the meats that they do have. Because I don't feel like they eat meat that often, and I feel that they did this periodically and it's always at this time, whatever this is they do.

JONES: Did they do this regularly every year, the same time every year, or just whenever they were in the mood to do it?

NIREN: I felt the full moon had something to do with this, maybe every full moon they did this, and I also think they eat these meats on the full moon for some particular reason...they feel like it gives their body something that it needs on the full moon...and I felt women especially.

JONES: Are there any symbols associated with these rituals?

NIREN: At these particular times I see the women dressed like in dark things, and I also see circles, I see things with circles on them, and to me that would signify the full moon, having something to do with that. There's something that has...I see like a main area where they have this, and on either side I see these long things with different colors, like going down. The colors are important to their...the way they go.

JONES: Long things with colors going down them?

NIREN: Yeah, like some kind of long pole; but thin ones, they're not real wide. But the colors have to be just right. I also see like rocks or things like this in this area. And the chief, he would be there in this area. I also feel like the childen were present at these times. The elders were watching them and they were sleeping. I really felt the moon was very important to their beliefs, almost like everything centered around it, very important to them.

JONES: Do you feel like this was an ultimate deity to them or was there something else or several other things or what?

NIREN: Well, I...I think there was something greater to them, but I think they looked to the moon to help them somehow, and for some reason I think of reproduction. They felt like if they were to do certain things, you know, that they would be able to conceive easily. That's what they need. They need, they need to have more people among them. I feel their numbers getting smaller and they're praying to the gods, or whatever, to help them...to do certain things. This is...I think the meat comes in with this for some reason...maybe the blood of the meat has something to do...and the full moon has something to do with the cycles of the women...I don't know. I feel like this is this main man, almost like he is getting...he gets insights as to what these people should do and...like if he said that you should do this, then they would go out and do this, or gather these certain things that they would need for their ritual type thing. I definitely feel it has something to do with the reproduction. I do. In between the man and the female, in between I see like this grass type mat going up there to the rocks.

JONES: Grass mat going to the rocks?

NIREN: Yeah, like well...the female on this side (south), and the males on this side (north), and the rocks are over here (east), and there is not just dirt, they have put some kind of grass things, thatching of some kind going up to this alter or whatever this thing is over here.

JONES: The rocks were an altar?

NIREN: Yeah, that type of thing...they offer things upon it...and also I feel like this is where the chief is (east side).

JONES: Do you see him there?

NIREN: Yeah. I feel...quite amount of things on him, like...painted different colors. I see red and...something down the legs, feathers of some kind or something...some kind of...you know that white bird...what do you call them ...some sort of a white bird with skinny little legs.

JONES: Like a heron or egret or...?

NIREN: Yeah, one of those, like the egret-type thing. I see white feathers along both of his legs, and...

JONES: What do you see around his head? On his face?

NIREN: There's a lot of things on his head, and I feel very decorative and...
this is strange...I see rabbit on it, and why they used the rabbit was because of
reproduction, how they reproduced so fast, and...because I felt this was their
major concern was to repopulate the area, because I see it almost like dying
away. They were very concerned...the rabbit also played some kind of role in
this.

JONES: In this same scene are these colored sticks, is that right?

NIREN: Yeah.

JONES: What role did they play? What did they mean, do you think?

NIREN: Like I see red at the ends, and this I felt signified life...blood, life, and
after that I see yellow, and this was like the sun...or the moon...having to do
with that. I just feel that everything has to do with getting the population
going again...and I think it's like a main thing in their whole environment
there.

JONES: Was that the only kind of ritual they did in this area?

NIREN: This is the main thing, I'm sure of it. They were very interested in
getting the population back to where it should be, and this was very important.

JONES: Does this relate to that sickness you were talking about? Is the sickness depleting them and are they trying to act to build up the population or
where those two different things?

NIREN: I think...that before the sickness came this was a big part. They
wanted to keep all this stuff going and it was important for them to have children, but I also see like a...I don't feel that they lived too long, you know...
that's why they feel it's very important to get these children going, to get
these children out. I also feel that there were more men than women, and this
is a concern of theirs also. Their whole thing here is for the population. This
isn't something new, because of the sickness...I feel it's been going on. I feel
more male children being born than female, and so they want to take steps before...they feel they have to put more children out to keep the thing going.

JONES: These huts, how big would you say they were?

NIREN: About as big as this room (12' x 12'). Some this big, some smaller,
and it seems they liked to put little huts over a lot of stuff...you know, like
covering things, to protect things. Just not for people to sleep in. Like they
had huts that they kept food in, and things like that, just not for sleeping purposes. I also feel that their beds were not on the ground. I don't...because of
snakes. They were safer up a little bit, and it was really just more practical.
They had all the trees around them to do it, so why not.

JONES: When people would die, what would they do with them?

NIREN: Well, over in this area (east of the site). I feel burial. I feel like
grounds of some kind that they would use. I don't feel them like digging
graves, I don't feel that. I also feel like they would lay them out for awhile and
...I don't see them going under the ground. Like maybe they would put something over them, you know. Over them. I see like a mound type of thing, you
know...I don't see it under the ground, like they would bury them.

JONES: Do you think they had a feeling of an afterlife?

NIREN: Yeah, I think that they did...because...something about...I think
they felt that everything had...like all animals had spirit and I think that is
why they didn't eat meat all that much. I think...something about reference to
the spirit of a snake. I don't know what that means. All I get is "spirit of a
snake," like they would say...I don't know..it's hard to explain. Like when
people got sick or something like that, they would come by with the reference
that the spirit of the snake is in you, or something like that.

JONES: An evil idea, an idea of sickness?

NIREN: They didn't have regular names for this stuff, you know, like "jaun-
dice" or something like that, it's like they referred to something they knew. If
they had to give a name they would say something they knew.

JONES: **What would they consider images of evil? Or what to them was the ultimate evil or symbol of it?**

NIREN: I think sickness, in a way, and I feel like they always blame something else for it, you know, like it wasn't theirs...like this person would bring in, it would be his fault, you know, even if he didn't bring it in, it would still be his fault.

JONES: **What do you think they feared most? What would really terrify these people?**

NIREN: I was seeing like a black panther. I think this type of animal...it being black somehow, would frighten them, like I almost feel like a bad omen type thing, if they were to see one of these. They feel like it would bring them bad luck of some kind.

JONES: **Are there any major environmental or geographic features around this place that would help understanding where this place was? Let's say I had no idea where this material came from. Are there any other things you could tell me to help me know where it came from?**

NIREN: I see...I feel in Florida, I see water all around, and of course the palm trees and that kind of scrub stuff. Like a stream going by. I don't feel mountains. The water is very close to the ground, very damp kind of feeling.

JONES: **If I asked you how far away is it from where you are sitting right now, what would you say?**

NIREN: I got twenty-five miles.

JONES: **What about age? How long ago? What time do you feel these people were doing this?**

NIREN: I feel around...like the 17th...16th, 17th century.

JONES: **Do you think these people are the first people who came to this area?**

NIREN: As far as they were concerned, like when they moved and when they went to these areas it was new to them, you know...not like coming into somebody else's territory. I feel that it was clean coming in there, but before that...I am not...I think that there was others there but...quite aways away...long ago. I don't see anyone new, I don't feel newness with this area. It looks like it's just old. Like nothing's been there when they move into it...

JONES: **But there was a long time ago? Is that what...?**

NIREN: Yeah, I feel like a long time ago there was. But not real recently.

JONES: **What about after these people (artifacts)? Where these the last people there?**

NIREN: I don't think it would be settled in these area. I think...it's like when they come into a new area it's cleared off and behind them somebody comes. I don't feel, like staying there, I feel like passing through, that type of thing.

JONES: **"Passing through" is after these people (artifacts)?**

NIREN: Yeah. I don't feel...

JONES: **Who were these people passing through?**

NIREN: I feel this is also one of the reasons why they moved southerly. (artifacts). I just...it's like they're running, they're going and...all they do is want to have a place to stay and stay there. And I feel all these kinds of anxieties, and people being killed and trying to reproduce and have more children and they just can't seem to find a place to settle down.

JONES: **Are these the people passing through?**

NIREN: It's like they feel they're going to be gone, and there's just nothing they can do about it. They fear these people that are coming through. It's like they know that this was their territory, and these people coming through were just going to push them out. And I feel like a need to...just stay here and try to get things going but I just don't feel that...like they are always being pushed out somehow, and these people...I see uniforms on them and some with blond hair, and...

JONES: **Where are we now? With the people associated with the ritual or with these later people?**
NIREN: The people that are coming into their sites as they move.
JONES: **Associated with those people with uniforms?**
NIREN: Yeah.
JONES: **What kind of feeling do you get about them?**
NIREN: I feel like...I'm in sympathy with the Indians. I feel that...like I'm being threatened by these people. I don't like them. I don't want to have anything to do with them. They won't leave me alone. They just want to...and I feel like with these people coming through, I see drinking...just wanton destruction. They just don't care. I see these people really appalled by the sight of them. They can't imagine people being like this.
JONES: **What kind of language were the men in the uniforms speaking?**
NIREN: I feel like it's a foreign language of some kind, and this adds to the Indians' fear of them... They can't understand them, and they just see what's going on. They really don't know what to make of all this, you know. It just kind of frightens them. I see a foreign language there, but I also see English there, too, not that many. I see mostly some kind of foreign language.

The clothes I see on these guys are like...not pirate looking but fancier, you know—fancier than being a pirate or something like that but dirty...dirt, kind of messed up. I see one guy there who is kind of a loudmouth type. I guess he's like the leader of this soldier-type thing...and I see like a wide-rimmed hat on him, not a safari type hat, but kind of wavy, you know, and I see like ruffles on him (neck), but really dirty, really dirty and...scroungy people. I didn't like them at all. I'm with the Indians, probably because I'm holding their things I feel in sympathy with them. It's like the soldiers want to take over everything and I just feel so sorry for the Indians. They just want to get away and live peacefully and not have them bothering them. (Holding bone) I feel this belongs to a woman and...I see her sitting there with her legs crossed and then just going backwards, just keeling over dead (she is holding mandible fragment). At this time...when this person died, I don't feel there were too many left. I also think that at this site there isn't like a main burial ground and I also think there is going to be scattered people, like people scattered around this area. Because they were the last ones to go, they were just left there, they were not buried.
JONES: **Scattered, buried around the area?**
NIREN: Not buried, but they had that mound, that burial mound, I don't feel everybody was there. You know, I feel like the last ones were just wherever they were at the time they died. I felt this woman just sitting back and dying and she wasn't put on the mound or anything like that, so I think you'll find people's bones scattered. I don't see a whole bunch of them...just a few of them...scattered around—that were not on the mound. I feel that...this person, I feel the age was somewhere in the thirties. Also feel like at the time of their death, it was like a release, like being so sick and just being too tired to care, that type of thing.
JONES: **Does this person here (mandible) have that sickness or is this another thing?**
NIREN: I'm talking about that sickness, yeah.
JONES: **Would this person have been alive to see that ritual you described?**
NIREN: Yeah, I think so, because I think they did it quite often. It was a part of their thing; it just wasn't something they did for when they got sick, I don't think. I think it was going on for quite a while. This was important to them. I keep seeing like a young man, like he was away from the camp coming back and seen that somebody has died, kind of mourning that person...crying, that type of thing. Like—sorry that he had gone, you know, not knowing what was happening. I feel like a lot of the men were always out watching what was

going on around them...where these other people were, these soldiers, some other people were. They always come back and say what was happening and what they should be doing, like confer with the chief on what they should do next.

JONES: Are there any other villages or camps near this place?

NIREN: I would go north and northwest. Like two sites...one up this way and one further that way (west) a little bit. I also feel these other sites were wiped out first, and I feel like these young men would see this and watch what was happening and then come back and say what was going on, and then the chief would decide if they would move on or not. I feel like a real weary feeling with these people. Like "why can't they leave us alone? Why can't they just go someplace else?" Really kind of sad.

JONES: Who is the "they" in "why can't they leave us alone?"

NIREN: These other strangers that are coming in. This other camp that I feel is north of this one, they were like totally...all of a sudden these soldiers came in and wiped them out—that type of thing. They just didn't have no idea, you know, what these people were like. I feel like they were friendly, the Indians were friendly towards them, and they were just wiped out. I feel like a few of the young boys ran to the next camp, and this is how they found out that this was going on, otherwise they would have been totally unsuspecting not knowing what was going on around them...these ones that got away came down to warn the other ones so this camp here (artifacts) were always on the lookout sending these people out to search and to see just where these soldiers were...kind of like kept an eye on them

JONES: Are there any other villages or camps in the vicinity of this mound?

NIREN: I see...like these two other places here...like they were once all together and they had branched out. And further south—further south I feel like there is somebody, but not these...not the same people, not these same people here. I don't know who they are.

JONES: Could they speak to each other?

NIREN: No, I don't even think they know they existed down there...whoever these people were. I feel it was somebody from across the sea somehow that were there. I don't feel like a large number of them or anything like that but I don't think...these people even knew that they were down there. They never got down there that far anyway.

JONES: From across the sea? Where do you feel they were from?

NIREN: Spain, or some place like that, or France, or some place like that area, but I don't see a whole of people there. I feel like kind of new...new...new to Florida...new experience, but I don't think these Indians even knew that they were down there.

I don't feel everybody in this camp died, either...well, I'm sure they died... but I feel that some of them moved, some of them got away, and...so I don't think that was the end of their race...completely.

JONES: What is the relationship between the people associated with the ritual and then the later people passing through? Did they know one another or were they in any way at any time related to each other or no relationship?

NIREN: I don't feel any relationship. You mean these soldiers? Is that what you are talking about? Which ones are you talking about?

JONES: Let's see, you felt there were real, real early people...

NIREN: Oh, I see what you mean.

JONES: ...and then come these people (artifacts), and then later on, with reference to some group that was just passing through...

NIREN: Those, I felt, were the soldiers...those people that had come through. But I don't feel they settled there or anything like that...just went through the area. I don't think they really wanted...as far as they thought, it wasn't the best place in the world to live...that type of thing. So after they went through, they found some place else.

I saw this woman giving birth, but it wasn't like in her hut, it was some place off...perhaps when they were getting ready to deliver they went off to a certain area.

JONES: I was wondering what you might pick up with this piece of flint here?

NIREN: Like little sticks...perhaps, like it was some kind of a tool or something...I feel like little sticks and things attached to it. I feel it was some kind of tool. I feel there were different tools, not just one tool. I see bigger ones and smaller ones.

JONES: What do they look like?

NIREN: There's one that's like flat and used for pounding...pounding things out. I see like a pointed one and used with colors, like to hit and to color something. Like a small...you know, color.

JONES: I don't understand, to hit and to color something?

NIREN: Say like this was the point of something, they would dip it in the color and then they would...this was like a stick or something...you could hit and color...like leave a mark of the color.

JONES: On what?

NIREN: Whatever...this...like...stuff from the trees, bark, not the bark but the other stuff from the trees, things that their clothing would come from. Just like making different kinds of designs of some kind. They'd dip it and hit it and dip it and hit it, and just...make like different designs of stuff.

JONES: Where did they get the flint? Do you see them getting it some place, or picking it up off the ground?

NIREN: I don't think it was...it's like it's there, but it's not...I don't know how that works...like...I don't really feel it around the area there. I feel like it's brought in, or that it was there, but...

JONES: Brought in? From where?

NIREN: I saw like a hunk of it, but it's not like it was there...I just don't feel like it belonged there for some reason.

JONES: Do you get a feeling of where it might have come from? How it got there?

NIREN: That's weird. I just see it there, but I don't feel it's from that area. I want to say, from the south of there, but I don't know how it got there. It just seems like it was brought up, but I don't know how.

JONES: What kind of art do you see with these people? Designs? Drawing? Carving?

NIREN: Yeah, I felt they were very artistic. Like I see some kind of things with...I see circles, color, like...and I think color played a big role with these people and they used color for a lot of things. This piece (flint) here, I see a big piece of it, and I don't feel there was a bunch of it around, I see like one big hunk, and that's what I say about that.

With this (potsherd), I don't know what this is, but I feel lighter somehow, when I hold this. The other things were kind of heavy to me (the piece she was holding elicited some of the more elaborate readings from Bowes and Davis)... not in their weight but in the feeling I got when I held it. Whatever this...I get a happy feeling when I hold this. I don't feel sickness or...I feel like a period of time before all this bad stuff happened. If this is a bone, I don't feel like this person died of this sickness, I feel that life was kind of normal, there wasn't all that upheaval feeling. I see people working around the camp site doing things, happy. There's no fear. They're relaxed...like everybody's doing their job. Like 'one-big-happy-family' type of thing.

JONES: What about if I asked you about stories they would tell? Myths or folk tales? Do you have any feelings about what they might talk about?

NIREN: I think, like animals were a big part of their entertaining stories and things like that. Like I think they would tell stories that would have actually happened, but also they would make things up to make it sound good. I don't see like a whole lot of play to their activities, because I think that why they enjoyed, whether it was picking berries or working on...whatever...all these different things that they did, they enjoyed doing that. It wasn't like work to them. It was just a part of life, a part of living. I do think...the elders sitting around telling the children tales and things about the woods, the forest type things, and, you know, like funny things that would happen to them, because they were a happy people. I see a lot of laughter, and there was like a different kind of humor than we have.

JONES: How long do you feel it was between the time that you feel that they were happy until they started running into trouble?

NIREN: I feel like about two years.

JONES: You mentioned fish. How did they get fish?

NIREN: I see pieces of wood together, like dropped down into the water. Used like as a bucket, or a net type thing, with these pieces of wood.

JONES: Pieces of wood as a net?

NIREN: Like...a little bucket-type thing, and I could see it laying down in the water, and the fish would get into it and they would scoop it up.

JONES: How big was it?

NIREN: I see one about like that (indicates about two feet in diameter). The one I'm seeing right now...I don't see any huge ones, but I do feel they have larger ones, but the one I see right now is a smaller one. (Makes round shape with her arm.)

JONES: How did they get it out of the water?

NIREN: Like they would hold it down, it would go down, and when they would see a fish would go in...because I feel the water was clear, they could see...and they would just scoop it up and all the water would run out through the holes and it wasn't heavy, you know, for them to do it.

JONES: And you said you thought there were bigger ones?

NIREN: Yeah, I feel like...there might have been some bigger ones. I feel that wherever this water was, a man could get on the other side, and they would use this, and I see like a basket-like effect and then having two...this would be like handles and one man would stand on one side and one man would stand on the other side and they go like that and scoop up, like that.

JONES: You mentioned that you felt there were some people here before these people came. Can you get to them?

NIREN: I see women in long dresses and...like there...like they came from across the...water, and I don't know why women...I don't understand this...I don't know all this history and like that...

JONES: Just tell me whatever you feel like.

NIREN: Like I see women in flowing dresses and like with a parasol and she is fair. I wouldn't figure that she would be there, like this doesn't really make sense.

JONES: What about this bead?

[Tape ends: Continued from notes] NIREN: I see bracelets on their ankles and arms...necklaces. I see a woman using a bone and making circles in through here...like bones of a fish. I feel colors and decorations as designs...decorations on the side of something like little "V" shapes. They made a lot of stuff for the chief. He wore more than anybody. Even the children had jewelry. I feel there was an older woman who worked with child birth...being more experienced. Certain people were in charge of different things...some in charge of food gathering, another in charge of...but the chief was the main one. All these others went to him. I see the chief and two men on either side of him. They have some degree of being in charge. Whether they were his sons or not they were

important...they had their say and the chief would decide. I want to go back to
the ceremony. He was really decked out then. At other times he looked normal,
but more jewelry. I felt the more you had, the more important it meant you
were. If some young man did something heroic, he got jewelry. It was important, and colors...a certain color meant certain things. These men were of the
chief's family...some kind of kinship with him. His family was very important.
they are not young...the men on each side of him. I feel that one was a brother...I feel like a brother-in-law. There are two on each side of him. I don't know
what the others are. These men would never leave. These men had more children
than others...that was really important to them...the population problem. The
leadership was in the family...the chief's brother-in-law and two others were
not in the family. Alligator eggs were sacred somehow. Shells were used as
medicine of some kind. Eggs were very important to them. The alligator was
important because it could go on water and land; it was food, the skins could
be used. Because it went on water and land, it was somehow singled out to
them. They felt it was very strong. Same kind of feelings with Indians and the
buffalo. They would use the alligator egg shells in their food...or they would
just grind it up. It was given to males in particular. It was supposed to do
something for them...the alligator was a big part of their environment. They
could see its great strength...the males felt they would get strength by eating
the shells. It wasn't medicine exactly. It was like a superstition. They felt it
was the alligator's land as well as their land. They didn't hunt alligators...it
was sacred. If they found a dead one they would use it, but I don't feel they
would kill one. They could defend themselves from them but I don't feel they
would actually hunt one to kill it.
JONES: How did they feel about bears?
NIREN: I see panthers...they really feared them. They saw panthers more
then bears. Bears, they might hunt, but it was different with alligators. The
bear stood on two feet and that was important...that's what the special feeling
toward the bear was based on. Alligators were awesome. Also there were traps
around the camp...holes in the ground covered. Everyone knew where they
were. They were for protection of the camp. This is why they slept above the
ground...alligators and snakes. The traps were all marked so nobody would
fall in. It was their little security system.

NIREN. BLIND READING OF 8SE32 MATERIALS

NIREN: I see people carrying quite a few of these (Conch Shells). Some kind
of...not like a basket, but some kind of pouch that they carried over their
shoulder. I feel that it's been brought from another place, like a little bit further north than where they are...like it's been brought down. I'm not sure if it
would be trading or what, but...bringing it in. I see about ten of them...like in
the guy's thing here (pouch)...carrying them, walking.
JONES: Do you have a feeling about who they are traded from?
NIREN: I feel some place up north. They are brought down with them...
JONES: What does he look like?
NIREN: I see long dark hair, and I don't see a shirt on him, and barefoot. I
only see one man carrying these. I don't see a lot of group of people around, I
just see one person.
JONES: What do they do with them? What are they getting them for?
NIREN: I feel like they were used as a decoration of some kind. Something
that would be very beautiful. It would mean something to them. I almost feel
like they would put the...I see like a stick. (the shells have a hole in one end
and are presumed to have been used as hoes.)
JONES: A stick on these things?
NIREN: Yeah.

JONES: I don't understand?
NIREN: It's like they are on a stick (laughs), but then I see them also laid...
like I see one here, one on one side and one over here, but there is something in
the middle (makes a small mound shape with hands). Adornment purposes...
decorating them, like when they move or something like that, these go with
them.
JONES: There is another one (conch shell) here. Do you get similar feelings
with it or do you get something different?
NIREN: Like it would become kind of musical thing...blowing into them. Here
again, I see like one man...what he had to do with this or what he had to do
with these?
JONES: What do you feel is in between them?
NIREN: I'm not sure if its a burial mound or...I just feel there is something
there and...between them.
JONES: How far apart are they?
NIREN: Like about six feet, or something like that. Here again I see one down
here and one up further and one up like that (in a line). I just feel...I seen them
on sticks and there's a space between them, but whatever these were used for I
feel it was to put on the sides of things (laughs). Because I always feel like a
space between them. (she picks up large shell piece or fragment) I see like the
front end of a canoe, and a bank.
JONES: What does the canoe look like?
NIREN: The end is kind of rough...and it's kind of narrow at this end that I'm
seeing. I see smooth, too, so...
JONES: How does that thing you are holding right now relate to that (canoe)?
NIREN: (Laughs) I don't know. That's just the first thing that I saw...I'm
picking up animals...like I see a bear in the woods by the water.
JONES: Do these people see this bear?
NIREN: I don't know...it's like I'm seeing a man in a canoe and then I'm
seeing like a bear in the woods there.
JONES: What kind of water is this? Stream?...or lake, or river or what?
NIREN: It's like...a river. I see a very large circular something...I don't feel
it's all like that though. I feel like it's narrow, but right now I'm seeing like a
round...not huge or anything like that, but roundish.
JONES: Roundish what?
NIREN: Lake, or river part...comes around, you know, that part.
JONES: Relative to that roundish lake or river part, where is the site?
NIREN: It's like...I see this round thing here, and I don't...I don't know like
how I'm seeing it, but it's back that way...a little bit.
JONES: Which way would the sun rise? Do you get a feeling of that?
NIREN: I see the lake or river over this way, and then the campsite over here,
and then a little trail kind of thing that slightly goes back that way.
JONES: Which way does the river run?
NIREN: This way. (North).
JONES: So, then the camp is sort of below the circular area?
NIREN: At least this pathway that I feel goes back to the campsite.
JONES: How far below?
NIREN: Not too far away. I don't think miles...more like yards. I don't feel
too far. I'd say an eighth or a quarter of a mile. I see another path going this
way...north, I guess...above it.
JONES: How big is this circular body of water?
NIREN: It's hard to tell. I mean I can see it but how do I...I don't...it's like
your average...
JONES: Your average body of water?
NIREN: (Laughs) You know, with little shores along the side.

JONES: Well, like there is the little lake—like Lake Hodge out there—and then there's the big lake—like Lake Monroe or Apopka.

NIREN: I feel like the smaller one. I keep seeing this bear standing there. I don't feel alarm with this guy. I don't know if he sees it or not. Back in the woods there is some kind of traps for animals.

JONES: Do you see what kind of traps?

NIREN: You know, like holes of some kind for animals in that area.

JONES: Are we talking about large animals or small animals? What kind of animals?

NIREN: I'd say large animals. Those are the ones they had to worry most about. (Picks up metal fragment) I see...that couldn't be. I don't feel these Indians had this...like it was...I kept on seeing a belt, and...but it wasn't the Indians, it was somebody else's...like it was on these other people's belt.

JONES: Who were these other people?

NIREN: Someone who was in some kind of army type thing. By looking at it (metal) I don't see how that could be, but...

JONES: How does that piece of metal go with the belt? What is that?

NIREN: It's like...it's like on the belt, it's like a part of the belt...like a decoration? I don't feel...I believe it is a part of a knife. That's what I'm seeing.

JONES: How are you seeing this belt and this knife? Is it on somebody or what?

NIREN: I was seeing this soldier-type guy, and I could see his belt and this is why I didn't see how this would fit because it wasn't like...I just on kept getting "belt" I kept seeing a belt but I couldn't see how this (metal) was in there exactly. Then, like a sword-type of thing kept popping into my view. I felt this belonged to that gentleman...the guy with the belt that I saw.

JONES: Do you know what it is doing with these Indian material?

NIREN: I feel that they came through there and left their sword, because I see it like out, you know...just left behind.

JONES: Do you see any kind of uniform?

NIREN: It looks sort of like white...something like white-colored. Light-colored pants...more or less light-colored-type stuff.

JONES: What about a hat or anything on the head?

NIREN: When you first said that I saw kind of a hat with a feather, and then I felt "no" (laughs), so I don't know...what kind of hat.

JONES: What do you feel are the Indians relationship to the people who had the belt?

NIREN: I don't feel too good. I don't have a happy feeling when I hold this.

JONES: Where do you feel the owner of the sword came from?

NIREN: I felt from France, because like the dress that I saw was fancy. I'm getting the number 100, like a hundred soldiers or something were around there.

JONES: Do you feel like they stayed there very long?

NIREN: No, I don't. I don't feel like they stayed there for too long, and yet I don't feel there were too many people there when they came...like they had moved, but I feel there were some that were left behind...that didn't go.

JONES: Where were these soldiers stationed?

NIREN: From where the campsite is I feel like a northwesterly, then from there they came from like a northeasterly...I feel like a zig-zag.

JONES: Like they came from the northeast heading to the southwest and then turned to the southeast.

NIREN: Yeah.

JONES: Do you have any idea of why they made that zig-zag instead of just coming straight on down?

NIREN: No.

JONES: **What are they doing there?**
NIREN: I think they came over and...they were looking for...I don't know. They tried to run them out and...they wanted to make them into something that the Indians didn't want to be. And it's almost like I feel that they wanted to take some of them back with them to France or wherever they were from, but I don't feel they got anybody. There was talk of it...taking over, running them out. Almost like looking for treasure or something like that, but...that's all I get from that.
(Picks up white-glazed ceramic piece) I don't feel that this belonged to these Indians...I feel that outsiders brought it somehow. I almost feel like it belonged to something that was fancy.
JONES: **What do you mean, "fancy?"**
NIREN: I don't know. That was just the word I got. But it's like...some kind of container or something. It had a top on it that was kind of a little bit fancier.
JONES: **Outside influence?**
NIREN: Like from these other people.
JONES: **Who were these other people?**
NIREN: Now it seems like I'm going up into a different state.
JONES: **Where?**
NIREN: Georgia.
JONES: **How did you get to Georgia?**
NIREN: I don't know. It feels like...this came from outside of Florida, I feel. (Laughs) How about that! I don't know if it was...I'm not sure if it came down there from them to this campsite...
JONES: **From Georgia?**
NIREN: Yeah. I just don't feel like this is...it's got a foreign feeling.
JONES: **Did Indians make it?**
NIREN: I don't feel they did, no.
JONES: **Did the people in Georgia make it?**
NIREN: I don't feel Indians did, either one.
JONES: **Where did it originate?**
NIREN: It came to the Indians. It was either given to them, or...I see it like in ...I feel like from Georgia and it was brought down. In Georgia it was given as a gift somehow.
JONES: **What is the relationship between these people and the people in Georgia? In other words, why would it come here? Who would bring it and why?**
NIREN: I feel like a division of Indians, and...because of the population. Some moved further south. Like this was taken then.
JONES: **Where did they move south from?**
NIREN: From Georgia...Tennessee. I'm not sure about Tennessee. (Touches flint piece). I saw a pile of rock in a flash all of a sudden...a bunch of things like this.
JONES: **Shaped just like that or...?**
NIREN: Different shapes. I feel like they were used for something, you know ...like sanding or something. (shakes her head). Like sanding—something like that.
JONES: **What are they sanding?**
NIREN: Looked like a canoe type thing.
(She picks up orange projectile point) I see a white bird...a big white bird, and I felt it going right through my chest...as if I were the bird.
JONES: **Do you see the person who shot the arrow?**
NIREN: No. I just saw that white bird.
(Picks up large white point) I see a young man kind of running, holding like a spear-type thing this way (about waist level pointed forward)...running. I saw a band on his head like...

JONES: What else do you see about his body or what he is wearing or...?

NIREN: I didn't see any shirt...I see some baggy type pants.

JONES: What about decorations?

NIREN: I keep thinking he was in his teens...a young man. Kind of sweaty, like he'd been running.

JONES: Do you have a feeling of why?

NIREN: I feel like they're...I see two other men...and I think they're after something...something that they're after.

JONES: What do the other ones look like? The ones that are with him.

NIREN: Young men, too. I get the number fourteen, and...I see them running. There is an open space there, and there's a woods up ahead and they're going that way.

JONES: What are they running after?

NIREN: A fox...I don't think they were permitted to go after bigger animals. It's their age. They were still too young to go after the big ones, you know. I saw a rabbit.

(She picks up bone piece) I see a wild boar...I feel like this is a part of an animal...I seen a wild boar. Do they have tusks? O.K. That's all I get with that. (She picks up flint chips) They're cutting something with it. It's like animal skins, or rabbit skins, something like that, and they're cutting things. Doing things that need—like a very sharp edge, and I don't feel like straight lines, I feel curves. Using them to cut through things. (Makes tapping motion) They were doing something, and I just can't get what it was they were doing.

JONES: Is what they are doing making food, or making tools or is it artistic?

NIREN: Well, I felt, like food, like some kind of food being shredded—chopped up—but I feel they (chips) had a lot of different uses for different things. Like carving or cutting...cutting things into strips.

JONES: The stuff that they are shredding and the stuff that they are cutting into strips, is it the same stuff?

NIREN: They are shredding something white.

JONES: What size it is? Like maybe you can see their hands?

NIREN: Yeah. Sort of a flat kind of thing.

JONES: Animal or vegetable?

NIREN: When I first saw it, I thought animal...you know, white. I feel like fish, or something...cutting fish. Chopping it up real fine.

JONES: And then you mentioned something else being cut into strips?

NIREN: Yeah. Strips of...like used to cut strips of animals, rabbit, whatever, game. Like also tree bark, used for that. It's like what you would use for your knife, used for a lot of different things.

(Picks up larger bone, hollow, with wear around one end) Something around the head, and...there's something on the right side of my head. Maybe it's something that would go around their heads...I just keep on getting a feeling of around in here (right side of head), it was used for...

JONES: A piece of bone used for something around the side of the head?

NIREN: I just keep feeling around this side. I don't know. It doesn't make much sense.

JONES: You keep touching the right side, is it also both sides?

NIREN: I feel like my ear closed up, and I feel something would go in here (into throat on right side). I don't know—this is pretty strange. Maybe some kind of doctoring or something...like I really feel something in my ear.

(Picks up bone awl)? Making things. A small piece of something.

JONES: You mean this is a piece of something that was larger?

NIREN: Yeah. I see someting long (indicates about two feet in length)... wooden. Like a wooden box, even like a spear type thing.

JONES: A wooden box and then a spear?

NIREN: That doesn't go together (laughs). Like I feel a wooden surface... some kind of piece of wood that was hollowed out to put this thing into.

JONES: And that's (bone) a piece of it?

NIREN: I think it was a piece of something larger.

JONES: Do you see any decorations on this box?

NIREN: I...something...the last time you were here I saw this circle and then I saw a dot in the middle, and I felt...it had something to do with the sun. The box was smooth on the top, like sanded down or something.

JONES: So you feel the conch shells, the chips, and the points are from some place else?

NIREN: Yeah.

JONES: What about the material...what the points are made of? Is that from this area?

NIREN: I don't feel this was...from this area.

JONES: Do you get a feeling about where it might be from?

NIREN: I just felt it may have been traded somehow, or just gotten to some-how.

JONES: How long ago did you feel these people lived?

NIREN: Like 15th or 16th century...somewhere around there.

JONES: This may sound like a strange question, but what do you think these people would consider a crime?

NIREN: I think life was sacred to them, and like killing somebody would be bad.

JONES: How would they punish somebody who killed someone?

NIREN: I feel like they would send them...like across the river...like send him away... He would be left alone, that type of thing, like isolated somehow.

JONES: What about an afterlife belief?

NIREN: I feel like they felt that animals had an afterlife. I wouldn't feel so sure that they thought they did. I feel animals did.

JONES: And they didn't?

NIREN: I'm not sure. I don't feel they did. No, wait a minute. O.K. I'm thinking about two different things. I think...I was thinking about reincarnation for some reason.

JONES: Do you have any impression about what they think an afterlife would be like? Or where it would be?

NIREN: I feel like the sky and the sun.

JONES: What about the family? What do you get about family life?

NIREN: I feel they were hard workers. And they spent a lot of time with their children, and their children were a part of their life. I feel happiness with them.

JONES: How did they select a leader?

NIREN: I feel like it was part of the family...like a father would have sons, you know, and the sons would be kind of...like in the family somehow.

JONES: Inherited leadership?

NIREN: Yeah.

JONES: What about religion?

NIREN: I think they...the sun and the moon being very important...wor-shipping them and the weather—things like that.

JONES: What about the kinds of things they ate?

NIREN: Yeah, I feel they had corn...I don't feel a large variety of things. I think they had just a few things.

JONES: How many do you think there were of them?

NIREN: I think the number dwindled down.

JONES: From some earlier time to this time or from this time until after this time?

NIREN: From earlier, I think they were more 45, 50, 60 here. Like I don't feel a very huge campsite or anything.

JONES: What about people they could speak to? Where would those people be? People who spoke their dialect or their language?

NIREN: I feel further north than they are. Up in north Florida and Georgia you know, that area, the southern states up there. I feel they had come down from there.

JONES: Are there any descendants of these people still alive?

NIREN: Yeah, I feel they are further south. Like you have the Seminoles down...further down in the Everglades. I feel they just moved down. I think a lot of them were killed but I think a few got out.

NIREN: BLIND READING OF 8SE32 MATERIALS

JONES: This is Number Eight (Code indicating artifact and bone collection)

NIREN: I'm seeing a river bank...o.k. I also saw a skull of some kind...

JONES: 'Of some kind?' What do you mean?

NIREN: I just got 'skull', you know, and then my rational mind comes in and I see all things like that—and then I think of a burial site. But I don't see why there would be a burial site for animals or things like that...close to the water. Not too far away from the water.

JONES: What kind of animals?

NIREN: Birds...

JONES: Any other types of animals other than birds?

NIREN: What I'm getting...I feel there was a particular area where they... where certain animals were killed. I'm also seeing animal bones being broken, as if it was—like to release the spirit of it or something.

JONES: Do you see the people breaking the bones?

NIREN: Yes.

JONES: What do they look like?

NIREN: Like animal bones, you know, and...

JONES: The people.

NIREN: Yeah, the people breaking bones.

JONES: Do they have any distinguishing characteristics that you can describe?

NIREN: I see this man there, and he's bending down, and these animals that they had...I don't know what these particular things are (bone fragments), but like I see small animals and...any animal they used, the bones they broke. It was like to release the spirit of that animal or something...and they felt it was like a necessary thing to do. Like a particular area by the water. I can see like a large tree there...behind the tree. Like the water was here and then this tree and then this area here...where they would work with these animals...skinning them, or like using all the parts of it...eating and...and birds. I see egrets. I guess you'd call them...these white birds and different things. The feathers being taken out. It's like they had a separate area, where they did this.

JONES: Do you see what kind of clothing these people wear?

NIREN: I see this gentleman and he's wearing...a skirt. He's got beads on... not wearing pants, just wearing a skirt. He's an older gentleman...

JONES: What does his hair look like?

NIREN: It's black and it's forward...like it comes down like this...like bangs or something. Kind of greasy looking. Like some kind of pomade or something on it, you know. I get the feeling that they had separate places for certain things that they did. Like their work areas were separated, like one area doing a certain thing and another area over here did something else...their own little place.

JONES: Do you see what's happening in other areas?

NIREN: I see some women further back, and it's like one of those things they make butter with—but it's not butter—it's for mashing something. (She is making a churning motion with her hands.)

JONES: Like a mortar?

NIREN: Yeah, but it's a long one (indicates over four feet in length). I see them just working around and cooking things like that...in that area.

JONES: How many people do you feel around there?

NIREN: I—first off—I got thirty or fifty. But I feel that many people moved through that area...this camp. But the main ones...there was about thirty to fifty.

JONES: This is Number Six.

NIREN: As soon as I saw this, I felt a burial site of some kind. A grave site.

JONES: Can you give me any particulars about the burial?

NIREN: As I hold this, I get the feeling it's a male, and that this was a piece of jewelry that was decorated on him. And I feel as though when someone was buried they put many things with them.

JONES: Like what?

NIREN: I'm seeing this woman placing...like a piece of pottery in there with him. I just got the words...like I saw this woman putting pottery in there and then I got the words "listening to the sounds." And I was trying to figure out what kind of sounds? What are they trying to listen to, you know?

JONES: How do you see the body arranged?

NIREN: Like it's on its back and...I see beads and...this thing that I'm tuning into...there's a problem with the head...I feel...why this person died.

JONES: What kind of problem?

NIREN: I don't know. I feel something to the left side of my brain...or skull ...like a blow or something.

JONES: Did it kill this man or...?

NIREN: I feel it was suddenly and I see people wailing and I felt like they felt the loss of this person, but the wailing went beyond that. Their voices were to help the spirit of this person somehow. I just saw a child go up and put something down beside the person.

JONES: Why are they putting these things beside the body?

NIREN: I get the feeling that this is what this person will have to take with them when they go.

JONES: Where do they feel they are going to go?

NIREN: Like 'into the great spirit world' type of thing, and they need these things on their journey there. I feel like this person...I get the feeling that it happened away from their camp site, and that they did not expect this to happen.

JONES: How did it happen?

NIREN: What I'm getting...I see white men...like 'renegades'...that's the word I'm getting. But—like to these white men, it was a joke...it was funny. It was almost like these Indians wouldn't fight back...and they knew that they wouldn't. They just kind of laughed and then they left, and the Indians took him back. I feel, with these other two men, like utter despair. It was like they weren't quite sure if they should fight back. They weren't cowards, it was just that...it would have been an important step to do this.

JONES: What do you get from any of the other material?

NIREN: I first picked this up...I felt darkness...Like a very bleak type of feeling...cold. I'm also feeling sadness.

JONES: Do you have any idea what this is relating to?

NIREN: No.

JONES: This is Number Four.

NIREN: As I hold this I get the feeling of laying back on the ground and looking up at the sky. I almost get like a very restful feeling, and as I look up I see a bird going overhead. Like now I'm almost getting feelings, you know:
JONES: What kind of feelings?
NIREN: As I looked to the left I saw some people walking up...it was a woman and a child...they were carrying some type of pottery to hold water in, walking down towards the water. As I hold this I...it's real strange...today I'm mostly getting feelings. It's like a feeling of unity with the people, that they had for one another, like a family type feeling. I don't get any violent reactions to holding these things...just like a drifting feeling.
JONES: Did these people live at this place all the time or did they move around or are they recent-comers or have they been here for...
NIREN: I feel like this area is a place where a lot of people have passed through; but I also feel that there were times when they have to leave.
JONES: Do they come back or do they go some place else?
NIREN: It's really weird. As I'm looking here (to the front), my eyes go that way (south).
JONES: Is there something important that way?
NIREN: I guess it would be like they would have to move on. I feel like an anchor point at this...like it was the hub of something, do you know what I mean?
JONES: Why would this site be "the hub of something?" What would make it that way?
NIREN: I feel like these people traveled in the water there. It was like a stop-off. It was like a point between two other places, or it was...you know, the time of day when it would be time to rest and that would just be the place where everybody kind of went, and then moved on...traveling through there. But I feel they knew these people.
JONES: I don't understand. They knew these people?
NIREN: These people that lived there would know these people that traveled through...most of them. I would say. It would be their friends that would come through.
JONES: Do you have any feeling about where they originated?
NIREN: These people? (laughs)
JONES: The people at the site?
NIREN: The words I'm getting are like 'migration.' Like a southerly migration...moving...
JONES: This is Number Seven.
NIREN: As I hold this I feel a female vibration. I'm seeing a young girl.
JONES: What is she doing?
NIREN: I saw her standing next to a woman...I take to be her mother. It's very strange. All of a sudden I was seeing light and then dark. Like a dark shade being pulled. Like darkness...just coming down.
JONES: What do you feel that means?
NIREN: I would feel it would be her death. I feel like a sickness. I don't feel any kind of violent death or anything like that..violence. But the lights are going out.
JONES: What kind of sickness? Do you feel any symptoms?
NIREN: It's like a very tired feeling. All the energy is just depleted. It's like I'm seeing the moment before her death, I guess, and it's just like letting go. It was easy to do. Just let go, and...beyond.
JONES: What is the relationship between the dead girl and the mother?
(Margie starts sobbing hysterically at this point and the tape recorder was stopped.)
JONES: Do you want to stop?

NIREN: No, go ahead.

JONES: What happened?

NIREN: I don't know. It's like...I saw a picture of a little child, like a brother and you know how when people start to cry their face gets all screwed up? Well, when I saw it, I just felt the vibration I guess, and I just felt all the sadness and everything. It was the grief this brother was feeling for this other person in the family...you know, the death. It was like this child that died was very close to many of the kids there and they had felt a great love for her, and they felt very close. I felt like there hadn't been a death for a while, you know, among the children. It really upset them a great deal.

JONES: This is Number Four.

NIREN: The first thing I picked up was a picture of the cooking area. Like it was used as some kind of utensil or something.

JONES: Like how?

NIREN: I got the Spanish name of Juan. The only thing I'm picking up about this is that I feel that somebody outside of the camp brought it in. A Spanish individual, and it's like they call him Big John. But I'm not getting what it actually is.

JONES: This is Number Two.

NIREN: I'm not sure exactly what this means, but as soon as I hold this I get the feeling of going back and forth, like rocking sideways. I don't even know what that means really.

JONES: Do you have any feelings of why you are doing it?

NIREN: It feels like shaking or something...shaking something. I get the feeling of somebody holding something out and just shaking it. And then I see the same man, and he's like on his knees and he's going forward and working with his hands. I don't want to say stretching something out, but like working with something in front of him. It's about that long (two feet) whatever this thing is he's working on. I'm not sure what it is.

JONES: Is it hard or soft, or do you get the feeling of color?

NIREN: Like a brown color. I'm seeing him, but I can't tell what it is that he's doing. Shaking something, and then moving and going over something, like it's flat.

JONES: Do you have any feelings about the diet of these people at this time?

NIREN: I feel like there's agriculture of some kind. I didn't feel that too much before...with the stuff that I worked on earlier. I didn't feel there was as much. I feel like corn, and...I feel like a few crops. I saw an orange tree.

JONES: Do you get any feeling of other crops? You mentioned some others? Shape? Color?

NIREN: I see round things on top of the ground.

JONES: Was it with the material you've seen today or previously that you got the feeling about no agriculture?

NIREN: Previously. I feel like it's more important now than as they progressed they didn't have as many crops for some reason. I don't know. I just feel more agriculture at this time than before.

JONES: Do you see what their dwellings look like?

NIREN: I see what looks like cypress—pieces of cypress. I see a thatched roof, but that...like pieces of cypress going horizontal, too...not just like for pieces going upward, and then like a little hat (thatching?). But I feel there are some horizontal pieces of cypress that's in there, too. I feel more of a permanence. Like a feeling of putting roots down. Like they made their homes to last longer, or something. I feel...like permanence type of feeling. I'm seeing like a main house...a large one.

JONES: What are you talking about now? Like different types of houses, or...

NIREN: I feel like I'm centered somehow, you know, and there's just one place that feels permanent.

JONES: **Is the place like a house or the area?**
NIREN: Not stable. Not what I would consider a house...not solid, but whatever this is, I feel it's more permanent than the other ones. Longer lasting.
JONES: **Is this like a feeling the people have or is it an actual thing...there?**
NIREN: It's like this one building that I'm seeing. People felt permanent there. I'm seeing this...I don't know what you'd call it...like a...I don't feel anybody actually living there in this one house, or...I see like a bunch of different things in there...inside.
JONES: **What was inside it?**
NIREN: Looking down at the ground I see some shells, and some kind of smooth rocks...small ones.
JONES: **What does it feel like?**
NIREN: Like a store!
JONES: **Like a store? Like a "buy something" store? Like a storeroom? Like...**
NIREN: I feel like these people loved to trade and I see them giving things to people and people giving them things, and they put them into this little place there. I see them bringing things in from different places, and they would give these people..they would give them things.
JONES: **Do you see what kind of things?**
NIREN: I see like materials brought in.
JONES: **What kind of materials?**
NIREN: Different colored materials.
JONES: **Where are the people that the people at this site are trading with? Directions?**
NIREN: I feel like people come from St. Pete (St. Petersburg, Florida), you know, like from the west coast. That area, and a northerly direction. I also feel southerly, too.
JONES: **Do you have a feeling about what these people have that those other people might want?**
NIREN: Before that, I feel like crossing a body of water in a southerly direction. I feel like beads. These people that lived at this place...their jewelry, and feathers, and...I keep on getting a feeling about something shiny inside...
JONES: **What is it made of?**
NIREN: It's like a shell or something, like a polished looking shell. Right now, I just feel like busy and I see trading and things going on like that. A very busy place.
JONES: **This is Number Three.**
NIREN: The first thing I saw was like piles of bones...like a mound of them. All I'm gettting with this, like I said, was I saw a pile of bones about that high (three feet), with all the pieces of things like that...and nice and white. And then I started getting a pain in my shoulder. Like the left side of me started feeling kind of funny.
JONES: **Is there any relationship?**
NIREN: I don't know now.
JONES: **Do you get any feelings about the kinds of people who were here before these people came?**
NIREN: Yeah. I feel there was somebody else, but that was quite a while before. They had lighter colored hair. I feel as though these people were there for quite a while, but I do feel there were people before them.
JONES: **Did they know of each other?**
NIREN: I would say—like heard of these people. There might have been a few, but I don't feel like I move in and there they are. I don't feel that. There might have been a few descendants from these people, but I would say generally, no, they didn't...I feel like this is going back somewhat.

JONES: **How far back?**

NIREN: I got the number 'seven'. Maybe seven hundred years or something like that.

JONES: **This is Number Four.**

NIREN: The first thing I saw was a rifle. I do feel that whatever this is was used for a weapon of some sort.

JONES: **Do you know exactly how?**

NIREN: I get a weird feeling about it. I don't know if I can even describe it. It's like a...like this is just a part of what it was...like a heaviness to it, and smooth and it's like...like something that's heavy and dead.

JONES: **Is it a manufactured "something" or a kind of natural "something"?**

NIREN: I feel it was something long, and...I keep on seeing a side view of it... it's smooth, and...and the piece I'm seeing...I'm not sure what this thing (point) is yet...but it's like a greyish type of wood, and smooth, like dead...like a real hard type of wood.

JONES: **How big is it?**

NIREN: The part I'm seeing about about that big (app. 2 feet long).

JONES: **What do they do with it?**

NIREN: It would be used in your arm...you'd hold it in your hand (seems to suggest *atlatl*). I felt like the stuff that I handled before, there wasn't much permanency to it, but this stuff—I felt more like it had been in one place longer.

JONES: **Do you feel like these people are the ancestors of the other people? Are they different people?**

NIREN: The same people.

Noreen Renier: Blind Reading of
Packaged Materials from 8Se32

JONES: **I can tell you that this (bagged materials) is a collection of artifacts from a single site, and, in that I have access to things from all over, this material could come from anywhere. Tell me what you pick up while touching the bag.**

RENIER: The first image I picked up was of a utensil...broken. In fact, there may be more than one in there. I also felt bone. It's a flat bone and it's very sharp and shiny. Something in here is broken off of something else...into a very small useless piece. It might take them a little while to figure out the whole things from this piece.

JONES: **What do the people look like?**

RENIER: I feel long clothes on them. I feel more layered or more...clothes. Covered bodies. The woman I am seeing looks quite broad. I felt broadness. Not that short.

JONES: **Can you tell me something characteristic of her clothing?**

RENIER: Colored. A lot of color or brightness around this individual's clothing...different patterns, colors.

JONES: **What about the environment?**

RENIER: It's dry. I feel dryness around there...I don't think it rains all that much. If the rain comes, it comes in certain spurts. I feel an incline...I see this person and behind her I feel an incline (makes motion with the hands to indicate a dome shape.)...I don't know if that's a dwelling or just stone or...but I feel it is made of...probably clay, water...goes up, goes up. It is high. It is not like a little...more height to it. Structure. Tall.

JONES: **Can you give me any more about that?**

RENIER: It looks...good heavens! I'm switching to another scene. I'm sorry I'm loosing that...I'm switching to a statue. I feel it like a statue. I feel like an animal statue. I don't know if it's in the cat family or not, but I see its arms and legs and it is upright. Not four feet on the ground, but upright, upright.

JONES: How big?

RENIER: I don't know.

JONES: What would the people at this place eat? What would their diet be like?

RENIER: I feel sort of grainy stuff. It looks mushy. Maybe it's meal with some liquid in it. A mushy substance that they might do several things with. Let me see food, food, food. I feel like fish. There must be some distant large body of water, but I feel it is distant, distant.

JONES: A large body?

RENIER: It's more like a...it flows like a river. More like a river.

JONES: Do these people have enemies? Do you feel any intruders?

RENIER: I feel there has been a deception on these people. I feel like they were pulled out from this little village...pulled out deceitfully. Pulled out so that the others came into the village.

JONES: What about the time factor? What time are we involved in?

RENIER: I am doing 1400.

JONES: What about the religion of these people?

RENIER: More than one god. They aren't so happy right now. I guess the gods aren't doing too well, because I feel very...negative and downcast among the people. For some reason I feel very low energy. Very great sadness.

JONES: Who are they?

RENIER: I keep seeing that one woman all the time. I don't know where the rest of them are.

JONES: Ask the woman.

RENIER: Oh, that's a good idea. She is pointing in that same direction I saw them going. Why have they gone? They want to protect their people as much as they could. I feel they lack sophisticated weapons, compared to these other people. Against these other people I feel that they just don't have a chance.

JONES: Who are these other people?

RENIER: I keep seeing that scene of the horse people. I'm getting worried that I'm picking up...that other stuff. I don't know that I'm on the right track.

JONES: You are doing very well.

RENIER: O.K. Ask me another question.

JONES: See the very earliest people in this place. Try to feel when that would be and who that would be.

RENIER: With the very earliest inhabitants, there was much more water and rain in that period of time, because I'm seeing a lot of grass where there is not grass now. I feel more rain. I feel very short, but a great deal of strength, with ornaments or things near the ear (makes motion along side of head down jaw line). This area (upper jaw) seems very predominate on the male for some reason.

JONES: Along the side of the face?

RENIER: Yes. I don't know if it's something he has put on, or it's part of his hair, or if it's an ornament. I feel some of it is either ornaments that they do to the hair, or they put in the hair. I feel him up high. I feel there is some height to this land (touches bag)...could be height that he is standing on. This is a long time ago. I feel these people are going to be seeing things that they haven't seen before. Somebody is invading their land shortly...or coming into a territory where they never been before. I don't know...people from a different land invading. A different land invading, or from a different territory. No, I feel from a different land.

JONES: What land?

RENIER: I see the people across the ocean. I see an ocean. I feel waves lapping up. I feel more of...like from England.

JONES: What do the trees look like?

RENIER: A lot of them together...more bushy at the top. Lots of things at the top. I'm just getting a shot of a bunch of trees.

JONES: Do you see any animals?

RENIER: I feel the water...something running. What is it? What is it? I got an alligator, or crocodile. I don't know which.

JONES: What about numbers of people?

RENIER: At one time they are joined by another group and they get large. I feel growth or strength at an early period. Other tribes or other people getting with this group here, and making them strong. I keep getting 'four' and I don't know if it's 40 or 400. O.K. all of a sudden I got a shot and I am in the woods and there is this campfire. There are not too many people, maybe four or five people around there. I am high up and I can see them. They have some ornaments in their hair. I feel like they are eating a rabbit.

JONES: Do you see these people very clearly?

RENIER: No, because I am high up.

JONES: What color is their hair?

RENIER: Dark. Straight. Some of them might have bangs.

JONES: Since you have the feeling of hovering over the site, I would like you to look to the east of the site and tell me what you see.

RENIER: I see a lot of land then, at quite a distance, water—big water.

JONES: Still over the site, turn and face the west, what do you see?

RENIER: It is Florida. I don't know why, but I feel that I am blocked with structures more toward the west.

JONES: In what direction, from this spot where you are right now, is the site?

RENIER: That way (she points east).

JONES: You are pointing east. Do you feel that there is anybody living at this site now?

RENIER: I see people walking over something important.

JONES: What is it?

RENIER: I don't know. I just feel there is something underground but these people are very casual and walking across this one area, and they are not aware. I get 'under the ground'. I feel excitement about it, but these people, they are just walking. They don't know.

JONES: What is in the ground there?

RENIER: I feel some very distinct evidence of some history. I want to say 'history'.

JONES: Are the descendants of the people who made these things (touches bag) still alive?

RENIER: Very few, if any. They are pretty wiped out.

JONES: From what direction from the site would they be found?

RENIER: More toward the northeast.

JONES: Is there anything else you would like to add?

RENIER: No. I would like to get some feedback now.

JONES: O.K., but once that starts, then the experiment is over.

RENIER: O.K. Do you have enough then?

JONES: Yes. I guess so.

Appendix D—Chapter V

PHOTO: V-1: CLEAVER. ACHEULEAN CULTURE. CA. 200,000 YEARS AGO.
SITE: YOUNGER GRAVELS OF THE VAAL RIVER, RIVER VIEW, SOUTH AFRICA.

BOWES: (Photo still in envelope) First thing I picked up was something like a hollow log. I don't know why I picked that up. I keep seeing medicines. I don't know what it means. (Photo taken out of envelope) I don't know if there is volcanic action or a place where there is an earthquake but I see things trembling, like a lot of noise. I don't know if it was during a war, or a loud explosion, or on an island where there was a volcano. I didn't pick up much from it. I felt, in association with this, a lot of vibration.

JONES: Do you see the people?

BOWES: First thing I seen was blue eyes. But the feeling I had was that most of them were like natives, or Indians, or people who...not really Indians, but I felt they were dark skinned and their face was flatter. Not Oriental. Didn't look Oriental.

JONES: Do you have a feeling about the climate?

BOWES: I would have to touch that to really tell you much more. I don't know why but I feel very removed from that, like it's not important. Very hot.

PHOTO: V-2: STONE HANDAXE. ACHEULEAN CULTURE. CA. 200,000 YEARS AGO.
SITE: YOUNGER GRAVELS OF THE VAAL RIVER. RIVER VIEW, SOUTH AFRICA.

All related tape transcripts are included in Chapter V.

PHOTO: V-3: TRIMMED END-STRUCK FLAKE. ACHEULEAN CULTURE.
CA. 200,000 YEARS AGO.
SITE: YOUNGER GRAVELS OF THE VAAL RIVER. WINDSORTON, SOUTH AFRICA.

BOWES: The thing I picked up with that was that it was only partially made. That they found it where somebody had just started working on it. I don't know if it was something in the ground or in a pile of stuff, but I kept feeling someone was chopping at it. I just see it on the ground.

JONES: Where?

BOWES: I don't see any shoes. I see bare feet. I hear the roar of the ocean, and I don't know if these people are near the water but I keep hearing (makes sound), like the waves, like the ocean. I don't know if that's the wind whistling through the trees but I keep hearing this noise and the wind is creating it... whistling and kind of blowing, kind of like it's blowing through pine trees. But that's all I picked up. I felt this could be on the ground, on the floor or on the bottom of something, but I felt they were chipping at it. Trying to open something. Maybe they were trying to make an ax or something heavy. But I see a big, big man...big man. Very big man with big forearms. Real big.

JONES: What race is he?

BOWES: I couldn't tell you that. He may have had more hair on his arms than an Indian, but that's all I picked up.

JONES: Do you see any clothing they might have on?

BOWES: That's strange. I just picked up something about a gun, and I don't know if there was a gun involved with a wick on it...almost like a cannon ball, like you light the wick and it went (hissssss) and it went into the gun and went "boom." I don't know what it meant. Could have been a cannon but I felt it was more like a huge rifle that two men had to carry. Could even have been a small cannon. It could even be one of those with a big funnel on the outside, but I would say it was mounted inside a building. I would say that whoever associated with this or whoever they were shooting at could have been very afraid of this loud noise. O.K. I would say that if that piece (in photo) was from the west or mid-west, that there could have been the Spanish, or could have been people from the past. And they might not have known they were there, but I would say they were there. Could have been from Spain, or from another country.

DAVIS: I'm very much aware of water...a large body of water. I want to say west, and that's what I get. I don't get a lot more with it. I feel that there were settlers that came into this area at some time that would have been very industrious. I see water, as though possibly like gold mining, or sifting, or...some kind of exploration but I see...it looks like pans of water that you would sift with, and I see people shaking it back and forth.

I see before that a group of people who would have believed very much in darkness. I don't know how I mean that exactly, but I just get the word "darkness." As though they would have been very aware of things in the dark. I feel very superstitious and very much afraid, and I just get a very dark feeling. That's strange.

I see a man, and this would be a man who would be the prospector type. That's what he would look like. I'm not saying that that's what he did. He has like a shabby beard, and a little hat, and is dressed in grubby clothes. I see him kneeling down and he has like a watch fob, an old one, and funny kind of spurs. They're thick. They're not real pointed at the end, but they're thick and heavy. I see horses, and I feel that the countryside would have been sloping. I feel it would have been somewhat mountainous, but it also was a sloping kind of thing. It wasn't, you know, real high mountains all the time. Kind of like California where there are a lot of hills that go pretty steep but it's not anything like the mountains and canyons and things.

I see a lot of greenery, and I don't feel desert at all. I see a lot of trees. And I see animals. I see some sort of cattle but they're not the cattle that I know. They are not cows. I think perhaps they are some other type of cow. I see, like buffalo...something that would look kind of like buffalo to me. It's a dark animal, four-legged animal, and would be rather a horse shape. I don't get much further with that.

I feel that the people were rather to the extreme, as though very superstitious, very much aware of things, but very much to extremes, as though there wasn't a lot of balancing. I feel there was one point when they lost their continuity so to speak. When they were all involved in...I want to say, like liquor. That's kind of strange. Like over-indulgence kind of thing, where it happened and things lost their balance and eventually they were taken over by some group of people.

I do feel that there was a battle or there was some sort of stress placed on the group through some sort of...well, battle, or dissension among the people as though there was a splitting off and then some sort of dissension that occurred, because I do feel that a lot of the people were killed off, though I do feel that these people still exist in great numbers today.

The next thing I see is a dam. It's a highly constructed one. It's been built in the last thirty years. Longer than that. Fifty years. I feel that this dam is very close to the site where this was picked up...where maybe some of these people settled, and would have carried this type of thing with them.

PHOTO: V-4: TRIMMED QUADRILATERAL FLAKE. MIDDLE STONE AGE.
CA. 50,000 YEARS AGO.
SITE: UITLOOP, POTIETERSRUST, TRANSVALL, SOUTH AFRICA.

BOWES: (Photo still in envelope) I kept seeing something round. I almost felt like it was a piece of leather...probably stone, but this stone could have layed inside of leather, but I felt it had lines. White, but in real life it may have been brown. I felt it was a piece of leather with a stone inside it. It could be stone with pieces chipped off the side around it. (Photo out of envelope) The first thing I picked up with this was the north, or volcanic action. I felt as though this could have come from another country. I felt this was the floor of something, or it was on the floor, and I felt this was laying on top of it. Somebody was squatting down and they were doing something inside this leather. This leather was real stiff and weathered...almost like you could peel it off and crack it or break it off. I felt it was sitting in there and inside it was some sort of grain and they were pounding it...doing something, stirring it or something. But this I felt was like the floor of a building.

JONES: Do you have a feeling of what the building looked like?

BOWES: I felt it had open windows and it was built in blocks. I felt like the windows was open. I didn't know...big windows, big solid walls, real thick massive. This thing could have been on the floor or could have been a piece of the floor.

JONES: Do you get any feelings about the environment?

BOWES: I felt it could have been on an island, or like a volcanic rock or island, or a place where the ground is very desolate and drops off very quickly. To me this looks like a lookout, or like a stone building that wasn't natural to the environment. I felt it was a stone building and it was vacant, and the wind was blowing. I felt it was like on a volcanic rock or island. I would say that if it isn't on an island it could be on a mountain, or like this building was built into the walls of mountains, or it could be like those stone buildings that the Indians made into the walls, or shelves of the mountains. That's the feeling I picked up. But I would associate it more with the water, because I kept seeing people who looked like natives, like on islands, and they ran down naked with no clothes on or maybe had something around their head. I felt they all ran to the shore. I would say they were associated with volcanoes or earthquakes... such as that. Uncertain ground conditions.

I would say in that culture that the Indians...that the eye...I said "Indians," I don't even know why. But I see eyes of a fish, or like a fish head was like this. They talked about the eye, and the hole in the eye. Maybe these fish were hanging to dry because they looked dead. They looked rotten. They were hanging by the eye or they were hanging up. Drying out. Something with drying out. It could be meat, or fish, or something that stinks.

DAVIS: I feel with Number Seven...I'm sensing a man and he is dressed and he has a fur piece over his shoulders. The fur is, I want to say, fox fur, because it's reddish type of fur, and some sort of like a cowhide almost...it's a mixture of furs, but I definitely got fox fur. I see him standing. He's a tall man. He's rather lean. I see him standing and there's a fire and behind him is like a mud hut and it's made strictly I feel with mud and so forth and a straw-type of fiber substance. It's just sort of packed and dried. The walls are kind of thick. It's like an adobe kind of thing. I do sense like a mountain in this area. I'm seeing an area that is mountainous as well as flat. It looks dry. There is not a lot of greenery. More of a desert-type of terrain.

I sense buildings and things put up against the mountain. I don't know if they are in the mountain itself. I can't really distinguish that...like cliff-dweller or anything...I'm not sure, but then I see ladders going up to different...they look like cliffdwellers. Anyway, I see ladders and it's a checkerboard kind of set-up with these different places—living quarters and things. Then I

see a wooden structure that is a "T" formation, and underneath it a large circle
...I think it's inside the circle. I feel it was a ceremonial type place. There are
carvings on the "T" formation and it's very large and it looks almost like a
capital "T".

I see colors. I'm seeing red and blue and yellow that I think they would have
used somehow in color and in art, and it's around this pole somehow. There are
some colors on this pole. And then I get like white, or a light color that would
have been a fabric or a woven substance like a cotton that would have been
also wrapped around in strips. I feel like this person that I was referring to originally was not wearing like leather, but more of a woven cloth, a blanket-like
woven substance, and I see sheep and I see goats, and an animal that looks
like a cat, like a ringtail cat perhaps, but I feel a western direction. I feel a
familiarity with this somehow. I sense that the people were very scattered
before they drifted off. I feel that they drifted off in small numbers. Eventually
they either died out, or faded out, or blended with other groups, because I
don't feel that they are that strongly in existence at this time.

I want to keep moving. I don't want to stay with them at all.

* * *

PHOTO: V-5: TRIMMED QUADRILATERAL FLAKE. MIDDLE STONE AGE.
CA. 50,000 YEARS AGO.
SITE: SOUTHWEST CAPE PROVINCE, SOUTH AFRICA.

BOWES: I would say they scraped something with that. They used it to
scrape fat off of skins, or used it for scraping something. I keep seeing this as
being held in the hand. I do feel women would be using it. Men made it and
men have used it at first, but I see women using it last. O.K.? I see a wheel and
I see a stick. I see this wheel going around and around and I felt it was like
grinding something or...

JONES: In terms of environment...
BOWES: I see water or boats, but I don't know what it meant.
JONES: Generally similar to the last pieces?
BOWES: Yeah. Cold weather or stormy weather...lots of wind or waves. It
could associate with the Great Lakes or some great big round body of water.

DAVIS: I am more drawn to the east coast, or east in a way, and I am sensing
a northeast direction. Where it would be chilly in the winter, and I'm seeing a
large body of water, and I feel people that would have lived close to the water,
and the water is an ocean. I don't feel like a river, or anything...I feel like a
very vast body of water, and they were very superstitious about this body of
water. When the waves got very high I feel like they would have reacted
strongly and felt that these were like signs or omens or whatever. I feel that
they had difficulty within their group because of a lot of the moisture or
humidity in their bones. Of course they didn't quite understand this but I do
feel that this caused some type of sickness, and some difficulty with breathing
at times, and many of these people passed away with respiratory conditions or
serious breathing problems as well as heart problems and I felt that this was
somehow connected with the humidity, and the diet.

The diet seems to be a scattered one with nuts and berries, and barks and
sometimes meats, but I feel that they had some type of grain that is grown in
this area and even now I feel that this is being raised somehow. I feel that this
grain would have been o.k. in moderation but I almost feel that it would have

been almost harmful to their system had they had too much of it over a long period of time.

I see a woman and she is standing by a young child. I feel that these would be a very prolific people, and I do feel that they did produce many and that there is still a small group or culture...tradition...that has been carried on. I feel that these people would have traveled southeast...southwest of their location, where they first formed. And as they did travel south, I feel that there were more and more of them and eventually they became very, very strong.

I do feel that there is some sort of a little hut type of thing that looks almost like...it's round and it looks almost like a small igloo, or something, and it's made out of mud and some wood. I see like branches, leaves. They were very comfortable in these homes. I feel the homes provided them with warmth and coolness. I see a woven piece of something on the floor place, which I wouldn't expect, but it is, it's like a woven blanket or something and it's made from furs and from fiber. I don't want to say cotton. I want to say more like flax, or more like...I don't feel cotton, I feel something else.

I feel they would have produced a great many leaders as well, or there were many leaders within their group at that time.

* * *

PHOTO: V-6: TRIMMED BLADE. MIDDLE STONE AGE. CA. 50,000 YEARS AGO. SITE: MUDEN, NATAL, SOUTH AFRICA.

BOWES: Hmmm. This is very funny. I felt like he picked this as number one for a reason. O.K. I felt this was an unusual piece. I don't know why but I felt that somebody had pondered this picture before I looked at it. In other words, they looked at it and looked at it and thought about what it meant. I felt this was important to them. I don't know if this object came from Florida or a place where there was a lot of clay or shell, but I felt like it was in the ground for a long, long time. In relationship to this I see wet, marshy ground...like made of shell or broken rock or broken shell. I don't know if this is from Florida or near the water but I do feel it was what they thought it was. It could have been a spear or something that they spear fish or an animal with. I don't know if these people had a problem with wet ground but I keep seeing them putting something on their feet, or wearing some kind of a shoe, or some kind of a...almost like a snow shoe, or something to keep them from sinking. This could be a relationship of someone who is in the snow maybe, or maybe it was soft ground, but I kept feeling like it was muddy part of the time, or it was real soft.

JONES: Do you have a feeling about what the people looked like?

BOWES: I would say they were dark-skinned. I would say probably Indians, or...very black eyebrows, but I don't feel they looked like Indians...Oriental looking people, round face, but I felt they looked more like Indians from India...black skin, black hair. I did see them having something on their head and I felt it was cloth, striped cloth...or something striped.

JONES: What did they eat?

BOWES: I see them carrying grain or something they could grind up and cook, or something they mixed with something...I don't know if they made bread, but I felt that didn't sound like it makes sense...sounds like two different people...but I really couldn't tell you that. I did feel that they carried some kind of grain, or bag of something that looked like grain. Those people could have been in the west or where there was a lot of rocks at one time. I see moccasins or something made of leather but I don't know what it meant. I don't know if these people were from the north, but I would say they could have associated with a bear or somewhere there was very cold weather around water but I felt there could be pieces of ice or something. I almost felt like it was a bear that was walking up the stream. An otter or this animal was in the water. I felt this was thrown at this thing.

* * *

PHOTO: V-7: DISC CORE. MIDDLE STONE AGE. CA. 50,000 YEARS AGO.
SITE: MUDEN, NATAL, SOUTH AFRICA.

DAVIS: With Number Ten (number given this photo in group being used for test) I feel exasperation as though there was a difficulty working at the site, or there has been difficulty locating a lot about these people. I just get exasperated. That's the feeling I draw from it. I feel, too, that there is a woman who is very important to this group. I feel that she was more like a seer, a person who helped these people do what they need to do. She worked a great deal with herbs...almost a medicine woman...witchdoctor kind of thing, but not quite. I feel her very respected, but also feared by some people.

All of a sudden I got a flash, and this is very strange, of a black mammy, and I'm on a plantation and it's several years before the Civil War, but I'm in a southern area somehow, and that's an impression I just got. Let me go back and try to capture this woman now. I keep getting this black man, perhaps they are one in the same, I don't know. I see pottery. I see like pots and they are broken. A lot of the things are not very well taken care of, or perhaps are used so much that they don't hang around very long. I do feel very good with the people. I feel very calm with the people. As though they learned a great deal...they lived a great deal. I feel a lot of the people were artistic or creative in some way. A productive thing because it assisted the rest of the group. I see blankets and something made out of reeds, or a plant substance that was like a woven mat, like a sit-upon type thing. I see clothing and I see drawings being done. I think there was charcoal around them, and that someone learned to draw and they used to draw on rocks and on some sort of substance that would look like paper, but it would be like a skin, but it would only be a layer of skin that they wouldn't use. I don't even know what I meant by that. Anyway, that's what I'm getting. I'm still coming back to the Civil War era, so let me go with it.

I'm sensing a people who would have migrated from a northern direction, and I feel that they would have settled. Later there would have been a kind of interracial mixture of people, like I want to say black and Indian, somehow. There is a feeling though that maybe later these people were killed. I see fire. I'm seeing battle. I feel that this would have been war time. I see blue soldiers and I see grey soldiers. I feel there would have been a time when there would have been much destruction of where they were living.

I am getting like a plantation situation. I'm getting like a house with columns in the front...a very exclusive lovely home...very well-to-do. I see little tiny houses in the back and sides. I feel that I am in a southern state, but then I get "Carolina," maybe South Carolina. I get a feeling of work, as though I have to work very diligently to produce. I have to keep doing this. I see somebody with a whip, but there is a whip on the wall here. It's an antique and I was very drawn to look at it, and I saw a man with a whip, so...I don't know what the correlation is. There's a feeling I have of a group of people and they are not all the same people, somehow as though they were a conglomeration of people, so I don't know what this plantation thing all relates to. I am drawn to say that the area of this plantation was later...later produced another large settling of some sort. Years before that, I feel I want to go in a northeastern direction, there was a great settling of land and people, and there was a shift in the land at the time also. I get the figure 1,200. I feel that there was a man who would have been very, very prominent on this land, and his family would have carried it for several generations. Almost 150 years worth, or even longer for that matter, because I see these people and their name was carried out and they were very prosperous and they also had many slaves, and they would have fought very hard to keep that tradition going. I feel, too, that before this group of people was there there was a former group of people, and they were later shifted to the west...had to migrate west and that was due to settlers and due to explorers coming in. I see somebody who would remind me of Daniel Boone, and it's more of an explorer-type person. I see him hunting. He has his gun and I see him moving through a wooded area that would remind me of the Blue Ridge mountains, and I see him traveling through there and tracking down animals as well as people. Trying to move them out. Trying to get them to go in a different direction. I sense that he was later known, and I get the name "Sam," in the area for being so good at this. I do feel that the former group was more of the Indian-breed type that were here more originally than say the settlers or whatever. I sense a diet of corn or green type substance that would have been pounded into a bread. Then there's like fruit. There was some type of food that could be stored. I don't know how. It could be stored or seeds were stored or something. I don't know, but it was a workable type substance. The juice of it was often used for potions and pultices. There's a woman...now I'm coming back. Here's the woman that worked with the herbs and was very prosperous within her group and she is an earlier lady, but I feel, what I got before, was that her teaching had gone on through her people and had later gone into the black group that came in through someone and it's like ...I think though a woman, and it wouldn't have been anybody famous or anything like that. It was just something that was carried on. I feel that this is why some of the blacks in the south are more superstitious and aware. I feel that a part of the tradition comes from the spreading of it through the Indians. Hmmm, that's interesting. I would have thought it went the other way. I want to stop with that. I think that's enough for me right now. I hope its useful.

* * *

PHOTO: V-8: BORED STONE. LATE STONE AGE. CA. 5,000 YEARS AGO.
SITE: LITTLE ENGLAND, STEYNESBURG, ORANGE FREE STATE, SOUTH AFRICA.

[Davis' reading is included in Chapter V]

NIREN: I don't feel the vibrations of the U.S.A. on it. I see water and a ship. I feel it was used with another part, perhaps a stick running through the middle. I do see water with this. I also feel a lot of heat connected with this. I also felt it was used for grinding food. I'm not going into all the things I see because I have some kind of mental block.

* * *

PHOTO: V-9: CHIPPED STONE CELT.
LOHO LIANG, KOMODO, LESSER SUNDA ISLANDS, INDONESIAN REPUBLIC.
SURFACE FIND.

BOWES: (Photo still in envelope) The feeling I felt with this more than anything else was masculine...male. Metal. Heavy. Something physical, and I don't know what it was. I felt they would grow something. I don't know if they tried to grow something in terraces, but I felt that they had very poor luck. I felt with this other things.

JONES: **The last things?**

BOWES: Yes. Something about a stove. I picked it up twice and I said "no, that's not true" but then I felt it was almost like a pot-bellied stove. I felt it was round on the top or it was flat and had a round thing, but I felt up here was like this (indicates), and they put this handle in there and they picked it up to put more fire in there, more wood in there.

I'm going to go ahead and look at this (removes photo from envelope) I kept picking up pieces of brick but I didn't know what it meant. Pieces of brick or rock or stone...it was stone or brick. The feeling I had with this was that it was an axe, and I felt it was hand-chiseled or cut. I don't know why but I felt the people who lived there had hardship in the sense that they may have moved away. I don't know if this was in the north, north of Florida, or north of Georgia, but I kept seeing a lot of slate, or stone that was in layers. Almost looked like it came out of a cliff and it...you'd look at it and you'd see pieces of it broken. Pieces of it broken off and then there was another layer that came out and then more pieces like little square pieces broken off. The ground was like this and the rock formation was sticking out. Pieces of it broke off and some stuck out farther and...just in layers like that. I do feel these people had something around their head. I don't know if they are bandannas or something to hold their hair back, but that's what I seen.

JONES: **Do you see anything about the general environment?**

BOWES: I kept seeing them cutting trees with this, but I felt that they were trees...I don't feel they were familiar with the trees, and I felt that when they cut them they were kind of testing them for hardness. I felt that some of their trees when they chop into them, they got a lot of water out, like in the south... like a swampy area. Like they would cut into a tree and it could just be real juicy, and it wouldn't hold up... And when they try to use it for materials it would generally dry up and crack.

JONES: **What did these people look like?**

BOWES: This in here was almost like a vest. This was real puffy (shoulders), and this was leather in here.

JONES: **Was this puffy place him or the material?**

BOWES: I wouldn't know what it was. I would say it was like cloth or something. I seen this (vest) as brown leather...like a vest. There was a strap across. Could have carried a gun. I felt these people were chopping things to make a doorway. Like the two logs they were trying to find for the doorway had to be extra strong. They never used that beyond cutting that wood that was real soft, real wet.

JONES: **Do you have any feelings about the diet of these people?**

BOWES: I kept seeing bags of grain but I kept seeing them cussing and mad about it being polluted or like moldy or dirty or something. It wasn't any good.

* * *

PHOTO: V-10: SHELL PICK, AND SHELL PENDANT OR PLUMMET.
SITE: KEY MARCO, FLORIDA.

[Bowes' reading is included in Chapter V.]

PHOTO: V-11: SLATE GORGET, BAKED CLAY OBJECT.
SITE: POVERTY POINT, LOUISIANA.

[Bowes' and Renier's readings included in Chapter V.]

PHOTO: V-12: WORKED FLINT.
LE MOUSTIER, VALLEE DE LA VEZERE, PERIGORD DISTRICT, FRANCE.

[*Bowes' reading is included in Chapter V.*]

PHOTO: V-13: CLAM SHELL, BUTTON, SPIKE, COLUMELLA BEAD.
SITE: TAYLOR MOUND, ST. SIMONS ISLAND, GEORGIA.

[*Bowes' reading is included in Chapter V.*]

PHOTO: V-14: FOUR SHARDS, ST. JOHNS PLAIN AND CHECK STAMPED.
ONE SCRAPER, ONE KNIFE, ONE PROJECTILE POINT.
SITE: HAWTHORNE MOUND, FLORIDA.

[*Bowes' reading is included in Chapter V.*]

PHOTO: V-15: CLAY BIRD EFFIGY PIPE. LAMAR CULTURE.
PREHISTORIC CHEROKEE.

BOWES: I'm going to pick up photograph marked Number One and I feel very strong, with a feeling of people in a cold climate. The first impression I got was like Vikings, or Indians, or people of a cold climate. I keep seeing a relationship to something symbolic. I don't know if this thing is a tool or its significance is a religious purpose or use. I keep seeing the claws of a bear or like claws or something. The feeling I had with this is a bird, or something that's used like a goblet, or something that's used like something that carried something. The feeling I had was a bird's head. I would say that this could be a very old object. I would say that it would be made of brass, or there could be bone or ivory involved with it. I would say the front of it, or there's an end, almost like it's round and it's almost like a goblet or something round and then it comes up to a point, and on the end of the point there could be...the first thing I picked up was an arrow head, but then I picked up an Indian, or some person. I felt fur on them. Another feeling I picked up was a bird's head, or something with a beak. I kept feeling these people were traveling a lot. It could be in the northern part of the United States, or it could be something around where there's water, but that's what I picked up. O.K.?

In dealing with this I pick up a different thing. I kept feeling fur, hair. I don't know if this is a pipe, but I keep seeing something being put in here. I don't know if air goes through here, or something goes through here. I would feel that this was buried. O.K. Do you want to ask some questions about it? I don't know what that would be (pointing to effigy figure on pipe.) I don't know if that be a snake or a bird or what.

JONES: You said "fur," I don't understand that.

BOWES: I kept seeing fur. A person with a lot of fur, or clothing, like a big vest, or a big jacket with things across it, like a leather across it and like tied around. Like in Canada or a place...he had a fur jacket on.

JONES: What do the people look like?

BOWES: I didn't pick that up at all. But it could be like Viking people, but I would say it relates more to an Indian culture, or a culture in the north. I would say it relates to something where people are traveling. I would feel they were purposefully traveling in a direction. I do feel that if there were white people involved, or Caucasians, they were pulling a boat over land, or pulling something on the land.

JONES: So you do feel that there are Caucasians around?

BOWES: I wouldn't say they applied to this (object), but I would still feel that there was something dragged across the land...almost like a sand bar or mud flats or there was real miniature trees, about that high (indicates a foot and a half)...like mud flats...like a tree that looked dwarfed. I felt it was like barren ground, very cold, or hard. Like the everglades, muddy, real muddy, marshy ground and there was little trees like...that were dead. Like water flooded the area and killed these trees. But I would say it was very, very hard country, or cold or something. O.K.

This could have come from another country or a country where there was desert, but I still feel that this idea, this, whatever it is...it could have ended up in or something, but I don't feel it originated there at all.

JONES: You still feel very strong with the cold?

BOWES: Yes! Very strong with that.

Appendix E—Chapter VII

[*Bowes begins to read the pictures before they are taken from envelope.*]
JONES: These three pictures are of the same place.
BOWES: Well, just set them down here and maybe I can tell you about them.
JONES: Since these are slides and it may be difficult to get a visual fix I can tell you it's a natural setting with...
BOWES: Don't say anything, o.k.?
JONES: Sure.
BOWES: The first thing I picked up was something stone. I felt grey stone. I don't know if it's like a cliff, or something sticking out of a mountain. The strongest feeling was it was a cliff that stuck out, and then there's a stream down below it. Could be even like a building with a balcony sticking out. But I felt cold stone. That's what I was picking up. Could be a stream there. I don't know if it's in the mountains or looking down, but I felt one of the pictures could be from a mountain looking down, or something up high looking down. I don't know if there's a building in one of the pictures but I felt it had been vacant for a long time. Then I picked up something about a barn with hay in it. Can I look at the pictures now?
JONES: Yeah, sure. (I take the pictures out of the paper and place them in front of Bowes.)
BOWES? I don't know if this had to do with an Indian, or something that had to do with ceremony, but I kept feeling something was pushed into this hole. There's springs in this water, or water down this hole. I would say there was no way to come up. I don't know if they ever pushed a woman in there, but the feeling I had was a young girl or woman, or they put a basket with fruit and threw it in there with a rock on it. I don't know if there is a hot springs near there but that's what I picked up.
JONES: Do you feel what the people looked like who associated with this place?
BOWES: I felt like the woman could have even had blond hair. I kept picking up a very beautiful young woman. It looked like an Indian woman with blond hair.
JONES: Do you see any clothing on her?
BOWES: I would say she may have worn some kind of, like a cape over her head, or something that I felt it was hanging over her head. It may have been secluding her hair, but I felt she had blond or white hair. A young girl. Now I may have two things confused here. I would say that it was a religious place, and it had a ceremonial or religious background. If it was like England, I would say there was a lot of savage people there, like the Vikings. If it was not in England, if it was up north...I would say there is still something strange about the Indians or wild people. If this is South America, I would say there's something buried in the bottom of that water. Could be in any case. The feeling I had with this place is...desolate. I would say the people were afraid to go in the water...they couldn't get out, or there was something fearful in the water. Could be today. Like now people feel that way. I felt "northwest," like toward Gainesville or toward the north. "Northwest, northwest." I felt like people died out and there wasn't people around there for a long time. At one time it was all beaten down at one side.
JONES: How many people would get around this place?
BOWES: There could be two or three hundred. The feeling I had was they traveled a long way and carried gourds or things with water in them. They

could have come from South America, or from the south up into the west, like towards California.

JONES: **Why do you feel those people felt that place was important?**

BOWES: It was a place where they could put people in there, or put something in there and it wouldn't come out. And I felt at night the warmth of the water made steam...or you could go there at night and see a lot of...like power coming out of the water, or some kind of strength or some kind of smoke coming out of there. It was a natural phenomena. I would say that they may have thought there was a god in there. A god in the ground. I felt like they thought if they put things in the water that it would help the crops, or help things naturally because the water was in the ground.

JONES: **Do you see any designs or...**

BOWES: I would say that they could have built something and I don't know if they built things in the sides of mountains but the feeling I had was they were like Aztec or people who built things. I would say they were very religious and very organized.

JONES: **Do you get any more about the culture? About the kind of society they had?**

BOWES: Again, I'm working with a picture of a location and it's lately. Probably in the last few years is when this picture was taken, and I'm not speaking of the past here, I'm only talking about a place. I would say it is far removed from where the people were. I would say that they were pottery makers. People who made lots of things...may have made buildings, or made things that were structures. The feeling I had was that they stored things in clay pots. They may even have mummified, or cremated people...I see little jugs of ashes, or preserved things like a pyramid. Little bitty rooms...and caves. Does any of that make sense?

JONES: **I guess so.**

BOWES: I would say a king fell in there at one time, or somebody who was...I felt "king". Now I'm not talking about...I kept feeling like Vikings that kind of people...kind of aggressive like wanted to war all the time, wanted to fight all the time. To them, wealth was women. Women was wealth...how many women they had, and like young children. Women, twelve, thirteen...that's wealth to them. And I felt a king fell in there. Somebody of royalty...fell in there and I felt they felt that was a very bad omen...like it poisoned the water, and I felt they left. They may have never went back.

JONES: **What kinds of things would these people eat?**

BOWES: The first thing when you said that, I picked up berries. I felt they grew things in fields, and they may even have had irrigation. Like they may even had had canals or ditches where the water came into that ground. But I felt the ground was dry there now.

JONES: **Interesting.**

BOWES: Extremely dry.

JONES: **Are there any descendants of these people?**

BOWES: I don't feel so, but if it's true they went north. And if it's in South America or...in the west...I felt they went north and there may be a few distant, distant relatives, but that's what I picked up. Because I felt like they ran into opposition going north. I felt these people could have had boats...which is not common, which wouldn't be expected to happen.

JONES: **Did these people have metal?**

BOWES: There could have been an adversary, like the Spanish or adversary people who had something better than they did...like war materials...because I don't feel they won all their wars. I felt every year they lost a lot of people...in war.

JONES: What did the homes of these people look like?

BOWES: I would say their homes would be dwellings beside a mountain or that they were made of stone. I would say this was a long, long time ago.

JONES: Before or after the time of Christ?

BOWES: I would say it was the same time that the Vikings were in Great Britain. But that's all I picked up.

JONES: What about domestic animals? Do you see...

BOWES: I felt they had llamas.

JONES: These people had llamas?

BOWES: Yes. Or that they were something similar to that. I kept seeing it looking like a camel with a big lip but it was softer and more docile than a camel. I felt they herded them, like goats.

JONES: If I say "family", what do you pick up?

BOWES: I would say they had a group of people, and I felt like more women than men...always more women than men. I felt that one man was always at home with the women, and the other men traveled or went places or worked in the fields, but there was always one man who stayed with the women.

JONES: Do you pick up anything about the kinds of myths that they might have told?

BOWES: I felt they talked of like dragons from the ocean, or people from the south. I felt they talked of a dragon that came out of the ground or out of the water. I felt they talked about the sky becoming fire, like the lights from the sky...I would say that this was a real thing they seen. It may have been in Alaska or in the north, but this was...like people came from the north and went down south and then came back. Hundreds of years, or a hundred years later and talked of this...they seen fire in the sky. Like the sky was red with fire, and it could have been during a volcano, or a time when there was a lot of smoke in the air...like the sky was red!

JONES: Were there volcanoes in the area?

BOWES: There could be volcanoes in the area or volcanoes at the time they were there. Yeah. But I felt red smoke or the sun was shining through the smoke and it looked like the sky was on fire.

I felt like they took the insides out of lizards and threw them in there. They may have thought that was to get rid of the evil. To them snakes or lizards were evil and they were throwing that to the gods, or whatever it was down in there. I would say that it could tend to be foggy around there...at night or at certain times of the season.

JONES: Do you see them in terms of a...

BOWES: I felt like in a religious ritual, that they may have problems with hearing or they did things to their ears. I see them clapping sticks together, or doing something with sticks and then I felt they slapped each others' ears...or something they did that made problems with hearing. I didn't know what it meant.

JONES: Is there anything unique or characteristic of the kinds of outfits they wore?

BOWES: As soon as you start talking I pick things up...I was picking up something that was very strange and I kept feeling like they were almost...like cannibalistic, or that they had a lot of things around their...or like...bracelets around their legs. For some reason the bottom parts of their legs were empty of...clothes. I see these bracelets and scars on their legs. That's what I picked up. It could have been cannibalistic or it could have been...I felt that they... people bled or they bled people, or they sacrificed people, or...kind of ugly, ugly people. To them blood, war and blood and violence to them was religious ...religious things. Ugly. I would say the only thing you could find of these people was the rocks that was left, or the stones or the clay pots. Not very much more than that. I felt mainly with South America.

ALBERT BOWES: READING OF TWO NON-DIAGNOSTIC MAYAN PHOTOS
PHOTO: 6-56: (DOORWAY TO ROOM ON TOP OF THE TEMPLE OF
KULKULCAN AT CHICHEN ITZA.

BOWES: The first thing I picked up was something where this had been re-paired. Another feeling I had was that there was someone with a uniform. I don't know if it was a Spanish uniform, but I kept feeling a uniform. I keep seeing them walking through here (indicates doorway). The feeling I had was inside here I felt "cold"...or a cold feeling. I would say that there was something up here (indicates over doorway). It may have been some sort of statue or some sort of image, but it was in the doorway. I would say there was some drawing on the wall (indicates each side of doorway).

JONES: Was this room important? If you went in there, what would have been...

BOWES: I would say in there that there was a storage of something. I kept feeling "cool". Cool...cool. But I felt like a cold feeling. The strongest feeling I would say was that there was bodies laying in there. At one time, I would say there was storage. They stored wheat, or like stored bags or bowls of grain. But I felt there was a stack or a pile of bodies in there at one time. It might have been soon after a war and they didn't belong in there. I felt mass death. I see decomposed bodies.

JONES: What do you feel this total structure would look like?

BOWES: I would say that it could be underground or that it was below ground level. I would say that there was worry of leakage or water dripping. I would say that the soil was very dry...even though I picked up something about moisture, I kept feeling very dry in there. There could have been something that was kind of square. I kept picking up something like this...(draws flat topped structure). I felt there must be a lot of trees and things around the outside. I felt there was a vent or an opening in the top right here (indicates middle of structure)...kind of a hole. Of course it could be filled in.

JONES: The people who were going into this room what did they look like?

BOWES: I would say they had a lot of jewelry on. I would say they were dressed like this (draws human figure). They had some sort of hat on. They may have had feathers or something in their hat. I felt lots of jewelry, or lots of gold or something hanging down here like...I didn't feel they had much at the bottom. They may have had like a skirt or something hung down here, but I felt their legs were plain.

JONES: And these people, are the people who go in here (door)?

BOWES: In and out of there. I felt that they could even have something hanging down like a breech cloth, but I felt the ones that were important had lots of jewelry or things hanging around their neck. I felt big plumes or flowers or feathers...pink ones. I felt these little bumps here (indicates shoulders, or shoulders of vest-like garment in his drawing). The other one I felt was like a soldier, and I felt he was in uniform or in some sort of unusual regalia...could have been like Spanish...some sort of uniform. If this was on an island, I felt a ship definitely visited there...with cannons.

JONES: What kind of environment do you feel around this place?

BOWES: I felt sacred. I kept feeling "sacred". The feeling I had was "desolate". When I said "trees"...there could have been a lot of hills or dirt. The strongest feeling is that this could be on an island, or could be on a place where there was water nearby. I would say it's kind of high. It's high up from the water level, but that's what I picked up.

JONES: What kind of climate exists here?

BOWES: I would feel hot weather. It could be dry, but I felt cool and dry in there (indicates photo of door), but that's all I picked up. I see problems with people's teeth but I didn't know what it meant.

PHOTO 7-40: (INTERIOR OF OBSERVATORY AT CHICHEN ITZA)

BOWES: The first feeling I picked up with this, too, is storage...storage. I felt a well. The strongest feeling I had was that there was a lot more inside this building than it shows at this point. I kept picking up more wood and there was layers. And there was a ladder in there. Like right up here (indicates top of photo), this might have been a platform of wood right up here. Flooring. I kept picking up that there was things stored in there, or there was a well there. I don't know if this is a fort on an island again or there was a fort, but I kept picking up that this place was defended. That's the feeling I had. I kept picking up stored things and I felt an association with water or food or something. I kept feeling water in the background or like a well. I felt if you dropped a stick or a rock over it would fall down and go "Ploup, ploup,,. Like way, way far down.

JONES: **What did this entire structure look like? Like if you were standing outside?**

BOWES: (draws exterior) I can only see one side of it...for some reason. Could be something this way and that way (indicates a and b). Like it could be a corner of a fort or the corner of a building, but I felt it was high ground somewhere else. I felt illnesses. I see sickness. I would say people were dying. That they were ill. I keep feeling as though they could have been starved, or they were very ill. They were dying.

JONES: **What did the people who would enter this structure look like?**

BOWES: I keep seeing them walking up a path that goes back and forth. Like this (c) is a path that goes down and down like that. Could have even been a cliff here (d), or something but I didn't know what it meant. I don't know how much of that. I just see lines of people walking up there...like, up this path. I felt there was a fat man, like a heavy-set man which sounded strange to me. They could have been in robes or in long things that hung down, but that's all I picked up.

JONES: **The people around this place...**

BOWES: I felt that it had been a long, long time since people actually inhabited this...and I would say that people didn't use this because there was a story of illness, or that there was a lot of mosquitoes, or there was a lot of pestilence around there. I would say they totally ignored it. They left it alone.

JONES: **When the people did use this...**

BOWES: I would say there was a lot of people there. There was a lot of people...there was hundreds or even thousands. Groups...large groups of people there. I would say that this could have been a place where they could look out...a group of people looking for something, or watching for something. That's what I picked up. I would say this door was very secure at one time, or secured. It wasn't always open.

JONES: **With these two pictures (6-56 and 7-40), where do you think that is?**

BOWES: The first thing I picked up was island and then I picked up...I picked up island; then England, and then South America. The strongest feeling I had was that they were very primitive people and they were people who were like Vikings, or people who were like...very crude or hard. I feel they carried spears, but that's what I picked up. They could have been people who went by boat...like big boats, like Viking boats...long boats. (Draws boat) I'm uncertain about the front here. But there was oars, or things like this (a). This was a large boat (main body), and this was smaller (pontoon-like extension). And it was boards or something in here (interior).

JONES: **How many people could be in this boat?**

BOWES: Maybe up to twenty, or thirty...a large group.

JONES: **Do you feel any designs or decorations or...**

BOWES: Could be like wooden...like little diamond shapes. They weren't all the same. They were all along there (border and top)...carved into the wood. This here was not something people would ride on (indicates pontoon), but this in here (interior center of main canoe)...there could have even been something in here where people slept or went inside. But I felt it was pretty big. And they carried fruit. Might have been three sided and it was green.

JONES: How was this boat constructed?

BOWES: I would say long logs. That there was long logs, and there may have been bracing in here (interior). I still see them carrying spears. They may have had an interest in skulls. Skulls, skulls, or something.

PHOTO: 7-42 (CHAC MOOL AT CHICHEN ITZA)

BOWES: Hmm. This used to be a statue. Very interesting. This marked a boundary. This marked a boundary of a group of people. When you went into that area it was like a signpost. It was telling you that you were going into a different group of people. There was something that looked like...ah, something that looked...I'll show you what I see (draws his impressions related to Chac Mool). Their lips were thick for some reason. (*Note: The other photos in the series were still in my briefcase at this time. I was taking one out at a time and putting it back before I took out the next photo. My briefcase was behind me and blocked from Bowes' view.*) There was several statues of people or things sitting around. One of them was stolen. The one that was back here (*a*).

JONES: Did anything special go on around this place (touches statue picture)?

BOWES: I would say that it was a boundary marker and I would say that... the strongest feeling I had was that there may have been games around there...where people went along and kicked things. This part in here (*b*) is uncertain to me. But I would say that there was more than one statue.

JONES: Do you have any feelings about why it was broken?

BOWES: I would say it was broken because of war. I would say somebody destroyed it...because they were destroying the border.

JONES: Do you have a feeling of the destroyers?

BOWES: I would say they were local people. That over the years local people stole whatever they could, to try to sell...that they carried it away in a wagon. I would say that during a war or during a group happening that this was destroyed because of resentment of the border...saying that they didn't like the border of a particular area...that they wanted to take the whole place over. This (statue) was a warning of a sort, to say that you are now entering this country or this group of people. It was more like a county, not really a particular country...more like a county or a state.

JONES: What about the direction from...?

bowes; I would say there was much more there...much more of it there.

JONES: There were three statues you said?

BOWES: Yes.

JONES: All three of them were boundary markers?

BOWES: Yes. One of them might have looked something like a totem pole... may have had a lot of pictures of round things on it, or faces...stood up straight.

JONES: The people who were angry about the border, from what direction did they come?

BOWES: I felt they came from...the first word I got was "south". I feel they came from the north (laughs). I pick Mexico...going south...north to south. They may have not been from the south but they may have been going south.

PHOTO: 5-87 (STELAE AT COPAN)

BOWES: The feeling I got with this was that this was a priest...a very revered ruler, or someone that was very kind. They made this in a reverence to him. I would say he was possibly a psychic, or an astrologer, or a person who predicted the future. To them, he was very kind. And he was like a psychic or an astrologer, or a person who looked toward the heavens. I would say he could have been a ruler, but I would say that he was a kind ruler. Or maybe that's the way they would have liked to thought anyway. He was of a high position, and he may have had many wives. I felt he died young, or there was youth involved in there...he looked young for many years. I would say his reign or when he lived was very short. I would say this was colored, very colored and all pretty (indicates the statue)...colorful. Blues and oranges and all different colors. There could have even been stones up here (over the head), which were destroyed. I felt there was a big headdress up here.

JONES: Can you get more about this person? His life? His times? His culture?

BOWES: I would say he turned a lot of effort...instead of making war, he turned a lot of effort towards raising crops or making irrigation...making the people's life better. I kept feeling as though he predicted or talked of famine or dry weather. I would say that it came true. He died soon after it. I would say he talked about cattle, or talked about...animals that were grazing in a woods.

JONES: Were there any other manmade objects in the vicinity?

BOWES: Yes, there was a whole bunch of them...a lot of things that were made of wood...and these things were like the peasants' or lower people's homes. And they may have been things like this (draws house). They were three sided. These were actually like little log cabins or buildings, and they could have been on stilts...I felt wood, and this was all slated in here (indicates sides of structure)...where the air could come in, but the rain couldn't. The slates were at an angle like a jalousey window. The roof had a slight overhang to it. I would say they were all around there. A lot of people milling around. To the left as you are looking at the picture was a building or a temple, or some sort of building that stood straight up...looks kind of fragile to me. This (statue) may have been in front of a temple or in front of a place where you want to worship...or went to study. I seen them studying things...and I felt there was something written, like scrolls, or like pieces of parch cloth, or wood, or like a wood with writing on it. Like a waxed material that they wrote on.

JONES: Do you have a feeling of what they were studying?

BOWES: They were studying religion and culture. I would say they studied things about astrology, or about the planets. I would say they were pretty accurate in predicting things.

PHOTO: 7-36 (DEATHS HEAD WALL AT CHICHEN ITZA)

BOWES: I would say this depicts death. It is telling you that death is sacred. I would say that it is almost like a threat. I would say that these (faces) were depicted as skulls...and there is a burial around there somewhere, and it's in the ground. There may have been thousands or hundreds of people buried there...a graveyard. I would say inside this there was buildings that were like pyramids...at one time. The strongest feeling I had was that this was depicting death...almost glorifying it. I would say that what it was saying was, that the people who died...that their spirit or death was laughing...laughing at people who were living. In other words, like the people who were dead were better off than the people who were alive. They were laughing, but it was like giving power...almost like a threat. I would say that these people worshipped death. Death to them was very powerful. It was like the more people they had die, or who were in the spirit world dead, that was more strength. I would say they probably killed girls...killed women. They may have picked virgin girls, or young girls to die.

JONES: Would this death occur in association with this place?

BOWES: Yes. This was a place saying "don't go beyond this point", or "this is where death is." But I feel they worshipped death.

JONES: **Do you pick them up building this thing?**

BOWES: I don't feel they built it, but I felt they moved it. They moved these stones. A lot of these...I felt they moved these...they made these and then they moved them there as time went on. I see them dragging them along the ground on wooden sleds. I felt that they built it gradually...that they didn't build it all at once. They built it a piece at a time and it took a long time to build it and they built it...like they were counting. It was like a thing that they wanted to count...it wasn't all built at the same time. These different stones could have been built like within a year or in the same year or whatever, but I would feel that they were counting something, and they were building it. Each one of those faces signified something.

JONES: **Something different? Each of them?**

BOWES: Each one was an identity in itself. Each one meant something different. Like each one of those could signify a person, or ten people, or a family. A number or unit...not particularly a person...because I would say there were many more people buried there than it shows. In fact, I would say that they might find a place that was like ten foot deep in skulls or burials...like the ground was sunk down with so many thicknesses of bodies.

PHOTO: 6-36 (BALL COURT AT CHICHEN ITZA)

BOWES: This place was very, very busy at one time. A very busy place. There may have been hundreds and thousands of people around there at a time...lots of people. This was a pretty advanced place. Lots of things missing. There was waterfalls or fountains, or places where people could get water. There was all kinds of statues and there was even things that looked like marble or something shiny that came from the south. Like almost, like idols. There may have been games there. Like people played games, where people were milling around almost like a...there was a place where they collected a lot of food and they traded it. Down there at the end (structure in background of photo), they announced things. There was games going on. There was things where people wore leather things on their heads, and they kicked or hit sticks...or hit things along the ground and I would say that they could even butt heads...could hit each other in the head. I would say that there was large groups of people who came here...almost like an auditorium. There was a lot of people running around, lot of people there. Lots of people. I don't know if this signifies a snake (indicates snake-like border of lower wall), but I kept getting a water evaluation. This was something that had to do with water here. This could have even been a fountain or there was water somewhere. This may have been a storage tank (touches wall area), or when it rained it stored water. I felt something was storing water. This down here (little structure in background) was a place where they announced things.

JONES: **What do you pick up about this structure right here?** (Indicates ring on wall)

BOWES: This is part of the game. They hung people there, or there was something hung. They might not have actually hung people there, but I felt skin stretched.

JONES: **Let me just put all these photos back together again and see if you have any final observations to make.**

BOWES: O.K. I would say my major observation is that this was a very powerful group of people. There was more people there than what people say there was. I would say there was a lot of people there. I would say that this culture was based on an idea of life after death or the idea of death. It was valued that way. I would say that this (6-36) was the active, everyday sort of used, sort of thing...it was used everyday. Very, very active. This place (6-56) was more like used like once every ten years or something very removed...some place where things are stored or hidden. This (7-36)...people walked by there everyday. Skulls. This (7-40) seemed a distance away...seemed a little more secluded. This (5-87) was next. This is next (7-42) because it is kind of far out.

JONES: What do you mean 'far out'?
BOWES: It was kind of 'out in the country.' Kind of far away...or it's on the suburb of a city. Suburb area. This here (6-36) had the feeling of...like Rome...lot of competition, general hub-bub, lots of people. This (7-36) was more of a religiously based thing more like a cemetery or it was a signifying something that was like a memory...like a mausoleum type thing. This (5-87) was something religious. It was like a statue of Lincoln or something. It signified an ancient important person, ruler or religious person. I would say he was more religiously based, more like a religious figure, like Jesus or more like Buddha. I don't think there was anything in the statue that signified violent death. This (7-40) I would pick up like it was a fortification, or a building made for storage or it was more of a dull...not important. This (6-56) a political move, more like 'you are now entering' a certain city or area. This (7-36) was more barbaric, more violent, or more primitive...more like used at the first of the civilization or the last...when the people were becoming radical.
JONES: How far back in time do you feel this (6-56) existed?
BOWES: I feel the last time that people actually lived there, or the people who built it had it...I feel the actual last time may have been in the thirteen or fourteen hundreds. I would say before that. It could have been as much as a thousand years that they were in that general area, or like five hundred years. I kept feeling '1200' when these people were originally there or actually building this. A lot of disease there. Like death through pneumonia, or like a disease that made people very weak (indicates 7-40), or they breathed hard. They abandoned these areas, or they ran away, but I felt somebody was hiding out there (7-40), or like the last of the people or storage of...I don't know what it was. More like death. There may have been a last ditch stand there (7-40) or there was war there, or like people literally starved to death there. I felt they just abandoned this and ran away.
JONES: Why?
BOWES: Invasion.
JONES: Is this (7-42) related?
BOWES: Yes. Invasion. I would say these (7-42) were not that originally, totally destroyed...when they were pushed over. I would say this (7-42) signified a midget, or the little people, or strong man. When I first picked this up (7-42) there was something about an owl...night. Watchman over the night. Owl.
JONES: Why midget? Why strong man?
BOWES: I would say it was signifying a powerful midget or like somebody who was strong. Like supernatural or like in the spirit world. Midget. Little people. Powerful. Warrior.
JONES: Did these people have a supreme deity?
BOWES: Yes. The sun. The planets. Associated with like astrology, and I felt they talked of the earth and the sky. Like they felt the planets had a big influence on the people, time, and future. And these things (draws VII-9), it had arms like this and it was sitting up here (6-36), they carried these along. It was like their mascot. I felt they were made of...could be more like a lion, or like a thing that was like 'This is our team. Football. Bulldogs.' Then another one had this and another one had that. They carried these. They were huge and heavy and some of them stayed there (6-36), but I felt they were sitting all

over the place. They were made of like marble and they were pink and white. Very beautiful. Expensive looking. This glass or this marble was so well made that it was almost like you could see depth in it...almost like see through it. I felt a lot of them were broken. Crushed. They may have been pink and white or they may have been green and white.

JONES: Did the color have significance?

BOWES: No. That was just the way they were made. These were arms. Had claws on them.

JONES: The ultimate ball player?

BOWES: Yes. That is what I am saying. It was short and stumpy. It may not look exactly like that (drawing) but I seen it from a distance. Like I was standing here (indicates left background in 6-36) and watching. They were heavy. Some were moved and some stayed there. They had things that were like calendars too...like this (draws VII-10) and they had like tablets sticking up with faces on them.

JONES: In this place (6-36)?

BOWES: Yes. They were signifying when something was going to happen, or something was there...these tablets. This is something I kept picking up about this (7-40) and it was like parchment cloth that was like waxed...some kind of scrolls. This was the last place it was at. I still felt like this (7-40) was the last place where they were at. Like they were worshipping, or there—still trying to calculate things at the very last. There could be little things in the floor there (6-36). Like in the dirt there could be little bitty things. Little things in the ground. Little rings or little toys or something...little religious things. In the floor. Made of clay.

JONES: Did the people who made these structures develop this ability in this area or did they come from some place else and build at this site?

BOWES: They moved to this area. I would say they already had their culture established, but re-established it here. This was not where they started and grew up. If they dug in the ground they would find buildings underneath all this. There was layers of people. They, say, they been here so many thousands of years. I feel they been there longer than that. Other civilizations below. They brought their cultures there from (draws map)...I felt they were here (indicates site location by "X"). They came from this direction (south) and I feel they knew about the Gulf Stream. They went this way (northeast).

DOUBLE-BLIND READING OF NON-DIAGNOSTIC LATE MAYAN
CERAMIC FRAGMENTS: ALBERT BOWES

JONES: All of these (indicates pottery pieces) are from the same site. What can you tell me about them?

BOWES: These are pretty advanced people from what I can pick up. I mean...I picked up something about a trade route...or trade. It would be north of here. The first thing I picked up was something about Alabama...or toward ...I felt water near there. It may be a river, or maybe it was that at one time they used the water to travel. I picked up...towards the west, like northwest from here. I feel as though these people had a written language. I picked up something about a trade route. I felt they had a religion that was quite involved with the idea of planets or something having to do with trade or navigation. The feeling I picked up was that these people were actually relaying and based on an idea of trade...something having to do with trade. In other words, I don't see them being totally self-sufficient. I would say there may have been a group of these people who traveled but most of the people stayed in one area. The feeling I had with this (ceramic piece) was that it was used every day. I don't know if something was stored in this but I felt it hanging from a tent or a building and there was something stored or put in it. The feeling I had was that something was jammed down in there...could have been a stick, or something. I felt it was hanging...hanging...like a weight. I don't know if there was a stream or river near here, but I kept picking up water. I see them down near the water, and I see them digging into the sides of the bank. I kept picking up that they were digging clay, or digging something out of the banks of the water, or the side of a hill. I picked up this (shard) and I picked up something Spanish or Spanish speaking toward the south of where they lived. I feel as though these people may have traded this from a different location. I would say that some women may have come from a different location that may have had clothing on—like wool or heavy clothing. I kept picking up woven cloth. It could have been woven material, but I felt "black". This (shard) I picked up was tied...something tied onto it, or something separating...I felt it was stretched or dealt with...stretched. I picked up a man with this (shard), and I felt him smoking or smoke inside a building. With this (shard) I kept picking up more like...Spanish speaking people, or they may have spoken to someone from a Spanish speaking... It may not have been Spanish, but it may have been from the Mexico direction.

JONES: What do the people look like who associated with this piece of pottery?
BOWES: They may have worn unusual helmets or hats. I kept getting that they had visited—like on a trip—dignitaries or religious people. These people could have walked up on mounds. There could have been great huge mounds where they worshipped. I kept feeling very beautiful countryside. I see a lot of heavy vegetation. I don't feel desert with this. I do not feel desert. I pick up more lush countryside. This (piece of copal)...I don't know if this was from another country. I picked up volcanoes or something where...I kept hearing sound, like the ocean or some sound like the wind. Now this (shard) I felt came from a different group or people. I felt more with women with this (shard). I saw them carrying things. I kept seeing this great big blanket or this great big piece of leather or something, and I see them laying all these pots out there... almost like they were bringing somebody Christmas gifts, or bringing someone gifts, like tokens. I keep seeing somebody standing there and shaking their head (affirmative gesture). I kept picking up the absence of horses but I kept picking up something of a dog or a small animal that may have pulled things. What is unusual about this (shard) was that the marks or designs were on the inside signifying something that would relate to religion. Like whatever was inside these bowls was religious or ceremonial or valuable... like it was stored. This (shard) was everyday wear...it was used. This was like a plate...used everyday. All this has something to do with a peninsula going out into the water. Like the Baja peninsula or someplace where there was a peninsula sticking out in the water. Like the ocean was here or water was here (indicates) and then the ground went way up high. You could walk out to the edge and look down. It was real high. I kept picking up a woman with glasses on and I felt like she was a teacher or she could write a book...she is investigating this. I didn't feel very impressed with this (shard). It was round for some reason but I didn't pick up much with that...this stuff could have come from another country. May have come from somewhere other than the United States, but I just picked up something about that. What I'm dealing with is little statues and one of them was a statue of a man with his hands up, and the other one was like a little dog sitting down. I picked up an association with those statues and this piece (shard). I picked up a bunch of little artifacts, or a bunch of little statues, or little animals, or different objects.
JONES: You mentioned that the site was in this country and then you said it may not be.
BOWES: The reason for that is I picked up something from an outside influ-

ence, and I picked up a narrower part of this country, or a narrow part of another continent. I kept picking up traveling people.

JONES: What was the diet of the makers of these materials?

BOWES: The first thing I picked up was something about grain or something about things that were grown in fields. Then I picked up long strips of something that was stripped and I picked up strips of meat that were smoked. But I felt that these were pretty advanced people. They knew how to preserve food. They stored food in jars or in bowls. I felt they were capable of making stone buildings.

JONES: I was going to ask you about the structures they lived in.

BOWES: I picked up that the lower class people or the lower group of people could have lived in wooden or shack type things—things that were stacked or braced against each other. I kept seeing sticks or wood. I felt some of the higher priests...the higher people may have lived in mounds where there was stone. They would have stones in the front of it. I kept picking up that these were mounds...some mounds...piles of dirt—but I felt it say up, above the ground, and wind blew across it. The shacks of wood were like...it looked like it went up and then it went up again...with a small hole down here at the bottom...the priest's houses.

JONES: Could you draw a map to locate this place?

BOWES: You see, one thing that confuses me is the idea of trade.

JONES: Well, could you tell me who these people would trade with? What did the people look like?

BOWES: I felt they had either canoes or something that they would pull by animals...like pulled by a dog, or pulled by an animal. I kept picking up west and then I picked up "peninsula" or I picked up "west", and then something jutting out into...this could be a mountain range, but I picked up more like water. I keep getting up about Alabama and then saying "west," toward Mississippi, toward Mexico, toward the west.

JONES: What did the makers of these things look like?

BOWES: I kept feeling they were short and stocky and they had real round faces. They chopped their hair off right here (bangs across brow)...flat across and kind of round shape (shoulder length)...I felt the common, hard-working people had real heavy clothes down to here (wrist)...real heavy clothes (draws figure)...kind of chopped hair. Didn't have real long hair. They had kind of an oriental look to them. Round looking faces, and these long, heavy clothes... real heavy. The clothes came clear down to their hands. These were like workers. The priests wore much more beads, and jewelry and a lot of things hanging...like layers and layers of beads or jewelry. I would feel they wore something more like this (draws priest)...I saw a tie in front (touches picture of worker and makes little lateral lines down the median line on 'worker' figure.) ...but these people (priests) had something...lots of beads. Layers and layers of beads. This (priest) is more like a person who is very religious or of a high position. These (workers) people are like women or like workers. People who carry big baskets...big round baskets. They may have carried stones or carried clay, or carried things in big baskets.

JONES: How many people occupied this site?

BOWES: Could have been over a thousand. These people wore different shoes, too. These people (workers) wore a shoe more like...a rugged shoe, real coarse. These people (priests) wore more like a sandal, and it was more like something open. I can't explain it. It was like straps, where this shoe (workers) was like solid leather, and just tied together. Quite a difference between these two peoples. These people (workers) didn't go anywhere, they always stayed at home. These people (priests) would do some traveling. They (priests) would be studying things, and visiting and investigating. These people hid things...maybe gold, maybe valuables...in caves south of where they lived. I feel they sealed it up...probably still there. Things hanging from the walls skulls and skeletons, and like people hanging...like a burial cave or something, because I see a lot of skulls.

JONES: You mentioned another people when you touched one of these pieces?

BOWES: From a Spanish speaking place...or people of another language or another culture.

JONES: What did these people look like?

BOWES: The first thing I picked up was that they were naked...they just had breech cloth, or just...and they may not have...this piece of pottery may not have been made by them, but what they got came from them. This is...(draws trader)...they just may have had something tied around here (middle).

JONES: What about the hair of the traders?

BOWES: I felt black hair. They were more like in the water, or around the salt water, or...real nature people, outdoors types. These people (worker) were more like workers, or very much more serious. The people who associated with this were more like slaves or savage people. They got things out of the ocean, or things out of the water. They had bows and arrows and they shot under water, or shot fish. They did things more like in nature. These people (workers) were almost like slaves...where they all worked together carrying big baskets.

JONES: Who were the masters of these people (workers)?

BOWES: These people (priests). These people (traders) were...talked another language, and these people (priests) had very little respect for these people (traders) , but they did trade with them. They (traders) had long hair.

JONES: What was the nature of the climate?

BOWES: I would say humid, or hot weather. I would feel where these people were (traders) was cooler, or a wind blowing. There could have been...I still felt tropical. Heavy...especially the reason for why they built these buildings ...this mountain...this dirt up high was to get the wind...the wind blew. Get away from insects and such. These people (workers) lived in these shacks...these grass shacks, or these wood shacks. These people (priests) lived here on the mounds...these people (traders) lived on the river or on the water. They were more like savages, or more like people who were fishermen, or people who were close to nature. These people (priests) talked about religion. These people (workers & priests) did not live as long as them (traders).

JONES: As a culture?

BOWES: Yes. These people (traders) were much healthier. These people...

JONES: What is the relationship between all these heavy clothes and the humid climate?

BOWES: It sounds like it contradicts...but I kept seeing the heavy clothing as a cultural thing or as a worker, and I kept seeing it as heavy leather, or heavy clothing but I kept picking up that they were like suppressed...they were workers.

JONES: Where these people (priests) and the workers of the same racial background?

BOWES: Yes, they had the same racial background. These people (priests) may have actually looked different...in the face. These (workers) looked more like orientals. These people were oriental, but they had a longer-looking face (priests). They may have not even interbred. These people (priests) were like royalty.

JONES: The religion...

BOWES: Again, it has to do with direction in the stars, or dealing with something that has to do with religious...like something that has to do with talking to the gods, or they could sacrifice, or they would work with the gods. Whereas these people (workers) may have just stood there and watched these others worship. These people (traders) would worship nature, fish, and animals, and the tides, and health, and things more like nature. These people (priests) felt there was a god, gods.

JONES: Do you pick up anything about religious symbols?

BOWES: I felt kind of an ugly thing. I don't quite understand. It looks like a devil face. Almost like a...the face was not smiling...they had a lot of things...layers of things...of to them there was like layers that they spoke of that signified evolution or growth.

JONES: During the time that these people were making these things, what other kinds of things were going on in the world?

BOWES: I seen the North American coast, and I see people traveling up and down here (southeastern coast area). I would say they were Indians...to signify that the white man didn't live there.

JONES: Didn't live in North America at the time these people were making these things?

BOWES: Right. I would say this may have had an association with this area (draws VII-12), or this area (arrow in Mississippi area toward Mexico). It may have been from up here, but I felt down here (toward Mexico)...like down the Mississippi, and back this way (southwest). It could be a peninsula here, or an area were a river would divide, but I kept picking up this effect...where water was on both sides.

JONES: Did the makers of these artifacts have the knowledge of working with metal?

BOWES: I felt a little round disk...a little metal thing. But I felt...I didn't understand that. I felt it was added later. It was among this stuff (artifacts) but it was added later by a different people. It was gold colored or tarnished grey, like a black grey.

JONES: Do you feel the presence of domestic animals other than the dog?

BOWES: Yes. I picked up something that looked like a llama, or something that looked like a pack animal, or a burden animal. I see them milking it. It might have been like a goat. I would say that the territory or the countryside looked very different at that time than it does now.

JONES: What kind of difference?

BOWES: I felt cooler or different. This may have been like five hundred years ago, but I felt it was different. Again, it could be from another continent.

JONES: You are doing something unique in this reading. Never before have you been torn between continents. You have indicated this possibility of these materials originating on another continent...

BOWES: I would say South America, or there could have been a connection with these people from another continent—like South America. There could have been trade in that direction.

JONES: So you feel with these people that a crucial fact of their life had to do with...

BOWES: Trade.

JONES: Is that why they are where they are, or did the trade happen later?

BOWES: No. That was the reason they are where they are. I would say originally they came to farm, but as there came to be more and more people, they would relate to trade to keep the people going. I would say they depleted their soil.

JONES: Are these people living on this site today? Anywhere near it?

BOWES: I wouldn't say they are living there today. I would say there might be construction or new changes coming to that area, but I didn't pick up it was that prevalent. Now if there's a golf course or a place like that, there could still be considered woods...or desolate, but I didn't see it as being well accepted as a place to live. I didn't pick up too much from the time. For some reason I am not picking up that much with the time...or place. I keep desiring to know that place, but it seems foreign to me. I've not picked up this vibra-

tion that well before. Something is different about it. I may have never been
there physically...personally, or I may have never handled the objects from
that area.

JONES: I am interested in the nature of the family?

BOWES: I would feel that these people (workers) had a very poor family
group. In fact when they may have begun to get a family they may have been
used like slaves, or separated or sent to particular places to learn certain
trades...where people learned about wood or about dyeing wood, or like making
these houses. Others were learning to stretch things or make leather or do different things. There may have been a man and a woman, but I feel that the
children were sometimes separated. These people (priest) were considered as
royalty and when they had children they were very coddled or taken care of,
but young women from here (workers) may have taken care of these people
(priests), but they (priests) were considered kings or royalty.

JONES: Did these traders have vessels of any kind?

BOWES: I would say they had large canoes, or they had boats that had two
sections, and I felt like pontoons. I felt they went right out into the waves, or
going right out into the water in canoes. I see them spearing both fish and
turtles.

JONES: You are seeing the place where these people made these things. What
does it look like in their community? What are you seeing?

BOWES: I see a lot of people talking and milling around. I see a lot of trading
going on...outside. These buildings are off in the distance. I see people
carrying things in big baskets. I feel they even had monkeys, or had little
animals that they sell and trade. Again, this could be South America, or some
place that had an association with another influence from some other place. I
keep seeing them talking and carrying things...some are carrying them on
their head. Off in the distance I see smoke rising, like red smoke and different
colors...green and red smoke from these buildings off in the distance. Almost
felt oriental influence. Almost like they would have buildings that are real
peaked, again wooden buildings or something. I keep seeing a lot of people
walking with limps...like hip problems or knee problems. These people—the
workers—maybe like scurvy or something with the lack of nutrition. These
people were limited in the kinds of food they had and they were pushing for
trade. I would say...again, if this is from South America, and it may be, but I
picked up that these people (priests) could have rode, and they (workers) may
have carried them...in things like this (draws)...like a box on poles. The man
sat in here. The man is out of proportion. A lot of feathers, lot of plummage,
lot of color.

JONES: You mentioned baskets earlier. Do you see any designs on the
baskets?

BOWES: I felt brown. These people (workers) had baskets that were round.
What's funny is that they carried rocks and they carried clay...they carried
things, vegetables or fruits, or big green or yellow fruits, like gourds or something.

JONES: Also, in the beginning you were picking up a written language.

BOWES: This could be written or like a language (draws).

JONES: The "wedge" shape appears often?

BOWES: It would mean different things. It might be like a word, and then
they would add more to it to give it another meaning. God, this is strange! I
keep picking up them limping, limping. I felt joints...problems with their
knees, and their hips...like stiffness, like a problem with malnutrition. I didn't
see them eating right. I kept feeling that these people (priests) gave them
(workers) liquids to drink, and it wasn't particularly good for them. They
(priests) would mistreat these people (workers), like experimenting on them.
The liquid was like tea, or some kind of liquid and they gave it to them and

they acted like it was going to cure them, but they knew it didn't. Like these people (priests) would almost laugh, not laugh...almost like 'Give it to them and let's see what happens.'

JONES: Can you pick up any more about that? That sounds interesting.

BOWES: I see them squeezing something out of a vine, or like roots hanging and I see them (priests) squeezing this out. They had an apparatus that crushed it, or it was like pieces of wood...there was a root...they (priests) put this root in here and then turned this and it would crush the root, and then this liquid came out, and they (priests) gave it to them (workers). They might put berries, or purple or black colored berries, and cook it. I see them (priests) giving it to them (workers). I would say that it would keep them working. Keep them going, like a stimulant. But I would say they (workers) had a real sad look, their eyes was real tired. It would keep them going so they wouldn't tire very easily. I felt around their (workers) legs there was a lot of sores. I kept feeling their (workers) legs looked kind of purple. Lots of sores. Terrible. I didn't feel that many women. I didn't pick up that many women. Even though I felt women were carrying these baskets...I don't understand it. Sores. Like illness. May have to do with the female area (genital reference). I see them sick (workers). I may be progressing along with what happened to these people. I would say these people (traders) ate very well in comparison to us. They would get to the food.

JONES: You mentioned these (priests) people were traveling...

BOWES: Yeah. They would get away. Go places and meet other people...in other places. They even visited a place where people live up in the side of hills ...like they have adobe buildings, or buildings up in the sides of mounds or hills. I hear them saying they are going to visit the water, which to them was a sacred place.

JONES: When these people (priests) left what kept these people (workers) from leaving?

BOWES: All of them (priests) didn't leave. The workers were like cattle, or like dedicated or brainwashed or like robots...they were kept working. What's strange is that they kept carrying things. Trading is probably what it was...they were carrying things. I see lines of them going down through the woods carrying things. May not be woods. It may be swamps. Maybe jungle. I picked up 'woods'.

JONES: These people (priest and workers)—what do they have that other people would want in terms of trade?

BOWES: Pots. Things made of clay. These little idols, these little figurines, things made of wood where they were making things like clubs that were very, very polished...things hanging with little faces. I felt dark red wood.

JONES: What would these people want from other people?

BOWES: Fish, animals, things of trade. They may even have had baskets with monkeys in them...or mice. I don't feel that the people who dug this up realized the trade involved. What they got here may have only been like an outpost of the actual civilization. Like a colony of the original. Like Columbus, like the pilgrims came over from England. These people were like the pilgrims in this particular place.

JONES: Where would the central civilizations be?

BOWES: I would say South America, or another place where it was very tropical.

JONES: Were these people ever attacked?

BOWES: I would say from the south probably. Possibly groups of people who only attacked when they (priests and workers) were walking...carrying things through the swamp, or the woods...when they were carrying things from one place to another. I would say they would only attack them when they knew there was a few of them.

JONES: How would they attack? What would it look like?

BOWES: I would say they would be shooting arrows or using blowguns or darts. I kept picking up that they were coming from the sides, or would wait until they came to a valley or a place like that was real narrow, and they were walking down through there. I keep hearing drops of water...dripping water. I see them walking down through there and I see a lot of people coming from the sides.

JONES: You mentioned, when you were touching this piece, something about funny looking hats or helmets. Can you get back to that again?

BOWES: I lost that. I'm getting tired. I would say they had some form of money or a calendar, or something that they looked at. They would barter on this calendar. They may have even counted things with these beads. Like when they were bartering or trading, they may have had like a piece of wood on both sides and a lot of little beads that they shoved back and forth. I don't feel anyone knows about that. Or they had this round ring...this may have been what all these beads were around this guy's neck (priest). I kept seeing them counting beads, or pushing beads across...counting, like bags of wheat or baskets of things...counting them. Let me ask you a question. Do you know where that stuff is from?

JONES: No. The archeologist who provided me with these thing will tell me that later.

BOWES: I...could be an association with islands, because I picked up islands a lot of times...an association with jungle and beaches.

* * *

NOREEN RENIER: DOUBLE-BLIND READING OF
LATE MAYAN CERAMIC FRAGMENTS.

JONES: These materials are all from the same site. Do you want me to put them all together?

RENIER: It doesn't matter. I can just do them one at a time. I'm getting an impression already. Can I start? Talk?

JONES: Just start when you feel ready.

RENIER: I see a very broad-faced individual and I feel like there's a band, or bangs on this man's head. I feel like bangs...hair. Bangs. I'm going back to where this is. I want to see...land. I feel the land is flat but as it goes into the distance there's mounds...not like mountains, or not like flat desert all over... I see mounds in the distance...In the background I see like sand mounds or...I don't see any vegetation on it. There is a large body of water. I'm facing it this way. A large body of water and I feel small...more of a stream...river cutting across the land.

JONES: You said mounds?

RENIER: More like hills...sand hills.

JONES: Sand hills. What do you feel the air temperature to be?

RENIER: I feel like I would sweat. I feel sun...very bright.

JONES: Do you have any feeling about where this site is?

RENIER: I want to say 'in the east'. I don't know if it is Asia I'm seeing. I don't know.

JONES: Is there any kind of plant or tree or animal in this place?

RENIER: Very thick, thick leaves. I feel moisture in the plant. I feel thickness in the plant...thick, thick...bloom. Doesn't bloom that much. Must be a desert. Doesn't bloom that often.

JONES: Anything that would indicate location. Bird life? Animal life? What kind of animals lived around here?

RENIER: I see an animal that's more like on the ground...crawling. I feel like it might be some sort of a lizard. I feel it long and bulky with very short legs... animal...long body, short legs.

JONES: You mentioned hair. How long does the hair come down?

RENIER: About to the shoulder. It wasn't black hair. I'm not that good on hair color but I felt light. For a moment I thought I might have picked up on the man who touched it (shard). (Renier picks up a different shard) Oh, Wow! I get a totally different impression. Something strange here. I don't know what this is. I've got a person who has something very high that peaks at the top, but it is very solid. It looks like...this man looks like he might have been a priest...a religious individual at one time. I feel it might have been gold or heavy material in this cap. Alright, this man has more dark hair...dark hair and curls around his hair. Ouch, ouch, ouch. Can I tell you? He had a back-ache. Oh, dear, this is ridiculous. I'm getting a backache...lower back to my right side. I'm getting a lot of pain in my back.

JONES: Why don't you see what he is wearing?

RENIER: A long thing...ouch...long, long robe. Full sleeves. Indentation in the sleeves. It is not straight across on the cuff. I feel either embroidered or again...ouch...felts, riches. Can I do another one?

JONES: Yes, of course.

RENIER: Oh, dear. Everytime I pick up one I get something different. I got a woman this time. I feel her barefoot...and she is in this sandy place. I almost feel like different levels behind her. She is down near the water. I feel like she might be gathering water. I feel she would...I feel she would either put things on her head to carry them or whatever. Woman...

JONES: What does she eat?

RENIER: ...chews something a whole bunch of times. I see her chewing some-thing a great deal of the time. It has to be chewed a lot.

JONES: Do you see it before she puts it in her mouth?

RENIER: It's tough...tough, dried.

JONES: What do most of these people eat?

RENIER: Two basics...I feel like I got meat but it doesn't look fresh meat. I feel more dried meat. I also feel some green stuff around, too...some green stuff that can be...I feel, as I put it in my mouth, there is moisture in the thing. I don't feel like it's cooked...raw and freshness coming...she is picking something up by the water. It's still water. I don't know what she is picking up...I don't know what it is.

JONES: Is she pulling it out of the ground, or is it laying on the ground or is she picking?

RENIER: It is lying on the ground. There is a shore like shallow water, and I saw her picking them up. She seemed to know when to bend down to pick it up.

JONES: Do you see a color to it?

RENIER: I don't know.

JONES: Do these people plant or do they gather or...

RENIER: I don't feel like it's harvest crops. I feel like things that are growing wild or...I feel more wildness; I don't feel like a garden.

JONES: What kind of structure does this woman live in?

RENIER: I got something that is high up. I don't know if it's a ladder that she is going up or if it's steps. No, it's a ladder there, too...as though I could climb...Oh, good, good, good, I'm by this water again. I feel the slope down...the water must be down...of course, it's low...I feel a gentle sloping to this water. Oh, I have some people on horses now. I feel negative toward these people. I don't feel the people on horses live in this area. They are not from that town or that city. I feel destruction with them. I feel fight. I feel the people on the ground are helpless. I don't see any...they don't have any protection. These other people are coming in in force. I feel they are coming in from the...I don't see any men. Just women and children around there. Oh, Dear, I'm bleeding! I'm dark, not black. The features are flat and broad. I don't cry that much. I don't know why I'm not crying.

JONES: What do the people look like who just came in on horses?

RENIER: Dark hair. Dark eyes. I feel bigness in their size. Bodies very strong. Their head is wrapped with something.

JONES: What direction do they come from?

RENIER: They had to travel over a green and more mountainous area to get to where we are. I feel they live in a higher altitude and a cooler climate than we do. I don't know why they are hurting us.

JONES: What do they want?

RENIER: They are killing people, and they are looking for some male. But they are not there. The males are gone. This place is almost deserted now.

JONES: Are the people who are in trouble praying to anyone or anything?

RENIER: No. I don't see that with them. I feel water.

JONES: Let's work with something else (I hand Renier another potsherd).

RENIER: In touching this I feel more like a young boy. Again, the hair. The hair is that cut again (indicates bangs and shoulder length)...straight. A lot of activity around him. I feel there is something on his body. I don't know if it's a scar or if it's painted on. I feel a triangular shape on the side of his body. Like a sidewise triangle.

JONES: What is he wearing?

RENIER: His chest is bare. I feel color. He is not an American Indian, I don't think. He is wearing a brief thing on the lower part of his body, and his legs are bare, too. Most of the time there is nothing on the feet.

JONES: What would he wear for decoration?

RENIER: He has to be older to put the decoration on his face. I felt him gathering and placing things in one spot. I don't know what he is gathering but I felt he put it in a shady spot against part of the structure...shade. I'm not getting that much more.

JONES: Why don't we move on to the next one (artifact)?

RENIER: I feel this piece migrated to this place...or it got carried around a lot. I feel travel with this piece. I feel it traveled. I don't know where it went but I see bigger water.

JONES: Do you get any feeling of how it traveled

RENIER: Yes. It is by ship, or a large boat...maybe that's better...a larger boat. It looks like something you see around the Nile River, or something like that. There is very thick...I don't know if it's a bracelet or if it's a...something to chain, a person to, but I feel very thick on the wrist with no decorations on it. I just feel very plain and very thick and I can see it on one wrist in particular. His right.

JONES: The person who brought this piece?

RENIER: Well, he associated with it or made it...I feel a lot of poison around.

JONES: Did this piece come from the same locale as the men on the horses?

RENIER: I feel difference. With this one I feel colorful sails...not white...not that many sails, maybe one or two. Once they land there is going to be a long journey overland. I feel...ouch...I feel A.D....I feel a "4" involved in the time period. I don't know if it's one-four, or four whatever...several zeros. I feel "east". The horsemen again. I can see his boot. He has a boot on. But I feel lightness in the material. I feel lightness in texture. The horse is light colored. I feel a blanket or something before the saddle. I feel again nice colors. A nice weave or blend of colors. Thick belt, or something thick around him.

JONES: Are there any designs on his clothing that are important?

RENIER: One color. I just get one color.

JONES: Do you hear them speaking?

RENIER: I feel it would be some kind of funny...I see all kinds of twisted things. It is not English, or Italian, or French...it's a funny kind of language.

JONES: Spanish? German?

RENIER: It is something that I don't know...I've never seen before.

JONES: Do you get an origin for the people on the horses?

RENIER:There is a lot of traveling involved with these people. I still feel higher altitude around them, and I see green...green hills and green grass. I see some rock in the hills...heavy stones, thick stones. Might go down to the ocean, but I am higher up. I don't see the water, but I can feel it...feel the ocean.

JONES: And this is the home area of the horsemen?

RENIER: Yes...(long pause)...Here's a book. Thickness to it. And I see that funny writing again.

JONES: What would be in that book?

RENIER: I feel it is words and wisdom that is very secret, very private. I feel words of a private, secret...those funny lines going different ways. Private. secret. These people have a lot of money. The men on the horses. I don't know who they are but I feel more wealth than with those other people (ceramic collection) with the funny buildings or structures.

JONES: Could you draw those structures?

RENIER: (As she speaks she sketches) Let's see, the water is down here (makes rapid oval shape), and the hills up behind. I feel more squareness about it...openness. I feel like they are all together. It is almost like an apartment building but it is not modern. Shade is very important. Ah, there is something over here, something over here that I don't know what it is. Something that is here is very important. Very important. I'm going up. I keep going up. Go up, go up. That's wood (indicates diagonal lines on her sketch)...beams or something.

JONES: What are the walls made of?

RENIER: Cool, cool. Clay, mud, clay. Is it solid? It is not set rock, not stone. It is either clay or...smooth. It is cool inside. I feel shade.

JONES: When you see this from the outside, what color is the structure?

RENIER: I feel almost like a very dull orange, dull like yellow, orange. It is not painted. I feel this one place is important, this place to the right. Something happens over here...something important. Oh, I see a tree. It is bare. It doesn't have a lot of leaves on it. It is just sort of sticking up there bare. I feel like there is a big nest up there.It is not a little nest...big nest. This is higher up, as you go higher...a big bird.

JONES: Do the people think anything about this bird?

RENIER: Oh, it is a bird that likes death. I don't know why. A bird that likes death. I feel like they burned their dead people.

JONES: Do these people feel that something happens after death?

RENIER: They do feel their soul or spirit has to be released. Not that much sorrow. I don't feel that much sorrow. I feel very matter-of-fact...to what we have to do. I see a very old man. Very shirveled up...lots of lines...not very big...maybe 5'2" or 5'3". Again, I feel nakedness. I feel people listened to this old man. He knows he is going to die. Really helps himself die.

JONES: How is he going to do that?

RENIER: I feel like he is going to...the poison again. He is going to take that.

JONES: Do these people tell myths to each other? What would they speak of?

RENIER: They talked about something that came in the sky. Something that was up in the air. It came many, many years before the old man. He tells the younger people that something in the sky came...very big. They felt it was one of the gods. Gods. Not only one god. Gods. They believed that some animal holds the souls or the spirit of other people. An animal that looks more like a dog or a wolf. I see his stomach being cut open.

JONES: Why?

RENIER: He is dangerous...if he is skinny...he is not well-fed. I feel more skinnyness.

JONES: Being with these people...if you wanted to act in a religious manner, what would you do?

RENIER: Act. Birds. Fire is very important. In a house...before the men leave there is a ritual. The men have to leave at certain times. There is a ritual...women...second-rate...I see a woman giving birth. Let me watch. Older woman by her on the floor. It is dirt. There is something I am laying on. Something not going right. Not going right...(long pause)...this boy. Let me see how they do with this boy. I feel like they took a stick, a long thing, and did something to this baby boy. I don't know if it was to the cord or the boy. I felt long stick and I felt hot, and I felt a point on the stick. Very thin. They are making designs on a baby! I see designs being put on the baby. Maybe it's charcoal from the burned end of the stick. They are doing something on the baby.

JONES: Do you see the shape of the designs?

RENIER: I feel like they are fast...they are going fast. It is important to make...there are some circles...some circles, but I feel like a circle on the baby's stomach.

JONES: Why?

RENIER: It might be something to do with the religion. Symbolic for the child. For it's spirit as he enters into the world. I feel this circle is awfully important.

JONES: Does it show up in any other religious context?

RENIER: I don't see any.

JONES: What kind of designs would they associate with their religion?

RENIER: There's that triangle shape...like energy coming out of it, but it is an open triangle. I don't see this part (base of triangle) being closed. Oh, dear Jesus! Somebody's tongue is being cut out. He has done something. I feel punishment.

JONES: How many people lived at this site?

RENIER: Small. Like hundreds, or fifty. Not big, maybe fifty.

JONES: You indicated with one of these pieces that the people associated with it came from somewhere else. I am interested in that.

RENIER: When I pick up this I get travel, and I get that boat again. That same boat...the long, smooth lines of it. It is beautiful. I feel riches. It is not an ugly boat. It is very pretty. I am going on the boat. We are loading. There's food and things being put on the boat. I feel quietness. I don't feel hostility, I feel peace...around it. God, doesn't anybody wear clothes around here? I feel nakedness again. It is warm though. It is hot. The sun is very bright. There is sand. The boat is not that deep. It doesn't go down that far. I feel shallowness in the boat structure. It is wood. Very long planks. I see very defined lines going laterally. Long. I can...

JONES: Where is this boat going?

RENIER: Very peaceful water. I feel peace and quiet. Quiet water. I don't feel waves. I feel quiet water. How can it...oh, it's more by a city or something. It must be an important boat because I feel like people are sending it good wishes, or love. I feel that it is very important where it is going.

JONES: How long will it take to get where it's going?

RENIER: I feel several days at least. There will be one stop before we get to our destination. Our destination is more northeast. We will go up, not down. Up. I feel differentness from these people (artifacts).

JONES: How do these people (artifacts) feel toward the people in the boat?

RENIER: I feel the people in the boat are more privileged, more important. Again, men, no women, are in the boat. Just men.

JONES: You have mentioned several times that the men go off from time to time. Where do they go? What are they doing? What are the women doing?

RENIER: (She begins to raise and lower her hand with a pounding motion). I've got a long…I feel pounding…

JONES: What are they pounding?

RENIER: To make food with. Making meal or mush. They do this all the time. Everybody has to do it.

JONES: Can you see the women putting something underneath the pounder? What does it look like?

RENIER: It is gathered…from the more wooded or the more…not green, not green, not green. More like a brown. Not green. I don't see green. Fire is open. It is shallow. Shallow fire. Can I touch another one?

JONES: Yes.

RENIER: You know, they leave those houses and they go away. They are not going to come back. They've got to go.

JONES: Why?

RENIER: Maybe because of the men on horses. I don't know but they are not going to stay.

JONES: Where are they going to go?

RENIER: More north. Higher up too. It is going to be cooler up there. Not as hot, and not as dry.

JONES: Try to move forward in time with these people. They have left their houses and they have moved up…

RENIER: First a few, then more later. I feel they are a lone people. I don't feel sociable. I feel they are good with their own people, but they don't want to socialize with other people. They would hide or move up…(tape ends)…I keep feeling like these things related to two different locales. I felt like one was more in a very dry, hot climate…very dusty…almost barren. And then when I would go to the boat I would see more green, more lushness. I would feel more pretty things. I don't know if I am speaking of two different things or if they are somehow the same. I don't know. The people on the boat were the ones who had that high hat on. It is more flat on the top. I felt it had a lot of designs on it. The man had a beard, and I could see the curly dark hair coming out. This man's beard seemed very sinister looking. I'm not a good artist. I could tell it was curly hair, and he is the one who had the robe. The sleeve was like this (drawing)…not straight across. It just seemed to go up here. He had sandals. I could…but those other ones (artifacts) didn't have much clothes on. I could just keep seeing nakedness.

JONES: With these people (artifacts) do you feel the presence of metal?

RENIER: (Nods her head in a negative gesture.)

JONES: What about domestic animals?

RENIER: Maybe they had dogs. I wanted to see a cow but I couldn't.

JONES: Did they make baskets?

RENIER: I feel more with clay, but that might be because I'm touching it. I think wood was scarce. Very little wood. That one shot I keep getting of the houses going upward. I didn't see a lot of vegetation around. I didn't see much.

JONES: What about when you talked about the little clothing that they did wear, what was the material? What was it made of?

RENIER: It was something that they could sort of drape and tie, drape and hang.

JONES: To these people, what would be an extremely precious commodity?

RENIER: Water. Water is very important. I feel sharp things hanging on a necklace. I feel this group being more peaceful too. I feel them at peace. I don't know why I'm feeling peace around them. I don't know about these horse people…I don't know if I'm getting two different stories.

JONES: **What if someone is giving a friend a gift...these people** (artifacts) **...what would they give?**

RENIER: Flat, flat. I don't know. I want to smile. I know they are trying to show me something, but I'm not picking it up. First of all, they are small people. I feel smallness in their structure. Smaller than five feet. I almost feel like I would have to bend when I walk into their houses. I feel like a giant. Oh, they are rubbing something on my feet. Why the hell are they rubbing something on my feet?

JONES: **Imagine that it is a very fancy occasion. You are going to be with a bunch of these people to celebrate some good event. What would you wear if you were going to dress in your finest?**

RENIER: I feel a berry. A purple or a blue. I can't see it. Food is very important. I just don't see a lot of riches. I don't see gold or silver. I don't see things like that. I just feel...

JONES: **How long would those people have been at that site?**

RENIER: I keep getting fours whenever I pick this stuff up. Fourteen. Four hundred. I'm so sorry. I'm not answering your question. I feel a terrible storm. I feel mud sliding...sliding land, sliding buildings. I feel an unnatural disaster. I feel sliding. I feel crumbling.

JONES: **This sliding and crumbling, is that on this site** (Indicates artifacts)?

RENIER: Yes. The one we have been looking at.

JONES: **Before or after the men on horses?**

RENIER: After. I don't see people there. It's funny. I see belongings but I don't see people there during the sliding. There was a land slide and destruction. An earthquake and water. I don't know. I just feel...trembling. I felt they knew it was coming.

JONES: **Did they know it collectively, or...**

RENIER: I don't know. I didn't see any people. I didn't see them running around and screaming. The belongings...none of them personal. Things that they couldn't carry.

JONES: **How much time before the disaster did the people leave?**

RENIER: More like within days or weeks. I keep wondering where the men were. That bothers me. Bracelets. No, they are slaves. They weren't black. I don't see them as black.

JONES: **The men may have been taken?**

RENIER: Yes. This old woman says not to worry so much. The men go off all the time. They may go up to the higher ground to hunt, or to get things that they can't get at home. She says they go all the time. That I shouldn't worry. They come back. Many things to be done while they are gone.

JONES: **How long is it before the men come back?**

RENIER: Many weeks. Long periods of time that they are gone because they have to travel so far...to higher ground.

JONES: **When they return, do they bring anything with them that they didn't have when they left?**

RENIER: I keep feeling more with meat.

JONES: **What do the women do when the men are gone?**

RENIER: I see a lot of things to do around water. It is very sloping. Preparing and storing some strange grain. Mashing. They have either something they chew...they chew it and I feel like it sort of relaxes them. Maybe like some sort of a dope. What we might consider a dope. But I feel like they chew it. It is what I tasted before. I don't know why but I want to laugh. It just feels so good. I feel very relaxed. I feel very good. With the older women I feel some weight on them. Again, short men. Darkness with them. She has a very loose fitting thing. Animal skins. Oh, I see why they are doing that. They are going toward a colder climate.

JONES: **Do people still live at this site?**

RENIER: Ah, I'm picking up a volcano. This piece (touches a piece of copal) ...this piece has been hot.

JONES: Are there people living at this site today?

RENIER: It is not like it was. I feel a city or a town about twenty-five miles away...toward the south...I don't feel...I don't feel it close by. At least twenty-five to thirty miles away.

JONES: Do you have any feelings about the characteristics of this city?

RENIER: I feel it to be very flat-roofed buildings. I feel white. I feel more like a kind of Mediterranean-type of heat. White. They're modern. Again I feel the desert and very lush growth. I feel water is important although there is a large body of water near them. The sun goes down very quickly there.

JONES: Is there much seasonal variation?

RENIER: Except for the wind...It would be cold occasionally but I don't see snow. I feel mostly heat.

JONES: I want to ask you about the location again?

RENIER: I just want to say 'east'. I don't feel like it is in the United States.

JONES: Do you have to cross an ocean out of this country?

RENIER: That would be one way. But I feel you could get there by land, or you could at one time. I feel the land had changed since this time when the people were on this site. Some strange relationship about the land being replaced by water, or water by land.

JONES: At the time these people were alive and making these things, what kinds of things were going on in other parts of the world?

RENIER: It was so many years ago. I feel it was very hard to get to this place, too. I don't think it would be easy to find this place. Let's see...in Europe at this time I feel boats with sails that sort of remind me of Columbus. Europe was more or less in a dark state or dark ages.

JONES: We are about finished now. Is there any last observation you would like to make about these people?

RENIER: I don't think they had any writing...per se. I felt mostly that everything was verbal.

JONES: If these people were making a religious appeal of great importance, how would they do it?

RENIER: Sacrifice...to the different gods.

JONES: Do you feel any characteristics of these entities?

RENIER: They sacrificed to the gods to bring luck to the hunters, to have food. I see a very big pit, very deep. I don't know if I am on the edge of a volcano or not, but it could be. It had a very wide opening, very, very big, and very, very wide.

JONES: How many feet?

RENIER: Fifty feet at least. Very big.

MAYAN STONES. BLIND READING BY ALBERT BOWES.

[See Photo VII-13]

BOWES: I keep picking up something...someone who would have worn grass ...or something hanging from their legs.

JONES: These pieces are like rubble or rock from three different sites which are geographically and culturally related. Three sites are within ten or twenty miles of each other. Same culture.

BOWES: And it's gravel?!

JONES: Let's just lay back and see what we can see.

BOWES: (Stone # A-21) I already pick-up someting about it. The strongest impression is that I kept picking up something about a high cliff, and I kept picking up something about a well, or like a sink hole, or something that goes down in the water. I kept feeling water way down below. I kept picking up something about caves, or like somebody hiding something in holes, like little cubby-holes. Could have been round holes. I would say this associated with Indians (Stone #A-21), or someplace where somebody lived. I kept going north. I kept picking up a coastal area, but then I keep...I keep seeing coastal areas, but then it says "no." Coastal area, then "no." I would feel there is water underground in this area. I kept picking up somebody picking up a hatchet, or picking up like a tomahawk, but very crude. Like a big round river rock on a stick and he held it up like this (above his head). I kept feeling it round.

JONES: **Could you draw this for me?**

BOWES: Yes. (draws) I felt the wood was like birch. Could have been grey or like birch. These people were very primitive. This thing could have been swung. This stone was grey. I don't know if these stones were thrown down on an animal, like a mastodon, or some animal, but I kept feeling "down below." I kept feeling a long thing like this, a thing like ivory, or a long piece of stone, or bone, or rib of something, or like a tusk of something. I kept feeling "under ground in caves". I kept feeling that this (touches stones) was rubble and there was piles of rock there, and they were digging in the rock. I picked up North Carolina, but I would say south of there. I would say it was a place with underground limestone caves with water. I kept getting a smell of sulphur. The strongest feeling is...I would say there is much more in the mud. If there is grey mud there, there is a lot of artifacts, or something that might have settled down to stone. Like—if there was clay there, the artifacts, tools and things may have settled down into bedrock. Like a lot of stones and they would have to put a well-point system in there to take the water out. After I picked up this (stone A-21) I get a dry countryside. I would feel that...I don't get Florida, but I get Texas or south...going south..southern part of the United States. I really don't get much from rocks. I felt whoever...I felt piles of stones. I would say there was a structure near there but it would have been abandoned. I felt a lot of dust. I feel the structure was very low, and the doorway was very low, and there was no top on it. Like it may have been underneath a cave, or like this (draws), but there may have been a roof or wood. I felt that all that was left was just the structure. Like the walls were very low. Like white stone down low.

JONES: **What did the people look like who associated with these rocks?**

BOWES: I feel big round faces. I picked that up very, very...pronounced. Real round face, almost like Japanese, or Oriental, but I felt real round looking, and real kind of fatty face with kind of slit looking eyes. I would say they may have traveled previously by boat. I keep seeing them using ropes or pulling something.

JONES: **What do you feel about body decoration?**

BOWES: I don't know if there was something like armor, or something hanging, but I would feel that they would have had straps. I felt almost like straps that protected them or something hanging. I felt a lot of leather. Very round face and very dark skin. I feel whoever was doing that was working and there may have been someone else there dictating. I don't know if it was Spanish people, but I would say there could have been armor or something on them. I see them carrying things and...I just keep seeing "piles of stone"... that were dug out of a cave or a hole.

JONES: **What does their hair look like?**

BOWES: I felt short, cropped. Not that long.

JONES: **What color was the hair?**

BOWES: I felt black. Indian looking people, or Oriental looking...people. I can't say.

JONES: **What did these people eat?**

BOWES: I would say there could have been slaves involved. I would say they could have broken something...I don't know if they ate fish, but I felt berries and I see them breaking something and taking something out...I don't know if it's bones, but I see them taking something out of the middle of bones. I don't see them growing things—right where that was at—somewhere else, they may have grown things. I feel that that (A-21) is just leftovers, like thrown in piles ...residue. Not very valuable to me. I would feel these people were in a hurry to achieve something, and they may have been looking for something.

JONES: What impressions do you pick up about structures?

BOWES: The only thing I picked up was like that (draws). This could be wood, or something that is braced. I would say that there is something in caves or something in stone. These could have been very primitive people. The feeling I picked up was like people...primitive people...were being used either to work or that they were very primitive people...like they may have eaten things like very primitive animals. Again I am picking up mastodons, or old, things.

JONES: What do you feel the environment of A-21 was like?

BOWES: Everytime I pick this up, I pick up a cliff or a hole, or something down in the ground, but that's all I pick up.

JONES: What about A-13? (refers to other artifact)

BOWES: I would feel this one was nearer the water. I keep feeling a stream or someplace where people were digging in the ground. That (A-21) was where there was a cliff or a big hole, ledges, or cliff.

JONES: With Stone A-13 you said "digging in the ground." What is that all about?

BOWES: I would feel they were digging to extract something that they were using for building materials or they were using it to build something.

JONES: This one is Stone A-14.

BOWES: I feel a different feeling with this. I feel a different environment. I feel more like trees or more like where they were carrying wood or logs.

JONES: This one is A-B.

BOWES: I see someone with problems with their teeth or problems with their mouth. I would say that whatever these people were eating they did a lot of chewing because their teeth was worn down. I see them hanging something up in a tree. I may not be doing too well with these things but I don't feel these stones were handled that much.

JONES: This one is A-307.

BOWES: I felt a landslide or someone was buried...like things were falling on them. I keep seeing people cussing or mad, or like they were in a hurry, and they were trying to get people to uncover something, like grave diggers...or grave robbers.

JONES: This is A-5.

BOWES: I pick up another environment. I kept feeling "higher". Even higher than A-21. I don't have much feeling with this. I can't feel the feeling of the people. I picked up a skirt affair.

JONES: What is the religious inclination of these people?

BOWES: They may have had an established religion or idea. I would say they talked about the skies or weather, and I felt it was part of their religion. I would feel that they had an association with water, or when it rained, or weather. I would say there was, not like a Christian religion, but some sort of certain religion that was pushed on them by another group. I kept seeing a very heavy-set person who was very dark skinned. I see him being a leader or someone who they felt was almost like a god. I feel like they actually worshipped other people, like they may have worshipped the leader of this group after...like a king or a god. The biggest man. I felt it was very dark skinned. Almost like a black man, but not quite. I keep feeling as though he lived in the mountains or worshipped in the mountains. He lived in the mountains...or up high.

JONES: What did the people feel the characteristics of this man were?

BOWES: I felt a man like this (raises his arm to shoulder-height, extends arms horizontally with forearms pointing straight up)...his arms like pipes or out like this. I see them putting this man aside from everyone else. They may not have had a crucifix, but they had some sort of thing that stuck in the ground and they may have hung a person on it or there was something in the air. Almost like when they would put two logs or sticks together and then they go like this (apart) and pulled their arms off. I just kept picking up he was like this (same posture as described above).

JONES: Did this man...

BOWES: I keep seeing him doing like this (above posture) to the sky and talking to the weather, or to the sky. I would say that they really felt he had results. I keep picking up forests and stones or jungles and stones. Great differences. Not like Florida...I felt like 'jungle and stones,' and like 'high and low'...ground. I felt like he would go to the mountains, like that was where he was worshipped, or like going up high. It may not have been so much a mountain, but there may have been something built that was like a hill, but I felt "up high".

JONES: Do you get anything more about that thing? I don't understand.

BOWES: I don't know if it was like a pyramid, or like a stone pile, but I kept picking up them possibly carrying something in a basket or something like in turtle shells or something round and I see them dumping stones. I see a lot of dust...lot of dust. I kept picking up that they would go up high again. In some areas there was much high area, but I just keep picking up 'high'. Again, I can't relate that well to this stuff because it is so impersonal to me. I keep seeing them carrying like oil in the lamps like on a pole. I felt like they were going to punish someone. In my way of seeing it, I felt they were going to punish someone. They would get all frenzied...they could have had purple scars on their body.

JONES: Was there any feeling of enemies in their environment?

BOWES: I would say they were concerned about people from another area... that brought disease once before. They may have been superstitiously afraid of these people because they kept saying they were like pygmies or short people because they came from the jungle...they came from what they called 'a wild place'...where they wouldn't go. I felt they were afraid of the disease they could bring.

JONES: Do you feel from what direction these people came?

BOWES: I would say from the south...southwest. I don't pick up Florida now...when you ask about direction. I pick up another area...could even be South America, or I feel different. I didn't feel Florida. I see a peninsula. I feel stuck in the water. Cliffs near the water.

JONES: What kinds of symbols were important to these people?

BOWES: I pick up the old symbol of a bird again, and I picked that up once before and I pick it up again, and I don't understand it.

JONES: Was there any color associated with these birds?

BOWES: I felt red.

JONES: What did these birds mean?

BOWES: Like ethnic groups, or groups of people that belonged to a certain group. Both had to do with something that was flying.

JONES: What was their notion of...

BOWES: I would say if someone seen their religious ceremony or snooped on it in secret they may have blinded them...because I see them punching their eyes. I felt cactus or like a swampy type cactus being punched in their eyes.

JONES: What are these people's attitudes about death?

BOWES: I would say that they think when a person dies they fall into a dark pit, and the only way they can revive them is to awaken their body by carrying it, or making a ceremony, or praying over it, or making a lot of noise, especially at night. They may carry the body and make a lot of noise, like a lot of wood going 'tat, tat, tat, tat, tat.' They were trying to revive the person. Carrying the body and making a lot of noise. They would carry it and throw it in a fire or throw it in something...and this is what this fire is about. I would feel they feel they are going to purify the body, or purify the soul in the sense that they don't want it to go into darkness, but they want to awaken it and then it would go and fly...like birds would fly.

JONES: Do they have an afterlife idea?

BOWES: Yes. Yes.

JONES: What do they feel the afterlife would be like?

BOWES: Birds. I would say birds. If you were birds you would be flying. If you were ugliness you would be insects or snakes, or things close to the ground.

JONES: Which of these pieces has the strongest vibration to you?

BOWES: This one right here did (A-21). This had very strong emotional or spiritual feeling (A-5).

JONES: When you say emotional or spiritual...

BOWES: I felt spiritual feelings in the sense of it being in an unusual or spiritual place. Now it could be a place of religion.

JONES: How would these people relate to children?

BOWES: I would say they could put a blindfold on them and lead them somewhere. I would say children were separated from religion up to a certain age. Children were like a resource to them, but not something...like a tree when it began to bloom, or began to produce fruit, then it was valuable. They may have just left children with a woman or with a man or with old people, but I felt 'children and old people'. They could have beheaded a girl, or taken a virgin, or taken someone's head off, but I felt it was a young child. Especially if it was like an albino child, or someone very light skinned. I felt they were afraid of that. Felt people with dark skin had power.

JONES: What was the single most important religious ceremony in which these people would become involved?

BOWES: I would say it was something on top of this mountain or hill, and it could be like a cross or like something sticking up in the air. I kept feeling like they would climb up this mountain, or they would climb up this hill, or they would climb up this thing. They would be like climbing out of the water. Again, I kept seeing something in the ground, or hole, caves, or something. I felt they came out of there and then up on top of the hill. I would say it was a certain time of the moon, or like it was full moon or at a special time of the season. And I would say it was religious significance to animals or food, and to them it was the most important thing because of the value of eating. Again, they may have actually looked at the stars, or moon, or the sky. I would say that food was diminishing. Again, if this was like Florida, and I didn't feel so much Florida, but I felt it was near water. I feel two groups of people who went near the water and then a group of people who stayed behind and could have died of the illness. But I feel the ones who went toward the water continued... continued their life. But the ones who stayed just died out. I kept feeling an illness that caused their body to get very skinny. Problems with teeth again. I'm getting very tired now.

JONES: O.K. Let me ask you a series of short questions. Do you feel they had domestic animals?

BOWES: I felt like sheep or an animal that had long hair. Could have been like a pig. I felt they caught it and tied it by its back legs. It could have been like a sheep or a pig, or an animal with long fur on its body...on its back especially. I picked up 'goat' to start with.

JONES: **Did these people ever see or interact with Caucasian people?**

BOWES: I would say there was a chance of it, but only at the last of when these people were living. I would say that they could be afraid or be very unsettled with people with light skin.

JONES: **Did these people write their language or have an unwritten language?**

BOWES: I would say they had not a written language but sort of a symbolic thing that were added together. Now I picked up a tablet with writing on it so I would say they had something like a written language.

JONES: **About what time did these people live here** (touches artifacts)?

BOWES: I picked up '14', or '400' or '14,000' or '14-something'. I picked up people were migrating from South America to the north, and something was happening in Italy. A change in "owners" I say, but I don't know what it means. At the time these people were alive, the people in power were changing in Italy, or the Mediterranean Sea at that time.

JONES: **Did these people know how to weave cloth?**

BOWES: I would say leather, but that's all I picked up.

JONES: **Did these people use or know how to make metal?**

BOWES: I didn't see that. I would say they hung things that were made of... like something that was other than what they would find in nature. I don't know what that means.

JONES: **Did these people have or ever see firearms?**

BOWES: There was a possibility of them finding firearms or something that exploded, or made a bright fire, like a match. If they seen a gun, the gun was like this...very primitive gun with a wick on it. But I picked up that just instantly. Could have been something under here, like a big lever (indicates area around "trigger"). I felt the stock of the gun was vey big. Very big. They could find a lot more about these people in caves or...like sink holes...I would feel there is a lot of evidence in sink holes. I would say that they (archeologists) are missing out on the most valuable things. There could be like a hole and down below is water. And below that is grey sand or clay, and if they took a pump and took that out of there, used well-points, they could get numerous...I felt the layers were like this...like a sink hole down in the bottom there is a layer of real soft mud, and clay, grey clay...and then down below is silt and sand and dirt and then down here there is rock (he is going down the stratigraphy), and then gravel and just above the gravel is all kinds of artifacts.

JONES: **What kinds of things?**

BOWES: Jewels. Pottery. Things. This (top) could be real sharp or almost closed in, with just a little opening showing, or it could be like sunken in. It settled in one place. Does that make any sense? There is just much more stuff down there.

JONES: **You have mentioned "primitive". What do you mean?**

BOWES: I felt like "cave men". Then the more questions you asked the more I felt I was coming forward in time. I felt these people were down in where water comes out...down inside them caves. The water was real low down there ...very primitive. That's what I picked up at the start, and then I went up in time.

MAYAN STONES: BLIND READING BY DIANE DAVIS

DAVIS: I'm picking up water and mountains. A large body of water, and a large...wooded...mountains.

JONES: **What kind of water, woods, and mountains?**

DAVIS: Not a lot of growth, but sparser than say, North Carolina. It wasn't desert.

JONES: Do you want to see the first one now?

DAVIS: Yes.

JONES: This is A-13.

DAVIS: The first impression I get is like of a colonial period. The woman is wearing a long dress, tied at the waist, and there is an apron. She is standing behind a large pot, and she is stirring it. I got the feeling of civil war, and so... something about this area that there was one point...at one point a war or some form of battle. She is very strong.

JONES: Did you say "civil war" or "*The* Civil War"?

DAVIS: I just get "civil war". I feel confused. I want to get into Indians, but I feel a colonial period. I see a man with a musket. I am very drawn to say that there is a large body of water to the north...like a big lake. I see something almost like Lake Erie. It is like that. I see a man with a three-cornered hat on, and I see white stockings and shoes and a musket in his hand. Something about fiber to be woven...I get spinning wheel and fiber.

JONES: Would you like to try another one? Do you feel a problem with this one (A-13)?

DAVIS: No. It's just that I keep wanting to get into Indians.

JONES: What about if I ask about an important religious symbol in the minds of these people?

DAVIS: O.K. I just got a circle and I got the word "tree" and I feel a design in a little circle that was like a tree. I'm suddenly around big rocks. I'm with a male. I feel an Indian. I feel him on these rocks and there is some connection with this community. (A-13).

JONES: What is the nature of the connection? Positive? Negative?

DAVIS: The idea of the French and Indian War fluttered in and then I said, "No." Let's clear this all out. Let's see. I am with this Indian on this rock and he has lost his footing. He is small, slender. I don't get any description about him, but I sense that he was carrying something on him that breaks. It was a gourd or clay or made by hand and it was broken, and bits of it were all over. I am very aware of broken pieces all beneath these rocks. I am on this place of land and I see this circular thing, and I get these broken bits of stone.

JONES: Circular thing?

DAVIS: Yeah, with the design that looks like a tree, but it is not a tree.

JONES: Can you draw it?

DAVIS: (draws) Broken bits around here...either rocks or broken pieces of clay, and something is in there that sparkles. There is something in there... shells. Something that creates sparkles of some sort, or color reflections.

JONES: Excuse me. You picked up a colonial woman and then an Indian. When you said "their" who were you picking up?

DAVIS: What was interesting was that I got this colonial group and I got...what is it? a hexagram? You know with the Pennsylvania Dutch? I got a picture of that and then it shifted and I saw this Indian and the wood "tree" and this round thing and these patterns, but I couldn't see a clearly defined tree in the circle.

JONES: What are these points?

DAVIS: Here I am with the mountains and the water. And now I'm feeling pine trees, but I...but there's...still not woodsy...you know, thick. They are like sparse.

JONES: What does the climate feel like?

DAVIS: Cool. It is not real cold there. I don't see snow, but I get a real crisp effect, like in the fall. I see pine needles, and I see green. I don't feel like they are getting ready to die away like in the fall. But I do see green, and again, there's the water.

JONES: Is there some significance to that, other than environmental description. It seems you have mentioned that about four times.

DAVIS: I feel a log cabin and I come back to these colonial people, and I see them close to the water, close to these three points. The lake I was describing was kind of like that. I feel in an old cabin, or something, and I'm not real close to the water, but I'm not far away either...in footage. There are mountains or hills behind the house, and an occasional pine tree right around the house but the trees are tall.

JONES: Do you want to go on to another piece?

DAVIS: Yes.

JONES: This is A-21.

DAVIS: I got the feeling that these colonial people moved to this place because of a war, or revolution of some sort, and that they were killed. I see Indians sneaking up on a house, and because of something done to the land. I feel them being eliminated.

JONES: Because something was done to the land?

DAVIS: Yeah. They were trespassers at that point...but they didn't know it. It was done innocently, and yet there was no way of communicating and there was a fear of the Indians. They had to eliminate them. They are cutting trees. Cutting trees.

JONES: They? The colonists?

DAVIS: Yes. Because of this symbol, that was also against their beliefs. Because they weren't giving back life, they were taking it.

JONES: What about population? How many people were involved?

DAVIS: I see this couple and a small boy, about six or seven, and that's it. I don't see any...I saw a young girl coming out of the barn...but the barn wasn't like a barn you would have today.

JONES: What did these people eat?

DAVIS: Indians or colonists?

DAVIS: "Musk". What's musk?

JONES: Animal scent, I guess you would say.

DAVIS: Is musk also an animal?

JONES: Musk-ox?

DAVIS: I got the word "musk", and also something else that starts with an "m". I don't know how to pronounce it "Ma-"...(she tries to pronounce word).

JONES: Let's try something different...the people associated with this stuff. How long have they been there?

DAVIS: Two hundred years. I'm in the 1700s...I get 1778. Then I feel a change and suddenly the feeling of Louisiana/Missouri. I get 'connection' then I get 'French' then I get 'Indian'...the 'colonist'. I'm suddenly with a man who is old and his hair is long. I feel an Indian old man. A wise person. Something hanging around his neck with something sharp coming off of it, and then a feather every so often. I feel this was some sort of adornment that was given to him because of his wisdom, his knowledge...I get the word 'counsel'. I feel that his presence with this group of people is well-known. He was looked upon...

JONES: What did these people consider this man's method of knowledge, or source of knowledge?

DAVIS: Can I ask you some questions about this?

JONES: I don't know much and I can't answer certain questions, but go ahead and ask if you would feel better?

DAVIS: Is this an area that would have an overlap of history? A lot of history?

JONES: Any spot on earth would.

DAVIS: American history? Am I allowed to ask you that.

JONES: I can't comment one way or the other about location or time.

DAVIS: Well I just got something about the cavalry...on top of these Indians (she makes a negative gesture and stops).

JONES: Are you having difficulty with these things?

DAVIS: Yes, because I can't get validation and I am rusty. I can't get that feeling of "Yeah, go ahead, you are right on." And it's been so long since I done this kind of thing. I am picking up these different phases and I don't feel necessarily that anything I have said is wrong.

JONES: Well, let's try to go to another piece.

DAVIS: I just want to jump into an Indian culture and sit there.

JONES: I guess the only thing to say is trust whatever image you are getting. I can't help you.

DAVIS: Yeah, that's what I am trying to do, but like now, I just got the cavalry...men on horses, and I see a blue uniform and I see the gold braid around the hat, and the tassles on the end of it and stuff. That comes in with the Indians. I feel the overlap and that's why I asked about the period of history.

JONES: I could say—because it would be true for anywhere—Yes, a historical overlap. Let's go on to A-14.

DAVIS: I see an outline of a man's face. The way I got into this was, I said, "O.K. I'm going to decide to know," and I saw a bird and the bird was flying over the village and in the village there were...like tipis, but they weren't tipis. They were some sort of protective cloth built on natural foundations, like trees and bushes. Then I saw this man's profile, and I come back to this man I mentioned earlier with the long grey hair, and something around his waist that is thick, like a fur piece, or a belt or a pelt or something and it's got things hanging from it. I get the feeling of warmth with this man...wisdom comes out strongly.

JONES: If you ask this man where his wisdom came from, what would he tell you?

DAVIS: I get 'the great spirit' and I get the feeling of 'all nature.' There is a strong identity with fire and water. A very strong feeling of the elements, and especially fire. He would look into the fire. The fire was his focal point of concentration...to receive his guidance. There was a great deal of preparation that went into the fire, not only in the building of it, but the actually working and chanting...low chanting, and typical movements all the while he is building the fire. There is a feeling of real familiarity with the area he is working in, like he has lived there all his life. He has a real strong desire for the children...I feel that some of the children have been killed. When I say killed, I feel that there has been a natural disaster, as well as something to do with animals like wild animals, or animals that maybe...they try to...

JONES: Animals they try to...?

DAVIS: ...capture or take in. I get this feeling like a wild boar and again I come back to this...it's not a wild boar. It's like a...it's a small animal that starts with "m". I see the fangs of a boar, or the teeth, but I'm not clear (she indicates the "fangs" going straight down from the upper front portion of the mouth)...I'm questioning if this boar is...a boar I get 'starts with mos-'' or "ma-'' something.

JONES: It is interesting. Boars' teeth tend in time to curve. You were moving your hand straight down.

DAVIS: Boar doesn't sound right to me, but it is a wild animal...I don't feel this animal is in existence now. Almost like it either has changed somehow or ...o.k., it is a small brown animal that would be the size of a little pig, and I get "pig" which makes me wonder if it isn't associated in that family...like a wild pig, or something of that structure, because the body is big and cumbersome, and there is a smallness in the legs. Looks like a boar but it isn't a boar, but with that kind of structure to the body. I see a snout kind of thing on it. The fangs aren't real long. They would hang an inch below their lip...mouth. I see the gum line.

JONES: Why was this particular animal important?

DAVIS: I felt these were one of the types of animals that would be in the wooded area. It would thrive near swamp water, or water that was in a swampy area where there were heavy trees...dampness. There was something about the dampness. I feel these animals are nearly extinct if it isn't already...but I feel the children would see these and try to capture them or kill them. I don't feel their meat was particularly savory but I feel it was a form of meat at the times when they needed it. Plus they had to kill them because they would just charge or attack. They were not an animal that would run. They would charge. They...

JONES: What would this group consider the most valuable resource? What would worry them to no end to not have...crucial and key to their survival?

DAVIS: The first word to come to mind was "water". I wasn't sure what that meant. Then I got the feeling of dampness and that confused me a little bit. What I felt was it wasn't so much the water as it was the sunshine, the warmth and the air. Something about the air...because a lot of water around there was stagnant. That was one of the things I was talking about in terms of the natural killing off of some of the children. They did not know protection from stagnant water.

JONES: What do you mean by protection from stagnant water?

DAVIS: Yes. In other words, a knowledge of how to determine if their water was stagnant. I get a feeling of a ritual performed at about the age of twelve, when I see these little boys sent off, and that was when it happened. I feel like a group of five and they all went off in different directions but they were by themselves, and it was like a ritual for them to go off and come back after they spent so much time out...and producing something or bringing in an animal, or hunting trophy, things. There was some of them that hit upon this animal and there was some of them that hit upon this water. This water was not far away, and the water had not always been stagnant. This group of people was small. I feel this old man's concern with these young warriors—or boys—because the group was so small that they were needed very much by the group. It was also during a time of some sort of battle or conflict.

JONES: Who were their enemies?

DAVIS: I get 'other Indians'. Another group. It was something to do about the land.

JONES: Something to do about the land?

DAVIS: Just as I said that I saw cavalry again coming in...horses. I see someone pointing 'go,' and these people are walking or being marched away. I feel there was some sort of strife that took place or some period of time that was very stressful between two different groups of Indians, and then I felt that shifted and they were not...or later they were forced to leave and confined to a certain area.

JONES: What would these people consider a fun game?

DAVIS: Something to do with throwing stones, and there was a circle... Throwing...stones within a circle. Then I see marks almost like counting marks...something like little lines and they throw the stones between the lines. I feel a humor to these people that is kind of interesting. I can't really touch it. I feel it. It is more joyfulness than I have known with some of the things I touched with you before. Not that they had so much joy around them but their outlook was not one that was...totally fearsome.

JONES: What was their attitude concerning death?

DAVIS: Just as you said that, I saw a whole thing with lots of ghosts. I feel they would stay with the body. Somebody guarded the body while the person went out of the body. They let the body sit. It was up on a high place, and it went through a decaying process, and was not buried. At least it was not buried for a few days.

JONES: Did they have any notions of an afterlife?

DAVIS: They have gone back to the great spirit. They have gone back to...I get the words 'white eagle'. Gone back to fly like an eagle. That's the bird I saw before. I feel they were in an area where there would be white eagles. They looked on death as a beginning, like a chance to go back. Really a fairly progressive philosophy in terms of what we would think of now, as people are exploring the mind and afterlife...even though there were a lot of primitive kinds of things having to do with the practice of healing, the family, and some of those structures, but this thing about afterlife was pretty progressive in our sense. I feel something was formally done in terms of the body, or the spirit...or what they could call the spirit. It's like a ghost. The image is very strong. They would leave the body out so they could be exposed to this association. Then they were honored.

JONES: You said they leave the body out. What does that look like?

DAVIS: I see a platform thing like in the movies, except this is on a rock. Remember those rocks I was talking about? Well, this is with those rocks. That boy was there guarding somebody and that's when he dropped and broke whatever he had. Down below the rocks...this circle; and I saw this chipped stuff and it might have been just the way these rocks were formed...down around there...little pieces of stuff. It was like shell and things and pieces of clay. I wasn't quite sure of the substance, it was that kind of look to it.

JONES: What is the predominant feeling of color?

DAVIS: White and red—like that shell luminescence. It was here, around the edge of this circle. When you asked about the religion I felt that this symbol is somehow used with the death process, or was looked upon about life. I feel like "tree of life". This young fellow I felt was watching over someone's body. It was like a relatively high place, but it wasn't the highest point of these rocks. There was like a platform of some sort and it wasn't very wide...maybe three feet wide and six feet long. They weren't that tall. Short. The platform was between six and seven feet long because it allowed for room for walking around the body. Then I see a skin or a cloth laid over the body. I see something burned around the body like...a torch, or something to light the way home.

JONES: Can you see this body really clearly now?

DAVIS: No. The body is sort of...represented.

JONES: You mentioned your feeling about their stature. Do you have any feelings about facial features?

DAVIS: Strong skin lines. Strong wrinkle marks, like leather. Very weathered people. I have the old man again and he has some scars but there were marked. They were identification marks of some sort, or they weren't...they were identification marks. He had some on his body. I am touching the right shoulder and then along the shoulder blade. It was like...they were identification marks from some sort of ritual or something to do with his position. And then I got the word 'bleeding' as though at one point there is something to do with bleeding...bleeding to purify the soul, and where the body is cut. I feel that could possibly be the one on the shoulder. That one is not clear to me. I feel the process of purification. Bleed out the evil spirits and purify and it was done when he was very young because the scar is very strong, and the tissue is well mended overtime.

JONES: What was the most common and feared natural disaster that could come upon them?

DAVIS: Again I get 'water'.

JONES: Natural disaster?

DAVIS: I know, but I get "water"...Stagnant water.

JONES: This is A-15.

DAVIS: Reminds me of an arrow blade.

JONES: What is the environment of this piece?

DAVIS: I'm looking up at...more rocks. I am removed from those other rocks though I am looking up at them. I am used for...My first impression is someone cleaning a fish. Almost like a knife or...like scraping...a knife. I see a lot of rain and I'm back to the natural disaster...the water. I felt a lot of rain and wind, but I didn't feel hurricane or anything like that. I just felt storm and water. I feel a fear or what would happen to the natural water supply and a fear of a natural disaster concerning rain or water, and I sense again a large body of water that was nearby and the fact that I am around what looks like a steep incline or a mountain or a cliff or something that's not huge, like the Grand Canyon, or anything, but it's...I mean I can see the top of it if I stand and face it. It's not so over powering that I have to step from it to see it. It's...I feel there was a lot of concern over that and a lot of worry...

JONES: What...with the rocks...or...

DAVIS: Water. I get a feeling of other Indians or other groups coming to meet here. Like I just saw inside...underneath like a canopy type set-up that was made with wood sticks and like a canopy top, and something that was almost like woven, maybe like branches that were woven very tightly—very tightly. These people sitting underneath it...but many of them are strangers and they are not...with any group of people who live in this area.

JONES: What are they doing there?

DAVIS: They are talking about this trouble. Between these groups. There is concern over land. There is concern over...I want to say 'white face'...like the soldiers is...of some feeling of...interference by other types of people.

JONES: Can you see if these different groups can talk to each other?

DAVIS: They communicate. I see somebody like drawing in the ...ground.

JONES: Do the people of these different groups ever talk to each other?

DAVIS: They communicate, but I see somebody like drawing on the ground, or floor of this place, and that was one of the ways that they communicated. They really weren't talking a lot anyway. They are sitting together around a fire. The fire is smoky. It's not...it's not burning...it's like...smoky burn. There is some smoke that is also important to the group.

JONES: These men you see sitting and communicating, what would be on their persons? Things they would be proud of?

DAVIS: One man has a beautiful skin, like a deer skin that is fawn colored, and it's got...that was one of these things I was drawn to. It is smooth and wraps around his shoulders and it's like a buck or something. It's real pretty, and it has a large white spot on it and I felt that was important because it was perfect. It wasn't scarred and it wasn't cut in any way. I felt like...I felt he had something around his neck that...they were beads but they weren't long and...dagger-like like those ones on the other man I saw. These were round like beads, but large. I think they were bone.

JONES: What color do you get associated with the beads?

DAVIS: It is like white or bone colored. It's like peach. Some of them are round.

JONES: Did these people have a relationship with metal?

DAVIS: I'm not feeling any. I haven't seen that many women.

JONES: Do you have a feeling of why?

DAVIS: No. Almost like the women aren't there. Like...they are not at this group gathering. I didn't feel them before either...around these men and boys and old man.

JONES: Are these people involved with trade.

DAVIS: Yes.

JONES: What could they trade other people? What would be sought from these people?

DAVIS: I get 'skins'. I keep picking up dogs. Something about the importance of dogs. They used dogs.

JONES: Used dogs?

DAVIS: Yeah. I feel like watch dogs...like hunting dogs. I feel like they would keep dogs around them. I get a feeling of isolation or protection. I am very conscious of this cliff-type wall that I have been talking about...with the rocks, and this spot below it.... It's like an area of land within a protected setting. It's like a wall...this rock. And it's near this water.

JONES: This water you talk about—if you stood on the edge of it could you see the other side of it?

DAVIS: I feel there was a little stream they used daily, but I feel there was a large body of water that could be faintly seen on the horizon, but...it wouldn't be that people would stand there and (snaps her fingers) be on the beach.

JONES: Let's try another one. This is A-B.

DAVIS: I see this old man again and I see something on his face like a color, and I feel gold and red. They get color from a berry...color from a berry was on his face that was a reddish-bluish. I feel he put this one on for special occasions...to show his stature among his people. I feel him searching or looking for an answer to help his people. I feel that what is happening is something he has known about for a long time but something about the future of this group. This small group of people were being forced out of their homes. I feel like I am a few years later, and I feel like I am not at the same time when I was with the brave. Like I have moved up in time.

JONES: Do you feel it is related to that piece (A-B) or, psychically, have you moved?

DAVIS: I don't know. Again I feel something to do with soldiers or a group of people who would force these people to leave.

JONES: How would these people politically organize themselves?

DAVIS: I feel there was like a hierarchy-type set-up. Like I get three leaders and then two above them and one above them...a pyramid kind of thing. I get a strong feeling it wasn't one from one group and one from another. I get this old man and he is very important and I feel this old man is famous and written about or something. He was known for his contributions.

JONES: Do you feel this famous old man would be an identifying characteristic of these people—this leader would be known?

DAVIS: Yes. There is something around his neck. He has got a cape on, and... there is something around his neck...of feathers. I don't see a headdress on the head. I see feathers or something as a collar. Something that would force him to put his head up. I see it coming off the shoulders like sleeves. I feel they were created for a special...it is not something you wore very often...or it was something that was not worn that often. It was almost—like made for this special occasion.

JONES: You have mentioned water a lot. Did these people have any boats?

DAVIS: I see something like a canoe, but it's like a shell. It's like flatter than a canoe...flatter and not real deep. It's almost resting on top and almost...sort of a rim...around them.

JONES: How many people could get into one?

DAVIS: I get four to eight. I get that they used cross-beams.

JONES: What are these people going to do when they get in their boat?

DAVIS: I felt they fished somehow. Almost like a net effect where they would reach into the water and pull out. I also got the word 'hunt'. They would go in groups. There were a lot of wild animals. Somehow I get that this area is close to, or involved in, a natural preserve...conservation wildlife, forests...something now. It has gone through changes and transformations, but I feel there was a lot of really interesting animals in this area that are now extinct or practically extinct. I feel that part of this area has been created as a park or something to carry on. I got a word like "kumu". It is a word in their language. I get "kumu sa"...something.

JONES: What if these people wanted to get intoxicated, could they?

DAVIS: Yes. I'm picking up a plant. I'm looking at a little round thing that looks kind of like a berry but flatter and...something like a big watermelon seed. I am conscious of something like a little dish, and these seed-like things were placed in at this group gathering and there was smoky stuff. They were also used by the man sitting by the fire (referred to earlier)...when I said the fire was smoking. I feel it is applied to fire and then as the fire smokes, I don't know...somehow the fire would produce smoke.

JONES: **Where were these people before they were here** (touches artifact)?

DAVIS: Well, I said that man had been there all his life. I felt that. But then I felt they came from the west, as though coming from the west and south...like coming up from perhaps Mexico, or somewhere that way. I see Louisiana again.

JONES: **Feel like you are going back on their route?**

DAVIS: I am in central America. An orientation around a large body of water.

JONES: **What do you mean?**

DAVIS: My first impressions were of a large body of water, and I feel these people would always migrate around a place where there was lots of water.

JONES: **You mentioned conflicts several times. How did these people make war?**

DAVIS: I feel spears. I feel a ball type of thing was thrown by a rope or something...

JONES: **A ball and...could you draw it?**

DAVIS: I feel like a scoop. I feel like it was made out of a young branch so it was real pliable...and like stones...it was bent back and...like a sling shot almost.

JONES: **What finally put an end to these people?**

DAVIS: Well, I mentioned their migration They were forced to leave. There was a small group confined to an area, like a reservation. And I feel like there are still some of them carrying on this group.

JONES: **But in terms of these people** (touches artifacts) **you feel forced...**

DAVIS: Yes. I see these men on horses riding and this group of people walking...

JONES: **At the time these people were vital what other kinds of things were happening in the world?**

DAVIS: I get a feeling of Italy. I get the word "Magellan". I have no concept of time with that. Then I saw these people pushing and I saw this cavalry kind of. The association with Italy is...I seen a man with a telescope. I feel a lot of things happening in Italy. In and about Rome, but not way back. I see blousey-type clothing with a beret type hat.

JONES: **Do you feel that much is known about these people?**

DAVIS: I feel that this group of people might have infiltrated into a group that was more largely and widely known, eventually settling on some reservation or some piece of land. I'm having difficulty with that. Because the group of people I picked up were small, but I feel them connected to a large group of people. I get this land that has been set aside, or whatever, is something connected with their culture. I don't feel it is directly their name.

JONES: **What would be the major content of their mythology?**

DAVIS: I felt they would talk about...sensation like a lion...it was a cat. Stories having to do with hunters. And I think there was stories about birds. I feel a story about fire, a hunter and a cat, or an animal of some sort that was the size of a mountain lion. I felt a lot of their images had to do with animals or man...they didn't deal a lot with...you know, about plants or terrain.

JONES: **Question on trade again. What was it that people wanted from those they traded with?**

DAVIS: Grain. There was some difficulty because of the dampness.

JONES: **Where did they get the grain?**

DAVIS: These neighboring groups...groups very close in kinship. They were compatible though they didn't associate that often. Sometimes they would trade fish. They knew how to dry fish or preserve it.

JONES: Did their trade have any form of money or currency?

DAVIS: When you asked about metal before, the only sensation I got was a crude sensation of metal. Like they could distinguish some sort of metal in rock and like stone. When you said that I saw a little bag or money pouch and there was these little rocks in it.

JONES: What color?

DAVIS: I get green, like a malekite or a jade kind of thing that would have little lines through it.

JONES: Before we stop is there any final comment you would like to make about these people.

DAVIS: I don't understand why the women aren't there. I feel this area I've talked about was used mostly by men, and I want to go behind these rocks and away from some of the water, and I feel that there might be more women. They are some distance away. I don't see the sun shining a lot, and I don't see them out in a real clear area. I get this feeling about dampness, and this wall of rock, or whatever it was, and it wasn't like it was impregnable or anything like that.

Mayan Stones: Blind Reading by Noreen Renier

(Picks up first stone A-B and starts to read it before it is unwrapped) I feel dirt around this. Heat. I feel a lot of digging. I think I'm going. I feel a very large, a very large thing going downward, and the sand looks lighter on the top, and then I'm getting darker. Let me get myself up and see the scenery. I don't feel a lot of brush and trees right around this area, but I see more like tropical trees in the distance. Do you want me to see people? Give me...

JONES: Anything...people...structures...costumes...time.

RENIER: Let me see structures. I'm getting something more of...made of palm...like a thatched roof and it looks primitive, and very open. More to protect yourself from the sun. I don't see a lot of detail inside of it. Feel more protection. Let me see people. O.K. I'm getting a foot. I don't know why I'm getting a foot, and a big toe. I just see a foot and a big toe...must mean something. Let me see the person. Oh, dear. I feel so proper. Can I pick...I feel very deep water underneath the ground. I feel like there is some running water underneath the ground. Very deep. very cool.

JONES: Is this a natural occurrence or something...?

RENIER: As I go underground, I feel more...made. Man-made. There is water there. It is dark and damp, and...looks like hard stuff, rock or cement on the top, and this water is going through this area. I don't know where I am.

JONES: Why don't you open the pieces up and look at them.

RENIER: I won't look at it first. Oh dear. I have a great deal of activity of people running and yelling...got a whole bunch of people running around. I see people and they look like they are panicking. Something unusual, something very fast must have happened and it has taken these people by surprise. They look like they are going in all directions, and not understanding what is going on. I feel something very sudden happened. Very fast. Very quick. Some sort of disaster.

JONES: What is the nature of the disaster?

RENIER: I feel like it was...I don't see an enemy. I just see people running. A good amount of people. I'm not just alone. I see the sun about half way down near some water here, and there is higher stuff behind me (makes step-like motion with her hands behind her). Higher things...behind me. Hard stuff behind...rock...stone. Not gigantic but very hard...and it rises up.

JONES: Population...you said you see people. Under 100 or over 100?

RENIER: Over a hundred. Around a hundred. I'm getting a lot of burning. I'm getting a burning sensation...I almost smell burning. I don't know what I'm smelling.

JONES: What are you smelling? (She is sniffing constantly at this time.)

RENIER: I felt like leaves and wood and natural things are burning.

JONES: What do the people look like?

RENIER: I got a very large mouth on this person, and I see a lot of teeth. Maybe a little bit of protruding...lots of teeth. Shortness and broadness in the face itself. Broad features on this person. I'm seeing a man.

JONES: What is the hair color?

RENIER: Dark. Straight. I feel there is something they do with the hair, and it is something that they put in. (She is twisting her hair as she speaks.) Maybe a braid of hair around there. (Indicates back of head)

JONES: Eyes...nose...ears...what do they look like?

RENIER: Let me see the eyes. Dark. I feel intelligence with this person. Nose ...not sticking out. More on the face, but not spread out all over though. Oh, that's not defined enough, I can feel it. Oh, oh—wait a second. There is something with the ear. I don't know if it is like a hole in the ear, or they do something to the ear. I feel like there is a hole in my ear.

JONES: What is this man wearing?

RENIER: He wasn't wearing much when I looked at him. Let me check him out again. I see a very strong climber...more of, like a hill, not trees. More agility around him. I seem to be focusing on one individual in particular. I feel something going around him that could either be a cape or blanket...something of warmth, either a cape or blanket. I feel some form of metal in use (she makes a motion to her wrist), like a thing on their bodies. Not a lot, but it's just very neat looking. I felt around the wrist, I did, I don't know what it is though.

JONES: What is the climate and weather like there?

RENIER: I saw some storms coming up as you said that. They would have unusual storms and very strong winds. The winds are coming from the water ...they seem to be sweeping over a large body of water. I feel like there is a lot of destruction to this land due to weather conditions.

JONES: Let's go back to the man you saw.

RENIER: The first shot I got of him was naked. I don't know if this nakedness is all the time or not. I don't see much hair on his chest.

JONES: Is he wearing anything on his feet?

RENIER: Something that comes up around the ankle, and it would tie...I don't see a sandal. I feel more of an over-covering...I feel more covering. More covered. I feel it comes up quite close...low to the ankle in some way.

JONES: What about from the waist down?

RENIER: There are things that are hanging from his waist.

JONES: What are they made of?

RENIER: Seems like I got some feathers. Little feathers though, not big feathers. And it's got designs and looks intricate like...lots of them and they hung down.

JONES: What did this man do?

RENIER: I see this man outdoors. I see him climbing this (makes step-motions)...this hard thing...I don't know what it is. I feel like he is looking, or watching for other people to come. I feel just watching.

JONES: What does he eat?

RENIER: I feel something dried. I feel they must have knowledge of how to dry things, because I feel something dried. I feel that some of it is meat. There are also some fields out around there, that are being cultivated. Not particularly with this man, but I see some fields around there that...small fields...small farm or small gardens. Oh, I'm picking up the dirt and I'm dropping it again. It is not good dirt. Not rich. I'm feeling more like sand to... just falls through my fingers dead-like. Needs rain, or something. It just doesn't look good. It's got more grey than black or yellow.

JONES: What is in the garden?

RENIER: Berries. Whatever it is, it doesn't grow very good.

JONES: Is it big or little?

RENIER: When I first saw it I saw some tall plants growing. Now I get close and it seems that things are withered up and dried, and close to the ground. Looks like they might have (unintelligible)...but they're not. (Tape ends, begins side 2) Everytime I pick up these things I feel a very violent storm. I feel a lot of rain in this storm and I feel that for a long period of time rain came. I feel water rising too. I don't know what all this is (she is now holding rock A-14).

JONES: Describe the area where this rock was found?

RENIER: I'm getting some scraggly looking bushes and trees. They look thin and the leaves are flat. It's scraggly...not like a big, thick tree. It grows under very unusual conditions. How about religion? Let me see religion. I'm seeing night. I see a fire. I see a lot of people around it...but this is not a cook-out. Some sort of event is taking place. I'm low, but there are these high things again around me. I feel more low. Not that many people, maybe twelve or fifteen. There is a deer...some form of deer or something that looks like a deer that's been killed. I feel slaughtered or killed. There is more than one god.

JONES: What are the characteristics of these gods?

RENIER: These gods...there is either a statue or some symbolic thing that they pray to, or give to...maybe even giving sacrifices, offerings, or food on. I feel they moved something to look like a god.

JONES: What does the god look like?

RENIER: He is scary looking. He's big. I feel stone. He has a big nose...flat nose. A mouth that is closed. I feel something about his hands (she puts her hands together with palms up at her waist as if to receive something)...I feel the hands are open and there is an indentation about the waist, or around this area (indicates waist). I feel this is a statue or a thing of stone. I feel stone with this.

JONES: Did the people do anything in relation to this statue?

RENIER: I'm getting darkness...almost...I don't know right now.

JONES: We still haven't gotten a good description of clothing.

RENIER: I feel a piece of cloth...longer than it is wide with designs on it.

JONES: Can you see the designs?

RENIER: I feel symbols on the side of this cloth. I don't see a great deal of detail, but it almost blends in with the rest of it. I feel a blending in. (She indicates that this cloth is associated with waist or belt region.)

JONES: About, about...some of the other gods they worshipped? You mentioned "gods".

RENIER: Oh, dammit. They had this one leader, but he is very ferocious and he wears a lot of things on his head. I feel some ferociousness as his character trait. Wait, I am going to something else. I see a body lying down and I see this man who is dressed sort of funny doing things around it.

JONES: O.K. Let's stay with that for a minute. What kinds of things is the man doing?

RENIER: Well, he is dancing around and shaking something and sprinkling some stuff over this person.

JONES: Is this person alive? Is something wrong with him?

RENIER: Not very well alive. Alive, alive, alive. I smell something burning again. Let me go back. I don't know why I keep getting night. It is getting

398 Visions of Time

dark again. I can't tell what...
JONES: **Do you know if the man is breathing?**
RENIER: His eyes opened!
JONES: **The man dressed in the strange way, what is he going to do?**
RENIER: I think he is going to take care of his spirit or his soul, and I think this is why I'm smelling things, because he is putting some stuff in the fire to make things smell a color.
JONES: **A color?...**
RENIER: Yeah, I feel things went in the fire and small clouds would 'poof' up. Looks like a lot of theatrics to me, but I don't know. I shouldn't say that. I don't know. Where I'm at now, I would have to bend my head to one side. I feel a side coming down very low. I'm bending my head. Let me see dwellings. The dwellings are not for long terms. They are more for protection than to show, or be materialistic.
JONES: **You have mentioned several times about high things behind you. Could you be more specific about what you are talking about?**
RENIER: I feel like there is some sort of...certainly on one side, I felt height but I felt very hard, a little bit of dirt, and hardness going up. Might be like caves in this place, cave going in. Caves might lead down into where the water is underneath. Caves. Wideness. Lowness. Caves.
JONES: **In these caves can you see anything that may tell us more about who these people were or precisely where you are? Look for something man-made.**
RENIER: There is one cave that has a hole that goes up, and I feel they might have built a fire...I don't know if it is straw mats...something that wasn't in the cave but that they brought into the cave to lay on or to sleep on...something to cushion. Maybe grass but it is dried. Let me see food. Oh, dear...O.K. wait a second, I'm getting two things. I am getting a fish with...a funny fish...fish. Funny mouth to this fish. I don't know if this had teeth or some funny things (she makes motion along the sides of her mouth), and I saw a bird fly, just briefly, over at the same time...Oh, Oh, I think the fish with the (makes motion along the sides of her mouth) and the bird are symbolic. I almost feel symbol because I am seeing them both. I see the fish here, and it is like drawn or something...I see a fish, and part of the fish is gone. But the bird is light, white, it would go very high. It's white, it's light. Something strange about the fish's mouth. Something that came out side of it, or if they fish...I don't know anything about fish.
JONES: **You felt symbolic?**
RENIER: Yes. I felt this might have been drawn. The fish, and then the bird was up higher...it looked like it was in flight, a lot of scales on it.
JONES: **Let's move to another piece. This is A-13.**
RENIER: Again, I get wind and rain. Everytime I touch one of these things I get wind and rain.
JONES: **What are the relationships these people associated with A-13 had with their neighbors?**
RENIER: As you said that I got somebody holding something and shaking something. I feel...sparsely...I don't feel a lot of people. I don't think they caused wars, but they were very cautious of other people—other tribes. I just feel very cautious. I'm shaking something that looks bigger at the top. It has words here and then it is wider at the top.
JONES: **What is your feeling as you shake it?**
RENIER: This way, this way. Up front. I feel like something is on this man's upper arm, too. I feel caution with them, but I don't feel that much...I don't feel they would go around hurting a lot of people but I feel they would protect themselves.
JONES: **Did these people have, or did they not have, domestic animals?**
RENIER: As you said that I got a long-legged...it's not that high...it looks

like it has long legs and a medium sized body. I don't know if it's a dog or a goat, or what. It looks sort of scraggly. I don't know what that thing is. Got sort of long hair instead of short hair.

JONES: How long?

RENIER: Medium long. I can see some coming from the stomach area. As I'm looking at this animal I see the long legs and I see about this much hair (three to five inches).

JONES: Do you see horses here?

RENIER: Not now (touches stone)...not at this time (taps stones again).

JONES: What about cattle?

RENIER: Maybe more to the south. There are small herds of...I don't think we would call it a cow. It looks like a small...you use a stick to keep them in order. They don't look like cows that I know about...if it is a cow. Small quantities of them. I feel like these animals could almost be domesticated.

JONES: Any other animals?

RENIER: I feel a wolf-type of animal. Like a wolf, either dog, wolf. Runs fast and attacks.

JONES: Did these people trade with other people?

RENIER: When you said that, I felt water around me and I felt water on the east...side. I feel the water is where there is more activity and more people are around the water. When I get away from the land and go to the water I see more people and I feel more civilized...more people. More secure. I don't feel anything is going to happen. There are some long, long boats, but I don't see motors... The boats I am seeing are more for short distances. You put supplies in there and then go back to where you came from, but they are long and slender. Short distances.

JONES: How many people could fit into one?

RENIER: Maybe four. I see it filled with different things. Maybe food...looked like supplies.

JONES: What is this boat made of? Can you see how it was constructed?

RENIER: It is very handmade. You couldn't buy one. I feel a lot of rough texture...I don't know if it's wood or bark.

JONES: What is the water like?

RENIER: It has a tendency to stir up at times, though I feel like there is a place, an inlet where I am at now (touches A-13), an inlet where I feel more quiet at this time, but I don't trust it. I think this water could be rather treacherous at times. Right now they are O.K. A river nearby...maybe twice a year it might overflow causing floods.

JONES: Did these people who were associated with the things before you ever see a Caucasian?

RENIER: There was talk about those people. I feel like more talk. Although some of that stuff around the water looks very civilized...to me. I just feel like ...a lot of people come there. Might even be like a wharf. My back is hurting. Feels like I've worked a lot. Very tired. Very tired. I've traveled and come an awful long way.

JONES: Where from?

RENIER: North. More northward coming down. I don't feel well. I don't feel good. Very sick.

JONES: Let's move to another object?

RENIER: It's not me, it's the rock.

JONES: Let's see if we can find a well rock.

RENIER: I feel sadness there for a while. I felt a funeral process going on.

JONES: Let's look at this one. A-307.

RENIER: I'm going to check out what they are eating. I feel a lot of grain going into my stomach. There is some very fresh...let me look into his stomach and see what the heck is going on. They smoke. They smoke something. I feel smoke inside this man's lungs, and I don't think it is like a cigarette, but there is some form of inhalation or something that would be smoky. Oh, this is interesting. I feel more like a heart, and it looks like death. What are they cutting out? Oh, Lord!

JONES: What are you seeing?

RENIER: They got to cut out the enemy heart or liver...I don't know which it is but I feel it is very important. It's the heart! It's so the enemy...for this man I've killed...like a soul...I don't know, David, I'm getting confused. I just see them cutting out something.

JONES: Would they do this often or is this a rare event?

RENIER: I don't feel good about doing this. Somebody has negative vibes around me while we are doing this.

JONES: What do they look like?

RENIER: If I had to do a voice level I feel it would be a monotone voice. I feel more monotone voice. What do they look like? I do feel the ear, or something on my ear, or something done to my ear. I feel that very strongly. Children...I see designs going on young people. I'm very tired, I am, I am. Can I stop now? Do we have one more to do?

JONES: Yes.

RENIER: O.K. Let's do it (she picks up A-5). This was part of a weapon. Part of something. It was not just stone. Part of a tool.

JONES: What was done with it?

RENIER: Cutting. I still feel highness and the caves. I feel youngness and children. Like a young person. I'm cutting the bark with it. I'm making something. I am cutting...outside.

JONES: (A-21) This one.

RENIER: I felt with children...something on the lower part of my leg. Something on the leg area. There is some game they played with bones...fish bones maybe. Game that has both some skill and some luck. O.K. I will be one of the boys. The water is not that close. I don't think I can go to the water...just go to the water...this big water...everyday. I feel like I can see it. Maybe I'm too young, but I can see big water in the distance. There is smaller water that I can go to. Oh, my father was killed in a war to the north and I am very proud of him...being killed in that type of thing. Proudness with the boy that his father was killed in a war to the north. He dreams about...the bird. I don't know why he dreams about this bird.

JONES: Can you feel his dream?

RENIER: I just saw him dreaming of this bird flying. I don't know if he wants to fly or if this bird is again a symbol.

JONES: Is there any other kind of thing that these people did to their bodies? You have already mentioned something to do with the ear.

RENIER: I feel that this young person would have something done on his body. Might even be painful for a few moments. I felt pain would be inflicted for a few moments with what is being done to his body. I just feel pain on his body. It is something he looks forward to...not hides from. The feet, I keep getting the feet. Now I've got him barefooted. I feel I am a boy about twelve or thirteen years old.

JONES: Did these people write their language?

RENIER: There was some things...they look more like designs than words to me...not like the English language. I feel more...no books, if that's what you mean.

JONES: Did these people ever know or see something like a gun or a cannon?

RENIER: By the water that I saw before...by that wharf or whatever it was... there was guns at that point. I feel some sort of guns, with those people they seen...

JONES: Those people?

RENIER: I don't know...I just felt they were different.

JONES: What about weaving cloth? Did these people have or did they make clothing other ways?

RENIER: Something big in front of me...with a definite design in the middle. Feels like they were very...very nice things and lot of care. It feels heavy. I don't know if it's cloth or not, but it feels heavier.

JONES: The design in the center, could you describe that please?

RENIER: Yes. Round. Might be more round things coming out of it, but I felt round. I felt very strong with round.

JONES: You mentioned earlier about some sort of metal of some kind of these people. Did these people know how to make metal or did they acquire it in some other way?

RENIER: I feel like...making...more or less (she makes hammering motion). That one bracelet I picked up...it looks crude and heavy...I'm getting tired.

BIBLIOGRAPHY

Adams, Richard W.E. 1974. *The Civilization of the Ancient Maya and Its Collapse.* Norwalk: Reading Laboratory.

Asher, Maxine. 1976. "Digging into the Past with ESP". In *Psychic,* June, 1976.

Bennett, C.E., trans. 1964. *Laudonniere and Fort Caroline: History and Documents.* Gainesville: University of Florida Press.

_____ 1975. The Three Voyages of Rene Laudonniere. *Gainesville: University of Florida Press.*

Bernal, Ignacio. 1963. *Mexico Before Cortez: Art, History and Legend.* New York: Doubleday & Co.

Binford, L.R. 1962. "Archeology as Anthropology". In *American Antiquity,* Vol. 28, No. 2.

Bond, Geoffrey. 1966. "Pleistocene Environments in Southern Africa". In *African Ecology and Human Evolution.* Edited by Clark Howell and Francois Bourliere. Chicago: Aldine Publishing Co.

Bordes, Francois. 1968. *The Old Stone Age.* London: Weidenfeld and Nicolson.

Butler, W.E. 1971. *How to Develop Psychometry.* London: Aquarian Press.

Cavendish, Richard. 1974. *Encyclopedia of the Unexplained.* New York: McGraw-Hill.

Ceram, C.W. 1959. *Gods, Graves and Scholars.* New York: Alfred A. Knopf.

DeGarmo, G.D. 1970. "Big Game Hunters: An Alternative and An Hypothesis". A paper presented at the 35th Annual Meeting of the Society for American Archeology, Mexico City.

Dozier, Edward P. 1967. *The Kalinga of Northern Luzon, Philippines.* New York: Rinehart & Winston.

Furst, Peter. 1972. *Flesh of the Gods: The Ritual Use of Hallucinogens.* New York: Praeger Publishers.

Goodman, Jeffrey. 1977. *Psychic Archeology.* New York: G.P. Putnam.

Hey, Douglas. 1966. *Wildlife Heritage of South Africa.* London: Oxford University Press.

Howell, F. Clark, and Clark, J. Desmond. 1966. "Archeulian Hunters-Gatherers of Sub-Saharan Africa". In *African Ecology and Human Evolution.* Edited by F. Clark Howell and Francois Bourliere. Chicago: Aldine Publishing Co.

Hudson, C. 1976. *The Southeastern Indians.* Knoxville: University of Tennessee Press.

Inskeep, R.R. 1967. "The Late Stone Age in Southern Africa". In *Background to Evolution in Africa.* Edited by Walter W. Bishop and J. Desmond Clark. Chicago: University of Chicago Press.

Jones, David E. 1969. "The Medicine Kit of a Comanche Eagle Doctor". In *Bulletin of the Oklahoma Anthropological Society,* Vol. XVIII.

_____ 1972. *Sanapia: Comanche Medicine Woman.* New York: Holt, Rinehart & Winston.

Larson, L.H. 1953. "The Historic Guale Indians of the Georgia Gulf Coast". An unpublished manuscript.

403

_____. 1969. "Aboriginal Subsistence Technology on the Southeastern Coastal Plain During the Late Prehistoric Period". A dissertation, Dept. of Anthropology, University of Michigan, Michigan.

McReynolds, Edwin C. 1957. *The Seminole*. Norman: University of Oklahoma Press.

Moss, Thelma. 1974. *The Probability of the Impossible*. New York: New American Library.

Murry, Marian. 1975. *Florida Fossils*. Tampa: Trend House.

Olsen, Stanley J. 1959. *Fossil Mammals of Florida*. In *Florida Geological Survey*, Special Publication No. 6.

Pau, Frederick. 1934. *Florida: Old and New*. New York: G.P. Putnam's Sons.

Peterson, H.L. 1956. *Arms and Armor in Colonial America: 1526-1783*. New York: Brinhall House.

Pike, Kenneth. 1954. "Language in Relation to a Unified Theory of the Structure of Human Behavior". Glendale, California: Summer Institute of Linguistics.

Ripley, S. Dillon. 1964. *The Land and Wildlife of Tropical Asia*. New York: Time-Life Books.

Schmeidler, Gertrude. 1969. *Extra-sensory Perception*. New York: Atherton Press.

Sears, William H. 1959. "Two Weedon Island Period Mounds". In *Social Science*, No. 5.

Smith, M.A. 1955. "The Limitations of Inference in Archeology". In *Archeological Newsletter*, Vol 6.

Spencer, R.F. et al. 1977. *The Native Americans*, second ed. New York: Harper & Row.

Stearman, Allyn. 1978. *Personal Communication*. Orlando, Florida: Florida Technological University.

Stuart, G.E., Stuart, G.S. 1977. "The Mysterious Maya." In *National Geographic Society* Special Publication.

Swanton, J.R. 1946. "Indians of the Southeastern United States". In *Bureau of American Ethnology Bulletin*.

Thompson, J. Eric. 1970. *Maya History and Religion*. Norman: University of Oklahoma Press.

von Hagen, Victory. 1960. *World of the Maya*. New York: New American Library.

Wallace, Ronald. 1975. "An Archeological, Ethnohistorical and Biochemical Investigation of the Guale Aborigines of the Georgia Coastal Strand". A dissertation, Dept. of Anthropology, University of Florida.

Wedel, W.R. 1961. *Prehistoric Man on the Great Plains*. Norman: University of Oklahoma Press.

White, Frank, ed. 1959. "The Journals of Lieutenant John Pickell: 1836-1837". In *Florida Historical Quarterly*, Vol. XXXVIII.

Wilmsen, E.N. 1974. *Lindenmeier: A Pleistocene Hunting Society*. New York: Harper & Rowe.

More books on our QUEST list

CHILDREN OF THE RAINBOW
By Leinani Melville

Religions, legends, and gods of pre-Christian Hawaii including 34 full page drawings of traditional Hawaiian sacred symbols. The author is the grandson of a minister of King Lalakaua's court.

A HUMAN HERITAGE
By Dr. Alfred Taylor

Humanity, suggest Taylor, has a heritage of happiness. He then goes on to prove it. The author is listed among the new breed of "spiritual-scientists" who combine dead letter scientific conclusions with their own personal intuitional insights.

INTELLIGENCE CAME FIRST
By Dr. E. Lester Smith and Associates

Do we need a brain to think? That's the question Dr. Smith asks—and answers. He is a Fellow of the Royal Society, discoverer of vitamin B-12. He suggests that the brain is not the mind—that function precedes the organ through which it is to be exercised.

I SEND A VOICE
By Evelyn Eaton

A poignant and true story about the American Indian and his unorthodox, but effective healing rites. The author, a white American woman , is accepted into a Sweat Lodge, given a Pipe, and taught how to heal the sick.

These titles are available from:
QUEST BOOKS
306 West Geneva Road
Wheaton, Illinois 60187